Praise for
A Writer's Workshop, 1E
by Bob Brannan

"I must say that Brannan did a fabulous job putting together a textbook that covers every topic essential for developmental courses. CONGRATULATIONS!"

—Joanna A. Benavides
Laredo Community College

"Brannan's book is informative, illuminating, and the most logical resource for the new millennium. . . . I would adopt it and encourage my fellow colleagues to do the same. I believe this book will be an unequalled resource for building writing skills."

—Marilyn Garrett
Texas Southern University

"In the design of every chapter one sees the work of an experienced, gifted teacher of composition. . . . No text that I know of can match the depth of coverage that this one offers. I would describe this text to my colleagues as an outstanding, comprehensive instrument for teaching developmental students."

—Huey Guagliardo
Lousiana State University at Eunice

"The writing samples are really pretty wonderful and very effective. They far exceed the value of the writing samples in my own text and I would like to use them in my class next semester."

—Rebecca Busch Adams
Naugatuck Valley Community Technical College

"I would encourage my department to adopt Brannan's text because he explains and models the writing process very well and offers hands-on instruction in all areas, not just the areas he thinks need the most attention."

—Nita Wood
Tidewater Community College

"Brannan does an outstanding job of showing how to turn the paragraph into an essay."

—Jeannette Palmer
Motlow State Community College

"The revision coverage is excellent."

—Susan Brant
College of the Canyons

"Inclusion of prewriting, drafting, revising, and editing steps in the writing process and accompanying activities and examples is a real strength and has a direct appeal to me as a teacher. . . . I would assign each chapter a grade of 'A' because the chapters meet my course objectives and teaching style."

—Karen Sidwell
St. Petersburg Junior College

"This is the most thorough introduction to paragraph writing I have ever seen. There are plenty of examples and assignments. The attention to audience, along with sample paragraphs and activities is really nice to see. . . I find the use of previous paragraphs for development into essays remarkably effective. . . . The emphasis on revision that this text appears to offer is long overdue."

—Tracy Peyton
Pensacola Junior College

"The examples and exercises meet the students where they are, but instead of leaving them there, they lead students to the skill level needed for college writing. I also like the emphasis on meaning, especially in the comparison chapter, the diversity that does not call attention to itself, and the range of assignments that are varied and interesting."

—Maria A. Garcia
San Antonio College

"Brannan is very, very good at explaining the writing assignment."

—Marcia B. Littenberg
State University of New York—Farmingdale

"The author's use of a student paragraph from the appropriate chapter in the paragraph unit and its development into an essay is one of the outstanding features of this text-book. This is such a good technique!"

—Sandra Barnhill
South Plains College

"The author understands student concerns. The exercises and prompts are very well done. The author knows how to motivate students and the importance of clarity and organization when teaching at this level. . . . This text is excellent."

—Laura Kasischke
Washtenaw Community College

"The chapter on Taking Essay Exams is innovative and exciting."

—Joyce L. Maher
Eastern Shore Community College

A Writer's Workshop

Crafting Paragraphs, Building Essays

Bob Brannan
Johnson County Community College
Overland Park, Kansas

Boston   Burr Ridge, IL   Dubuque, IA   Madison, WI   New York   San Francisco   St. Louis
Bangkok   Bogotá   Caracas   Kuala Lumpur   Lisbon   London   Madrid   Mexico City
Milan   Montreal   New Delhi   Santiago   Seoul   Singapore   Sydney   Taipei   Toronto

McGraw-Hill Higher Education ℘

A Division of The **McGraw-Hill** *Companies*

A WRITER'S WORKSHOP: CRAFTING PARAGRAPHS, BUILDING ESSAYS
Published by McGraw-Hill, an imprint of The McGraw-Hill Companies, Inc.
1221 Avenue of the Americas, New York, NY, 10020. Copyright © 2003 by The
McGraw-Hill Companies, Inc. All rights reserved. No part of this publication
may be reproduced or distributed in any form or by any means, or stored in a
database or retrieval system, without the prior written consent of The McGraw-Hill
Companies, Inc., including, but not limited to, in any network or other electronic
storage or transmission, or broadcast for distance learning.

Some ancillaries, including electronic and print components, may not be available to customers
outside the United States.

This book is printed on acid-free paper.

3 4 5 6 7 8 9 0 QPD/QPD 0 9 8 7 6 5 4 3 2

ISBN 0-07-239329-7 (student edition)
ISBN 0-07-252267-4 (annotated instructor's edition)

President of McGraw-Hill Humanities/Social Sciences: *Steve Debow*
Executive editor: *Sarah Touborg*
Senior developmental editor: *Alexis Walker*
Senior marketing manager: *David Patterson*
Project manager: *Ruth Smith*
Production supervisor: *Rose Hepburn*
Senior designer: *Jennifer McQueen*
Associate supplement producer: *Vicki Laird*
Producer, Media technology: *Todd Vaccaro*
Photo research coordinator: *Jeremy Cheshareck*
Photo researcher: *Amy Bethea*
Cover illustration: *Paul Turnbaugh*
Typeface: *10/12 Sabon*
Compositor: *Electronic Publishing Services, Inc., TN*
Printer: *Quebecor World Dubuque Inc.*

Library of Congress Cataloging-in-Publication Data

Brannan, Bob.
    A writer's workshop : crafting paragraphs, building essays / Bob Brannan.— 1st ed.
        p. cm.
    Includes index.
    ISBN 0-07-239329-7 (student ed. : alk. paper) — ISBN 0-07-252267-4 (alk. paper)
    1. English language—Paragraphs—Problems, exercises, etc. 2. English
language—Rhetoric—Problems, exercises, etc. 3. English language—Grammar—Problems,
exercises, etc. 4. Report writing—Problems, exercises, etc. I. Title.
PE1439 .B69 2002
808'.042—dc21

www.mhhe.com

Bob Brannan

Bob Brannan is a professor at Johnson County Community College in Overland Park, Kansas, where he has taught composition for the past ten years. He received his M.A. in composition/rhetoric from Iowa State University and began his teaching career as a "freeway flyer," shuttling between community colleges and carrying his office in a bag. Over the years he has taught a number of writing classes—including developmental, first- and second-semester composition, business and technical, advanced composition, and honors seminars—but he focuses much of his attention on the pre-college-level writer. *A Writer's Workshop* is his first composition textbook.

When not working in a writing classroom, Bob spends much of his time with his family, frequently attending his daughter's tea parties, where his voice imitations are in great demand, and climbing trees with her in his backyard.

A Writer's Workshop is a text for developing writers that begins with three basic assumptions: Students learn to write best by writing, they need to revise their work significantly, and they deserve comprehensive instruction on why and how to revise to express themselves effectively. To this end, I have tried to create a text that provides many opportunities for students at all levels—from the least- to best-prepared—to write often within a rhetorical context and to critically evaluate their work.

You will probably notice as you work through *A Writer's Workshop* that it is quite assignment centered. In fact, no other pre-college-level composition text offers as much process instruction and support to students for developing their paragraphs and essays—almost three-fourths of the book. While many composition texts claim to thoroughly explore an assignment with students, they devote only a few pages to this instruction, preferring instead to focus on grammar, spelling, and punctuation. *A Writer's Workshop* has a thoroughly developed handbook section in Unit Five, well supported by Unit Four; however, neither of these units was developed at the expense of the critical process instruction in the paragraph and essay units.

A well-developed rhetorical apparatus is vital if a book is to be a valuable tool for both teachers and students. As composition instructors we have all found ourselves working up instructional material to supplement the textbooks that do a good job of outlining a writing project, but then fall short on the explanation, examples, writing models, and activities students really need to complete—or in some cases even to start—an assignment. *A Writer's Workshop* devotes most of its focus to answering questions students regularly ask about how to compose a specific paragraph or essay: "What do you mean by 'dominant impression'?" "How do you build toward a climax?" "How can I keep my examples from being underdeveloped?" From the chapter introductions, into the practical skills sections, on to the engaging and substantive student models, through the step-by-step process explanations, ending with the Annotated Student Models, *A Writer's Workshop* keeps the students who are struggling to improve a *specific* assignment in focus at all times.

Of course, no textbook can replace a talented and dedicated teacher, who in a single class session is apt to casually offer students more practical advice for solving their own immediate writing problems than a book manages in many pages. However, students *can* take the book home with them, so the clearer and more detailed the instruction, the better able students are to help themselves outside the classroom. My goal for *A Writer's Workshop* has been to design a composition text that can be of real help to students in the absence of their instructors and that can free teachers from a good part of their classroom drudgery. If we can spend less time tracking down models, creating heuristics, detailing checklists, and concocting editing practices, we can spend more time with our students' own writing—the true focus of a composition course.

ORGANIZATION OF THE BOOK

The book is divided into six units:

Unit One: Getting Our Feet Wet

Unit Two: Working with the Paragraph

Unit Three: Working with the Essay

Unit Four: Polishing Style

Unit Five: Practicing Sentence Sense

Unit Six: Additional Readings

UNIT ONE covers the writing and reading process.

- **Chapter 1** gives students many opportunities to practice essential writing strategies like prewriting and organizing and ends with several assignment options that instructors might use to assess student skill levels. Chapter 1 is useful the entire semester as students move from one part of the writing process to another.

- **Chapter 2** helps students who have difficulty effectively reading. This chapter is a logical extension of Chapter 1 and makes the reading/writing connection clear, framing the reading process in terms like locating thesis and topic sentences, focusing on primary examples, and working with the writer to actively understand a point. Activities help students practice reading/writing suggestions and are linked to Chapter 3 so that instructors can quickly move students into the assignment chapters of *A Writer's Workshop*.

UNIT TWO introduces the paragraph.

- **Chapter 3** offers a comprehensive treatment of paragraph structure and development.

- **Chapter 4** offers in-depth revision suggestions for rough, developing, and final *paragraph* drafts, explaining important distinctions in descriptive, narrative, and expository writing. As they revise drafts, students will appreciate being able to consistently refer to one chapter that gives them specific, well-illustrated suggestions for improving their work.

- **Chapters 5 to 11** cover seven patterns of development (definition and argument treated in Unit Three), taking students through all phases of the writing process.

UNIT THREE moves students into the essay.

- **Chapter 12** focuses on essay form and development, with special attention devoted to introductions and conclusions.

- **Chapter 13** offers thoroughly illustrated advice for revising rough, second, and final *essay* drafts, and includes useful editing practice.

- **Chapter 14** helps students either expand a former paragraph assignment or begin an essay focusing on one of the patterns of development. The three chapters that follow, **Chapters 15, 16, and 17**—definition, persuasion, and essay exam skills— stress combining the patterns of development that students have worked with in Unit Two.

UNIT FOUR helps students with many elements of style.

- **Chapter 18**, Creating Sentence Variety, works toward increasing students' syntactic fluency, using extensive sentence-combining exercises that also reinforce correct punctuation.

- **Chapter 19** helps students learn to control their tone, select language carefully, and eliminate clutter.

UNIT FIVE works on common problems developmental writers have with grammar, spelling, and punctuation, but does so without intimidating students, through the framework of a Writer's Basic Sentence Grammar. The operating principle in this unit is that less is more. Using a minimum of grammar and punctuation rules, students can learn to punctuate effectively, express themselves clearly, and achieve a degree of syntactic fluency. A number of basic stylistic options are also demonstrated, and there is a substantial chapter devoted to the special concerns of ESL students.

UNIT SIX offers fourteen professional readings that are appropriate to the course in length and complexity, modeling key principles introduced in the assignment chapters.

Appendix 1 is a guide to basic word processing using Windows and the common word processing software Microsoft Word. Even though we live in an increasingly computer-literate society, many of our students have difficulty with word processing, making their composition efforts that much harder. This appendix is largely illustrations—a simplified user's manual with some practical suggestions and warnings—to help students with the many questions they ask their instructors in class: "How do I double space, insert page numbers, spell check, word count . . . ?"

Appendix 2 is an Improvement Chart, which students can use to track their progress with mechanical correctness throughout the semester. The chart is particularly valuable for helping students isolate and overcome pattern errors.

FEATURES OF THE ASSIGNMENT CHAPTERS

The assignment chapters in Units Two and Three are the heart of this text. Here is a list of their key features:

- **Introduction:** The chapter illustration uses visual reinforcement to help focus students' attention on the main point of the chapter.

- **Setting the Stage** summarizes the chapter's goal in a paragraph.

- **Linking to Previous Experience** shows students what they already know about the chapter concepts, linking the material to their personal, work, and academic lives and to other material they have already practiced in the text. (This approach is tied to reading theory—activating a person's "schema"—and is used throughout the text.)

- **Determining the Value** shows students why they might want to care about the chapter information, linking the material to their personal, work, and academic lives and to larger concerns of personal growth.

- **Developing Skills, Exploring Ideas** helps students with concepts and skills essential for understanding and writing the chapter assignment. The activities are thoroughly explained, helping students understand the *why* and the *how* behind the activity and linking the specific concept to the general goal of effective communication.

- **Student Models** offer a Prereading paragraph to help students actively read the upcoming model and then a Postreading paragraph to help students analyze key composition elements, which they can apply to their own paragraph or essay assignment. The Questions for Analysis, which follow the student models, focus on organization, development, and style, helping students see how their own writing can be improved.

- **Explaining the Writing Assignment** prepares a rhetorical context for the students' writing assignment, including a clear focus on audience and purpose.

- **Topic Lists** are extensive and geared to student interests.

- **Prewriting** is modeled for each assignment.

- **Organizing Ideas** deals with overall arrangement and gives specific guidance with essential elements like topic and thesis sentences, complete with examples.

- **Drafting** offers several important reminders to help ease students into their first drafts.

- **The Annotated Student Model** treats draft development in four stages for the *specific* assignment students are working through. Students can readily see revision from more global matters of organization and development through polishing for style and mechanical correctness.

• **Alternate Writing Assignments** give students some specific options that incorporate chapter writing strategies and include topics drawn from students' personal, academic, and work lives.

HOW TO USE *A WRITER'S WORKSHOP*

This text is divided roughly 60/40 between paragraph and essay, and there are enough assignments in each unit to allow an instructor to teach mostly paragraph or essay or balance the two. If you focus primarily on paragraphs, teaching most of the patterns of development before moving into the essay, you may find Chapters 14, Expanding Paragraphs into Essays, and Chapter 15, Defining Terms, Clarifying Ideas, particularly useful as capstone writing projects. If you weight your course more toward the essay, you will find that a thorough treatment of narrative/descriptive and expository writing in Unit Two helps students quickly apply basic organizational and developmental strategies to the essay assignments in Unit Three. Working concurrently with the appropriate pattern of development from Unit Two, you can ease students into the essay by midterm or sooner. Whether your course is primarily paragraph or essay, you may appreciate the in-depth treatment of the essay exam in Chapter 17, one of the three essay chapters that stress combining the patterns of development.

Chapters 1 to 3 work well if presented during the first few weeks of class and are written to reinforce each other. You may want to begin Chapter 3 while students are reviewing the writing process, and you will notice several activities in Chapter 1 that introduce students to description, the assignment for Chapter 5. Also, if you plan to move students fairly quickly into the essay, Chapter 7 makes an effective transition point. Throughout the text you will find copious cross-referencing so students can easily link one chapter to another. However, the cross-referencing is used as *support* for instruction and examples provided in the chapters rather than as replacement for them.

Of course, you will use the handbook section as needed, but you might want to take students carefully through Chapter 20, Working with Sentence Parts, before progressing into the rest of the handbook or Unit Four. Chapter 18, Creating Sentence Variety, works best when visited frequently throughout the semester, particularly when students are polishing and editing drafts.

The skills section of each assignment chapter helps students practice key composition strategies needed to do well in the chapter assignment. Although many of the more challenging activities are labeled *collaborative*, students can manage most by themselves in or out of class. When time is pressing, you may also want to handle some of the activities orally. Aside from the skills section, you will find other writing possibilities in the chapter rhetorical apparatus:

1. Journal Entries (can be collaborative)

2. Prereading and Postreading Analysis Questions

3. Questions for Analyzing Paragraphs and Essays

4. Alternate Writing Assignments

A substantial section of each assignment chapter is devoted to the process breakdown of the assignment and the Annotated Student Model. The purpose of this material is not to hold students back who understand and can move more quickly into a writing project. Rather it is to help students move as quickly and painlessly as possible into their own writing. The operative principle from my perspective is "need-to-know." Some students will want to read most of the assignment and models before they feel confident about proceeding with their papers. Others will make successful creative leaps, quickly skimming for the gist and then plunging in. However you pace your classes, I think that you will find the draft/revise/draft/edit illustration a useful model for students who are still stuck in the "knock-it-out-the-night-before" mode.

KEY FEATURES OF THE TEXT

Aside from the points already listed, you might note these features that set *A Writer's Workshop* apart from the competition:

- *A Writer's Workshop* offers eleven fully illustrated assignments and fifty alternatives (*Instructor's Manual* contains two additional fully developed assignments with ten alternate assignments).

- Strong attention is paid to reading theory throughout the text: chapter introductions, summaries, prereading/postreading activities, essay analysis questions, and writing activities. Students are asked to think critically: to compare new information with old, to synthesize new concepts, and to apply them to their current writing projects.

- User-friendly tone, diction, examples, and models are geared especially toward a diverse student body: traditional, nontraditional, minority, and ESL students.

- *A Writer's Workshop* features a strong revision emphasis, with an Annotated Student Model illustrating revision stages in each assignment chapter and two chapters devoted to revision.

- Questions for Paragraph Analysis focus on the "nuts and bolts" of composition—how to effectively use the models presented.

- Writing activities serve as prewriting to step students through the process of writing their chapter assignment.

- Key composition concepts—such as unity, coherence, and development—are frequently reinforced and repeated in all assignments.

- Instruction in grammar and punctuation is reinforced at the most timely points in the students' writing process as they review draft stages in the two revision chapters.

- Writer's Journal prompts are integrated into the writing process, helping students with invention, organization, drafting, revising, and editing.

- An essay-exam chapter lets instructors build a thorough discussion of the strategies for successfully completing this common academic writing task.

- Unit Four gives teachers a wide variety of options for helping students polish their style.

- Chapter indexes at the front of each chapter make it easy to find and review material.

- Appendix 1 gives instruction on basic word processing.

- The index is particularly comprehensive and thoroughly cross-referenced.

- All instruction is grounded in a rhetorical context:

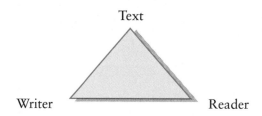

Text

Writer　　　　　　　Reader

SUPPLEMENTS PACKAGE

- *The Instructor's Edition* (ISBN 0-07-252267-4) consists of the student text complete with answers to all activities and marginal notes on using the text in class.

- The *Instructor's Manual* (ISBN 0-07-239330-0) includes comprehensive commentary on every chapter in the text, sample syllabi, alternative writing assignments, peer response worksheets, and more.

- A *website* accompanying the text (**www.mhhe.com/brannan**) offers instructional aids and resources for instructors, including the *Instructor's Manual* and online resources for writing instructors.

- *PageOut!* helps instructors create graphically pleasing and professional web pages for their courses, in addition to providing classroom management, collaborative learning, and content management tools. PageOut! is **FREE** to adopters of McGraw-Hill textbooks and learning materials. Learn more at http:/www.mhhe.com/pageout/.

- *WebWrite!* is an interactive peer-editing program that allows students to post papers, read comments from their peers and instructor, discuss, and edit *online*. To learn more, visit the online demo at http://www.metatext.com/webwrite.

Supplements for Students

- The *website* accompanying the text (**www.mhhe.com/brannan**) offers additional resources for students, including self-correcting exercises, writing activities for additional practice, guides to doing research on the Internet and avoiding plagiarism, useful web links, and more.

- *AllWrite! 2.0* is an interactive, browser-based tutorial program that provides an online handbook, comprehensive diagnostic pretests and posttests, plus extensive practice exercises in every area.

Please consult your local McGraw-Hill representative or consult McGraw-Hill's website at **www.mhhe.com/english** for more information on the supplements that accompany the first edition of *A Writer's Workshop*.

Custom Options

A Writer's Workshop can be customized for brevity or for courses that place different amounts of emphasis on the paragraph or the essay. The text can also be expanded to include your course syllabi, semester schedule, or any other materials specific to your program. Spiral binding is also available. Please contact your McGraw-Hill representative for details, or send us an email at english@mcgraw-hill.com.

ACKNOWLEDGMENTS

A Writer's Workshop has benefited from the input of many people, including the editorial team at McGraw-Hill. I thank Sarah Touborg, executive editor, who patiently listened to my early ideas for the book and who had the faith to bring me on board. Also, I am grateful to Alexis Walker, senior developmental editor, who has given me many suggestions for reorganizing and slimming down a manuscript that threatened on occasion to swamp us all.

A number of reviewers and class testers from across the country have helped me tighten and polish the ideas in this book, and I would like to acknowledge my debt for their many practical revision suggestions:

Rebecca Busch Adams
Naugatuck Valley Community Technical College

Linda Bagshaw
Briar Cliff College

Sandra Barnhill
South Plains College

Joanna A. Benavides
Laredo Community College

Karen L. Blaske
Arapahoe Community College

Susan Brant
College of the Canyons

Vicki Covington
Isothermal Community College

Crystal Edmonds
Robeson Community College

Marilyn Garrett
Texas Southern University

Eddye Gallagher
Tarrant County College

Maria A. Garcia
San Antonio College

Jeanne Gilligan
Delaware Technical and Community College

Huey Guagliardo
Louisiana State University at Eunice

Faye Jones
Northeast State Technical Community College

Laura Kasischke
Washtenaw Community College

Patsy Krech
University of Memphis

Eleanor Latham
Central Oregon Community College

Marcia B. Littenberg
SUNY, Farmingdale

Joyce L. Maher
Eastern Shore Community College

Sebastian Mahfood
St. Louis University

Randy R. Maxson
Grace College and Seminary

Aubrey Moncrieffe, Jr.
Housatonic Community College

Jeanette Palmer
Motlow State Community College

Myra Peavyhouse
Roane State Community College

Tracy Peyton
Pensacola Junior College

James Read
Allan Hancock College

Al Reeves
Montana State University College of Technology

Carole Rhodenhiser
Fort Valley State College

Lola Richardson
Paine College

ACKNOWLEDGMENTS

Linda C. Rollins
Motlow State Community College

Christina Vick
Louisiana State University at Eunice

Harvey Rubenstein
Hudson County Community College

Ted Wadley
Georgia Perimeter College

Patricia S. Rudden
New York City Technical College

Beverly Walker
North Central State College

Julia Ruengert
Ozarks Technical Community College

Fred Wolven
Miami–Dade Community College

Karen Sidwell
St. Petersburg Junior College

Nita Wood
Tidewater Community College

Pauline Simonowich
Pitt Community College

William W. Ziegler
J. Sargeant Reynolds Community College

Alvin Starr
Community College of Baltimore

I would particularly like to thank the following colleagues at Johnson County Community College who have helped me enormously by reviewing and class-testing chapters, and by giving many thoughtful answers to what must have seemed at times an endless stream of irritating questions:

Jay Antle

Monica Hogan

Andrea Broomfield

Pat Jonason

Mark Browning

Bill Lamb

David Davis

Mary Pat McQueeney

Kami Day

Ellen Mohr

Maureen Fitzpatrick

Paul Northam

Mary Grace Foret

Judy Oden

Keith Geekie

Larry Rochelle

Sandy Calvin Hastings

Marilyn Senter

Finally, I want to thank those friends and family members who have patiently put up with my many excuses over the past three years, who, though they may have grown tired of hearing "I'll be able to do that in a month or so . . . ," have had the good grace, if not good sense, still to include me in their lives. To my wife, Beth Johnson, and my daughter, Lauren, who bring me a great deal of joy every day, I want to say, "I love you. The computer is now off."

Bob Brannan

Walkthrough

Guided Tour

Welcome! The following pages illustrate how this book works. Spending a few minutes getting to know the features of the text will help you get the most out of *A Writer's Workshop*.

Chapter openers list key concepts and provide a chapter outline.

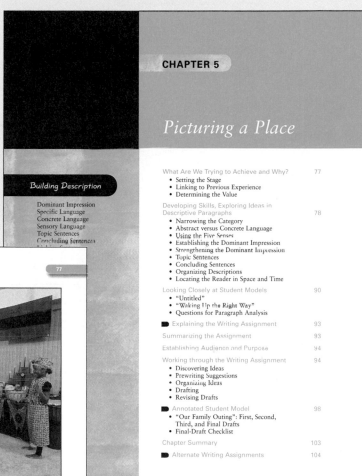

CHAPTER 5

Picturing a Place

Building Description

Dominant Impression
Specific Language
Concrete Language
Sensory Language
Topic Sentences
Concluding Sentences

CHAPTER 5 PICTURING A PLACE 77

▶ WHAT ARE WE TRYING TO ACHIEVE AND WHY?

Setting the Stage

Take a moment to look closely at the picture that begins this chapter. What do you notice about it? A family is celebrating Kwanza, smiling happily, standing and sitting close together as they focus their attention on the young girl, who has perhaps just performed for them. What feeling comes to you as you observe the family? If you had to find one or two words to sum up this picture, what do suppose they would be? If you said something like happiness or comfort or family togetherness, you have just identified a **dominant impression** and gotten to the heart of this chapter on description.

Describing is the process of relating details to help another person see what we have seen. It is the act of painting a picture with words. But more than just allowing a reader to *see* a scene, we can use the other senses (hearing, touch, taste, and smell) to involve the audience more completely. When we tell about and listen to subjective descriptions, we enrich our lives, communicating personal experiences and extending the boundaries of what we can know through our senses alone.

In this chapter we will learn about describing in general and of describing a place in particular.

Linking to Previous Experience

What kinds of describing have you done in the past—how about vacations? Maybe you have gone skiing. What did the mountains look like? How much snow fell while you were there; was there a deep base? What were the temperatures? How crowded were the lift lines? If you have not been on a vacation for awhile, when was the last time you tried to describe a scene or character closer to home? Talking to a friend,

The **assignment chapters** in Units Two and Three guide you step-by-step through the work of writing. **Setting the Stage** uses photos as visual texts that introduce the chapter's topic.

Journal Entries help you think through each step in the writing process on the way to completing each assignment.

Determining the Value

Aside from helping us get through our daily lives more easily, the ability to describe has other benefits. The act of carefully selecting words to create images will make us better readers and improve our writing on the job, at home, and in school. But perhaps the most value in learning to describe well is that it will encourage you to observe more closely. By the time you have worked through the activities in this chapter, analyzed the student model paragraphs, taken notes for your own description, and finally workshopped your own and other students' drafts, you will find yourself noticing more of the world around you—and seeing it more clearly.

JOURNAL ENTRY 5-1

List at least one example of describing that you have done recently, either orally or in writing, from school, work, and home and recreate one description for your instructor. What value do you see in being able to describe well?

DEVELOPING SKILLS, EXPLORING IDEAS IN DESCRIPTIVE PARAGRAPHS

As we work together through the following eleven activities, we will practice and come to understand the important composition concepts discussed in C___ 3, ultimately using the skills we learn in our own place descriptions.

Can there be *too much of a good thing?*

Note: The point of using sensory details is not to cram as many into a paper as possible, or even to represent all the senses, but rather to use these details selectively wherever they can enhance an image.

Collaborative

Activity 5-4: Using the Five Senses

Get together in groups of four or five and brainstorm sensory details for one of the following places. Be particularly alert to any details that might help illustrate a central focus or dominant impression/feeling. Also don't be surprised if you come up with more under sight and sound than any other.

Answers will vary.

1. **Cafeteria** at lunch hour (dominant impression = activity/fast pace, maybe even confusion or chaos!)

2. **Church wedding** (dominant impression = excitement/happiness, maybe even communal spirit of love)

3. **Zoo** (dominant impression = *either* depression/confinement, maybe even animals in misery *or* relaxation, maybe even contentment, animals happy to have a life so easy—try for one of these, remembering that, as always in focused description, you *choose* the details that you want your reader to see)

4. **Summer camp** (dominant impression = happy confusion/expectation/fun)

Activities—some designed for group work—give you a chance to practice the skills you'll need to complete each assignment.

Untitled

The most peaceful activity I know of on a clear, dry night is relaxing around an open campfire. There is an ideal spot just north of the pond on my grandparents' land. As the brilliant yellow moon shines down, reflecting off the pond, little waves ripple across the surface. Gazing at the sky, I can see millions of sparkling stars and, from time to time, even view a falling star. The blazing embers leave a smoke trail rising upward from the fire. Through the darkness, I can see the shadows of the trees, silhouettes of the horses, and swooping bats. The sounds of the night surround me: the murmur of voices in the distance, leaves rustling, and branches brushing against each other. From the nearby pond and surrounding trees, I can hear the unique chorus of the tree frogs and bullfrogs. As the train whistles by, the cries of howling coyotes drift on the wind. From time to time, I can even hear the lonesome hooting of an owl. When the popping and crackling of the fire dies down, the embers are ready for cooking. The hotdogs sizzle as they begin to cook and drip their juices off the end of the stick. Refreshing aromas of trimmings from the apple and pear trees add sweetness to the oak branches as they burn. Nearby, the smell of the horses is carried in the breeze. While fire heats the hotdogs, I can smell the meat cooking. The hot, white melting marshmallows fresh from the fire stick to my fingers. After eating and being contentedly full from the hotdogs and sticky chocolate/nut smores, I have time for solitude. While the chilly breeze blows, the radiating warmth of the fire draws me in. This is my favorite time around the campfire—a truly peaceful time in which I feel a sense of oneness with nature as she embraces me.

Andrea Turner

Student Models—three to four in each chapter—give you ideas of how others have approached an assignment; the **Annotated Student Models** show a student's progress through three drafts.

___st rough drafts of illustration papers often have difficulties with overall ___, development, and relevant material. Note how much explanation and how ___ more examples were added to this draft to help clarify meaning. As you ___ through your own draft, keep asking the question "What do I mean by that ___atement, example, or idea?" Also be alert to the overall structure of topic, ___pic, and concluding sentences. Help your reader find her way through your ___ with the least possible effort. She will appreciate your efforts.

___ult students with spouses and children have a difficult time balancing ___l with the rest of there lives.

___ey don't have much time for a social life, but everyone needs some relax-___. Even struggling with classes, most students want to see an occasional ___e with a friend, catch a ball game, or have diner out. *When students take ___ for rest & relaxation, they are looking over their shoulder at the clock.

Subtopic sentence revised	But socializing is often the least of the distractions for returning students. They constantly face the money battle. With families to care for the students have to worry about rent and mortgage payments, utilities, car payments, car repair bills, general property maintenance, food, clothing, medical, insurance of various kinds, school (their own included), and even squeezing in a few presents for their loved ones occasionally. *The stress of dealing with the money drain sometimes makes focusing on textbooks difficult.	Second-level examples added / *Explanation added

| Subtopic sentence revised | In order to meet the financial demands, of course, most nontraditional students are full-time workers as well. Often both husbands and wives financially support the family. Though sometimes only one brings in a paycheck while the other works at home. Spending forty hours a week, and more outside the home selling insurance, repairing cars, waiting tables; or spending the same amount of time inside the home cleaning house, fixing meals, and chasing children around—*nontraditional students often have a kind of frazzled look around the edges. | Second-level examples added / *Explanation added |
| Subtopic sentence revised—to show *most important problem* | But the other stresses and distractions aside, for nontraditional students coming back to school, the family might be the biggest obstacle. Most mothers and fathers love there children and each other. But the daily drag of diapering, feeding, carting to school, and soothing fears and hurt feelings can drag a person | Second-level examples added |

Topic Lists and **Alternate Writing Assignments** offer you a chance to write about everyday issues that are important to you, including dating, work, family life, politics, and entertainment.

Discovering Ideas

Assuming that your instructor is not simply assigning you a particular place to write about (i.e., "Let's all describe our bathrooms"), your choice of topics is virtually limitless. The good news is that you can select a place that you know well and have a real interest in. The bad news is that lots of freedom can be paralyzing. It is all too easy when faced with almost every possibility "out there" to feel overwhelmed and either put off choosing a place till too late or settle on the first choice that comes to mind, whether you have a real interest in it or not. Because you will be working on this project for several weeks, why not take the time to select a topic that you care about enough to invest some energy in? (Learning to become involved in a writing project is a trick of the writer's trade that will help you have a lot more fun with your writing and will usually produce better work.)

The following topic lists may help get you off to a good start:

Writer's Tip: Try to get involved with your project.

Choose several possible places before you fix on one.

Topic Lists

Places to Describe Inside

1. Any room in your house	15. Riverboat	29. Bus depot
2. Attic	16. Dance studio	30. Airport
3. Tool shed	17. Church/synagogue	31. Subway station
4. Restaurant	18. Pet store	32. Train station
5. Tavern	19. Pawn shop	33. Boxing arena
6. Department store	20. Music store	34. Doctor's office
7. Museum	21. Hospital	35. Police station
8. Gym	22. Movie theater	36. Grocery store
9. Bowling alley	23. Art gallery	37. Florist's
10. Arcade	24. Recording studio	38. Furniture store
11. Library	25. Beauty salon	39. Tire warehouse
12. Cafeteria	26. School (any level)	40. Recycling center
13. Office	27. Day care	41. Funeral home
14. Hardware store	28. Foundry	42. Cemetery

---

104   UNIT TWO   WORKING WITH THE PARAGRAPH

■ ALTERNATE WRITING ASSIGNMENTS

While the focus of this chapter has been on illustrating a place, there are many other uses for description. As you consider the following assignment options, keep these points in mind:

- Decide on a dominant impression.
- State the dominant impression in your topic sentence.
- Rely on specific words and sensory details to develop your dominant impression.
- Conclude with a sentence that links to the topic sentence and expands the thought.
- Connect your sentences with time and place words.

1. **Describe a person:** Find someone you know reasonably well or someone you come in contact with regularly enough to observe her appearance (physical look and clothing) and actions (how she walks, stands, and sits; body language; mannerisms). Listen closely to the person and try to record some characteristic dialogue. Your goal is to create a verbal portrait of this person so that someone who has not met your person would recognize her from your description. Focus your description with an overall dominant impression, such as sloppy, well groomed, athletic, lazy, talkative, shy, funny, angry, and so on.

2. **Describe an object:** Select an object that you can observe closely and take notes on. This object could range from the small and ordinary (salt shaker, toaster oven, wrench) to the large and more unusual (construction crane, new Corvette, office building). Your goal is to capture the dominant impression of the object through description. For instance, your salt shaker might be exceptionally functional. You could describe its look as well as how well the shaker performs its job, dispensing salt. The construction crane might suggest power. You could describe the large metal parts and then show the machine in action.

UNIT SIX

Additional Readings

Unit Six, Additional Readings, offers fourteen texts by professional writers illustrating various writing strategies and followed by questions for discussion and writing.

of its arms as ferociously as a charging cat. It leaps savagely on the crab, there is a puff of black fluid, and the struggling mass is obscured in the sepia cloud while the octopus murders the crab. On the exposed rocks out of water, the barnacles bubble behind their closed doors and the limpets dry out. And down to the rocks come the black flies to eat anything they can find. The sharp smell of iodine from the algae, and the lime smell of calcareous bodies and the smell of powerful protean, smell of sperm and ova fill the air. On the exposed rocks the starfish emit semen and eggs from between their rays. The smells of life and richness, of death and digestion, of decay and birth, burden the air. And salt spray blows in from the barrier where the ocean waits for its rising-tide strength to permit it back into the Great Tide Pool again. And on the reef the whistling buoy bellows like a sad and patient bull.

Questions for Analysis

1. What is the dominant impression of these two paragraphs? Does the author state it in a topic sentence, if so where?

2. Name five specific words. How do these words contribute to the description?

3. Choose any image that seems clear to you and tell how the details and explanation make the image appealing.

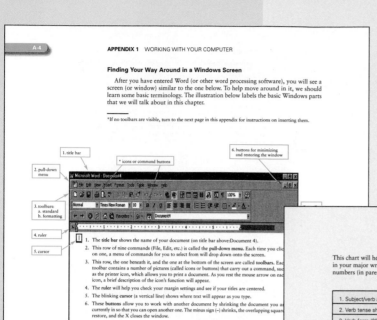

Appendix 1, Working with Your Computer, is an illustrated overview of word processing procedures—a practical user's manual—to help you with nuts-and-bolts questions: "How do I double space, insert page numbers, spell check, count words . . . ?"

IMPROVEMENT CHART

Name: _____

This chart will help you track and correct errors in your major writing assignments. Chapter numbers (in parentheses) follow each error.

	1	2	3	4	5	6	7	8	Spelling	Sound-alike
1. Subject/verb agreement (23)										
2. Verb tense shift (23)										
3. Verb form (23)										
4. Pronoun agreement (24)										
5. Pronoun shift (24)										
6. Pronoun case (24)										
7. Pronoun reference (24)										
8. Parallelism (21)										
9. Misplaced and dangling modifier (25)										
10. Adverb form (25)										
11. Run-on sentence (22)										
12. Comma splice (22)										
13. Sentence fragment (22)										
14. Unneeded comma (26)										
15. Comma to introduce (26)										
16. Comma to enclose/end (26)										
17. Comma to divide (26)										
18. Comma with a series (26)										
19. Comma with coordinate adjective (26)										
20. Comma for contrast (26)										
21. Comma with numbers, dates, addresses, place names, direct address (26)										
22. Semicolon (26)										
23. Quotation marks (26)										
24. Apostrophe (26)										
25. Capitalization (26)										
26. Hyphen (26)										
27. Spelling (27)										
28. Sound-alike (27)										
29. Wrong word (19)										
30. Missing word (1)										

Appendix 2 offers an **Improvement Chart** where you can record your progress across the semester.

These features will serve as familiar guideposts as you make your way through the book. The structure they create will help you in understanding the book's content, even as the activities and exercises assist you in learning and remembering the material.

We hope that your experience using this first edition of *A Writer's Workshop* will be entirely successful.

Trust us—it works.

BRIEF CONTENTS

CONTENTS

UNIT THREE
Working with the Essay   259

Chapter 12
Introducing the Essay   260

Chapter 13
Revising Essays   294

Chapter 14
Expanding Paragraphs into Essays   306

Chapter 15
Defining Terms, Clarifying Ideas—Combining Patterns of Development 334

A Writer's Workshop

Crafting Paragraphs, Building Essays

Getting Our Feet Wet

CHAPTER 1

Practicing the Writing Process

▶ HOW DO WE BEGIN TO WRITE?

The first step in beginning to write is to think of ourselves as writers—not necessarily easy to do. Depending on past experiences, we have often already labeled ourselves as OK, not so hot, or downright terrible. Many of us view the act of writing as mysterious and the successful writer as someone who has lucked into a wonderful talent. But most people who write are not geniuses. Just like you, accomplished writers have to work hard at their craft. They often begin in confusion, uncertain and anxious about where the ideas will come from, produce some genuinely bad writing in their experimental drafts, and agonize over the final shape of their words—and what others will think of the work.

Whatever your past experiences with writing, you share in the common experience of everyone who seeks to commit words to paper. When you write, be it a brief paragraph or long essay, *you* are a writer, with all the hard work, the aggravation, and the satisfaction that comes with it.

How do writers get started? To focus your efforts even before the process of gathering, arranging, and writing out ideas begins, ask yourself the following questions:

Questions to Ask at the Start of a Writing Project

1. **What is my purpose?**

People write for many reasons, often mixing several purposes in one writing project. One purpose usually predominates. Primary reasons for communicating with one another are to entertain, to explain ideas and information, and to persuade someone

Teaching Idea
Developmental students generally need a great deal of encouragement to overcome their initial self-definition as incapable of success at writing. To dispel this false impression, we can discuss it in class.

that a particular point of view or action is the best one. There are, of course, other reasons for writing: you might, for example, write a note to yourself, a letter, or a diary entry simply to record information or work through an idea or an emotion.

2. Who is my audience?

In school many of you have had only one reader: your teacher. However, in "real-world" writing, you will be expected to communicate effectively with different readers, ranging from a fairly general audience to a very specific one. Having a clear sense of who your audience is will help you make decisions about what and how much to say.

3. What, exactly, is the project?

If you are writing for yourself, you may have a fairly clear idea of what you want to say, but writing out what you want to accomplish will still help focus your work. In class your instructor will give you an assignment guide, or you will follow the assignment instructions in the text. In any case, from the outset you should determine what the writing project calls for: purpose, audience, overall organization, length, and due dates for drafts.

4. How can I develop a real interest in the project?

Teaching Idea
It is important to establish from the outset that students must take responsibility for their own success in the course. Committing themselves to success in writing is the same as striving to do well in any other activity they prize: sports, cars, dance, music.

Perhaps the worst approach for producing good writing is to take the passive, I-don't-care, what*ever* attitude toward your topic. Sometimes you will have to write to specific boundaries, sometimes not. When you have your topic preselected, it is still worthwhile to find some part of the topic that appeals to you. When you can choose from a wider variety of topics or select your own, take the time to find one that truly interests you, rather than going for the first or seemingly easiest topic. If you can develop a commitment to the project, you will find that the long road toward the final paper can be enjoyable and ultimately fulfilling, beyond a mere grade.

Good writing is not easily accomplished; it takes time. Along the way it will help you to develop a clear overview of the project and then to use all the tools for writing success to your advantage. In class you can develop the habits of listening carefully, asking questions, and taking notes, especially when your instructor writes the information on the chalkboard or uses the overhead projector. When handouts are offered, take them home and study or complete them. During class activities and discussion, participate as fully as possible: this kind of behavior will help you understand every writing assignment. Your instructor will often give the class supplemental instructions to help clarify the writing assignments in the text, and, of course, you should read the textbook student models that demonstrate what kind of paper to shoot for.

▶ AFTER BREAKING GROUND—INTO THE WRITING PROCESS

Teaching Idea
Rather than prescribing *the* writing process, we can talk of many writing processes and try to help students improve on the habits they bring to class.

We all have written paragraphs and essays in the past, and we all have gone through several steps to produce that work, so it is safe to say that we all have *a* writing process. For some of us the process has worked well, for others . . . not so well. The rest of this chapter explains a more formal version of the writing process that many of us already unconsciously practice, at least in part. However, this writing process varies with each individual, and you should freely adapt it to what works best for you.

▶ STEPS IN THE WRITING PROCESS

Gathering ideas, shaping them, and getting the words on paper are parts of a natural sequence for most of us, but writers seldom move through them like a train fixed on a track, beginning at one end and progressing to the final station. You will often find yourself brainstorming for ideas in the middle of your paper, editing a sentence as you notice an error, and sometimes substantially reorganizing when you thought the work was nearly complete. Formalized steps are meant as a helpful guide, and you will probably find yourself comfortably using many of them by the end of the term.

The Writing Process

1. Discovering ideas

2. Organizing ideas

3. Drafting

4. Revising

5. Editing

6. Proofreading

Discovering Ideas

How many times have you been faced with a writing project and found your mind blank, with nothing to say? It is a common, frustrating occurrence. Instead of taking your frustration out on the keyboard (which can hurt your hand, and quickly become expensive) or simply giving up, you can try one or several of the following methods for discovering ideas.

Freewriting

If you have never heard the term *freewriting* (rapid, uncensored writing) before, you still may have practiced it as a quick rough draft. The primary value in fast drafting or freewriting is that we are moving forward and getting ideas on paper, some of which may be usable. The danger in freewriting is mistaking what we have produced for a solid first draft—or even a final draft!

If you have no idea about what to write, you can freewrite to uncover a few usable ideas. If you already have a topic in hand, then you can try **focused freewriting.** In either case you will want to set aside a designated time, say five to ten minutes, and write nonstop, without censoring your ideas or worrying about grammar, spelling, and punctuation. If you run out of thoughts, still try to keep your pencil or keyboard active. It is not uncommon in a freewrite to produce sentences like the following:

> *Well I don't know what to say at this point and I think this freewritng stuff isnt going anywhere fast. Whose idea was it for me to try this king of writing anyway. May be Ill humor the teacher and keep it going for a few more minutes. Geez I just looked at the clock and I've got seven motre minutes to write!*

The point is to keep producing words, even when it might seem there is no hope of getting anywhere. Although no one has been able to adequately explain it yet, just the act of writing triggers more words and then, often, usable ideas. The following example is a brief **focused freewrite:**

> *I get to chose from a list of places or come up with my own place. I don't k ow what the best way is. Maybe I'll try some of the outside places on the list I like the outdoors fishing. hnting. hiking in themountains. I like being around the trees and plants. I seem to have always liked being outside ever since I was a little kid. How about that trrehouse my brother and I built when we were how old? About 11 and 13. Eric was pretty good at figuring out how to get the main platform built and braced into the trees. He was always better at building stuff than I was but we worked preety ell on that job. Let's*

Teaching Idea
To help students overcome resistance to prewriting methods like freewriting, try some in class, writing and sharing your efforts with students.

Caution: Freewriting is not a draft!

No ideas at all? Try freewriting.

Focused freewrites can help after you have some direction.

see I'm supposed to be comeing up with a descriptionof something. May be the treehouse could work. I wonder if it's still there? I could drive back into the oldneighborhood and look I guess. How many trees, 3. We had to nail on to those big old catalpa trees in our backyard in South Bend. Dad would only let us put it up about ten-twelve feet from the ground. No way to get up high into those huge branches. . . .

In this freewrite, the author discovers several potential ideas for a descriptive paper—the backyard itself, the tree house, or the author's former house might make interesting subjects to explore further.

Activity 1-1: Focused Freewrite

Select a topic from the following list and write nonstop on it for five minutes. Remember not to worry about grammar, spelling, or punctuation, and don't be concerned if the ideas get tangled.

Teaching Idea
The prewriting methods in Chapter 1 are slanted toward description, a common jumping off place for developmental writing courses. You might want to combine some of the chapter activities with Chapter 5, "Picturing a Place."

airport	football field	restaurant
attic	gym	swimming pool
beach	interstate	wharf
cafeteria	kitchen	woods
car wash	library	zoo

Clustering

Clustering is another good prewriting technique. This method asks you to write a single word or phrase in the center of a piece of paper and then to write down around it any word or phrase that the center word brings to mind. After you have one or several words connected to the original word, try to connect additional words to the second set. Keep extending your network of connected words until you find a grouping that seems of interest. Consider the following cluster aimed at finding a place to describe:

General cluster

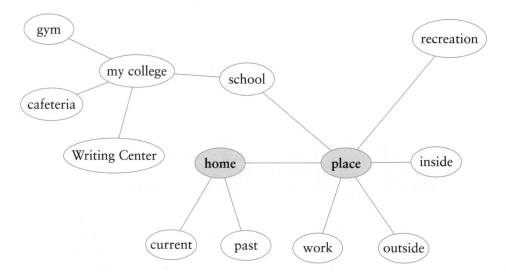

If the author wanted to select the home cluster to begin a more **focused cluster,** the next step might look like this:

Focused cluster

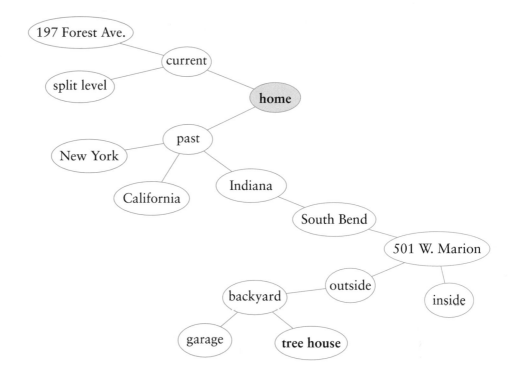

Now the author has arrived at the tree house as a possible topic for his description paragraph. He might choose to cluster again for specific details, or he might decide to try another method for generating ideas, like brainstorming or listing.

Activity 1 2: Focused Clustering

Select a topic from the list in Activity 1-1 (or continue with the one you have already chosen) and create a focused cluster like the one above. Work for five minutes, trying to fill a page with word associations.

Brainstorming (Listing)

In brainstorming, either by yourself or with others, you list in a word or phrase every idea that occurs to you when you think about the general topic at hand. If we extended the tree house topic from our clustering activity, we might end up with this sort of list:

Teaching Idea
Students who resist formal outlines often see the value in brainstorming to create a loose list. If we don't scare students with the Roman numerals, we can often help them into an outline by condensing and arranging ideas on the board.

Tree House

General brainstorming list

mine and my brother's	*dad got the shingles*
no one else allowed	*climbing the rope*
sturdy	*sleeping outside*
good in rain	*water balloon fights*
our gang	*creaking in the wind*

If we **focused** the list, we could concentrate primarily on the specific words and sensory details that make for good description (for more on description, see Chapter 5):

Tree House

Specific words	**Sensory details**
10–12 feet off the ground	*Sight—colors: red shingles, gray boards,*
three catalpa trees	*green leaves*
backyard	*Sound: boards creaking, wind in the branches,*
by redbrick patio	*cars passing in the alley, mower,*
rope to climb—no stairs or ladder	*boys laughing and shouting*
rope to swing from	*Touch: rough feel of bark, splinters,*
red shingles	*rope in my hands, heat and humidity*
white pine walls	*Smell: fumes from the cars passing,*
painted slate gray	*cut grass, clean air after rain*
	Taste: baloney sandwiches on white bread
	with mustard, potato chips

Often after you have created a list that is somewhat focused, you will find your-self with a rough or scratch outline that you can then begin to work with, looking for patterns to arrange and ideas to delete or expand.

Activity 1-3: Brainstorming (listing)

Choose a new topic from the list in Activity 1-1 (or use the topic you have already chosen) and create a list of descriptive phrases that apply to your topic. Try to include words that help you visualize the place and any other words that suggest sound, touch, taste, or smell.

Journalist's Questions

After you have a fairly clear idea of your writing topic, you can ask yourself the classic journalist's questions *who, what, when, where,* and *why.* You should also add *how* and *what was the result.* To continue with our tree house example:

Who: *my older brother Eric, me, and our "gang"*
What: *our tree house, building it and playing in it*
When: *summer of 1979*
Where: *South Bend, Indiana, backyard of our house*
Why: *for a place of our own and besides tree houses are just fun*
How: *built it mostly by ourselves with some help from dad*
What was the result: *closer feeling between Eric and me and good times*

Activity 1-4: Journalist's Questions

Select a topic from the list in Activity 1-1 (or continue with the one you have been working with) and create a list of answers to the questions above.

Patterns of Development

Another way to generate material for your paper is to turn the patterns of develop-ment into questions and then apply them to your topic.

Teaching Idea
Using the patterns of development as a prewriting method is a good way to painlessly introduce students to a core element in the course.

Narration: telling a brief story to make a point

What kind of story could I tell to show someone the tree house?

Description: using vivid details to paint a picture

What details do I remember that could help show someone the tree house?

Illustration: giving examples to illustrate some point

What examples could I give to show the tree house?

Comparison/contrast: showing how your subject is like and unlike similar subjects

What could I compare or contrast the tree house to that my reader would know?

Classification/division: putting your subject into a group, separating it from others like it

What group does the tree house fit into? What other related group is the tree house different from?

Cause/effect: telling what actions can affect your subject, what effects can flow from it

How did the tree house come about? What were its effects on me?

Process analysis: telling how your subject works

How did the tree house work? What were regular activities I did there?

Definition: telling the essential characteristics of your subject

What makes the tree house unique?

Persuasion: trying to move someone to agreement with you or to some action

How could I persuade someone of the value a tree house can have for a child?

Activity 1-5: Patterns of Development

Select a topic from the list in Activity 1-1 (or continue with the one you have been working with) and create a list of questions like the ones above. Next, answer each question in a sentence or two.

Journal Entries

Keeping a journal in which you write for a few minutes every day can be a good general source of ideas. If you decide to keep a personal journal, or your instructor assigns one, you can benefit by additional daily writing, getting valuable practice in organizing and expressing your thoughts and perhaps gaining some insights into yourself and the world around you.

However, the journal entries in *A Writer's Workshop* are aimed at helping you complete major writing assignments, paragraphs or essays. If you answer them carefully and thoughtfully, these entries will help you discover, focus, organize, and develop ideas for writing. As you respond to the entries, remember that your ideas are what count: although it is never a bad idea to spend some time editing your writing (even journals), grammar, spelling, and punctuation should be a low priority.

Teaching Idea
The journal entries in *AWW* are most useful to students and instructors if the entries are checked frequently. They can help teachers stay in touch with students' progress on their major writing assignments.

Keeping a writer's journal

Considering Your Audience

While we sometimes write only for ourselves, we frequently write for others. These "others" may be a relatively general audience (though not the entire planet—not everyone on earth is interested in a particular piece of writing), or they may be quite

Let your audience help focus your material.

specific. And we may be directing our work toward several kinds of readers, often a more specific group within a larger secondary audience. When you consider a subject to write about, you will usually find that knowing who you are writing to will help you *generate* and *select* interesting ideas.

If you were describing an action/adventure film like *Armageddon* to two friends, one who is a sci-fi fan and the other who prefers more serious, "literary" films, which of the two following paragraphs would you be more likely to match with your friends' interests?

1. This movie makes you think an asteroid is really going to slam into earth. The opening special effects are great! Blazing chunks of rock rain down on New York City, exploding cars, tearing craters in the streets, punching holes through sky scrapers, and throwing people all over the place. The action is nonstop. From the meteorite bombardment, to Bruce Willis finding his daughter in bed with one of his oil drillers and then chasing after him with a shotgun, through the astronaut training and mission to blow up the asteroid—you can't even get up to hit the restroom, or you'll miss too much.

2. There's plenty of action in the film, but not all of it is explosions. The relationships really make the movie interesting. Bruce Willis plays a loving father who is having difficulty communicating with his daughter and accepting that she has become a woman. To complicate matters, she is in love with one of Willis's employees, who returns her love, and their relationship adds tension to the film. The audience is not sure how Willis will ultimately react to the young man. As the film progresses, several characters must make difficult personal decisions, ultimately testing their loyalty, courage, and sense of self-sacrifice.

Clearly, the first version tries to capture the attention of the action fan whereas the second goes for the friend who favors more serious films.

Writers must constantly create and then select material based on what they think would interest their readers. Although much writing appeals to a fairly large "general" audience, even within that group you can discover similarities and differences that will help you write in a way that captures the reader's attention. Notice some of these possible defining characteristics of potential readers:

What are they like— your audience?

Describing Your Audience

age	hobbies	prejudices
city	level of intelligence	race
country	needs	region
education	neighborhood	religion
ethnicity	occupation	social groups
gender	particular knowledge of a subject	special interests
general knowledge	personality	sports
goals	political affiliation	wants

Human beings are a diverse group. If you can develop a real sense for your audience, you are much more likely to write in an engaging way—and come closer to enjoying the process of the writing.

Teaching Idea
To help students with the concept of audience, you might want to work through Activity 1-6 in class or simply generate a discussion about a current popular film. Why do some students like it? What parts of the film interest them, and which don't—why? What could (or did) an advertisement say about the film to persuade them to see the movie? What would they say about the film to persuade a friend to see it?

Help focus your paper with a central point.

Teaching Idea
Some instructors object to the term *opinion* used in a topic or thesis sentence; others approve. We might say *opinion, attitude,* or *feeling*—any statement that will limit the topic sufficiently.

Activity 1-6: Considering Your Audience

Assume that you have rented the film *The Wizard of Oz* for the evening, and you are trying to persuade two friends to join you. One friend doesn't mind children's stories but thinks a sixty-year-old movie would be boring. The other friend doesn't much like children's stories but does like horror and supernatural films. List three points you could make or examples you might choose to help convince your friends to watch the movie with you. (If you have not seen *The Wizard of Oz*, choose any film you have enjoyed, list two friends who might not like it for different reasons, and then list three examples/points that would help persuade each person.)

ORGANIZING IDEAS

If you have tried prewriting, you should now have some ideas for your paper. Before moving ahead, though, you must decide on a central point—a **rough topic sentence** for a paragraph or a **working thesis sentence** for an essay—in the form of the topic plus a statement that expresses an opinion, attitude, or feeling about it. For instance, in our tree house description the author might want to focus on adventure, in which case many of the examples and details he chooses would point toward the fun and excitement he had: "My brother and I had a world of good times in our backyard tree house."

Now you could just plunge into the draft, writing furiously and hoping for the best. Sometimes this approach works well, especially if the material falls into a natural order or if you are fortunate enough to have "a feel" for the best method of organizing the writing. But often we are not sure how to handle all the words sitting in front of us. This is the time to reconsider your purpose (to entertain, explain, or persuade), review the assignment instructions for suggestions, and try some informal or formal **outlining**.

If we chose to describe a place, we might use a spatial method of organizing material (moving from one side to another, inside to outside, top to bottom) and then create a rough or "scratch" outline. Look again at the brainstorming we did for the tree house example:

Tree House

I. Specific words	**II. Sensory details**
10–12 feet off the ground	*Sight–colors: red shingles, gray boards,*
three catalpa trees	*green leaves*
backyard	*Sound: boards creaking, wind in the branches,*
by redbrick patio	*cars passing in the alley, mower,*
rope to climb–no stairs or ladder	*boys laughing and shouting*
rope to swing from	*Touch: rough feel of bark, splinters,*
red shingles	*rope in my hands, heat and humidity*
white pine walls	*Smell: fumes from the cars passing,*
painted slate gray	*cut grass, clean air after rain*
	Taste: baloney sandwiches on white bread
	with mustard, potato chips

The author might choose to arrange the material in a description of the tree and the tree house from bottom to top:

Rough Outlines

1. *by redbrick patio (base of tree)*

2. *three catalpa trees (focus on lower trunks)*

3. *rope to climb*

4. *10-12 feet from ground (bottom of tree house)*

5. *white pine walls*

6. *red shingles (on roof)*

7. *rope to swing from (tied over the tree house)*

Once this structure is established, additional details (for example, were there windows?) and some or all of the sensory details (the chalky smell of the brick, the rough feel of the bark, the deep yellow of the rope) from the other list can be integrated.

Creating a "scratch" outline by arranging descriptive details of the tree house, moving from the bottom of the tree to the top of the house

Activity 1-7: Rough Outlines

Look back at your list from Activity 1–3 and rearrange the examples/details, moving from one side of your place to another, inside to outside, top to bottom, or front to back.

Formal Outlines

More formal outlines are particularly useful for longer writing projects, and when you move into essay writing, you might try one. Below notice the pattern of a formal outline:

Thesis Statement (Controlling Idea of Essay)

Formal outline for an essay

I. First topic sentence (first main supporting idea)   } paragraph one
   A. First supporting example
      1. First specific supporting detail
      2. Second specific supporting detail
         a. Additional supporting detail
         b. Additional supporting detail
   B. Second supporting example
II. Second topic sentence (second main supporting idea)   } paragraph two

This pattern continues for the length of the essay. (To see a detailed informal essay outline, turn to p. 282.)

▶ DRAFTING

Preparing a Workspace and Moving Ahead

With your material in hand and the overall shape of your paper determined, you can confidently begin the *first* draft (remember that more drafts will come).

However, before jumping into the writing, take a moment to prepare your surroundings. If you feel comfortable working in the middle of noise and activity, great, but many people do not compose well in this situation. If you are a person who needs quiet for concentration, find a place that will give you this (admittedly, difficult sometimes). Try to set aside ample time to complete whatever writing goal you have determined. Perhaps thirty minutes is enough; perhaps several hours is more like it. Take a few minutes to decide what you need to be comfortable while you write: soft (loud?) music, a window, a glass of juice, food, a relaxing chair? Are you more productive

Create a comfortable writing space.

Teaching Idea
If students do not have home computers or are not comfortable composing on them, you might remind them of your college's computer facilities and encourage them to try drafting on a computer. *We* know how helpful computers can be for drafting. (Remind students of Appendix 1, a practical guide to using Microsoft Word.)

In drafting, keep self-criticism to a minimum.

Teaching Idea
"Bad" writing, a second cousin of freewriting, in which students deliberately misspell words, create sentence fragments, let thoughts digress or obsess, can be a positive first step for breaking out of writer's block or writer's inertia.

curled up in bed, or do you get more done in the library or a computer lab? Try to create whatever environment helps you work most efficiently.

As you begin to write, stay focused on your main idea (topic or thesis sentence), purpose, and audience. In the first draft your goal is to produce a usable paper for the upcoming revision, so try not to concern yourself too much with grammar, spelling, and punctuation (though it is common for writers to occasionally backtrack to correct minor errors as they go). Because you are trying to get ideas on paper, constantly interrupting yourself to fine-tune phrasing and sentences often breaks the rhythm of your writing. That flow of words is important in several ways, including helping ideas blend into a solid unit of thought. Start-stop writing can lead to problems in unity as too many related ideas come piling into your paragraph. However, rereading your work in progress, especially for content, can also keep you connected to each unfolding idea.

Try to keep at your work for the scheduled time (going beyond if you find the words coming easily), and resist the impulse to be negative about the draft. There will be ample time to look more critically at your writing later. If you are usually a fast writer but find your draft on this particular occasion becoming scattered, force yourself to slow down and be a bit more reflective. If, on the other hand, you typically write slowly and are not having good luck with a draft, try speeding up. Be willing to experiment with different approaches. Many people are comfortable composing at a keyboard; others prefer to draft on paper. But if you are not moving well with either medium, try switching. Finally, if you have difficulty resuming a draft after you have ended a writing session, you might try leaving an idea or even a sentence unfinished and then beginning at that point. Your former idea and sentences can help move you forward.

If you reach a place where no words are coming (writer's block), you might try one or several of the following solutions:

Breaking Out of Writer's Block

1. Return to your central point. Be sure that you have written out a working topic or thesis sentence at the top of the page, where you can reread it frequently as you compose.

2. Try any of the discovery methods listed in this chapter (clustering, listing, etc.).

3. Talk to yourself on paper. Begin a conversation about the problems you are encountering.

4. Talk to yourself out loud, or have a conversation with another person. Often just having someone else listen can help clarify a fuzzy idea or give you a new direction.

5. Read what others have written. *A Writer's Workshop* offers many models of the assignments you will be working on. See how other writers have solved the problems.

6. Try some bad writing. To get around the "perfection syndrome" that sometimes freezes us in our tracks, deliberately write the worst sentences you can think up as you move through your paper. Say to yourself, "I know this is junk writing, but that's what I'm trying for." You might be surprised at how many usable ideas and even sentences result.

7. If you are writing an essay and the introduction is a problem, just jump into the body paragraphs. If your first body paragraph is not working, move on to the next.

8. Finally, take a break. Sometimes a ten-minute trip to the kitchen is just what you need, consciously avoiding any thought about the paper. At other times you may need a day or so, thinking about the paper on occasion, to let the ideas sort themselves out.

Activity 1-8: Drafting

Following the guidelines listed under drafting above, select any of the topics you have developed so far, write a topic sentence to focus it, and then rough out a draft of 200 to 300 words. Remember not to be overly concerned with grammar, spelling, or punctuation at this point in the process.

▶ REVISING

> Revision =
> adding, cutting, and
> rearranging material.

If giving yourself a break was the operating principle during the first rough draft, now we need to adopt a different attitude. The process of revision requires a critical (as opposed to negative) frame of mind, a willingness to look closely at what we have written, knowing that it can be improved. As you move through your draft, by yourself and with others, you will be looking to add, shift, and delete material.

Nothing about revision is easy; in fact it may be the hardest part of the whole writing process. It requires practice in learning what to look for, insight into the meaning you are trying to communicate, and the ability to let go of hard-earned words. Sometimes it even calls for you to throw out much or all of that first rough draft and start over. But if you are truly interested in seeing your writing improve, you will join all the professional writers who may gripe and groan and mutter under their breath about how miserable they are as they revise their work, but who do so religiously until they shape a product they can be proud of.

> Try putting your
> reactions to your
> draft on paper.

If you are determined to improve your writing, you can. After you have given the draft some time to "cool off" (try for at least a day), remind yourself again of your purpose and audience, and look closely at your topic or thesis sentence. Taken as a whole, does your paper feel like it grows from your main point? Take a moment to jot down any reactions you have, positive as well as negative, and then begin to reread the draft, following this list of priorities:

Revision Priority List

1. **Material:** The content of your work is the most important feature. First check your ideas for clarity: Can you and other readers understand your point? Next, be sure you have enough examples and details to convey your meaning and satisfy the reader's curiosity. Finally, check for unneeded material. Any point, example, or detail that is unnecessarily repetitive or distracting from the central idea should be cut.

2. **Organization:** Your topic or thesis sentence is crucial to helping your paper stay on track. Check to see if the working sentence you previously wrote will hold the paper together. Next, review the overall organizational pattern. If, for instance, you have chosen a spatial arrangement, be as consistent with ordering your details as possible. Look closely at the way sentences and paragraphs flow together. If transitions or other connectors are needed, put them in place. Finally, check your ending. Does it link to the main point of your paper, and does it leave the reader with something to reflect on?

3. **Style:** The words you choose and how you arrange them in sentences can make your writing easy or difficult to read. As you reread your draft, be alert to words that are not working well. Is your meaning fuzzy? Do you repeat words unnecessarily? When you look closely at your sentences, check for sentence variety in length, type, and beginnings. Finally, tighten sentences, eliminating words that serve no purpose.

4. **Mechanics:** The last element to check in your paper is mechanics (grammar, spelling, and punctuation). When you move into more polished drafts, you will edit out important errors that keep you from communicating clearly.

As you become more comfortable with and practiced at revising, you will be able to move more quickly through your papers and be able to handle several categories of revision at once. But until you have built up some experience, don't rush it. Move methodically and limit what you expect your eyes to find.

Group Revising

But what if you have tried to revise in the past and have not had much luck? It can be especially difficult to see your own work clearly. Fortunately, yours are not the only eyes that will be on your papers. In class you will collaborate with other students as well as your instructor.

To profit most from collaborative work, you need to open yourself to constructive criticism. Although none of the students in your group is an English teacher, you don't have to be an expert to respond effectively to each others' drafts. Just letting a student author know that some idea is unclear or that a paragraph seems to be drifting can be important help.

In each assignment chapter in this book, you will find advice on discovering ideas, organizing, and drafting, and for beginning to revise. In the revision chapters of Units Two and Three, you will find thorough step-by-step suggestions for working through your drafts. For guidelines on how to respond to your own and your fellow students' papers during group revision, note the following lists.

How to Approach Group Revision

How the Writer Can Help the Reader

1. At the top of your draft in a sentence or two, write out your audience and purpose.

2. Clearly tell your reader your main point.

3. Direct the reader to any part of the paper you have *specific* concerns about. For example: "I'm not sure about my topic sentence. Does it tell you what I think is the main point?" Or: "Do you think I might have too many details of sound in the first half of the paragraph?"

4. After your paper has been read, listen carefully to the reader's responses, and then ask for clarification of any point you didn't understand.

   Remember not to let a reader overwhelm you. Be selective in the advice that you follow. Have several other readers respond to any suggestions for revision, especially if the suggestion seems to take your paper in a direction you are not comfortable in going.

How the Reader Can Help the Writer

1. Ask about the audience, purpose, and main point.

2. Read the whole draft quickly. Next, respond to what you *liked* or thought the author did well.

3. Answer any questions the author might have about the draft.

4. Reread the draft again, this time slowly, using the revision checklists in each revision chapter. Jot notes in the margins of the paper. A helpful shorthand is to draw a straight line under words, phrases, and sentences that you particularly like and a wavy line under any part that seems like it could be a problem.

Revising with others

You don't have to be an English whiz to help others revise.

Teaching Idea
It helps to meet head-on the misconception of many students that they don't know enough to help each other in group revision.

Teaching Idea
Some students will accept almost blindly any suggestion another student makes about their writing. It is important for students to learn to evaluate each other's feedback.

5. Talk to the writer. Share your reactions as honestly and openly as possible. Remember, neither one of you should expect the other to be the "teacher." Your job is just to give the best response you can as you understand the requirements of the assignment instructions.

6. Remember to role-play the designated audience as you read, and respond as you think that person or group would.

Collaborative

Activity 1-9: Revising

Get together with one or more group members and trade drafts. Using the above suggestions, help each other produce a better-developed and more clearly written draft.

 EDITING

After you have revised your paper several times for material, organization, and style, you must focus on mechanics: grammar, spelling, and punctuation. Hopefully, hearing the word *grammar* doesn't make your eyes begin to glaze over or, worse, make the sweat start trickling. The object of close editing is simply to make your writing more readable, to help a reader better understand and enjoy your interesting ideas.

Our purpose this semester is to gain control over the *majority* of the mechanical problems that plague good writing, not to eliminate every one. So don't despair. Even if you currently think that you can't figure out where all the commas and other "stuff" go, you will have learned most of what you need to know to write clearly and correctly by the end of the term.

The following are some pointers to help with effective editing:

How to Edit

1. Go *slowly*, stopping often. There are no green lights while we edit; think only yellow and red. The problem in editing is that we see whole word groups as we are *used* to seeing them, rather than how they may actually be written on the page in front of us. Our minds fill in the blanks for the missing words, registering the *there* as a *their* and creating or eliminating pauses for commas in an unpredictable fashion.

   To help with editing, try putting your finger or pencil point on each word of your printed draft. Move line by line, sentence by sentence, stopping frequently at the end of completed thoughts. If you are not sure about a possible mistake, write a question mark and continue. But don't just ignore it, hoping the question will go away. It won't. You might find it useful to cover with a sheet of paper the line after the one you are editing, to keep your eyes from jumping ahead.

2. Plan on reading through your paper many times, each time focusing on only one or two kinds of errors.

3. Begin an **Improvement Chart** after your instructor hands back your Diagnostic writing sample. The chart, which you will find in Appendix 2 in the back of this book, will list the errors most common to your papers, allowing you to track them and then learn the appropriate rule to eliminate the error. Does it make more sense to memorize all the rules in a 500-page handbook or to figure out the handful of mistakes that cause *you* the most problems?

4. Be willing to use Unit Five, (the handbook section in this text) and a supplemental handbook if your instructor requires one. As you write papers, your instructor will mark many errors, at least some of which will be pattern errors. Use your handbook to locate examples that demonstrate the error and show how to correct it.

You *can* learn to edit effectively.

Teaching Idea
Encouraging students to track their errors from paper to paper is a good teaching strategy. You might want to frame the issue as upgrading each paper by using the Improvement Chart in Appendix 2. The chart can be especially useful to remind students of their pattern errors, including homonym and spelling problems, during editing sessions.

Learn your pattern errors.

5. Finish your drafting and revising with enough lead time to have others look at your work with you: consider asking your classmates, friends, family members, writing center tutors, and composition instructor.

6. Take the time to word process your draft. Errors are generally more noticeable on a cleanly word-processed page, and you have the advantage of using spell and grammar check.

Unit Five examines problems with grammar, spelling, and punctuation in detail, but the following list will give you an overview of common errors:

Major Categories of Mechanical Errors

1. Grammar

   A. Subject/verb agreement (pp. 539–544)

   B. Verb tense shift (pp. 538–539)

   C. Correct verb form (pp. 531–538)

   D. Pronoun agreement (pp. 549–551)

   E. Pronoun shift (pp. 554–555)

   F. Pronoun case (pp. 551–552)

   G. Pronoun reference (pp. 546–549)

   H. Parallelism (pp. 514–516)

   I. Misplaced and dangling modifiers (pp. 560–562)

2. Punctuation

   A. Run-on sentences/comma splices (pp. 518–524)

   B. Sentence fragments (pp. 524–529)

   C. Unnecessary commas (pp. 573–576)

   D. Commas to introduce main clauses (pp. 565–569)

   E. Commas to enclose nonessential words or set them off at the end of main clauses (pp. 569–570)

   F. Commas to divide main clauses (pp. 570–571)

3. Word

   A. Spelling (pp. 582–586)

   B. Sound- and look-alike words (pp. 587–591)

   C. Wrong words (pp. 451–454, 464–472)

   D. Missing words (p. 71)

   E. Capitalization (pp. 578–579)

Teaching Idea
Proofreading as a final step can be a useful distinction for students to learn. A final proofreading in class on a paper due date can also help with common problems like misspelled instructor names, capitalization errors in titles, and missing words.

▶ PROOFREADING

Proofreading is the last step in the preparation of a paper. Assuming that you have closely edited your last draft and caught all the mechanical errors possible, you will print out a final copy, the one you turn in for a grade. At this point you might think the last copy is as finished as you can make it. But there are still common problems that appear in the last draft, ones that you can catch and correct—before your instructor does.

CHAPTER 2

Making the Most of Reading

Building Reading Skills

Prereading
Reading
Postreading

🔲 IS THERE A METHOD TO EFFECTIVE READING?

When we were children, struggling with the alphabet and the first few words we learned to recognize—*c-a-t, d-o-g, p-i-g*—reading was a mysterious and difficult process. But as we progressed through school, the process became comprehensible. However, as we have matured, our reading tasks have become more difficult than in the Golden Book and Marvel comic days. As adults, like those in the illustration above, we are expected to read, understand, and evaluate complex texts. When we confront large, abstract ideas in college, though, we sometimes feel like we are back in elementary school struggling with those first few words, trying hard to untangle the mysteries of language: "Is it *i* before *e* or the other way around?" To make the demanding task of college-level reading more rewarding, we can benefit from once again becoming conscious of the reading process to learn some of the *techniques* that help effective readers remember, comprehend, and evaluate ideas.

This chapter will focus on methods for reading. We will divide the process into these three stages:

Methods for Reading

1. Prereading: preparing to understand

2. Reading: processing and recording ideas

3. Postreading: retaining ideas

Teaching Idea
Helping students see reading and writing as a process with methods that can be learned will reinforce both important concepts in the course. This chapter stresses *organization* and *development* of a text, using writing process terminology.

Teaching Idea
If you teach this chapter, you can do so in conjunction with Chapter 3, helping students focus on critical points in their introduction to the paragraph. Several of the activities can be used as a quiz.

▶ PREREADING: PREPARING TO UNDERSTAND

Reading, like writing, is best understood as a process. Just as we spend time initially discovering and organizing ideas before we write our first drafts, so too should we spend some time sizing up a text before we begin reading it, especially a work heavy with information like a textbook. Here are three useful approaches:

1. **Skim** all *signposts:* titles; chapter previews and summaries; headings; subheadings; analytical questions; text boxes; and highlighted, bolded, and italicized print.

2. **Skim** *beginnings* and *endings*.

3. **Link** new information to previous knowledge.

Signposts

All textbooks use visual aids to help students focus on the points the authors are most anxious to communicate. The title itself will usually contain the main idea of the chapter. After the title you will often find chapter previews, sometimes as bulleted lists or brief summaries. Within the chapter you will notice major headings and subheadings, which form, in essence, a chapter outline. At the ends of chapter sections, you may find brief summaries or numbered lists of essential points, and often a chapter concludes with a summary or questions that help you analyze the chapter's primary ideas. Text boxes and marginal notes reiterate significant points and ask questions to help readers reflect on the material. Finally, you will notice words and passages that have been bolded, italicized, or shaded to emphasize a point. Skimming through a chapter and noting these reading aids may take a few minutes, but it is time well spent.

> Signposts create a chapter outline.

Beginnings and Endings

Chapters in textbooks are organized in much the same way as paragraphs and essays. Each chapter has a central focus (thesis), which divides into several topics. These are in turn divided into subtopics, all of which are then developed through examples, details, and explanations. Before you read the supporting material within the body of the chapter, it will pay off to read the chapter introduction (usually a paragraph or two) and concluding paragraphs or chapter summary. To gain more in-depth knowledge, you can skim some or all of the body paragraphs of the chapter, focusing on the first and last sentences of each paragraph. Just as in your own careful writing, all paragraphs should contain a unifying idea, and that idea will frequently be stated as a clear topic sentence at the beginning of the paragraph and may be reiterated as a summary sentence at the end.

Linking New to Previous Knowledge

After you have previewed a chapter, noting the signposts and perhaps skimming paragraphs for beginnings and endings, pause for a moment of reflection. What have you just read? What does it mean to you at this point? How do the larger terms and ideas about to be discussed fit into your previous experience? Because we all have led rich lives, we have a large store of experience and knowledge to draw from. When we can link new knowledge to what we already know, we can remember more efficiently. For example, in learning about the Internet, you may have initially had difficulty grasping the concept of this sort of global communication. However, after you began to relate the Internet to a vast *net* or *spider web* of telecommunication lines connecting people's computers all over the world, the World Wide Web probably made more sense. Within almost all new material, we will find something that we are familiar with to help fix the new information in our minds. If we have little actual experience with a topic, we will still have associations with it and can make useful comparisons that will help us understand and remember it.

Activity 2-1: Previewing a Chapter

In this activity we will practice prereading to see how well it can work. Turn to Chapter 3, Introducing the Paragraph. Now quickly scan the signposting devices and the beginning and ending. Remember that you are not reading the body of the text, rather sampling what the chapter is about to present in more depth. After about five minutes of skimming, return to the questions below and try to answer them without reading any further in Chapter 3. You may need to flip back to one page or another, but try to avoid in-depth reading so that you can decide for yourself whether or not prereading will be a valuable habit to develop.

1. What is the chapter focus? *Learning about body paragraphs*

2. What are three essential parts of a body paragraph? *Topic sentence, body sentences, and concluding sentence*

3. What are three ways of organizing ideas within a paragraph? *Spatial, chronological, importance*

4. What is a topic sentence? *Sentence containing the main idea of the paragraph*

5. What are the three ways of developing a paragraph? *Examples, details, explanations*

6. What does it mean when we say that a paragraph is *coherent*? *All the sentences are linked by connectors*

7. What are five ways to achieve coherence in a paragraph? *Transitions, repetition, synonyms, pronouns, reference to main idea*

8. On the basis of your prior knowledge, how would you describe the concept of *coherence* in a paragraph? What does the word *coherence* mean to you? What image or association comes to mind when you think of it? For example, the text uses the image of glue or tape. *Answers will vary. Possible responses: coherence means making sense. Images: thread stitching fabric together; nails holding two-by-fours together; rivets holding sheet metal together*

▶ READING: PROCESSING IDEAS

After we have previewed a chapter, we move into the next step of active reading where we move through the body of the text, fleshing out our initial internal outline of the material. During the reading we can expect to pause many times to think about what the author is saying, sometimes needing to back up and reread. Complicated material requires careful reading; seldom can we sprint through a college textbook. As an active reader moves through a text, consciously or unconsciously, she interacts with the book, asking questions, anticipating the author's next point, agreeing or disagreeing with the ideas, and linking the new information to her established knowledge.

Teaching Idea
Some students mistakenly believe that all effective readers can understand even difficult material quickly and retain it easily. We can help them to see that there is virtue in sometimes reading slowly.

Active reading is a deliberate, often slow process.

Active readers interact with the text.

Teaching Idea
Encouraging students to interact with an author's text is another step in moving them to interact with their own writing.

Here are three useful habits to develop as you move through any text:

1. **Anticipate** and **react** to the author's points.

2. **Visualize** what the author is explaining or detailing.

3. **Link** new ideas to previous ones.

Anticipating and Reacting

In previewing a chapter, we guess at what the body of the text will present more fully. Then as we read through the text, we can react to the more-detailed information. For example, if an author makes an arguable statement like "The Second Amendment provides for militias, not individual gun ownership," we can at least tentatively agree or disagree with it, depending on the examples and explanations that follow. In a passage where the author wanted to develop an extended comparison between school and a prison, a reader might respond to the text in ways like these:

- **Uncertainty:** "*What in the world does the writer mean by this comparison?*"

- **Guesses:** "*I wonder if he means school before college, when education is still mandatory?*"

- **Disagreement/agreement:** "*I don't see many similarities here.*"

- **Comprehension:** "*Oh, I see. He means the teachers are like prison guards.*"

Experienced readers carry on a running *internal* conversation with themselves and the text but also sometimes express themselves *aloud*.

It might help you to remember that all writing—from the Sunday comic section to a calculus textbook—comes from people, most of whom are doing their best to communicate ideas that are important to them. Authors are not always right, and they do not always make themselves clear, so readers should expect to have to puzzle out meaning on occasion. Interacting with a text is the most important habit you can develop to help you become a more effective reader.

Visualizing

Teaching Idea
Encourage class discussion about visualizing by having students continue to add details to the park picnic scene, either orally or in writing.

Another technique for becoming an active reader is to **visualize** what the author is saying. To one degree or another, we all have the ability to form images in our minds. For example, what kinds of pictures do you see in the following description of a family picnic?

- The redwood table was covered with summer picnic food just right for the park: bowls of potato salad, cold pasta, baked beans, deviled eggs, sweet pickles, and potato chips. Hot dogs sizzled on the grill alongside hamburgers, soaking up flavor from smoking mesquite chips. Mom and dad rested on the bench for a moment, sipping iced tea and gazing fondly at their three children laughing as they pushed their swings higher and higher still into the clear blue sky.

Although this brief paragraph does not include many of the details we could see if we were there or had taken an actual picture of the scene, if we work with the writer, we can start with the details provided and then fill in others that might be there, making the scene come alive. For example, does the picnic table have a tablecloth? If so, what kind and color—possibly plastic covered with a red-and-white check pattern? Maybe there are trees nearby, other families spread out on blankets in the grass, or other children climbing monkey bars and sliding down slides. Writers select details to help stimulate a reader's imagination. As active readers we then do most of the work ourselves to make the images satisfying.

Even when a writer is not directly building a description, she uses many detailed examples to illustrate points. Active readers encourage pictures to form in their minds as key words trigger images. For example, you might read a passage like the following:

- In mid-September of 1835, the *Beagle* arrived at the Galápagos Islands, a volcanic archipelago straddling the equator 600 miles west of the coast of Ecuador.

Even though several of the words may be unfamiliar, words like *island, volcanic,* and *equator* create pictures in our minds. Perhaps you visualize sandy beaches and palm trees, maybe you picture a volcano in full eruption, spewing molten lava and hot gases, possibly you see a black line circling a globe in your local library. We all form images differently, but creating vivid pictures can help us remember material— and make the reading more interesting.

Linking New to Previous Knowledge

Just as in our prereading, and similar to visualizing, connecting new ideas to previous knowledge is essential in active reading. Connecting the *Beagle*'s arrival at the Galápagos Islands to some other event of the mid-1800s you might be familiar with— say, the beginning of Queen Victoria's reign—can help you put Darwin's voyage *in context*—an important step toward understanding. Whenever you can link previous knowledge to new ideas through associations and comparisons, you help yourself understand and remember.

Activity 2-2: Developing Active Reading Habits

In this activity we will return to Chapter 3 but this time to read several sections in more depth. Turn to the page numbers listed for each of the three topics below. Read the material carefully, and then practice the three active reading habits that we have discussed: *anticipating and reacting* to the text, *visualizing* (creating a mental picture), and *linking previous knowledge* to new ideas.

Example: Turn to p. 40 to see the information on Revising Topic Sentences.

A. **Anticipate and react:** "Oh, jeez, more about topic sentences. Now I'm supposed to make the topic sentence more interesting? What if I'm not even all that interested in my topic?"

B. **Visualize:** When I think of a tool, I see hammers, saws, rakes, pliers, wrenches, drills—I just need to create a picture in my mind of my garage.

C. **Link to previous knowledge:** I see that specific words are words that fall into a "more limited category" than ones like them. This makes sense to me if I think of cars in general or my own Toyota Corolla. My Corolla is more specific than the hundreds of other kinds of cars on the road.

Answers will vary.

1. Examples and details versus explanations (pp. 41–42)

   A. Anticipate and react: _Possible response: "This writing stuff doesn't seem so hard. Give examples and then tell about them, big deal."_

   B. Visualize: _Possible response: "I can picture the little girl in the bathroom, but I wouldn't have worried about her either until I heard the explanation."_

C. Link to previous knowledge: _Possible response: "I have had to explain myself with examples many times like with the baseball example. I agree with the writer about boring games."_

2. Layering examples (p. 43)

A. Anticipate and react: _Possible response: " I can see how this 'layering' can make my sentences grow."_

B. Visualize: _Possible response: "I would rather have a three-layer cake than one layer."_

C. Link to previous knowledge: _Possible response: "This sounds like the upside down triangle we learned my sophomore year in high school."_

3. Unity (pp. 44–45)

A. Anticipate and react: _Possible response: "How am I supposed to write anything that's interesting if I have to cut every little idea that isn't related to the topic sentence?"_

B. Visualize: _Possible response: "I can picture the woman mowing the yard, and I don't think her paragraph would be unified if she started talking about how hot and sweaty she got while mowing."_

C. Link to previous knowledge: _Possible response: I've mowed my lawn enough to know what the advantages are. A disadvantage that would break the unity of the paragraph would be getting a sunburn."_

▶ READING: FOCUSING AND RECORDING MAIN IDEAS

Knowing a few organizational and developmental patterns will make your reading easier and more efficient the first time through. Also, using a *pencil* and *highlighter* will fix the material in place for review.

Here are several points to help focus your reading and methods for recording the information you have located:

1. **Look** for *thesis, topic,* and *summary sentences.*

2. **Focus** on *primary (essential) examples.*

3. **Look** for *repeated material.*

4. **Notice** the *patterns of development.*

5. **Learn** to *annotate, outline, summarize,* and *paraphrase.*

Looking for Thesis, Topic, and Summary Sentences

Thesis sentences contain the main idea of an essay; topic sentences contain the main idea of a paragraph. Both sentences state, "This is my topic, and this is what I'm going to say about it." When beginning an essay or a textbook chapter, you will usually find a thesis statement in the opening paragraphs. Within body paragraphs you will often find a topic sentence as the first or second sentence; and at the end of the paragraph, you may also find a summary sentence—used to reiterate the main idea. Look for these sentences when you preview a text, and then concentrate on those areas while you are reading. In the following paragraph from Chapter 3, the topic and summary sentences are shaded. (For more on thesis, topic, and summary sentences, see pp. 278–279.)

Developing Body Paragraphs

After a writer has established a workable topic sentence, he must next move into the heart of his paragraph, the support sentences. Depending on the writer's purpose, the audience's expectations, and the topic itself, these supporting sentences might range from several to several dozen. "Twenty-four sentences!" you might think to yourself when faced with a lengthier paragraph or essay assignment. "How in the world am I ever going to fill up all that white space?" The answer is the same way that writers have been filling up paragraphs, essays, books, and other kinds of writing since words were first pressed into wet clay. After you have declared your main point, you will illustrate it with **examples, details,** and **explanations.** These are the simple tools of the trade. And no matter how long the writing project runs, writers use the same kinds of material over and over to "fill up the space," sometimes artfully, sometimes not. During the next few pages we will take a look at exactly what solid support is: what it consists of, how much is enough, when it is relevant, and how to be sure it is clear to your reader.

Focusing on Primary (Essential) Examples

Paragraphs are built from detailed examples and explanations. However, not all of these are critical to a reader's understanding of the paragraph's main idea. Writers often use secondary examples and explaining to illustrate their most important ones, trying to help every reader understand the paragraph's central focus. When we read for information, we should concentrate on the primary examples and most important explanations, not being distracted by the less-important ones. In the paragraph excerpted above, the main points for support of the topic sentence happen to be in bold font (not unusual in a textbook). The other supporting points—the possible text length, a writer's reaction to a long project, and the reference to clay tablets—are secondary and useful primarily to develop the main statement.

Expecting to Find Repeated Material

Textbooks in particular will repeat and elaborate important ideas, providing multiple examples and explanations. Within a paragraph or section of a chapter, when you notice repeated material (often highlighted in lists, charts, summaries, headings,

Teaching Idea
To help students understand essential versus nonessential examples, have them read the student model "Dangers in a Deli" in Chapter 3 before and after the second-level examples were removed.

and text boxes), pay special attention; it is probably important. In the paragraph excerpt Developing Body Paragraphs on p. 27, you will notice the idea of support, in the boxed phrases, repeated several times.

Noticing the Patterns of Development

In Chapter 1 we looked briefly at the patterns of development, which writers use to expand and clarify their ideas. Although detailed examples are the core of all development, writers apply them in predictable ways. For example, in the paragraph excerpt on the preceding page, we find imagined dialogue, which is a narrative element. Then the paragraph begins to tell how writers develop their ideas—the process analysis or how-to pattern. Illustrating through examples, using vivid descriptive details, making comparisons, speculating about causes and effects, defining terms—when we begin to recognize these patterns, the ideas and information contained within them become easier to understand and to recall.

Learning to Annotate, Outline, Summarize, and Paraphrase

After we have isolated the most significant information in a text, we need methods for preserving it so we can review without having to reread from the beginning. When we **annotate** a text, we underline or highlight the important points that we have already located and then write notes to ourselves in the margins to record our reactions to the material. It is common to write questions, agree/disagree with a point, express surprise, link an idea with one found elsewhere in the text, and so forth. You might number examples, star passages, circle prominent facts, and connect information with arrows.

There is no one way to annotate, but a general principle is to highlight selectively. It will not help you to focus on critical parts of the text if you highlight three-fourths of it. Less is better.

Annotating a Text

After a writer has established a workable topic sentence, he must next move into the heart of his paragraph, the <u>support sentences</u>. Depending on the writer's purpose, the audience's expectations, and the topic itself, these supporting sentences <u>might range from several to several dozen</u>. "Twenty-four sentences!" you might think to yourself when faced with a lengthier paragraph or essay assignment. "How in the world am I ever going to fill up all that white space?" The answer is the same way that writers have been filling up paragraphs, essays, books, and other kinds of writing since words were first pressed into wet clay. After you have declared your main point, you will <u>illustrate it with **examples, details, and explanations**</u>. These are the simple tools of the trade. And no matter how long the writing project runs, <u>writers use the same kinds of material over and over</u> to "fill up the space," sometimes artfully, sometimes not.

Informal "scratch" outlines can also be useful for retaining information. Here is how we might outline the paragraph above:

> ### Scratch Outline
>
> Topic sentence: <u>After a writer has established a workable topic sentence, he must next move into the heart of his paragraph, the support sentences.</u>
>
> Supporting points:
>
> 1. *There is no set length to paragraphs.*
>
> 2. *Examples, details, and explanations develop paragraphs.*

Teaching Idea
Although *AWW* does not encourage students to research, paraphrasing and summarizing are critical skills. Asking students to read and then summarize selected passages from the text in class will give them summarizing practice and help them learn important concepts.

Paraphrase and Summary

Paraphrasing and summarizing help us remember material because they require that we put the ideas in a text into our own words. A paraphrase retains both primary and secondary examples and is therefore longer than a summary, which keeps only the main idea and an occasional significant example. Here is how we might paraphrase or summarize the excerpted paragraph:

Sample Paraphrase

- The main point of this paragraph is how to develop paragraphs. The author says that paragraphs have no set length, but that their size depends on what the writer wants to accomplish, what his reader expects to hear, and maybe how complicated the subject is. Support sentences consist of "examples, details, and explanations."

Sample Summary

- This paragraph states that developing paragraphs relies on "examples, details, and explanations."

Activity 2-3: Focusing and Recording Main Ideas

Read through the paragraph excerpt below, underlining the topic sentence and any primary examples. (Remember that topic sentences are usually the first or second sentence, but they can be located elsewhere in a paragraph.) Next, annotate in the margins to show your reactions. Finally, write a brief scratch outline and a one-sentence summary.

Organizing Body Paragraphs

So far we have looked closely at the parts of a body paragraph and discussed a number of important ways to focus and develop them. <u>But paragraphs and essays also benefit from an overall organizational plan, and there are several methods that are useful, depending on what you want to accomplish.</u> If your primary goal is to <u>describe</u>, you might choose a **spatial** method of arrangement, organizing the parts of your description from side to side, front to back, near to far, inside to out, or bottom to top. If your primary goal is to <u>tell a story</u>—to entertain, explain, or persuade—you would choose a **chronological** pattern, relating events as they unfold in time. If you are most interested in <u>communicating information</u>—telling how something works, defining an idea, giving some history—or persuading, you might select **order of importance,** that is, beginning with your least-important or interesting idea and ending with the most significant. Whatever overall method you choose, keep in mind that, especially in writing longer papers, you will often combine methods. For instance, a persuasive essay with reasons primarily arranged from least to most convincing might include a story that is arranged chronologically, or the essay might need to arrange some scene spatially.

Scratch Outline

Topic sentence (main point): _But paragraphs and essays also benefit from an overall organizational plan, and there are several methods that are useful, depending on what you want to accomplish._

Supporting points:

1. _Spatial arrangement is good for descriptive writing._
2. _Chronological order is good for narratives._
3. _Order of importance is useful for informative and persuasive writing._
4. _Essays often combine these methods._

Summary (one sentence): _Paragraphs can be arranged by space, time, or importance._

▶ POSTREADING: RETAINING IDEAS

Teaching Idea
You might relate postreading to the revision or editing stage of the writing process. Postreading requires patience too, but it pays off by completing the job and fixing knowledge in place.

When we finish a reading assignment, part or all of a chapter, we can just slam the book shut and run from it, or we can take a few more minutes to review what we have concentrated on so carefully. Taking the extra time for that final review of key points will pay off. Here at the end of the process, you can continue to apply the critical strategy of interacting with the text. What do you think about the material you have just covered? How does it fit into your experience? Were there any special points that you agreed or disagreed with, an idea or suggestion that you plan on using from now on or that strikes you as useless? Forming opinions will help fix important ideas in your memory.

There are many ways to review effectively, and you have probably tried them at one time or another: silently skimming main points, stating them aloud, or organizing your thoughts on paper. Here are some specific suggestions for helping with your review:

1. **Repeat the prereading step,** especially focusing on signposts (chapter previews and summaries, headings, etc.).

2. **Summarize or outline the main points** of your reading session. This may only require pulling together the paragraph summaries you have already written or listing the main points that you underlined when you annotated.

3. **Quiz yourself** over the material as if your instructor were asking the questions. If you can't answer your own questions, you know you have to reread.

4. **Try to define any important term or idea** in a sentence of twenty words or less. Can you remember (or come up with) an example?

5. **List** what you feel are the three most important points from your reading.

Activity 2-4: Practicing Postreading Strategies

Using any of the five suggestions above, review Chapter 2, and then list the *essential* points for making the most of your reading. Limit your list to ten to twelve points.

CHAPTER SUMMARY

1. There are techniques to help people read more effectively.

2. Most people can read more efficiently if they practice reading techniques.

3. Reading can be divided into three stages: prereading, reading, and postreading.

4. Interacting with the text is the most important habit a person can develop for improving comprehension and recall.

5. Three useful ways to preread are to look for signposting devices, skim beginnings and endings, and link new to previous knowledge.

6. Three habits to form while reading are to anticipate the author's points and react to them, form a mental image from points in the text, and link new to previous knowledge.

7. Four points in a text to focus on while reading are thesis, topic, and summary sentences; primary examples; repeated material; and the patterns of development.

8. Four methods to help record information in a text are annotating, outlining, summarizing, and paraphrasing.

9. People who practice postreading retain more information.

10. Five ways to postread are prereading, summarizing, self-quizzing, defining important terms, and listing important points.

Working with the Paragraph

CHAPTER 3

Introducing the Paragraph

WHAT IS A PARAGRAPH?

In the illustration above, a young woman seems interested in solving her puzzle, putting the many pieces together to make a complete picture. We too need to work on our writing puzzle, looking closely at the pieces that help make writing effective. So far we have discussed the writing and reading process, reviewing in general how compositions grow. Now we need to look more specifically at one fundamental writing unit—the paragraph—to see how it works in relation to larger units of writing.

A paragraph is a collection of related sentences that are clearly connected to one another and that make some point. Paragraphs come in several varieties:

1. Introductory

2. **Body**

3. Concluding

4. Transitional

Although each of these "specialty" paragraphs serves its own purpose, our focus in this chapter will be the body paragraph, developing it as a single unit of thought but remembering that paragraphs generally work together in essays. We will practice focusing paragraphs through a **topic sentence;** developing that main idea with specific, relevant **support;** and **concluding** the paragraph forcefully.

Paragraphs usually
work together.

There is no set length for a paragraph, the kind of writing and audience for it usually determining the number of sentences. For example, newspapers favor shorter paragraphs, whereas academic journals often produce paragraphs that fill a page. Our papers in Unit Two will usually run to 250 to 300 words, or around fifteen sentences.

Paragraph = focused topic, interesting development, decisive conclusion

To see a student model paragraph with the parts labeled, turn to pp. 42–43.

Caution: A body paragraph is not an essay.

To contrast the paragraph with an essay and to help with our discussion of paragraph parts, take a look at the following diagram:

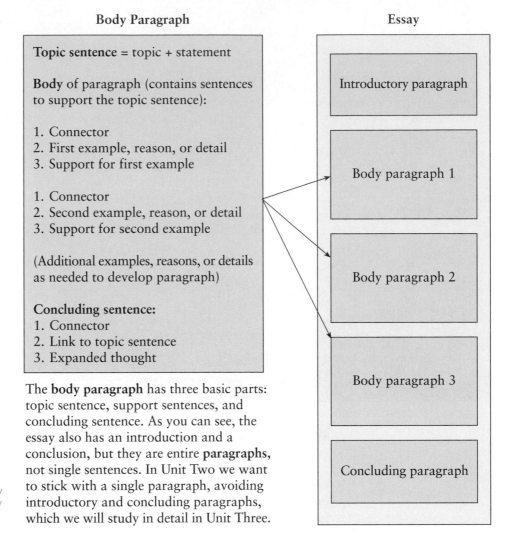

Body Paragraph

Topic sentence = topic + statement

Body of paragraph (contains sentences to support the topic sentence):

1. Connector
2. First example, reason, or detail
3. Support for first example

1. Connector
2. Second example, reason, or detail
3. Support for second example

(Additional examples, reasons, or details as needed to develop paragraph)

Concluding sentence:
1. Connector
2. Link to topic sentence
3. Expanded thought

Essay

Introductory paragraph

Body paragraph 1

Body paragraph 2

Body paragraph 3

Concluding paragraph

The **body paragraph** has three basic parts: topic sentence, support sentences, and concluding sentence. As you can see, the essay also has an introduction and a conclusion, but they are entire **paragraphs,** not single sentences. In Unit Two we want to stick with a single paragraph, avoiding introductory and concluding paragraphs, which we will study in detail in Unit Three.

Teaching Idea
It helps to stress that you know students have written essays in the past but that the current focus is on the body paragraph. Students usually see the sense of writing in smaller units when there is a lot to learn, particularly when you remind them that they will be tossing out lots of words in their rough drafts.

▶ WRITING A TOPIC SENTENCE

All effective paragraphs have a main point, that is, some reason for their author to put those particular sentences together. In body paragraphs writers frequently state explicitly what the paragraph will be about, and they often make this statement the first sentence. This is called a **topic sentence.** Topic sentences focus the direction of the author's and the reader's mental travel. Like a compass guiding a backpacker through unfamiliar terrain, the topic sentence can help people find their way from one end of a paragraph to the other, without taking needless detours along the way.

Consider the three following sentences. Which both *limits* the topic and makes a *statement* or expresses an *opinion* about it that you think the author could develop in a single paragraph?

1. I have a brother named Jason.

2. Many families have more than one boy.

3. My brother Jason is a great guitarist.

Teaching Idea
To help students understand focusing a topic sentence, you can begin with a general statement (such as, "Many young people like to play sports") and then progressively limit it. Often, asking them to state an *opinion*, make a *comment*, or tell their *attitude* will help them avoid presenting general topics as topic sentences.

Sentences 1 and 2 are simply factual observations that give the reader no sense for what else the writer might want to say about them besides "So what?" Sentence 3, on the other hand, limits the topic ("Jason") and makes a clear statement or assertion about it ("is a great guitarist") that we would expect the author to discuss further. With a clearly expressed opinion or statement combined with a well-focused topic, we give ourselves and a reader the necessary direction to move into the rest of the paragraph. As you begin to write topic sentences, keep in mind several important points as indicated in the following box.

How to Write a Topic Sentence

1. **Limit the topic.**

   Remember that we are only working with paragraphs at this point, so the scope must be fairly narrow. For example, instead of trying to take on the topic of global environmental problems, you might discuss a personal commitment to recycling.

   Sometimes writers list several parts of their topic in a **forecasting statement** like this: "If people want to begin to recycle, all they need to do is <u>call Deffenbaugh Waste Disposal</u>, <u>make a bit of extra room in their garage</u>, and <u>be prepared to separate the 'hard' from the 'soft' trash.</u>"

2. **Make a clear statement about it.**

   Simply mentioning a topic does not give your reader much sense of direction. Your topic sentence should state an opinion or controlling point. For instance, don't say, "Many people recycle in the United States"—a general factual statement that could lead in many directions. Instead express a point, like this: "I learned the hard way how important it is to recycle."

3. **Use specific word choices.**

   Strive to make your topic sentence interesting, since it is your introduction to the rest of your paragraph. You may begin with a rough topic sentence like "My brother is a great guitarist," but before you are through revising, you might end up with a more focused and interesting sentence like this: "My brother Jason toured all last summer with Pearl Jam, playing some terrific solo riffs."

Activity 3-1: Recognizing the Parts of Topic Sentences

In the following group of topic sentences, underline the topic once and the statement being made about it twice.

Example: My dad, Charlie Martin, had a way of making us smile in the middle of difficult situations.

1. My best friend had a horrible experience in a pawnshop last week.

2. Hot air balloon rides are fun but more dangerous than most people think.

3. Once they are behind the wheel of their cars, some people become too aggressive.

4. More businesses ought to provide on-site day care for working mothers and fathers.

5. I think cemeteries are very restful places.

Teaching Idea

If you work through Activity 3-1 in class, you might have students orally add an example or two to these sentences, warming them up for paragraph development.

Focusing Topic Sentences

Topic sentences need to fall somewhere between relatively general and relatively specific. They must be broad enough to let the writer develop a subject with specific examples, explanations, and details but narrow enough to allow the subject to be covered in a paragraph. Notice how the following examples of broad topic sentences can be narrowed:

Unfocused: Most people look forward to holidays.

Workable: I always look forward to spending Thanksgiving with my relatives in Dallas.

Unfocused: Fall is the season in which nature slows down and prepares for winter.

Workable: While much of nature slows down in the fall, squirrels seem to be in perpetual motion as they prepare for the long winter months ahead.

Activity 3-2: Focusing Topic Sentences

Revise the following topic sentences to narrow their focus. Imagine that you will have to write a paragraph based on your revised topic sentence. How can you limit the general statement being made? Consider personalizing the sentences through your own experiences or general knowledge and making a specific point about each topic.

Teaching Idea
In Activity 3-2 you might want to help students begin to see the distinction between paragraphs developed through personal experience versus general knowledge. Possible answers in this annotated edition for sentences 2 and 3 lean toward development through general knowledge versus personal experience in 1 and 5.

Example: Having to stay in the hospital can be a miserable experience.

Revised and limited: _One of the most miserable experiences of my life was being hospitalized for knee surgery last June._

Answers will vary.

1. Many people enjoy rock concerts.
   Possible response: The most fun I have had at a concert was at the Rolling Stones' Kansas City performance in the summer of 1973.

2. Education costs a great deal in this country.
   Possible response: Fifty dollars a credit hour is too much to charge at Johnson County Community College.

3. Computers are often used by students to word process their writing assignments.
   Possible response: Computers are especially helpful to students when they revise and edit.

4. There are many SUVs on the road today.
   Possible response: Because most SUVs are larger than passenger cars, SUVs put many drivers at risk.

5. Most people take precautions when they learn that a tornado has been sighted in their vicinity.
   Possible response: Last summer when a tornado was sighted near K-10, my wife and I began preparing the house for high winds.

Often when we reread our paragraph drafts, we see that the material has taken us in a slightly different direction than what we stated in the rough topic sentence. Sometimes this requires deleting or modifying examples, and sometimes it means reshaping the topic sentence.

Activity 3-3: Deducing Topic Sentences

For further practice with topic sentences, read the following groups of example sentences that would come from the body of a paragraph, write out a *possible topic* to match the given sentences, and then write a suitable *topic sentence* on the lines provided.

Example: • Jinyi opened her first present and clapped her hands in delight.

• Her parents, brothers and sisters, and the rest of the family wished her well.

• Jinyi's mother brought the cake, with ten candles blazing, into the room.

• Her father hugged her and whispered, "You are the best daughter a father could ever hope for."

Possible topic: _Jinyi's tenth birthday party_

Possible topic sentence: _Jinyi had a wonderful time on her tenth birthday._

Answers will vary.

1. • One major mistake for new college students is too much partying.

• Another problem many students have is zoning out in class.

• Whereas cramming used to cut it in high school, daily study is now required.

• It is difficult to balance schoolwork with our jobs.

Possible topic: _Problems for college students_

Possible topic sentence: _Students new to college will soon find out the pitfalls that stand in the way of their education._

2. • I never realized that marriage would have so many bumps in the road.

• Being a good partner requires more than giving fifty-fifty.

• A couple must communicate on a daily basis.

• Another important ingredient is regularly showing your affection.

Possible topic: _Problems in marriages_

Possible topic sentence: _To help a marriage succeed, a couple must work hard at it._

3. • Dad told us to burn the leaves, and my older brother Jim thought gasoline would help.

• After we had the leaves raked in a big pile, Jim poured on a mayonnaise jar full of gas.

• "Go ahead and light them," he ordered me.

• When the leaves exploded, I was knocked flat on my back.

Possible topic: _A story about a yard accident_

Possible topic sentence: _Following orders one day without thinking about them nearly put me in the hospital._

Revising Topic Sentences

After you have selected a topic and devised a *rough* topic sentence, you can confidently move ahead with the writing process. But when polishing our work, we should review the topic sentence to see if it is as clear, precise, and interesting as we can make it. One way to improve a topic sentence is to use *specific* words wherever possible. Selecting specific words simply means choosing a word that fits into a more limited category than another that is similar to it. Consider the following word lists and decide which list is more general (the larger category) and which is more specific (the smaller category).

A	B
tool	hammer
plant	rose bush
person	Thomas Jefferson
energy source	coal
animal	horse

If you decided that column B is more specific, you can see that these words are part of a larger group the words in column A represent. For instance, the first word, a tool, includes such things as a screwdriver, wrench, paintbrush, shovel, and more, including a hammer. The more specific the word we choose, the sharper the image it creates—and the more interesting the sentence becomes for a reader.

Take a look at the following topic sentences. The first one in each pair is the rough topic sentence, and the second has been polished by adding specific words (underlined).

Rough topic sentence: My vacation didn't turn out too well.

Revised topic sentence: My vacation to <u>Ft. Lauderdale</u> was a <u>disaster</u>.

Rough topic sentence: Our day care has had a problem recently.

Revised topic sentence: <u>Peppermint Patty's</u> day care has sent <u>six children</u> home this week with <u>pinkeye</u>.

Rough topic sentence: My family's table manners need some work.

Revised topic sentence: <u>Elbows on the table, arms stretched across plates as hands reach for the salt shaker, brothers and sisters outshouting one another to be heard</u>—my family's table manners need some work.

(For more on specific language, see pp. 78–79, 451–452)

Activity 3-4: Polishing Topic Sentences

Rewrite the five following sentences, making them more interesting by adding specific words where appropriate.

Answers will vary.

1. Rough topic sentence: I like working on my car.

   Revised topic sentence: _*I like working on my '66 convertible Mustang.*_

   _____

2. Rough topic sentence: I didn't much care for some teachers in high school.

   Revised topic sentence: _*The most boring teacher I had to suffer under in*_ *high school was my American history teacher, Mr. Armor.*

Teaching Idea
Activity 3-3 introduces the concept of specific language that will be revisited in Chapter 5, Picturing a Place. You might also encourage students to add sensory details and active verbs to the topic sentences.

3. Rough topic sentence: I know now why I am finally back in school.

Revised topic sentence: _After breaking my back digging holes in rotten weather for too long, I'm leaving landscaping behind as soon as I finish college._

4. Rough topic sentence: My husband has to work too much.

Revised topic sentence: _Because my husband is now working sixty hours a week, our family life has suffered in many ways._

5. Rough topic sentence: Living in a new country is difficult.

Revised topic sentence: _Moving to the United States from Korea, I have faced three special challenges._

DEVELOPING BODY PARAGRAPHS

Teaching Idea
To help students understand development in a paragraph, ask one or two of them to say something about a vacation they have recently taken. If they reply with a laconic "awesome," you can ask what they did that was such fun, building on their responses until the vacation begins to come clear. Separating examples from supporting explanation can help students see the importance of both.

After a writer has established a workable topic sentence, he must next move into the heart of his paragraph, the support sentences. These sentences are developed with **examples, details,** and **explanations**—the simple tools of the trade. No matter how long the writing project runs, writers use these tools over and over to "fill up the space," sometimes artfully, sometimes not.

During the next few pages we will take a look at exactly what *solid* support is: what it consists of, how much is enough, when it is relevant, and how to be sure it is clear to your reader.

Kinds of Support

Examples

An example seeks to illustrate some part of a statement by showing the reader a specific instance of it. Whenever you are asked for additional information to help someone understand an idea, chances are that you will provide an example. For instance, you might say to a friend, "Baseball is a boring game." Your friend, who is a baseball fanatic, immediately replies, "What do you mean by that?" When you respond by telling her that there is not enough action, that the pitcher and the catcher have most of the fun, that half the time the infielders and outfielders might as well be asleep for all the moving they do, and that you would like to see a little more body contact, like in football, you have just provided a list of examples.

Personal examples are those based on your own experiences. When you talk about how frustrating preschoolers can be and illustrate your point with the time your four-year-old sister locked herself in the bathroom, refusing to come out for two hours, you are using a personal example.

Examples outside your personal experience include some of the possibilities listed below:

- **Facts:** commonly accepted truths. Example: Some trees lose their leaves in the fall.

- **Statistics:** numerical facts. Example: The earth is 93,000,000 miles from the sun.

- **Information** gathered from print sources (books, newspapers, magazines, etc.), electronic sources (including the Internet), interviews, TV, and radio

- **Second-hand anecdotes:** stories that happened to someone else

- **Comparisons** (including metaphor/simile): Example: The flute is basically a pipe with holes drilled in it.

- **What-if? situations:** speculating about what *could* happen (e.g., what would happen if you decided to stop working on Fridays?)

- **Dialogue** created to express a point

Details

Just as we need examples to illustrate general statements, we need details to make examples more interesting. Details help sharpen an image or clarify an idea. To make the example of your little sister's locking herself in the bathroom more vivid, we could **name** some parts of the scene, then add **modifiers** and **sensory details:**

> My <u>four-year-old</u> sister slammed the <u>hard wooden door</u> of the bathroom, and I heard the <u>lock click</u> shut. Then she <u>shrieked</u> at me, "I hate you!" When I tried to calm her down, she turned on both <u>taps</u> of the <u>sink full blast</u> and began <u>flushing</u> the <u>toilet</u> to drown me out.

Explanations

Examples can develop much of our writing, but sometimes we need more. What if the reader does not understand the example or how it relates to a point? We can offer **explanations**—*reasons* that justify behavior, tell how things work, and anticipate possible outcomes. Explanations are vital in developing a main point because they fill in the gaps between examples and guide readers through our ideas.

Suppose a reader's reaction to the detailed example of the preschooler's behavior above was "That doesn't seem so frustrating to me. Why didn't you just walk away and forget it?" The writer would need to *explain* that the child was his responsibility and that it would have been too dangerous to leave her locked in a bathroom by herself, especially while she was having a tantrum.

Explanations work with details and examples to "fill up the white space." In the following paragraph you will find three major **examples** to support the topic sentence, **explanation** following each major example, and **details** throughout to make the examples and explaining more vivid for the reader.

Dangers in a Deli

Key:

Topic sentence

Examples

Details

Explanations

More frequently than people realize, there are dangers in deli work. [1.]One concern for potential deli workers is <u>slippery floors</u>. If the <u>counter</u> is packed with <u>anxious customers,</u> and <u>workers</u> are hustling about taking care of their orders, a <u>wet floor</u> is not going to take top priority. During the <u>rush</u> what's going to stop an employee from running too fast, which could result in a serious <u>wipeout</u>. [2.]In addition to <u>slippery floors</u>, working around <u>chemicals</u> should not be taken lightly. When cleaning the <u>glass</u>, you might end up with <u>ammonia</u> sprayed in your <u>eyes</u>. Both <u>pan degreaser</u> and <u>sanitizer</u> are used at <u>dish time</u>, and it only takes one <u>splash</u> in the <u>sink</u> to send someone on her way to the emergency room. ³·But the part of the job that is most dangerous is using the meat and cheese slicer. Whether operating the slicer or simply cleaning it, you risk cutting yourself. With just one careless slip near the sharp blade, you could end up with one less finger. **A new person on the job might be a little nervous because of the possible injury that deli work entails, but luckily safety training is a requirement.**

| **Concluding sentence**

Sufficient Support

Knowing what kinds of support to work toward is important, but we must also be sure when developing paragraphs to use **sufficient support.** All too frequently inexperienced writers fall into the trap of thinking a topic has been fully presented when in fact the development is thin or merely repetitive.

You might want to think of paragraph and essay writing as following a descending level of generality: the further you progress into the body of your work, the more specific it should become. For each major point you raise, you will immediately begin to clarify it with examples, details, and explanations that become increasingly specific or limited until you feel the reader should understand your idea. Practically speaking, in our one-paragraph papers you will regularly be descending only one or two "levels."

> Layer examples from general to specific.

> **Teaching Idea**
> For a closer look at this "layering" principle, refer students to the Chapter 7 Prewriting Suggestions for the Annotated Student Model. In addition to the terms *first level/second level*, you might simply ask students to explain a statement by answering the questions "What do you mean by that? Can you give me an example?" This will often open up a student's ideas wonderfully.

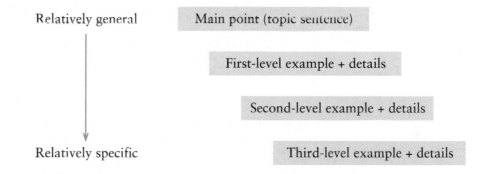

Relatively general — Main point (topic sentence)

First-level example + details

Second-level example + details

Relatively specific — Third-level example + details

Read below to see what the deli paragraph from our last example sounds like once we strip away the second-level examples, details, and explanations:

More frequently than people realize, there are dangers in deli work.

¹One concern for potential deli workers is slippery floors. ²In addition to slippery floors, working around chemicals should not be taken lightly. ³But the part of the job that is most dangerous is using the meat and cheese slicer. **A new person on the job might be a little nervous because of the possible injury that deli work entails, but luckily safety training is a requirement.**

> Only three major examples remain to support the topic sentence.

Does this version of the deli paragraph read more like a paragraph or an outline? The main ideas are there but nothing more.

Activity 3-5: Creating Sufficient Support

The five sentence groups below begin with topic sentences followed by a first-level example. To further develop the topics, create a second-level example that adds more specific information (details and explanation).

Examples: • Topic sentence: People should avoid jogging because it hurts more than helps them.

First-level example: For instance, jogging can be bad for a person's joints.

Second-level example: *I have had problems with my knees, and my ankles swell if I run for more than half an hour.*

Answers will vary.

1. Topic sentence: Making it to class on time is difficult for several good reasons.

   First-level example: First, students have difficulty finding a parking space.

   Second-level example: *Fifteen minutes before any class is a nightmare as students stalk one another, trying to snatch the prized space close to the classroom buildings.*

2. Topic sentence: I learned how to budget my money the hard way.

   First-level example: One lesson was to stop eating out so often.

   Second-level example: *I love fast food and used to make the daily rounds at Burger King, the Sub Shop, and Pizza Hut.*

3. Topic sentence: My family's annual trip to Silver Dollar City was fun this year.

   First-level example: I most enjoyed my time on the lake.

   Second-level example: *My sister and I went jet skiing every day, each of us trying to beat the other on the slalom course.*

4. Topic sentence: Painting my house this spring was a valuable experience.

   First-level example: Another way I profited was by saving money.

   Second-level example: *The three painting companies I contacted gave me bids ranging from 2000-3000 dollars.*

5. Topic sentence: Though some people hate it, I love doing yard work.

   First-level example: My work outside gives me a great chance to observe nature.

   Second-level example: *It seems like I never really notice how busy the squirrels are until I am out in my back yard watching them at work near me.*

Relevant Support—Achieving Unity

> Unity = all examples and explanations clearly relating to a paragraph's main point

Even when paragraphs seem fully developed with enough major examples and secondary support, we can sometimes be fooled. It is not uncommon, especially in a first rough draft, to have included material that may be interesting to us, accurate, and

Teaching Idea
Using students' own work to demonstrate unity, you might either have them freewrite on a topic for a few minutes in class or have them bring a freewrite that they have done out of class.

Writer should show that all ideas in a paragraph are relevant.

Teaching Idea
The paragraph model "What's the Rush" can be used as another example of description for Chapter 5, Picturing a Place.

worthwhile but that still distracts the reader from the main point. When our paragraphs contain material that does not clearly develop the topic sentence (main point), we have a problem with **unity**.

Consider: If someone were writing about the advantages of mowing her yard herself, talking about fresh air, communing with nature, exercise, and so forth, but then stopped for a moment to mention the durability of the mower's engine, would this be a digression? Perhaps, but what if she then included the idea of learning more about two-cycle engines and how the knowledge is useful to her? If the author can make the connection for her reader between the material she is offering and her main point, the paragraph is probably *unified*.

If you write out a controlling topic sentence and then look at it *often* as you work, you will limit trouble with unity. Always consider your audience and try to gauge whether they would view any of your material as distracting or unnecessary.

Notice in the following descriptive paragraph the shaded clause "I am relaxing" in the first (topic) sentence. Because relaxation is supposed to be the main point of this paragraph, do you think the underlined sentences reinforce or detract from the feeling?

What's the Rush?

It's eighty degrees on a pink-sand beach, and I am relaxing in the shade of a thatched umbrella. The breeze blows cool from the north off the ocean, just enough to keep the temperature comfortable. I suppose that I should count myself lucky since the weather forecast for tomorrow is rain and high winds. From behind me I can hear the clink of bottles and glasses from the bar, and I wonder whether or not I'm feeling too lazy to go get another drink. In a minute, I think. What's the rush? But maybe I ought to speed it up a bit to catch the office back home before they close. I should check the McWard portfolio this afternoon. A white seagull eyes me hopefully, standing on the sand about ten feet away, anticipating another piece of the sandwich that I have been sharing. Other seagulls circle overhead squabbling and attacking each other over what looks like a piece of trash. About fifty yards down the beach, I can see a young couple—newlyweds?—laughing and drawing shapes in the wet sand. Beyond them the surf is gentle, breaking softly on the flat shelf of the beach. In the distance, rocking gently in the swells, a boat heads out to sea, its red flag with white diagonal stripe flapping. I glance down at the snorkeling gear I brought and think maybe it's time for a little action, but then the bartender is standing by my chair, another glass of soda and lime in hand. "Michael," he says smiling, "how about a little refresher?" There goes my resolve. "Thanks, I think," I tell him. As I flop back onto the lounge chair, I remind myself that this is my vacation. There is a time for work and a time for rest, and a wise person knows when each is right.

Activity 3-6: Determining Relevant Support

Look closely at the following paragraph and then underline any material that seems to stray too far from the topic sentence. In the space provided after the paragraph, explain why each sentence that you marked seems like it does not belong.

Primary audience: American college students ages eighteen to twenty-two.

When I was ten years old, I used to live for baseball. Summer signaled the time school was finally over, and my friends and I could hit the park. We never wasted any time. Eight boys ranging in age from seven to fifteen met at our house for breakfast, filled up their water bottles, and headed down to the park.

Teaching Idea
Activity 3-6 might generate
some discussion about the
sentence with the overly
competitive brother. Students
can successfully argue for or
against the sentence,
demonstrating the need for
the author to control unity by
his or her clear explanations.

We almost always had it to ourselves. Of course, there was one time when the city held their Fourth of July celebration there. Down went the Frisbees to mark the bases, out came the gloves, bats, and balls, and then began the all-day games. You might think that a group of kids couldn't stay focused on anything all day, but we did. This was like our little World Series. Part of it was just love of the game; part of it was the competitive spirit. We all wanted to win. My brother was the most competitive of all of us and would fight over the strikes and the foul or fair balls. After countless innings, balls chased into the street, and blisters from swinging the bat too many times, we would call it a day. I knew that later in the evening I might sneak a quick game of basketball in with my brother in our driveway. The sun would finally set on the eight of us, sweating, dehydrated, and covered in dirt from sliding into bases and diving for grounders. Whoever had the most wins, it didn't really matter. We went home happy, knowing that the next day we could play baseball again.

1. *Of course, there was one time. . . . This sentence is a clear break in the narration.*

2. *My brother was the most competitive. . . . Some students will leave this in, citing the preceding sentence mention of competition. Others will point out that the paragraph's focus is on love of the game, not winning. This discussion can help with the sometimes slippery nature of paragraph unity.*

3. *I knew that later in the evening. . . . This sentence, too, is a clear break in the narration.*

Clear Support

After working through your paragraph, revising it for kinds of support, sufficient support, and relevant support, you might think that you were home free. But there is still one important element to watch for—**clarity.** Clarity (explaining your examples, reasons, and word choices completely) is essential if readers are to follow the material you have worked so hard to accumulate. One of the surest ways to check for clarity in your own writing is to imagine a specific audience reading your work so that you can anticipate and answer their questions.

Clarity = clear
explaining and precise
word choices

For example, in the baseball paragraph from Activity 3-6, there are a number of words, phrases, and ideas that might puzzle someone unfamiliar with American culture. Consider the phrase "my friends and I could hit the park." This is an idiomatic expression that native speakers understand but that could easily be misinterpreted. (Why would young people want to beat the ground at the park?) In the next sentence from the baseball paragraph, even members of the intended audience might wonder about seven-year-olds playing baseball with fifteen-year-olds. Are the ages accurate; is any more explaining needed here? When we look at the words chosen, we can see that the stated audience would not have any difficulty with *Fourth of July, Frisbees, World Series, foul or fair balls, strikes, sliding into bases,* and *diving for grounders,* but other readers might.

Role-playing your
audience can help
with clarity.

As you reread your work, checking it for clarity, try to role-play your audience. And as you get input from other readers when you share your papers, ask these questions as frequently as possible: "Do you understand all of my ideas? Are my examples and explanations clear? Do any of the words puzzle you or seem to need further explaining?"

Teaching Idea
Activity 3-7 is oriented toward process instruction and is a good one to revisit if you teach the process analysis chapters. Audience is, of course, especially important in process instructions.

Activity 3-7: Clarity in Word Choices

In the following brief paragraphs think about who the audience is and what they might know, and then underline any word or phrase that you think might need additional explanation.

Example: Audience: twelve-year-olds learning about fly fishing

First you must select the proper fly for the weather and water conditions. I would suggest a dry fly #12, perhaps a Royal Wulff. Your leader should be tapered, with no more than a 3 X tippet, and you must be particularly careful using the improved clinch knot with which you will attach the fly to the tippet.

1. Audience: continuing education class learning basic word processing

   Make sure the floppy is out of drive A, and then turn on your computers and monitors. Numbers and words will quickly flash across the dark screen as the computer boots up, and then your desktop will appear. Double left click the mouse on the Word icon, and you will see the basic Word window.

2. Audience: person training as a waiter

   Be careful on Friday and Saturday evenings during the rush. Orders are coming fast off the wheel, and the servers will blow past you pretty quickly coming off the line. Always check with the manager to see if any menu items have been 86ed, and be sure to check the special.

3. Audience: a young uncle who has volunteered to baby-sit (but who has no experience with toddlers) getting instructions on changing a diaper

   Be careful not to use the Kleenexes; they're too rough. Use the wipes. And don't wipe her from back to front. Go the other way. If it's before bedtime, use a day diaper. If she's ready for bed, don't use the old night diapers because we want her to start using the pull-ups now. You will find the cloth diapers and all the other diapers in the drawers under the changing table, but don't try to use the cloth diapers for anything but padding the table. And, oh yes, don't use the Diaper Genie; it's a holdover from Alexis's baby days.

Teaching Idea
To generate some discussion over clarity in explanation, ask students if they remember ever reading instructions like those in Activity 3-8.

Activity 3-8: Clarity in Explanations

In the following brief paragraph think about who the audience is, and then underline any phrase or sentence that you think fails to explain its point clearly. In the space provided below the paragraph, explain what more you would want or need to know to follow the registration instructions.

Teaching Idea
The last sentence of the
paragraph in Activity 3-8 is
particularly difficult to decipher
because of the negatives. You
might ask students about this
sentence to reinforce the value
of writing with positive
statements.

Audience: first-year community college students beginning the registration process
Answers will vary.

    All new students must attend a preadvising session, so set some time aside and <u>find the right room for the session.</u> Next, <u>go get an application, fill it out, and turn it in.</u> Be sure to create a <u>PIN</u> and record it for future use—this is important! If you want to enroll in <u>credit classes</u>, you must take the <u>assessment tests</u>, but not everyone has to take all the tests, and not doing well on the tests will not keep you from attending the college, but not taking the tests at all will.

Which "right room," where do we get the application, how do we fill it

out, where do we turn it in? Would we want to enroll in any other

kinds of classes (non-credit?)? What's this about an assessment test?

▶ WRITING A CONCLUDING SENTENCE

Teaching Idea
It can help to reinforce the
structure of a concluding
sentence by writing this on the
board: connector + link to topic
sentence + expanded thought.

    As important as it is to begin a paragraph with a clear, focused, interesting sentence, and to substantially develop the body, writers need to end their paragraphs with equal care. Although many short and medium-length body paragraphs in essays do not use summary or "clincher" sentences, it is a common and useful tactic to do so with longer body paragraphs. In our one-paragraph papers this semester, we will always end with a sentence (sometimes two might seem necessary) that brings the paper to a full sense of completion, and we will learn several ways to do this effectively. Working with well-shaped final sentences will also help us ultimately to create more interesting concluding paragraphs in our essay writing.

How to Write a Concluding Sentence

1. Use a connector.

Remember to use a transitional word (*finally, aside from, on the other hand, consequently,* etc.) or other sentence connector in the first part of the concluding sentence (for more on sentence connectors, see p. 52–57).

2. Link to the topic sentence.

Always remind your reader of the topic and the statement you have made about it in your topic sentence. You may simply repeat a word or phrase or, better still, find a synonym or alternate phrase. Some paragraphs benefit from a brief mention (only a word or two) of some important example, reason, or strong image from the body.

3. Expand the thought.

Try to leave your reader with something to think about in addition to your topic sentence statement. This added thought should be an *extension* of your discussion in the supporting sentences of the paragraph. Any of the following methods can work:

A. Express an emotion.
B. Give a judgment or opinion.
C. Ask a related question.
D. Make a reflective statement.
E. Say how something has affected your behavior or outlook on life.
F. Make an ironic observation.

What to Avoid in Concluding Sentences

1. Do not simply repeat the topic sentence or a slightly altered version of it. Show your reader that you have some good reason for writing the paragraph and for her to have read it.

2. In trying to find an interesting expanded thought, don't drift off into the *Twilight Zone*. Your final thought should grow logically from the paragraph.

3. Do not end with a cliché or worn phrase, for example, "So, as you can see, I was caught between a rock and a hard place." (For more on clichés and worn phrases, see pp. 474–475)

4. Do not announce to your reader that you are ending the paper, for example, "Well, it's time for me to end this paragraph, so. . . ." A brief summary of any important examples or points (just a few words), your expanded thought, *and* the fact that there are no more words on the page will all let the reader know that you have finished.

Expanded Thought

There is no one "right" way to conclude a paragraph or essay, although there are some poor choices. Actually, conclusions, like introductions, are often detachable parts of the larger writing project. As you change one, you will frequently need to change the other. Take a moment to examine the six possible concluding sentences that *could* end the following paragraph. Each ends with a different final thought. Which do you prefer?

An Oak Deeply Rooted—or a Tumbleweed?

Many people would define the ideal life as one in which a person can live where she wants to, when she wants to. The Midwest appeals to people from all over the country who want housing that is still affordable, a small city with lots of green spaces, and an environment that is relatively low in crime. But when summer comes, people head for the mountains in droves. In an ideal situation, a couple would have a small, well-furnished cabin in a rugged mountain chain like the Rockies and spend time there from July through September. They could spend time backpacking, fishing the lakes and streams, rafting the rivers, horseback riding, and putting the mountain bikes to the purpose for which they were made. However, mountain winters are rugged, so there comes a time when what many people feel is the most desirable destination is the one to head for—the beach. In January when the temperatures in the middle and northern part of the country are dipping well below zero, there is a mass exodus of winter-shy crowds heading for the southern rim of our country and beyond. And why not? Who wants to bundle up in four layers of clothes and a down coat just to waddle outside to check the mail? Beach residents can look forward to sailing, motorboating, jet skiing, windsurfing, fishing, snorkeling, diving, and leisurely strolling along the beach. Aside from the gentler weather and fun activities, it seems easier to find large groups of like-minded people of various ages to socialize with: _____

_____

Possible Concluding Sentences

A. It would be fun to have the freedom and money to live wherever a person wanted to, and it is a shame that more people in this affluent country of ours can't do it.

Teaching Idea
If you want to show students a connected theme, "the ideal life," treated as description, narration, exposition, and persuasion paragraphs, see pp. xx in the *Instructor's Manual*.

Any of the sentences A–F could be inserted here.

ORGANIZING BODY PARAGRAPHS

So far we have looked closely at the parts of a body paragraph and discussed a number of important ways to focus and develop them. But paragraphs and essays also benefit from an overall organizational plan, and there are several methods that are useful, depending on what you want to accomplish.

If your primary goal is to *describe,* you might choose a **spatial** method of arrangement, organizing the parts of your description from side to side, front to back, near to far, inside to out, or bottom to top. If your primary goal is to *tell a story*—to entertain, explain, or persuade—you would choose a **chronological** pattern, relating events as they unfold in time. If you are most interested in *communicating information*—telling how something works, defining an idea, or giving some history—you might select **order of importance,** that is, beginning with your least important or interesting idea and ending with the most significant.

Whatever overall method you choose, keep in mind that, especially in writing longer papers, you will often combine methods. For instance, a persuasive essay with reasons primarily arranged from least to most convincing might include a story that is arranged chronologically, or the essay might need to arrange some scene spatially.

For more complete explanations of these organizational methods and to see paragraph examples, turn to the following pages:

- Spatial: pp. 87, 101–102.

- Chronological: pp. 124, 129–130.

- Order of importance: pp. 138, 156–157.

CONNECTING SENTENCES—ACHIEVING COHERENCE

After you have established an overall pattern for your paper, formulated a working topic sentence, and written your first draft, you should read your paper for **coherence.** As we learned earlier in this chapter under Developing Body Paragraphs, a paragraph or an essay must be *unified;* that is, all the material must clearly relate to one main idea (topic or thesis sentence). If unity relates to **ideas,** then coherence relates to the paper's **structure,** what holds the sentences together. It might help to think of the link between cohesion and the word *adhesive,* a useful sticky substance (like tape or glue) that can keep your sentences from falling apart.

There are a number of ways to link sentences and paragraphs, and most of us use them quite naturally even as we churn out rough drafts. But when we miss necessary connectors, confusion often follows. Consider the following two sets of sentences, and decide which seems most clear to you:

A. ___ I prepared for surgery _____ the vet clinic _____ I work, I was administering anesthesia to a miniature black poodle _____ respiration stopped _____ the heart _____ beating. I quickly scrambled _____ the side of the small _____ to start _____.

B. **As** I prepared for surgery at the vet clinic **where** I work, I was administering anesthesia to a miniature black poodle **when** respiration stopped, **and** the heart **stopped** beating. I quickly scrambled to the side of the small **poodle** to start **respiration.**

The omission of several transitional words and three repeated words in version A means that we have difficulty even following the writer's information, much less enjoying what he has written. In our own work, we want to become aware of the devices listed below, which will help our writing "stick together":

Essays often combine organizational patterns.

Coherence = linking sentences with connecting words

Linking sentences is a natural habit that writers learn to control during revision.

Methods for Achieving Coherence

1. Transitions

2. Repetition

3. Synonyms

4. Pronouns

5. Reference to a main idea

Teaching Idea
It can be a bit misleading to refer to all the methods for linking sentences as transitions (although they certainly function this way). You may find the term *connectors* useful to refer to the five methods listed in *A Writer's Workshop*.

Transitions

The use of **transitions** (also called "connectors" in this text) is the most common technique for creating coherence in writing. Transitional words and phrases guide a reader through our writing like street signs help us to find our way in the city.

TABLE 3-1	List of Common Transitions		
For Locating or Moving in Space (particularly useful for descriptive writing)			
above	east (west . . .)	In front of	over
against	elsewhere	inside	surrounded by
alongside	far off (away)	into	there
around	farther on	near	through
at the side (end)	forward	next to	to
backward	from	off	to the right (left)
behind	here (close to here)	on	under
below	in	on the other side	up
beyond	in the back	onto	upstairs
by	in between	opposite	
down	in the distance	out of	
For Moving in Time (particularly useful in narrative writing)			
after	first (second, etc.)	next	suddenly
afterward	immediately	now	then
at last	in the meantime	often	time passed
awhile	in the past	once	until
before	later	previously	when
earlier	long ago	recently	while
finally	meanwhile	soon	

All references to calendar time and calendar events

ago (days, weeks, months, years)

one day (days of the week, months of the year, seasons, holidays)

that morning (afternoon, evening)

today (tonight, yesterday, tomorrow)

All references to clock time	**All references to regular meals**
any clock numbers used with A.M./P.M. (12:00 A.M., 1:00 P.M., etc.)	during breakfast (brunch, lunch, dinner)
a few minutes (seconds, hours)	

TABLE 3-1	List of Common Transitions *(concluded)*		
For Adding Material (particularly useful in writing that explains how something works)			
again	as well as	furthermore	likewise
also	besides	in addition	moreover
and	further	last	next
For Giving Examples and Emphasis (particularly useful in explanatory and persuasive writing)			
above all	especially	in particular	one reason
after all	for example	in truth	specifically
another	for instance	it is true	surely
as an example	indeed	most important	that is
certainly	in fact	of course	to illustrate
For Comparing (particularly useful in writing that focuses on similarities and differences)			
alike	both	like	resembling
also	in the same way	likewise	similarly
For Contrasting (particularly useful in writing that focuses on similarities and differences)			
after all	dissimilar	nevertheless	though
although	even though	on the contrary	unlike
but	however	on the other hand	whereas
differs from	in contrast	otherwise	yet
difference	in spite of	still	
For Showing Cause and Effect (particularly useful in explanatory and persuasive writing)			
accordingly	because	hence	then
and so	consequently	since	therefore
as a result	for this reason	so	thus
For Summarizing and Concluding (particularly useful at the end of body paragraphs and at the *beginning* of concluding paragraphs)			
finally	in conclusion	in short	that is
in brief	in other words	largely	to summarize

Teaching Idea
To help students through Activity 3-11, you might have them focus on space and time transitions first and then the others.

Activity 3-11: Coherence through Transitions

Using the lists above, locate and underline all the transitional words that you can find in the following paragraph excerpt. The first sentence has been marked as an example.

Paddling <u>down</u> Kansas <u>and</u> Missouri rivers is one of my favorite pastimes, <u>but</u> I have had some awful experiences <u>on</u> them. One aggravation I have learned to deal with is bad weather. Our <u>first</u> night <u>on</u> the river, everybody is excited <u>and</u> raising hell—till the rain comes. <u>For some reason</u> the rain clouds seem to follow us <u>down into</u> the river valleys <u>and then</u> open up. Fellow campers and I usually wake up <u>in</u> a huge mud puddle, <u>and</u> we are lucky if we don't have to swim <u>to</u> the trucks to get clean, dry clothes. <u>While</u> uncertain weather might seem bad enough, having a friend get hurt is worse. <u>Once</u> my friend Matt flipped his canoe <u>in front of</u> mine, <u>and</u> I couldn't stop <u>in</u> time. Matt caught the bow <u>of</u> my canoe <u>in</u> his right eye. The cold, clear spring water <u>of</u> the Current River did not stop the huge purple lump <u>above</u> his eye from swelling.

> Repeating a word or phrase is a common and useful connector.

Repetition

Repeating a word or phrase is the second most common technique for creating coherence in writing. However, you should be careful not to repeat needlessly. There is a point where successful coherence ends and boring repetition begins. Take a look at the following sets of sentences and judge which uses repetition most effectively:

A. Every summer, after school was over in Venezuela, two of **my cousins** used to come to my parents' house to spend their vacation time with us. **My cousins and I** didn't realize at that young age that **my grandfather,** who lived with us, was having a hard time trying to sleep. Kept awake every night by **my cousins'** loud voices and laughter, **my grandfather** decided to play a joke on **my cousins and me** that didn't turn out to be as funny as **my grandfather** thought it would be.

B. Every summer, after school was over in Venezuela, two of my cousins used to come to my parents' house to spend their vacation time with **us.** We didn't realize at that young age that my grandfather, who lived with **us,** was having a hard time trying to sleep. Kept awake every night by our loud voices and laughter, **he** decided to play a joke on **us** that didn't turn out to be as funny as **he** thought it would be.

If version A seems a bit awkward, it is because the writer has overused repetition, instead of offering some variety as she does in version B.

Synonyms

Using **synonyms** (words with identical or nearly identical meaning) or short phrases in the place of another word or phrase is a good alternative to simple repetition. For example, in the excerpt above, the author could have created variety by naming her two cousins and using the word *children* to refer to herself and her cousins.

> **Teaching Idea**
> Sometimes students think that they must find a single synonym to replace an overly repeated word, forgetting that a brief phrase can also be effective.

> **Teaching Idea**
> Activity 3-12 can also show that some repetition is not just permissible but desirable.

Activity 3-12: Coherence through Repetition and Synonyms

In the following brief paragraph cross out any unneeded repetition, and then write in any necessary replacement words in the space above the line. Do not cross out every repeated word, though—remember that some repetition is useful.

Answers will vary.

Everyone has experienced the thrill of victory, but I have yet to see a comeback as sweet as the 1997 Chapman vs. Abilene football game. Chapman and Abilene are two class 4A high schools located in north–central Kansas, and ~~Chapman and Abilene~~ *they* have one of the fiercest football rivalries in the state ~~of Kansas~~. At first, the game seemed like any other ~~football rivalry~~ game.

Chapman would get a touchdown, and then ~~Abilene~~ *my team* would ~~answer with~~ another touchdown. Both ~~Chapman and Abilene~~ *teams* had a strong passing game, but Chapman could run the football better ~~than Abilene could run it~~.

Pronouns

Pronouns (words that stand in the place of nouns) are used by most of us so unconsciously that we might overlook them as strong coherence devices. Whenever we use words like *he, she, him, her, them,* we are using pronouns and helping to hold our sentences together (for more on pronouns see Chapter 24). As with synonyms, however, we must be careful not to overuse pronouns, and, to avoid confusion, we must be sure that a pronoun clearly refers back to a specific noun. Read the following two sets of sentences and decide which is most coherent and clear:

A. Bill's boss told **him** that **his** office would be relocated while major renovations were completed on their building. The rest of **his** staff were worried that **his** office relocation would put **him** too far away to stay in touch with day-to-day problems. But Jim assured everyone that **his** office project would be handled quickly, and **he** would be back on the front line with **his** co-workers before they knew it.

B. Bill's boss told him that **Bill's** office would be relocated while major renovations were completed on their building. The rest of **Jim's** staff were worried that **Bill's** office relocation would put him too far away to stay in touch with departmental business. But Jim assured his employees that **Bill's** office project would be handled quickly and that **Bill** would be back on the front line with his co-workers before they knew it.

Always check pronouns for clear reference.

If version A seems difficult to understand, you might notice the overuse of *his.* Pronoun reference becomes especially tricky when within a sentence or immediately preceding it there are several nouns a pronoun could be referring to, as is the case above with Bill and Jim. A good general rule of thumb to follow when revising for both coherence and clarity is to be suspicious of *all* pronouns, checking them several times to be sure the noun that they refer back to is clear to your reader. (For more on pronoun reference problems, see pp. 546–549.)

Activity 3-13: Coherence through Pronouns

In the following paragraph excerpt cross out unneeded or confusing pronouns, and write in the replacement words in the line above.

Teaching Idea
Activity 3-13 will help students see the importance of clarity and also tone in pronoun reference. The reference errors (head removed, put the mother down?) seem laughable, damaging the author's serious, sad tone.

Smokey lived with me for eight and a half years and was my good friend. But then she contracted a feline virus comparable to AIDS in humans. During the time she was sick, she also got cancer, which caused a lump on her neck just behind her head. We had ~~it~~ *the lump* removed once in hopes that ~~it~~ *the operation* would save her life, but instead ~~it~~ *the lump* came back. When it returned, it was twice as big as ~~it had been~~ *before*, and ~~it~~ only took half the time to form. My mother and I decided that it would be best to put ~~her~~ *Smokey* down. It was the hardest decision of my life, but I loved ~~her~~ *my cat* too much to see her in such pain.

Reference to Main Ideas

Another useful method for achieving coherence between sentences and paragraphs is by linking main ideas or examples. For instance, notice how the following paragraph excerpt begins to develop the idea of *merciless teachers* in the topic sentence, continues with the synonym *cruel*, and reinforces the idea of cruelty with the word *punish*.

As I think back on middle school in Korea, I remember that I was afraid of the <u>merciless</u> teachers who wanted me to enjoy studying by forcing it on me. One of my teachers, for moral education, was short and fat, just like the whip he carried. "I see you haven't done your homework, Jeong," he said. With my palms up, he began to whip my hands harshly. Somehow the pain ended with me crying and begging, "I will do it next time, teacher!" Another <u>cruel</u> man, my history teacher, liked to use his green baby bamboo stick to <u>punish</u> me when I didn't score more than 80 percent on his exams.

Well-connected writing relies on all five methods to achieve coherence, often using several in the same sentence.

◼ SELECTING A TITLE

Teaching Idea
During their final revising sessions you might have students review the pointers on writing effective titles and then compare theirs. Next have several students read their titles aloud to get some feedback from the class and from you.

Your title may already be lurking as a phrase within the sentences of your draft.

With your paper well in hand, topic and concluding sentences in place, and body well developed, it is time to expend one last bit of creative energy. Now is the time to focus on the title. But why do we need one in the first place? Especially if it is a short paper, why not let the reader just jump right in? Well, think for a moment of all the writing you have read over the years—the books, stories, poems, newspaper and magazine articles—and the television programs and movies you have seen. How many did not have a title? If professional writers spend a great deal of thought on what to call their work, there may be a good reason for it.

A title's primary purpose is to attract a reader. In "real-world" writing authors are competing for their readers' attention, their time and money; so any device that might increase the authors' chances of success is welcome. You, too, are competing for your audience's attention. Whether you are working on a personal project, a business proposition, or a paper for a professor, capturing your readers' interest sets up a positive expectation as they move into your work. The title can predispose the reader in your favor.

As you work through the writing process, discovering ideas, organizing, drafting, and revising, be alert to any image or phrase that might make a good title. If nothing seems promising, you can brainstorm alone or with others when the paper is complete. Whenever you decide to create your title, remember that it should accomplish two goals: interest a reader and predict something about the coming topic.

If you had to choose one of the following papers to read on the basis of the title, which would most interest you?

1. A profile of a hard-working mother:

   A. *My Mom the Worker*

      or

   B. *She Kept the Ship Afloat*

2. A story about a child sneaking one too many cookies:

   A. *Children Should Mind Their Parents*

      or

   B. *Slamming the Lid on Andrew*

3. A personal narrative about a serious accident:

A. *A Bad Wreck*

or

B. *Crawling through the Wreckage*

If you preferred the B versions, you can work on creating titles that are more like them by following some of the suggestions listed in the boxes below.

How to Write Effective Titles

1. Keep them short (roughly 1 to 8 words). Some longer titles work well, but people can read and process a shorter title more efficiently than a longer one. Making a reader labor over a title may make him think that the paper to follow will also be hard work.

2. Link the title to your main idea or dominant impression.

3. Create an image:
   A. Use a metaphor or other comparison. Notice the first title example above. What do you suppose the *ship* refers to? (For more on metaphors, see pp. 473–474.)
   B. Use specific words, sensory details, active verbs, and *-ings*. Notice the second and third title examples use the *-ing* to convey action. (For more on action-oriented *-ings*, see p. 68.)

4. Use a question. Look back at the paragraph "What's the Rush?" (p. 45).

5. Make a play on words. Notice in the second title example that "slamming the lid" might mean something besides the literal top of a cookie jar. Consider the slang expression "to put a lid on it," meaning to stop some behavior. Word play can add a humorous touch to a paper when the topic and tone warrant it.

6. Refer to something that your audience might know and find engaging: sports; world, national, or local news; literature; religion; social groups; life roles (employer, employee, parent, brother, sister, etc.); a joke or song lyric reference; and so on. (For more on audience profiling, see p. 10)

What to Avoid in Titles

1. Clichés and worn phrases: Recycled comparisons are boring. If you are tempted to title a paper "The Wait That Seemed an Eternity" or "The Night That Sent Shivers Down My Spine," don't do it. These kinds of clichés *will* "send shivers down your instructors' spines," may make them "break into a cold sweat," and will certainly make them feel like they have been reading your paper "for an eternity." (For more on clichés, see pp. 474–475.)

2. Inappropriate tone: The tone of your work is the feeling you have about your topic and the feeling you want your reader to sense (happy, playful, sad, bitter, angry, formal, etc). If, for instance, your topic and your treatment of it are serious, sad, or angry, don't use a light-hearted title. (For more on tone, see pp. 464–473.)

3. Waiting until five minutes before class to write it: If the title can really contribute to the overall impact of your paper, why gamble on inspiration at the last possible moment?

Formatting

1. Capitalize all words in your title—even small ones like *do, is, can,* etc.—except articles (*a, an, the*), prepositions (*in, on, to,* etc.), and coordinating conjunctions (*and, but, or, nor, for, so, yet*). However, the first and last words of the title and a word following a colon should be capitalized no matter what kind of words they are.

2. No quotation marks or underline is needed for a title placed on a title page or at the heading of the first page of text.

3. Be sure to center the title on the page.

CHAPTER SUMMARY

1. A paragraph is a unified and coherent collection of sentences that is most often grouped with other paragraphs.

2. Body paragraphs must have a central point—often a topic sentence located as the first sentence in the paragraph.

3. A topic sentence consists of the topic plus a statement of opinion or attitude. It should be focused and as interesting as you can make it.

4. Paragraphs are developed with examples, details, and explanations.

5. Paragraph support should be sufficient, relevant, and clear.

6. Paragraphs almost always benefit from specific word choices and specific examples.

7. Concluding sentences should end a paper decisively. One way to do this is through an expanded thought.

8. Three types of overall organizational patterns for paragraphs are spatial (description), chronological (narrative), and order of importance (explanatory and persuasive). These methods often overlap.

9. A paragraph is unified when all examples, details, and explanations, relate to a central point (topic sentence).

10. Paragraphs become coherent when sentences are clearly linked using transitions, repetition, synonyms, pronouns, and references to main ideas.

11. A title is an important part of a paper, and there are strategies for writing effective ones.

CHAPTER 4

Revising Paragraphs

Re-visioning Paragraphs

Material
Organization
Style
Mechanics

◨ REVISING PARAGRAPHS

This chapter is a practical guide to help you with the difficult task of revising. You will soon see that it pulls together many concepts already mentioned in Chapters 1 and 3 and also asks you to recall important principles you have practiced in the Skills section of each assignment chapter. In addition, you will be focusing closely on some common editing problems that are explained in greater depth in Unit Five.

To help focus your writing before drafting, you might want to skim through the rough-draft questions in this chapter that apply to your paragraph assignment. Even more important, after you complete a draft, the questions will help you think critically about it, focusing your energy on revision priorities: content and organization first, style and editing second. If any question seems unclear and the examples/explanation in this chapter are not enough to help, turn back to the pages referenced and read a bit more. Effective revision is a skill that can be learned, but it is not easy, and most people do not have a natural talent for it. However, if you are willing to invest the energy, you will gradually become your own best editor.

You will notice that Picturing a Place and Telling Your Own Story have individual first-stage draft questions. The five Expository patterns of development—illustration, classification, cause and effect, process analysis, and comparison/contrast—have their own first-stage draft questions as well. But all the paragraph assignments in Unit Two use identical suggestions for handling **second**-stage and **editing** drafts.

Whether you are beginning the revision process on your own or within a group, turn back to Chapter 1, pp. 14–16, for reminders about overall revising strategy.

▶ FIRST-STAGE DRAFTS (FOR DESCRIPTION)

List for helping with first-draft problems in **descriptive** writing

Focus on:

- **Content:** the substance of the scene being described
- **Organization:** arranging and connecting ideas

1. Are you really describing a place and not slipping into a narrative (story)?

   While a well-told story will have lots of action leading to a high point or climax, a descriptive paragraph may have little or no action. A story follows a person through a series of actions and has an uncertain outcome. Your description, on the other hand, should be completely predictable, from the topic sentence that states your main point onward.

2. How effective is your topic sentence?

   If you have included the place you are describing and some limiting statement about it, you are probably in good shape. Now to make the topic sentence even stronger, include a word or two of **sensory detail** to interest your reader (a color, sound, or touch detail works well), and look closely for ways to make a word or two more **specific,** particularly the name of the place you are describing. (Glance at the topic sentences in the student paragraph models in Chapter 5 to see general and specific word choices: for example, family fun center = Incred-A-Bowl.) Also, consider writing a medium-length topic sentence (fifteen to twenty-five words) rather than a shorter one (five to ten words) or a longer one (twenty-five to forty words). (For more on topic sentences, see pp. 36–40, 85–86.)

3. Does your description have an overall point (dominant impression)?

   Many rough drafts add sight, sound, and other details to a description almost at random. Remember that you are not merely a camera recording any picture that comes in front of your lens. You are a person with a point to make about your place. Do most of your details cause a reader to feel one way or another about the location? For example, if you want a person to feel that your bedroom is a relaxing place, do not include the details of your piled up textbooks and overdue homework assignments on your desk, both of which are making you nervous. (For more on the dominant impression, see pp. 82–84.)

4. Are you occasionally telling your reader what to think about the details?

   Readers often need some brief explanation within a sentence to help clarify part of a description or reinforce a dominant impression. For example, in "Our Family Outing" (pp. 101–102) the author mentions the pool tables and batting cages but then notes that parents bring their children to practice there, adding to the paper's focus on family togetherness. (For more on clarifying the dominant impression, see p. 83.)

5. Are you occasionally letting your reader know how you feel about the place?

   Because this is a subjective description, you should let your reader know what you feel and think about what you are describing—as long as the thoughts and feelings help to reinforce the dominant impression. (For more on thoughts/feelings in description, see "Waking Up the Right Way," p. 93.)

6. Are you using enough specific language?

   One of the primary goals of practicing the descriptive paragraph is to help you think more about relatively specific versus relatively general words and how to use them both. Your second draft can almost certainly be improved by making some of your images more specific. (For more on specific words, see pp. 78–79.)

7. How well are you using sensory details?

Remember that we often overrely on sight and use too few of the other senses in building image, especially sound and touch. Sometimes, too, we overdescribe, cramming too many details into a sentence. (For more on sensory detail, see pp. 80–81.)

8. How effective is your concluding sentence?

If the concluding sentence contains a connector word or phrase, a word or phrase that echoes the dominant impression, and possibly a thought or comment about the place you have described, then you have a strong final sentence. Sometimes, influenced by our urge to write concluding *paragraphs,* we end with three or four sentences that break from description and move more into speculation, which would be fine to add to the concluding paragraph of an *essay.* But we need to limit the paragraph paper to one or at most two sentences that let the reader know the description has come to an end. (For more on concluding sentences, see pp. 48–51, 86–87.)

9. How well connected are all the sentences within the paragraph?

This first rough draft will probably profit from more time and space connectors, especially the space locators. Take a few minutes to carefully reread each sentence, pretending that you are directing someone with a video camera who is filming the place. You will need to tell the photographer what she is supposed to shoot, so you will be using phrases like "*to the left of* the mirror," "*in front of* the picture window," "*next to* the refrigerator," and so on. (For more on connectors, see pp. 52–57.)

> **JOURNAL ENTRY 4-1 (CONTINUES JOURNAL ENTRIES FROM CHAPTER 5)**
>
> To help you focus on the revision process and to alert your instructor to your progress, list three *specific* changes you have made or feel you ought to make from your first to second rough draft. Refer to the First-Stage Draft questions and answer as specifically as possible. (Example: Question 2: "I felt like my dominant impression was a bit weak. I had to cut [list details] because the details were off the main point.") Next, in a sentence or two say what you like best about your draft.

FIRST-STAGE DRAFTS (FOR NARRATION)

1. Has your narrative gotten out of hand and grown into a "sort of" essay?

Once you get rolling, it is easy to begin including many interesting side details that nonetheless distract the reader and diminish the impact of your main point. Locate the center of your tale—the high point of action and its meaning—and then cut anything that doesn't get your reader there in a hurry. Use no more than a sentence or two to supply any necessary background. Move immediately from the high point of action to the concluding sentence (or two). Remember to limit the overall duration of the narrative (a few minutes to a few hours usually work best for a paragraph).

2. How effective is your topic sentence?

Personal narrative and fiction can effectively begin with an action sentence like the following: "After finishing a lunch of greasy fries and hamburgers, I dashed through the parking lot toward room 130." However, this sort of beginning does not give your reader (or yourself) a clear sense of where the paper is headed. So

Teaching Idea
Journal Entry 4-1 is a good first checkpoint to see if students are beginning to understand revising. It is worth the time to pick the entry up, check, and return it. All of the journal entries are useful for stimulating discussion about specific revision strategies.

List for helping with first-draft problems in **narrative** writing

Move straight from your topic sentence into the action.

for our brief stories, to help with focus, it would be best to begin with a topic sentence. Often you will include a hint of the climax here or simply state it outright, and you might link the topic sentence to the significance of the event. (For more on topic sentences, see any of the Chapter 6 student models and pp. 36–40.).

3. Does the story have conflict, suspense, climax and resolution?

> Conflict and movement are crucial to your story.

For your narrative to work, it must have conflict: person versus person, person versus the external world (forces of nature, animals, machines), person versus herself (an internal struggle). In order for the story to have suspense, it must keep the reader wondering what will happen next. If the action is well organized, it will move chronologically up to some high point, at which moment the action stops. As you reflect on the action in the final sentence (or two), you can resolve the story by highlighting some significant point or meaning. (For more on these points, see pp. 109–110, 122–123.)

4. How well have you sketched the setting?

You don't need to go overboard describing the one or two scenes in the setting, but you should create enough details to orient your reader. When you describe, remember what we practiced in the Picturing a Place chapter: *specific* word choices Mustang vs. car) and *sensory details* (sight, sound, touch, smell, taste). (For more on specific language and sensory details, see pp. ___–81.)

5. Have you described people sufficiently?

Although the focus is on people's actions, thoughts, and emotions, do give your reader some sense for who any important person is (brother, sister, wife, etc.). Notice how the brief description of the grandfather in "What a Joke" (pp. 117–118) adds to our appreciation of the tale: "Toothless, his hair ruffled from sleep, and wearing loose white pajamas, he was standing in front of me, leaning forward to scratch on the door again and continue his joke." Also, be sure to show how your important people move—their gestures and how they walk, sit, or stand.

6. Have you included effective dialogue?

Because dialogue is a powerful device for showing what people feel and think, it is used frequently in stories. You may not need dialogue in your story, depending on the topic (see the student model "Death Strikes," pp. 74–75, for an example), but your story would probably benefit from it. Check to make sure the dialogue sounds convincing. (For more on dialogue, see pp. 113–114.)

7. Have you revealed your thoughts and feelings?

As the narrator you are in the unique position to tell the reader what is going through your mind and what you are feeling, and you can speculate on the other characters' thoughts and emotions. While you can do too much telling and not enough showing, you should take the opportunity to share relevant thoughts and emotions.

8. Is the significance of the event clear?

Remember that your event may have several meanings. There is no one right interpretation. However, since the assignment calls for you to share some insight about yourself or the world around you, you should decide what you want the reader to see and then make it clear to her. (For more on significance, see p. 111.)

9. How effective is your concluding sentence?

Your concluding sentence should contain a connector word or phrase (transitional word, repeat word, etc.) and a clear indication of the significance of the event. But try not to conclude with a cliché or worn expression, which we sometimes do when hard pressed for a substantive thought. (For more on concluding sentences, see pp. 48–51.)

10. How well connected are sentences within the paragraph?

This first rough draft will almost certainly benefit from more time and space connectors, especially time transitions. Keep in mind that there are several ways to link sentences to maintain coherence, and remember that summarizing phrases can speed up the pace of the story. (For more on sentence connectors see pp. 52–57.)

> Summarizing actions can link scenes and speed up the pace of the story.

JOURNAL ENTRY 4-2 (CONTINUES JOURNAL ENTRIES FROM CHAPTER 6)

To help you focus on the revision process and to alert your instructor to your progress, list three *specific* changes you have made or feel you ought to make from your first to second rough draft. Refer to the First-Stage Draft questions and answer as specifically as possible. (Example: Question 1: "My story was slow to take off, so I had to cut out the first three sentences and use the fourth one as my topic sentence.) Next, in a sentence or two say what you like best about your story.

FIRST-STAGE DRAFTS (FOR EXPOSITION)

> List for helping with first-draft problems in **expository** writing

1. Have you used three or four examples, or have you only developed one?

Coming from our narrative projects, you might still be in the single-place, single-story mode. But it is time to break from this. For now, try to use three to four examples. Resist the temptation to cram five, six, or ten examples into the paragraph. Too many examples mean too little development.

2. How effective is your topic sentence?

Your topic sentence has two functions: to identify a topic and limit it with a statement or assertion. For example, you might want to deal with rock-and-roll as a topic. Instead of trying to handle the past forty-some-year history of rock, you might limit the topic to one group, say, the Beatles. Your statement to limit the topic could be "My favorite group of ancient rock and rollers is the Beatles." If you prefer, you could also use a **forecasting statement** as in "The Beatles are my favorite vintage rock group *because their music is simple yet inventive, and their lyrical themes are largely positive.*" In this brief paragraph assignment, however, you may find that a forecasting statement makes your subtopics sound repetitive. Decide what works best for your topic and audience.

Be sure to add **specific words** to your topic sentences like this: "Paddling down *Kansas and Missouri* rivers is one of my favorite pastimes, but I have had some awful experiences on them." (For more on topic sentences, see pp. 36–40.)

3. Have you clearly arranged your main examples—either by time or importance?

Chronological order can work well in illustration paragraphs, but order of importance is more emphatic. Determine which method works best for you and then remain consistent. By the way, you may find that your material follows both patterns, which is fine. (For more on order of importance see, p. 138.)

4. Have you written a subtopic sentence to introduce each main example?

While not all paragraphs that use examples also use subtopic sentences, many do, and they can help your work in several ways. First, subtopic statements are a clear guide for your reader. Second, they are a clear guide for you. Third, they create emphasis. (For more on subtopic sentences, see pp. 136–138 and any of the Unit Two student models.)

5. Are your main examples adequately developed?

Each major example should be developed with second- and perhaps third-level examples and the details that go along with them. Notice how in "The Jobs from Hell" Eric Latham developed one of his subtopic sentences:

The **worst job** I have ever had was in my sophomore year when I applied for work at Fritz's Meat House. **(Subtopic sentence)**

The store was absolutely gross, filled with rotting meat from days ago, hanging pig carcasses waiting to be chopped, and an overflowing grease bin. The bin was located on the bottom floor of the two-story building, and all the animal parts ended up in it—chicken heads, legs, and feathers; pig feet; cow ribs; and gray intestines slippery from blood and yellow fatty tissue. **(Second- and third-level examples with details)**

Remember to ask yourself the question "What do I mean by that?" just as Eric did to help his example grow.

Q: What do I mean by "worst job"?

A: "Gross store"

Q: What do I mean by "gross"?

A: "Meat, pig carcasses, grease bin, etc."

Q: What do I mean by "meat, pig carcasses, and grease bin?"

A: "Rotting meat, hanging pig carcasses, overflowing grease bin." (Details are underlined.)

Remember the principle of becoming increasingly specific as you move through each example, and use the elements of vivid scene building where appropriate (specific word choices, sensory details, active verbs, "-ings," dialogue, setting and people description).

6. Are your examples thoroughly explained?

Each example should not only be vividly presented but also clearly explained. Often you must *tell* your reader what an example is supposed to represent or how it connects with your main point. Notice how in "Teaching with Whips" Jeong included a sentence of explanation with his descriptive example of the black stick.

The most memorable of all these tyrants was the despised art teacher nicknamed Poisonous Snake. **(Subtopic sentence)**

None of the students got along well with him. He seemed to dislike all of us equally. The black tape wrapped around the long, powerful stick that he used so frequently increased all our fear. **(Second-level example—explanation underlined)**

(For more on clarity in examples, see pp. 46–47.)

7. Are your examples relevant?

In first drafts, especially, material can slip in that might be interesting but that nevertheless distracts from the main point. For instance, in the student model "Dangers in a Deli" (p. 146), while it might be both true and noteworthy that deli workers often get along well together and have many good times on the job, these facts distract from the main point of what dangers to watch out for. (For more on relevance in examples, see pp. 44–45.)

8. How well connected are sentences within the paragraph?

This first rough draft will probably benefit from transitional words for adding material, giving examples, and emphasizing a point. Also within narrative/descriptive examples you may need more time and space transitions. For achieving overall coherence, remember the other connectors besides transitions: repeat words, synonyms, pronouns, and reference to main ideas. (For more on sentence connectors see pp. 52–57.)

9. How effective is your concluding sentence?

Ideas for expanded thoughts in the conclusion often occur while you are drafting.

Your concluding sentence should use a connector word or phrase, refer back to the topic sentence statement, and expand the main idea of your paragraph. While you were drafting, if you saved any of the ideas that seemed too digressive in the body, this might be a good place to use them. For example, we noted in question 7 that "good times" would be distracting within the body of the deli illustration paragraph, where the author is developing the idea of dangers, but coming at the end, this observation could work well. (For more on concluding sentences, see pp. 48–51.)

> **JOURNAL ENTRY 4-3 (CONTINUES JOURNAL ENTRIES FROM CHAPTERS 7 THROUGH 11)**
>
> To help you focus on the revision process and to alert your instructor to your progress, list three *specific* changes you have made or feel you ought to make from your first to second rough draft. Refer to the First-Stage Draft questions and answer as specifically as possible. (Example: Question 1: "I realized that I was only developing one example, so I added two more.") Next, in a sentence or two say what you like best about your draft.

SECOND-STAGE DRAFTS: ALL PATTERNS OF DEVELOPMENT

List for helping with second-stage draft problems for all Unit Two paragraph assignments

Depending on your writing habits, you may find yourself with a fairly complete draft at this stage, or you may still need to spend more time on major content and organizational concerns. But assuming that you are comfortable with most of the material in your draft, we can work a bit more with **word-** and **sentence-level** revision possibilities.

1. How well have you used specific language?

Teaching Idea
If class time runs short, you can combine selected questions from the First- and Second-Stage Draft lists, emphasizing the ones that are most significant to you.

Your paragraph will include both relatively *general* and relatively *specific* terms, but now is the time to double-check for places where specific words could sharpen an image. We could use the relatively general term "old clothes," or focus the reader with more specific language, "old blue jeans and a sweatshirt," or, even more specific, "faded Levis ripped out at the knees and a baggy KU Jayhawk sweatshirt." (For more on specific language, see pp. 78–79.)

2. How thoroughly have you explored sensory details?

All writing can benefit from sensory details (sight, sound, touch, smell, and taste), but description and narration thrive on it. If you are using personal examples and trying to create an image, remember to use as many of the senses as possible, without overrelying on sight. Compare the following two sentences. Which creates the sharper image in your mind?

A. Eating a dessert in the country can make it taste better than at home.

B. The hot, white melting marshmallows fresh from the fire, stick to my fingers and almost burn me as I pop them too quickly into my mouth.

If you think sentence B creates a sharper image, revise your own sentences, adding sensory details wherever they will help.

> **Caution:** Avoid *over*detailing, which can make your writing sound forced. Especially try not to "stack" modifiers in front of words, for example, "a sleek, shiny, turbo-charged, gas-guzzling black Mustang." (For more on sensory details, see pp. 80–81.)

3. Are you choosing the most "active" verbs to describe action?

Almost all of our sentences require verbs to make them complete, often conveying a sense of action or movement. But some verbs show action less efficiently than others (*be, do, have, make* are common culprits). Compare the following two sentences. Which creates the sharper image in your mind?

A. The children <u>are having</u> a good time bowling.

B. The small children <u>are jumping, clapping, and screaming</u> as their balls <u>hit</u> the pins.

If you think that sentence B creates a more vivid image, revise your own sentences, adding active verbs wherever they are needed. (For more on active verbs, see p. 451.)

4. Are you using any "-ing" words?

Participles (a verb form with an "-ing" ending) can also convey action well. Compare the following two sentences. Which creates the sharper image in your mind?

A. I can hear the trees move.

B. I can hear the leaves <u>rustling</u> and branches <u>brushing</u> against each other.

If you think sentence B creates a more vivid image, revise your own sentences, adding "-ing" words wherever they are needed. (For more on "-ings," see pp. 494–495.)

5. Are the sentences in your paragraph varied in length?

Writing can become more or less interesting based on the structure of sentences alone. After you have polished word choices, look at the length of your sentences, counting the words in each one. If you find more than three or four sentences in a row roughly the same length (say, 14, 17, 12, 15 words), either combine two of them or divide any longer ones. (For more on overall sentence variety, see Chapter 18.)

6. Are the beginnings of your sentences varied?

If even two sentences in a row in your draft begin with the same word or phrase, such as *the,* you might need to change an opening or combine sentences to break up the pattern. Also be alert to using too many similar openings, even if the sentences are widely spaced. (For more on variety in sentence openers, see pp. 435–446.)

Teaching Idea
Questions 3 and 4 ask students to focus on action without insisting on grammatical terminology, such as participles and progressive tense. Students are sometimes more comfortable using terms like "-*ing* words" to describe the action elements in their sentences.

Teaching Idea
Sentence variety is discussed at length in Chapter 18, but it is a good idea to introduce this concept early in the semester, and then revisit it as students revise for style.

7. Have you repeated a word or phrase so often that it becomes noticeable?

   While some repetition of a word or phrase is fine, too much of the same word group becomes boring. Compare the following two sentences. Which sounds repetitive?

   A. I like to spend time at the **pond** because the **pond** is a relaxing place. Of all the **ponds** I have visited in the last twenty years, this **pond** is the one that will forever live in my memory.

   B. I like to spend time outdoors in relaxing surroundings, and there is one **place** in particular that I enjoy. Of all the **ponds** I have visited in the last twenty years, this is the **one** that will forever live in my memory.

   If you think that version B is more readable, revise your own sentences, cutting or replacing words too often repeated. (For more on unnecessary repetition, see pp. 479–480.)

8. Have you included words that serve no purpose?

   Everyday speech is full of nonessential words, but writing should not be. Cluttered writing can bore and confuse while concise writing involves a reader and clarifies ideas. Compare the following two sentences. Which is concise; which is cluttered?

   A. The **meat** hotdogs, **long and thin,** sizzle **with a sizzling sound** as they cook, **roasting,** and drip **meaty hot dog juices** off the end of the **wooden stick.**

   B. The hotdogs sizzle as they cook and drip juices off the end of the stick.

   If you think that sentence B is more readable, revise your own sentences, cutting nonessential words. (For more on unneeded words, see pp. 454–464.)

> **JOURNAL ENTRY 4-4 (CONTINUES JOURNAL ENTRIES FROM ASSIGNMENT CHAPTERS 5 THROUGH 11)**
>
> To help you focus on the revision process and to alert your instructor to your progress, list three *specific* changes you have made or feel you ought to make from your second draft. Refer to the Second-Stage Draft questions and answer as specifically as possible. (Example: Question 4: "I noticed that although I am describing people in a restaurant, I hadn't used any "-ing" words, so I found a good place for these in my fourth and eighth sentences.") Next, in a sentence or two say what you like best about your draft so far.

EDITING: ALL PATTERNS OF DEVELOPMENT

The editing stage of preparing our work for final presentation to an audience is one that we often hurry through. This is understandable considering how long a journey it has often been from brainstorming to final draft. We fall down at the end of the journey much like the over-excited backpacker who has survived uninjured in the mountains for a week and a half, and, seeing the lodge just down the trail, hurries too quickly, trips, and sprains her ankle.

Of course, aside from just being overanxious to complete the writing excursion, we often just don't know what to look for in the draft. After all, if we don't know the rule that tells us where to put the comma, how are we supposed to recognize the spot where the comma is missing?

Well . . . it would be great if there were a quick fix for grammar, spelling, and punctuation errors, but the simple truth is that you will be grappling with them for a long time. All writers do. But it sometimes helps to remember that the mechanics of writing are truly the least important element (though still significant), and even if you are not a "comma whiz," you can quickly catch some, perhaps many, mistakes if you are willing to read your own and others' work slooowly and carefully.

The following brief paragraphs have a number of these common mechanical errors:

- Apostrophes
- Capitalizations
- Comma splices
- Missing commas
- Missing words

- Misspelled words
- Pronoun agreement
- Pronoun reference
- Run-on sentences
- Sentence fragments

- Sound-alike words
- Unneeded commas
- Verb tense shifts
- Wrong words

Take a moment to read through each paragraph *slowly* and carefully, putting your finger on every word if necessary, and see how many of the mistakes you catch.

Editing Review

Editing these practice paragraphs will help you with your own revision.

Effective editing requires a person to slow her reading to a crawl.

Teaching Idea
These editing review paragraphs can be especially useful if reviewed on a day when students are preparing to edit their own papers.

1. As I glance down at the windowsill I often, think, about the many dead insects, lying their one can only assume that the bugs want there last moments alive too be my porch. Its small body makes quite a feast, for the two Barn Spiders that share my porch with me. The webs' are always filled with one delicacy, or anothr, one spider, in particular has, woven quite a spectacular web, against the old, paint-chipped corner. While I am inhaling, my first cup of morning fuel. A magnificent gust of wind blows thru. The sweet smell my neighbors freshly cut grass fills the air so flagrantly, that I can barely notice the thick humidity building for the day ahead.

(To see the corrected version of this excerpt, turn to page 92 and look at the first half of "Waking Up the Right Way.")

2. When I went to Middle School in korea. I was afraid of sevral merciles teachers, who seemed too want me to enjoy studying forcing it on me. My Moral Education Teacher was one of these crule educators, he was short, and fat like the whip he carried to enforce there every whim. "I see you have'nt done your homework Jeong", he would say. He orders me to hold my palms up and, then he begins to whip my hands harshly.

(To see the corrected version of this excerpt, turn to page 143 and look at the beginning of "Teaching with Whips.")

3. Panick and fustration our a sure fire recipe, for tears but I fought them of and strugled too remain calm, for my girls. Suddenly I hear a voice, say "Listen I have a cell phone, do you want to call someone to come pick you up". As I turned toward the voice I saw an older gentleman, who looked a lot like my dad. Begining to cry I explained how helples I felt.

(To see the corrected version of this excerpt, turn to page 130 and look at the middle of "Do Unto Others. . . .")

4. In order too help customers shop more efficiently, in Toys R Us, the store is divided into three overall categories: areas for older children, toddlers, and babies. The older chidren have four major areas. Blue, Pink, R-Zone, and Silver piles of toys for everyone. Boys mostly head for the blue section, and items like the GI Joe's Hotwheel's and Lego's. In no time, at all, the boys can have Lego race tracks assembled, on he floor, and be racing miniature batmobiles after the "bad guys."

(To see the corrected version of this excerpt, turn to page 169 and look at the beginning of "Shopping the Easy Way.")

5. Marrying, while still teenagers, can be a bad decision creating many problems for young couples. First when teens marry in or just out of highschool. They're relationships often change drasticaly instead of spending with there individual former friends newlyweds often find that that there spouse did not like some or all of the others friends' so the husband, or wife has to chose—"them or me."

(To see the corrected version of this excerpt, turn to page 192 and look at the beginning of "Making the Promise Last.")

6. Living in the country as a child a sling shot is what I longed for to play, and hunt with and finally decided would make one. Collecting the materials' for my treasure through did not come eazy. It recquired the most perfect forked branch form a Pine tree. A square of leather to hold the stone and a peice of rubber band. Any old rubberband will not do, though, it has too be surgical tubing light brown, and hose shaped, for the power I wanted.

(To see the corrected version of this excerpt, turn to page 217 and look at the beginning of "A Boy's Best Friend.")

7. Raisin hell, and living for the moment where all I use to care about but now that Im moving in my thirties life has change. When I was just entering, my twenties, I was still living at home. Although you never would have known it, by the way I come and go, telling none any thing. But, I have come along way sense then.

(To see the corrected version of this excerpt, turn to page 242 and look at the beginning of "Breakin' Through.")

Well, how did you do? If you caught all but two or three errors, congratulations; you are a careful editor! If you missed more than five or six, try to slow down even more. The following are a few reminders of what errors to look for in your own draft:

Editing Problems for All Patterns of Development

1. **Spelling:** Use your spell checker first, and then try to find at least one other reader who is not afraid to say she is a fairly good speller. Remember, too, that the dictionary is not that painful to use. (For help with spelling problems, see pp. 582–586.)

2. **Sound-alike words:** (*there/their/they're, to/too, then/than, your/you're*, etc.) Keep adding to your **Improvement Chart** (Appendix 2), and try to memorize these repeat errors. Writers usually keep repeating the same handful of mistakes—unless they identify and correct them—till doomsday. (For help with sound-alike words, see pp. 587–591.)

3. **Missing words:** Read slowly. Sometimes reading a sentence backward—admittedly, a tedious process—can help, and covering the sentence ahead of the one you are editing can keep you from jumping ahead too quickly.

4. **Wrong words:** Be suspicious of words that sound too "writerly." If you often find yourself thumbing through a thesaurus for word choices, you might be using the words incorrectly. You probably already have plenty of vocabulary to express yourself well, and smaller, more common words are frequently the best choices anyway. Your readers can be especially helpful in alerting you to *possible* poor selections, and then you can work with a dictionary and yet another person to make the final decisions. (For more on clarity through small words, see pp. 465–466.)

List for helping with editing problems for all Unit Two paragraph assignments

5. **Sentence fragments:** Remember two common types:

   a. Phrase: "Running to the store for bread and a six-pack of Coke." (See pp. 525–526.)

   b. Subordinate clause: "Because he is the kind of man we want for mayor." (See pp. 527–528.)

6. **Comma splices/run-ons:** There are at least five easy ways to fix these:

   a. Comma splice: "The cement is freezing, it instantly numbs my feet."

   b. Run-on: "The cement is freezing it instantly numbs my feet." (See pp. 518–524.)

Note: In dialogue be careful to avoid this kind of comma splice:

Roxanne shouted, "Get out of here, nobody gives a damn about you anyway!"

Instead write: Roxanne shouted, "Get out of here! Nobody gives a damn about you anyway!" People frequently speak in short sentences and in fragments. Don't be afraid to show this in your dialogue.

---

7. **Capitalizations:** Rule of thumb: capitalize a proper noun (a specific/unique person, place, or thing, see p. 578). In your title capitalize most words, even little ones like *is* and *one*. But do not capitalize articles (*a, an, the*), prepositions (*to, on, of, in,* etc.), and coordinating conjunctions (*and, but, so,* etc.) unless these words begin or end a title or follow a colon.

8. **Apostrophes:** Use to show ownership or mark the omission of a letter in a contraction: "Maria's calculator isn't working." (See p. 578.)

Teaching Idea
If you have students edit in class, it is useful to list the three major comma categories on the board along with some "cue" words: *because, who/which, and/but*. You will also find selected editing review sheets in the Instructor's Manual.

9. **The Big Three comma categories:** These categories govern perhaps half of our common uses of the comma:

   a. Use commas to introduce some single words, phrases, and the subordinate adverb clause before a main clause (cue words: *because, as, if, when,* etc.). (See pp. 565–566.)

   b. Use commas to enclose *nonessential* words, phrases, or clauses within a main clause or set them off at the end of a main clause (cue words: *who/which*). (See pp. 567–569.)

   c. Use commas to divide main clauses joined by *and/but* (*or, so, yet, for, nor*). (See pp. 570–571.)

10. **Unnecessary commas:** As you learn the handful of rules that help with comma placement, you will begin to move away from the old standby "I put commas where I hear the pauses." Using your ear can be a good help with punctuation, but it is only useful about half the time. Most of us don't want a 50 percent average, so learning a few rules is the way to go. Try to avoid the ear/pause mistakes of the unneeded comma in the following examples:

    A. I went to Burger King for lunch, and then to McDonald's for dinner.

    B. I eat three thirteen-ounce bags of potato chips every day, because I want to have a heart attack. (See pp. 573–575.)

After you have done the most thorough job of editing that *you* can do on your draft, it is time to get some help. Every writer—professional and beginner—benefits from having others look closely at her work. You will undoubtedly spend some class time in collaborative editing sessions, but don't stop there. Be willing to work with your instructor, and remember that many schools have writing centers that specialize in helping students through all phases of the writing process.

How to handle two past actions?

A Special Note on Verb Tense in Narrative

Verb tenses can be tricky in all languages, but native speakers generally do not have a great deal of trouble with the workhorse categories of past, present, and future. However, when we write narrative, it can get more complicated, because we frequently dip into two kinds of past situations and sometimes a present in one sentence. Consider this:

> We **had talked** for hours when suddenly Fernando <u>whispered</u>, "What is that sound?"

In the sentence above, the people had talked in the *more distant* past—before Fernando whispered—so we use the past perfect tense, which requires the helper verb *had* (for more on this, see pp. 532–533). Also, note that it is common to shift verb tense from past to present in direct dialogue, as the shaded verb *is* in the example sentence above illustrates.

JOURNAL ENTRY 4-5 (CONTINUES JOURNAL ENTRIES FROM ASSIGNMENT CHAPTERS 5 THROUGH 11)

Your draft should be in good shape at this point, with all the important details in place, words carefully chosen, and sentences flowing in smooth, varied patterns. Review your **Improvement Chart** to focus on pattern errors and then slooowly edit your paper, word by word, line by line. List at least three errors from the list that you found in your draft, and then write out the corrections.

PROOFREADING

Proofreading is the last step in the preparation of your paper. This is where we put on the final polish. Assuming that you have closely edited your last draft and caught all the mechanical errors possible, you will run off your final copy, the one you turn in for a grade. At this point you might think the last copy is as finished as you can make it, because, after all, you have just spent several hours editing. But there are still common problems that appear in the last draft, ones that you can correct—before your instructor does.

Teaching Idea
Proofreading is just another name for final editing, and it is amazing how many students skip it. In particular, you might stress number 3, spell checking additional required material and title pages.

How to Proofread and Prepare Your Final Manuscript

1. Check for typographical errors such as misspelled, run-together, and omitted words. Often when fixing errors in the editing stage, we slip up in small ways on the keyboard. *Be sure to spell check once again.*

2. Check the following items carefully: font size (12 point), line spacing (double space), margins (1 inch), and title (see capitalization of words in Editing Problems 7, above).

3. Spell check any additional required material, such as outlines and audience profiles.

4. Staple or paper clip your pages. Avoid putting the paper in a plastic sleeve. (Most instructors don't want to fish around in the sleeve and then try to stuff the paper back into it when they are finished evaluating the paper.)

Below you will find both a title page and a one-paragraph paper without a title page. Check with your instructor to see which format he or she prefers. Notice that the title in both cases is neither underlined nor enclosed in quotation marks, and all information is double-spaced.

Sample Title Page

Title centered
12-point font
No underline
No quotation marks
All information
double-spaced

Death Strikes

by

Terry Gwin

Composition 100, Section 37

Professor Brannan

September 28, 2002

Sample Paper (No Title Page)

Double-space heading *and* paragraph.

1/2-inch

1-inch

Gwin 1

Terry Gwin

Professor Brannan

Composition 100, Section 37

September 28, 2002

Death Strikes

Title centered
No underline
No quotation marks

1-inch

1-inch

There were many people in the water waiting to put their boats on their trailers at Hillside Lake on that tragic July afternoon. I felt hot and sticky waiting on the lake, frantically maneuvering my small aluminum boat closer to the ramp, but I knew my turn was still a long way away. Slowly, ominous black clouds that had been building on the horizon rolled closer and closer. Thunder shook the huge lake as if it were a glass of water, vibrating, nearly ready to fall off some gigantic rock and shatter on the ground. Suddenly, the sky began to pour, as if someone had opened a faucet. I remember looking at the old man in the boat next to me and how his head turned so quickly. I can remember hearing a high-pitched hum, like a camera flash charging up. Quickly, instinctively, I jerked my head around to my left toward the shore and saw the massive bolt of lightning fly down from the sky into a man's chest. He arched his back and was thrown into the water. The lightning hit him as though a refrigerator had been dropped on him. He was only thirty-three years old, and he died right in front of me, a sight that will stay in my memory, like a stain, forever. Death can strike anyone at any time, and I know now that eighteen does not mean immortal.

at least 1-inch margin

JOURNAL ENTRY 4-6 (CONTINUES JOURNAL ENTRIES FOR ASSIGNMENT CHAPTERS 5 THROUGH 11)

Reflecting for a moment over your work in and out of class in producing this paragraph assignment, take five minutes to write a paragraph telling your instructor about the challenges you had to overcome, how you dealt with them, and what strategies you think might be most important to apply to your upcoming writing assignments this semester.

Picturing a Place

WHAT ARE WE TRYING TO ACHIEVE AND WHY?

Setting the Stage

Take a moment to look closely at the picture that begins this chapter. What do you notice about it? A family is celebrating Kwanza, smiling happily, standing and sitting close together as they focus their attention on the young girl, who has perhaps just performed for them. What feeling comes to you as you observe the family? If you had to find one or two words to sum up this picture, what do suppose they would be? If you said something like happiness or comfort or family togetherness, you have just identified a **dominant impression** and gotten to the heart of this chapter on description.

Describing is the process of relating details to help another person see what we have seen. It is the act of painting a picture with words. But more than just allowing a reader to *see* a scene, we can use the other senses (hearing, touch, taste, and smell) to involve the audience more completely. When we tell about and listen to subjective descriptions, we enrich our lives, communicating personal experiences and extending the boundaries of what we can know through our senses alone.

In this chapter we will learn about describing in general and of describing a place in particular.

Linking to Previous Experience

What kinds of describing have you done in the past—how about vacations? Maybe you have gone skiing. What did the mountains look like? How much snow fell while you were there; was there a deep base? What were the temperatures? How crowded were the lift lines? If you have not been on a vacation for awhile, when was the last time you tried to describe a scene or character closer to home? Talking to a friend, perhaps you have found yourself detailing another person's clothing or have described your child for a casual acquaintance who also has a child in your preschool. Perhaps you have tried to create a favorable image of that "blind date" you were trying to set a friend up with? We describe things daily, and being able to do it well is a useful skill.

Determining the Value

Aside from helping us get through our daily lives more easily, the ability to describe has other benefits. The act of carefully selecting words to create images will make us better readers and improve our writing on the job, at home, and in school. But perhaps the most value in learning to describe well is that it will encourage you to observe more closely. By the time you have worked through the activities in this chapter, analyzed the student model paragraphs, taken notes for your own description, and finally workshopped your own and other students' drafts, you will find yourself noticing more of the world around you—and seeing it more clearly.

Teaching Idea
Journal Entry 5-1 can get students talking about description as they use it in their own lives and can be done in class on the day that you introduce this chapter.

> **JOURNAL ENTRY 5-1**
>
> List at least one example of describing that you have done recently, either orally or in writing, from school, work, and home and recreate one description for your instructor. What value do you see in being able to describe well?

Teaching Idea
This chapter introduces several concepts crucial for developing students' writing: specific and concrete words and sensory details.

▶ DEVELOPING SKILLS, EXPLORING IDEAS IN DESCRIPTIVE PARAGRAPHS

As we work together through the following eleven activities, we will practice and come to understand the important composition concepts discussed in Chapters 1 and 3, ultimately using the skills we learn in our own place descriptions.

Groundwork for Activity 5-1: Narrowing the Category

One of the most important ideas in creating memorable description is the concept of **general versus specific language** (for more on this, see p. 40). If the writer wants to make a general statement (as in topic sentences and the lead-in material for important examples), she should do so, but when she wants to support a point or create a vivid picture, the author will choose the most specific words she can get her hands on. The larger the group that contains a word, the more general the word is. And, conversely, the smaller the group, the more specific the word is—not unlike the nested ovals below:

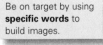

Be on target by using **specific words** to build images.

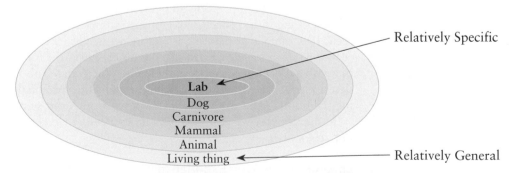

Relatively Specific

Lab
Dog
Carnivore
Mammal
Animal
Living thing

Relatively General

The same concept is illustrated by the Language Line below:

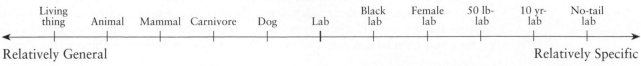

Language Line

Living thing — Animal — Mammal — Carnivore — Dog — Lab — Black lab — Female lab — 50 lb-lab — 10 yr-lab — No-tail lab

Relatively General   Relatively Specific

You will probably notice that as we move along the Language Line, choosing more specific nouns, the group the word belongs to shrinks, in the process creating an image. To make the image even sharper, we begin to add details (adjectives), and the result is a fairly clear picture of an old female black lab that is not too big and that lost a tail at some point. This is a dog that we might be able to pick out of a group of other dogs running in a park, and she is a far cry from the opposite end of the spectrum called merely a "living thing." We can easily apply this process of **narrowing the category** to our own descriptions.

Teaching Idea
The Language Line works well for many words, particularly nouns. You might draw the line on the board, have the class suggest a word, and then have them help you develop the word. Try having students begin by making the word more *general.*

Activity 5-1: Narrowing the Category

For each of the five words in column I below, select a word for columns II and III that becomes increasingly specific, and then add two modifiers to the words in column IV.

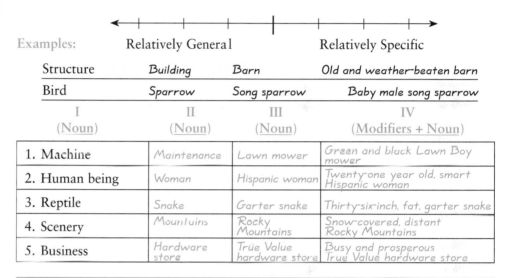

Examples:	Relatively General		Relatively Specific
Structure	*Building*	*Barn*	*Old and weather-beaten barn*
Bird	*Sparrow*	*Song sparrow*	*Baby male song sparrow*
I (Noun)	II (Noun)	III (Noun)	IV (Modifiers + Noun)
1. Machine	*Maintenance*	*Lawn mower*	*Green and black Lawn Boy mower*
2. Human being	*Woman*	*Hispanic woman*	*Twenty-one year old, smart Hispanic woman*
3. Reptile	*Snake*	*Garter snake*	*Thirty-six-inch, fat, garter snake*
4. Scenery	*Mountains*	*Rocky Mountains*	*Snow-covered, distant Rocky Mountains*
5. Business	*Hardware store*	*True Value hardware store*	*Busy and prosperous True Value hardware store*

Groundwork for Activity 5-2: Abstract versus Concrete Language

Abstract words are those that refer to qualities, processes, or ideas (goodness, photosynthesis, freedom) and emotions (love, fear, pity). Concrete words represent things that we can experience with our senses (chair, car, hamburger—cement or concrete is also "concrete"!). Like relatively general words, abstract words have a necessary place in writing; they allow us to talk about large ideas and states of being. For instance, when we discuss "democracy," most of us understand that it means self-rule through elected officials within a society that guarantees certain freedoms. However, as soon as people become unclear about a term or when they disagree with basic assumptions about it, the abstraction needs to be clarified with specific examples, which are often illustrated with concrete terms. In our descriptive papers we will select fairly specific and concrete places to show a reader, but we will also make clear a relatively abstract feeling or overall **dominant impression** by favoring specific and concrete words.

Teaching Idea
Making an abstract term more concrete is, of course, another way of making it more specific. You might point to common items found in a classroom (pencil, lights, soda can), and ask students to name a more abstract term into which the term could fit (i.e., pencil = writing = communication).

Activity 5-2: Abstract versus Concrete Language

Look at the abstract words in column I, and then try to write a more concrete word or phrase in column II. Remember that concrete words are often a specific example used to show what a person *might* mean by the more abstract term.

I. **Abstract** (idea, quality, emotion)	II. **Concrete** (knowable through senses: has weight, color, smell, texture, etc.)
Example: Happiness	*a smile*
Example: Love	*a kiss*
Example: Football defense	*a sacked quarterback*
1. Comfort	*resting in a warm bath*
2. Activity	*hockey game*
3. Tranquility	*dad rocking his baby to sleep*
4. Death penalty	*a convict in the electric chair*
5. Transportation	*'69 Firebird*

Teaching Idea
Ask students to close their eyes and listen carefully for half a minute. Now have them write a single sentence that contains one or two sounds that they heard. You might remind them that silence also gives a "sound" impression.

Groundwork for Activity 5-3: Using the Five Senses

All description benefits from using our senses. Because people come to know their environment best through their senses, it stands to reason that we would want to come as close as possible in our writing to duplicating what we saw, heard, felt, smelled, and tasted in a setting. With this in mind, consider the following two paragraph excerpts, and decide which one makes you feel more a part of the scene:

1. I am back at the pond again tonight, relaxing and noticing the stars. As I listen, I can hear the sounds of the woods around me. Animal noises tell me that I have truly made it back to my favorite spot. I can see that the fire is about ready, so I get out the food I brought and settle down for some late night snacks.

2. As the brilliant, yellow moon shines down reflecting off the pond, little waves ripple across the surface. While gazing at the sky, I can see millions of sparkling stars and, from time to time, even view one falling. The blazing embers leave a smoke trail rising upward from the fire. Through the darkness of the night, I can see the shadows of the trees, silhouettes of the horses, and swooping bats. The sounds of the night surround me: the murmur of voices in the distance, leaves rustling, and branches brushing against each other. From the nearby pond and surrounding trees, I can hear the unique chorus of the tree and bullfrogs. As the train whistles by, the cries of howling coyotes drift on the wind. From time to time I can even hear the lonesome hooting of an owl. As the popping and crackling of the fire dies down, the embers are ready for cooking.

The second paragraph benefits from two senses primarily, sight and sound, as you can see by the shaded sight and boxed sound details. Although the author has not called on taste, smell, and touch, she has still created a memorable scene that many of us would probably like to join in.

Collaborative

Activity 5-3: Using the Five Senses

With group members locate all the sensory details you can find in the following paragraph excerpt, and then list them under the appropriate columns on the sensory chart. Specific words are *sight* details, colors included (see Activity 5-1). Sound and touch details are represented but few smell or taste details. If you removed all the sensory details, would this description be less interesting to you?

Jumping feet first off the gently rolling boat, the salty taste of seawater in my mouth, I feel the warm Caribbean waters close over my head. Sinking slowly in a swirl of frothy silver bubbles, I look back up to the surface to see the dark hull of the dive boat steadily receding. Beneath me broken shafts of sunlight filter past the tips of my black fins as I kick back and forth, keeping the descent under control. At thirty feet I begin to kick harder and inflate my BC, the sudden sound of compressed air rushing past my ear. Another ten, twenty, thirty feet, and there I hover, weightless, over the plateau. Spread out to a hundred feet in all directions, green and purple sea fans bend gently in the mild surge as rainbow-colored parrotfish graze on the reef, the sound of their teeth grinding chunks of coral audible even under sixty feet of water.

Sensory Chart

Sight	Sound	Touch	Smell	Taste
Bout/ dark hull	Compressed air	Warm water	None	Salty
Silver bubbles	Teeth grinding	Sinking		
Shafts of sun		Weightless		
Black fins		Rolling		
Green and purple sea fans				
Rainbow-colored parrotfish				

Teaching Idea
To supplement Activity 5-3 by showing cluttered writing, have students write two or three sentences that include as many sensory details as they can cram in. Then have them trim the sentences back so they are effective.

Can there be *too* much of a good thing?

Note: The point of using sensory details is not to cram as many into a paper as possible, or even to represent all the senses, but rather to use these details selectively wherever they can enhance an image.

Collaborative

Activity 5-4: Using the Five Senses

Get together in groups of four or five and brainstorm sensory details for one of the following places. Be particularly alert to any details that might help illustrate a central focus or dominant impression/feeling. Also don't be surprised if you come up with more under sight and sound than any other.

Answers will vary.

1. **Cafeteria** at lunch hour (dominant impression = activity/fast pace, maybe even confusion or chaos!)

2. **Church wedding** (dominant impression = excitement/happiness, maybe even communal spirit of love)

3. **Zoo** (dominant impression = *either* depression/confinement, maybe even animals in misery *or* relaxation, maybe even contentment, animals happy to have a life so easy—try for one of these, remembering that, as always in focused description, you *choose* the details that you want your reader to see

4. **Summer camp** (dominant impression = happy confusion/expectation/fun)

up at the corners, leaving the ancient mattress staring back. I like to snack in bed, so you'll find the remains of old meals: there's an old pizza crust with the red sauce . . . well, kind of *dark* red sauce now, a Big Mac box, an old French fry or two (they may still be good; I'll try them in a minute), and some kind of crumbs—no, I think it's sand. A red and green quilt is lying in a pile by the end chest where it slipped off a month ago, in May, when the weather got too warm for me to need it anymore, and I'm afraid to look under the bed for what I might find there. My desk is littered with papers and old Kleenexes (some used some not, but, hey, at least I'm ready for the next blow), and you'll usually find an open can of Coke on it, sticky at the bottom (someday I'll learn how to drink without spilling). I'll get around to taking out the wastebasket someday, but in the meantime I can still cram a little more trash into it.

Write out the dominant impression for "The Late Night Place to Be":
Dominant impression: activity

Underline details that distract from the dominant impression.

The Late Night Place to Be

I enjoy spending time at the gym because of all the different activity going on there. The bright lights of the place shine through plate glass windows, illuminating the parking lot as I arrive at 1:00 a.m. After checking in, I head to the mezzanine on the left side of the gym where the cardiovascular area is located. As I walk upstairs, I start to identify the different sounds of the room. I can hear the heavy breathing of the sweaty runners as their feet pound strongly against the treadmills, which are lined up against the back wall. The room is carpeted in dark pink and is full of cardiovascular equipment such as NordicTracks, stair steppers, and stationary bicycles, and most of the machines are, surprisingly, in use. The carpet feels good on my feet after a hard night working in the restaurant, and I wonder if the other people here appreciate it too. Management has kept up the physical surroundings: the walls are freshly painted, the mirrors clean, and all the resistance machines look practically brand new. This all improves my attitude and makes it somehow easier for me to work out harder. Although there are plenty of people, the place doesn't look too crowded, but it is noisy. The beeping sound from various machines marks people getting on and off and setting different resistance levels. Looking down to the main area of the gym, across from the reception desk, I can see two girls talking and hear part of their conversation as they work out. Near the back wall, about sixty feet away from the reception desk, there are three men working with the free weights. I can hear the clink and clank of the metal weights as they lay them down. Although it might seem strange to some that all this activity is going on so late at night, to me, and maybe the rest of the people in the gym, this is the best way to relax at the end of a long day.

Groundwork for Activity 5-7: Topic Sentences

As we learned in Chapter 3, most body paragraphs in essays and single-paragraph papers should begin with a topic sentence. In this descriptive paper we will want to include these two parts in our topic sentence: the **place** and the **dominant impression.**

Beyond this, the topic sentence can be made more interesting by adding a **sensory detail,** an **action,** and **specific words.** Take a look at the following basic topic sentence:

Place + Dominant impression (statement)

- **Rough** topic sentence: The bar & grill is noisy.

This is a perfectly acceptable working topic sentence, but as you begin to polish your draft, you might want to make the sentence a bit more interesting:

Action/Sound specific word   Specific word

- **Revised** topic sentence: If I fired a .44 magnum in the Longbranch Saloon on a
Specific word   Dominant impression
Friday night, there is so much noise that no one would notice.

Activity 5-7: Topic Sentences

Read the following sentences and circle the number of each one that you think would make a good *rough* topic sentence for a place description:

1. My kitchen has a linoleum floor.
2. My house has a relaxing place to spend time in.
3. My home office measures twelve by eighteen feet.
4. For a memorable place to vacation, skiing is the best.
5. Farm ponds are pretty busy places.

Now take any one of the rough topic sentences that you chose and try to make it more interesting by adding a sensory detail (color, sound, touch), an action, or specific word.

Your choice of rough topic sentence: *Answers will vary: Farm ponds are pretty busy places.*

Your revised topic sentence: *On warm Saturday afternoons in May, I love to watch my uncle Sam's farm pond come alive with leaping bass, croaking bullfrogs, and fluttering red-winged blackbirds.*

Groundwork for Activity 5-8: Concluding Sentences

Just as topic sentences are vital to introduce many paragraphs, so too are concluding sentences essential to wrap up the main point. In an essay, of course, you will have room to expand a concluding thought into a full paragraph, but with single-paragraph papers we should try to limit ourselves to one (or two) forceful, final sentence with these parts: a *connector*, mention of the *place*, and link to the *dominant impression*.

As we learned in Chapter 3, we can make the final sentence even more effective by adding **details, specific words,** and an **expanded thought** linked to the dominant impression. Here is a rough concluding sentence followed by a more polished version:

- **Rough** concluding sentence: <u>After</u> last call the <u>volume</u> begins to drop, <u>and everyone heads out from the Longbranch for home</u>.

  Connector — Dominant impression — Place

- **Revised** concluding sentence: <u>After</u> last call the <u>shouted conversations and the banging together of beer mugs</u> begin to die down, and <u>everyone heads out from the</u> bar into the night, <u>alone again till the next time they come back to their home away</u> from home.

  Connector — Sound detail — Dominant impression — Sound detail — Action — Action — Place — Expanded thought

Activity 5-8: Concluding Sentences

The following groups of paired sentences contain rough topic sentences that *could* work to begin a paragraph of place description and rough concluding sentences that *might* work to end a paragraph. Choose a sentence that could work to conclude a paragraph that describes a place.

1. My kitchen is an easy place to work in. (Rough topic sentence)

   <u>With all this equipment to work with, my kitchen is efficient</u>. (Rough final sentence)

2. My house has a relaxing place to spend time in. (Rough topic sentence)

   <u>If I plastered and repainted, all the rooms would look better</u>. (Rough final sentence)

3. My home office is well organized. (Rough topic sentence)

   <u>I really don't use my home office very much</u>. (Rough final sentence)

4. For a memorable place to vacation, skiing is the best. (Rough topic sentence)

   <u>Snow skiing in the mountains is great fun</u>. (Rough final sentence)

Now take the rough concluding sentence you chose and create a more complete (and interesting) ending, being sure to include these three parts: a connector, the place, and the dominant impression.

To create an even stronger concluding sentence, include an **expanded thought, specific words, sensory details,** or an **action.**

Example:
Farm ponds are pretty busy places. (Rough topic sentence)

<u>*With so much going on, farm ponds are fun to spend time at.*</u>   (Rough final sentence)

          <u>Connector</u>   <u>Dominant impression</u> <u>Place</u>

- **Revised** concluding sentence: *With all the frantic <u>animal</u> <u>action</u> at my <u>uncle's pond</u>, you might think no one could rest there, but, for me, it's one of the <u>most relaxing places I can</u>*
  <u>Expanded thought</u>
  <u>spend time on a late spring afternoon</u>.

Your choice of rough concluding sentence from the list of four: _____*Answers will vary: Snow skiing in the mountains is great fun*_____

Your revised concluding sentence: _____*Having finally mastered the bunny hill, I now love skiing and can't wait to challenge myself on the blue slopes next year.*_____

Groundwork for Activity 5-9: Organizing Descriptions

All writing that is easy to read follows some sort of organizational strategy. In writing description, an author will often choose "spatial arrangement," which simply means to organize details from one point in space to another so the reader can more easily visualize the scene. In describing a person or an animal, you might progress from the head to the feet; for an object like a car, you could proceed from the outside to the inside; for a place like a room, you might begin at the ceiling and work your way down to the floor or perhaps begin at the entrance to the place and then move inward.

There is seldom only one right way to approach spatial description. As in so much of what we write, an author needs to choose a direction that seems sensible and then remain as consistent as possible.

Activity 5-9: Organizing Descriptions

The following place lists have descriptive details that are not arranged in any logical order. Take a moment to read through the lists, and then number the details to show a simple, one-step-at-a-time progression, beginning with 1 as the first detail in a descriptive paragraph and progressing to 6. (It might help to visualize the places being described as if you were operating a video camera, or shooting a movie!)

Example: Topic sentence: My attic is the dirtiest place in the house. (Arrange details from bottom to top.)

  __2__ The floorboards are covered with dust.

  __4__ Two small windows are streaked and smeared.

  __6__ The rafters have cobwebs hanging from them.

  __1__ I can feel grit beneath my feet on the stairs going up.

  __3__ Old furniture has the dust of ages accumulating on it.

  __5__ Boxes of ancient books are piled high.

1. Topic sentence: First Watch on a busy Sunday morning is a study in efficiency. (Arrange details from front to back.)

  __1__ Outside the restaurant there is a host taking names for seating.

  __6__ At the far end of the line, I can see the cooks efficiently cranking out the food.

Teaching Idea
Some students become so concerned with getting every piece of a spatial description in the "right" order that their writing becomes mechanical. You might remind students that spatial organization should support not control their material. The paragraph "What's the Rush?" in Chapter 3 is another model that demonstrates a clear yet not rigid spatial arrangement.

_2_ In the lobby coffee and tea are set up to help with the wait.

_3_ At the front desk a manager greets people while checks are being orderly processed.

_4_ Busboys clear, wipe, and reset tables quickly.

_5_ Behind the food line I can hear the dishwashers hard at work.

2. Topic sentence: The poolroom grew quiet, and time seemed to slow as everyone around the table concentrated on the last shot of the game. (Arrange details from bottom to top.)

_5_ The TV sets on the walls seemed to blur out, and the sound became just so much white noise.

_6_ Overhead, the blades of the ceiling fans were frozen in place.

_1_ People stopped shuffling their feet.

_3_ Lucky Ed was draped over his cue—the stick, cue ball, and eight ball his whole universe.

_4_ As Ed's right hand drew the cue back, the crowd leaned forward in anticipation.

_2_ Bottles of Budweiser were dangling at their sides—no one dared to move before the shot.

3. Topic sentence: Monastery Beach on a hot July afternoon is full of activity. (Arrange details from distant to closer as you stand in the parking lot at the edge of the beach.)

_4_ Scuba divers are putting their fins on at the edge of the surf.

_5_ In the middle of the beach, a handful of giggling kids tries to get a kite up into the air.

_1_ In the distance a fishing boat loaded with tourists chugs along.

_2_ Forty yards out from shore a sea otter floats on his back in the kelp, banging away at an abalone he has wrenched from the ocean floor.

_3_ Waves pick up height ten yards from the beach as they curl and break over the few brave swimmers.

_6_ Where the beach meets the parking lot, seagulls cluster around trash cans, squabbling among themselves for scraps.

Groundwork for Activity 5-10: Locating the Reader in Space and Time

As we know from Chapter 3, linking sentences within and between paragraphs is essential if the reader is to follow a flow of ideas smoothly. In description, because we are building a scene, which consists of people, objects, and sometimes animals, it is important to help the reader see where these elements fit in relation to one another. The act of locating a reader within a scene contributes to well-organized writing.

To link sentences, we use repeat words, synonyms, pronouns, references to main ideas, and transitional words. **Time** and **space** transitions are particularly useful in description.

For Locating or Moving in Space			
above	by	in the back of	over
against	east (west . . .)	into	there
alongside	far off (away)	near	to the right/left
around	in	next to	under
at	in the back	on	upper
For Moving in Time			
after	first (second, etc.)	next	suddenly
afterward	immediately	now	then
at last	in the meantime	often	time passed
awhile	in the past	once	until

- All references to calendar time and calendar events: last week, a few months ago
- All references to clock time

(For a more complete list of transitions, turn to pp. 53–54.)

Activity 5-10: Locating the Reader in Space and Time

In the following descriptive paragraph, "Ground Zero," underline all the **space connectors** once and any **time connectors** twice (there are only a few time connectors). Use the lists provided to locate many of the linking words and phrases, but use your own common sense and experience to find any not already given.

Ground Zero

My bedroom is a mess. I can't seem to hang a picture straight on the walls, and my poster of The Dave Matthews Band has come untaped at the upper right corner so that it sags a little. The queen-sized bed is a disaster; it looks more like an animal's nest than a place for human rest. There are three pillows up against the oak headboard and two lying on the carpet. The elastic has worn out around the pale-blue bottom sheet, so it has curled up at the corners. I like to snack in bed, so you'll find the remains of old meals: there's an old pizza crust with the red sauce . . . well, kind of *dark* red sauce now, a Big Mac box, an old French fry or two (they may still be good; I'll try them in a minute), and some kind of crumbs—no, I think it's sand. A red-and-green quilt is lying in a pile by the end chest where it slipped off a month ago, and I'm afraid to look under the bed for what I might find there. My desk is littered with papers and old Kleenexes (some used some not, but, hey, at least I'm ready for the next blow), and you'll usually find an open can of Coke on it, sticky at the bottom. I'll get around to taking out the wastebasket someday, but in the meantime I can still cram a little more trash into it.

Activity 5-11: Locating the Reader in Space

Using the space locators on p. 89, fill in the blanks with a word or words that make sense.

Answers will vary

1. After walking into the movie theater, you have to go _____to the right_____ or _____left_____ to get to the film you came to see.

2. Driving _____into_____ the garage, I could see my work cut out for me.

3. The weight room is located _____in the back_____ of the club.

4. In most houses you can find a mirror _____above_____ the vanity.

5. The boathouse is _____next to_____ the dock.

▶ DESCRIPTIVE PARAGRAPHS: LOOKING CLOSELY AT STUDENT MODELS

The following models show how you might approach both outside and inside description: how to develop and arrange material, and how to polish sentences to make a paragraph readable. As you focus on each model, take a few extra minutes to read through the Prereading and Postreading commentary and then to carefully answer the questions for analysis. All of this material will help you better understand why the writing is successful, the goal being to help *you* write stronger descriptive paragraphs.

▶ Prereading Exploration for "Untitled"

The following descriptive paragraph was written in response to the assignment instructions for picturing a place. The author's purpose is to communicate a special feeling she has about an activity and a place to her classmates so that they might get to know her a bit better. Before you jump into the reading, think for a moment about the elements of effective descriptive writing that we have discussed. Next, answer these questions:

1. How should the author try to focus the paragraph? _____Through a dominant impression_____

2. What kinds of details do you suppose the author will use to develop the paragraph? _____Sensory details_____

3. What is the difference between a relatively general and a relatively specific word, and which tends to create the most vivid image? _____General words belong to larger categories. Specific words create the most vivid images._____

Before you continue with the rest of the paragraph, carefully read the first and final sentences, and then look for descriptive detail and explanation that reinforce the **dominant impression**.

Teaching Idea
The student model "Untitled" is
a fine example of description
without any people interaction.
You might want to contrast it
to both the other Chapter 5
models, which use people as
part of the description.

Untitled

The most peaceful activity I know of on a clear, dry night is relaxing around an open campfire. There is an ideal spot just north of the pond on my grandparents' land. As the brilliant yellow moon shines down, reflecting off the pond, little waves ripple across the surface. Gazing at the sky, I can see millions of sparkling stars and, from time to time, even view a falling star. The blazing embers leave a smoke trail rising upward from the fire. Through the darkness, I can see the shadows of the trees, silhouettes of the horses, and swooping bats. The sounds of the night surround me: the murmur of voices in the distance, leaves rustling, and branches brushing against each other. From the nearby pond and surrounding trees, I can hear the unique chorus of the tree frogs and bullfrogs. As the train whistles by, the cries of howling coyotes drift on the wind. From time to time, I can even hear the lonesome hooting of an owl. When the popping and crackling of the fire dies down, the embers are ready for cooking. The hotdogs sizzle as they begin to cook and drip their juices off the end of the stick. Refreshing aromas of trimmings from the apple and pear trees add sweetness to the oak branches as they burn. Nearby, the smell of the horses is carried in the breeze. While fire heats the hotdogs, I can smell the meat cooking. The hot, white melting marshmallows fresh from the fire stick to my fingers. After eating and being contentedly full from the hotdogs and sticky chocolate/nut smores, I have time for solitude. While the chilly breeze blows, the radiating warmth of the fire draws me in. This is my favorite time around the campfire—a truly peaceful time in which I feel a sense of oneness with nature as she embraces me.

Andrea Turner

Postreading Analysis

This paragraph is easy to follow, from the opening sentence, which clearly states the dominant impression, to the final sentence, which reinforces the main point and then adds a thought for brief reflection. Turner does a good job of orienting the reader in the beginning of the paragraph ("just north of the pond on my grandparents' land") and continues to use plenty of place connectors ("across the surface"/"in the distance") to locate us in space. To help us see the scene around the pond and fire, the author favors many relatively specific words (owl vs. bird/marshmallows vs. dessert) and selects many strong sensory details without overloading her work. You might also notice how effectively Turner conveys action through active verbs ("waves ripple"/"train whistles by") and "-ings."

Description often
includes action.

Teaching Idea
"Waking Up the Right Way" is
a good model to introduce the
importance in description of
having the narrator reveal
thoughts and emotions.

▶ Prereading Exploration for "Waking Up the Right Way"

So far we have practiced important elements of description like specific word choices, sensory detail, and clear focus (dominant impression). But we have not much discussed how the narrator (meaning you) can contribute to the overall impression of the place by simply revealing her thoughts/feelings in relation to the description. Take thirty seconds to skim the upcoming paragraph, noting the topic and concluding sentences; then look closely at the highlighted passages, which reveal the author's thoughts and feelings.

How would you describe these thoughts/emotions?

1. *Answers will vary: They project a positive feeling.*

How do they link to the stated dominant impression of tranquility?

2. *Positive thoughts and feelings reinforce the dominant impression.*

After you have read the paragraph more carefully, respond to these questions: How accurate was your judgment of "Waking Up the Right Way," based only on the quick skim? What value do you see in skimming as a prereading technique?

3. *Answers will vary.*

Waking Up the Right Way

With my morning cup of coffee in hand, I head toward the most tranquil part of my house, my front porch. Sometimes I feel that nothing comes alive until I walk out—little do I know. The sun has already started its astonishing daily routine of creating sunshine. Everywhere I look I see all the different foliage around stretching upward, hoping to grasp everything that the incredible fireball in the sky has to offer. Families of blue jays and cardinals live together peacefully in the walnut trees to the west. They seem to be chatting away with each other's family, like most neighbors do. Could they possibly be discussing the upcoming events of the day? The family of squirrels in the next tree starts conversing as well. By the way their mouths and bellies are rapidly filling, I can sense they are pleased with the cashews I left for them last night. As I glance down at the windowsill, I often think about the many dead insects lying there; one can only assume that the bugs want their last moments alive to be on my porch. These small bodies make quite a feast for the two barn spiders that share my porch with me. The webs are always filled with one delicacy or another. One spider in particular has woven quite a spectacular web against the old, paint-chipped corner. While I am inhaling my first cup of morning fuel, a magnificent gust of wind blows through. The sweet smell of my neighbor's freshly cut grass fills the air so fragrantly that I barely notice the thick humidity building for the day ahead. As I am taking in the fresh aroma of the morning dew, my attention is drawn to a group of young children who are eagerly on their way to the first day of school. My next-door neighbor waves to me and hollers, "Morning to ya!" and then starts his trek to work. As he pulls his pickup from our shared driveway, the gray dust from the gravel leaves a chalky taste in the morning air. Like clockwork (at 7:20 A.M.), Rex, the German shepherd who lives in the backyard behind me, starts his morning barking routine. So, along with most experiences in life, my morning relaxing time has come to a temporary halt. Heading back inside to get dressed, I know that I'm ready for the challenges awaiting me in my day. I'm ready to face each one confidently because I started in my favorite place— my porch.

Stacey Becker

Postreading Analysis

In this descriptive paragraph the author does a fine job with sensory details, in several places playing one off the other to enrich an image ("sweet smell of cut grass . . . thick humidity"/"inhaling . . .fuel . . . wind blows"). Both first and last sentences clearly telegraph the central point of the paper, and the author is especially careful with time connectors ("morning cup of coffee," "until I walk," "As he pulls his pickup"). Because Becker is writing a *description* of a place, you might think that she wouldn't pay much attention to action, but she does. Notice how so much of the movement in the paragraph—the animals interacting, the children, the next-door neighbor—contributes to the overall impression the author is trying to convey.

Questions to Help You Analyze and Write Effective Descriptive Paragraphs

1. What is the dominant impression of the paragraph?

2. What two important points do we learn from the topic sentence?

3. How does the concluding sentence link to the topic sentence?

4. Name at least one instance of action within the paragraph that helps reinforce the dominant impression, and then explain how the action does this.

5. Name at least five instances of specific word choices (a word that belongs to a smaller group or category of words).

6. Locate and list as many sensory details from the paragraph as you can find: sight, sound, touch, smell, and taste.

7. After looking at your list from number 6 above, which sensory details seem easier to show and which more difficult?

8. List at least three time and three space connectors (see p. 53).

9. Name three active verbs and three "-ings" words the author uses to convey motion (note how the "-ings" can enhance a sensory detail). (Active verbs show the most specific kind of action, i.e., the horse *gallops* vs. moves; the cardinal *sings* vs. makes a song.) (For more on active verbs, see p. 452.)

10. What is your favorite image in this paragraph? Why do you like it?

11. Can you name three additional sensory details or specific words that would add to the dominant impression?

12. In the seventh sentence of "Waking Up the Right Way," the author uses a question. Is there any value in asking the reader an occasional question? Why do you suppose Becker does it? (For more on question sentences, see p. 433.)

13. Can you suggest a title for Andrea Turner's paragraph? Why do you think your title would make a good one? (For more on titles, see pp. 57–58.)

■ EXPLAINING THE WRITING ASSIGNMENT

▶ SUMMARIZING THE ASSIGNMENT

In this writing assignment we will paint a verbal portrait of a place. This place can be indoors and more or less surrounded by four walls (a room in a house, a store in a shopping mall, a library, etc.), or outside (a park, a favorite fishing hole, a basketball court, etc.). Our goal is to focus a single paragraph of description, roughly 250 to 300 words, through some general feeling or overall impression we want our reader to have about the place. This **dominant impression** will help shape and develop the paragraph.

ESTABLISHING AUDIENCE AND PURPOSE

You may select any person or group that you think might be interested in the location that you want to describe. For instance, if you chose a favorite fishing pond, say on a friend's farm in southern Miami County, KS, you could gear your description specifically toward your friend, knowing that you would both share memories of the place, or you could choose a larger audience, say the readership of a conservation magazine like *Kansas Wildlife & Parks,* in which case you would expect the audience to share some common interests and to know the general lay of the land but not actually to have visited your spot. (Note: Your composition instructor is always at least a secondary audience, so write to show him or her that you are learning descriptive strategies.)

Your overall purpose is to convey information and a feeling about a place, to help a reader see it through your eyes.

WORKING THROUGH THE WRITING ASSIGNMENT

Discovering Ideas

Assuming that your instructor is not simply assigning you a particular place to write about (i.e., "Let's all describe our bathrooms"), your choice of topics is virtually limitless. The good news is that you can select a place that you know well and have a real interest in. The bad news is that lots of freedom can be paralyzing. It is all too easy when faced with almost every possibility "out there" to feel overwhelmed and either put off choosing a place till too late or settle on the first choice that comes to mind, whether you have a real interest in it or not. Because you will be working on this project for several weeks, why not take the time to select a topic that you care about enough to invest some energy in? (Learning to become involved in a writing project is a trick of the writer's trade that will help you have a lot more fun with your writing and will usually produce better work.)

The following topic lists may help get you off to a good start:

Topic Lists

Places to Describe Inside

1. Any room in your house	15. Riverboat	29. Bus depot
2. Attic	16. Dance studio	30. Airport
3. Tool shed	17. Church/synagogue	31. Subway station
4. Restaurant	18. Pet store	32. Train station
5. Tavern	19. Pawn shop	33. Boxing arena
6. Department store	20. Music store	34. Doctor's office
7. Museum	21. Hospital	35. Police station
8. Gym	22. Movie theater	36. Grocery store
9. Bowling alley	23. Art gallery	37. Florist's
10. Arcade	24. Recording studio	38. Furniture store
11. Library	25. Beauty salon	39. Tire warehouse
12. Cafeteria	26. School (any level)	40. Recycling center
13. Office	27. Day care	41. Funeral home
14. Hardware store	28. Foundry	42. Cemetery

43. Toy store
44. Veterinary clinic
45. Kennel
46. Auto repair shop
47. Ski resort
48. Cable car

49. Dive boat
50. Fishing boat
51. Cruise ship
52. Barn
53. Trade show
54. Nature center

55. Art gallery
56. Hotel room
57. Casino
58. Stable
59. Tattoo/piercing shop
60. Greenhouse

Places to Describe Outside

1. Your property
2. Beach
3. Park
4. Mountains
5. Pond
6. Stadium
7. Lake
8. Zoo
9. Field
10. Interstate (at rush hour)
11. Parking lot
12. Car wash
13. Fountain
14. Trailer court
15. Municipal landfill
16. Pig or cattle pen (corral)

17. Woods
18. Summer camp
19. River
20. Rock quarry
21. Strip mine
22. Construction site
23. Wharf
24. Race track (car, horse, dog)
25. Tree house
26. Basketball court
27. Football field
28. Tennis court
29. Outdoor racquetball court
30. Swimming pool
31. Wildlife sanctuary
32. Rose garden

33. Historic site
34. Cemetery
35. Rodeo
36. Outdoor concert
37. Hot air balloon
38. Amusement park
39. Orchard
40. Nursery (for plants)
41. Field (corn, wheat, milo, etc.)
42. Jogging path
43. National park
44. Airport
45. City market
46. Outdoor art fair
47. Plaza or town square
48. Hot tub

Teaching Idea
Some students write terrific descriptions from memory, but most need the immediacy of the scene and focused note taking to create substantive descriptions.

Limit your location.

Visit your place and take notes!

Aside from these lists think of the places where you regularly go—home, work, school. Also consider some of your interests. What kinds of hobbies do you enjoy? Do you target shoot, play in a band, collect rare books, prepare gourmet meals? How about sports—team and individual? We all lead varied lives that carry us through a world of possible places to choose for topics.

Caution: Whatever place you select, be sure to limit how much of it you try to describe. For instance, a college campus is too much to handle in this brief paragraph assignment, but the school cafeteria could be just right. The Lake of the Ozarks is, again, too large, so settle for a particular arm, cove, or dock that you know well.

After you have decided on a possible topic, try to go there, sit down, and take a few notes. While you might be able to draw all the necessary detail for this assignment from memory, your description will probably be stronger if you actually go to your place. Even professional storytellers, who are paid to create scenes from their imagination, often visit a place and take notes. Assuming that you can visit your place, here are several suggestions to help generate material:

Prewriting Suggestions

Looking for a
dominant impression

1. Go to the place and sit quietly for a few minutes. Look around, listen carefully, and open your senses—all five—to the surroundings. Remember that you are looking for a single point of focus (dominant impression). Is the place obviously busy and loud, slow and quiet, full of angry people, full of pleasant people? Are you outside in the middle of one of nature's spectacles—sunset/sunrise, snowstorm, fog, electrical storm, animal migration. . . ? If a dominant impression does not suggest itself to you at that moment, think about coming back at another time.

Listing is one of
several useful
prewriting methods.

2. Whether or not a single focus is clear yet, you still need to take notes. One way to gather valuable details is to create a list of sensory impressions, including *sight*, *sound*, *touch*, *smell*, and *taste*.

   You will probably find that sight and sound are the easiest sense impression to record, but you may be able to find several in the other categories, especially touch.

3. Jot some brief notes to yourself on the people present and how they interact. Pay attention to their actions. Are they friendly, cooperative, competitive, angry, isolated, quiet, busy, rowdy . . . ?

4. Jot down physical dimensions of the area, and be prepared to tell your reader where one object is in relation to another.

5. Include **colors** under the sight column on your sensory list.

6. Try to create a comparison while you watch your place, perhaps as a metaphor or simile (i.e., "the waiter was as busy as a squirrel burying acorns in autumn). (For more on metaphor/simile, see pp. 473–474.)

7. Try to catch a few lines of dialogue as close to word-for-word as possible.

Working with others
can save you work.

If a dominant impression is not yet clear, it is probably time to get someone else involved. Of course you will meet with group members and spend time discussing your notes in class, but you can often talk to a family member, friend, writing center staff member, or your instructor to help focus the description before class.

Teaching Idea
Journal Entry 5-2 is important
because it helps clarify the
problematic concept of
"dominant impression" for
students. Incorporating the
Journal into the regular class
curriculum is one way to stay
in touch with student progress
on the assignment.

JOURNAL ENTRY 5-2

How can you describe the overall feeling of your place in a sentence or two? Does there seem to be a lot of activity, are people in a good mood, does the action seem chaotic? Perhaps your place is restful or has a soothing quality? Maybe you have selected an outdoor area that impresses you as rugged and wild? Review your prewriting notes, and then write out in one sentence the overall feeling you think you can communicate to your audience about the place. (Remember, a place can feel different to another person, and there are often several similar words useful for describing the overall impression.)

Organizing Ideas

Keep details that
show the dominant
impression—delete
distracting details.

After gathering sensory details, listing the names of specific things in your place, and recording actions, now is the time to select and arrange the material most related to the overall feeling you want to give about your place. You will probably find a few unneeded details in your lists and some that even contradict the dominant impression, so this is a good time to weed out the junk. But as you begin to draft, other useful details will come to you, so don't limit yourself to your prewriting notes. Good ideas come to writers throughout the process of drafting and revising.

Below you will see a prewriting list for Jo Lucas's place paragraph, "Our Family Outing" (pp. 101–102), with several details crossed out that distract from the overall impression she wanted to show of activity and family fun:

Sight	Sound	Touch	Smell	Taste
40 lanes: kids having fun, black bumper pads, computer scoring, Cosmic Bowl (dark with black lights), smoke	Noisy games		Lane oil smell	All the food
Bowling balls: blue, pink, orange, green, yellow				
Wall: red, blue, green, yellow	Laughing children	Hot cheese	Hamburgers,	
Arcade games: blue print carpet	People talking		French fries	
Main service desk	Game tokens clatter		Popcorn	
Snack bar	Sizzling hamburgers		Chili, cheese	
Backstop restaurant: TVs, pool tables, batting cages, birthday parties		~~AC too cold~~		~~Taste of spearmint gum~~
~~Lazy food servers, husband and wife arguing, dad yelling at his son~~				

Teaching Idea
You might ask students why they think the author of the Annotated Student Model chose to delete the details of "lazy food servers" and so on under the sight column.

The details that you keep you will arrange in a roughly spatial order, as we practiced in Activity 5-9. Jo Lucas chose to organize her description as she progressed into and through the family fun center. However you arrange your material, top to bottom, front to back, and so forth, remain reasonably consistent in the ordering of details.

After organizing your material, write at least a rough **topic sentence** that names the place and states the dominant impression, as in the following topic sentences from the chapter student models. The <u>place</u> is underlined once and the <u><u>dominant impression</u></u> word twice:

Move from the topic sentence directly into description.

1. The most <u>peaceful</u> activity I know of on a clear, dry night is relaxing <u>around an open campfire</u>.

2. With my morning cup of coffee in hand, I head toward the most <u>tranquil</u> part of my house, my <u>front porch</u>.

Teaching Idea
Despite your strong emphasis on a focusing dominant impression, some students will still leave it out of their topic sentence. You might spot-check for the dominant impression at this point by having students read their topic sentences aloud.

Move straight from the topic sentence into the description, and be sure to locate your reader within the scene by using plenty of space and time transitions (words like *above, near, next to, first, after, finally*). (For more transitions, see pp. 53–54).

JOURNAL ENTRY 5-3

How will you organize the details of your place description: from top to bottom, from outside to inside, from one side to another, from far to near? Can you picture yourself in a fixed spot inside a room, or do you see yourself walking through the place? After you have reviewed your notes, write a paragraph explaining how you will organize and why this method makes sense to you.

Teaching Idea
Although you may have already covered drafting in Chapter 1, it helps to review this material again the day before student drafts are due.

Drafting

With the preliminary work done, you are almost ready to write your first draft. But before you plunge in, take a moment to review the Drafting suggestions in Chapter 1, pp. 12–13, and to think about the following points:

1. Describe a place; do not tell a story. A story, which we will write in Chapter 7, is a series of actions connected by time, leading to a high point and resolution of the action. Your description may have plenty of action in it, as all our chapter student models do, but the actions will only be to illustrate the dominant impression.

2. Do feel free to include action description along with dialogue.

3. Occasionally tell the reader what to think about your details and how you feel about them (for more on this, see the chapter student models).

4. Add more, not less. Specific words and sensory details are essential. Even if you overdescribe in the first draft, you can always cut unneeded material later.

JOURNAL ENTRY 5-4

After you have completed the first rough draft, take a moment to reflect on your work, and then write two brief paragraphs of four or five sentences each. In the first paragraph tell what you like most about the draft and why; in the second, tell what you like least and why. Be as specific as possible. This self-assessment can help you decide where to begin revising.

Revising Drafts

To review the detailed lists for revising first, second, and final drafts, turn to Chapter 4.

■ ANNOTATED STUDENT MODEL

Teaching Idea
If you assign the Annotated Student Model in stages that parallel students' progress through their own papers, you can use the annotated drafts to ease students into their peer revising groups.

Let's look closely at how another student successfully completed the assignment, working through the writing process: gathering ideas, drafting, revising, and finally editing to create an interesting, well-focused, vivid description of a family fun center. To see a prewriting list for this paragraph, turn to p. 97.

Keep in mind that revision seldom occurs in tidy, well-defined packages. You will sometimes edit early in the revision process and change content in a later draft. The following draft stages, however, will help *focus* your revision efforts.

First-Stage Draft

These first four sentences deleted to tighten topic sentence

It's Friday night, and the whole family is wondering what to do. We could go catch a movie or save some money and just rent a video. They just built a new Blockbuster down the street, so it's easy to pick one up. After a little debate, we finally decide on bowling. We all pile in the car and my husband drives and soon we are there—Incred-a-Bowl. And it is pretty incredible, there's so much there for a family to do. As you walk in the place you can see all kinds of activity. People are laughing and talking, employees are busy checking out bowling shoes, and you can see the balls rolling down the alleys into the pins. There is a huge arcade with brightly lit and noisy arcade games. You can also see people helping customers. Further along is the snack bar. You can smell the aroma of freshly popped popcorn and hamburgers on the grill. If you keep looking, you will see the Backstop restaurant with televisions mounted around the room, near the ceiling. Each television is on a different sports channel, so you don't miss a play of any sport. They have put the bumper pads in the gutters for the small kids so they can knock over a few pins. Tonight is the Cosmic Bowl. This is where they turn the regular lights off and turn the black lights on. They turn the smoke machines on and it gives the effect of outer space. The bowling balls glow as they are rolling down the lanes. Everyone is laughing and enjoying themselves.

Teaching Idea
You might want to point out to students that they will find lots of mechanical errors in the rough drafts.

Teaching Idea
To help demonstrate second-draft revising, have students focus on several sentences of the Second-Stage Draft, comparing them to the First-Stage version. Ask them to explain why they think the revisions are worthwhile or not.

Second-Stage Draft

It's Friday night, and we are at the Incred-A-Bowl, which is the largest and busiest family fun center in Johnson County. As we walk through the main entrance of the fun center, you can immediately detect the scent of the lane oil. The wall above the pins, of the forty shiny synthetic lanes, is painted in florescent red, blue, yellow, and green colors. Off to the left is the huge arcade, with its blue print carpet, and brightly lit and noisy arcade games. There are children everywhere laughing and screaming, as they play there games and collect their tickets. You can hear the clatter of tokens, as parents get change for their bills in the token machine. To the right of the entrance, where we came in, is the control desk. Here, people are talking, laughing, and helping customers. Further down the crowded concourse is the snack bar. You can smell the aroma of freshly popped popcorn, and hamburgers sizzling on the charbroil grill. To the left of the snack bar, is the Backstop restaurant. It is decorated with all kinds of sports memorabilia. There are thirteen inch televisions mounted around the room, near the white ceiling. Each television is on a different sports channel, so you don't miss a play of any sport. Upstairs in the restaurant are pool tables and batting cages. Back downstairs there are some birthday parties going on. They have put the bumper pads in the gutters for the small kids. They are now jumping, clapping, and screaming as their pink, blue, yellow, green, and orange balls hit the pins. Tonight they are having a Cosmic Bowl. This is where they turn

Sensory details added: colors, smells, sounds

Specific words added

Locator phrases added

Topic sentence revised

Action through "-ings"

Another location added

Action through "-ings"

the regular lights off and turn the black lights on <u>above the lanes</u>. They turn the smoke machines on and it gives the effect of outer space. The blue, pink, orange, green, and yellow bowling balls glow as they are rolling down the lanes. Everyone is laughing and enjoying themselves. *This is a great place to keep family ties close.*

Closing sentence added

Expanded thought in conclusion

> **Special Points to Check in Revising from First to Second Drafts**
> 1. Added sensory details are shaded.
> 2. Added specific words are boxed.
> 3. <u>Added locator phrases are underlined.</u>

As you work through your own first draft, watch for these problem areas:

- Unfocused dominant impression
- Too many sentences leading into the description
- Weak concluding sentence
- Too few specific words and sensory details

Moving into a third-stage draft, Lucas polished her work for word choices and sentence variety.

Teaching Idea
Many students who write drafts at the A and B level resist revising a strong draft to make it even better. The Third-Stage Draft can be particularly beneficial to them.

Teaching Idea
To prepare students for editing, you might want to have them group edit the third-stage draft and then check themselves against the final edit.

Third-Stage Draft

Our Family Outing

Title added

It's Friday night, and we are at the Incred-A-Bowl, which is the largest and busiest family fun center in Johnson County. As we walk through the main entrance ~~of the fun center~~, you can immediately detect the scent of the lane oil. The wall above the pins, of the forty shiny synthetic lanes, is painted in florescent red, blue, yellow, and green colors. Off to the left is the huge arcade, with its blue print carpet, and brightly lit and noisy arcade games. There are children everywhere laughing and screaming, as they play there games and collect their tickets. You can hear the clatter of tokens, as parents get change for their bills in the token machine. To the right of the entrance, where we came in, is the control desk. Here, seven people are talking, laughing, and helping customers. [Further down the crowded concourse is the snack bar where you can smell the aroma of freshly popped popcorn, and hamburgers sizzling on the charbroil grill.] Someone has just purchased an order of chili cheese fries. It looks so sinful, with its homemade chili and hot nacho cheese. [To the left of the snack bar is the Backstop restaurant, which is decorated with all kinds of sports memorabilia.] There are thirteen-inch televisions mounted around the room, near the white ceiling. Each **tv** is on a different ~~sports~~ channel, so you don't miss a play of any sport. Upstairs in the restaurant are pool tables and batting cages. This is where many parents take their sons and daughters to practice batting the upcoming

Material added

Material added

baseball season . Back downstairs there are some birthday parties going on.

Material added

[They have put the black bumper pads in the gutters for the small kids, who are now jumping, clapping, and screaming as their pink, blue, yellow, green, and orange balls hit the pins.] The computerized scoring is a nice feature, because it allows the parents to participate in the fun instead of having to keep score. [Tonight they are having a Cosmic Bowl, which is where they turn the regular lights off and turn the black lights on above the lanes.] They turn the smoke machines on, and it gives the effect of outer space. The ~~blue, pink, orange, green, and yellow~~ **multicolored** bowling balls glow as they roll down the lanes. Everyone is laughing and enjoying themselves. This is a great place to keep family ties close.

Special Points to Check in Revising from Second to Third Drafts

1. Added sensory details are shaded.
2. Added specific words are boxed.
3. [Combined sentences are in brackets.]
4. **Synonyms for repeated words are in bold.**
5. ~~Unneeded words are lined through.~~

Here is the last draft of "Our Family Outing," the one where Jo Lucas will work closely on editing. This is the time to slow down, focusing on each word and applying the grammar and punctuation rules we have learned so far, especially for commas.

Final-Editing Draft

Our Family Outing

It's Friday night, and we are at the Incred-A-Bowl, which is the largest and busiest family fun center in Johnson County. As we walk through the main entrance, [9a] ~~you~~ [4] I (or we) can immediately detect the scent of the lane oil. The wall above the pins, of the forty shiny synthetic lanes, is painted in ~~florescent~~ [1] fluorescent red, blue, yellow, and green colors. Off to the left is the huge arcade, with its blue print carpet, and brightly lit and noisy arcade games. There are children everywhere laughing and screaming, as they play ~~there~~ [2] their games and collect their tickets. ~~You~~ [4] I (or we) can hear the clatter of tokens, as parents get change for their bills in the token machine. To the right of the entrance, where we came in, is the control desk. Here, seven people are talking, laughing, and helping customers, [6]. Further down the crowded concourse is the snack bar. ~~You~~ [4] I (or we) can smell the aroma of freshly popped popcorn and hamburgers sizzling on the charbroil grill. Someone has just purchased an order of chili cheese fries. It looks so sinful, [6] with its homemade chili and hot nacho cheese. To the left of the snack bar is the Backstop restaurant, which is decorated with all kinds of sports memorabilia. There are thirteen-inch televisions mounted around the room, near the white ceiling. Each ~~tv~~ [7] TV is on a different sports channel, so you ~~dont~~ [8] don't miss a play of any sport. Upstairs in the restaurant are pool tables and batting cages. This is where many parents take their sons and daughters to practice batting [3] for the upcoming baseball season. Back downstairs there are some birthday parties going on. They have put the black bumper pads in the gutters for the small kids [9b], who are now jumping, clapping, and screaming as their pink, blue, yellow, green, and orange balls hit the pins. The computerized scoring is a nice feature because it allows the parents to participate in the fun instead of having to keep score. Tonight they are having a Cosmic Bowl [9b], which is where they turn the regular lights off and turn the black lights on above the lanes. They turn the smoke machines on [9c], and it gives the effect of outer space. The multicolored bowling balls glow as they are rolling down the lanes. ~~Everyone is~~ [4] All the people are laughing and enjoying themselves. This is a great place to keep family ties close.

Jo Lucas

Teaching Idea
It is worth the time to take students back to Chapter 4 as they revise and edit their first several assignments. The Final-Draft Checklist is mirrored in Chapter 4, so if students need more in-depth reminders than the checklist provides, they will not have to search through the text. The information is packaged and accessible in a few consecutive pages.

Special Points to Check in Editing Final Drafts

1. Spelling	5. Sentence fragments	9. Common comma categories
2. Sound-alike words	6. Comma splices/run-ons	a. Introduce
		b. Enclose/end
3. Missing words	7. Capitalizations	c. Divide
4. Wrong words	8. Apostrophes	10. Unneeded commas

Final-Draft Checklist

Before you turn your final draft in for a grade, take a few minutes to review this checklist. You may find that, as careful as you think you have been, you still have missed a point or two—or three. (For more on any of these points, see Chapter 4.)

__ 1. Are you really describing a place and not slipping into a narrative (story)?

__ 2. Does your description have an overall point (dominant impression)?

__ 3. Are you occasionally telling your reader what to think about the details?

__ 4. Are you occasionally letting your reader know how you feel about the place?

__ 5. Are you using enough specific language?

__ 6. How well are you using sensory details?

__ 7. How effective is your topic sentence?

__ 8. How effective is your concluding sentence?

__ 9. How well connected are all the sentences within the paragraph?

__10. Are you choosing the most "active" verbs and "–ings" to describe action?

__11. Are your sentences varied in length and beginnings?

__12. Have you repeated a word or phrase so often that it becomes noticeable?

__13. Have you included words that serve no purpose?

__14. Have you written a title for the paper? (Check capitalizations)

__15. Have you prepared your paper according to the format expected by your instructor? (Check to see if you need a title page, be sure to double-space, leave at least 1-inch margins, use a 12-point font, and be sure to type or word process.)

__16. Have you edited your work as closely as you know how to (including having at least one other person—classmate, friend, family member—proofread closely)? Have you checked your **Improvement Chart** for your pattern errors so that you can look for them specifically?

__17. Have you looked specifically for the following errors: spelling, sound-alike words, missing words, wrong words, sentence fragments, comma splices/run-ons, capitalizations, apostrophes, and the Big Three comma categories?

CHAPTER SUMMARY

1. Describing is the process of relating details to build vivid images.

2. Descriptive writing relies on specific words and sensory details.

3. Words can be relatively general or relatively specific—the more specific a word, the clearer the image.

4. Description is often found in narrative, expository, and persuasive writing.

5. Writers often focus their description through a dominant impression.

6. A topic sentence in a paragraph of description usually includes the place and dominant impression.

7. Descriptions are often organized spatially.

8. Descriptions are strengthened by transitional words that locate readers in time and space.

9. Subjective descriptions can be strengthened by the writer revealing his or her thoughts and emotions.

10. Action is often part of description, including people moving and speaking.

11. Writing is never complete until it has gone through several revisions and careful editing.

■ **ALTERNATE WRITING ASSIGNMENTS**

While the focus of this chapter has been on illustrating a place, there are many other uses for description. As you consider the following assignment options, keep these points in mind:

- Decide on a dominant impression.

- State the dominant impression in your topic sentence.

- Rely on specific words and sensory details to develop your dominant impression.

- Conclude with a sentence that links to the topic sentence and expands the thought.

- Connect your sentences with time and place words.

1. **Describe a person:** Find someone you know reasonably well or someone you come in contact with regularly enough to observe her appearance (physical look and clothing) and actions (how she walks, stands, and sits; body language; mannerisms). Listen closely to the person and try to record some characteristic dialogue. Your goal is to create a verbal portrait of this person so that someone who has not met your person would recognize her from your description. Focus your description with an overall dominant impression, such as sloppy, well groomed, athletic, lazy, talkative, shy, funny, angry, and so on.

2. **Describe an object:** Select an object that you can observe closely and take notes on. This object could range from the small and ordinary (salt shaker, toaster oven, wrench) to the large and more unusual (construction crane, new Corvette, office building). Your goal is to capture the dominant impression of the object through description. For instance, your salt shaker might be exceptionally functional. You could describe its look as well as how well the shaker performs its job, dispensing salt. The construction crane might suggest power. You could describe the large metal parts and then show the machine in action.

3. **Describe an animal:** You could focus on the domestic scene, selecting a household pet (dog, cat, hamster, iguana); the rural, choosing, say, a farm animal (cow, horse, pig, chicken); or the outdoors in your neighborhood, noting some of the typical wildlife (squirrel, rabbit, bird, garter snake). Again the trick is to focus the description through a dominant impression, some defining trait of the animal. It might be easy and obvious to choose a trait like sloppiness for a pig. But it could be more challenging to try to show the intelligence or loveable qualities of the pig.

4. **Describe an event:** Rather than create a story with organized action leading up to a high point, you would try to capture the overall feeling of an event. Perhaps you have been to a concert that impressed you as chaotic, or as full of human warmth, or as a disaster (complete with bad performances, a rotten sound system, and a violent crowd). Maybe you were in the delivery room when your wife gave birth and noticed how casual the attending physicians seemed—everything under control, just business as usual.

5. **Describe a product:** There are a zillion possibilities for products to describe, but you could limit the field by sticking to one you use regularly. For instance, you might describe your favorite breakfast cereal. Why do you find it appealing? You could focus your description on characteristics like taste, texture, and length of time it stays crunchy.

CHAPTER 6

Telling Your Own Story

WHAT ARE WE TRYING TO ACHIEVE AND WHY?

Setting the Stage

People have been in the storytelling business for a long time, perhaps for as long as humanity has existed. A universal impulse, spanning all cultures and time, moves people to share their experiences with one another. Just as the Native Americans above are drawn closer together by the tales of the tribe's elder, so too are we drawn together by the stories of our own culture. Whenever we tell someone what we have done during the day—the bargain we got while shopping, the algebra exam we aced, the ticket we got speeding to school—we are telling a story or **narrating.**

Narration comes naturally to us. Beginning about the time we could speak, we have been telling those around us about our lives, telling stories that have helped us release emotion, reveal some part of ourselves, influence others, and entertain. In this chapter we will work more consciously with the elements of personal narrative, learning how to fashion them into a focused and interesting story. As we begin to discover material for our papers, we will become alert to the **significance** within our stories, and test this definition of personal narrative: *Someone doing something somewhere for some reason.*

Linking to Previous Experience

What experience do we already have with narrative? Consider film and television. Movies begin as screenplays, and almost everything we see on TV is scripted. Much of what we read for entertainment is fiction, beginning with Golden Books in our youth and progressing into short stories and novels as we grow older.

Teaching Idea
To introduce personal narrative, you can begin asking questions about the students' experiences with storytelling. Often they don't realize that TV and films are largely narrative, and with at least this medium they have *lots* of experience.

Purposes for telling our own stories

We also create our own narratives. Though few of us have the skills of an accomplished fiction writer, we all talk about ourselves, work associates, friends, and family members (perhaps *too* much sometimes!). Whenever we begin a conversation with a line like "You'll never guess who I saw Ted Wilson's wife with last night," we are launching into a narrative.

In addition, many of us write narratives on occasion. If you have ever kept a diary or e-mailed a friend, you were probably writing narrative. In elementary, middle, and high school, you have probably been asked to write about your life. If you have worked through Chapter 5 in *A Writer's Workshop,* you have written a description of a place, an assignment that contains many elements of narration: specific language, sensory details, active verbs, clearly linked sentences, and a unified dominant impression. In this chapter, we will learn more about **telling** and **showing** in narrative and continue to polish our descriptive skills.

Determining the Value

Getting better at telling stories can help us in many ways. For example, on the job we might have to defend ourselves by describing a conflict with a customer or fellow employee. In school we narrate events in our classes: in political science, we might be asked to tell about the 2000 presidential campaign; in sociology, we might need to illustrate with personal examples a discussion of violence in movies and its effects on teens; and in composition, we might be asked to tell about an event that has helped us see ourselves in a different light.

Improving narrative skills will also enrich our personal lives. Knowing more about storytelling can increase our enjoyment of stories and films. Talking through our stories in class will help us speak more comfortably in front of people. And as each of us works through the process of remembering an event, we will reflect on our behavior and the behavior of others, thinking about the meaning of our story and how it has helped make us who we are.

Teaching Idea
As for many of the journal entries, Journal Entry 6-1 can be written in class and used to stimulate whole-class or group discussion of personal narrative. Students will often want only to summarize their stories, so it is useful to stress their purpose in telling the story and to ask them about possible significance.

We tell stories for many reasons.

JOURNAL ENTRY 6-1

Think back over the past week or so and try to remember three instances when you told someone about something that happened to you. List each occasion and summarize in a sentence or two what happened. Next, list who you told your story to and what you think your purpose was: to release frustration, to communicate information, to help someone understand how you were feeling, to persuade, or simply to make someone laugh. How well did you succeed in each instance?

DEVELOPING SKILLS, EXPLORING IDEAS IN NARRATIVE PARAGRAPHS

To write effective personal narrative, we can keep the following points in mind:

1. Create a narrative that has conflict and tension.

2. Choose a story that has clear significance or meaning.

3. Build a story that often shows as well as tells.

4. Use effective dialogue.

5. Include metaphor and simile to add clarity and interest.

Groundwork for Activity 6-1: Conflict, Suspense, Climax

Perhaps it is human nature to be more interested in narratives that involve conflict than those that do not. As a species surviving millennia of struggle with other species and the planet, we may well have no choice in the matter. Our genes might simply tell us, "Look out: possible negative outcome. Pay attention!" Whatever the case, you will find some sort of potential for events to go wrong (**conflict**) critical to your story, and you will want to arrange the action so as to keep your reader wondering (**suspense**) what the outcome will be (**climax**).

The central *conflict* in your story might be one of these:

A. Person dealing with another person or group: Example: Your boss treats you unfairly.

B. Person dealing with herself: Example: You are learning to control your temper.

C. Person coping with the environment: Example: Your air conditioner is broken and it is 100 degrees outside.

In example A above, we might have two very different stories to tell.

1. My boss is a great guy who treats me wonderfully

   a. I am paid more than I am worth.

   b. I get four annual merit bonuses.

   c. I have all the time off a person could want.

   d. My boss insists that I leave the office every day by 3:00 P.M.

   e. I have a beautiful office.

2. My boss is a tyrant who makes my life a living hell.

   a. I am working for next to nothing.

   b. No matter how hard I work, I have never gotten a raise.

   c. I am lucky to get part of the weekend off, much less a vacation.

   d. My boss insists that I work a minimum of ten hours a day.

   e. I work in a cramped cubbyhole with poor lighting and ventilation.

Most of us might envy the fortunate soul in version 1, but we would probably be more interested to know how the poor stiff in version 2 is going to improve his life.

If we were to fashion the action elements of a brief narrative based on version 2, we might choose a few hours in—let's call him Oscar Jamieson—Oscar's day when it looked like his life was going to take a sudden turn from bad to worse. We will have Oscar arriving at 7:30 A.M. at the Sprint building where he works.

Action Outline

Conflict: Oscar has a confrontation with his boss today.

Worrying about the big billing statement he completely mishandled yesterday

- Hearing through a co-worker on the way to his office that he is in big trouble

- Finding a brief "come-see-me" note in his in-box from his boss

- Wondering, worrying, and avoiding the confrontation all morning

- Getting a phone call from the boss that says, "Get in here now!"

- Seeing the boss's secretary look up, shake her head, and look down at her desk

- Entering the boss's office and having him scowl from behind his desk

Teaching Idea
To help students with the idea of suspense in narrative, you might have them discuss some especially suspenseful moments in a popular film.

Teaching Idea
Students often see narrative conflict as a confrontation between people, forgetting about internal conflict and a person coping with his or her environment.

Lead-in

Developing the conflict: actions to build suspense

- Standing helplessly while the boss lays into him about the billing statement mess

- Hearing and seeing the boss get angrier as he begins shouting

- Listening to the dreaded words, "You're fired!"

Climax

Seeing his boss suddenly fall back in his chair, clutching his chest
Calling the secretary, but, too late (darn it), the boss has dropped dead from a heart attack

Resolution

Finding out that Oscar's best friend has been promoted to the boss's position and that Oscar, too, is in for a promotion

   Hurray for Oscar! What looked like a horrible day for him (the good guy) turned out to be a terminal day for his boss (the bad guy). Although this action outline is a simplistic rendering of people, who are seldom simply good or bad, it demonstrates several important elements in story crafting:

- Lead-in: a brief introduction to arouse interest and set the stage

- Conflict: the problem a person encounters in the story

- Suspense: the reader's uncertainty about the outcome of the conflict

- Climax: the high point of the action

- Resolution: the result of the climax—the point of the story (significance)

Teaching Idea
You might have students compose their own "action outlines" using participial phrases to encourage action (a side benefit is the illustration of parallelism in outlining).

Activity 6-1: Conflict, Suspense, Climax

Collaborative

With members of your group, choose a topic from one of the three categories listed below (or turn to the topic lists on pp. 120–121), and decide what kind of conflict might be represented. If you choose to work on an event that actually happened to a group member, ask questions about the event. Next, write a description of the conflict in a single sentence, and then create an **action outline** as illustrated above.

Teaching Idea
Activity 6-1 may take twenty minutes or so and is a good way to get students thinking about specific action in their own narratives.

- An embarrassing moment: speaking in public, asking for a date, having forgotten your wallet or purse in a restaurant when the bill is presented, being caught in a lie

- An unpleasant moment as a consumer: returning defective merchandise, being overcharged in billing, suspecting mechanics of pulling a fast one

- A public confrontation: handling a traffic accident, being pulled over by a police officer, arguing in a restaurant, dealing with a neighbor, protecting your property

Answers will vary
Action Outline

Topic: *A person eating at a restaurant has forgotten his wallet.*

Conflict: *Alex is on his first date with Sonya, and as the bill comes, he realizes that he has no money!*

Lead-in: *Alex has finally found the courage to invite Sonya, who he is infatuated with, out on a date. They are finishing a pleasant dinner.*

Actions to develop conflict and build suspense:
A. *Alex telling Sonya what a good time he has had*

B. *Sonya responding similarly, saying how glad she is that Alex finally invited her out*

C. *Both exchanging soulful looks*

D. *Waiter leaving check at the table*

E. *Alex frantically searching for wallet*

F. *Alex desperately trying to think of a solution: "Did I leave my wallet in the car? Did I leave it some place in the restaurant? Do I know anyone here I can borrow some money from?"*

Climax: *Alex tells Sonya about the problem.*

Resolution: *Sonya laughs about the affair, says no problem, and uses her own credit card to pay the bill. She shows her sympathetic nature and proves her quality of character to Alex, who falls even harder for her.*

Groundwork for Activity 6-2: Significance

For a story to have substance, it should have some point. Without a point, the narrative deteriorates into a mere collection of actions that leaves the reader wondering why she bothered to read it. In Oscar Jamieson's story from Activity 6-1, we see that he has been freed from a tyrant who has been making Oscar's life miserable. There is a clear progression from the anxious beginning of his day to the triumphant end. But even in a story that clearly resolves the conflict, there is room for a direct statement of the **significance** of the action. For example, here are several possible points that could emerge from Oscar's story:

A. After people have suffered enough, if they have faith and can hang on, like Job, they may eventually be rewarded.

B. There is justice after all.

C. Bullies and tyrants will come to a bad end.

D. Avoid feeling too worried or depressed about a possibly bad situation before you know the outcome.

E. Having experienced cruelty, Oscar resolves to become a kinder person.

Any one of the ideas above or a combination could be the main point of a story. It is the author's privilege to choose. The main point should, however, emerge as naturally from the event as possible. Most readers would scratch their heads if the writer used Oscar's story to try to point out that people ought to eat better and exercise regularly if they want to avoid heart trouble. And it would seem contrived if the point were how Oscar helped his friend to prosper in the company. In your own narratives the significance will not always be clear in the beginning, but as you begin to recreate the event, *a*, if not *the*, meaning the event has for you should emerge.

> Writers choose the meaning of their stories.

> Significance is not always clear to a writer at first.

Collaborative

Activity 6-2: Significance

Whereas skillful writers of serious fiction often deliberately imply many shades of meaning, as beginners, we want to be as explicit in our brief stories as possible. The following story, "The Death of a Dog," provides many opportunities to express significance, but fails to do so. If the student writer were part of your group, what suggestions could you give him to reveal meaning? Read the model, discuss it among yourselves, and then write out three possible main points the story *could* be making.

The Death of a Dog

As I prepared for surgery at the vet clinic where I now work, I was administering anesthesia to a miniature black poodle when respiration stopped, and the heart stopped beating. I scrambled to the side of the small poodle to start respiration, also giving epinephrine (adrenaline) and dopram, trying to get the heart beating again. Not sure what else to do, I yelled frantically for Dr. Erickson, and he came into the room saying, "What the hell is going on in here?" After assessing the situation, he began to assist me in trying to revive the limp, almost lifeless poodle lying on the surgical table. It seemed there was no hope for the small black poodle when a single breath came from its lungs, then another, and another. However, the battle had just begun, for the dog had no heartbeat, but it was breathing. The doctor and I had never seen anything like it before. Often there will be a heartbeat and no breath, but never the other way around. After a few more minutes, we got the dog's heart beating, but the big question then was whether we should go ahead with the exploratory surgery as planned or let the animal come out of anesthesia, in which case it would risk dying from the abdominal swelling. We decided to go ahead with the surgery, trying to save the poor poodle from certain death. As we cut open the body cavity to find out what was causing the swelling, the uterus expanded and swelled out of the animal's body cavity. We immediately removed the infected uterus, sutured the body cavity, and quickly brought the dog out of anesthesia to observe it for other difficulties.

List of Possible Meanings

Example: ___*It amazes me to see how tenacious life can be.*___

Answers will vary

1. *Teamwork can save a life.* _____

2. *Remaining calm is important in a crisis.* _____

3. *Making the right decision under pressure can be difficult.* _____

Groundwork for Activity 6-3: Showing and Telling

Creating a scene for a reader to participate in requires the ability both to show and tell. When we **show** the reader something, we allow her to make her own evaluation or interpretation of whatever is being discussed or described. When we **tell** a reader about something, we make the judgment for him. Look at the two following passages and see if you can determine which one tells and which shows.

1. We were growing more frightened by the moment.

2. As late as it was, one of my cousins, my brother Tama, and I were still up, talking over some gruesome scenes from *The Exorcist,* in our minds once again hearing Linda Blair roar out "MERRIN!" in her demon voice and seeing her head turn completely around. Suddenly we all heard a scratching sound at the outside of the door and an awful noise that sounded like someone groaning in pain. "Ooohhh-aaaghh!"

If you selected number 1 for telling and 2 for showing, you are correct. You might notice that telling is more economical; it gets the point across fast. However, telling often only involves the mind, leaving out the heart. And while showing requires more words, if done well it can involve your reader on several levels as she *reacts* to the characters' speech and other actions and *experiences* the sensory details you have provided. Good writers typically interweave both showing and telling as they create scenes, using one to clarify and reinforce the other, as illustrated in the passage below:

As late as it was, one of my cousins, my brother Tama, and I were still up, talking over some gruesome scenes from *The Exorcist,* in our minds once again hearing Linda Blair roar out "MERRIN!" in her demon voice and seeing her head turn completely around. **We were growing more frightened by the moment** when suddenly we all heard a scratching sound at the outside of the door and an awful noise that sounded like someone groaning in pain. "Ooohhh-aaaghh!"

Rough drafts often suffer from too much telling and not enough showing. But if you realize the power showing lends to writing and are willing to work a little harder, you can create narratives that truly move an audience.

> **First drafts often tell too much and show too little.**

Activity 6-3: Showing and Telling

The following sentences *tell* a reader how to interpret a situation. Write a sentence that *shows* the same statement. (You can show with sensory details, by describing a person's actions, and by having him speak.)

Example: **Telling:** My brother was concerned about my grandfather lying on the floor.

Showing: _My brother screamed, "Mom, help, grandpa is dying!"_

Answers will vary

1. Telling: Josh felt sick again today.

   Showing: _After throwing up three times in thirty minutes, Josh crawled back to his bed._

   _____

2. Telling: The whole family felt sad as they gathered around the casket.

   Showing: _Grandfather quietly cried while his three granddaughters placed roses in the casket with their father. The older man looked down at his forty-five-year-old son and muttered again, "The old should not have to bury the young. It just ain't right."_

3. Telling: The customer service representative did not appear interested in my story.

   Showing: _Stifling a yawn and turning for the third time to laugh at a joke from his friend behind the counter, the customer service representative at Best Buy did not seem much interested in my story._

4. Telling: Now I finally understood that Adrian was a bigot.

   Showing: _"It's the damn Jews who own all the banks. They're the ones who control the interest rates in this country." Hearing this from Adrian, I finally realized that he was a bigot._

5. Telling: Batur was overjoyed when his semester grades arrived.

   Showing: _Kissing his grade report, Batur danced a little jig and shouted to his wife, "Another 4.0—I'll get the scholarship for sure!"_

   _____

Groundwork for Activity 6-4: Dialogue

Dialogue is an integral part of **showing**. While narratives can be written without any dialogue, almost all stories benefit from it. Allowing people in your story to speak can show their qualities, add information, and enhance the mood or feeling of the

ESTABLISHING AUDIENCE AND PURPOSE

You may select the primary audience for this paper, a person or group who you think might be interested in what you have to say (for more on audience profiling, see pp. 9–10). You might want to tell a story that involves family members and so would be particularly meaningful to them. Perhaps you want to relive some special moment with a good friend and think that she would also enjoy the tale. Often your audience will be people who can identify with your experience because they have lived or are living through something similar. For example, while many people might be interested in and sympathize with the author of "Do Unto Others . . ." (pp. 129–130), mothers with several young children might best be able to identify with the story.

Another way to describe your audience is by what they read. For example, would your story interest someone who subscribes to *National Geographic* or *Car and Driver?* Your audience should affect the content of your story, the action description, explanation, and word choices. (Note: Your composition instructor is always at least a secondary audience, so also write to show him or her that you are learning narrative strategies.)

Your overall purpose may be to inform, persuade, or entertain, but the significance of the story should be clear.

WORKING THROUGH THE WRITING ASSIGNMENT

Discovering Ideas

You can begin your prewriting by looking for several topics that you feel strongly about and that clearly involve conflict (person with person, person within herself, person with some external force). Any of the following categories might give you a useful idea:

Teaching Idea
To help students understand the concept of audience in narrative, you might start a class conversation about movies they have recently seen and see how the class divides its opinion on various films.

Topic Lists

Personal Life

1. A situation that made you feel good (or bad) about yourself: helping a person in need, reacting quickly in an emergency, donating to a charity, completing a big project

2. An experience of winning or losing some important prize or contest: athletic, scholastic, job or hobby related, lottery or drawing

3. A special experience within a group: sports team, choir, band, club, Boy Scouts/Girl Scouts, fraternal organizations (Kiwanis, Rotary, Elks, etc.), military, PTA

4. An embarrassing moment: speaking in public, asking for a date, having forgotten your wallet or purse in a restaurant when the bill is presented, being caught in a lie

5. A "first" experience: infatuation, love, fight, "A," honor roll, speeding ticket

6. An experience with altering your appearance in some significant way: tattoo, body piercing, hair coloring, cosmetic surgery, weight loss, body building

7. An event that made you see yourself or someone else in a new light: realizing that a friend is a bigot, understanding why someone dislikes you, losing respect for a hero, discovering an unlooked-for quality in a person you know

8. An event that you especially looked forward to: rock concert, symphony, trade show, sporting event, fashion show, art exhibit, mall opening

9. A memorable vacation: at the lake, ocean, or mountains; a special time spent at home; a stay at a bed and breakfast, a hotel near home, a relative's, or a good friend's

10. A life-threatening accident: involving an automobile, motorcycle, airplane, or boat; drowning, falling, freezing, or suffocating

11. A moment when another person has badly frightened you: thief in your house, someone on the street, stalker, phone caller, friend, family member

12. A moment when frustration turned to anger with consequences that you later regretted: shouting at or demeaning a loved one, breaking an appliance, driving dangerously, punching a wall, provoking a fight with a stranger

13. A moment when you experienced great pain: childbirth, broken bone, burn, kidney stone, migraine headache, dislocated shoulder, muscle spasm, heart attack

14. A relationship going badly (or well): girl friend/boy friend, marriage, parent/child, friendship, employer/employee, work associate, doctor, lawyer, clergy

15. A time when someone died: family member, friend, co-worker, personal hero

16. An unpleasant moment as a consumer: returning defective merchandise, being overcharged in billing, suspecting mechanics of pulling a fast one

17. A public confrontation: handling a traffic accident, being pulled over by a police officer, arguing in a restaurant, dealing with a neighbor, protecting your property

18. A childhood prank: throwing snowballs at a car, soaping windows, throwing firecrackers, calling strangers on the phone, frightening a friend

School

1. A moment of comprehension: any breakthrough in learning: algebra (factoring, the quadratic equation, negative exponents), biology (mitosis vs. meiosis, the carbon cycle, Mendel's law), composition (sentence fragments, audience, persona)

2. A moment that helps decide a career path: becoming interested in a course; being influenced by a teacher, counselor, or fellow student; shadowing a career professional

3. A moment of despair: failing the exam, feeling swamped by the work, finding yourself in the class from hell (teacher is a monster or a bore, fellow students are automatons, the material is over your head)

4. A moment of triumph: acing the exam, achieving a high GPA, graduation

5. A moment that helps you get back on track: forming a study group; finding a tutor; going to your writing center, math center, or learning lab

Work

1. A particularly pleasant (or unpleasant) experience: raise, promotion, decrease in work load, more authority, disliked boss or co-worker leaves, vacation increase

2. A moment when you decide to leave the job

3. A moment when you realize that you truly value your job

4. A creative breakthrough

5. A moment within a childhood job that affected your future plans: babysitting, lawn mowing, bailing hay (any farm work), landscaping, house painting, walking dogs, volunteering (candy striping, etc.)

Brainstorm
with others to
discover ideas.

After you have read through the lists, if you have no idea for a story, try reading the student models in this chapter and some of the other paragraph models in the Skills section. Think back over your life of the past several years. Has there been a time when you were particularly depressed or happy? Have you made any major life changes: moving from one school, city, or country to another; becoming part of a new group of people; switching careers? If ideas are not coming, talk to others about stories they would tell. If all else fails, simply choose a topic from the lists and begin one or more of the prewriting methods listed in Chapter 1.

Prewriting Suggestions

Here is an example of how using the journalist's questions with a topic from the Personal Life category might generate some useful ideas:

Frame the questions like this: Who was involved in the event? What happened? When did it happen? and so forth.

Event: a childhood prank

Who: My brother Nat, a friend, me, and old lady Swanson were involved.

What: We soaped Mrs. Swanson's windows out front and then got both mirrors in her hall before we rang her bell and called, "Trick or treat."

When: It was Halloween night in 1981.

Where: We were in Cleveland, Ohio, six houses down the street from our house.

Why: We were looking for excitement.

How: Nat and I brought the soap with us. We had premeditated.

What was the result: Mrs. Swanson came to the door with a bowl of mini Hershey bars and was handing them out to us when she suddenly noticed the soaped mirrors in her hallway. She confronted us—not in a mean way; she was hurt—saying she had just been out there a few minutes before we had come. We were caught but felt forced to lie. I could see that she didn't believe us. I felt guilty about it and stopped soaping windows after that. But the worst part was being forced into the pointless lying.

Try several topics
before you commit
to one.

When using a prewriting technique like this one, try not to get too carried away with it, unless you feel like material is just pouring out. It is usually a good idea to try two or three topics before you commit much energy to one. But after you have decided on one event, you can extend your prewriting material by asking more *specific* questions of it. For example, what were the boys' ages and Mrs. Swanson's? Further details could help set the mood (a cold rainy evening), and sharpen the setting (details of the hall). If one prewriting method is not helping, switch to another.

To focus your invention practice even further, think about one piece of your story at a time, setting aside half a page for each and listing memories as they surface. The following are some important areas to gather material on:

Teaching Idea
You might want to help
students through part of their
prewriting in class by having
them choose an event, answer
the journalist's questions, and
then list or freewrite on one or
more of the six narrative points.

- **Setting:** In narrative the setting or scene is just a backdrop against which your characters move, so you will seldom go into great detail. However, some detailing is always a good idea to show the characters in relation to one another and to help set the mood. For example, consider how the darkness and silence of the house in "What a Joke!" (p. 118) contribute to the children's feeling of fright. As you recall details of physical objects (car, chair, tree), their size and location, and remember details of color, sound, smell, and so forth, jot them down. You won't use them all, but it is good to have them to draw on.

- **People:** Your event will feature you and perhaps one other person as important enough to describe in any detail. But you only need to provide a brief sketch

Teaching Idea
You might remind students that *approximate* dialogue is fine.

Teaching Idea
Because some students have difficulty discovering the point of their narrative (and, of course, sometimes there simply isn't one), you might model a Q/A exchange with one student, using the prompts under Significance. Then the class can group up and do the same with each other.

Get reactions from others.

(approximate age, overall physical look, maybe hair or eye color, some article of clothing), and then focus on the action; your thoughts and feelings; and realistic, brief dialogue.

- **Dialogue:** While not all of your narratives will include spoken dialogue, most should. Dialogue is a powerful device for *showing* what a person feels and thinks. It is an important method for varying the narrator's voice (yours) and of providing additional information useful to the story. As you prewrite, try to list word-for-word dialogue or a close approximation of what the person would say.

- **Action:** Without action narrative dies. The action does not have to be dramatic or violent (Arnold Schwarzenegger firing another Stinger missile to blow up a helicopter), but it does have to exist. Remember that there can often be compelling mental and emotional action as well. However, as you gather ideas, try to recall physical movement. How did you cross the room? Where did the other person sit? Did you lean back on one arm, slouch in your chair, or slice the air with your hand as you emphatically said, "No!"?

- **Thoughts and feelings:** As you reflect on the event, try to recall what you thought and felt immediately before, during, and just after the action. Often you will only capture a piece of the thought or feeling and then elaborate on it based on your current thoughts and feelings.

- **Significance:** In our personal narratives we need to discover why the memory is important enough to *want* to write about it. The significance or meaning may not be clear at first or even limited to one point, but it is important, and answering the following questions will help you discover it:

  - How did my behavior reflect on who I was at the time?
  - How did my behavior reflect on who I am now?
  - What did the other person's (people's) behavior indicate about him?
  - What were the positive or negative effects of the action?
  - What *could* have resulted?
  - Have I learned anything about myself, another person, or how the world works?
  - Have I changed my behavior, thinking, or feeling as a result of the actions?

  (For more on significance, see p. 111.)

Whether you have definitely fixed on your topic or not, this is a good stage in the writing process to get some input from others. Talk to people in or out of class about your event. If they think it can be shaped into an interesting final story, you may feel more confident moving ahead.

Prewriting—Summing Up

1. Decide on several events or choose several from the topic lists.

2. Use a prewriting technique (like the journalist's questions) to get an overview of your events.

3. Choose an event and briefly summarize it.

4. Use another prewriting method to generate ideas for the setting, people, action, and significance.

5. Summarize your story for someone else to see the person's reaction.

> **JOURNAL ENTRY 6-2**
>
> Review your prewriting notes, particularly the ones that deal with the significance of the event. Do you feel that your story has a point yet? Does it seem that some of the material you have gathered reveals something of who you are to your reader? In a brief paragraph write out the meaning your narrative has for you.

Organizing Ideas

Try hinting at the significance of your event in the topic sentence.

Before you plunge into your draft, here are several points to help shape and focus it. First, be sure to write out at least a *rough* topic sentence. The topic sentence does not have to reveal the outcome of your story, but it should hint at the outcome and give the reader a clear sense of your direction (for more on topic sentences, see pp. 36–41). It often works well to tie the significance of the story into the topic sentence. In the following topic sentences, taken from student models in this chapter, you will see the topics underlined once and the limiting statements twice.

1. At the Civil Air Patrol Encampment of 1996, when I was only sixteen, I learned how satisfying it can be to lead a group successfully.

2. At 3:00 A.M. one morning my grandfather decided to play a joke on us that didn't turn out to be as funny as he thought it would be.

Teaching Idea
Emphasizing that they limit the lead-in to their narratives will save some students from major first-draft cutting and refocusing.

Organize your paragraph chronologically (as the clock or calendar moves), beginning close to the high point of action, keeping your lead-in to the climax as compact as possible. A one-paragraph story that wants to focus on the birth of a child should begin on the day of the delivery, leaving out the other nine months.

Here are two ways to manage time problems in one-paragraph narratives:

Limit the total **time** of your narrative.

- Limit the time of the event. Many terrific short narratives cover only a few *minutes*, as do the student models in this chapter. If you try to cover more than a few minutes, be sure to summarize, using time transitions like *the next morning, when we got there*, and *by 8:00*.

Limit the total **scenes.**

- Stick with one or two scenes in which all the action occurs. For example, in the student model "What a Joke!" the story is set entirely in Anna's room.

Teaching Idea
If you worked through Chapter 5, you might remind students that the time and space transitions are the same they have already used.

Remember the value of strong connectors between sentences. Here is a list of time and space transitions as a reminder (for more on connectors, see pp. 53–57).

For Locating or Moving in Space			
above	east (west . . .)	in the back	over
against	elsewhere	in the distance	surrounded by
alongside	far off (away)	into	there
around	farther on	near	through
For Moving in Time			
after	first (second, etc.)	next	suddenly
afterward	immediately	now	then
at last	in the meantime	often	time passed
awhile	in the past	once	until

- All references to calendar time and events: one day, days ago, tonight, afternoon

- All references to clock time: a few minutes, 12:00 A.M., three hours

- All references to regular meals: during breakfast, lunch, dinner

Teaching idea
If students limit their "action" outlines from Journal Entry 6-3 to, say, six to eight major actions, they will be less likely to write 500-word paragraphs.

JOURNAL ENTRY 6-3

To help focus your draft, try a "scratch" outline (for more on outlining, see pp. 12, 282) that lists the major actions of your event as they occurred. For example, in the student model "What a Joke!" you might list the primary action like this:

1. Talking late with the family
2. Frightening ourselves with a scary movie
3. Opening the door
4. Hearing noises
5. Seeing grandfather fall into the room
6. Seeing the family rush into my room
7. Being reassured that grandfather was all right

(To see an action outline for this journal entry, see pp. 109–110 .)

Drafting

With the preliminary work done, you are almost ready to write your first draft. But before you plunge in, take a moment to review the Drafting suggestions in Chapter 1, pp. 12–13 and to think about the following points:

Teaching Idea
Although you may have already covered drafting in Chapter 1, it helps to review this material again the day before student drafts are due.

1. Visualize the setting. Close your eyes and try to see the setting of your story. If the narrative occurs inside, what does the room look like? What kind of furniture is there? How is it arranged? Is it day or night, warm or cold, summer or winter? Sometimes it helps to establish a larger frame for the picture before moving into the smaller parts. Imagine that you are hovering in a helicopter filming from a hundred feet above the scene. What do you see?

2. Use your "creative memory." Few people can remember everything they want to put into a story. Feel free to fill in the blank spaces of your memory with details and dialogue that *could* have happened.

Summarizing increases the pace; detailing slows it.

3. Summarize action whenever you want to move the reader quickly through your story.

4. Detail a scene when you want the reader to slow down and pay attention. In particular, carefully detail the few sentences close to the climax of your story.

Teaching Idea
To help students understand how summarizing and detailing affect narrative pace, you might have them skim the first few sentences of the Annotated Student Model to show summarizing and then skim the detailing of the author's thoughts and emotions. They should be able to see that the detailing slows down the pace and emphasizes the material.

JOURNAL ENTRY 6-4

After having written your first draft, take a few moments to reread it and determine the high point of the action. Where do you think the climax occurs? Write a brief paragraph explaining where the climax is in your story and why you think it is there.

Revising Drafts

To review the detailed lists for revising drafts, turn to Chapter 4.

■ ANNOTATED STUDENT MODEL

To help you with your narrative, take a few minutes to read through the Annotated Student Model that follows. In examining the drafts that the author, Chris Potts, wrote, you can profit from her hard work and head off some of the problems that are likely to creep into your own drafts.

Keep in mind that revision seldom occurs in tidy, well-defined packages. You will sometimes edit early in the revision process and change content in a later draft. The following draft stages, however, will help *focus* your revision efforts.

First-Stage Draft

First drafts are for getting words on paper, so, naturally, there will be plenty to change. While many narratives initially leave out important parts of the story, other first drafts include too much. Notice in this first draft how much of the lead-in was unneeded.

Total words = 538 (need to focus)

> "Come on, Joelle, we need to hurry up," I said, trying to motivate my three-year-old girl toward the car. "Coming, mommy, I gotta get my babies!" Oh, no, I thought, this could take forever, and I don't have forever. I had to get to the bank to pick up some papers for the house. Jordan, her nineteen-month-old sister, looked on, playing with her "babies." She was not getting ready to move any faster than her big sister. "Listen, sweetie, we are in a hurry, like a race. Ready. Set. Go!" Neither of my girls were cooperating today, so I scooped them both up and headed for the garage. After wrestling the girls into their car seats, I slowly backed down the driveway. It was getting more difficult each day to maneuver the car with my ever-increasing midsection—the girls' little brother, four weeks till delivery—getting in the way. But we made it into the street and were on our way to the bank. What I hadn't counted on was taking a turn too hard. I flattened a tire. I didn't know what to do since there was no one around to help me, and I couldn't do the job anymore myself. Panic and frustration are a sure-fire recipe for tears, but I tried to stay calm and composed so my girls wouldn't catch my mood. Suddenly, I heard a voice. "Listen, I have a cell phone. Do you want to call someone to come pick you up?" As I turned toward the voice, I saw an older guy who looked a lot like my dad. I explained to him that everyone who could help was out of reach and I wasn't sure what I was going to do. As I spoke, I had no control over the tears. "Are you sure you've thought through all your options?" he asked. "How about Triple-A? Do you have any other family or friends who could help?" I just shook my head. "Well, then," he said as he rolled up his sleeves I still no how to fix a flat. If you don't mind me taking a run at it? Show me where the jack and spare are, and I'll see what I can do. "Why don't you wait inside the bank while I put the spare on?" I nodded yes, and opened the door to get the keys. Then I unbuckled the girls and ushered them out of the car. As Joelle jumped out, she called the man "Papa," thinking he might be my dad, but she wasn't sure about it. To really confuse her, the man, said, "Hi, Peanut," which is the name my dad calls her. The girls and I went into the bank, retrieved our papers, and headed to check on the man's progress. "Well, you're back in buisness," he said. "It's just a spare tire. You shouldn't go over forty-five miles per hour with it." As he spoke, I offered the cash envelop to him. Then I attempted to utter a profound thank-you. Gratefulness was still caught in my throat, and I

Teaching Idea
If you assign the Annotated Student Model in stages that parallel students' own progress through their papers, you can use the annotated drafts to ease students into their own peer revising groups.

Teaching Idea
This First-Stage Draft clearly alerts students to the overlong lead-in problem.

Lead-in summarized to get closer to the climax more quickly

was crying again. He said that he didn't want the money in the envelop and added, "You don't have to do that, but I will ask you to do a favor for me. The next time you see who needs help, stop and help them." I said "I will" and a few "thank-yous" and we headed our seperate ways.

Second-Stage Draft

Teaching Idea
This Second-Stage Draft points out the common narrative problem of insufficient showing.

First rough drafts of narratives often have unneeded material, so watch closely for too much of a good thing. Also be alert to the other material and organizational concerns listed under First-Stage Draft Problems (pp. 63–65). Try to refine your topic and concluding sentences, realizing their strong connection. Remember that you are trying to build suspense/tension within the overall conflict and that action is crucial for involving your audience. Double-check dialogue to make sure it is believable and economical—cut any that is not. Finally, look closely at your setting and people. Are all pieces of your scene adequately described to help your reader follow the action?

Teaching Idea
Here is another clear reminder to students to revise for suspense/ tension.

Topic sentence revised

Examples added to *show* helpless condition

Explaining added to *show* emotion

Have you ever been stuck, needing help, with no place to turn? One day several years ago, I found myself in a rush to get to the bank. I needed to sign papers vital for the closing of our first house. We desperately needed a larger house for our growing family. With my two girls in there car seats in the back, we neared the parking lot of the bank. I thought we would make it before the bank closed but I hadn't counted on the accident. Bang! A nasty metallic sound told me what to expect. As I got out I could see it, yes, the tire was flat. The rim touched the ground. What was I going to do? I ran through my options quickly. My husbands plane wouldn't land for another hour and a half. My friend Angie had left town with her family that morning. I knew how to change flat, but, I was pregnant. And then what would I do with my daughters in the back seat? Panic and frustration are a sure-fire recipe for tears, but I tried to remain calm and composed so my girls wouldn't catch my mood. Suddenly I heard a voice say, "Listen, I have a cell phone. Do you want to call someone to come pick you up?" As I turned toward the voice, I saw an older guy, who looked a lot like my dad. I explained to him that everyone who could help was out of reach and I wasn't sure what I was going to do. As I spoke, I started crying. ***** "Well, then," he said as he rolled up his sleeves, "why don't you wait inside the bank while I put the spare on. You have a spare, don't you?" I had no words. Gratefulness had swallowed panic and frustration but had gotten caught in my throat as I simply nodded yes. The girls and I went into the bank, retrieved our papers, made a cash withdrawal, and headed back outside. The man had just shut the trunk, and was rolling down his sleeves. "You're back in buisness," he said with a smile." As he spoke, I offered him the cash envelop. Then I attempted to utter a profound thank-you. Gratefulness was still caught in my throat, and I was crying again. He said that he didn't want the money in the envelope and added, "You don't have to do that, but I will ask you to do a favor for me. The next time you see who needs help, stop and help them." I said, "I will" and a

Lead-in condensed from first draft.

Material added to increase tension

Added: sound, action, specific details

Teaching Idea
Although the pronoun "you" is frequently overused in student writing, it can be effective when the writer actually intends to speak to her audience as Chris Potts does in her topic sentence, using a question to draw her reader in.

*Unneeded dialogue deleted

Specific detail added for clarity

Action added

Conclusion revised to reinforce the significance

few "thank-yous," and we headed our seperate ways. Later, after I had returned the favor I understood why he hadn't excepted the money I had offered. *No reward could be as satisfying as the good deed itself.*

Special Points to Check in Revising from First to Second Drafts

1. ~~Delete unnecessary material~~
2. Add material to increase tension/suspense
3. *Show* as well as tell
4. Describe physical actions
5. Check time and space connectors
6. Tighten topic and concluding sentences

Third-Stage Draft

By this point in the process, Chris has her draft in good shape. The content is almost entirely in place, and she will not change any of the organization. Topic and concluding sentences are working well, and the time and space connectors have her reader firmly anchored in the story. Now is the time to look closely at sentence- and word-level problems that can keep a good narrative from becoming an excellent one.

Do Unto Others . . .

Have you ever been stuck, needing help, with no place to turn? [One day several years ago, I found myself in a rush to get to the bank to sign papers vital for the closing of our first house, a house we desperately needed for our growing family.] [With my two girls in there car seats in the back, nearing the parking lot of the bank, I thought we would make it before the bank closed] but I hadn't counted on the accident. Bang! I had hit a curb hard and a nasty metallic sound told me what to expect. As I got out, I could see it. [Yes, the tire was flat the rim touching the pavement.] What was I going to do? I ran through my options quickly. My husbands plane wouldn't land for another hour and a half. My friend Angie had left town with her family that morning. I knew how to change flat, but, eight months pregnant, I was lucky still to be tying my own shoes. And then what would I do with my daughters in the back seat? Panic and frustration are a sure-fire recipe for tears, but I fought them off and struggled to remain calm ~~and composed~~ (~~so my girls wouldn't catch my mood~~) **for my girls.** Suddenly I heard a voice say, "Listen, I have a cell phone. Do you want to call someone to come pick you up?" As I turned toward the voice. I saw an older gentleman who looked a lot like my dad. (~~I explained to him that everyone who could help was out of reach and I wasn't sure what I was going to do. As I spoke I started crying.~~) **Beginning to cry. I explained how helpless I felt.** "Well, then," he said as he rolled up his sleeves, "why don't you

Metaphor added

wait inside the bank while I put the spare on. You have a spare, don't you"? I had no words. Gratefulness had swallowed panic and frustration but had gotten caught in my throat as I simply nodded yes. The girls and I hustled into the bank, retrieved our papers, (~~made a cash withdrawal~~) **withdrew cash,** and headed back outside. Our good samaritan had just shut the trunk, and was rolling down his sleeves. "You're back in business," he said with a smile." **[As he spoke, I offered him the cash envelop, and attempted to utter a profound thank-you, but gratefulness was still caught in my throat, and the tears were in full force again.]** He (~~said he didn't want the money in the envelope~~) **declined** the envelope **saying**, "You don't have to that, but I will ask you to do a favor for me. The next time you see who needs help, stop and help them." I squeaked out an "I will" and a few "thank-yous," and we headed our seperate ways. Later, after I had returned the favor I understood why he hadn't excepted the money I had offered. No reward could be as satisfying as the good deed itself.

Special Points to Check in Revising from Second to Third Drafts

1. Added specific words are boxed.
2. [Sentences combined for variety are in brackets.]
3. Synonyms and phrases replacing clutter and repeat words are in bold.
4. ~~Unneeded words are lined through.~~
5. Active verbs and "-ings" are shaded.

Final-Editing Draft

Teaching Idea
To prepare students for editing, you might want to have them group edit the third-stage draft and then check themselves against the final edit.

Here is the last draft of "Do Unto Others . . . ," the one where Chris Potts will work closely on editing. This is the time to slow down, focusing on each word and applying the grammar and punctuation rules we have learned so far, especially for commas.

Do Unto Others . . .

Have you ever been stuck, needing help, with no place to turn? One day several years ago, I found myself in a rush to get to the bank to sign papers vital for the closing of our first house, a house we desperately needed for our growing family. With my two girls in ~~there~~ [2] their car seats in the back, nearing the parking lot of the bank, I thought we would make it before the bank closed [9c], but I hadn't counted on the accident. Bang! I had hit a curb hard [9c], and a nasty metallic sound told me what to expect. As I got out, I could see it, [6]. Yes, the tire was flat [9b], the rim touching the pavement. What was I going to do? I ran through my options quickly. My ~~husbands~~ [8] husband's plane wouldn't land for another hour and a half. My friend Angie had left town with her family that

Teaching Idea
Although we teach our students to avoid fragments most of the time, they can be used to good effect as Chris Potts does with the one word "Bang!" You might ask students to compare her intentional fragment to the two unintentional ones later in the draft to see which fragment they feel accomplishes a special purpose.

Illustrating through Examples

WHAT ARE WE TRYING TO ACHIEVE AND WHY?

Setting the Stage

What is it about amusement parks that appeals to people in general? What activities appeal to you specifically? If a friend asks you what you like best about a local theme park—Disney World, Six Flags Over Texas, Worlds of Fun, Coney Island—and you say "the rides," or, more specifically, "Roller coasters, especially the wooden ones like the Timber Wolf!" you have just given an example. Whenever people make a statement and then follow it with an example to show their meaning, they are clarifying and illustrating a point. Examples are the building blocks of all writing. This is the heart of the assignment in Chapter 7.

Building on the narrative/descriptive skills we have practiced so far, we will continue to value specific word choices, sensory details, comparisons, focus, and well-connected sentences, but we will move one step further. Instead of developing a single place or story, this time we will work with *several* examples, each introduced by a **subtopic** sentence. In addition to personal examples, some of us will develop our paragraphs through general knowledge of the world and close observation, achieving a slightly more formal tone.

Linking to Previous Experience

What experience do we already have using examples? If you have worked through Chapters 5 and 6, you have already focused closely on examples that can help a reader feel a dominant impression or understand the significance of an event. And, of course, our own lives are full of examples that we create for people. Any time that we narrow and clarify a statement, we are probably doing so with an example. You might say, "I can't stand my job," and a friend responds, "Why?" As soon as you mention

Teaching Idea
You might begin Chapter 7 with a brief review of examples from Chapter 3 under Developing Body Paragraphs.

Teaching Idea
Some students have difficulty breaking from the single place or single narrative assignments from Chapters 5 and 6. It helps to stress three to four examples.

the long hours, monster of a boss, and low pay, you have given examples. If you discuss a similar topic, bad jobs in general, you might leave your personal experience out of it altogether, instead using examples that *typify* bad jobs: a rotten boss, low pay, long hours, unpleasant co-workers, and a poor work environment. We often give examples to explain ourselves or defend a position, based on what we have read, heard, or deduced.

Determining the Value

If we want to share our experiences, discuss ideas, and plan for the future, we need the clarity that specific examples bring. Without being able to give examples, we have a world filled with unsupported statements like "I can't stand Shannon," "The Royals are a second-rate ball club," and "George W. Bush will lead the country to ruin." We want to know why people feel these ways, and examples can help us understand their positions.

Examples also help us clarify our own feelings and thoughts. Why do we trust one co-worker and not another? What examples can we recall to explain these feelings? When we are preparing for an exam in school, we gather as many examples as we can remember. Why is Martin Luther King, Jr., considered a pivotal figure in the Civil Rights movement in this country; why do some people believe in the conspiracy theory behind the assassination of John F. Kennedy? If we can offer specific examples along with clear explanations, we will probably do well on the exam.

As we work at developing examples in Chapter 7, we will not only learn to communicate with one another more effectively, but we will also clarify our own thinking.

JOURNAL ENTRY 7-1

Take a few moments to recall occasions during the past week when you have used examples to explain, defend a position, or entertain. List one instance from work, school, and home, summarizing the situation in a sentence or two. Was one example in each situation enough to achieve your purpose, or were more needed? How much detail did you go into? Did you try to recreate part of a scene using specific language, sensory detail, dialogue, and so on, or did you explain at length, perhaps using some comparisons to help?

DEVELOPING SKILLS, EXPLORING IDEAS IN ILLUSTRATION PARAGRAPHS

To more effectively illustrate our work with examples, we will practice the following:

1. Use subtopic sentences to introduce each major example.

2. Arrange major examples by order of importance.

3. Link all sentences, especially subtopics.

4. Develop examples with specific words, details, and explanations.

Groundwork for Activity 7-1: Organizing through Subtopic Sentences

We know that most paragraphs should begin with topic sentences, which tell what the paragraph will be about. When we develop a paragraph with *several* major examples writers often use **subtopic** or minor topic sentences, in addition to the topic sentence, to tell what each major example will be about. Each subtopic sentence will begin with a connector word or phrase (shaded in the following examples), state the example (underlined once below), and then make a limiting statement about it (underlined twice).

Topic sentence: How I <u>survived</u> my <u>adolescent years</u>, I will never know.

The topic sentence predicts a paragraph about the writer's dangerous youth.

First subtopic sentence: Although I was never more than <u>bruised</u> at it, <u>jumping onto the top of boxcars</u> from a low bridge was one of my earliest idiot moves.

The first subtopic sentence gives the first major example, jumping onto boxcars, to show a dangerous act. This sentence would be followed by several more sentences filled with details (sights, sounds, smells, etc.) to show what jumping onto boxcars was like.

Second subtopic sentence: More <u>dangerous</u> and even stupider than train jumping was my sixteen-year-old's effort at <u>flying a '69 convertible Firebird</u> from an off-ramp.

The second subtopic sentence gives the second major example, "flying" a Firebird, to show another dangerous act. More details would follow to develop the scene: explanation of how the driver lost control, sensory details, thoughts, and feelings.

Third subtopic sentence: But the closest I came to <u>death</u> was when I was just thirteen and thought the <u>ice on Granite Lake would support me</u>.

The third subtopic sentence gives the third major example, being on weak ice, to show another dangerous act. More details would follow to develop the scene: action of walking onto the ice, sound detail of hearing the ice crack, touch detail of being immersed in freezing water.

The subtopic sentences signal subsections within the paragraph, as you will see in all the student models in this chapter. These subsections could easily be developed in greater detail to become separate body paragraphs within an essay, with the subtopic sentences then becoming topic sentences (for more on this, see Chapter 14).

Note: Many paragraphs rely on only one main example and therefore do not need subtopic sentences.

Activity 7-1: Subtopic Sentences

After reviewing the groundwork for this writing activity, think about the topic sentences listed below, decide on three major examples that could illustrate a paragraph about them, and then complete each of the subtopic sentences with your examples.

Example: Topic sentence: To be a <u>good parent</u>, a person must either be born with or develop <u>several essential personality traits</u>.

Subtopic sentence 1: *The first trait a parent should have is a love of play.*

Subtopic sentence 2: *Another important quality is a vivid imagination.*

Subtopic sentence 3: *However, the most necessary ability for a parent is patience.*

Answers will vary.

1. **Topic sentence:** When people <u>lose control of their anger</u>, there are often severe <u>consequences</u>.

   Subtopic sentence 1: One negative effect is *that they damage property.*

Teaching Idea
To practice development, you might ask students to give a few additional examples or details for any one of the subtopics under Groundwork in Activity 7-1.

Teaching Idea
Activity 7-1 can also help students with connecting subtopic sentences, including indicating order of importance.

Subtopic sentence 2: Angry people will also _hurt themselves._

Subtopic sentence 3: The worst result of losing control is _when we hurt other people._

2. **Topic sentence:** Some people love <u>fall</u> with the trees glowing brilliant red, orange, and gold, but it is <u>my least favorite</u> season.

Subtopic sentence 1: Autumn depresses me because _it is the end of the summer._

Subtopic sentence 2: Another reason I don't like fall is _the beginning of school._

Subtopic sentence 3: But I least like this season because _life slows and becomes more difficult for all living things._

Groundwork for Activity 7-2: Arranging by Order of Importance

Teaching Idea
Activity 7-2 can begin
discussion of the writer's
role in ordering examples
by importance. Only topic
3 has a "correct" sequence.

The main examples in illustration paragraphs may be arranged in several ways: spatial, chronological, and order of importance. Of these, the last method works particularly well for achieving emphasis. When you order examples by importance, beginning with the least interesting or dramatic and progressing to the most, you tell the reader what to pay special attention to and leave her with your strongest point, an effective way to conclude. Notice that the last subtopic sentence in the example for Activity 7-1 signals ordering by importance:

> But the closest I came to death was when I was just thirteen and thought the ice on Granite Lake would support me.

When you begin to arrange your primary examples, sometimes the order of importance is obvious, but sometimes it is not. Often the author determines whether, for instance, a house burning down is more or less significant than a much-loved pet getting sick.

Activity 7-2: Arranging by Order of Importance

The following sets of subtopics are ordered randomly. Rearrange them by putting a number in the spaces provided, beginning with what you feel is the *least* important or dramatic (1) and moving to the *most* (5).

Answers will vary.

1. Alexander's vacation was a disaster.

    _3_ The prices at Disney World were outrageous.

    _4_ One of his suitcases was stolen.

    _5_ He was mugged in the parking lot.

    _1_ The weather was mostly gloomy.

    _2_ People were rude at his hotel.

2. Some people invite accidents when they drive.

   _5_ They drive drunk.

   _1_ They change lanes without signaling.

   _4_ They drive too fast in bad weather.

   _2_ They race along residential streets with children nearby.

   _3_ They slow down to a crawl on the highway to gawk at accidents

3. Jobs within a restaurant can be ranked according to status.

   _1_ Dishwasher

   _3_ Manager

   _4_ General manager

   _5_ Owner

   _2_ Wait person

4. The Internet is not an unqualified blessing.

   _5_ Some people become Net addicts, losing the other parts of their lives.

   _1_ It allows advertisers into the house in yet another way.

   _2_ E-mail eats up time.

   _3_ Much information on the Internet is questionable.

   _4_ The Internet gives children access to pornography.

Groundwork for Activity 7-3: Linking Sentences

Teaching Idea
Before students complete Activity 7-3, you might have them review Creating Coherence in Chapter 3, particularly connecting with repetition and synonyms.

We know that linking sentences within and between paragraphs is important to help readers more easily follow our ideas. As we have practiced in Chapter 4, we can make these connections in five ways: transitions, repetition, synonyms, pronouns, and reference to a main idea (for more on this, see pp. 52–57). It is especially important when structuring subtopic and concluding sentences to help your reader move smoothly from one main example to another to the final thought.

Notice the shaded transitions in the example below. The author has indicated **order of importance** by using several transitional words ("more" and "closest"), and has referred back to boxcar jumping with a repeat word ("jumping") and a synonym ("train").

Topic sentence: How I survived my adolescent years, I will never know.

Subtopic sentence 1: Although I was never more than bruised at it, jumping onto the top of boxcars from a low bridge was one of my earliest idiot moves.

Subtopic sentence 2: More dangerous and even stupider than train jumping was my sixteen-year-old's effort at flying a '69 convertible Firebird from an off-ramp.

Subtopic sentence 3: But the closest I came to death was when I was just thirteen and thought the ice on Granite Lake would support me.

As you construct subtopic sentences in your own paragraphs, use connectors to link main examples and signal order of importance.

Collaborative

Activity 7-3: Linking Sentences

Rewrite each subtopic sentence in the three paragraph outlines that follow so that the sentence clearly connects with the example that precedes it. Use any of the transitional words in the lists provided and/or any other connector that works. (For more on connectors, see pp. 52–57.) Circle all connectors.

For Adding Material			
again	as well as	furthermore	likewise
also	besides	in addition	moreover
and	further	last	next
For Giving Examples and Emphasis			
above all	especially	in particular	one reason
after all	for example	in truth	specifically
another	for instance	it is true	surely
as an example	indeed	most important	that is
certainly	in fact	of course	to illustrate

Example:

Topic sentence: To be a good coach, a person has to know how to relate to his players.

Subtopic sentence 1: He should be patient.

Rewrite with connectors: *One important quality in a coach is patience.*

Subtopic sentence 2: He should be a good listener.

Rewrite with connectors: *Another ability a coach needs is to be a good listener.*

Subtopic sentence 3: He should be sympathetic.

Rewrite with connectors: *While being a good listener is important in coaching, being sympathetic is the most important trait of all.*

Answers will vary.

1. Topic sentence: James Hanson is one of the most boring people alive.

    Subtopic sentence 1: He speaks in a monotone
    Rewrite with connectors: *One boring habit of his is speaking in a monotone.*

    Subtopic sentence 2: All he ever talks about is football.
    Rewrite with connectors: *Besides a monotonous tone, James is always stuck on one topic—football.*

    Subtopic sentence 3: Once he has someone cornered, he won't let the person go.
    Rewrite with connectors: *But the worst habit he has for putting people to sleep is holding them in one spot.*

2. Topic sentence: Fishing is a relaxing sport for many people.

    Subtopic sentence 1: Tossing a line in the water and reeling it back in is simple.
    Rewrite with connectors: *One example of relaxing is that tossing a line in the water and reeling it back in is simple.*

Subtopic sentence 2: The natural surroundings are pleasant.

Rewrite with connectors: *Besides the ease of fishing, the natural surroundings are pleasant.*

Subtopic sentence 3: A person can get away from routine distractions.

Rewrite with connectors: *But the most pleasant part of fishing is that a person can get away from routine distractions.*

3. Topic sentence: Urban living has a number of disadvantages.

Subtopic sentence 1: Pollution can be a problem.

Rewrite with connectors: *First, pollution can be a problem.*

Subtopic sentence 2: Traffic is often frustrating.

Rewrite with connectors: *Also, traffic is often frustrating.*

Subtopic sentence 3: The crime rate is often high.

Rewrite with connectors: *However, even more than the previous examples, crime can be a big problem.*

Groundwork for Activity 7-4: Developing Examples

As we discussed in Chapter 4, writers develop their points through detailed examples and explanations. If we have too few, we risk losing our readers. Take a moment to compare the following two paragraph excerpts about the liabilities of owning an older car. Which example seems most interesting and most clearly makes its point?

A. <u>But none of these troubles is more important than unexpected breakdowns, and used cars are more likely than new ones to leave a driver stranded</u>. When the car breaks down, the driver is left without transportation. He is going nowhere. This situation is frustrating and can be dangerous, depending on where a person finds himself.

B. <u>But none of these troubles is more important than unexpected breakdowns, and used cars are more likely than new ones to leave a driver stranded</u>. Imagine driving alone down a deserted country road in the middle of nowhere at midnight when a loud bang from the engine compartment and a horrible grinding noise tells you to pull over fast. You are stuck, going nowhere. It's creepy and cold, and the trees and shrubs crowd up close to the nonexistent shoulder of the road. You can't pull safely off, even if the car would start. Luckily, you have a cell phone, and help will arrive—within the next *hour!* Being at the mercy of a used car this way is frustrating and sometimes dangerous, and whether a person is left stuck at a stoplight in the middle of a busy intersection or stalled out on a road trip, she must wonder just how good that "good" deal was when she decided to buy used instead of new.

Specific words, sensory details, and action description help to develop paragraphs.

If you decided that version B is more interesting, there are several reasons a reader might prefer it. Version A says little after the initial subtopic sentence that introduces the main example. The second and third sentences merely repeat the statement made in the first sentence, and the final sentence only makes general statements about "frustration" and "danger." On the other hand, version B develops the statement about unexpected breakdowns with a "what-if" example that includes action, specific word choices, sensory details, and explanation. Adding another level of examples and details helps clarify how unpleasant being stranded could become. The final sentence reinforces the main point of the paragraph excerpt, providing several more specific examples. (For more on developing body paragraphs, see pp. 41–48.)

Collaborative

Teaching Idea
If you have students work in groups on Activity 7-4, you might encourage them to include more examples/details than they would actually use. Each group member can write his or her own examples, and then they can compare, select, and combine into one subtopic.

Activity 7-4: Developing Examples

If you agree that paragraph A above sounds *general* and *repetitive,* you will find the same problems with the two paragraph subtopics that follow. Rewrite the sentences in each of the subtopics using more specific examples and details. As you revise them, ask the questions "What does the writer mean by these statements?" and "What kinds of examples, details, and explanations can I add to make the statements more clear?"

Example: Topic: What constitutes a healthy diet?

Subtopic sentence: An important part of a healthy diet is eating low-fat foods.

Poorly developed subtopic:

Vegetables are in a low-fat category, unlike other food. They will not put weight on a person because they do not have much fat in them. Vegetables are low in calories and so do not cause a person to gain weight; therefore they can keep a person healthy.

Revised subtopic with specific, detailed material:

Most vegetables, such as broccoli, asparagus, and cauliflower, have no fat but plenty of fiber and essential nutrients. In fact, snacking vegetables like carrots and celery have so few calories that a person burns most of the calories off just by chewing. On the other hand, dairy products like whole milk, cheese, and ice cream are loaded with fat and low-density cholesterol, which can clog arteries and cause heart attacks.

Answers will vary.

1. Topic: What makes for an interesting person?

   Subtopic sentence: One way for a person to be interesting is to be a good listener.

   Poorly developed subtopic:

   A good listener is someone who knows how to listen well. He or she pays attention and tries to hear what a person is saying. Paying close attention, a good listener follows a conversation and does not drift away from what is being said.

   Revised subtopic example with specific, detailed material:

   A good listener is not just someone who stays in the same room with you while you are talking. He will often sit close to you, frequently make eye contact, nod his head, and respond in other ways. A good listener asks questions occasionally to clarify what the speaker is saying, but he does not try to control the conversation.

2. Topic: What fears did I have as a child?

   Subtopic sentence: The most terrifying moments for me came at night.

   Poorly developed subtopic:

   I especially hated being alone in my dark room. Because the room was so dark, I could too easily imagine things that were not there. Seeing imaginary creatures always frightened me and made me want to be anywhere but in my bedroom.

Revised subtopic example with specific, detailed material:

I especially hated being alone in my dark room. As soon as my mom and dad kissed me good night and closed the door, I would begin seeing monsters. A chair with my jacket on it became a bear; my model airplanes hanging from the ceiling became spiders slinking down their threads; the closet door creaked, and I knew a demon was ready to leap out on me.

ILLUSTRATION PARAGRAPHS: LOOKING CLOSELY AT STUDENT MODELS

The following student models will help you write effective illustration papers. "Teaching with Whips" and "Dying to Have Fun" are paragraphs developed through the "I" voice of personal experience. "Dangers in a Deli" and "Nothing Worthwhile Comes Easy" demonstrate the "they" voice that shifts the reader's focus away from the author and toward the material. As you read, you will gain more insight into the models by working through the Prereading and Postreading commentary and the questions for analysis.

Prereading Exploration for "Teaching with Whips"

The author, Jeong Yi, wanted to share some of his personal experiences with fellow classmates so they might compare their own education with his and learn something of the cultural differences between them. Jeong also noted that teachers might be interested in the paper because of his discussion of the effectiveness of using force to make students learn.

Having read through the chapter introduction and worked through several of the activities, how many **main examples** might you expect this paragraph to contain? What kind of sentence would you expect each major example to begin with?

Three or four

A subtopic sentence

Teaching with Whips

When I went to middle school in Korea, I was afraid of several merciless teachers who seemed to want me to enjoy studying by forcing it on me. My moral education teacher was one of these cruel educators. He was short and fat like the whip he carried to enforce his every whim. "I see you haven't done your homework, Jeong," he would say. He ordered me to hold my palms up, and then he began to whip my hands harshly. Somehow the pain ended with me crying and begging, "I will do it next time, teacher. I promise!" Another spiteful man was my history teacher, who liked to use his green baby bamboo stick to punish me when I didn't score more than 80 percent on the exams. When I would see him headed my way with that certain glint in his eye, slapping the stick into his own hand, I knew what was about to happen. "Why," I wanted to shout at him, "why don't you let us feel some interest in history. Maybe then we would be more responsible!" But these words never left my lips, although his did. "If you don't study, you won't succeed," he barked as he dealt quick whips. I muttered curses with his final blow. The most memorable of all these tyrants was the despised art teacher nicknamed Poisonous Snake. None of the students got along well with him. He seemed to dislike all of us equally. The black tape wrapped around the long, powerful stick that he used so frequently increased all our fear. I could only anticipate the pain I would feel the day I scored poorly on an exam I'd just taken. Burning with

Teaching Idea
Ask students before or after they have read this paragraph model how they feel about corporal punishment in schools. Is it justified? Is there a better way to maintain discipline in school and if so what? The examples students give of their own school experiences will reinforce the idea of specific development.

anxiety, I thought the only way to prevent these pains would be to study more diligently. If the goal of Poisonous Snake and the rest of my teachers was just to make me study harder, they succeeded. But if they were concerned at all whether or not I learned to like education, then they all failed miserably.

Jeong Yi

Postreading Analysis

Coming directly to this illustration assignment from working on narrative, Jeong decided to rely heavily on his narrative/descriptive skills for development. Each main example uses elements like dialogue, character and scene description, active verbs, "-ing" words, specific words, and sensory details—in short, he has created several "ministories." But notice that Jeong is careful not to let any example get out of hand, instead remembering his larger purpose of presenting several examples forcefully. The paper is well organized with topic and concluding sentences that clearly reinforce each other, and each subtopic sentence is equally well crafted (connector + subtopic + statement). The author takes care to develop each main example with second- and third-level supporting examples. Finally, notice how well linked the title, "Teaching with Whips," is with topic, subtopic, and concluding sentences. Why do you suppose the writer bothered to add details about the teachers' sticks?

▶ Prereading Exploration for "Dying to Have Fun"

Tom Kellogg wrote this paper for himself as a way to think through the tragedy mentioned and for an audience of people who like the outdoors, especially river floating. If you are not particularly attracted to outdoor activities, does it seem odd that some people might like them, particularly in light of the author's statement about "awful experiences" in the topic sentence? Are there any pastimes you enjoy that others might consider dangerous, exhausting, uncomfortable, or just plain tedious? Take a moment to brainstorm for topics. Next, list an activity, make a statement about it, and then write out three or four examples to illustrate your statement.

Answers will vary.

_____

_____

_____

_____

Dying to Have Fun

Paddling down Kansas and Missouri rivers is one of my favorite pastimes, but I have had some awful experiences on them. One aggravation I have learned to deal with is bad weather. Our first night on the river, everybody is excited and raising hell—till the rain comes. For some reason the rain clouds seem to follow us down into the river valleys and then open up. Fellow campers and I usually wake in a huge mud puddle, and we are lucky if we don't have to swim to the trucks to get clean, dry clothes. While uncertain weather might seem bad enough, having a friend get hurt is worse. Once my friend Matt flipped his canoe in front of mine, and I couldn't stop in time. Matt caught the bow of my canoe in his right eye. The cold, clear spring water of the Current River did not stop the huge purple lump above his eye from swelling. After ten years of floating, I thought I had experienced all the problems a person could run into on a river until one trip on the Niangua three years ago. My partner and I pulled up onto a gravel bar alongside a crowd gathered in a circle. At first I thought they were only having a party. But then I saw my friend Mitch kneeling in the sand, pushing on a man's chest. "What happened?" I asked. "Is there anything I can do?" He shook his head. "It's too late for this guy. No one knows what happened. He just keeled over and stopped breathing." Mitch kept trying, anyway, to jumpstart the man's heart, but it was a losing battle. I walked back to my canoe and sat down on the soggy, vinyl-covered seat cushion, for once not feeling my butt itch from it. A line from the miniseries *Lonesome Dove* ran through my mind: "The best thing you can do with death is just walk away from it." This guy had started out his trip like I had, expecting only to have a good time, ending up having his last time. I thought to myself, "It could just as easily be me lying there." Despite the problems over the years, even the death, I still enjoy floating, but I am more prepared now than ever to deal with the bad times that too often are waiting just around the next bend in the river.

Thomas Kellogg

Postreading Analysis

This paragraph on a favorite pastime has many strengths. Tom uses personal examples developed through scene building, action, dialogue, sensory details, and specific language. From the opening mention of Kansas and Missouri rivers (relatively specific) through the naming of the Current and Niangua rivers (very specific), the author pays close attention to language and helps us believe that he really has floated many rivers over the years.

The first two major examples are brief but interesting and lead into the most thoroughly developed one. Aside from the good story *showing* here, the author does quite a bit of explaining, helping readers see the significance of the event to him. Mentioning a movie, *Lonesome Dove*, (as well as other references that a reader might know—to books, current news, sports, music, etc.) works well to develop the author's mental and emotional state. Many readers in the target audience may have seen the miniseries or read the book and would recognize the quoted line, which follows a boy's death in a river. As you work through your own drafts, if you find transitions and other connectors difficult to create (or if they sound too mechanical), look at how Tom manages the link in his third subtopic sentence.

▶ Prereading Exploration for "Dangers in a Deli"

Catherine Denning chose to avoid the "I" approach in this informative paragraph about dangers in her workplace. Having selected her topic and brainstormed for examples, she felt that a target audience of new employees reading an orientation booklet might listen more closely to a somewhat more objective, even authoritative, voice.

Have you ever been in a situation where you were responsible for someone else's safety, where the person depended on your knowledge and experience? Perhaps as a mother or father you have helped your children avoid danger through clear explanations (what not to touch in the kitchen, for instance!). Try to remember a situation where you alerted someone to possible dangers. Using clustering (or another prewriting method you like), try to remember three or four main examples of danger and then write them below. Did you choose to explain using the "I" of personal experience, or did you choose a less-informal voice—why?

Answers will vary.

_____

_____

_____

_____

Teaching Idea
To stimulate some discussion of proportional development, ask students if the last example seems relatively overlong or about right and whether either of the other two examples would benefit from additional developing.

Teaching Idea
"Dangers in a Deli" can be linked with the chapter Annotated Student Model to illustrate the third-person perspective that some students will choose for their paragraphs.

A. Topic = smoking: The day I climbed a short flight of stairs to my apartment and stood there leaning on the door so winded that I almost passed out, I knew <u>smoking</u> was <u>hurting</u> me.

B. Topic = smoking: The <u>ill effects</u> of <u>smoking</u> have been well documented.

All of these topic sentences limit a subject, and you might notice that the A sentences predict an "I" paper whereas both B sentences predict a slightly more formal "they" tone.

Remember that you may still need to trim several examples, keeping only the three or four strongest ones, which you will probably arrange from least to most important and link with connectors, including transitional words like those below (for more on connectors, see pp. 52–57).

For Adding Material

again	as well as	furthermore	likewise
also	besides	in addition	moreover
and	further	last	next

For Giving Examples and Emphasis

above all	especially	in particular	one reason
after all	for example	in truth	specifically
another	for instance	it is true	surely
as an example	indeed	most important	that is
certainly	in fact	of course	to illustrate

JOURNAL ENTRY 7-3

Take a moment to write out your working topic sentence. Is it focused enough to help you select examples? Now list your main examples in order of importance, moving from the least important to the most. Cross out several and leave four. Next, write out a brief explanation of why you chose to order in this way. Do you have a clear "least" and "most" important example?

Drafting

With the preliminary work done, you are almost ready to write your first draft. But before you plunge in, take a moment to review the Drafting suggestions in Chapter 1, pp. 12–14 and to think about the following points:

1. You can get quick results by writing each major example at spaced intervals down the page and beginning to write on the one (probably the last one) that you have the most to say about. Polish your subtopic sentences later.

2. Remember to layer examples within each subtopic. Keep asking the question "What do I mean by what I have just written?"

3. Your examples do not need to be perfectly balanced, though all should be developed. In fact, your final, most important, one may be several sentences longer than the others.

4. To replace "I" in papers using a more-formal "they" voice, try pronouns like *their, they, them, those,* and so forth, and nouns like *people, men, women, young adults, students, consumers, athletes, applicants,* and so on.

Sidebar notes:

Choosing "I" or "they" approach to the paper

Arrange examples from least to most important.

Teaching Idea
You might want to link Journal Entry 7-3 to Activity 7-2 and remind students that order of importance in examples is often determined by the writer.

Teaching Idea
It can help students to see their subtopic sentences (and the support they are giving each example), if you ask students to highlight the subtopic sentences in each draft.

Try placing each main example on the page before drafting.

Use sensory details: sight, sound, touch smell, and taste.

Substitute words for "I"

> **JOURNAL ENTRY 7-4**
>
> Respond to this journal entry soon after writing your first rough draft. Skim through the draft and ask yourself whether or not it feels like the assignment that Chapter 7 is asking for. Do you supply three or four examples? Are they arranged effectively? What part of this draft do you like best? What part do you dislike most? Answer in a paragraph.

Revising Drafts

To review the detailed lists for revising drafts, turn to Chapter 4.

■ ANNOTATED STUDENT MODEL

Teaching Idea
To prevent students from writing an underdeveloped essay with weak introductory and concluding paragraphs, point out that the division of the Annotated Student Model is only to more clearly demonstrate the paragraph parts.

Help yourself to avoid obstacles in the writing process and to overcome road-blocks in your own drafts by reading through the Annotated Student Model as carefully as possible. Doing this will save you at least a few headaches and probably help clarify questions you didn't even know you had.

First-Stage Draft

Bill Ross decided to explain how difficult college can be to those who have never gone to college and those who have gone but forgotten how rough it can be. He used listing to discover eight major examples, which he then trimmed to four. As you will see, he was not sure what tone to adopt initially, so the draft skips back and forth between "I" and the more formal "they."

First drafts often give a new direction to your ideas.

After completing the first draft, Bill made two important decisions. First, he decided that the "I" voice might make him sound like he was merely complaining, so he decided to try for a more objective, reporter's voice. Second, he discovered that he wanted to shift the *focus* of his topic from the experience of college students in general to that of nontraditional students like himself who attend community colleges.

Note: This rough draft is separated into topic and concluding sentences and four subtopics *only* to illustrate the connections among the pieces of this *paragraph*.

First-Stage Draft

Topic sentence

Some college students have a difficult time with school and the rest of there lives.

We all want to relax sometimes, but it's hard to have a social life and still get

First subtopic

the studying done. And if you are a partier, look out! Its hard to make grades and have fun.

Refocus of paper will create <u>material cuts and additions.</u>

Second subtopic

Bills are another problem. Some students have it easy, scholarships or a free ride from there parents, but most community college students, anyway, are working their way through. If you have children, it's even worse. Just think of all bills having a house and family can rack up like mortgage payments, utilities, food, clothing, doctor bills, etc. Stressing out over money makes studying difficult.

Need overall developing of main examples with specific support, details, and explanations

Third subtopic

Having to work to pay the bills is another problem. Of course, almost all adults have to support themselves but most people aren't running in three different directions at once. With college students trying to study, have some kind of social life and then work forty hours a week, it can be to much.

And then there's the family hassle that students like me have to worry about. I'm a returning student who hasn't been in college for fifteen years. Along the way I accummulated a wife and three children, so its especially hard for me. But I am not alone. Just look around in your classes and you will see lots of older students struggling to make it all work out. As much as I love my family, they take the biggest chunk of my time, after work. And you probably know how much a family can just wear you out. By the time my wife and I get the kids to bed, it's hard to hit the books.

College is not easy for most people, but I think it has to be harder for the older returning student with a family.

Second-Stage Draft

First rough drafts of illustration papers often have difficulties with overall focus, development, and relevant material. Note how much explanation and how many more examples were added to this draft to help clarify meaning. As you move through your own draft, keep asking the question "What do I mean by that last statement, example, or idea?" Also be alert to the overall structure of topic, subtopic, and concluding sentences. Help your reader find her way through your paper with the least possible effort. She will appreciate your efforts.

Adult students with spouses and children have a difficult time balancing school with the rest of there lives.

They don't have much time for a social life, but everyone needs some relaxation. Even struggling with classes, <u>most students want to see an occasional movie with a friend, catch a ball game, or have diner out.</u> *When students take time for rest & relaxation, they are looking over their shoulder at the clock.

But socializing is often the least of the distractions for returning students. They constantly face the money battle. With families to care for the students have to worry about <u>rent and mortgage payments, utilities, car payments, car repair bills, general property maintenance, food, clothing, medical, insurance of various kinds, school (their own included), and even squeezing in a few presents</u> for their loved ones occasionally. *The stress of dealing with the money drain sometimes makes focusing on textbooks difficult.

In order to meet the financial demands, of course, most nontraditional students are full-time workers as well. Often both husbands and wives financially support the family. Though sometimes only one brings in a paycheck while the other works at home. <u>Spending forty hours a week, and more outside the home selling insurance, repairing cars, waiting tables; or spending the same amount of time inside the home cleaning house, fixing meals, and chasing children around</u>— *nontraditional students often have a kind of frazzled look around the edges.

But the other stresses and distractions aside, for nontraditional students coming back to school, the family might be the biggest obstacle. Most mothers and fathers love there children and each other. But <u>the daily drag of diapering, feeding, carting to school, and soothing fears and hurt feelings</u> can drag a person

---

Margin notes (left):

Fourth subtopic

Teaching Idea
The First-Stage Draft shows a clear example of pronoun shifting from "I" to "you."

Concluding sentence

Teaching Idea
This model clearly illustrates subtopic sentences along with connecting words. Here, again, students can see layered development.

Topic sentence revised

Subtopic sentence revised

Subtopic sentence revised

Subtopic sentence revised

Subtopic sentence revised—to show *most important* problem

Margin notes (right):

Avoid tone shift from "they" to "I"

Second-level examples added

*Explanation added

Second-level examples added

*Explanation added

Second-level examples added

*Explanation added

Second-level examples added

down and wear him or her out. *Even the most dedicated student has a hard time studying after a full day. And those who do jam the late-night studying in are often beat in class the next day.

Concluding sentence revised

While other students also have difficulties, dealing with their education, and community college students in particular, the returning adult student with family responsibilities might just have the toughest job of all.

*Explanation added

Note the expanded thought.

Special Points to Check in Revising from First to Second Drafts

1. Check topic sentence: topic + statement
2. Check subtopic sentences: connector + main example topic + statement
3. Check concluding sentence: connector + link to topic sentence + expanded thought
4. ~~Delete unnecessary material~~
5. Add material for clarity, completeness, and emphasis
6. Check connectors: transitions, repeat words, synonyms, pronouns, reference to main idea

---

Third-Stage Draft

Many of us are tempted to call the paper complete by the time we have done a thorough second draft. After all, we have reorganized; deleted material; added new examples, details, and explanations—shouldn't the paper be done? But if you want your work to move beyond good to excellent, this third draft gives you that opportunity. With most of the major material and organizational concerns taken care of, you can now improve your word choices and sentence variety and get rid of the clutter words that so often slip into rough drafts.

Teaching Idea
The Third-Stage Draft shows sentence combining for variety and elimination of unneeded repetition.

Nothing Worthwhile Comes Easy

Nontraditional students with spouses and children have a difficult time balancing school with the rest of there lives.

More accurate words substituted

[Although many of them don't have much time for a social life everyone needs some relaxation.] Even struggling with a twelve-hour course load, most students want to see an occasional movie with a friend, catch a ball game, or have diner out. Most of the time when they take time for rest & relaxation, ~~students~~ **they** are looking over their shoulder at the clock—classes start at 8:00 a.m.!

Sentences combined, specific words added, repetition reduced through pronoun

[But socializing is often the least of the distractions for returning students, as they constantly face the money battle.] ~~Students~~ **Their** families add to the financial worries with **parents** footing the bills for rent or mortgage, utilities, insurance, general property maintenance, food, clothing, medical, car, school (their own included), and even the occasional present for a loved one. The stress of dealing with the money drain sometimes makes focusing on textbooks difficult.

Sentences combined, repetition reduced through synonym and pronoun

In order to meet the financial demands, of course, most nontraditional students are full-time workers as well. Often both ~~husbands and wives~~ **spouses** financially support the family. Though sometimes only one brings in a paycheck

Synonym replaces phrase

while the other works at home. Spending forty hours a week, and more outside the home selling insurance, repairing cars, waiting tables; or spending the same amount of time inside the home cleaning house, fixing meals, and chasing children around—nontraditional students often have a ~~kind of~~ frazzled look around the edges.

Clutter phrase deleted

But the other stresses and distractions aside, for ~~non-traditional students~~ **mom's and dad's** coming back to school, the family might be the biggest obstacle. [As much as most mothers and fathers love there children and each other, the daily routine of diapering, feeding, clothing, carting to school, soothing fears and hurt feelings, explaining, teaching, and just generally loving family members can ~~drag a person down and~~ wear **a person** ~~him or her~~ out.] Even the most dedicated student has a hard time studying at 2:00 a.m. after a full work and family day. And those who do jam the late-night studying in are easy to spot as they work to keep their heads propped up in class the next day.

More appropriate word substituted

Sentences combined, specific words added, redundant expression deleted

While other college students also have difficulties, dealing with their education, and community college students in particular, the returning adult student with family responsibilities might just have the toughest job of all.

More accurate word added

> ## Special Points to Check in Revising from Second to Third Drafts
> 1. Added specific words are boxed.
> 2. More precise or audience-appropriate word substitutions are shaded.
> 3. [Sentences combined for variety are bracketed.]
> 4. **Synonyms and phrases replacing clutter and repeat words are bolded.**
> 5. ~~Unneeded words are lined through~~.

Final-Editing Draft

By this point Bill's draft is in great shape. Now is the time to shift into low gear, moving slowly line by line, looking for every error in grammar, spelling, and punctuation. Keeping an **Improvement Chart** (see Appendix 2) will help you focus on your own **pattern errors,** an efficient way to finish this step in the process.

Nothing Worthwhile Comes Easy

Nontraditional students with spouses and children have a difficult time balancing school with the rest of ~~there~~ [2] their lives. Although many of them don't have much time for a social life [9a], everyone needs some relaxation. Even struggling with a twelve-hour course load, most students want to see an occasional movie with a friend, catch a ball game, or have ~~diner~~ [1] dinner out. Most of the time when they take time for rest & relaxation, they are looking over their shoulder at the clock—classes start at 8:00 ~~a.m.~~ [7] A.M.! But socializing is often the least of the distractions for returning students, [10] as they constantly face

Topic, subtopic, and concluding sentences are merged to show a single, complete paragraph.

Teaching Idea
You might want to focus on a single error in the Final-Editing Draft, such as the unneeded comma, to help students review.

the money battle. Their families add to the financial worries with parents footing the bills for rent or mortgage, utilities, insurance, general property maintenance, food, clothing, medical, car, school (their own included), and even the occasional present for a loved one. The stress of dealing with the money drain sometimes makes focusing on textbooks difficult. In order to meet the financial demands, of course, most nontraditional students are full-time workers as well. Often both spouses financially support the family[5], though sometimes only one brings in a paycheck while the other works at home. Spending forty hours a week[10] and more outside the home selling insurance, repairing cars, waiting tables; or spending the same amount of time inside the home cleaning house, fixing meals, and chasing children around—nontraditional students often have a kind of frazzled look around the edges. But the other stresses and distractions aside, for ~~mom's and dad's~~ [8] moms and dads coming back to school, the family might be the biggest obstacle. As much as most mothers and fathers love ~~there~~ [2] their children and each other, the daily routine of diapering, feeding, clothing, carting to school, soothing fears and hurt feelings, explaining, teaching, and just generally loving family members can wear a person out. Even the most dedicated student has a hard time studying at 2:00 ~~a.m.~~ [7] A.M. after a full work and family day. And those who do jam the late-night studying in are easy to spot as they work to keep their heads propped up in class the next day. While other college students also have difficulties[10] dealing with their education, and community college students in particular, the returning adult student with family responsibilities might just have the toughest job of all.

William Ross

Teaching Idea
It is worth the time to take students back to Chapter 4 as they revise and edit their first several assignments. The Final-Draft Checklist is mirrored in Chapter 4, so if students need more in-depth reminders than the list provides, they will not have to search through the text. The information is packaged and accessible in a few consecutive pages.

Special Points to Check in Editing Final Drafts

1. Spelling	5. Sentence fragments	9. Common comma categories
2. Sound-alike words	6. Comma splices/run-ons	a. Introduce b. Enclose/end
3. Missing words	7. Capitalizations	c. Divide
4. Wrong words	8. Apostrophes	10. Unneeded commas

Final-Draft Checklist

Before you turn your final draft in for a grade, take a few minutes to review this checklist. You may find that, as careful as you think you have been, you still have missed a point or two—or three. (For more on any of these points, see Chapter 4.)

___ 1. Have you used three or four examples, or have you used only one?

___ 2. How effective is your topic sentence?

___ 3. Have you clearly arranged your main examples—either by time or importance?

___ 4. Have you written a subtopic sentence to introduce each main example?

___ 5. Are your main examples adequately developed?

___ 6. Are your examples relevant and thoroughly explained?

___ 7. How well connected are all the sentences within the paragraph?

___ 8. How effective is your concluding sentence?

___ 9. How well have you used specific language?

___ 10. Are you choosing the most "active" verbs and "-ing" words to describe action?

___ 11. Have you tried using a metaphor or simile?

___ 12. Are the sentences in your paragraph varied in length and beginnings?

___ 13. Have you repeated a word or phrase so often that it becomes noticeable?

___ 14. Have you included words that serve no purpose?

___ 15. Have you written a title—an interesting one—for the paper? (Check capitalizations.)

___ 16. Have you prepared your paper according to the format expected by your instructor? (Check to see if you need a title page, be sure to double-space, leave at least a 1-inch margin, use a 12-point font, and be sure to type or word process.)

___ 17. Have you edited your work as closely as you know how to (including having at least one other person—classmate, friend, family member—proofread closely)? Have you checked your **Improvement Chart** for your pattern errors so that you can look for them specifically?

___ 18. Have you looked specifically for the following errors: spelling, sound-alike words, missing words, wrong words, sentence fragments, comma splices/run-ons, capitalizations, apostrophes, the Big Three comma categories, and unnecessary commas?

CHAPTER SUMMARY

1. Expository writing primarily communicates ideas, information, and opinions. After a relatively general statement is made (topic sentence), examples, explanations, and details are used to develop and clarify that statement.

2. Examples may be based on personal experience or otherwise. Writers often develop examples through close observation, accumulated knowledge, "what-if" situations, generalized or typical instances, and research.

3. Narrative/descriptive elements are often found within examples, especially those based on personal experience.

4. Tone in writing is the attitude or feeling the author has toward his subject and the relationship he wants to establish with his audience. Writers vary their tone based on their material and audience.

5. Writing that adopts a more-formal tone seldom uses "I" and relies heavily for development on close observation, accumulated knowledge, "what-if" situations, generalized or typical instances, logical reasoning, and research.

6. To most clearly guide a reader through a paragraph using multiple examples, introduce each main example with a subtopic sentence.

7. Expository writing and persuasive writing often organize examples from least to most important or dramatic.

8. Transitional words and other connectors are especially important in linking subtopic and concluding sentences to the rest of the paragraph. The transitional phrases "for example" and "for instance" are invaluable in illustration paragraphs.

9. Examples are most adequately explained by following the principle of increasing specificity: each example supports the previous one by limiting the category to which the previous example belongs.

10. Writing is never complete until it has gone through several revisions and careful editing.

ALTERNATE WRITING ASSIGNMENTS

Here are a few more assignment options that may be of interest. As you consider them, keep the following points in mind:

- Use subtopic sentences to introduce each major example.

- Arrange major examples by order of importance.

- Link all sentences, especially subtopics.

- Develop examples with specific words, details, and explanations.

1. Although the chapter assignment asks for several examples, you will often write paragraphs within essays that rely on only one major example. Rethink any *one* of the *major examples* you chose for the chapter assignment and then develop it further. Be sure to use plenty of second- and third-level examples, and if you are drawing on personal experience, you might review Chapters 5 and 6 for reminders on the dominant impression and significance of the event. Remember to rework your topic sentence to reflect the narrowing of your scope.

2. After having written the Chapter 7 assignment, rewrite it shifting the tone. If you were especially warm and chatty, in the new version try for a more distant, reporter's voice. If you had chosen an objective tone, try for a more personable voice. Remember that your audience influences the tone, so you may need to rethink your designated reader. If, for instance, you were writing to young adults about great places to vacation and were emphasizing the partying potential, you may have chosen personal examples and relatively informal diction. Changing the audience to parents who might be interested in their sons' and daughters' vacation plans would affect not only the tone but probably the content of the main examples as well.

3. Write a biographical sketch of a person, focusing on a single personality trait and using three to four anecdotes (brief stories) as major examples. For instance, you might characterize your brother as exceedingly selfish. What three to four instances of selfish behavior can you remember that would show this character trait to a reader?

4. Choose a topic that relates to your cultural heritage or to any group with which you closely identify. Perhaps you are of Irish descent and are interested in the mythology or music of Ireland. Coming from a western-European background, you might be attracted to events like Renaissance festivals. Perhaps there are some elements of pop culture with which you especially identify. As in the main chapter assignment, select a topic, create a working topic sentence, and choose three to four examples to illustrate your point.

5. Select a work-related project that you will use on the job. If, for example, you work in retail sales, you could characterize three or four types of customers that a new employee should be able to identify. Maybe you work at a business like Kinko's and can identify several potential problems for a person new to the job. Or perhaps you are writing a job evaluation for yourself or another employee and need to supply several examples to justify a statement such as "Jasmine has great communication skills." Give your supervisor or prospective employer several specific examples demonstrating these skills.

CHAPTER 8

Creating and Explaining Groups

Building Classification

Single Organizing
   Principle
Inclusive Groups
Purpose for Categorizing
Framework
Development
Revision

◗ WHAT ARE WE TRYING TO ACHIEVE AND WHY?

Setting the Stage

Imagine a grocery store that did not divide its merchandise in some orderly fashion. If you were a shopper new to a supermarket, like the woman above, trying to find a bar of soap and a loaf of bread, how would you find them? In a store that had no merchandise signs or that lumped items together in a random way, it would be hard to do. How long would you be willing to spend trying to figure out a store's logic that grouped bread with, say, butter because these two food items often are used together or that shelved the bar soap with drain openers because they are both used with water? Most of us probably wouldn't spend much time, and the store would soon be out of business—a victim of its own disorder.

But in reality all major supermarkets, and other businesses, do organize their products systematically, using a method called **classification.** As we work through the upcoming chapter, we will practice classifying, learning to select a logical **single organizing principle** (SOP) to group topics, which we will then develop through examples, explanations, and details.

Linking to Previous Experience

What kind of experience do we already have with classification? Well, in the supermarket illustration above, we can see how the store manager does it. The right side of aisle 3—containing spices, cooking oil, cake mixes, and more—is devoted to baking necessities, the basis for shelving all these items together. How about your local True Value hardware store? An aisle or part of an aisle will be devoted to, say, locks—padlocks, chain locks, bolts, hooks and eyes. At home most of us sort laundry from time to time—socks, underwear, pants, shirts, blouses, washcloths, towels: we classify and group these items on the basis of how we use them. If you have ever moved your own personal belongings or an entire household, you have undertaken a major classification project. Unless you grouped and labeled items according to the room you wanted them in, you might have found a mess on the other end.

In school, of course, we see classifying all around us and the SOP at work. The campus is divided into buildings that contain a gym, faculty offices, cafeteria, academic departments, maintenance, security, and so on. It would be unlikely (though perhaps not unpleasant) to find a lone English instructor plopped down among a department full of math teachers. And our textbooks are full-length examples of classification based on material closely related and grouped by units, chapters, and subsections.

Determining the Value

How useful is classifying? We have already seen examples from our personal lives, but we also need this ability in school. For example, in a history class, of the many causes leading to the Civil War, you might be asked to focus on economics (the SOP), to list reasons for the conflict, and then to develop those reasons with examples and explanations. In a biology class you could be asked to classify a particular plant or animal on the basis of how it reproduces (the SOP). Being able to organize *ideas* in school and out is at least as important as being able to organize objects.

At home, on the job, and in school, classifying is valuable because it helps us make sense of the world. We depend on the ability to streamline our physical and mental space and often use it unknowingly. But we should be aware that our natural inclination to simplify can create problems. We often create categories without examining them critically, tossing things and people into them too quickly. *Stereotyping* is one result. When we oversimplify complex issues and people, classification can create rather than solve problems for us.

Teaching Idea
Because this chapter stresses grouping similar things, in effect, minimizing difference, it is worth spending a few minutes discussing what makes things and people unique, sometimes impossible to classify. Your conversation can easily lead to the danger of unwarranted classification— stereotyping.

Misusing classification can create stereotypes.

> ### JOURNAL ENTRY 8-1
>
> Think for a moment about instances during the past week when you have classified or seen classifying at work. Try to list one example from school, work, and home. What was classified? Was an SOP used? For example, perhaps you recently reorganized a clothes closet. Did you group clothing according to how it is worn (shirts with shirts, pants with pants, etc.)? Or perhaps you subdivided a group, say shirts, based on another standard (frequency of use, maybe?).

DEVELOPING SKILLS, EXPLORING IDEAS IN CLASSIFICATION PARAGRAPHS

To divide and classify successfully, there are several important points to keep in mind:

1. Use a single organizing principle.

2. Avoid overlapping categories.

3. Include all of the important members of the group.

4. Have a reason for the classification.

The following activities will help you practice these points, and as you gain more experience with them, you will be able to move more comfortably into your own paper.

Groundwork for Activity 8-1: Using a Single Organizing Principle

If we want to group items logically, we should choose some standard for doing so. For example, when we open a menu in a restaurant serving dinner, we might find food items grouped as appetizers, entrées, side dishes, and desserts. Using the principle of

Teaching Idea
The activities lead students through the prewriting they need to produce their first draft. You might remind the class to be alert to possible topics as they do this work.

the *usual order* in which food is presented (appetizers before the main course), we can quickly find the general category of food we want. Within each food group we would expect to find only items that are similar to each other—desserts would feature ice cream and pie but not pork chops. Or in choosing a restaurant for the evening, you might decide on Italian cuisine. As you discuss possible destinations with a friend, using the SOP of Italian food, you might mention several Italian restaurants but leave out Thai cooking.

   As you settle on a topic for this assignment, you will need to decide on a single organizing principle to help you select and group the material contained within it.

Activity 8-1: Using a Single Organizing Principle

The following groups have been established using a single principle of organization, but one of the items does not belong. Put an "X" by the item that does not seem to fit or that "overlaps" with other members of the group, and then write out in a few words what you think is the SOP of the group.

Example: Topic: holidays

Categories: ____ Spring ____ Summer ____ Fall ____ Winter __X__ Christmas
Organizing principle: *seasons of the year*

1. Topic: parties

   Categories: ____ Home ____ Friend's house ____ Park __X__ Boring ____ Hotel
   Organizing principle: *place that parties are held*

2. Topic: first dates

   Categories: ____ Relaxed __X__ Cheap ____ Tense ____ Exciting ____ Funny
   Organizing principle: *emotional responses to*

3. Topic: love

   Categories: ____ Spouse ____ Child ____ Friend __X__ Erotic ____ Parent
   Organizing principle: *kinds of people to love*

4. Topic: cooking

   Categories: ____ French ____ Greek __X__ Spicy ____ Mexican ____ Vietnamese
   Organizing principle: *cooking of different countries*

5. Topic: commercials

   Categories: ____ Explosions ____ Gun fire ____ Punching __X__ Humor ____ Falls
   Organizing principle: *grouped by violence*

Groundwork for Activity 8-2: Selecting an Organizing Principle

   As people classify, they often rely on predictable standards to form their groups. For instance, in buying a car, most of us are concerned with price and would naturally list that as one essential standard for deciding which ones we seriously look at and which ones we only dream about. And there are many standardized categories for things, people, and areas of knowledge. For example, when we mention major

Teaching Idea
Activity 8-2 encourages students to notice the many possibilities for grouping. It helps students see the possibilities if they can compare responses in class.

domestic car manufacturers in the United States, we know that we are talking about General Motors, Ford, and Daimler Chrysler. If we think about insurance, most of us would list categories like life, medical, auto, and homeowner.

But often we deal with subjects that can be thought of in many ways and grouped accordingly, based on our interests and those of an audience. For instance, if we chose children as a topic, we might group them by any of these categories:

Age	Health	Personality
Creativity	Height	Physical abilities
Gender	Intelligence	Responsibility
Growth rate	Math and reading skills	Weight

Things can be grouped using many SOPs.

Each one of these could be a valid standard of measure, depending on the writer's purpose. After you have chosen a topic for your paper, you too will need to choose among several organizing principles.

Collaborative

Activity 8-2: Selecting an Organizing Principle

After reviewing the groundwork for this activity, discuss with group members the principle of organizing groups. Next, look at the following topics and write out three different organizing methods for each.

Example: Topic: drivers

Possible organizing principles:

a. _Temperament_   b. _Experience_   c. _Responsibility_

Answers will vary.

1. Topic: relatives

   Possible organizing principles:

   a. _age_   b. _sex_   c. _closeness_

2. Topic: leaders

   Possible organizing principles:

   a. _personality_   b. _profession_   c. _effectiveness_

3. Topic: weddings

   Possible organizing principles:

   a. _seasons_   b. _expense_   c. _religion_

4. Topic: sports

   Possible organizing principles:

   a. _levels of violence_   b. _levels of fitness required_   c. _longevity of the players_

Groundwork for Activity 8-3: Dividing and Developing Topics

After selecting a topic and an organizing principle, you will separate your topic into groups and then *develop* the groups with detailed examples, as in the following example:

Topic: *drivers*

Organizing principle: *temperament*

Three groups: *aggressive, moderate, and cautious*

Specific examples for each group:

1. *Aggressive: weaves in and out of traffic at high speeds, honks the horn frequently, tailgates, cuts other drivers off*

2. *Moderate: drives the speed limit and/or adjusts to the general flow of traffic, lets cars onto the highway, signals when changing lanes*

3. *Cautious: drives the speed limit or less, stays in the slow lane, constantly checks all mirrors, keeps both hands on the steering wheel at all times*

In order to develop your groups, you will use the same principles of detailed examples and explanations that we practiced in Chapter 7.

Collaborative

Activity 8-3: Dividing and Developing Topics

With members from your group, choose any one of the topics from Activity 8-2, select *one* of the organizing principles you listed, and write out three possible categories to explain it (as in drivers: <u>temperament</u>: aggressive, moderate, cautious). Next, list at least one example to show what each category means. You may draw on personal experiences or use more general observations to create your examples.

Answers will vary.

Topic: *sports*

Organizing principle: *levels of violence*

Three groups:

1. *baseball   least violent*   *this grouping scheme might include*
2. *basketball or moderately violent*   *examples of several sports, i.e. most*
3. *football   most violent*   *violent: football, rugby, hockey*

Example (s) for each group:

1. *baseball: baserunners sliding and/or colliding with infielders, fights*
2. *basketball: fouls, other body contact, fights*
3. *football: tackling, blocking, fights, etc.*

Groundwork for Activity 8-4: Completing the Group

Some topics are conventionally divided into such well-established categories that all of the groups should be represented in a classification. For example, a discussion of the major professional team sports in the United States would be incomplete if you mentioned only baseball and football; basketball belongs as well. Or if you wanted to classify entertainment or informational media—listing newspapers, magazines, and radio—what else might a reader expect to be mentioned? Omitting obvious categories sends a message to readers that the writer has not carefully thought through the topic, an impression that we all want to avoid.

Teaching Idea
You might remind students that, without saying so, Activity 8-3 has them creating a working outline for a classification paragraph.

Activity 8-4: Completing the Group

Think for a moment about the five groups that follow, and then write in a likely category needed to complete each list.

Teaching Idea
If any student answers number 1 in Activity 8-4 with "swimming pool"—a valid response—you might want to discuss how well it fits the other outdoor places to swim and steer students toward a tightening of the SOP (*naturally occurring* places to swim).

1. Places to swim outdoors: pond, lake, river, _ocean (swimming pool)_

2. School levels: preschool, kindergarten, _elementary_, middle school, high school, college, graduate school

3. Common gems: rubies, sapphires, emeralds, _diamonds_

4. Food groups: meat, fish, poultry; fruits and vegetables, grains, _dairy_

5. Continents: Africa, Asia, North America, South America, Europe, Australia, _Antarctica_

CLASSIFICATION PARAGRAPHS: LOOKING CLOSELY AT STUDENT MODELS

Teaching Idea
This paragraph is a good model for showing students how to take an interesting slant on a topic. Ask students to classify shoppers using another SOP, such as level of enthusiasm or efficiency, and see what groups they come up with.

The student models that follow will help you write effective classification paragraphs. Both "Mall Crashers" and "Shopping the Easy Way" are developed through generalized experience, whereas "I Do" includes several personal examples. Either method can work well. As with any writing models, be careful not to simply reproduce what the authors have done, but try to apply the principles you discover within their work to your own.

Prereading Exploration for "Mall Crashers"

During a class discussion about types of shoppers, Chanthan decided he wanted to take the topic in a different direction, so this paper on nonshoppers emerged. Using the members of his writing group as the target audience, he also felt that his paragraph would appeal to a larger, more general audience, especially middle-class Americans who frequent malls.

Before you read ahead, think about your own experience with mall shopping. What kinds of people have you seen who are not shopping but are there for some other reason? List four possible categories of nonshoppers below, and then compare your list with the author's. What kind of paragraph might you have written on this same topic?

Answers will vary: window shoppers, parents bringing children for rides, diners, people walking for exercise

Mall Crashers

Malls across America attract thousands of people every day who are not there to buy anything, but all of them have their own special reasons for being there. The first, and maybe most satisfied, of these nonshoppers is the classic window shopper. These people are the ones who only browse, looking at and trying out merchandise, but seldom buying anything. They may try on four pairs of shoes or half a dozen sweaters, but they mostly just leave the salesclerks with no money and plenty of mess. The next nonshoppers, generally teens and young adults, are the ones looking to meet a member of the opposite sex. They can be found cruising the aisles of stores, sometimes pretending to be interested in merchandise; but usually when they are spritzing cologne around or feeling fabric, their eyes are on the attractive man or woman who is really shopping. Standing in a store, sitting on a bench, or sipping a soda in a food court, they are the ones who are not much interested in picking up merchandise, but who would love picking up a date. The remaining non-shoppers, the least happy, are those who accompany the serious shoppers. This group might include friends who are dragged along for company, children who have no choice, or the reluctant spouse of a shopaholic wife or husband. These nonshoppers are easy to spot because they are often the package carriers and protectors. While their determined partners are attacking the sale racks, the poor tagalongs can be seen draped with shirts, pants, and blouses as they obediently follow the leader; or they spend their time pacing back and forth on mall sidewalks, muttering to themselves as they glance back and forth from their watch to the store. As closing time for the mall stores nears, the nonshoppers will be the last ones to leave, many having achieved their ends, but few carrying any purchases of their own.

Chanthan Srouch

Postreading Analysis

Beginning with a topic sentence that clearly states the subject and single organizing principle, the author moves into a well-organized and developed paragraph. Notice that each category is announced by a subtopic sentence and then supported through general observations, clear explanations, and specific examples.

Because Chanthan is dealing with human behavior, his examples particularly benefit from action description. For example, his nonshoppers are "spritzing cologne," "feeling fabric," "attacking the sales racks," and "pacing back and forth." Also you might find the paragraph readable, in part, because specific language supports the action: "cologne, fabric, sales racks." The concluding sentence repeats the phrase "mall stores" as a link to the rest of the paragraph, refers back to the SOP, and ends with a final comment (expanded thought).

Do you think wordplay can add to the readability of writing? Notice how Chanthan uses "shopaholic" (in place of what other common word?) and mentions "picking up merchandise" versus "picking up a date." (For more on figures of speech, see pp. 473–480.)

Teaching Idea
"Mall Crashers" gives the class an example of wordplay and how it can affect tone in writing. You might focus students on the last paragraph of the Postreading Analysis to begin a discussion on wordplay and humor in their work.

▶ Prereading Exploration for "Shopping the Easy Way"

Ann Nall works in a local Toys "R" Us and so decided that it would make a good topic for her classification paper. Although many of her fellow students had been in this toy store, she thought that new parents might most appreciate her information, especially the listing of items in the baby section. Would you expect the author to include personal experiences to help illustrate the subsections in her store? Do you think personal experiences are necessary in a classification paper? If you had to divide and classify the space where you are currently employed, how would you do it? Write out a single organizing principle and three or four subsections that might grow from it.

Teaching Idea
For students who have difficulty writing outside the first-person perspective, "Shopping the Easy Way" is a good model.

Answers will vary. Personal experiences are not necessary, although Ann could easily have included some.

Shopping the Easy Way

In order to help customers shop more efficiently in Toys "R" Us, the store is divided into three overall categories: areas for older children, toddlers, and babies. The older children have four major areas—Blue, Pink, R-Zone, and Silver—with piles of toys for everyone. Boys mostly head for the Blue section and items like the GI Joes, Hotwheels, and Legos. In no time at all, the boys can have Lego racetracks assembled on the floor and be racing miniature Batmobiles after the "bad guys." Girls, on the other hand, usually go for the Pink section, where there are Barbies, Cabbage Patch Kids, and tea sets to help them build fantasies and pretend they are older. Both sexes are interested in the video games and bicycles in R-Zone and Silver. The next group of children, the toddlers, has the Red and Green areas. Customers shop in Red to find smaller toys such as Play Dough and building blocks to help their children develop fine motor skills. Large outdoor play sets with swings, slides, and gliders are located in the Green section. For the smallest children, babies, moms and dads shop in Purple. This part of the store contains most of what parents need to get children through their first year. Each aisle is clearly marked, guiding shoppers to shelves of diapers, formula, bottles, clothes, and many other items. After the baby's immediate needs have been met, the store can still help with important items like baby carriers, car seats, and strollers. Because Toys "R" Us does such a good job of labeling and grouping its merchandise, customers can be sure to find what they need right away, minimizing the wasted time and frustration that often come with shopping of any kind.

Ann Nall

Postreading Analysis

As in the other student models, Ann's paragraph begins with a topic sentence that clearly states the SOP used for dividing and grouping store merchandise. Her major divisions are again introduced by subtopic sentences, and the concluding sentence is well constructed, including a strong connector (Toys "R" Us), link to the SOP, and interesting final observation (expanded thought). The major groups are arranged by age, from oldest to youngest, which is logical but not necessarily least to most important. Notice that Ann does a good job with specific examples of the items found in each part of the store, for example, "Batmobiles, Barbies, and Cabbage Patch Kids."

> Specific words make your writing interesting.

> **Teaching Idea**
> You might point out that "Shopping the Easy Way" is not organized in any of the three ways we have discussed (spatial, chronological, importance) and ask if the paragraph seems well organized nonetheless. Also, ask if it could just as easily have been ordered by space or importance.

Questions to Help You Analyze and Write Effective Classification Paragraphs

1. What is the topic of this paragraph, and what statement does the author make about it? In which sentence do you find this information?

2. What SOP does the author use to classify the paragraph topic?

3. What statement does the author make in the concluding sentence that links to a statement made in the topic sentence?

4. What is the expanded thought in the final sentence, and how does it add to the overall point of the paper? (For more on expanded thought, see pp. 49–50.)

5. Write out each of the subtopic sentences. Next, underline the <u>subtopic</u> to be discussed once and the <u>statement</u> made about it twice. Circle any connecting words. (For more on connecting sentences, see pp. 52–57.)

6. How does each subtopic sentence reinforce the topic sentence?

7. How are the main examples arranged: spatially, chronologically, or by order of importance? What connector words reveal this?

8. How does the explaining in any one of the groups contribute to your understanding of the example?

9. Is action described in any of the groups, and if so how does the action description contribute to the quality of the writing or your interest in it?

10. List at least five uses of specific language (a word that belongs to a smaller group or category of words). (For more on specific language, see pp. 78–79.)

■ EXPLAINING THE WRITING ASSIGNMENT

■ SUMMARIZING THE ASSIGNMENT

Our goal for this paper is to write a well-developed paragraph of 250 to 300 words that groups things in a logical fashion. In order to create the groups, we must choose a topic that can be broken down into at least three categories according to a logical standard or **single organizing principle** (SOP). Just as in Chapter 7, we will begin with a topic sentence that clearly introduces the subject, end with a concluding sentence that expands our main thought, create several subtopic sentences, and develop each grouping in the paper with specific, detailed examples and explanations. Asking and answering the question of our examples "What exactly do I mean by these?" will continue to help us communicate clearly.

■ ESTABLISHING AUDIENCE AND PURPOSE

Who might be interested in reading this paper besides your composition instructor? If you find after some brainstorming that you would like to write about, say, jewelry, what then might you want to say about it? You might be impressed by its beauty, price, history, or effect on people. You could choose an objective voice and convey information about the historical importance of jewelry to a like-minded audience of jewelry lovers. Or you might want to use the more informal voice of personal experience to illustrate for a friend how different types of jewelry have affected people you know. Whatever topic you choose, you will find that writing with a fairly specific group of readers in mind will help generate and focus your ideas. (For more on audience profiling, see p. 10.)

You may have several purposes in mind as you write—to entertain, persuade, or inform—but communicating your ideas clearly should take top priority.

■ WORKING THROUGH THE WRITING ASSIGNMENT

Discovering Ideas

We know writing that sorts information, objects, and ideas is necessary, but it can also be dull. Classifying certainly helps a customer in a hardware store to locate a number 2-size Phillips head screw by designating a section for screws; however, nuts, bolts, nails, and screws may not make the most fascinating paper. As you think about topics, try to creatively explore them. What would you like to discuss about a subject? What do you think might interest a reader? Would including some personal experience be useful (for instance, the time you were in the hardware store, dropped a handful of tiny screws into the wrong bin, and learned about sorting and classifying the hard way), or will you use the less-informal "they" voice and generalize your examples? Whichever voice you choose, try to include detailed examples and lively explanations.

The following categories can all be subdivided in several ways, based on the SOP you select. For example, in the People category below you might select *students* and choose to classify them according to their study habits: *studies night and day, prepares most of the time, occasionally cracks a book,* and *never bothered to buy a book.* Or you might choose the topic *weddings,* from the Events category, dividing and grouping according to the standard of expense: *outrageously expensive, expensive, affordable, and inexpensive.* Using another standard, you might have some fun with the prevailing emotional state of the bride and groom: *blinded by love, happy, uncertain/anxious,* and *panicky.* There are many possibilities.

Having a *point* to make about your topic will focus your groups and guide the examples.

Teaching Idea
Try to head off the meaningless classification paper by asking students in class about their topics and why they have chosen them. For students who do not yet have a point, ask the rest of the class to help out with points that *could* be made.

There are many ways to divide and classify topics from the list.

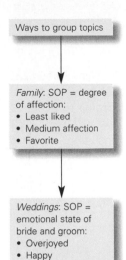

Ways to group topics

Family: SOP = degree of affection:
• Least liked
• Medium affection
• Favorite

Weddings: SOP = emotional state of bride and groom:
• Overjoyed
• Happy
• Doubtful
• Panicky

Teaching Idea
Have the class pick a subject or two from the Topic List, decide on an SOP, and give you three or four groups to list on the board.

Teaching Idea
Another activity for discovering an SOP is having students create grocery lists of twenty items and then group the items in any way that seems logical to them. Next, have them compare lists and explain why they grouped the items as they did.

Topic List

1. **People:** immediate family, relatives, neighbors, students, drivers, shoppers, dates, white-collar professionals, blue-collar professionals, criminals, friends, enemies, sleepers, babies, toddlers, teenagers, adults, men, women, musicians, vocalists, losers, winners, leaders, followers, etc.

2. **Places:** zoos, parks, sports arenas, rivers, lakes, beaches, swimming pools, cemeteries, amusement parks, national parks, websites, hotels, vacation spots, radio stations, retail stores, restaurants, libraries, schools (any kind), homes, office buildings, arcades, apartments, automobile dealerships, etc.

3. **Events:** embarrassing moments, funerals, weddings, holidays, accidents, practical jokes, painful moments, stages in your life, sales calls, parties, etc.

4. **Services:** dating, moving, pest control, hair styling, equipment rental, bail bonds, landscaping, employment, travel, phone, heating and air conditioning, adoption, counseling, auto repair, body shops, insurance, etc.

5. **Emotional states:** happiness, sadness, love, hate, contentment, discontent, enthusiasm, boredom, desire, revulsion, depression, fear, anger, etc.

6. **Behavior:** kind, cruel, responsible, irresponsible, truthful, deceptive, generous, selfish, etc.

7. **Personal adornment:** jewelry, makeup, tattoos, piercing, hair coloring, hair styling, fingernail polishing, etc.

8. **Clothing:** shirts, pants, shorts, dresses, blouses, jackets, coats, sox, shoes, etc.

9. **Expenses:** home, work, school, recreational, etc.

10. **Academic school subjects:** history, math, English, science, art, music, philosophy, business, accounting, computer science, economics, foreign language, journalism, etc.

11. **Career programs:** nursing, welding, heating ventilation and air conditioning, paralegal, emergency medical technician, dental hygiene, fashion merchandising, hospitality management, etc.

12. **Art:** drawing, painting, sculpture, pottery, metal work, textiles, photography, etc.

13. **Musical instruments:** strings, wind, and percussion

14. **Energy sources:** renewable and nonrenewable

15. **Sports:** team sports, individual sports, spectator sports

Prewriting Suggestions

After you have chosen several topics, the next step is deciding on an SOP. If we used the wedding topic mentioned just before the Topic List, we might create a focused cluster like this one to discover possible ways to group:

Focused cluster to find SOP

Expense, religion, ethnicity—any of these could be used to classify weddings, so it is up to the writer to decide which she might be interested in. Using clustering or another prewriting method, we could develop categories for several of the boxed terms. For example, we could choose *seasons* and list spring, summer, fall, and winter. But then the question becomes, "What do I want to say about these kinds of weddings?" If you want to write for, say, a trade magazine that specializes in weddings, you could choose *seasons* as the standard for grouping and communicate information in a straightforward, businesslike tone. But if your purpose is to entertain and reveal something about your experiences and opinions, you might go with a less-conventional standard, like the one we began earlier, the "prevailing emotional state of the bride and groom."

Here is how Richard Bailey, the author of the student model paragraph "I Do," listed different types of weddings a person might encounter, based on how the bride and groom feel.

1. *Blinded by love*

2. *Joyful*

3. *Happy*

4. *Content*   Brainstorming list of possible
                                                  categories for grouping
5. *Uncertain and anxious*   weddings by emotional states

6. *Panicky*

7. *Horrified*

After brainstorming on each of the possible types of weddings, Richard decided that he had something to say about three of them: *joyful, content,* and *uncertain/anxious.* To see how he developed each of these groups, turn to the paragraph model "I Do" on pp. 178–179.

Prewriting—Summing Up:

1. Choose several topics from the list, or create several of your own.

2. Use a prewriting method to generate several possible organizing principles.

3. Use a prewriting method to generate categories and examples for each principle.

4. Reflect on your purpose, knowledge, interests, and audience to choose an SOP.

JOURNAL ENTRY 8-2

Having selected a topic, list several possible organizing principles, and then choose one that most interests you. Explain in a few sentences why this principle interests you more than the others, is appropriate to your topic, and might interest an audience.

Organizing Ideas

At this point we can begin to focus and arrange categories. As always, a rough topic sentence will help you stay on track. When we classify, the topic sentence should state the organizing principle, with or without using words like *categories, groups, kinds, types, sorts, varieties, classes,* and *divisions.* Some writers also prefer to use a forecasting statement that mentions their groupings. The following topic sentences illustrate these points:

Margin notes:

You must decide on one organizing principle among many.

Link the SOP to your point or reason for writing the paragraph.

Teaching Idea
You might encourage students to list as many groups as they can think of in their prewriting (the Annotated Student Model began with seven) and then trim them to the three or four that they have the most to say about.

Teaching Idea
Journal Entry 8-2 is a good checkpoint to see if students are on track. You might have them share their work in groups or in general class discussion.

Words to show classification.

Topic sentence =
topic + SOP

Grouping words
are boxed.

Follow the same
order in the paragraph
as in the forecasting
statement.

Try a scratch outline
before you draft.

1. The <u>weddings</u> I have attended over the years fall into several distinct categories based on the <u>emotional state</u> of the bride and groom.

2. <u>Weddings</u> can be divided into the four following types based on the <u>emotional state</u> of the bride and groom: joyful, content, uncertain, and panicky. (forecasting groups)

3. The <u>weddings</u> I have attended over the years often reflect the <u>emotional state</u> of the bride and groom. (no grouping word mentioned)

You can see in each rough topic sentence the topic underlined once and the SOP underlined twice. Sentence two illustrates forecasting categories with the four groups shaded, and sentence three shows how to avoid using a grouping word if you wish.

For overall organization you might choose space, time, or importance:

- **Space:** for a topic that requires physical grouping of objects (books in a library)

- **Time:** for a topic that uses brief stories to group (stages of your life)

- **Importance:** for a topic using groups that are clearly less and more dramatic (dangerous weather: thunderstorm, blizzard, tornado)

Remember to introduce each of your three or four groups with a subtopic sentence and to link them with connectors like the transitions listed below (for more on connectors and a complete list of transitions, see pp. 52–57).

For Adding Material			
again	as well as	furthermore	likewise
also	besides	in addition	moreover
and	further	last	next
For Giving Examples and Emphasis			
above all	especially	in particular	one reason
after all	for example	in truth	specifically
another	for instance	it is true	surely
For Comparing			
alike	both	like	resembling
also	in the same way	likewise	similarly
For Contrasting			
after all	dissimilar	nevertheless	though
although	even though	on the contrary	unlike
but	however	on the other hand	whereas

Organizing—Summing Up:

1. Create a rough topic sentence to help focus your material.

2. Eliminate the least-promising categories and any that overlap. Keep only three or four.

3. Arrange the categories by space, time, or importance.

4. Try a scratch outline.

5. Review the list of transitions above (and remember the other connectors).

> **JOURNAL ENTRY 8-3**
>
> Write out your rough topic sentence. Does it contain a single organizing principle? Next list your categories in whichever order you have chosen. In a few sentences explain why you think this arrangement will work well.

Drafting

With the preliminary work done, you are almost ready to write your first draft. But before you plunge in, take a moment to review the Drafting suggestions in Chapter 1, pp. 12–14 and to think about the following points:

1. Remember to use an SOP and avoid overlapping categories. If, for example, you are categorizing movies by genre, you might include action/adventures, romantic comedies, westerns, and musicals, but not also films by Arnold Schwarzenegger, most of which would fall into the action/adventure category already mentioned.

2. Include all of the important members of your group. Whether you are creating personal categories or working with ones more commonly recognized, you should include all obvious groups. For example, a paper dealing with winter sports in the mountains might list cross-country skiing, ice skating, sledding, and snow shoeing, but it should also mention downhill skiing.

3. Focus your SOP so you do not create an "endless" list. For instance, an SOP of *sports played with a ball* is too general, producing a list that goes on and on: *baseball, basketball, football, softball, soccer, racquetball, handball, tennis, ping pong. . . .*

4. Have a clear reason for the classification. If you are not trying to make a point with your classification, you are likely to bore your reader and yourself. For example, merely talking about a pet parakeet, gerbil, iguana, and guinea pig because they all live in cages (the SOP) might well make your reader respond, "So what?"

Teaching Idea
If you don't have time to pick up the students' first rough drafts, consider collecting Journal Entry 8-4 to give you a quick glimpse into their progress.

> **JOURNAL ENTRY 8-4**
>
> Respond to this journal entry soon after writing your first rough draft. Skim back through the draft and ask yourself whether or not it feels like the assignment that Chapter 8 is asking for. Are there three or four categories in place? Are they arranged effectively? What part of this draft do you like best or think best fulfills the assignment instructions—why? What part do you dislike most or feel is drifting from the assignment—why? Answer in a paragraph.

Revising Drafts

To review the detailed lists for revising drafts, turn to Chapter 4.

■ ANNOTATED STUDENT MODEL

Help yourself to avoid difficulties in your own drafting by reading through the Annotated Student Model as carefully as possible. Doing this will save you at least a few headaches and probably help clarify questions you didn't even know you had.

Teaching Idea
You may find the Annotated Student Model most useful in showing the many changes often needed from a first to a second draft.

First-Stage Draft

Richard Bailey had been to several weddings in the recent past and so thought that he might have some fresh memories to use for a classification paragraph. He decided that young adults thinking of getting married in the near future would be a good target audience.

You will see how after limiting his list of groups to three—*joyous, content,* and *unhappy* weddings—he wrote a *fast* draft to get some ideas down on paper.

The groups are in place, but need to be developed with detailed examples and further explanation.

Weddings come in all shapes and sizes but not all of them are happy. I have been to half a dozen over the last 10 years, and I can tell you that some were great, some were so-so, and others were disasters. One of the happiest weddings I have ever been to was my older brother's best friend. He married a terrific woman of about the same age (they were in their forties), and the church was full of teary eyes as they walked down the aisle with some old fifties tune in the back ground. Not all people getting married can be ecstatic. Some fall into another group. These kinds of weddings are with people who have grown up as childhood sweethearts and then they become friends and then they get married. Weddings like these are full of people who already know each other because of the couple's history together the conversation in the church is among people saying the wedding is long overdue. Another bad wedding to be in is the confused and panicky kind. Weddings like this are often between two people who don't belong together in the first place. Sometimes accidents force the issue, sometimes familys pressure people, and sometimes two people just chose the wrong partners. My younger brother's first marriage was this sort, and the problems were obvious even to the wedding guests. His bride's people took one-half of the church and Marks took the other half of the church. The ceremony was over fast. No one seemed sure what was happening and Mark ended up dropping his wife on the floor! As awful as Mark's wedding was and despite high divorce statistics in this country, I will probably get married someday.

Unneeded sentence between topic and first subtopic sentence.

The second and third subtopic sentences need further focus.

Second-Stage Draft

First rough drafts of classification papers often have difficulties with overall focus, development, and relevant material. Note the explanations and examples that were added to this draft to help clarify meaning.

Teaching Idea
You might want to skim the first and second drafts in class before students begin working on their first drafts to help them head off several potential problems.

Topic sentence revised

Subtopic sentences have been revised (and shaded to help you identify them).

The weddings I have been to over the years can be grouped into several categories based on how the bride and groom feel. When many people think of weddings, they think of deliriously happy young couples. These are the people who can't wait to get the wedding over, and the honeymoon started. I have been to several like this. However, the happiest couple I have ever seen were not young, but in their early forties. Neither Jack nor Fran had any doubt. As they stood at the altar reciting their vows to the sound of some old fiftys tune and the church was full of teary eyes as they completed their vows with a kiss. If not all marrying couple are lucky enough to be overjoyed, there are still many who are happy and content. Often these weddings are between people like

Supporting examples and details added throughout

my older brother and his wife. Bruce and Julie grew up together, became friends, and then fell in love. Weddings like these are often full of people who already know each other, because of the couple's history together. The conversation in the church is full of people saying stuff like "Well . . . it's about time" and "at last." The worst kind of state for a couple to be in is in confusion and panic. Weddings like this are often between two people who don't belong together in the first place, shouldn't be together, and who will never last. Sometimes accidents force the issue, sometimes familys pressure people, and sometimes two people just chose the wrong partners. My younger brother's first marriage was this sort, and the problems were obvious even to the wedding guests. Evelyns people took one-half of the room and Marks took the other half of the room. No mixing it up between the families. The ceremony was quick and the reception was short. No one seemed sure what was happening, and Mark, who had been drinking too much made matters worse when he dropped Evelyn as he tried to carry her across the threshold. As awful as the panicky marriage can be and despite all the divorces in this country, I expect to get married one day, and I hope that mine lasts.

Transitional word worst *added to show order of importance*

Dialogue added

Explanation added

Explanation added

Concluding sentence revised

Special Points to Check in Revising from First to Second Drafts

1. Check topic sentence: topic + statement of SOP
2. Check subtopic sentences: connector + group + statement
3. Check concluding sentence: connector + link to topic sentence + expanded thought
4. ~~Delete unnecessary material~~
5. Add material for clarity, completeness, and emphasis
6. Check connectors: transitions, repeat words, synonyms, pronouns, reference to main idea

---

Teaching Idea
Whereas some students may not see the value in the sentence combining of the third-stage draft, most will recognize the improvements from added specific words and synonyms and the concision effort.

Title added

Third-Stage Draft

Many of us are tempted to call the paper complete by the time we have done a thorough second draft. But if you want your work to move beyond good to excellent, this third draft gives you that opportunity. With all of the major material and organizational concerns taken care of, you can now improve word choices and sentence variety and get rid of the clutter phrases that so often slip into rough drafts.

Teaching Idea
To reinforce style revision, you might want to assign selected pages from Unit Four on the days the class is discussing the Annotated Student Model third-stage draft and working on their own developing drafts.

I Do

The weddings I have been to over the years can be grouped into several categories based on how the bride and groom feel. [When many of people think of weddings they think of young couples', deliriously happy, who can't wait ~~to get the wedding over~~ **to get the rings** and the honeymoon started.] [I have been to several like this, however, the happiest ~~couple~~ **people** I have ever seen were not young, but in their early forties.] Neither Jack nor Fran had any doubt

Within this text we have already worked with the principles of cause and effect. In Chapter 5 when you established your dominant impression (effect), you needed to show what elements in your place brought about (caused) the feeling. The Chapter 6 personal narrative was full of cause/effect relationships as your story unfolded, event A adding to event B and so forth. The significance of the event (effect) was created (caused) by the people and their actions. In Chapter 7 we made a statement (often the effect) and then used examples (causes) to illustrate it. And the categories of Chapter 8 were frequently developed with cause-and-effect examples.

As we move ahead in this text, we will continue to see cause and effect operating, one of many interdependent and overlapping strategies for developing our ideas.

Determining the Value

As we have already discussed, finding solutions for problems and predicting outcomes in our daily lives are important benefits of understanding cause and effect, but the academic world makes its demands too. In a nursing class you are presented with the problem of a patient with "rolling" veins. How will you handle the injection? In an interior design class you must solve the problem of making a tiny room appear larger. An economics class asks you to predict the outcome on mortgage loans of raising the prime interest rate by one point. Your Composition I instructor asks you to support an argument by illustrating the probable negative effects of an action.

Being able to handle the academic demands of causal thinking is an important step toward earning a degree, but perhaps more significantly toward helping establish a critical frame of mind. The world is complex, people multifaceted. As we practice clear causal thought, we take a giant step backward from the superficial thinking that oversimplifies complicated issues and tries to pass off snap judgments as reasoned conclusions.

Teaching Idea
If you teach the persuasion chapter, you might want to link clear cause/effect thinking to avoiding the post hoc fallacy.

Teaching Idea
Journal Entry 9-1 is a good in-class discussion tool to help students understand how much a part of our lives cause-and-effect thinking is.

JOURNAL ENTRY 9-1

Think for a moment about instances during the past week when you have used cause-and-effect thinking to understand a situation, solve a problem, or predict an outcome. Try to list one example from home, work, and school, summarizing the situation in a sentence or two. Perhaps the in-laws came for the weekend. What effects did they have on your household? Maybe you just received a brand new MasterCard with a $3,000 limit. If you don't immediately cut it in two, what effects might you predict? After listing the situations, write out what you think are the important causes and/or effects for each one.

▶ DEVELOPING SKILLS, EXPLORING IDEAS IN CAUSE OR EFFECT PARAGRAPHS

To determine causes and effects successfully, there are several important points to keep in mind:

Teaching Idea
You might point out to students that Activities 9-1 and 9-2 can be used as prewriting for their own topics.

1. Explore all the likely causes and effects.

2. Develop causes or effects thoroughly.

3. Choose only the real causes and effects.

4. Avoid oversimplifying by thinking critically.

The following activities will help you practice these points.

Teaching Idea
In Activity 9-1 rather than focusing on the terminology of "primary, secondary," and so on, you might emphasize the various causes and effects these terms can reveal.

Kinds of causes and effects

There are often several primary causes and effects.

Primary/ secondary cause? Often the writer's judgment

Teaching Idea
Activity 9-1 is more challenging to students if they list *possible* rather than far-fetched causes and effects.

Groundwork for Activity 9-1: Discovering Causes and Effects

It is rare for there to be only one cause or one effect of an action, so we should not settle on the first possibility that comes to mind. For example, in trying to understand why a student did poorly on an algebra exam, we might immediately say, "Too little studying." This is *one* likely *primary* or main cause, but perhaps there are other significant reasons. If we devised a list of questions to explore the causes, it might look like this:

Questions for Exploring Causes and Effects

Primary: What causes would certainly bring about the effect?

Secondary: What causes might reasonably bring about the effect?

Contributing: What causes might develop or add to another cause?

Immediate: What is the cause closest in time that produced the effect?

Distant: What causes might be separated from the effect by time or space?

Hidden: What causes might not be readily apparent?

Minor: What causes might be mistaken for significant ones?

Applying these questions to the failed algebra exam, we might come up with this kind of list:

1. **Primary:** insufficient studying

2. **Secondary:** argument with parents the night prior to the test

3. **Contributing:** work demands cutting into study time

4. **Immediate:** answering only half the problems

5. **Distant:** not grasping fundamental arithmetic concepts from earlier grade levels

6. **Hidden:** undiagnosed attention deficit disorder

7. **Minor:** student nearby whistling through the exam

Now we can see that there are a number of possible reasons to account for a poor grade, and we would select the ones best suited to our purpose, interest, and audience. Notice that what might be only a secondary reason for one person might be a primary reason for another. For example, the argument might have been so severe or the student so upset that she could not think clearly during the exam. Also, a distant or hidden cause might be crucial to creating the effect, so be aware that the list of questions can produce overlapping responses. You must determine which causes or effects are most significant.

Collaborative

Activity 9-1: Discovering Causes and Effects

After reading the groundwork information above, discuss with group members one or more of the following topics, brainstorming for possible causes *or* effects. The Questions for Exploring Causes and Effects above may help you discover ideas. Next, list six possible causes or effects. Now, decide which *three* are the most likely, and tell why you decided to eliminate the other possible causes or effects.

Example: Topic: Being elected valedictorian of your graduating class

Possible Causes

1. Having overall highest GPA	2. Making As on all final exams
3. ~~Having a parent as the principal~~	4. ~~Getting early computer training~~
5. Having good study habits	6. ~~Being rewarded by parents for every A~~

Reason for cutting causes: _Number 3 is not likely because GPA, not the principal,_
determines the valedictorian. Both 4 and 6 could contribute to student success but are
not as significant as causes 1, 2, and 5.

Answers will vary.

1. Topic: Requiring all high school students to take a course that educates about
   addictive substances

Possible Causes

1. Governmental mandate	2. ~~A few students getting caught with marijuana~~
3. A trend in drug overdoses at a school	4. ~~Several students talking about smoking pot~~
5. The well-publicized death of a student	6. ~~The mayor's campaign promise from last year~~

Reason for cutting causes: _Reasons 2 and 4 are insufficient, and 6 is unlikely, given how often_
politicians follow through on campaign promises.

2. Topic: Switching careers in midlife

Possible Causes

1. Being discredited in one job and losing it	2. ~~Secret childhood fantasy (rock star?)~~
3. Being caught stealing (other major infraction?)	4. ~~Friends from high school doing better~~
5. Realizing that a job is being phased out	6. ~~Being tired of a job and wanting a change~~

Reason for cutting causes: _Number 2 seems least likely, though still possible, because most_
middle-aged people do not make major life changes based on adolescent fantasies. Number 4 does
not seem sufficient, though it could contribute. Because most people cannot justify the time, money,
and energy a career switch takes, based on boredom, number 6 is out.

3. Topic: Marrying while still teenagers

Possible Effects

1. Starting a family early	2. ~~Seeing the world~~
3. Beginning to lose touch with unmarried friends	4. ~~Maintaining a burning infatuation~~
5. Divorcing early in life	6. ~~Graduating from college with honors~~

Reason for cutting effects: Most teen marriages are caused by pregnancy, and young people (or those of any age) struggling with children have a difficult time achieving 2, 4, or 6.

4. Topic: Watching too much television

Possible Effects

1. Studying less	2. ~~Being driven into depression~~
3. Missing out on social activities	4. ~~Learning the secret to instant success~~
5. Reading less	6. ~~Committing a "copycat" crime~~

Reason for cutting effects: TV is unlikely to account for either 2 or 6 without some significant contributing causes. And despite late-night television real estate schemes and "psychics," 4 is also unlikely.

5. Topic: Falling in love "at first sight"

Possible Effects

1. Feeling wonderful	2. ~~Remaking a person's character~~
3. Increasing self-confidence	4. ~~Remaining forever unrequited~~
5. Marrying	6. ~~Abandoning friends and family~~

Reason for cutting effects: Few people manage radical changes in behavior even over many years, so number 2 seems unlikely. Most people who fall in love manage to let the other person know, so 4 is out. It is unusual, though not unheard of, for people to break from their society and close support group for any reason, including "love" at first sight.

Groundwork for Activity 9-2: Developing Causes and Effects

   After you have chosen likely causes or effects for your paragraph assignment, you will develop them with detailed examples and clear explanations. (For more on developing paragraphs, see pp. 41–48.) You may decide to use the "I" of personal experience or the more formal "they" approach. Remember to include specific words, sensory details, active verbs, "-ings," and dialogue to make your examples more lively and clear. Also, be sure to introduce each cause or effect with a subtopic sentence.

Collaborative

Activity 9-2: Developing Causes and Effects

Choose one of the topics you worked with in Activity 9-1 (or choose another topic if you prefer). Now, brainstorm with group members for examples, details, and explanations that you could use to develop each cause or effect. You can personalize each cause/effect, using your own experience or discuss it from your general knowledge. After you have decided on one specific example for each cause or effect, write a subtopic sentence that includes the cause or effect and makes a statement about it, and then write two or three sentences to explain your point. The example below uses personal experiences to develop its point.

Example: Topic: Watching too much television

- **Possible effect:** _Too little time for studying, causes poor grades._

- **Subtopic sentence:** _When I was a sophomore in high school, my grades took a nosedive_ _when my parents gave me a TV for my room._

   It was great to have some privacy to watch TV and not have to fight with my older brother over who got to see what program. But I started watching the tube nonstop from the time I got home from school till bedtime. After failing three out of five classes, even I saw a problem, and my parents took the set till my grades improved.

Answers will vary.

Topic from Activity 9-1:

_____

- **Possible cause or effect:** _____

   _____

- **Subtopic sentence:** _____

   _____

Subtopic developed: _____

_____

_____

_____

_____

_____

_____

_____

_____

_____

_____

Groundwork for Activity 9-3: Choosing Real Causes and Effects

When we observe events casually, it is not uncommon to make quick judgments about them. Children who hear thunder and notice rain following might conclude that thunder causes rain. An adult caught in slow highway traffic might conclude that the driver in front of him is the problem—and so the honking begins—when in fact the slowdown is caused by the two hundred rubberneckers ahead of both drivers who cannot resist gawking at a stalled car on the side of the road. But if we slow *ourselves* down and begin to think more critically, we are more likely to arrive at real causes and effects, solving many life problems—and writing more effective cause-and-effect papers as well.

Activity 9-3: Choosing Real Causes and Effects

Look closely at the columns of causes and effects, and then put an X in front of the cause/effect that seems *least* reasonable, given the topic. Next, briefly explain in the space provided why you think the cause or effect is unlikely. (If you think all causes or effects are likely, explain why the *least* likely one seems reasonable to you.)

Teaching Idea
Some students will think all of one cause or effect list is likely, for instance that "liking the taste of beer" might cause alcoholism. This reaction can create some lively discussion, especially when the student explains her reasoning. (You might refer students back to Activity 9-1 and the "minor" cause.)

1. Topic: Becoming addicted to alcohol

Causes	Effects
_____ Having heavily drinking parents	_____ Losing a job
_____ Having heavily drinking friends	_____ Losing nonaddicted friends
_____ Suffering from overstress	_X_ Leading a happy life
_X_ Liking the taste of beer	_____ Becoming malnourished
_____ Being genetically predisposed	_____ Developing cirrhosis of the liver

Unlikely cause: _Liking the taste of beer may be a contributing cause, but it is not a significant reason._

Unlikely effect: _Few alcoholics lead happy lives, at least until they give up drinking._

2. Topic: Overusing pesticides and herbicides on a lawn

Causes	Effects
_____ Being ignorant of the problem	_____ Killing unintended plants and animals
_____ Being indifferent to the problem	_____ Polluting water
_____ Having no real laws prohibiting	_X_ Eradicating all insect pests and weeds
_____ Revering a beautiful lawn	_____ Polluting soil
_X_ Reacting to environmentalists	_____ Making animals and people sick

Unlikely cause: _Few people would protest against environmentalists by poisoning their own yard._

Unlikely effect: _Lawn battles are constantly fought and never won._

3. Topic: Attending the funeral of someone you never liked

Causes	Effects
_____ Fulfilling a family obligation	_____ Feeling good about the decision
__X__ Trying to meet new people	_____ Feeling horribly bored
_____ Acting kindly toward the family	_____ Making family members happy
_____ Fulfilling a moral obligation	_____ Reassessing feelings toward deceased
_____ Fulfilling a work obligation	__X__ Realizing deceased was a saint

Unlikely cause: _Not many people go to funerals to fill their social calendar._

_____

Unlikely effect: _A person might view the deceased more favorably but is_
unlikely to canonize her.

_____

4. Topic: Learning to cook

Causes	Effects
_____ Wanting to save money	_____ Saving money
_____ Wanting to eat in a more healthy way	_____ Becoming more healthy
_____ Wanting to gain more control of life	_____ Becoming more creative in the kitchen
_____ Wanting to eat better tasting food	_____ Learning more about food
__X__ Needing to follow a spouse's order	__X__ Saving a marriage

Unlikely cause: _I hope there aren't many marriages left like this._

_____

Unlikely effect: _Cooking might enhance a relationship but is not likely_
to save it.

_____

Groundwork for Activity 9-4: Thinking Critically

Teaching Idea
You might want to link
Activity 9-4 to the fallacy of
oversimplifying if you teach
the persuasion chapter.

Teaching Idea
Letting students compare their
responses to Activity 9-4 in
class will reinforce the message
that causes and effects can be
complex.

When we look for a quick explanation or solution for a problem, we often fall into the trap of oversimplifying. Sometimes we find one important cause or effect and stop thinking there, and sometimes we don't even find one that is significant or true. For instance, when you see a young person in a $50,000 automobile, you might conclude that she has plenty of money. But there are several other plausible explanations: (1) She is leasing the vehicle. (2) She has little personal wealth but is driving her parent's car. (3) She has a five-year loan and barely makes the payments. In order to write and think critically, we often need to slow ourselves down and continue to ask the question "Is this the only or best explanation possible?"

Activity 9-4: Thinking Critically

Read through the following statements and list at least five other plausible causes or effects that a critical thinker might include to complete the oversimplified statements.

Answers will vary.

1. Television is the reason so many college students do not perform better in school.

    Other causes for poor academic performance:

    A. *Dealing with family problems*

    B. *Working too much*

    C. *Missing classes*

    D. *Avoiding homework*

    E. *Partying*

2. If the driving age were raised to eighteen, there would be fewer accidents.

    Other causes of accidents:

    A. *Anyone driving drunk*

    B. *Driving when a person is too old*

    C. *Careless driving by middle-aged adults*

    D. *Anyone driving in bad weather*

    E. *Anyone coping with difficult road hazards*

3. If a person switches careers in midlife, he is probably failing at his job.

    Other causes for a career change:

    A. *Moving*

    B. *Wanting more money*

    C. *Failing business*

    D. *Wanting more opportunity for advancement*

    E. *Having achieved financial security and looking for creative fulfillment*

4. People exercise mainly to feel good about themselves.

    Other effects of exercise:

    A. *Increasing health*

    B. *Increasing longevity*

    C. *Increasing quality of life*

    D. *Contributing to a person's social life*

    E. *Helping an athlete perform better in an organized sport*

5. Rap music makes people behave violently.

    Other effects of rap music:

    A. *Helping people feel happy*

    B. *Creating a good beat to dance to*

    C. *Bringing a group of people closer together*

    D. *Introducing people to part of a different culture*

    E. *Allowing people to vent frustration without hurting anyone*

▶ CAUSE OR EFFECT PARAGRAPHS: LOOKING CLOSELY AT STUDENT MODELS

The student models that follow will help you write effective cause or effects paragraphs. "Making the Promise Last" is developed through generalized experience whereas "The Thousand-Dollar Lesson" and "Building Memories" are centered around personal examples. Either method can work well. As with any writing models, be careful not to simply reproduce what the authors have done, but try to apply the principles you discover within their work to your own.

▶ Prereading Exploration for "Making the Promise Last"

Gebdao polled her collaborative group while she was prewriting and found that the two young men and two young women agreed with her about the danger of early marriage. They shared several stories from which the author was able to gather some specific examples for her paper, and her group's response helped her decide on a target audience: young people considering early marriage.

Though this paper is not a formal argument, part of the author's purpose is persuasion. Before you read further, to help with your perspective on this issue, take a moment to list four *positive* effects on young adults who decide to marry right out of high school.

Answers will vary: Possible positive effects: two people support and nurture one another; two lives are enriched by joining; two people become even more responsible as they chart out a life together; no longer needing to play the dating game, the couple can move ahead with life goals, such as building a business or continuing their education.

Teaching Idea
To promote causal thinking and to stimulate an interesting discussion, have students talk over the *positive* effects of early marriage before they read "Making the Promise Last."

Making the Promise Last

Marrying while still teenagers can be a bad decision, creating many problems for young couples. First when teens marry in or just out of high school, their relationships often change drastically. Instead of spending time with their individual former friends, newlyweds often find that their spouse does not like some or all of the other's friends, so the husband or wife has to choose—"them or me." Even when the old friends are accepted, many times friendships die out because a married couple's interests can be so different from a single person's. While some young couples continue to go to the same parties, concerts, and vacation spots, many more find themselves having to try to have fun with each other's in-laws instead. As the years pass, another problem begins as young couples often find themselves becoming increasingly cut off from the rest of life and dependent on one another. They have already been seeing less of old friends, many of whom are off at college or trade school or simply doing other things, but after that first baby arrives, the young couple's life becomes really hard. If they had been thinking about more school, with the new load of bills, forget it. The newest priority becomes baby food and diapers. When the normal stress of raising a baby is added to life goals put aside and relaxation time vanishing, many young marriages begin to crumble. Now the couple experiences one of the worst effects of hasty marriage—divorce. Even without the added tension of a baby, many young adults, who are still finding out who they themselves are, soon learn in their time living together that they are not right for each other. If a child *is* involved, then the baby's life and the parents' lives, are inevitably changed for the worse. The childless couple may split finding a better life for themselves one day, but divorce with a baby heaps extra bills for separate maintenance and guilt on the parents. While some early marriages work out well, so many end poorly that maybe teens should wait until they know and can take care of themselves better before they stand at an altar and promise to take care of someone else.

Gebdao Kaiwalweroj

Postreading Analysis

This paragraph is clearly constructed with topic, subtopic, and concluding sentences that serve as a solid framework. The author uses her general knowledge and observations to discuss the negative possible outcomes of early marriage, distancing herself somewhat from the topic by using the "they" approach.

Qualifying cause/effect relationships is important.

Notice how careful Gebdao is to qualify throughout the paper with phrases like *often, many, maybe, some, may.* When a writer describes cause-and-effect relationships, qualifying is essential, particularly when the writer stakes out a position with which an audience might disagree. Notice too how the author carries the qualifying into her final sentence, conceding that "some early marriages work out well," even as she reiterates her opinion as part of the expanded thought.

Do you think this paragraph would be more persuasive if Gebdao had included personal examples, or do they not matter much?

Prereading Exploration for "The Thousand-Dollar Lesson"

For this essay, Luke Eimers targeted an audience of young adults who have themselves received a speeding ticket or two and who have had trouble with their auto insurance. Before you read ahead, consider: If you were to write a paragraph on this subject, would you lean more toward causes or effects? Do you think that some topics might be better handled as causes, or effects, based on the topic itself and the reader's likely interest? Take a moment to list below four possible reasons why a person might speed.

Answers will vary. Some topics are better handled as causes or effects.

Possible reasons: (1) enjoyment. (2) emergency. (3) drunk. (4) test driving

a new car.

Teaching Idea
Because "The Thousand-Dollar Lesson" focuses on effects, you might also want to discuss possible causes, encouraging students to see that their own topics might be better handled as either causes or effects.

The Thousand-Dollar Lesson

While traveling last spring, I learned about the miserable consequences of speeding. My first unpleasant experience was actually getting the ticket. I knew I was in trouble from the moment I saw the red flashing lights in my rearview mirror and looked down at the speedometer to see the needle on eighty-five. I thought I might be able to talk my way out of it until I saw the Clint Eastwood look-alike Texas highway patrol officer step up to my window. "All right, boy, let me see your license and proof of insurance," he drawled, cutting off my "Gee-I-didn't-realize-I-was-going-that-fast" line. The officer seemed to enjoy every second it took him to write that ticket out, and with an evil smirk he handed it to me, saying, "Have a nice day." I'm pretty sure he was the only one having fun. The next problem was paying the ticket. I didn't want it on my record because it would crank up my insurance rates, so I knew it would cost plenty, and it did. The ticket was only seventy-five dollars but it cost three hundred to have it "disappear" from my record. But as puppy would probably involve the causes for bringing it into the household or the effects it has on the family and surroundings (chewing table legs, dragging out the trash, etc.). So in this sense many of your choices will be about events or things that happen. To help you focus, it might help to remember these reasons for writing a cause/effect paper:

1. To understand a situation

2. To solve a problem

3. To predict an outcome

4. To entertain

5. To persuade

   The following topic lists might also help generate a few ideas. As you skim through the topics, remember that you may deal with either causes or effects, but that a single paragraph can lose focus if it tries to deal with both. However, be open to creating a brainstorming list of causes *and* effects initially so you can discover which you would prefer to write about. For instance, making it onto the varsity basketball team undoubtedly had several important *causes,* such as diligent practice, self-sacrifice, innate ability, and support from others. But making the team would also have important *effects*: building self-esteem; establishing loyalty to a new group; reinforcing the principles of hard work and self-sacrifice; and opening new possibilities for competition, travel, and athletic scholarships.

Create a list for *both* causes and effects.

Com
your
what

Teaching Idea
To encourage students initially to explore both causes and effects, you might refer them back to Activity 9-3, which includes both, and the List of Causes and Effects under the chapter Prewriting Suggestions.

Topic Lists (Causes or Effects)

Personal Life

- Taking a child to a museum (zoo, baseball game, swimming pool, movie, etc.) for the first time
- Attending the funeral of someone you never liked
- Having parents choose a spouse for their child
- Becoming a parent (grandparent)
- Making it onto the varsity football team (basketball, baseball, soccer, swimming, golf, etc.)
- Being chosen valedictorian of your graduating class
- Shopping only when articles are on sale
- Learning to cook
- Using steroids to bulk up
- Limiting TV viewing to one hour per day
- Finding a role model early in life

School

- Making financial aid to students easier to qualify for
- Graduating from high school (college)
- Dropping out of high school
- Making poor grades

- Enlisting in ROTC
- Requiring exit exams for graduating high school or college seniors
- Working toward a skilled trade in high school rather than preparing for a four-year college
- Enrolling a four-year-old in preschool
- Requiring all high school students to take a course on auto maintenance and repair

Work

- Joining the military after high school graduation
- Letting work pile up at your home or office desk
- Taking a three-day weekend once each month
- Telling your supervisor what you really think of her
- Being promoted to supervisor in your department
- Reporting a fellow employee's misconduct to a superior
- Becoming significantly more productive than your fellow workers
- Losing your job
- Writing a memo to your supervisor detailing the reasons why you deserve a raise

Community

- Raising the drinking age to twenty-five
- Raising the driving age to eighteen
- Eliminating the speed limit on U.S. interstate highways
- Driving recklessly
- Reporting reckless driving to the police
- Requiring counseling before a couple can divorce
- Providing a pet to any person in an assisted-living situation who wants one
- Abusing a child or spouse
- Marrying while still teenagers

Prewriting Suggestions

With several topic ideas in hand, the next step is to list some causes and effects. One way to uncover these is to use the Questions for Exploring Causes and Effects (primary, secondary, contributing, etc.) listed on p. 185.

Or you might try any prewriting methods you are comfortable with. A focused cluster and listing can both work well. Brian Peraud, the author of the chapter Annotated Student Model, chose "taking a child somewhere" from the Personal Life category in the Topic List and then focused the topic using his own experience with taking his daughter to the zoo. He brainstormed for both causes and effects, creating the lists below:

> Creating a list of causes and effects

List of Causes and Effects

Causes	Effects
1. Help daughter learn about animals	1. Learn about exotic animals
2. Fulfill a promise to her	2. Overcome her fears
3. Have fun with her	3. Encourage kind treatment of animals
4. Enjoy zoo myself	4. Have fun together—bond
5. Enjoy cheap entertainment	5. Reduce boredom
6. Escape from the house	6. Teach her about the larger world
7. Enjoy good weather	7. Increase environmental awareness

Causes or effects? Choose a direction.

After thinking about both lists, Brian decided that he had more to say about the effects side.

Prewriting—Summing Up:

1. Choose several topics from the list, or create several of your own.

2. Use a prewriting method to create a cause/effect list for each.

3. Brainstorm to discover detailed examples for the causes and effects.

4. Choose either causes or effects to focus your paragraph.

JOURNAL ENTRY 9-2

Write a brief paragraph telling why you have chosen your topic and focus. What is your purpose? Who is your target audience? How well have you been able to detail the examples in your prewriting? Are you leaning toward examples developed more from personal experiences (the "I" tone) or more from general knowledge (the "they" tone)? (For more on tone, see pp. 464–473.)

Teaching Idea
Journal Entry 9-2 asks students about their purpose, which may be mildly persuasive, as in "Making the Promise Last," or informative/entertaining, as in "The Thousand-Dollar Lesson." It helps students at this stage to let them discuss their topics in groups.

Organizing Ideas

Now we can begin to focus and arrange the major points. To help direct the work, you will need a topic sentence that states the subject and focus, either causes *or* effects (recalling that paragraphs within essays and longer works often deal with both). You could state directly that you will deal with causes, using words like *reasons, explanations, problems, factors,* or you might choose phrases like *to bring about* or *to create.* To announce effects, you could use words like *results, outcome, consequences, occurrences, solutions, instances, examples,* or you might choose phrases like *what follows* or *what happens to.* Some writers also prefer to use a forecasting statement that mentions the causes or effects to be explained. The three following topic sentences will show you several different approaches:

Topic sentence = topic + statement of cause or effect

Words to show cause and effect

Forecasting statement

1. Taking my daughter to the zoo last Sunday had three important consequences.

2. Our trip to the zoo last Sunday taught my daughter a lot about exotic creatures, helped her to overcome her fears of large animals, and helped us grow closer together.

3. Before our trip to the zoo last Sunday, I would not have believed so many positive experiences could come from one place.

Targeting an audience will help focus your material.

The topic of each sentence is underlined once, and the words that indicate effects are underlined twice. Sentence two uses a forecasting statement, which is shaded.

After you have written out a topic sentence and chosen your list of causes or effects, you will need to limit the list. Brian crossed out several effects that he did not have room enough to develop in a paragraph and then combined 2 with 3 and 4 with 5 to leave a manageable working outline of these three points:

Teaching Idea
You can have several students write their lists on the board while the class discusses ways to combine and arrange the causes or effects.

Working outline for "Building Memories"

1. *Learn about exotic animals*

2. *Overcome her fears*

3. *Encourage kind treatment of animals*

4. *Have fun together–bond*

5. *Reduce boredom*

6. ~~*Teach her about the larger world*~~

7. ~~*Increase environmental awareness*~~

A. *Learning about exotic animals*

B. *Overcoming fear of large animals*

C. *Bonding with a parent*

Finally, remember to introduce each cause or effect with a subtopic sentence linked to the paragraph by connectors like the transitions listed below (for more on connectors and a complete list of transitions, see pp. 52–57).

For Adding Material			
again	as well as	furthermore	likewise
also	besides	in addition	moreover
and	further	last	next
For Giving Examples and Emphasis			
above all	especially	in particular	one reason
after all	for example	in truth	specifically
another	for instance	it is true	surely
as an example	indeed	most important	that is
certainly	in fact	of course	to illustrate
For Showing Cause and Effect			
accordingly	because	hence	then
and so	consequently	since	therefore
as a result	for this reason	so	thus
For Summarizing and Concluding			
finally	in conclusion	in short	that is
in brief	in other words	largely	to summarize

Organizing—Summing Up:

1. Create a rough topic sentence to help focus your material.

2. Decide on the main causes or effects (only three or four).

3. Try to combine closely related causes/effects, delete unneeded ones, add any needed ones, and arrange the rest either chronologically or by order of importance.

4. Create a working outline.

5. Review the list of transitions (and remember the other connectors).

JOURNAL ENTRY 9-3

Take a moment to write out a working topic sentence. Is it focused enough to help you select causes or effects? Now list your main causes or effects. Does chronological order or order of importance seem the best arrangement for the material—why?

Drafting

With the preliminary work done, you are almost ready to write a first draft. But before moving ahead, take a moment to review the Drafting suggestions in Chapter 1, pp. 12–14, and to think about the following points:

Qualifying can reduce over-simplifying.

1. Remember to qualify where necessary. Because events are often complicated, it can be difficult to point to a single cause or effect and say, "That's the one that caused it!" You will frequently soften statements in causal writing (and argument) with terms like *often, many, sometimes, usually, frequently, seldom, might, could, possibly,* and others. (For more on qualifying, see pp. 371, 459.)

2. Be careful not to omit likely causes or effects. For instance, if the author of "Building Memories" had left out the bonding experience between parent and child as an important effect but included increased environmental awareness, the reader might need an explanation as to why environmental awareness overshadows the parent-child connection.

   With a less-personalized topic, say, the effects of using steroids, you should be even more alert to obvious omissions. For example, a paper focusing on the negative results of steroid use should include intense mood swings and outbursts of anger.

3. Remember that closeness in time or space does not necessarily create a cause or effect. Does thunder really cause the rain?

Complete all points or thoughts.

4. Complete all thoughts so a reader can see the cause/effect relation. If, for instance, you say that because your parents were on vacation you almost lost your job, a reader has the right to respond, "What are you talking about?" If you complete the thought by explaining that your folks usually wake you in the morning so you won't be late for work, then a reader can understand the causal connection.

JOURNAL ENTRY 9-4

Respond to this journal entry soon after writing your first rough draft. Skim back through the draft and ask yourself whether or not it feels like the assignment that Chapter 9 is asking for. Are there three or four causes or effects in place? Are they arranged effectively? What part of this draft do you like best or think best fulfills the assignment instructions—why? What part do you dislike most or feel is drifting from the assignment—why? Answer in a paragraph.

Teaching Idea
You can use Journal Entry 9-4 to help focus group revision, as each student directs the readers to parts of the draft that the author is concerned about.

Revising Drafts

To review the detailed lists for revising drafts, turn to Chapter 4.

■ ANNOTATED STUDENT MODEL

Teaching Idea
You may find it helpful to assign the Annotated Student Model in stages paralleling the students' own drafting and revision.

Help yourself to avoid difficulties in your own drafting by reading through the Annotated Student Model as carefully as possible. Doing this will save you at least a few headaches and probably help clarify questions you didn't even know you had.

First-Stage Draft

Brian Peraud used listing (see p. 198) to uncover several effects to write about in this first *fast* draft and decided that parents with school-age children might be especially interested. He stresses how important it is for parents to spend time with their children.

I had a great time with my daughter the other day. The drive over to the zoo took longer than it should have, but that didn't keep us from having a good time. First, we both learned more about foreign animals like lions and elephants. Katy learned that they live in families called prides and the females do almost all the hunting. Then the female lions bring home the food to the head of the pride and the other lions. Another good thing about our trip together was that it helped my daughter overcome fear of big animals. When she was three, she was knocked down by a dog, and she has been nervous around dogs since. Being close to calm animals like the elephants, made her feel more relaxed. She enjoyed seeing the mother caring for her new baby. After we had been at the zoo for awhile, Katy was relaxed enough to help me feed a giraffe. It was fun watching my little girl feed the animal. The giraffe was so tall and she was so small. She held the grass out to it standing so high above the ground. As the tongue curled around the grass, Katy squealed, yet she fed the giraffe even more. Another good thing about our trip was spending playtime together. It was fun to run around, laughing at the prairie dogs and creeping up on the peacocks shimmering in the sunlight. We both had our hands slimmed by the baby goats, and Katy got a big kick out of seeing me butted from behind. We had to keep up our strength by eating. This gave us an excuse to eat all the junky zoo food we could get our hands on: hotdogs, cheese nachos, and rainbow bomb pops. This trip to the zoo helped me realize how important it is to keep building happy memories.

Topic sentence needs focus

Second sentence is unneeded.

The subtopic sentences need further focus.

The main effects are in place but need to be developed with detailed examples and further explanation.

Second-Stage Draft

Teaching Idea
In the Second-Stage Draft have students evaluate the revised subtopic sentences and the added detailed examples. Ask in what way they contribute to the draft.

First rough drafts of cause/effect papers often have difficulties with overall focus, development, and relevant material. Note the explanations, details, and examples that were added to this draft to help clarify meaning. As you move through your own draft, keep asking the question "What do I mean by that last statement, example, or idea?" Also pay special attention to your topic, subtopic, and concluding sentences.

Topic sentence revised to clarify effects and add specific words

***Explanation added**

Taking my daughter to the <u>zoo</u> last <u>Sunday</u> had three main consequences. ~~The drive over to the zoo took longer than it should have, but that didn't keep us from having a good time.~~ One important effect was that we both learned more about foreign animals. *<u>Both Katy and I have been around dogs and cats.</u>

Unneeded second sentence deleted

Supporting <u>examples and details added throughout</u>

But neither of us has spent much time near wild animals. Going to the zoo gave us a chance to be close to and read about the big cats, elephants, rhinos, hippos, zebras, seals, and others. Katy learned that lions, for instance, live in families and that the females do almost all the hunting. They bring home the food to the dominant male and the cubs. Another benefit to our trip together was helping my daughter overcome her fear and anxiety of large animals. When she was a little girl of three, Katy was knocked down by a dog, and she has been nervous around even small dogs since. Being close to large, calm animals like the elephants, peacefully flapping their ears and grazing, made her feel more relaxed. She especially enjoyed seeing the mother caring for her new baby. After we had been at the zoo for awhile, Katy was relaxed enough to help me feed a giraffe. It was fun watching my little girl—all forty-one inches of her—holding grass out to the giraffe. This is an animal standing sixteen feet above the ground! As the tongue curled around the tuft of grass, Katy squealed, "Ooh, its slimy!", yet she was willing to feed the giraffe even more. But for me the most important result of our trip was just that we got to spend some playtime together. It was fun to run all over the zoo, laughing at the prairie dogs in their burrows and creeping close to the male peacocks shimmering in the sunlight. We both had our hands slimmed by the baby goats as we fed them those smelly little green pellets, and Katy got a big kick out of seeing me butted from behind. We knew we had to keep up our strength by eating. This gave us an excuse to eat all the junky zoo food we could get our hands on: hotdogs, cheese nachos, rainbow bomb pops, and a wad of cotton candy that would have choked a hippo. Besides being great fun, our trip helped me again to realize how important it is in any relationship—but especially for a parent and child—to keep building happy memories.

Special Points to Check in Revising from First to Second Drafts

1. Check topic sentence: topic + statement of cause or effect

2. Check subtopic sentences: connector + cause or effect word + statement

3. Check concluding sentence: connector + link to topic sentence + expanded thought

4. ~~Delete unnecessary material~~

5. Add material for clarity, completeness, and emphasis

6. Check connectors: transitions, repeat words, synonyms, pronouns, reference to main idea

---

Third-Stage Draft

This draft gave Brian the opportunity to polish his work at the word and sentence level to move his draft beyond good to excellent. Notice in particular how he has added more *specific* words to clarify images.

Title added

Building Memories

Taking my daughter to the zoo last Sunday, had three main consequences. One important effect was that we both learned more about exotic animals. [While Katy and I have been around dogs and cats neither of us has spent much time near ~~foreign~~ wild animals.] Going to the zoo, gave us a chance to be close to and read about the big cats, elephants, rhinos, hippos, zebras, seals, and others. [Katy learned that lions, for instance live in families called prides, and that the females—"the girls," as she said—do almost all the hunting, bringing home the ~~food~~ kill to the dominant male, and the cub.] Another benefit to our trip together was helping my daughter overcome her fear ~~and anxiety~~ of large animals. When she was ~~a little girl of~~ three Katy was knocked down in the park by a Chow and she has been nervous around even small dogs since. Being close to large, calm animals like the elephants, peacefully flapping their ears and grazing, made her feel more ~~relaxed~~ **at ease.** She especially enjoyed seeing the mother caring for her new calf. After we had been at the zoo for ~~awhile~~ an hour. Katy was relaxed enough to help me feed some grass to a giraffe. [It was fun watching my little girl—all forty-one inches of her—holding grass out to an animal standing sixteen feet above the ground!] As the dark-purple tongue curled around the tuft of grass in her hand, Katy squealed, "Ooh, its slimy!" yet she was willing to feed the giraffe even more. But for me the most important result of our trip was just that we got to spend some playtime together. It was fun to run over the zoo, laughing at the little prairie dogs in there burrows and creeping close to the male peacocks shimmering blue-green in the sunlight. We both had our hands slimmed by the ~~baby~~ pygmy goats, as we fed them those smelly little green pellets, and Katy got a big kick out of seeing me butted from behind. [To keep up our strength, we just had to eat all the junky zoo food we could get our hands on: hotdogs, cheese nachos, rainbow bomb pops, and a wad of cotton candy that could have choked a hippo.] Besides being great fun, our trip to the zoo helped me again to realize how important it is in any relationship—but especially for a parent and child—to keep building happy memories.

Special Points to Check in Revising from Second to Third Drafts
1. Added specific words are boxed.
2. More precise or audience-appropriate word substitutions are shaded.
3. [Sentences combined for variety are bracketed.]
4. **Synonyms and phrases replacing clutter and repeat words are bolded.**
5. ~~Unneeded words are lined through.~~

Final-Editing Draft

By this point Brian's draft is in great shape, and he can shift into low gear, moving slowly, line by line, looking for every error in grammar, spelling, and punctuation that still exists. (Keeping an **Improvement Chart** will help you to focus on your own **pattern errors,** an efficient way to finish this step in the process.)

Building Memories

Taking my daughter to the zoo last Sunday, [10] had three main consequences. One important effect was that we both learned more about exotic animals. While Katy and I have been around dogs and cats, [9a] neither of us has spent much time near wild animals. Going to the zoo, [10] gave us a chance to be close to and read about the big cats, elephants, rhinos, hippos, zebras, seals, and others. Katy learned that lions, for instance, [9b] live in families called prides, [10] and that the females—"the girls," as she said—do almost all the hunting, bringing home the kill to the dominant male, [10] and the cubs. Another benefit to our trip together was helping my daughter overcome her fear of large animals. When she was three, [9a] Katy was knocked down in the park by a Chow, [9c] and she has been nervous around even small dogs since. Being close to large, calm animals like the elephants, peacefully flapping their ears and grazing, made her feel more at ease. She especially enjoyed seeing the mother caring for her new calf. After we had been at the zoo for an hour. [5], Katy was relaxed enough to help me feed some grass to a giraffe. It was fun watching my little girl—all forty-one inches of her—holding grass out to an animal standing sixteen feet above the ground! As the dark-purple tongue curled around the tuft of grass in her hand, Katy squealed, "Ooh, ~~its~~ it's slimy!", yet she was willing to feed the giraffe even more. But for me the most important result of our trip was just that we got to spend some playtime together. It was fun to run all [3] over the zoo, laughing at the little prairie dogs in ~~there~~ [2] their burrows and creeping close to the male peacocks shimmering blue-green in the sunlight. We both had our hands ~~slimmed~~ [1] slimed by the pygmy goats, [10] as we fed them those smelly little green pellets, and Katy got a big kick out of seeing me butted from behind. To keep up our strength, we just had to eat all the junky zoo food we could get our hands on: hotdogs, cheese nachos, rainbow bomb pops, and a wad of cotton candy that could have choked a hippo. Besides being great fun, our trip to the zoo helped me again to realize how important it is in any relationship—but especially for a parent and child—to keep building happy memories.

Brian Peraud

Special Points to Check in Editing Final Drafts

1. Spelling	5. Sentence fragments	9. Common comma categories
2. Sound-alike words	6. Comma splices/run-ons	a. Introduce
		b. Enclose/end
3. Missing words	7. Capitalizations	c. Divide
4. Wrong words	8. Apostrophes	10. Unneeded commas

Final-Draft Checklist

Before you turn in your final draft, take a few minutes to review this checklist. You may find that, as careful as you think you have been, you still have missed a point or two—or three. (For more on any of these points, see Chapter 4.)

___ 1. Have you listed three or four causes or effects?

___ 2. How effective is your topic sentence?

___ 3. Have you clearly arranged your causes or effects—either by time or importance?

___ 4. Have you written a subtopic sentence to introduce each main example?

___ 5. Are your main examples relevant, adequately developed, and thoroughly explained?

___ 6. How well connected are all the sentences within the paragraph?

___ 7. How effective is your concluding sentence?

___ 8. How well have you used specific language?

___ 9. Are you choosing the most *active* verbs and *ing* words to describe action?

___ 10. Have you tried using a metaphor or simile?

___ 11. Are the sentences in your paragraph varied in length and beginnings?

___ 12. Have you repeated a word or phrase so often that it becomes noticeable?

___ 13. Have you included words that serve no purpose?

___ 14. Have you written a title—an interesting one—for the paper? (Check capitalizations.)

___ 15. Have you prepared your paper according to the format expected by your instructor? (Check to see if you need a title page, be sure to double-space, leave at least a 1-inch margin, use a 12-point font, and be sure to type or word process.)

___ 16. Have you edited your work as closely as you know how to (including having at least one other person—classmate, friend, family member—proofread closely? Have you checked your **Improvement Chart** for your pattern errors so that you can look for them specifically?

___ 17. Have you looked for the following errors: spelling, sound-alike words, missing words, wrong words, sentence fragments, comma splices/run-ons, capitalizations, apostrophes, the Big Three comma categories, and unnecessary commas?

CHAPTER SUMMARY

1. The process of cause and effect asks about reasons and outcomes. It helps us explore the "why" behind events, ideas, people, places, objects, and animals.

2. Developing a sense for cause-and-effect thinking can help us solve immediate and future problems.

3. Events are complex, rarely having only one cause or effect.

4. Closeness in time or space of a cause/effect to an event does not necessarily mean that the cause/effect is significant.

5. Without carefully considering many causes and effects, we risk oversimplifying.

6. The writer often determines which causes/effects are most important, based on her topic, interest, and knowledge, and the interest and knowledge of a reader.

7. The writer is responsible for completing all ideas and making all points. He should not expect his reader to make any but obvious connections.

8. A topic sentence for a cause or effect paper must interest the reader, mention the topic, and make a clear statement about it (pointing toward causes or effects).

9. Each major cause or effect should be introduced by a subtopic sentence.

10. Each sentence in a paragraph should be clearly linked, with subtopic and concluding sentences the most well connected of all.

11. Writing is never complete until it has gone through several revisions and careful editing.

■ ALTERNATE WRITING ASSIGNMENTS

The following assignments represent a few of the many ways we regularly use cause-and-effect analysis and may help you focus more quickly on a paper topic. If you select one of these options, feel free to modify it to your situation and interest. However, remember the essential elements of the assignment that we have practiced throughout the chapter, keeping these points particularly in mind:

• Choose either causes or effects and mention your focus in the topic sentence.

• Beware of oversimplifying and underexplaining.

• Introduce each main cause or effect with a subtopic sentence.

• End with a concluding sentence that expands the main idea of the paper.

Teaching Idea
Ask students to carefully consider their purpose if they choose Alternate Writing Assignment 1. A paragraph that is essentially venting frustration will be handled differently than one with a persuasive intent.

1. Write a letter of complaint that deals with a situation, service, or product. We all have other people occasionally work for us: auto repair, home maintenance, lawn care, and so forth. Try to recall an instance when you were unsatisfied with some service, identify the service, and then discuss the outcome (effects). You might focus your effects merely on reporting, say, the stalling out of your car after a tune-up or mention in detail what you intend to do about the poor service if the situation is not remedied (i.e., call the Better Business Bureau, sue, go to small claims court, spread the word to friends about the shoddy work). If you have ever had bad luck with a product (tape deck, TV, computer), you could follow the same procedure as for the service.

2. List the causes or effects of a trend (something steadily changing). If you have recently noticed a trend in society, you could comment on the causes or effects. For example, you might notice an increase in young women smoking and speculate on why

(advertising targeting young women, schools cutting back education on ill effects, role models also smoking, people seeking an early grave?). Or you might notice a decrease in concert or sports attendance. What is causing it? What might be the results? Think of trends affecting entertainment, sporting events, employment, education, interpersonal relationships, consumer products, child care, health care, and more.

3. Write about the long-term effects someone has had on you. Think about a person who has been or still is important in your life—a teacher, coach, boss, parent, child, and so on—and tell about the effects he or she has had on you. For instance, a parent might discuss how she developed patience, humility, and appreciation for the little things in life (effects) from her child. Or you may remember a coach who was a tyrant—overly demanding, belittling, verbally abusive—causing you to consciously avoid such behavior in your life.

4. Choose a problem and find a solution. Think about a problem that has been troubling you recently, one that you have already found a solution for or one that is unresolved. For example, tuition costs might be hard for you to meet. How did you or will you handle this? You might continue to work part- or full-time, pick up more hours, ask for a loan from a parent or friend, apply for a bank loan, apply for a Pell Grant, buy ten more lottery tickets and hope. . . . The solutions will be the effects generated by the problem or cause.

5. As an exercise in critical thinking, choose a seemingly trivial cause and look for dramatic effects. In exploring ideas, consider the old saying "For want of a nail, the shoe was lost. For want of a shoe, the horse was lost. For want of a horse, the battle was lost. For want of a battle, the war was lost." When you build your chain of effects, think about how each action affects the one that follows it. For instance, many imported species of plants and animals have ravaged their new environment. In the late 1800s rabbits were introduced into Australia to provide sport and additional meat but rapidly decimated the local animal population by eating most of the vegetation they survived on. Common dandelions, another European import, have prompted many lawn lovers to pour herbicides onto their grass, and when the chemicals run off or seep into the water table, another chain of destruction begins. On a more personal level you might construct a causal chain beginning with an argument or kind act and then pursue the effects that could follow.

CHAPTER 10

Explaining Activities

Doing Them, Understanding Them

Building Process Analysis

Selecting Audience
Listing All Steps
Explaining Steps
Defining Terms
Giving Warnings
Polishing Sentences

◼ WHAT ARE WE TRYING TO ACHIEVE AND WHY?

Setting the Stage

In the illustrations above, you will notice a boy preparing to focus his telescope on a full moon. But before he can bring the image into focus, he will have to follow a few simple steps, loosening several lock knobs, using the view finder to target the moon, tightening the lock knobs, and then adjusting the focus knob. If you have never handled a telescope, do you think you could follow a brief set of clear instructions that detailed how to focus one? When we try to explain or understand an activity, how something happens or is done, we are involved in process analysis—the assignment for Chapter 10.

As we move further into the chapter, we will discuss both aspects of process analysis: how to do and how to understand something. In our picture above, learning the steps involved with physically moving the telescope, pointing the lens, and making the fine adjustments would be an application of how-to-*do*. If instead we wanted to comprehend how a telescope works, how the lenses and mirrors reflect and refract light, for instance, we would be involved with a how-to-*understand* process analysis.

Linking to Previous Experience

Every day we are surrounded by thousands of processes: in nature—the rising and setting of the sun, the movement of the wind, the growth of plants; among people—working together, maintaining households, striving for an education; and individual behavior—getting out of bed in the morning, fixing a meal, showing affection for a loved one. The business world is full of ongoing processes, every occupation features its own activities, and machines by definition serve a function and therefore involve a process. We are enmeshed in ordinary activities and seldom think about the steps involved in them, until an accident makes it difficult for us to accomplish the task (How *do* you shower with a cast on your leg?) or until we need to learn a function or explain it to another person.

Also consider the experience we have with *process* in school, learning both how to *do* and *understand*. From the history class that asks you to list the major events (steps) leading to U.S. involvement in the Vietnam War to the algebra class that asks

2. Process (to perform): How to housebreak a puppy.

Audience: Ten-year-old who has never owned a dog or cat.

Decide if you will paper train or train for outside	Take puppy on a twenty-minute walk each night
If training for outside, be ready to walk dog a lot	If puppy messes in house only scold him if you catch him in the act or immediately thereafter
Provide food and water at times you can watch dog	If he messes, scold, and then take outside
Right after puppy eats or drinks take him outside	Be alert to signs that puppy wants to go outside
Wait outside for dog to pee or poop or both	Take puppy outside for brief outing many times each day
Praise puppy and give him a treat	
Never feed close to bedtime	

3. Process (to perform): How to buy a used car

Audience: Sixteen-year-old the day after she has gotten her driver's license.

Decide whether or not to consider a dealership	Size up the owner—responsible/credible?
Call ads in the newspaper	Check car carefully on inside and outside
Ask all necessary information about vehicle	Ask owner questions about maintenance and accidents
Determine how much you can afford	Test drive
Have the money in your checking account	Have inspected
Pay cash	Negotiate price
Visit the owner	Have cash but be ready to walk

4. Process (to understand): How gasoline is converted to energy within an engine

Audience: Class of students beginning automotive training

Gas is pumped into tank	Piston moves up forcing exhaust out of cylinder
Engine starts	Moving piston transfers energy to crank shaft
Fuel pump and gravity pull fuel from gas tank through fuel line into carburetor (preinjectors engines)	Crankshaft passes energy along through drive train to wheels
Gas is metered from carburetor into cylinders on the intake cycle	
Gas and air are compressed by the pistons	
Electrical spark ignites the air/gas mixture	
Piston is pushed downward	

5. Process (to understand): Childbirth

Audience: First-time expecting parents

Uterine contractions begin and the cervix begins to dilate	The child emerges from the mother's vagina
Contractions progress, becoming more regular	Physician cuts the umbilical cord
The cervix continues to dilate, averaging 13 to 14 hours for first pregnancies	Baby takes her first breath
When dilation reaches 9 to 10 centimeters the baby begins to move out of the uterus	Within a few minutes the placenta is expelled
The placenta breaks and the amniotic fluid escapes	
The baby slowly moves through the cervix with each contraction and "push" of the mother	
Pain increases with the infant's passage	

Groundwork for Activity 10-2: Explaining Steps Thoroughly—Giving Reasons and Warnings

Teaching Idea
If students are still uncertain about warnings and explanations, you can ask them about several steps/suggestions in buying a used car, from Activity 10-1. For example, ask why a person should try to avoid a dealership, or why it might be important to have the used car inspected before negotiating a price.

After we have listed all the steps necessary for a specific audience to do or understand a process, we must next be sure to explain the steps fully. It does little good to give an instruction, for instance, from our tire-changing example, like "locate the correct jacking point" if the reader has no clear idea what we mean by "correct jacking point." If we clarify our meaning by saying one of four areas on the vehicle specially reinforced to bear the weight of the car and then either list the likely spots or refer the reader to an illustration, then he might be able to accomplish the step.

Aside from clarifying the meaning of a step, we must often explain the "why" behind it for a curious reader, who wants to know why *this* way and not another. For instance, why would a person changing a tire want to remove the top lug nut last? If we explain that it is to keep the wheel centered so that it will not slip off from one side or the other, we satisfy our reader's curiosity and bring her closer to following our suggestions.

Also we will frequently include **warnings** to reinforce a reason, especially when the reader might be endangered if he fails to execute a step as written. For example, we might warn a person not to fully tighten the lug nuts on a tire while the vehicle is suspended because he risks knocking the car off the jack, damaging the car or crushing his foot.

Collaborative

Activity 10-2: Explaining Steps Thoroughly—Giving Reasons and Warnings

After reading the groundwork for this activity, look back at any process you described in Activity 10-1. In the spaces provided below, write out an explanation, reason, or warning for every step that you think might need clarifying for the stated audience. (You may find that one clarification requires another, especially when establishing a possible cause/effect relationship.)

Answers will vary.

Process: _____ buying a used car _____

Audience: _____ sixteen-year-old _____

Explanations/Reasons:

Why bring cash (check), negotiate, and be ready to walk away?

People selling used cars often don't want to spend any more time on the process than they have to. If you are ready with the money, it can help the owner to decide in your favor.

Always negotiate because this is part of the buying/selling game. Most people ask for more than they think they can get and expect to take somewhat less. Being prepared not to buy strengthens your position in the negotiation game. Also, you may need some time to cool down, if you are overly excited by the deal.

Warnings:

Why avoid dealerships, have an inspection, and size up the owner?

Dealerships have a lot more experience selling cars than you have buying them. They are selling for a profit and often simply lie, so you get stuck with the bad deal.

Even if the vehicle looks and sounds good, it might have many problems. An expert inspection increases your chances of buying smart.

Some people are more inclined to lie than others, and many people will simply withhold information—caveat emptor.

Groundwork for Activity 10-3: Defining All Terms

Process instructions call for clearly defining all terms. Just because a word is familiar to you or many other people does not mean that everyone else knows it. For example, would we expect someone who has never changed a tire to be able to identify a lug wrench, lug nuts, or wheel block? Further, could we expect the person to know how to use the lug wrench or set the wheel block? Because we cannot know whether readers understand all our terms, we must define any that we think might be a problem for them. (For more on defining terms, see pp. 336–342.)

Collaborative

Activity 10-3: Defining All Terms

Look back at the process you used for Activities 10-1 and 10-2. Decide which terms *probably* and which terms *might* need to be defined for the stated audience, and then list them in the spaces provided below. Next, explain why you separated the "maybes" from the "probablies." Remember that you are using your best judgment when you decide which terms to define and which would already be known by your audience. There is no absolute way to predict what a reader might know.

Teaching Idea
The example in Activity 10-3 will give students another idea for writing about a process to understand. Students might also choose one of their own topics here.

Example: Process: *earthquake*

Audience: *seventh-grade earth science class*

Probable terms to define: *plate tectonics, seismic activity, crust, magma, faults, Richter scale, seismograph, epicenter*

Possible terms to define: *shock, aftershock, earth's core*

Why I separated the terms: *The probable terms to define are common in the scientific community, and many adults would know them, but most twelve- and thirteen-year-olds would not. The possible terms to define are more familiar and likely to be understood through the context of the process-analysis discussion.*

Answers will vary.

Process: *buying a used car*

Audience: *sixteen-year-old*

Probable terms to define: *Blue Book value, caveat emptor, title transfer, potential mechanical defects: "valve job," "frame realignment," "losing compression," "worn timing chain," etc.*

Possible terms to define: *notary public, cash, credible owner*

Why I separated the terms: *Probable terms to define: Many sixteen-year-olds have heard these terms, but most have not had to learn yet what they mean. Possible terms to define: Notary: The reader has probably heard the term and knows that notaries certify legal documents, but the reader may not know where to find a notary or why one might be important. Cash: Some readers will not realize that "cash" does not necessarily mean dollar bills and might have a problem carrying, say, $5,000 in hundred-dollar bills around. Credible owner: Some young people will need more than a word or two to warn them away from a seller who is likely to lie to them, for example, a professional small-time dealer working out of his or her home.*

Groundwork for Activity 10-4: Avoiding Monotonous Sentence Patterns

How often have you found yourself reading through a process explanation, say, instructions for assembling a bookcase, passing your driver's license exam, or learning to factor in an algebra class, and said to yourself, "Hey, this is exciting stuff. I can't wait to get to the next paragraph!"? Probably not often enough. In part this is because most process instructions try to be no-nonsense, let's-just-get-this-done documents—but even the driest subject can be made more or less interesting on the basis of sentence structures alone. Consider the following paragraph excerpt on putting up a wall shelf:

> First, I gather all my supplies. Second, I set them within reach. Third, I begin to attach the shelf brackets to the wall. Fourth, I pencil in each hole in the mounting brackets against the wall. I do this so I can drill in the correct spots. Fifth, I choose a bit one size smaller than the bracket screws. Sixth, I drill holes about half the length of the screws. I do this to help the screws grip more firmly. Seventh, I screw the brackets into the wall. Eighth, I begin the steps for attaching the shelf.

If your response is "Fairly clear writing but boring," how then can we make the information more readable? Suppose we combine some of the sentences in the next example to vary their **length** and **beginnings**—and eliminate the monotonous string of first, second, third, and so forth.

> **Once** I have gathered all of my supplies, I set them within reach **and** begin the process of attaching the shelf brackets to the wall. **First,** I place the mounting brackets on the marks **that** I previously measured for the height of the shelf, **and then** I pencil in each bracket hole **so** I can drill in the correct spots. **With** a bit the next size smaller **in** diameter than the bracket screws, I drill holes about one-half the length of the screws (the smaller holes help the screws grip the wall more firmly **and** eliminate the problem of making holes too big for the screws). **Now** I line up the brackets with the holes **and** screw the brackets into the wall, **being** careful not to overtighten the screws **so** I don't pull them out of the soft drywall. **With** the brackets secure **on** the wall, it's time to attach the shelf.

Now we have a paragraph that reads more smoothly and is, consequently, more interesting for a reader. Although Chapter 18 will work in more depth on the principle of sentence variety, you already unconsciously know many useful patterns and can apply them if you see the need.

Collaborative

Activity 10-4: Avoiding Monotonous Sentence Patterns

Read through the following paragraph and then rewrite it in the space provided. In place of the ten short sentences of roughly the same length, try to combine some. Also feel free to add information or explanations that would contribute to the spirit of the paragraph. You may read ahead in Chapter 18 for additional information if you wish, or just try some of the following words to help you combine sentences:

because, although, as, if, since, when, where, while
and, but, so, or, for, nor, yet
who, which, that
first, second, third, last, next, then, now, after, as a result, later, soon, before, especially

Teaching Idea
If you want students to begin focusing on grouping steps, you might ask them to separate the steps in Activity 10-4 into three groups, each introduced with a subtopic sentence, as the suggested answer in this instructor's edition demonstrates.

Answers will vary.

Process: how to guarantee that you will get a ticket after being pulled over for speeding

Audience: a younger brother or sister

Monotonous version:

> *First, act like you are trying to hide something. Second, avoid eye contact with the officer. Third, loudly protest that you weren't speeding. Fourth, refuse to show your driver's license. Fifth, throw your license at the officer. Sixth, accuse the officer of harassing you. Seventh, accuse the officer of just trying to fill a ticket quota. Eighth, try to bribe the officer. Ninth, swear at the officer. Tenth, act like you want to punch the officer.*

Rewritten version with greater sentence variety:

Topic sentence: *If you want to be sure to get a ticket after you have been pulled over for speeding, just follow these easy steps. You can begin by mildly annoying the officer. Act like you are trying to hide something under the seat as he or she approaches the car. If the officer fails to ask about the suspicious behavior, still be sure to avoid eye contact and loudly protest that you weren't speeding (you might want to begin swearing). Now that you have the officer annoyed, guarantee the ticket with these pointers. First refuse to show your driver's license; then change your mind and throw the license out the window. Next, accuse the officer of harassing you, that you were only keeping up with the traffic and that you think he is just trying to fill his monthly quota. Now, of course, the ticket is assured, but if you want to push for more, like jail time, try these pointers. First, try to bribe the officer, and when that doesn't work, begin calling him names. Finally, get out of your car and try to hit the officer. Congratulations, you have just earned not only a ticket but also a ride to jail.*

▶ PROCESS ANALYSIS PARAGRAPHS: LOOKING CLOSELY AT STUDENT MODELS

The student models that follow will help you write effective process papers. If you choose the "how-to-do" approach, you will find "A Boy's Best Friend" and "Recipe for a Red-Hot Sunday" particularly helpful. Both of these paragraphs illustrate the hands-on explanation of steps required to complete a task. The Annotated Student Model, on the other hand, demonstrates one way to write about a process to be understood. As with any writing models, be careful not to simply reproduce what the authors have done, but try to apply the principles you discover within their work to your own.

▶ Prereading Exploration for "A Boy's Best Friend"

Teaching Idea
To help with their invention, remind students about the many things that children build, such as "forts" made of cardboard boxes or pillows, bird feeders/houses, tree houses, doll houses, animal cages, and so on.

Steve Oh chose a manageable how-to-do topic in this memory from his childhood in rural Korea. He thought his paragraph might appeal most to young men in any culture who have had similar childhood experiences, wanting to use "weapons" for fun and to gain a bit of control over their environment.

Do you remember building anything as a child that was particularly special to you also? In the space below list one thing that you remember building as a child, and then list at least six steps that went into it.

Answers will vary.

A Boy's Best Friend

Living in the country as a child, I longed for a slingshot to play and hunt with, and finally decided I would make one. Collecting the materials for my treasure, though, did not come easy. It required the most perfectly forked branch from an oak tree, a square of leather to hold the stone, and a piece of rubber band. Any old rubber band would not do, though; it had to be surgical tubing, light brown and hose shaped, for the power I wanted. To obtain this rarity, I biked half an hour into town to the drug store, after begging the money from my older brothers. My brothers also helped me find the best-shaped and healthiest-looking branch from a nearby forest. Because the only leather I could find was my dad's belt, I secretly cut off a two-inch length from the end of it, praying that he would not notice. Finally, I was ready to construct my prize. With instructions from my brothers, I sawed the three ends of the oak branch to form a capital Y, each section approximately 6 inches long. Next, I peeled away the rough brown bark and sanded it with a medium grade of sandpaper until it was smooth as silk. Using the Korean equivalent to a pocketknife, on the side of the Y facing away from me, I carved notches roughly 1/8 inch deep and 1/4 inch wide about 1/2 inch from the tips. Then I wrapped the ends of the rubber band around the notches, being extra careful to tie the bands securely. (I didn't want to lose an eye if the tubing slipped from the branch when I had the slingshot fully drawn back!) With my knife I drilled a small hole in the ends of the leather patch, slipped one inch of the tubing through each hole, folded it over, and tied it together with a square knot so it, too, would not slip. My slingshot was complete. I pulled back the band to test it, let it go, and heard the best "Snap!" I could have hoped for. My childhood dream was realized, and I was ready to chase after those terrible little sparrows that had been ruining our rice crop.

Steve Oh

Postreading Analysis

The author manages a personable tone in this process paragraph, overcoming one of the problems common in how-to writing—reader boredom. By using "I" and personal experience, Steve is able to include some interesting points about his character and background. For example, we learn that he is from a rural area, his folks are probably farmers, and money is scarce. We also gain some insight into the author's character: he is inventive, determined, and bold enough to risk annoying his father to achieve his ends.

Using chronological organization, as is typical of most process descriptions, Steve begins with a clear topic sentence, includes two subtopic sentences to introduce the two major step groupings in the paper, and concludes with a sentence that strongly links to the topic sentence. Throughout, the reader is helped to move easily between sentences with connecting words, including transitions. When we move into the actual construction, Steve is careful to use plenty of specific language, which includes measurements and locator words. Notice, too, several explanations for his actions (for example, why he cut the belt) and one important warning to anyone wishing to build a slingshot.

▶ **Prereading Exploration for a "Recipe for a Red-Hot Sunday"**

Jeff Coburn was stuck for a topic idea until a group member suggested cooking, and Jeff decided to write about the only dish he knows how to make. Because he does not care much about cooking, he thought he might focus on readers who would share his general lack of enthusiasm for it but who might appreciate a quick dish in a party

Teaching Idea
You might stress that process instructions do not have to be dry, although there are many circumstances where outline instructions are preferable to livelier writing.

setting. As you prepare to read these process instructions, imagine that you do not know much about cooking, and ask yourself if the explanations seem complete and all the terms understandable.

Recipe for a Red-Hot Sunday

If you are looking to spice up those cold November football Sundays, try my easy recipe for nuclear hot chili. The first step is to gather the ingredients. With the friends who are going to be watching the game with you in mind, you will need at least two pounds of ground beef (90 percent lean lets you avoid draining the grease after browning). Next, pick up two 14-ounce cans of kidney beans, one of chili-hot beans, one of whole stewed tomatoes, and two 6-ounce cans of tomato paste (these items are generally located in the same aisle). Your trip through the vegetable section should produce two green peppers, two habaneros (the rocket fuel!), two garlic cloves, celery, and one white onion. For spices, try a package of McCormick's Ground Beef Chili Seasoning; the salt and pepper are probably already on your shelves. With the ingredients assembled, you are ready to prepare the kitchen and veggies for cooking. Locate a sharp serrated knife and cutting board, a 1-quart bowl for holding the chopped veggies, and a large pot like a Dutch oven (12 inches across and 6 to 8 inches deep). Now slice the green peppers, celery, and onion into bite-sized chunks. Mince the garlic and slice the habaneros into slivers, being careful not to touch your eyes, especially, until after washing your hands, unless you enjoy feeling like you are being scalded! Open the canned ingredients, and you are ready to cook. First, brown the meat (draining it if you want to), and then add the chili seasoning along with salt and pepper to your taste. Next, add the garlic, peppers, tomatoes, and paste, and stir them all thoroughly. Let this mixture simmer for about thirty minutes, and then add the three cans of beans (they are precooked, so you don't want to overcook them to mush). That's it. You're done. Now just let the pot simmer till you hear the doorbell ring, and get set for a good, *hot* game.

Jeff Coburn

Postreading Analysis

Recipes are a common use of process instructions and are often done in a bare outline form, so it is especially difficult to make them readable. If you choose a similar topic, you might try some of the same tactics that Jeff used to make his chili recipe more interesting.

First, target a reader and give him a reason to be interested in the paper as Jeff does with the football fans. A simple, quick dish might be useful to this audience on a Sunday afternoon. Second, try to vary your sentences, especially in beginnings and length. Notice, for example, the two-word sentences near the end of the paper. (For more on sentence variety, see Chapter 18). Third, try to vary your connectors. It is all too easy to fall into a clear but monotonous pattern like "first, second, third, fourth,"—as the preceding three sentences do—or to repeat too often transitional words like *next*, *now*, *after*, *before*, and so forth. If ever a type of writing calls for word and sentence variety, it is process analysis, and recipe explanations in particular.

Questions to Help You Analyze and Write Effective How-to-Do Paragraphs

1. What is the topic of this paragraph, and what statement does the author make about it? In which sentence do you find this information?

2. What statement does the author make in the concluding sentence that links to a statement made in the topic sentence?

3. What is the expanded thought in the final sentence, and how does it add to the overall point of the paper? (For more on expanded thought, see pp. 49–50.)

4. Write out each subtopic sentence, underlining the grouping of steps. Circle any connecting words. (For more on connecting sentences, see pp. 52–57.)

5. How does each subtopic sentence reinforce the topic sentence?

6. List at least three transitional words used in the paragraph.

7. What warning (s) does the author include?

8. List two instances of the author explaining the reason for some action or step.

9. Where has the author taken special care to describe an object or define a term? Is the description/definition helpful to the reader—why/why not?

10. List any sensory details in the paragraph (sight, sound, touch, smell, taste).

11. List at least five uses of specific language (a word that belongs to a smaller group or category of words). (For more on specific language, see pp. 78–79.)

12. Assuming that you are part of the target audience for this paragraph, based on the information and explanations provided, could you now perform this process—why/why not?

Teaching Idea
You might point out the common organizing device in process instructions of a major group of steps devoted to gathering supplies, a device used in both these student models.

EXPLAINING THE WRITING ASSIGNMENT

SUMMARIZING THE ASSIGNMENT

This chapter assignment calls for a paragraph of 250 to 300 words that explains a process or activity. Rather than illustrating a statement as we did in Chapter 7, now we will focus on *performing* a task or *understanding* how something happens. Instead of making a statement like "Home-cooked meals are far superior to restaurant food," and then explaining your belief through various examples, you might find yourself saying, "Anyone can make a great home-cooked meal if he can read a cookbook and has an hour for preparation time." Our emphasis is on doing something or understanding how it can be done.

Because we want an audience to be able to follow our instructions, specific examples, clear explanations, and well-defined terms become especially important. We will work to discover all the necessary steps for completing a process, organize the steps chronologically (usually), create controlling topic sentences, help the reader follow the steps by grouping them where appropriate, use subtopic sentences, and conclude with an expanded thought.

ESTABLISHING AUDIENCE AND PURPOSE

Teaching Idea
To reinforce the importance of audience awareness and defining of terms, you can remind students of Activity 10-3 as they read through these two process explanations. Also, you might ask students if the comparisons in the second version help with clarity.

Which of the following two process explanations is easier for you to understand?

A. Most pelecypods move by extending the slender muscular foot between the valves. Blood swells the end of the foot to anchor it in the mud or sand, and then longitudinal muscles contract to shorten the foot and pull the animal forward. In most bivalves the foot is used for burrowing, but a few creep. Some pelecypods are sessile.

B. Most creatures like clams and oysters move by extending a slender muscular part of their bodies called a foot. The foot is often smaller than a person's little finger and works a bit like a rubber band. As the animal stretches the foot from between its two shells, it digs into the sand with one end, and then moves its body forward as the "rubber band" contracts. Most of these creatures use their foot for burrowing, but a few can move across the ground. Some are permanently fixed in one spot.

If you are more comfortable with version B, it is probably because you are not a biology major and so are unfamiliar with several of the terms used in A: *pelecypods, valves, bivalves, sessile.* Whenever we write process explanations or instructions, it is critical to have a clear idea of who will be trying to follow the ideas. If terms are unfamiliar or concepts difficult to grasp, they should be defined and simplified until the reader understands them.

You may have several purposes in mind—to entertain, persuade, or inform—but explaining the process clearly should take top priority.

▶ WORKING THROUGH THE WRITING ASSIGNMENT

Discovering Ideas

As you begin to gather topic ideas for your paper, look to your own life for material. Most of us enjoy hobbies (needlepoint, baseball card collecting, surfing the Internet), sports (as participants and spectators), and special interests. We work, go to school, have families, and belong to organizations. Think about what you know well enough to explain to a person or something that you would like to know more about.

Also, because this is just a one-paragraph paper, you will need to limit the scope of your subject, often carving a smaller slice from a big topic. For instance, explaining how a space shuttle is built is too large a task, but discussing the installation of heat-shielding tiles on the nose might work well. Remember too that after you have chosen a topic, your audience definition will help you to further focus.

The topic lists that follow may help you choose a subject. Keep in mind as you skim through them that you can write a how-to-do *or* how-to-understand paper.

Caution: Limit your topic.

Teaching Idea
Try having students skim these lists and write down six topics that they know well enough already to write about. They are often surprised by how much they know.

Topic Lists

Personal Life

- How to decide on the right pet for you
- How to break a bad habit (smoking, drinking alcohol, eating unhealthy foods, etc.)
- How to ski moguls
- How to pitch a tent
- How to get up on a surfboard
- How to prepare your favorite meal
- How to get along with a neighbor you don't like
- How to handle an embarrassing moment in public
- How to organize a garage sale
- How to hold a guitar (strum a chord, fingerpick, learn a scale)

- How to housebreak a pet
- How to perform some small function with any musical instrument (hold it, clean it, tune it)
- How to lose (or gain) weight
- How to build a birdfeeder
- How to plan a great vacation
- How to find a deer in the woods
- How to get along with backpacking/hiking partners
- How to condition yourself for any demanding sport
- How to deal with losing (or winning)
- How to catch a trout (bass, bluegill, crappie, catfish, bonefish, grouper, cod)

- How to detail a car (remove a dent, tune an engine, adjust the headlights)
- How to fix a broken vacuum (or any other appliance/machine)
- How to avoid a speeding ticket after you have been pulled over

Work

- How to write a résumé
- How to fire an employee gracefully
- How to ask for a raise
- How to handle fellow employees after you have received a raise or a promotion
- How to deal with angry customers
- How to handle a "rush" of customers on the job
- How to dress appropriately for work
- How to reduce boredom on the job
- How to receive a promotion
- How to increase your gratuity as a restaurant server
- How to get along with a fellow employee you don't like
- How to protect yourself from work-related dangers

School

- How to prepare for an exam
- How to participate in class
- How to show that you are a serious student
- How to show that you don't care for the course, your fellow students, or the instructor
- How best to contribute to group work
- How to always be on time for classes
- How to select a major or certificate program
- How to take notes
- How to create a good excuse for tardiness or absence
- How to gain on the job experience through school
- How to apply for college admission or transfer
- How to balance your schedule as an athlete and student

If you have discovered several possible topics by this point, great. But before you proceed, keep the following two points in mind:

1. Be sure to work toward a process, not just an explanation. You do not want your paper to move in this direction: "Several funny things happened to our household while we were housebreaking Fluffy." Here is a better approach for a process analysis: "Housebreaking a puppy requires patience, planning, and time."

2. Choose a topic limited enough to handle in a paragraph and/or choose some small part of a larger process and/or select only the most important points. For example, do not try to instruct someone on how to play guitar, but help her learn a scale, a chord, or a method for strumming.

Prewriting Suggestions

Continuing with your prewriting activity, you will need first to decide whether to write instructions to be performed or a process to be understood. If we chose a hobby like aquariums as a general topic, we could focus it with a **how-to-do list** of possible topics—any one of which could be a separate paragraph topic, like this:

Teaching Idea
Students often try to describe too much when initially choosing a topic. You might head off their frustrated reaction of abandoning a topic by showing them how to narrow it.

Decide on how-to-do or how-to-understand.

List steps in the process.

How to

- Clean salt water/ freshwater
- Set up
- Choose fish for
- Create one without a pump
- Choose all invertebrates
- Keep children safe around

However, we might be more interested in a process paper that explains how the aquarium *functions*. In this case, we would use a prewriting method to create a list of steps in the process like the following:

- *Aquariums run on air pumps.*
- *Aquariums sometimes use external filters.*
- *Aquariums often use lights (sometimes lights simulating sunlight to stimulate plant growth).*
- *Aquariums need the correct chemical balance to keep fish alive.*
- *Air runs to a gang valve.*

- *Air pushes water up the tubes.*
- *Air runs down tubes to an undergravel filter.*
- *Air bubbles breaking at the surface of the aquarium help mix oxygen with the water.*
- *Water carries waste from the fish, trapping it at the bottom.*
- *Water moving up the tubes draws water down through the filter.*

With a list of steps in hand, we can now delete, add, and arrange material.

Prewriting—Summing Up:

1. Decide on several topics, on your own or using the Topic Lists.

2. Focus on a process limited enough to discuss in one paragraph.

3. Select a real process—one involving a sequence of steps—not a general explanation.

4. Decide on a how-to-do or how-to-understand approach to the assignment.

5. Decide on an audience.

6. Use a prewriting method to create a list of steps needed to explain your process.

JOURNAL ENTRY 10-2

List your topic, approach (to do or to understand), audience, and steps. Is the topic limited enough to handle in one paragraph? Have you mentioned all the steps your audience needs to understand this process? What steps are you not sure are needed, and/or what other steps do you think might be useful to include? Explain in a brief paragraph.

Organizing Ideas

The topic sentence is crucial in focusing process explanations and can help us weed out unnecessary steps. If we continue with our aquarium example, we might simply state: "This paper is about how an aquarium works," which would get the point across but is not terribly interesting. Instead, we might try one of the following:

1. An aquarium is a simple closed environment that can keep fish alive for many generations.

2. Have you ever wondered how fish can survive trapped in such a small space as an aquarium?

Forecasting statement

Arrange material by time (or by order of importance).

Teaching Idea
If students have listed steps in minute detail, they may have lengthy lists by now. It helps to choose several of their topics to organize on the board.

Subtopic sentences may be useful for ordering and clarifying your steps.

Grouping supplies is often needed in process instructions.

3. The watery world that captive fish survive in depends on two primary elements in a working system: an air pump and an undergravel filter.

Notice that all three topic sentences mention the topic (aquariums) and indicate that a process will be discussed while sentence three forecasts two important points.

After deciding on a rough topic sentence, we arrange steps *chronologically* and delete or add steps where needed. If we use the third topic sentence, which includes a forecasting statement, we would then decide which steps are truly part of the functioning of the aquarium and within the scope of our topic sentence.

1. Aquariums run on air pumps.
2. ~~Aquariums sometimes use external filters.~~
3. ~~Aquariums often use lights (sometimes lights simulating sunlight to stimulate plant growth).~~
4. ~~Aquariums need the correct chemical balance to keep fish alive~~
5. Air runs to a gang valve.
6. Air runs down tubes to an undergravel filter.
7. Air pushes water up the tubes.
8. Water moving up the tubes draws water down through the filter.
9. Water carries waste from the fish, trapping it at the bottom.
10. Air bubbles breaking at the surface of the aquarium help mix oxygen with the water.

Steps 2 to 4 are valuable information but are not essential to the discussion of the undergravel filter and air pump, so we would set them aside temporarily, perhaps including the information in a draft if the information seems necessary to explain or clarify one of the other steps.

The next question is whether or not to divide the material into groups. While many simple process explanations can be written with a single topic sentence followed by a list of steps to the conclusion, it is often helpful to create several **subtopic sentences** to emphasize what stage of the process you want the reader to focus on. Because the previous topic sentence has already announced two points, the air pump and undergravel filter, they would easily fall into two subtopic sentences.

If you find that your material will benefit from subtopic sentences (as the student models in the chapter have), you may find one useful grouping to be *preliminary steps* or the gathering of necessary supplies. When we set out to complete a task like baking a cake, tearing apart a carburetor, or hanging a picture, we need tools and ingredients. These are commonly listed at the beginning of process instructions. Notice how the student model "Recipe for a Red-Hot Sunday" handles this first major step.

Remember to link your sentences securely with transitions like those in the following lists and other connectors (repeat words, synonyms, pronouns, and reference to main ideas). (For a more complete list of transitions, see pp. 53–54.)

For Moving in Time			
after	first (second, etc.)	next	suddenly
afterward	immediately	now	then
at last	in the meantime	often	time passed
awhile	in the past	once	until

(continued)

For Adding Material			
again	as well as	furthermore	likewise
also	besides	in addition	moreover
and	further	last	next
For Giving Examples and Emphasis			
above all	especially	in particular	one reason
after all	for example	in truth	specifically
another	for instance	it is true	surely
For Showing Cause and Effect			
accordingly	because	hence	then
and so	consequently	since	therefore
as a result	for this reason	so	thus

Organizing—Summing Up:

1. Create a rough topic sentence to help focus your material.

2. Eliminate steps that are not essential to the process.

3. Add any steps that might still be needed.

4. Arrange the steps chronologically (or by order of importance).

5. Consider using two or three subtopic sentences to group and clarify steps.

6. Review the list of transitions (and remember the other connectors).

JOURNAL ENTRY 10-3

Write out your working topic sentence. Does it clearly indicate that your paragraph is about a process? Arrange your steps chronologically (or by order of importance), and divide them into two or three groupings if you think that your topic would benefit from this organization.

Drafting

With the preliminary work done, you are almost ready to write a first draft. But before moving ahead, take a moment to review the Drafting suggestions in Chapter 1, pp. 12–14 and to think about the following points:

1. Remember that this assignment calls for process description, explaining how some activity is actually physically performed or understood.

2. If all the steps are not included and clearly explained, you may lose your reader.

3. People need to know the why behind steps and warnings so they can follow the steps.

4. Define any word that you think might puzzle your reader.

5. The word *you* can be inappropriately used in writing, but process instructions often require this pronoun, either directly stated or implied like this: "Keep the heat at 350 degrees"—meaning *you* the reader, keep the heat under control. Another approach is to use *I* throughout. If you choose *I* instead of *you*, be careful not to switch back and forth between the two. Refer to "A Boy's Best Friend" for using *I* and "Recipe for a Red-Hot Sunday" for using *you*. The Annotated Student Model shows how to write about a process to be understood, largely avoiding both *I* and *you*.

Teaching Idea
Before students begin drafting, you might reiterate that explanations and warnings are crucial to well-written process instructions.

Teaching Idea
This is a good place to remind students to avoid omitting the article *the,* as in: "When [the] butter, sugar, and cocoa are combined. . . ."

Be consistent with pronoun use.

> **JOURNAL ENTRY 10-4**
>
> Respond to this journal entry soon after writing your first rough draft. Have you written about a process rather than simply given examples unrelated by sequence or time? Have you included a series of steps that may or may not be grouped using subtopic sentences? What part of this draft do you like best or think best fulfills the assignment instructions—why? What part do you dislike most or feel is drifting from the assignment—why? Answer in a paragraph.

Teaching Idea
Journal Entry 10-4 can give you some insight into the students' progress and is also useful to help focus group revision.

Revising Drafts

To review the detailed lists for revising drafts, turn to Chapter 4.

■ ANNOTATED STUDENT MODEL

It can be particularly useful to see where someone else has struggled through the whole process of producing a well-written paper, from the first undeveloped draft through the last polished version. If you carefully read through the Annotated Student Model, you will be able to head off many problems common to process instructions.

First-Stage Draft

Teaching Idea
You might point out that Schumann defines her audience as having little knowledge of aquariums and have students assess the clarity of her explanations based on this.

Carla Schumann decided to write about her hobby of keeping an aquarium. Although she has one twenty-gallon and two fifty-five gallon tanks at home, she realized that including this, and similar information, would distract readers from her effort to explain how an aquarium functions. To help her focus the paragraph, she selected an audience of people who do not know much about keeping fish as pets but who might like to do so.

Teaching Idea
The day before or on the day first drafts are due, try having one student read the First-Stage Draft aloud and then have another student read the Final Draft. Ask the class to characterize the two versions. What do they like about each?

Avoid shift to *you* in process to be understood.

If you have ever wondered how fish can stay alive in an aquarium, the answer is, "Easily." Almost all aquariums use a pump to push air that it sucks in from around it into the water. This pumping action helps mix the air with the water and gets rid of fish waste. You can see how the air travels first thru one or two small tubes that are attached to the pump and end up in the water. The tubes can run directly into the water but are usually connected to a valve that splits the air into separate channels. Then the plastic tubing runs down to the undergravel filter. After the air is pushed down through the risers to the bottom of the aquarium, it immediately moves upward, making it rise up the tube. As the water rises, the water nearest the undergravel filter is drawn through the gravel and filter on the bottom of the tank. This pulls all the junk out of the water and traps it within the gravel and under the filter, so the water stays clear and the bacteria down enough for the fish to live. As the water comes from the risers, it splashes around on the surface of the water in the aquarium, which in turn speeds up the mixing of oxygen into the water. This process of air mixing with water keeps the tank clean and the fish lively.

Need more specific words

Need to define terms and explain more thoroughly

Missing a step

Second-Stage Draft

When drafting process explanations, we often leave out steps or include unneeded ones, as is the case with Carla's first draft. Another common difficulty is underexplaining steps and not defining important terms. Role-playing your audience and/or having another person read the draft will help you with these common problems.

Topic sentence revised

*Explanation added

If you have ever wondered how fish can stay alive in a small glass case the answer is, "Easily." The process begins with a pump to push *ordinary room air* that it sucks in from around it into the water. This pumping action helps mix the air with the water and gets rid of fish waste. You can see how the air travels first thru one or two small tubes that are attached to the pump and end up in the water. The tubes can run directly into the water but are usually connected to a valve that splits the air into separate channels. These channels have a short length of plastic tubing connected to them. The tubing is in turn connected to thin, plastic rods that descend through larger plastic tubes that attach to the filter on the floor of the aquarium. The undergravel filter is the second most important piece of equipment in the process of keeping the water livable for the fish and clear enough for pleasant viewing. *(This simple piece of plastic covers the bottom of the aquarium, resting against the glass and is covered with a layer of gravel.) After the air is pushed down through the risers to the bottom of the aquarium, it immediately moves upward. *This creates a slight pull on the surrounding water, which causes it to rise upward through the tube. As the water rises, the water nearest the undergravel filter is drawn through the gravel and filter on the bottom of the tank. This pulls all the junk out of the water and traps it within the gravel and the filter, so the water stays clear and the bacteria down enough for the fish to live. As the water comes from the top of the risers, it splashes around on the surface of the water in the aquarium, which in turn speeds up the mixing of oxygen into the water. This simple cycling of air down to the bottom and up to the top does not account for all aquarium maintenance), but it is the most essential process in keeping captive fish alive and healthy.

Subtopic sentence clarified

Step in the process added and explained

Subtopic sentence added

*"Filter" defined

*Explanation added

Concluding sentence revised

Note the expanded thought.

Special Points to Check in Revising from First to Second Drafts

1. Check topic sentence: topic + indication of process
2. Check subtopic sentences (if applicable): connector + major step grouping
3. Check concluding sentence: connector + link to topic sentence + expanded thought
4. ~~Delete unnecessary material~~
5. <u>Add material for clarity, completeness, and emphasis (remember definitions)</u>
6. Check connectors: transitions, repeat words, synonyms, pronouns, reference to main idea

Third-Stage Draft

Teaching Idea
This Third-Stage Draft clearly illustrates how many specific words might still be needed in a developing draft to improve clarity and readability.

If you want your work to move beyond good to excellent, this third draft gives you that opportunity. With all the major material and organizational concerns taken care of, now you can improve your word choices and sentence variety and get rid of the clutter phrases that so often slip into our rough drafts.

Staying Alive

Title added

You used to connect with reader in topic sentence.

You removed to cut pronoun shift in body.

If you have ever wondered how fish can stay alive in a small glass case, for years, the answer is—easily. The process begins with a pump to push ordinary room air into the water of an aquarium. **[This air travels first thru one or two narrow clear plastic tubes that are attached to the pump, and end up in the water.]** The tubes can run directly into the ~~water~~ **aquarium,** but are usually connected to what is called a "gang valve" that splits the air into several outlets. **[These outlets have a short length of plastic tubing connected to them and the tubing in turn is connected to thin hollow plastic rods that descend through larger plastic tubes called risers , ~~connected~~ attached to the undergravel filter on the floor of the aquarium.]** The undergravel filter is the second most important piece of equipment in the process of keeping the water livable for the fish and clear enough for pleasant viewing. (This simple piece of slotted plastic covers the bottom of the ~~aquarium~~ **tank** from side to side, resting against the glass, and is covered with a one- to two-inch layer of gravel.) **[After the air is pushed down thru the risers to the bottom of the aquarium, it immediately ~~rises~~ bubbles upward, causing the surrounding water to rise ~~upward~~ through the tube.]** As some water moves toward the surface that water nearest the bottom of the tank is slowly drawn downward through the gravel layer and undergravel filter. This continual movement of water pulls all the fish waste and excess food out of the water, trapping it within the gravel and under the filter, keeping the water clear and the bacteria level low enough for the fish to survive. As the water emerges from the top of the risers, it agitates ~~and splashes~~ the surface of the water in the aquarium, in turn speeding up the absorption of needed oxygen into the water. This simple cycling of air down ~~to the bottom~~ and up ~~to the top~~ does not account for *all* aquarium maintenance (regular feeding, examining fish for illnesses, scraping algae, water changes—to name a few other chores) but it is the most essential process in keeping captive fish alive and healthy.

Sentences combined for variety and flow

More accurate words substituted

More specific words added

More specific words added

Special Points to Check in Revising from Second to Third Drafts

1. Added specific words are boxed.

2. More precise or audience-appropriate word substitutions are shaded.

3. [Sentences combined for variety are bracketed.]

4. **Synonyms and phrases replacing clutter and repeat words are bolded.**

5. ~~Unneeded words are lined through.~~

Teaching Idea
If you want to use the Final Draft as an editing aid, you can isolate several sentences in the Third-Stage Draft and have students edit them.

Final-Editing Draft

By this point Carla's draft is in great shape. Now she needs to shift into low gear, moving slowly, line by line, looking for every remaining error in grammar, spelling, and punctuation. Keeping an **Improvement Chart** will help you focus on your own **pattern errors,** an efficient way to finish this step in the process.

Staying Alive

Audience: People who might want to begin keeping fish as a hobby

Dash added for emphasis

If you have ever wondered how fish can stay alive in a small glass case, [10] for years, the answer is—easily. *The process begins with a pump to push ordinary room air into the water. The air travels first ~~thru~~ [1] through one or two narrow clear plastic tubes that are attached to the pump, [10] and end up in the water. The tubes can run directly into the water, [10] but are usually connected to what is called a "gang valve," which splits the air into several outlets. These outlets have a short length of plastic tubing connected to them, [9c] and the tubing in turn is connected to thin hollow plastic rods that descend through larger plastic tubes, [9b] called risers, attached to the undergravel filter on the floor of the aquarium. *The under-gravel filter is the second most important piece of equipment in the process of keeping the water livable for the fish and clear enough for pleasant viewing. (This simple piece of slotted plastic covers the bottom of the aquarium from side to side, resting against the glass, and is covered with a 1- to 2-inch layer of gravel.) After the air is pushed down through the risers to the bottom of the aquarium, ~~it~~ [4] the air immediately bubbles upward, causing the surrounding water to rise through the tube. As some water moves toward the surface, [9a] that water nearest the bottom of the tank is slowly drawn downward through the gravel layer and undergravel filter. This continual movement of water pulls all the fish waste and excess food out of the water, trapping it within the gravel and under the filter, keeping the water clear and the bacteria level low enough for the fish to survive. As the water emerges from the top of the risers, it agitates the surface of the water in the aquarium, in turn speeding up the absorption of needed oxygen into the water. This simple cycling of air down and up does not account for *all* aquarium maintenance (regular feeding, examining fish for illnesses, scraping algae, water changes—to name a few other chores), [9a] but it is the most essential process in keeping captive fish alive and healthy.

Parentheses used to add definition

Italicizing a word for emphasis

Carla Schumann

Key: Special Points to Check in Editing Final Drafts

1. Spelling	5. Sentence fragments	9. Common comma categories
2. Sound-alike words	6. Comma splices/run-ons	a. Introduce
		b. Enclose/end
3. Missing words	7. Capitalizations	c. Divide
4. Wrong words	8. Apostrophes	10. Unneeded commas

Final-Draft Checklist

Before you turn in your final draft, take a few minutes to review this checklist. You may find that, as careful as you think you have been, you still have missed a point or two—or three. (For more on any of these points, see Chapter 4.)

— 1. Have you chosen a process—either how-to-do or how-to-understand?

— 2. How effective is your topic sentence?

— 3. Have you listed enough steps for your reader to complete or understand the process?

— 4. Have you clearly arranged your main examples—either by time or importance?

— 5. Have you written a subtopic sentence (if needed) to introduce each step grouping?

— 6. Are your examples relevant and thoroughly explained, giving reasons, warnings, and definitions

— 7. How well connected are all the sentences within the paragraph?

— 8. How effective is your concluding sentence?

— 9. How well have you used specific language?

—10. Are you choosing the most active verbs and "-ing" words to describe action?

—11. Have you tried using a metaphor or simile?

—12. Are the sentences in your paragraph varied in length and beginnings?

—13. Have you repeated a word or phrase so often that it becomes noticeable or included words that serve no purpose?

—14. Have you written a title—an interesting one—for the paper? (Check capitalizations.)

—15. Have you prepared your paper according to the format expected by your instructor? (Check to see if you need a title page, be sure to double-space, leave at least a 1-inch margin, use a 12-point font, and be sure to type or word process.)

—16. Have you edited your work as closely as you know how to (including having at least one other person—classmate, friend, family member—proofread closely? Have you checked your **Improvement Chart** for your pattern errors so that you can look for them specifically?

—17. Have you looked for the following errors: spelling, sound-alike words, missing words, wrong words, sentence fragments, comma splices/run-ons, capitalizations, apostrophes, the Big Three comma categories, and unnecessary commas?

CHAPTER SUMMARY

1. Process analysis examines an activity so that we might understand or perform it.

2. There are countless activities surrounding us, and knowing how to understand, explain, and do them is a basic survival skill.

3. Writing for a specific audience is critical in process analysis.

4. Process instructions require a complete list of steps.

5. Each step or suggestion must be explained clearly and thoroughly.

6. Wherever needed, be sure to provide warnings.

7. Clarifying terms is essential in process analysis. When in doubt, define.

8. Avoid "Dick-and-Jane" sentence patterns. Polish your draft for sentence variety.

9. Most process instructions are organized chronologically.

10. Grouping steps within a larger process is often necessary.

11. The topic sentence in a process analysis should interest the reader, mention the topic, and indicate that an explanation of how to do or to understand is forthcoming.

12. Writing is never complete until it has gone through several revisions and careful editing.

■ ALTERNATE WRITING ASSIGNMENTS

As we have discussed, there are countless processes to write about and many ways to approach them. If you choose one of the following topics, keep these points in mind:

- Process papers can be either practical instructions for physically completing a task or a somewhat more general explanation of how something functions.

- Process analysis requires listing and thoroughly explaining all necessary steps and giving warnings.

- Any words unfamiliar to your audience should be defined.

- Begin with a clear topic sentence, connect your sentences securely, and end with a concluding sentence that expands the thought.

1. Write a how-to-do paper for a child. Writing for children is particularly challenging because they have not yet reached an adult's level of knowledge and most of the time cannot comprehend adult-level instructions. So decide on a target age group, say, four to six, seven to nine, or ten to twelve, and then tell them how to complete an age-appropriate task. For example, how would you explain to a five-year-old "straightening up" his room? Do you expect him to put every toy away in its place—toy box, drawer, shelf? Are all clothes to be neatly folded, hung, and shelved? Or would this be expecting too much from the audience? For small children a more modest goal might be enough, perhaps just getting the big toys into one box and the small toys into another.

2. Write a process paper that tells someone how to fail at something. You might handle this assignment in a humorous way. For example, you could give someone advice on how to fail his composition class (!), lose a job, or break off a relationship the wrong way. Instead of giving someone *else* instructions, you could describe something that you have done poorly, giving all the "steps" that went into the failing. If you choose a topic like a mishandled breakup, you might want to illustrate it in part by detailing a scene from your life. For instance, perhaps you took your significant other out to dinner and dropped the bomb on him or her there, hoping the public location would help ease you out of it, but then watched as the situation escalated out of control. Be sure not just to tell a story. Include steps that led to the disaster.

3. Help a reader to annoy someone. We all have people in our lives who irritate us, people who we would like to irritate back. This could be your chance. Decide on someone you have been bothered by for awhile and now would like to repay the favor. For example, you might have a next-door neighbor who deserves to hear your stereo rattle his windows at 3:00 A.M. every weekend or to hear you mow the lawn several times a week around midnight. If your process for annoying involves only one prank, be sure to detail how to prepare it step by step, probably in chronological order. If you have several evil ideas in mind, consider arranging the paper from least to most dramatic.

4. Give someone *how-to-do* advice on getting a job or help someone *understand* how she might prepare herself for a career. In the first instance you would select a job that you know something about, perhaps your current one. Try to remember how you prepared yourself to get the job. How did you present yourself? Did you write a cover letter and résumé? Did you just walk in off the street? How did you handle the interview? What advice might you give on researching a company, rehearsing for the interview, dressing, or presenting yourself during the interview?

If you would rather discuss general preparation for a career, you could help someone else prepare for the career you are currently working toward.

5. Taking either a how-to-do or how-to-understand approach, help someone plan a special occasion. Most of us have been involved—either voluntarily or by being drafted—in the planning process of a special event. Perhaps you put together a graduation party; maybe you organized a birthday party for your five-year-old son and twelve friends at Chuck E. Cheese's; perhaps this year your extended family will descend on your house for Thanksgiving? To prepare for the event, you need to know who will be there so you can anticipate what food, entertainment, and activities to provide. Here are some factors to consider in organizing your event: preparing a guest list; contacting the guests; arranging a location; deciding what, if anything, the guests should bring; deciding on a time limit; buying and preparing food and beverages; figuring out seating; and bribing people to help with the cleanup.

CHAPTER 11

Explaining Similarities and Differences

Building Comparison and Contrast

Discovering Comparisons

Having a Point

Organizing Comparisons

Developing Comparisons

Connecting Examples

Polishing Examples

 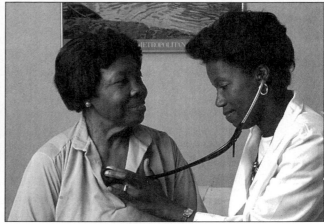

WHAT ARE WE TRYING TO ACHIEVE AND WHY?

Setting the Stage

In the pictures above do you notice any similarities or differences? Both illustrations show a medical examination underway. A doctor uses a stethoscope to check a patient's heart. Both physicians are African American, both patients appear relaxed, and both pairs are alone in their office. On the other hand, there are some obvious differences: adults versus children, female versus male, two African Americans versus mixed racial pairing, and a real doctor versus a child who is role-playing. Whenever we notice similarities and differences between two people, places, events, objects, or ideas we are comparing and contrasting them—this is the assignment for Chapter 11.

Linking to Previous Experience

We all have a wealth of experience with comparing and contrasting. From the two-year-old child who compares two video covers and picks the one that most resembles her much-loved *Aladdin* film, to the married couple comparing and contrasting houses as they search for their first home, we use comparison and contrast daily. On the job we discover similarities and differences as quickly as possible when we meet people. If the new boss begins to seem like the tyrant from a year ago that you would rather forget, you might soon find yourself looking for another place to work. In school you are asked to compare historical figures like George Washington to Thomas Jefferson, Ulysses S. Grant to Robert E. Lee, or Elizabeth I to Mary Queen of Scots. And in this text you have already practiced comparison in several ways, including the use of metaphors and similes.

As we move through *A Writer's Workshop*, we will continue to see how comparison/contrast works with the other patterns of development to help us explore our ideas and communicate more effectively with others.

Determining the Value

Comparison and contrast skills help us every day to avoid poor choices, like buying overripe bananas or avocados at the supermarket. In larger, more important ways, too, we need to compare and contrast critically to live a happier life. If we judge correctly from the start, we are more likely to avoid that unsuitable college, dead-end job, or failing marriage.

Developing the habit of close comparing also improves our thinking and broadens our perspective. Recognizing that the numbers 0 to 9 are to arithmetic what the notes A to G are to music, we might feel less intimidated trying to read music. Seeing ice-skating's similarities to a sport we already practice, like roller-skating, might help us decide to try it for the first time. As we move into the wider world of human experience, we can see how similar people are: African, Asian, Hispanic, European, and Native Americans in our own country, all the nationalities and ethnic groups around the earth. Learning to compare, to see ourselves in other people, can help us become more tolerant human beings.

Teaching Idea
You might use Journal Entry 11-1 in class to discuss how common comparison/contrast is and to reinforce the value of having a point to make.

JOURNAL ENTRY 11-1

Think for a moment about instances during the past week when you have compared or contrasted something or when you have heard someone else doing so (a friend, a radio announcer, a teacher). What was being compared—two people, places, events? What was the reason for the comparison—to give information, to entertain, to persuade? Did the comparison accomplish its purpose? Summarize one instance of comparison or contrast from school, work, and home.

DEVELOPING SKILLS, EXPLORING IDEAS IN COMPARISON/CONTRAST PARAGRAPHS

To write successful comparison/contrast papers, you will find the following suggestions helpful:

1. Make a meaningful comparison or contrast.

2. Make an interesting comparison or contrast.

3. Develop each topic thoroughly.

4. Use transitions and other connectors.

The following activities will give you some practice with these points so that you will be able to move more easily into your own papers.

Groundwork for Activity 11-1: Making a Meaningful Comparison or Contrast

In all of our writing projects, we want to establish a purpose and point as quickly as possible. Lacking either or both, we are likely to wander all over the landscape, getting nowhere fast. Can you determine the writer's point from the following outline?

Topic sentence: Ford and Chevy pickup trucks have a lot in common.

- Fords have engines, and so do Chevies.

- Fords have four wheels and so do Chevies.

- Fords have beds in the back and so do Chevies.

- Fords have cabs in the front and so do Chevies.

- Fords have windshield wipers and so do Chevies.

- Fords come in many colors and so do Chevies.

Concluding sentence: I think you can see that Ford and Chevy pickups are similar.

If you said, "Yes, yes, I see what the writer is trying to say—many times over. Now, so what?" your reaction is understandable. Merely choosing a topic and compiling a list of similarities is not enough. You must have something to say about the comparison if you want to hold a reader's interest. In the Ford/Chevy comparison the author could focus his paragraph with several main points, including one of the following:

Teaching Idea
Activity 11-1 uses several examples with a persuasive intent, but you might remind students that their purpose may also be to inform or entertain.

- Ford and Chevy trucks are so similar that price should decide which you buy.
- Although Ford and Chevy trucks are similar in many ways, Ford has a better warranty.
- Although Ford and Chevy trucks are similar in many ways, Chevies have a better maintenance record.

Collaborative

Activity 11-1: Making a Meaningful Comparison or Contrast

After reading the groundwork for this activity, discuss the topics below with group members, and then list several similarities and differences. Now, write out three different statements that would give each topic a point. After you have listed three possibilities, compose a topic sentence based on *one* of them. (Be sure to indicate in the topic sentence that you intend to compare *or* contrast.) (For more on topic sentences, see pp. 36–40.)

Example: Topic: jogging vs. bicycling

Pointless topic sentence: Both jogging and bicycling are forms of aerobic exercise.

Points that *could* be made about this topic:

A. *Jogging is worse for a person's body than bicycling.*

B. *Bicycling is more dangerous than jogging.*

C. *Bicycling requires more dedication than jogging.*

Possible topic sentence: *Although jogging is a convenient and inexpensive form of exercise, it is far harder on a person's body than bicycling.*

(paragraph of ____*contrast*____)

Answers will vary

1. Topic: men vs. women

   Pointless topic sentence: Men are a lot different than women.

   Points that could be made about this topic:

   A. *As a rule men assert themselves more in conversation than do women.*

   B. *Overall, women have better manual dexterity than men do.*

   C. *Most men have a different management style than women.*

   Possible topic sentence: *Whereas many men have a confrontational, authoritarian management style, women tend to manage their subordinates through dialogue and consensus.* (paragraph of ____*comparison*____)

2. Topic: college classes vs. high school classes

   Pointless topic sentence: Both college classes and high school classes require homework.

   Points that could be made about this topic:

   A. *Colleges offer a dangerous freedom seldom found in high schools.*

   B. *College professors are less concerned about student success than are high school teachers.*

   C. *A good student in high school is likely to be a good student in college.*

   Possible topic sentence: *The freedom in college classrooms as opposed to high school classes makes a college education much more difficult.*

   (paragraph of ____*contrast*____)

3. Topic: infatuation vs. love

Pointless topic sentence: Infatuation is different than real love.

Points that could be made about this topic:

A. _Infatuation requires a blindness not found in real love._

B. _Infatuation creates a fantasy image of the opposite sex that real love does not need._

C. _Infatuation insists that two people cling to one another whereas love allows them to live separately._

Possible topic sentence: _While infatuation sometimes leads to love, the former thrives on self-deception while the latter grows through honesty._ (paragraph of ___contrast___)

4. Topic: college vs. a business

Pointless topic sentence: Colleges are much different than businesses.

Points that could be made about this topic:

A. _Colleges and businesses are alike in that both produce a product._

B. _Colleges and businesses are similar in that both have an operating budget and must stick close to it to keep functioning._

C. _Colleges are similar to businesses in that the "consumers" must be satisfied or both institutions will fold._

Possible topic sentence: _The primary difference between colleges and businesses is their goal—businesses exist to make profit; colleges exist to help people learn._ (paragraph of ___contrast___)

Teaching Idea
You might point out to students that choosing a less-obvious comparison may make the paragraph more interesting not only to read, but also to write.

Avoid obvious comparisons.

Groundwork for Activity 11-2: Making an Interesting Comparison or Contrast

Once we have a topic, it is sometimes tempting to settle for the obvious list of likenesses or differences. For instance, in comparing a rowboat to a canoe, we might easily list points of similarity, such as that both vessels carry people on water, require muscle power to move, can be used for fishing, are easy to transport, and are found on lakes and rivers. However, as in Activity 11-1, choosing an obvious list of points to compare or contrast often leads to boring reading.

To minimize a possibly dull approach to a topic, follow this rule of thumb: If two topics seem alike, try to contrast them. If two topics seem different, try to compare them. If we made a point about the rowboat/canoe comparison, say, that rowboats are superior to canoes for fishing, then we could build a list of interesting differences to help support that claim: rowboats are more stable, provide more room for casting, will support more powerful motors, hold more gear, and are easier to anchor in moving water.

Collaborative

Activity 11-2: Making an Interesting Comparison or Contrast

For each of the following paired topics, create a list of similarities and differences, decide which list could make the most interesting paragraph, and then write out a topic sentence that expresses some point.

Example: Topic: winter vs. summer

Differences		Similarities
Winter	Summer	Winter and Summer
Cold	Hot	Extreme temperatures
Snow	Rain	People need shelter
Plants sleep	Plants awake	Some pleasant days
Short days	Long days	School break
Animals scarce	Animals plentiful	Drought

Most interesting list: similarities

Topic sentence: Although there are some obvious differences between winter and summer, the weather extremes affect people in much the same way.

Answers will vary.

1. Topic: high school vs. college

Differences		Similarities
High School	**College**	**High School and College**
Few electives	Many electives	Both four years
Long class days	Short class days	Both have teachers
Parental supervision	Self-supervision	Both have a core curriculum
Less expensive	More expensive	Both award valuable credentials
Less freedom	More freedom	Both receive governmental financial support

Most interesting list: differences

Topic sentence: Although both high schools and colleges deal in paper, pencils, and textbooks, the degree of freedom in each makes them different in some fundamental ways.

2. Topic: beach vacation vs. mountain vacation

Differences		Similarities
Beach	**Mountain**	**Beach and Mountain**
Warm	Cold	Night life
Lazy	Active	Dangers—sunburn
Sea level	Altitude	Beautiful scenery
Swimming	Skiing	Distant locations
Wildlife	Wildlife	Expensive

Most interesting list: similarities

Topic sentence: Although some might think that a beach and a mountain vacation have little in common, the exotic locations, beautiful scenery, and night life make them seem similar in significant ways.

3. Topic: river vs. lake

Differences		Similarities
River	**Lake**	**River and Lake**
Running water	Still water	Activities: boating, swimming, fishing
Narrow	Wide	Animal life: fish, reptiles, amphibians, insects
Shallow	Deep	Purpose: relaxation
Current	Seldom a current (dams)	Proximity
Vessels	Vessels	Inexpensive to enjoy

Most interesting list: _similarities_

Topic sentence: _On the surface a lake and a river may not seem to have much in common, but in the most important way—how people enjoy themselves—they are much alike._

4. Topic: smoking cigarettes vs. standing in a burning house

Differences		Similarities
Smoking Cigarettes	**Standing in House**	**Smoking Cigarettes and Standing in House**
Pleasurable	Frightening	Smoke inhalation
Voluntary	Involuntary	Burns
Less expensive	Major expense	Disfiguring of the body
Social	Non-social	Foul smell
Addiction	Accident	Painful death

Most interesting list: _similarities_

Topic sentence: _Being trapped in a burning building—aside from being involuntary—has much in common with smoking cigarettes._

Teaching Idea
Remind students that any of the activity topics could serve as paper topics and that working through the activities is useful prewriting.

Groundwork for Activity 11-3: Developing Topics Thoroughly

After we have a meaningful and interesting comparison or contrast topic, we need to develop it through layering examples, details, and explanations (for more on this, see Chapter 3, pp. 41–43). To expand the winter/summer comparison from Activity 11-2, we would first list the topic sentence:

- *Although there are some obvious differences between winter and summer, the weather extremes affect people in much the same way.*

The topic sentence predicts a *comparison* paragraph, so we need a list of *main* examples to show how "weather extremes affect people" and then a list of *second-level* examples to develop the main examples.

Main Examples

1. *People are uncomfortable from weather extremes.*

2. *People avoid strenuous outdoor exercise.*

3. *People hide indoors where there is heating or air conditioning.*

4. *People become sick or even die from heat or cold.*

Teaching Idea
To help get students more
actively involved in Activity
11-3, as you read through the
Groundwork, ask them to
extend any of the second-level
examples.

Second-Level Examples ("How can I further explain each main example?")

1. *Uncomfortable: profuse sweating or itching; dry, chapped skin*

2. *Avoid outdoor exercise: few joggers or cyclists, working out on treadmills*

3. *Hide indoors: going to shopping malls and movies, eating indoors*

4. *Sickness and death: dehydration and heat stroke, frostbite and freezing to death*

These examples offer some solid raw material for a comparison paragraph. When we begin drafting, of course, we may add additional examples along with supporting details (how hot? 105 degrees; how cold? 20 degrees below zero; etc.).

Collaborative

Activity 11-3: Developing Topics Thoroughly

After reading the groundwork for this activity, choose one of the topics you worked with in Activity 11-2. Discuss with group members what kinds of examples would help develop your topic sentence, and use an invention strategy such as listing to create several main supporting examples. Next, list at least one second-level example for each main example. (For more on developing examples, see Chapter 3, pp. 41–48).

Answers will vary.
Topic from Activity 11-2: *cigarette smoking vs. being trapped in a burning building*

Topic sentence from Activity 11-2: *Being trapped in a burning building—aside from being involuntary—has much in common with smoking cigarettes.*

Main examples:

1. *Foul smell*

2. *Smoke inhalation*

3. *Burns and disfiguring of the body*

4. *Painful death*

Second-level examples:

1. *Foul smell: smoke saturates clothing, hair, furniture; smoke smell clings to body*

2. *Smoke inhalation: clouds of hot, toxic gases breathed in; painful coughing; lungs damaged*

3. *Burns and disfiguring of the body: burns on clothing, hands; discoloration of skin; lines in face*

4. *Painful death: causes: lung cancer, anoxia, burns; hospitalization, lingering as friends watch helplessly*

Groundwork for Activity 11-4: Using Transitions and Other Connectors

Comparison and contrast writing particularly needs transitional words and other connectors to signal the move from one part of a comparison to the next. While many kinds of transitions will be useful in your paper, those listed below apply especially to comparison/contrast. (For more on sentence connectors, see Chapter 3, pp. 52–57.)

Teaching Idea
You might want to point out the tone difference in using transitions like *nevertheless,* *on the contrary,* and *however* versus *but, yet,* and *though.*

For Comparing			
alike	both	like	resembling
also	in the same way	likewise	similarly
For Contrasting			
after all	dissimilar	nevertheless	though
although	even though	on the contrary	unlike
but	however	on the other hand	whereas
difference	in contrast	otherwise	yet
differs from	in spite of	still	

Activity 11-4: Using Transitions and Other Connectors

In the sentences that follow, select a suitable transitional word or words from the two lists above, and then write the transition in the blank.

Answers will vary.

1. I liked going to camp when I was young, _____even though_____ I missed my family a lot.

2. _____Although_____ living on my own has its advantages, it _____also_____ has its downside.

3. _____Nevertheless_____ living with a roommate can be a problem.

4. _____Still_____ many people prefer to live on the Plaza.

5. _____In spite of_____ all the preelection promises, I still don't expect much government reform.

6. The helicopter, _____however_____, is superior to the plane in at least two respects.

7. Most of my friends don't like museums, _____yet_____ I do.

8. _____Unlike_____ Carlo, Tony is more energetic and enjoys being around people.

9. Bruce thinks I prefer electric guitar. _____However_____ I would rather hear acoustic.

10. Eleanor is going to medical school _____in the same way_____ her mother did.

▶ COMPARISON AND CONTRAST PARAGRAPHS: LOOKING CLOSELY AT STUDENT MODELS

The three paragraphs that follow will help you write effective comparison/contrast papers. As you read through them, look for the four points we have practiced in the Developing Skills section. You will notice that the first model, "Two Different Worlds," illustrates the **block** method of organizing while both "Breakin' Through" and "The Joy of Simple Living" illustrate the **point-by-point** method of overall arrangement. (These methods are discussed at greater length under Organizing Ideas, pp. 247–249.)

▶ Prereading Exploration for "Two Different Worlds"

Dave Harrison chose a topic that he felt strongly about for this paragraph contrasting the work demands in high school versus those in college. He thought that college-bound high school seniors would be most interested in the information.

Teaching Idea
The prereading questions for "Two Different Worlds" can stimulate some interesting class discussion and help students with topic ideas.

Before you begin the paragraph, think for a moment about your expectations of what college would be like, comparing them to your current reality. Have there been any great surprises this semester? Have you changed your views about education, other people, or yourself since you started? If so, list your viewpoint—before and after—and consider exploring the differences in a paragraph of contrast.

_____

_____

_____

Two Different Worlds

I never realized how easy high school was until my first semester in college—that's when I hit the wall. High school, for the most part, was a breeze. I had no worries about homework, papers, or tests. When I knew a test was coming, I would read my notes and then ace the exam. At that time I thought I had it rough, although I probably only spent thirty total hours on homework my whole senior year. The only paper that was semidifficult was my government research essay. As a junior I was assigned a paper to write on any topic, the only requirements being to make it five to seven pages long and cite my work. I chose to do my report on the extinction of the dinosaurs. This was an acceptable topic for my *government* research paper. I had an entire semester to finish the paper, and it still about killed me. Looking back now, I see just how easy high school was, but the level of work amplified when I started college. I had fewer classes but ten times the homework of high school. I now know what work is. Every week I have completed lab reports for Intro to Electronics, done Internet research projects, or turned out papers for my writing class. On top of doing my lab reports, I spend from six to eight hours a week doing the labs. Late nights are not uncommon anymore. Some nights I have been known to stay up till two in the morning, and sometimes I never sleep, period. Adjusting to the workload from high school to college has been a shock, and I have learned that if a student wants to learn and do well in school, he or she has to be committed.

David Harrison

Postreading Analysis

Teaching Idea
Throughout the discussion of comparison/contrast as a controlling form for a paragraph or essay, it is worth reiterating that writers often *briefly* compare or contrast along with the other patterns of development to clarify ideas.

Comparison and contrast papers use either point-by-point or block organization (see Organizing Ideas, pp. 247–249). The point-by-point method discusses one major example for each topic and then moves on to the next major example. The block method states one or more major points or main examples for one topic and then switches to the other topic, repeating the discussion of main points.

"Two Different Worlds" uses the block method, as you will see in the roughly fifty/fifty split between high school in the first half of the paragraph and college in the second half. In this paper Dave focuses on one primary point—workload—developing his **single focus** in some depth through several examples. However, he might have chosen several main points to contrast between high school and college, for instance, workload, kinds of teachers, and friendliness of students, still using the block method (see "The Joy of Simple Living" Block Method, p. 248). If you want to develop a single point in depth for each topic, the block method is the best choice for arrangement.

choose one or the other, decide on the block or point-by-point method of arrangement, and then develop the topics with specific examples and vivid details.

As in our other assignment chapters, we will begin with a topic sentence that clearly states what will follow in the paragraph—in this case two subjects being compared or contrasted for some *reason*—and then we will introduce each major example with a subtopic sentence. The final sentence should link to the topic sentence and expand the paragraph's main point.

ESTABLISHING AUDIENCE AND PURPOSE

By this point in the semester, you may feel that thinking about an audience before drafting is a good idea. While almost anyone can gather a few related ideas and arrange them in a passably clear paper, to select the most interesting and revealing examples is more challenging. If you have a point to make in your comparing and contrasting and a sense for someone who might care to read your paragraph, then you stand a better chance of making the work exciting—both for you and your audience. As you read the student models, look closely at the target audiences mentioned in the Prereading Explorations. Do you agree that the papers would be interesting to the stated audience?

As usual you may have several purposes in mind as you write—to entertain, persuade, or inform—but explaining the similarities or differences should be your top priority.

WORKING THROUGH THE WRITING ASSIGNMENT

Discovering Ideas

Because comparing and contrasting are such everyday processes, there are many topics to draw from. You might be interested in two people, places, or events. Or you might want to look closely at two objects, say, an oak tree and a rose, and think about their relationship to one another. Perhaps you feel like doing some introspection and want to compare one period of your life with another? The topic choices are limited only by your imagination and what you can develop in a single paragraph.

Try to resist the temptation to choose the first or easiest-sounding topic. Look for one that you care about enough to make interesting. If you really want to discuss two similar family pets, say, a German shepherd and a Labrador retriever, surprise your reader by contrasting the animals. Because a dog and a cat on the surface seem so different, try comparing them.

However, be careful not to choose two subjects that are so unlike that a person cannot make a reasonable comparison between them. For example, a TV and a blender have little in common except that they both need electricity to run. A horse and a horsefly share some common characteristics of all living creatures, but it would be a stretch to compare them in a paragraph. It is all right to work with an "apples and oranges" comparison—and may make for a more interesting paper—but be cautious of choosing topics so unrelated that you cannot make a meaningful point about them.

The Topic Lists that follow may help you choose a subject. Remember that you might compare *or* contrast.

> Search for an interesting topic, and try for a surprising slant on it.

> Caution: choose topics that can reasonably be compared.

> **Teaching Idea**
> Some students will enjoy the creative challenge in trying to make unlikely comparisons seem likely. It is worth a few minutes of class time to model how an "unlikely" comparison can be developed.

Topic Lists: Compare or Contrast

Personal Life

- Pets: dog/cat, fish/turtle, parakeet/boa constrictor
- Cars: Camry/Taurus, SUV/van, Miata/MG
- Clothing: down jacket/fiberfill, silk blouse/cotton, Adidas tennis shoes/Reebok

- Jewelry: man's/woman's, child's/adult's, expensive/cheap, tasteful/garish
- Hair styles: long/short, man's/woman's, labor intensive/easy
- Consumer services: MCI/Sprint, two cable providers, Yahoo/Web Crawler
- Films: <u>Armageddon</u>/<u>Deep Impact</u>, <u>Mission to Mars</u>/<u>Armageddon</u>, <u>Alien</u> /<u>Abyss</u>
- Cultural traditions: Italian wedding/Jewish wedding, Irish funeral/Japanese funeral
- Family members: brother/sister, mother/father, aunt/uncle
- Food: Vietnamese/Thai, Creole/Italian, German/French, baseball park/movie theater
- Homes: childhood home/current home, house/apartment, mobile home/fixed home
- Locations: town/city, United States/Korea, East Coast/Midwest, California/Kansas

School

- Stages of education: high school/college, elementary/college, K/high school
- Groups: football team/soccer team, marching band/choir, athletes/debate team
- Colleges: your college/any other, community college/university
- High schools: your high school/any other, U.S. high school/any other country
- Teachers: senior English/college composition, geometry/algebra, history /speech
- Courses: composition/speech, nursing/nutrition, travel/hospitality management
- Examinations: multiple-choice/short essay, midterms/finals, pop quizzes/take-home

Work

- Jobs: mowing lawns/waiting tables, military/civilian, clerical/manual labor
- Employers: hard driving/easy going, friendly/distant, generous/penny pinching
- Employees: talented/bumbling, friendly/aloof, responsible/unreliable
- Potential careers: electrical engineering/computer science, nursing/respiratory therapy, elementary education/secondary education
- Working conditions: current job/past job, indoors/outdoors, stress level for job A/B
- Losing a job: easy way/hard way, justly/unjustly, one that mattered/one that did not
- Part-time to full-time employment: pluses and minuses of any part- to full-time job

Prewriting Suggestions

After you have selected several topics from the lists and/or from your own imagination, the next step is to prewrite to generate ideas and focus. It is important to have a point to make in your comparison or contrast, and you might find that a general cluster will help you determine what you want to say. For example, if we chose a topic like town versus city living, we could begin with the question "What comes to mind when I think about both towns and cities?" and then fashion a general cluster like the following:

A pointless comparison is painful to write and to read.

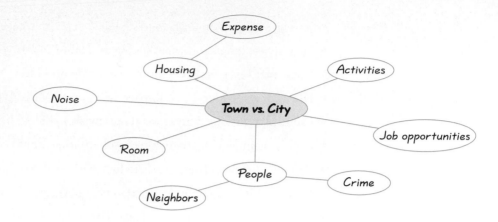

With some ideas in hand, we might then use listing to look at both the differences and similarities.

Differences		Similarities
Town	**City**	
Quieter/peaceful	More noisy	Both can be noisy
Fewer people	More crowded	People can be a problem in both
Friendlier people	Less friendly	People can be helpful in both
More living space	Less living space	Can be room enough in both
Less crime	More crime	Some crime in both
Lower cost of living	Higher cost of living	People cope with expenses in both
Lower salaries	Higher salaries	People earn an income in both
Fewer activities	More activities	Many similar activities

These kinds of lists can help focus your paper. Think about both similarities and differences, and then choose the list that seems most interesting to you. The author of the Annotated Student Model, "The Joy of Simple Living," chose differences for her paragraph, focusing on three primary examples to contrast her experiences with towns and cities.

Prewriting—Summing Up:

1. Decide on several topics, on your own or using the Topic Lists.

2. Ask yourself if you have a reason or point to make about the topics.

3. Use a prewriting technique to discover both similarities and differences.

4. Look to your lists to see if they help you with focus and a point.

5. Choose a topic interesting to you and to an audience.

6. Choose either to compare *or* contrast your topic.

JOURNAL ENTRY 11-2

List the topic that you are leaning toward. Write out lists of differences and similarities. Which side will make the most interesting paper to you and an audience? Who besides your instructor do you think might like to read about your topic? Why would the audience be interested? How will you limit the subject so it can be sufficiently developed within a single paragraph?

Organizing Ideas

Words for indicating comparison or contrast in your topic sentence

If you have not done so, now is the time to write out a topic sentence, one that includes the topic, your point, and an indication of contrast or comparison. Words like the following help indicate likenesses—*same, similar, alike, resembling, both, also*—or differences—*different, unlike, dissimilar, opposite, although, whereas*.

If your first rough topic sentence reads like this: "Towns are different than cities," be wary. You probably have not yet decided on a point for the comparison. Instead, go back to your prewriting lists and see if the examples suggest a point. Using our town/city list, we might compose topic sentences like the following:

Topic sentence = topic + point + comparison or contrast

1. City living offers <u>cultural advantages</u> that cannot be duplicated in small towns.

2. Although cities offer many cultural advantages, small towns offer a <u>sense of community</u> that a city cannot easily duplicate.

3. Although small towns often offer a strong sense of community, cities offer many more <u>economic opportunities</u>.

Forecasting of three main examples

4. Both cities and small towns have their merits, but <u>for raising a family</u>, a small town is better in at least three ways: more room, more peace and quiet, and friendlier people.

Notice that each topic sentence predicts a different focus, each of which is underlined, and each sentence tells the reader to expect, in this case, a paragraph of contrast. If you prefer, you might try a forecasting statement, shaded in sentence four.

Usually arrange main examples by order of importance.

Your overall organizing of examples will probably be by order of importance, but you also need to decide on **block** or **point-by-point** arrangement. A block form calls for all points stated about one subject first and then, roughly midway through the paragraph, the same ones restated for the second subject. The point-by-point method mentions one point at a time about each subject, in effect creating several subsections or units of thought in each paragraph. When you begin each major example for either organizational method, you should use a **subtopic sentence**, just as we have done in Chapters 7 to 10. Below you will see an example of both block and point-by-point organization, using the town/city topic.

Teaching Idea
To help students understand block versus point-by-point comparison, put one or two of their topics on the board and have the class arrange them using both methods.

Small Town vs. City

Block	Point by Point
Topic sentence: _____	Topic sentence: _____
I. Small town	I. Space for the children to play
1. Space for the children to play	A. Small town
2. Peaceful for the whole family	B. City
3. Relationships with the neighbors	
	II. Peaceful for the whole family
II. City	A. Small town
1. Space for the children to play	B. City
2. Peaceful for the whole family	
3. Relationships with the neighbors	III. Relationships with the neighbors
	A. Small town
	B. City
Concluding sentence: _____	Concluding sentence: _____

The block illustration above divides a paragraph, the first half discussing three points about *small town* living and the second half discussing the same three points about *city* living. The point-by-point method takes the same three points and discusses them one at a time in relation to both town *and* city. For a one-paragraph assignment you might use either method. However, when you begin writing longer essays, you are more likely to choose the point-by-point method over block for the sake of clarity. Imagine a reader trying to follow both sides of a comparison when the first half of the paper is 1,000 words long! By the time he is part way through the second half of the essay, the reader may well have lost track of important ideas in the first half. You will also notice either point-by-point or block order *within* various paragraphs of longer essays, rather than arranging the entire essay as one or the other.

One reason for selecting a block pattern is to develop only a single point in more depth for two subjects, rather than developing several points in less detail. The student model "Two Different Worlds," p. 241, illustrates this block approach.

In the Annotated Student Model at the end of this chapter, you can read the fully developed version of "The Joy of Simple Living." But to help us understand the two basic patterns for arranging examples in a comparison/contrast paper, we can look closely at the two simplified forms below, the first block, and the second point by point.

Block Arrangement

Mentions all points about *one* subject and then switches to the other subject, again mentioning the same points.

Having had the opportunity to live in both cities and small towns, I find that I prefer town living for raising a family.

First, my children need space to run and play. In the town of Acton, Massachusetts, I found a spacious home on three-fourths of an acre with additional surrounding land. Also, life in Acton was peaceful and quiet. With fewer cars, we rarely heard "city" noises. Instead, the nights seemed filled with soft breezes in the treetops. But what the whole family liked most about Acton were the friendly people. The children found playmates lined up on our front sidewalk, and my husband and I mixed easily with the townsfolk. They were good people who would go out of their way to help.

On the other hand, when I found my home in Geneva, Switzerland, it was small with a tiny backyard. The children had to play in a parking lot, which frightened me, thinking of the accidents that could happen. Geneva was filled with the sounds of people coming and going in the streets, talking loudly, and sometimes shouting. Also, I found that people in the city were less helpful.

Of course I have had many good experiences in cities as well as these bad ones, but for anyone raising a family, I recommend the slower pace and neighborliness of a town over a city anytime.

Point-by-Point Arrangement

Mentions a point about both subjects *together* and then moves to another point about both subjects together.

Having had the opportunity to live in both cities and small towns, I find that I prefer town living for raising a family.

First, my children need space to run and play. In the town of Acton, Massachusetts, I found a spacious home on three-fourths of an acre with additional surrounding land. On the other hand, when I found my home in Geneva, Switzerland, it was small with a tiny backyard. The children had to play in a parking lot, which frightened me, thinking of the accidents that could happen.

Block pattern works particularly well for single-focus papers.

Teaching Idea
Remind students that the paragraph models illustrating organization on pp. 248–249 are *shortened* versions of the final draft.

Topic sentence

Space, peace, neighbors in the **town**

Space, peace, neighbors in the **city**

Concluding sentence

Topic sentence

Space example: **town and city**

Peaceful example:
town and city

Also, life in Acton was more peaceful and far quieter. With fewer cars, we rarely heard "city" noises. Instead, the nights seemed filled with soft breezes in the tree-tops. In contrast, Geneva was filled with the sounds of people coming and going in the streets, talking loudly, and sometimes shouting.

Neighbors example:
town and city

What the whole family missed most, however, were the friendly people of Acton. The children found playmates lined up on our front sidewalk, and my husband and I mixed easily with the townsfolk. They were good people who would go out of their way to help. In contrast, I found that city residents were less helpful.

Concluding sentence

Of course I have had many good experiences in cities as well as these bad ones, but for anyone raising a family, I recommend the slower pace and neighborliness of a town over a city anytime.

After you have decided on either the block or point-by-point method for organizing, remember to introduce each major point of comparison or contrast with a subtopic sentence linked to the paragraph by connectors like the transitions listed below (for more on connectors and a complete list of transitions, see pp. 52–57).

For Comparing			
alike	both	like	resembling
also	in the same way	likewise	similarly
For Contrasting			
after all	dissimilar	nevertheless	though
although	even though	on the contrary	unlike
but	however	on the other hand	whereas
differs from	in contrast	otherwise	yet
difference	in spite of	still	

Organizing—Summing Up:

1. Create a rough topic sentence to help focus your material.

2. Look to your prewriting lists for help with focusing and selecting your most important examples. Limit primary examples to three or four.

3. Arrange the examples by order of importance (occasionally by space or time).

4. Plan on using a subtopic sentence to introduce each major example.

5. Select either block or point-by-point organization.

6. Review the list of transitions (and other connectors).

JOURNAL ENTRY 11-3

Write out your topic sentence. Does it mention two subjects, tell whether you will compare or contrast, and express an opinion/reason for making the comparison or contrast? Now list your three or four main examples by order of importance, following either a block or point-by-point format (see the paragraph outlines above).

Drafting

With the preliminary work over, you are almost ready to write a first draft. But before moving ahead, take a moment to review the Drafting suggestions in Chapter 1, pp. 12–13, and to think about the following points:

1. Choose either comparison or contrast.

2. Include all the main examples for one topic that you have for the other and develop each point with at least one specific, detailed example.

3. Be sure your paper makes a point. Remember, the fact that both Ford and Chevy pickups both have engines, transmissions, exhaust systems, and wheels does not mean that anyone cares to read through the comparison. The topic and *especially* concluding sentences can help clarify why the comparison or contrast has meaning for you.

4. If you want to develop one point extensively, then choose the block method for organizing (see "Two Different Worlds," p. 241).

5. Metaphors and similes (comparisons of unlike subjects—"the sun *was* a blast furnace/ *like* a blast furnace") work especially well in comparison and contrast papers.

Teaching Idea
This is a good time in the writing process to reiterate that all points of comparison should be included for both topics.

Teaching Idea
Encourage students to include an occasional metaphor or simile (see Chapter 19).

Teaching Idea
Journal Entry 11-4 encourages students to interact with their writing and can be useful to focus peer revision sessions.

> **JOURNAL ENTRY 11-4**
>
> Respond to this journal entry soon after writing your first rough draft. Are you working with *two* subjects? Have you focused on comparing *or* contrasting? Have you introduced each major example with a subtopic sentence? What part of this draft do you like best or think best fulfills the assignment instructions— why? What part do you dislike most or feel is drifting from the assignment— why? Answer in a paragraph.

Revising Drafts

To review the detailed lists for revising drafts, turn to Chapter 4.

■ ANNOTATED STUDENT MODEL

Help yourself avoid difficulties in your own drafting by reading through the Annotated Student Model as carefully as possible. Doing this will save you a few headaches and probably help clarify questions you didn't even know you had.

Teaching Idea
To stress that a point is needed for focus, you might refer students back to Ana's prewriting lists (p. 246) to show what else she could have written about.

First-Stage Draft

Ana Maria had moved with her family a number of times and felt like some part of the moving process would make a worthwhile comparison or contrast paragraph. After some brainstorming she decided to focus on town versus city living, using examples from two of several locations she had lived. Although she also found many similarities between towns and cities, because she wanted to emphasize that towns are superior for family living, she chose to contrast the two. Thinking that other people with young children might be especially interested in her work, she began drafting with a specific point in mind and audience to help her focus, select examples, and organize.

Teaching Idea
Refer students to Chapter 24 for help with pronoun shift errors.

Avoid *you*

Need more connecting words to move between town and city points

Some people go for small towns and some for cities but I would rather live in a small town. Some people just need more space around them than others, especially if you have kids. When we lived in Acton, we had plenty of land and a large house. There was a ton of room for the kids to play, and I loved watching them playing games in the neighborhood. In Geneva we were cramped. There wasn't much room in our house and the children ended up playing in the streets, with all the problems that meant. Life in Acton was quieter than in Switzerland. We weren't bothered by car noises. Instead, we heard the sounds of the wind moving through the tree-tops. But, in Geneva we heard way too much racket. People shouted and cars raced their engines on a regular basis which disturbed all our sleeping. I think that I most missed the good friends and even acquaintances I made in Acton. Maybe we were just lucky to find such a good group, but the townsfolk were almost always friendly and willing to help. In Geneva people seemed to want to ignore you. They were standoffish, and none of us really made any lasting relationships. Cities are depressing places and I'm glad we will be moving once again; you guessed it, back to Acton.

Need to develop examples with more specific supporting examples and details

Second-Stage Draft

First rough drafts are often underdeveloped, needing further detailed examples and explanations. Also, topic, subtopic, concluding sentences, and connecting words usually need work. Notice how Ana Maria strengthened her paragraph of contrast by working on these points in particular.

Teaching Idea
Ask students to compare the first example from drafts one and two and say what they like about the revision.

Topic sentence revised—contrast is *implied*, not mentioned directly

Having had the opportunity to live in both cities and small towns I find that I prefer town living to city living for raising a family. In the town of Acton I found a spacious home with additional surrounding land. During my walks through the neighborhood, I would smell the fragrance of the blossoming trees. I would also enjoy watching the kids playing ball. They looked happy and glad to be with each other, shouting to each other, "Throw me the ball, here, here!" On the other hand, when I found my home in Geneva, it was small with a very tiny back-yard. The children had to play in a parking lot. This frightened me as I thought of the accidents that could happen. Sure enough, one day my daughter Anina came weeping and crying to me. Making me long for are safe home in Acton. Also, life in Acton was more peaceful and far quieter, with so few cars, we rarely heard "city" noises. Instead, the nights seemed filled with soft breezes the wind whispering through the treetops. In contrast, Geneva was filled with the noises of people killing time in the streets, talking loudly and sometimes shouting. Sirens, backfiring, and racing engines disturbed all our sleep, especially my daughter Sandra's. What the whole family missed most, however, were the friendly people of Acton. The kids easily found playmates and my husband and I also found friends. They were good people who would go out of their way to help. Once when I locked my keys in car, one of the people I barely knew took me home, waited for me to locate my spare key, and then drove me back to my car. In contrast, I found that people in the city were less helpful. Once when

Supporting examples and details added throughout

Dialogue added

Transitional words *in contrast* and others added

Subtopic sentences revised (and shaded to help you identify them)

Concluding
sentence
revised

my battery died, none of the people I asked for help would bother. <u>I ended by
calling a tow service and I lost a day waiting for them to come get my car.</u> Of
course I have had many good experiences in cities as well as these bad ones,
but for anyone raising a family I recommend the slower pace and neighborliness
of a town over a city anytime.

Note the
expanded
thought

Special Points to Check in Revising from First to Second Drafts

1. Check topic sentence: topic + point + indication of comparison or contrast

2. Check subtopic sentences: connector + subtopic + point

3. Check concluding sentence: connector + link to topic sentence + expanded thought

4. ~~Delete unnecessary material~~

5. <u>Add material for clarity, completeness, and emphasis</u>

6. Check connectors : transitions, repeat words, synonyms, pronouns, reference to main idea

---

Teaching Idea
Try selecting only
one point at a
time for students
to focus on in the
third-stage draft,
such as specific
words.

Third-Stage Draft

We might be tempted at this second-draft stage to call a paper complete. But
this is the point at which we can concentrate on word choices, sentence variety,
and concision—polishing a good draft to make it a great one.

The Joy of Simple Living

Title added

Clutter phrase
deleted

Having had the opportunity to live in both cities and small towns I find that
I prefer town living ~~to the city living~~ for raising a family. First, my children need
space to run and play. In the town of Acton, Massachusetts I found a spacious
home on three-fourths of an acer with additional surrounding land. [During my
leisurely walks through the neighborhood in spring , I would smell the fragrance
of the blossoming apple trees , and enjoy watching the children playing ball.]
They looked happy ~~and glad to be with each other~~ with their flushed faces' ,
shouting to each other, "Throw me the ball, here, here!" On the other hand
when I found my home in Geneva, Switzerland , ~~the house~~ **it** was small with a
~~very~~ tiny backyard. [The children had to play in a parking lot frightening me as
I thought of the accidents that could happen.] Sure enough, one day my daughter Anina came ~~weeping and~~ crying to me with her knee bleeding. Making me
long for are safe home in Acton. Also, life in Acton was more peaceful and far
quieter, with so few cars, we rarely heard "city" noises. Instead, the nights
seemed filled with soft breezes the wind whispering lullabies through the tree-
tops. In contrast, Geneva was filled with the ~~noises~~ **sounds** of people coming,
and going in the streets, talking loudly and sometimes shouting. Sirens from
police cars and ambulances , backfiring from cars and motorcycles , and racing
engines disturbed all our sleep, especially my daughter Sandra's. What the

More specific
words added

Sentences
combined and
specific words
added

Clutter phrase
deleted

More
appropriate
words
substituted

whole family missed most, however, were the friendly people of Acton. The children found playmates lined up on our front sidewalk and my husband and I mixed easily with the townspeople. They were good people who would go out of their way to help. [Once when I locked my keys the car in the grocery store parking lot, ~~one of the people~~ **a neighbor** I barely knew took me home, waited for me while I rummaged around to locate my spare key, and then drove me back to my car.] In contrast, I found that people in the city were more detached, less helpful. Once when my battery died while I was parked downtown, none of the people I asked for help would bother. I ended by calling a tow service and I lost a day waiting for them to come get my car. Of course I have had many good experiences in cities as well as these bad ones, but for anyone raising a family I recommend the slower pace and neighborliness of a town over a city anytime.

[margin note: Sentences combined and specific words added]

[margin note: Synonym replaces phrase]

Special Points to Check in Revising from Second to Third Drafts

1. Added specific words are boxed.

2. More precise or audience-appropriate word substitutions are shaded.

3. [Sentences combined for variety are bracketed.]

4. **Synonyms and phrases replacing clutter and repeat words are bolded.**

5. ~~Unneeded words are lined through.~~

[margin note: Teaching Idea To help them edit their own papers, ask students to explain the difference between the 9c and 10 errors in the Final Draft.]

Final-Editing Draft

By this point Ana's draft is in great shape. Now she needs to shift into low gear, moving slowly line by line, looking for every error in grammar, spelling, and punctuation that still exists. Keeping an **Improvement Chart** will help you to focus on your own **pattern errors,** an efficient way to finish this step in the process.

The Joy of Simple Living

Having had the opportunity to live in both cities and small towns, [9a] I find that I prefer town living for raising a family. First, my children need space to run and play. In the town of Acton, Massachusetts, [9b] I found a spacious home on three-fourths of an ~~acer~~ [1] acre with additional surrounding land. During my leisurely walks through the neighborhood in spring, I would smell the fragrance of the blossoming apple trees, [10] and enjoy watching the children playing ball. They looked happy with their flushed ~~faces'~~ [8] faces, shouting to each other, "Throw me the ball, here, here!" On the other hand, [9a] when I found my home in Geneva, Switzerland, it was small with a tiny backyard. The children had to play in a parking lot, [9b] frightening me as I thought of the accidents that could happen. Sure enough, one day my daughter Anina came crying to me with her knee bleeding, [5] making me long for ~~are~~ [2] our safe home in Acton. Also, life in Acton was more peaceful and far quieter. [6] With so few cars, we rarely heard "city" noises. Instead, the nights seemed filled with soft breezes, [9b] the wind whispering lullabies through the treetops. In contrast, Geneva was filled with the sounds of people coming, [10] and going in the streets, talking loudly and sometimes shouting. Sirens from police cars and ambulances, backfiring from cars and motorcycles, and racing engines disturbed all our sleep, especially my daughter Sandra's. What the whole family missed most, however, were the friendly people of Acton. The children found playmates lined up on our front sidewalk, [9c] and my husband and I mixed easily with the townspeople. They were good people who would go out of their way to help. Once when I locked my keys [in 3] the car in the grocery store parking lot, a neighbor I barely knew took me home, waited for me while I rummaged around to locate my spare key, and then drove me back to my car. In contrast, I found that people in the city were more detached, less helpful. Once when my battery died while I was parked downtown, none of the people I asked for help would bother. I ended by calling a tow service, [9c] and I lost a day waiting for them to come get my car. Of course I have had many good experiences in cities as well as these bad ones, but for anyone raising a family I recommend the slower pace and neighborliness of a town over a city any time.

Ana Maria Sauer

Special Points to Check in Editing Final Drafts

1. Spelling	5. Sentence fragments	9. Common comma categories
2. Sound-alike words	6. Comma splices/run-ons	a. Introduce
		b. Enclose/end
3. Missing words	7. Capitalizations	c. Divide
4. Wrong words	8. Apostrophes	10. Unneeded commas

Final-Draft Checklist

Before you turn in your final draft, take a few minutes to review this checklist. You may find that, as careful as you think you have been, you still have missed a point or two—or three. (For more on any of these points, see Chapter 4.)

___ 1. Have you chosen either a comparison *or* contrast?

___ 2. Do you have a clear reason for making the comparison or contrast?

___ 3. How effective is your topic sentence?

___ 4. Have you chosen either a block or point-by-point method of arrangement?

___ 5. Have you clearly arranged your main examples—probably by order of importance?

___ 6. Have you written a subtopic sentence to introduce each main example?

___ 7. Are your examples relevant, adequately detailed, and thoroughly explained?

___ 8. How well connected are your sentences, especially beginning main examples?

— 9. How effective is your concluding sentence?

—10. How well have you used specific language?

—11. Are you choosing the most *active* verbs and "-ing" words to describe action?

—12. Have you tried using a metaphor or simile?

—13. Are the sentences in your paragraph varied in length and beginnings?

—14. Have you repeated a word or phrase so often that it becomes noticeable?

—15. Have you included words that serve no purpose?

—16. Have you written a title—an interesting one—for the paper? (Check capitalizations.)

—17. Have you prepared your paper according to the format expected by your instructor? (Check to see if you need a title page, be sure to double-space, leave at least a 1-inch margin, use a 12-point font, and be sure to type or word process.)

—18. Have you edited your work as closely as you know how to (including having at least one other person—classmate, friend, family member—proofread closely? Have you checked your **Improvement Chart** for your pattern errors so that you can look for them specifically?

—19. Have you looked specifically for the following errors: spelling, sound-alike words, missing words, wrong words, sentence fragments, comma splices/run-ons, capitalizations, apostrophes, the Big Three comma categories, and unnecessary commas?

CHAPTER SUMMARY

1. Comparison and contrast is the act of discovering similarities and differences between two people, places, events, objects, or ideas. When we are asked to compare/contrast, especially in school, we may be expected to compare or contrast or do both.

2. Comparison and contrast is a fundamental mental process by which we explore and evaluate unfamiliar things and circumstances in the light of those we already know.

3. Comparison may take the form of an analogy, metaphor, or simile.

4. Comparison/contrast, as in all the patterns of development we have worked with in this unit, is often used to develop a single point within a paragraph in which other patterns are also used (i.e., process analysis, cause/effect, description, etc.).

5. Comparisons should be meaningful and interesting and between two topics that are similar enough to be compared.

6. Two ways to organize comparison/contrast are block and point by point.

7. Transitional words and other connectors are especially important in introducing each new point under discussion and in signaling the shift from one block topic to the next.

8. Comparison and contrast papers can be organized spatially or chronologically but are frequently arranged by order of importance.

9. Subtopic sentences are useful for introducing each new point of comparison or contrast.

10. The topic sentence should mention the topic, make a statement about it, and indicate that a comparison or contrast paper is forthcoming.

11. The concluding sentence should begin with a connector, link to the topic sentence, and expand the main point of the paper.

12. Writing is never complete until it has gone through several revisions and careful editing.

■ ALTERNATE WRITING ASSIGNMENTS

To give you some options to the chapter Topic Lists and perhaps a bit more focus, you might be interested in the following alternate writing assignments.

Remember to observe these points as you begin any of the options:

- Think about both similarities and differences.

- Have a reason for your comparison or contrast.

- Choose either comparison or contrast.

- Develop each side of your topic relatively equally.

- Use transitions and other connectors.

1. Write a paper comparing or contrasting some part of your life to the life of someone you know well. Talk to an older member of your family, a parent or grandparent, an aunt or uncle, and ask her about her life growing up. Focus on some point in the person's life that you might compare to your own. For example, if your person has a lot to say about her early childhood, you might focus your paper on the period from, say, five to twelve and think about some of the following points for comparing:

- Location: town, city, state
- Home
- School
- Work
- Friends
- Recreation
- Hopes/dreams/aspirations
- Worries/fears

As you talk to your subject, ask her to tell whatever stories she remembers about the time period. Encourage the person to expand on any of the above suggested points and/or add to the list. You may find that you gather a lot of material on one point and then decide to focus your paper on that single topic.

2. Write a paper comparing or contrasting yourself with someone from another country or someone from another culture within our own country. To gather information, interview a fellow student in your writing class, other classes, or one who you know socially, asking him questions about his home and culture and how he feels they compare to your own. You could begin your interview by asking questions about some of the following points and then ask any others that occur to you:

- Country
- Area in the country
- Occupation of parents
- Work he/she has done
- School
- Recreational activities
- Music
- Sports
- Clothing
- Dating
- Friends
- Hopes/fears

After you gather your material, choose a comparison or contrast approach, and then be sure to focus the paragraph. What point do you want to make?

Teaching Idea
You might caution students about overdoing the extended metaphor, a potential pitfall with this assignment.

3. Create an extended metaphor or simile. Metaphors and similes, as we have discussed, are comparisons of two unlike things. When we say that Shannon lost her tennis match because she moved like a slug, we have used a simile. For this assignment you would simply add several more layers of examples to a metaphor or simile. For example, you might have found your summer job of lawn maintenance to be hellish. You could compare elements of the job with what you envision eternal damnation to be like. Your boss might be a demon, co-workers could be the other lost souls, the 103-degree temperatures could be the unforgiving flames, and so on.

4. Write a paper that examines some commonly held stereotype. For example, you might be tired of hearing that rap music is a negative form of expression that always glorifies drug use, denigrates women, and incites violence. You might first explain the stereotype or "commonly held wisdom" and then contrast three or four points with those from your own experience or general knowledge.

Some other possible stereotypes:

- Teenagers are bad automobile insurance risks.

- Men want sex while women want love.

- Asian-Americans are great at math and science.

- Anyone with a high GPA must be a nerd.

- High school and college athletes don't care much about academics.

5. Write a paper that creates a profile of yourself matching the specifications for a job you would like. (This kind of comparison has the practical value of helping you prepare a cover letter and a résumé.) You might either locate an actual job description—from your current employer, for instance, or from your school career center—or create your own, based on a job you would like. For example, if you have always wanted to work in film, and can imagine yourself working as a special assistant to Steven Spielberg, what do you suppose would be the qualifications for the job, and how do you fit those requirements?

An alternative to the more realistic approach to the assignment is to match your imagined qualifications with a fantasy job. Perhaps you have always wanted to be a philosopher king, a ruler of your own small country—or maybe the universe! Lay out the necessary skills of the position, and then show how you are particularly well suited for it.

Working with the Essay

CHAPTER 12

Introducing the Essay

Building Strong Essays

Thesis Sentences
Introductions
Body Paragraphs
Development
Conclusions
Organization
Coherence
Titles

Teaching Idea
Although students have written essays in high school, they are often initially intimidated by the move from the paragraph. It reduces their anxiety to discuss their essay writing experiences, including the essays many students will write in other classes this semester.

Teaching Idea
If you are having students expand a former paragraph assignment, you might work them through Chapters 12 and 14 concurrently, using examples from their former papers to help illustrate essay form and development.

WHAT IS AN ESSAY?

Although we have already worked through a number of challenging single-paragraph assignments in Unit Two, the essay may still seem a bit intimidating. Like experienced hikers who have climbed many foothills but are finally confronted with a mountain, we might think, "Too steep, too rugged, the air's too thin—I'm not goin' *there!*" But, in truth, the essay is not overwhelming; it does not even have to be all that big. In fact, you will soon see that an essay is largely an expanded paragraph, written for the same reasons (to entertain, inform, or persuade) and complete with parts you already know: an introduction, body, and conclusion.

While essays may include dozens of body paragraphs—and use several more paragraphs to introduce and conclude them—many are also relatively brief, as will be the ones in this unit. As we work through our short essays of five to six paragraphs, we will continue to practice all the discovery, organizational, and developmental strategies we began earlier in the semester, and we will acquaint ourselves with the single controlling statement that governs all essays—the **thesis.**

Essay Form

In Chapter 3 we noted that the body paragraph and an essay have many similarities. Both should begin with a controlling point; grow through supporting explanations, examples, and details; and end decisively. The following illustration shows how body paragraphs and essays are related:

Body Paragraph	Essay

Body Paragraph

Topic **sentence**: topic + statement

Body sentences
• Subtopic sentence one: connector, subtopic, statement
• Development: examples, details, explanations

• Subtopic sentence two: connector, subtopic, statement
• Development: examples, details, explanations

• Subtopic sentence three: connector, subtopic, statement
• Development: examples, details, explanations

Concluding **sentence**
• Connector
• Link to topic sentence
• Summary
• Expanded thought

Essay

Introductory **paragraph**
• Hook
• Development
• Thesis: topic + statement

Body paragraph one
• Topic sentence: connector, subtopic, statement
• Development: examples, details, explanations
• Summary sentence (optional)

Body paragraph two
• Topic sentence: connector, subtopic, statement
• Development: examples, details, explanations
• Summary sentence (optional)

Body paragraph three
• Topic sentence: connector, subtopic, statement
• Development: examples, details, explanations
• Summary sentence (optional)

Concluding **paragraph**
• Connector
• Link to thesis
• Summary
• Development (expanded thought)

The body paragraph often begins with a topic **sentence** (main point) while the essay begins with a **paragraph** that usually contains a thesis sentence (main point), often positioned as the *last* sentence in the paragraph. Notice in the illustration above how the first arrow shows this relationship. Topic and thesis sentences are comparable, except that because essays are longer and more fully developed, the thesis is often a little roomier to accommodate that development.

Body paragraphs that develop several primary examples begin each example with a **subtopic** sentence to introduce the main point. Similarly, body paragraphs in essays usually begin with a **topic** sentence to introduce the main point (see the second, third, and fourth arrows in the illustration above). Both subtopic and topic sentences are then developed with additional examples, explanations, and details.

Body paragraphs end with one or two *sentences* while brief essays end with one *paragraph*, as you will notice from the fifth arrow above. In both cases a writer concludes by referring back to the main point of the paper—contained within the topic or thesis sentence—and offering an idea or statement that lets the reader feel that the paper has ended decisively. Body paragraphs sometimes include a few brief summary words in the conclusion while essays frequently use a few words, a sentence, or more for summary.

Student Models: Paragraph and Essay

To take a closer look at how a paragraph might grow into an essay, we can compare the two versions of the student models below, "Dangers in a Deli," paying particular attention to the beginnings and endings and to the development of main points.

Teaching Idea
You might remind students that the topic and concluding sentences of the deli paragraph model are only separated here for instructional purposes.

Paragraph Model

Length: 200 words

Topic sentence

Subtopic sentence one

Sentences for development

Subtopic sentence two

Sentences for development

Subtopic sentence three

Sentences for development

Concluding sentence

Dangers in a Deli

More frequently than people realize, there are dangers in deli work. One concern for potential deli workers is slippery floors. If the counter is packed with anxious customers, and workers are hustling about taking care of their orders, a wet floor is not going to take top priority. During the rush what's going to stop an employee from running too fast, which could result in a serious wipeout.

In addition to slippery floors, working around chemicals should not be taken lightly. When cleaning the glass, you might end up with ammonia sprayed in your eyes. Both pan degreaser and sanitizer are used at dish time, and it only takes one splash in the sink to send someone on her way to the emergency room.

But the part of the job that is most dangerous is using the meat and cheese slicer. Whether operating the slicer or simply cleaning it, you risk cutting yourself. With just one careless slip near the sharp blade, you could end up with one less finger.

A new person on the job might be a little nervous because of the possible injury that deli work entails, but luckily safety training is a requirement.

Catherine Denning

Essays require an introductory **paragraph:** hook, development, thesis.

Length: 575 words

Hook: first sentence arouses the reader's curiosity

Sentences for development

Thesis sentence: last sentence in first paragraph

Topic sentence one

Sentences for development

Essay Model

Dangers in a Deli

1 Would you like to keep all of your body parts intact today? How about your eyesight, how much do you value it, or that brain that keeps your body functioning? With all of the activity in a deli, employees rushing about, impatient customers pressuring you to hurry, and management barking orders, accidents can happen when you least expect them. Smashing your head on a slippery tile floor, splashing caustic chemicals into your eyes, and slicing off fingers are just a few of the dangers you can encounter. If you don't want to end up in the emergency room on your first day here, you need to be aware of the potential dangers in working at a deli.

2 One common hazard for deli workers is slippery floors. Often, especially during the lunch rush, the place gets jammed. Anxious customers crowd into one another and lean over the stainless in your face to call out three more changes to their already late orders. Trying to manage the rush, employees hustle about, carrying checks, prepping sandwiches, carting plates back and forth. When scurrying from the salad case to the register, you might not notice that freshly mopped floor, and before you know it, you are crashing into a wall and banging your head on the slick, hard tile. And if you don't trip yourself up, there are always other employees to run into you, which can also cause a serious wipeout.

Topic sentence two

Sentences for
development

Topic sentence three

Sentences for
development

Essays require
a concluding
paragraph:
connector, thesis
link, summary, and
development.

Sentences for
development

Besides the slippery floors, workers also need to be cautious around chem-   3
icals. Even when business is slow, it is easy enough to be careless when
cleaning the grease and handprints off all the glass, suddenly spraying yourself
in the face with ammonia. But it gets worse when the rush begins, and the
owner goes into his panic mode: "Get these dishes done! Now, now—we're
filling up!" You might think you have a good grip on that slippery platter, until it
squeezes out of your hands and splashes into a sink full of pan degreaser and
sanitizer. It only takes one faceful of that hot, soapy water to send someone on
her way to the emergency room.

But the part of the job that is most dangerous is using the meat and cheese   4
slicer. Whether operating the slicer or simply cleaning it, you risk cutting yourself. The shiny circular blade on the machine is as sharp as a surgeon's scalpel,
and you will be using it all the time, your hand just inches away from the cutting
edge. Everyone knows the kind of damage that can happen; everyone is extra
careful, but then business picks up or someone is just too tired to pay attention.
The blade doesn't know the difference, a piece of ham or four fingertips. Just
one careless slip and you could end up with one less finger.

Cuts, chemicals, concussions, and other dangers—with all these ways to   5
injure himself, a new person on the job might feel a little overwhelmed. But
deli work doesn't always make you feel nervous and frazzled; in fact, it can
be enjoyable. Whether you are talking to interesting customers or spending
time with friends, the deli is usually a fun place to work. It can even be a great
place for keeping your mind off problems at home or that algebra exam on
Friday. Although accidents can happen, you are a lot less likely to have one if
you keep the worst of the hazards in mind.

Catherine Denning

Teaching Idea
This is a good place to
stress *developing*
examples. If
students are expanding a
former paragraph, in particular,
many will want to write an
introduction and conclusion,
while not paying enough
attention to their body
paragraphs.

As you glance back and forth between the paragraph and the essay models, you might immediately notice their primary differences: **length, introduction,** and **conclusion.**

Increased *length* can be accomplished in two ways: adding more main examples and developing examples that already exist. The deli paragraph of 200 words grew into an essay of 575 words not by using any more primary examples but by adding to those the author had already chosen. In the paragraph unit we have practiced using examples, details, and explanations to add substance and interest to our topics. Essays require exactly the same strategies for development.

While the deli paragraph could rely on a single topic sentence to draw the reader in and mention the topic, the essay *introductory paragraph* is a bit more complex. Even though the main point (thesis) is almost identical to the paragraph topic sentence, the author added a lead-in sentence to "hook" the reader's interest (not unlike baiting a hook for a fish) and then used several more sentences to ease her reader into the thesis and, hence, the body of the essay.

Rather than relying on a single sentence to end, as the paragraph does, the deli essay supplies a *concluding paragraph*. Here again you will find much that is famil-iar. The lead sentence provides a connector (as do the body paragraph lead sentences), a brief summary of the essay's main points, and a link to the thesis (dangers in a deli). Rather than just trailing off, . . . the author wisely chooses an expanded thought to leave her audience with a sense that the essay is really finished. You might note that the expanded thought has changed in the essay—as yours may—from the paragraph's mention of safety training to the good time deli work can be.

In developing a
paragraph, you might
change the expanded
thought.

As we move ahead in Chapter 12, we will explore these three essential elements that help transform simple paragraphs into more complex essays: introductions, body development, and conclusions.

Teaching Idea
Stressing this three-part approach to introductory paragraphs will help make them seem less mysterious to students and more learnable.

INTRODUCTORY PARAGRAPHS

Many of us, sometimes unknowingly, have already been writing partial introductory paragraphs this semester. If you began some of your one-*paragraph* papers with two or three sentences and then trimmed them back during revision, you fall in this camp. Often the sentences were on their way to becoming a full-fledged introductory paragraph but were merely distracting to the reader in the shorter paper. Now, however, we can develop those sentences and see how to arrange them for greater interest and force.

Introductory paragraphs in all forms of writing serve an important function: they engage a reader's interest. If a reader is disappointed in the first few sentences of an essay, why should he read further? With so much to keep us all busy, a poor introduction is a good indication that reading further will be a waste of time, and so the article ends up ignored—or in the trash. To avoid this reaction, we can learn to use these basic strategies for creating clear, interesting, and lively introductions:

1. **Hook:** one sentence (*first* sentence in the introductory paragraph)

2. **Development:** three to four sentences (middle sentences)

3. **Thesis:** one sentence (often the *last* sentence in the introductory paragraph)

THESIS SENTENCE

The thesis sentence is the most important part of your introduction, the focusing statement that will guide your reader through the rest of the essay. Often when composing a thesis for an essay, a writer will allow a bit more room in it to develop more or different points than might be contained within a single paragraph. Practically speaking, if you are expanding a paragraph from Unit Two, and you have created three or four main examples to illustrate your overall point (topic sentence), your thesis may not have to grow much. However, if you want to add additional points or change a primary example, you may need to significantly alter your former topic sentence so it will focus your essay. Even if you do not change main examples, you may still rework the thesis to polish the wording. Consider the topic sentence from "Dangers in a Deli" versus its thesis:

Topic sentence: More frequently than people realize, there are dangers in deli work.

Thesis sentence: If you don't want to end up in the emergency room on your first day here, you need to be aware of the potential dangers in working at a deli.

Clearly, both sentences express the same main point; however, the thesis targets an audience more precisely (a potential deli employee) and uses a more specific phrase (emergency room) for emphasis.

Sometimes writers use several sentences to express their thesis; sometimes they locate that thesis in various paragraphs spread throughout an essay; occasionally, writers only imply the thesis. For example, in persuasive prose, when arguing an issue to a fairly resistant audience, a writer might choose to delay mentioning her thesis. However, for the sake of clarity and to keep ourselves and readers oriented within our own essays, it would be helpful to position the thesis as the *last sentence* in the *first paragraph*—as you will find all the student model essays in this text have done.

Teaching Idea
It is worth reiterating the various places thesis sentences *can* be placed and showing several examples of this (several of the Unit Six essays will help here).

Position the thesis as the last sentence in your first paragraph.

When composing your thesis, remember the points you have applied to your topic sentences all semester:

1. Limit the topic.

2. Make a clear statement about it.

3. Refine the statement through clear explaining, specific words, action words, and sensory details.

Limiting the Thesis Sentence

Even long, complicated essays grow from humble beginnings. A twenty-page research paper might begin with a single word (a topic) that the author explores until he can find the right size piece to fit his interest, his reader's interest, and the length requirements of the assignment. But, once the topic is narrowed, a writer is obligated to express his focus and direction as clearly as possible, which he does in the thesis sentence.

The thesis falls somewhere between a relatively general and relatively specific statement. It must be roomy enough to allow for the examples and explanations that follow in the body of the essay but focused enough not to require twenty-five main examples if three are all the writer intends to give. Our Language Line from Chapter 5 can help us see the "relativity" principle:

Relatively General	**Thesis**	Relatively Specific
"Lots of things"	"Hard, dangerous work"	"Serious dangers"

Limiting a thesis sentence is often a matter of trial and error, the writer beginning with a fairly general topic and discovering more focus as she moves through the prewriting, organizing, and drafting process. Notice how the following thesis sentence becomes increasingly focused until it reaches a point where it can usefully guide the drafting of the essay "Dangers in a Deli":

1. *There are <u>lots of things</u> that go on in a <u>deli</u>.*

2. *A deli job takes plenty of time and can be hard, dangerous work, but there are good times too.*

3. *Working in a deli can be hard and dangerous.*

4. *<u>Working in a deli</u> involves some <u>serious dangers</u>.*

Now the author has moved from the fairly general statement of "lots of things" (see the Language Line arrow above) to the fairly specific statement of "serious dangers," giving her a good jumping-off point for her first rough draft. If she had wanted to include a **forecasting statement,** she could have specified the primary kinds of dangers like this:

- *Working in a deli involves several serious dangers: the slippery floors, some harsh chemicals, and the meat and cheese slicer.*

Making a Clear Statement about the Topic

Even after we have narrowed a topic, we sometimes have difficulty expressing our meaning within a thesis sentence. Sometimes this is merely a problem with wording, but other times it is a problem with clear thinking. Consider the following thesis:

- *Television is full of violence that affects children in ways that no one will ever be able to fully understand.*

Where is this thesis going? We can see that the topic is violence on TV, and it seems like the writer wants to discuss some part of how that violence affects children—a reasonably limited topic for an essay—but perhaps the author has another essay in mind. To clarify the meaning, we could revise the thesis in these ways:

- *Violence in children's programming can cause children to behave violently.*

  or

- *Though psychologists and psychiatrists think they understand the impact of television violence on children, they have only learned part of the picture.*

Aside from the thesis that goes astray through faulty wording or thinking, sometimes one will meander, like an old lazy river, winding around in great looping oxbows in and out of itself until it finally arrives at the end—sort of. Consider the following thesis:

- *The medical profession offers many exciting career possibilities for young people who want to fully explore their potential and work within an industry that helps other people in the same selfless way that a member of the clergy might, especially if a person decides to go into an area that some would avoid because of unpleasant working conditions or patients who suffer too much, areas like respiratory therapy or geriatric care.*

Besides simply being too long for a thesis sentence, this example includes too many ideas, though most are worthwhile and could be useful elsewhere in the essay.

How long is too long, or too short, for a thesis? While there is no set "rule," a medium-length sentence works well, say fifteen to thirty words. Some can be quite short for dramatic impact while others can effectively run to forty words or more. As long as your thesis is *clear*, the word count should not be much of a problem.

While clarity in thesis sentences can suffer from fuzzy thinking, poor word choices, and too many ideas, we should not mistake a well-crafted thesis that *implies* its focus with one that merely obscures it. For example, in an essay dealing with effects, a writer might construct either of these two thesis sentences:

A. *Joining the navy right out of high school had four positive effects on my life.*

or

B. *I have come to appreciate the unconscious wisdom of my decision to join the navy right after my high school graduation.*

Version A clearly states the topic and even uses the word *effects*. But version B also clearly states the topic while implying that the essay will develop effects. Contrast either of these two thesis sentences to the following one:

- *I had to decide what to do with my life after high school, and I thought about joining the military because so many young people go that route.*

Undecided or "waffling" thesis sentences like the one above make it difficult for a reader to know where the essay they are supposed to predict is headed.

Polishing the Thesis Sentence

Few of us this semester will immediately hit upon the "perfect" thesis sentence and then go tearing into an essay. Instead, most of us will treat the thesis just like the rest of the draft as we rework and refine, polishing for clarity and expression. The elements that we worked with in Unit Two to improve style—**specific words, action words,** and **sensory details**—still apply to the essay, and we can create more interesting thesis sentences by using some of them.

Looking back at the deli essay, we can see one example of a writer upgrading a thesis:

- *More frequently than people realize there are dangers in deli work.*

- *If you don't want to end up in the <u>emergency room</u> on your first day here, you need to be aware of the potential dangers in working at a deli.*

In the second sentence, aside from more directly addressing her reader, the author has included the "emergency room" to show the reader more specifically where he might be headed if he does not pay attention to the information in the essay.

Could we add an **action word** to this thesis? How about "bleeding?"

Sidebar notes (left margin):

Watch out for the meandering thesis sentence.

Thesis sentences are often between fifteen and thirty words long.

Teaching Idea
Remind students to save their brainstorming and drafting material because, as with the "meandering" thesis, good ideas can often be salvaged.

Thesis sentences may artfully *imply* the focus of an essay.

Teaching Idea
Ask the class to compare the thesis sentences that forecast, imply, and "waffle." Let them put in their own words why the waffling sentence is ineffective.

Polish thesis sentences through **specific words, action words,** and **sensory details.**

- *If you don't want to end up your first day here <u>bleeding</u> all over yourself on the way to the emergency room, you should be aware of the potential dangers in deli work.*

Could we also add a **sensory detail** (sight, sound, touch, smell, or taste)?

- *If you don't want to see <u>bright red</u> arterial blood spurting from a severed index finger, you should be aware of the potential dangers in deli work.*

Teaching Idea
If students wince a bit at this last thesis sentence, point out that specific language and action words evoke responses in a reader and so are valuable rhetorical strategies.

This thesis sentence adds a visual detail, "bright red," two action words, "spurting" and "severed," and includes two specific words, "arterial" and "index." However, the point in trying to refine your thesis sentence is not to cram as many action words or sensory details into it as possible. In fact, sensory details may not even be appropriate for your topic and treatment of it. The point *is* to look critically at your work with an eye to making a passable thesis sentence a powerful one.

Activity 12-1: Polishing Thesis Sentences

After reading the introductory material that precedes this activity, revise the following rough thesis sentences, <u>underlining</u> any specific words, action words, or sensory details that you add. Use your imagination, have some fun, and remember that even small additions can be significant improvements.

Teaching Idea
In Activity 12-1 you might invite students to mention several examples they would use to develop their revised thesis sentences into essays. Number 2 can generate some interesting responses.

Example: Rough thesis: A sense of humor is a useful human trait.

Revised thesis: *Being able to <u>laugh</u> at myself in <u>embarrassing situations</u> has saved me from some awfully <u>depressing moments</u>.*

Answers will vary

1. Rough thesis: Winter is hard on the world.
   Revised thesis: *With its Arctic wind and subzero temperatures, winter drives plants, animals, and people into hiding.*

2. Rough thesis: I know how to make my wife (husband, girl/boyfriend) happy.
   Revised thesis: *While my wife enjoys receiving presents on established occasions like birthdays, if I want to make her truly happy, I bring her small, unexpected presents throughout the year.*

3. Rough thesis: There is one kind of party that is sure to attract the police.
   Revised thesis: *Whenever I have Eric's band over to play at a keg party in my backyard, the police usually show up before midnight.*

4. Rough thesis: Buying gifts that will be well received is not easy.
   Revised thesis: *To buy a special gift for someone, you have to know the person well and buy her what she, not you, would value.*

5. Rough thesis: Extreme sports fall into several different categories.
   Revised thesis: *Leaping from a bridge with a piece of rope attached to my ankle, clinging to a sheer rock face 2,000 feet above the ground, or jumping out of a plane at 15,000 feet—my favorite extreme sports can be classified by the element of risk in each.*

Teaching Idea
Let students know that there are other ways to develop introductions besides these, but if students learn several reliable methods, they will seldom be stuck for an introduction.

Note: These methods are often combined.

Teaching Idea
Some students feel that it is "wrong" not to begin an essay by writing the introduction first, consequently blocking themselves from getting the body on paper because they are stuck at the start. It helps to discuss this problem and how ideas for the introduction may be waiting undiscovered in the body examples.

Some writers prefer to begin an essay draft with only a thesis, composing the introduction later.

Teaching Idea
See Chapter 12 in the Instructor's Manual for the introductory paragraph method each essay in *AWW* uses.

Note how the hook (first sentence) blends with the rest of the paragraph.

Thesis sentence

Hook is underlined

DEVELOPING INTRODUCTIONS

With a clear thesis sentence to end your introductory paragraph, you are on your way to a strong start to your essay. But now we need additional material to help involve and direct the reader.

To generate interesting material to fill out the introduction, writers use many techniques, including the ones listed below:

1. Description

2. Narration

3. Comparison/contrast

4. Cause and effect

5. Definition

6. Persuasion

7. Question (s)

8. Background information/history (including why the topic is important to *you*)

9. Startling information

10. Reversal

11. **Combination of several**

To help us see how to apply these methods, and to see how detachable an introduction often is, we can create different beginnings for "Dangers in a Deli," each one leading to the same thesis sentence.

Note: The word *you* is appropriate in these introductory paragraphs because of the author's intended audience. However, *you* is frequently overused in student writing, so only use it when you are sure of the context. (For more on *you* and pronoun shift problems, see Chapter 24.)

Methods For Developing Introductory Paragraphs

1. **Description:** Create a series of vivid images—perhaps three or four. Consider these images to be quick snapshots rather than a continuous story. Use one sentence for each image, and develop each picture with people/things in action, specific words, and sensory details (sight—colors!—sound, and touch, especially).

   <u>Irritated customers shouting orders, pans clanging together, shirts soaked through with sweat—another shift at the deli is well under way</u>. Employees are racing to keep up with the orders. Ben is slicing bread too fast for safety, the bread knife barely missing his palm as he opens one loaf after another. Ellen slips on a wet spot on the tile floor and jams her wrist against a wall. Ramon mutters, "Damn it!" as he scalds himself in the sink. A delicatessen in a lunch rush can be a hectic, nerve-wracking place. If you don't want to end up in the emergency room on your first day here, you need to be aware of the potential dangers in working at a deli.

2. **Narration:** Tell a brief story.

   <u>Shawn came into the restaurant cracking jokes, kidding customers and fellow employees alike, and generally having a good time</u>. Everyone liked him right away and could see that he would be fun to have around. But in the middle of his third day on the job, during the lunch rush, we lost him for good. I was taking an order at table seven, when all the loud talking, jostling, and eating stopped abruptly. Everyone in the restaurant heard Shawn scream as

he lost the first joint of his little finger to the meat slicer. He learned the hard way how dangerous this job can be. If you too don't want to end up in the emergency room on your first day here, you need to be aware of the potential dangers in working at a deli.

3. **Comparison/contrast:** Compare or contrast your topic to something your reader would be familiar with. You might also compare through a metaphor or simile.

Thesis sentence

Hook is underlined

Although I have never been on a cattle ranch, I think I know what it feels like to be caught in the middle of a stampede. I don't usually think of my customers as cows (though some *do* eat like animals), but in the middle of a lunch rush in our deli, with the restaurant packed from the front door to the counter and frustrated people calling out orders, you too might feel like you are about to be trampled. The pressure during a rush from customers and management alike can cause employees to move faster than what is safe. If you don't want to end up in the emergency room on your first day here, you need to be aware of the potential dangers in working at a deli.

Thesis sentence

4. **Cause and effect:** Explain causes leading to your topic or effects leading away from it. Or create a fictional scenario, what *might* happen relating to your topic.

Hook is underlined

Let's talk about Allen, a fictitious new employee at the deli, who is not paying much attention to his trainer as she talks about procedures and hazards on the job. He halfway listens as she tells him about how fast he will be expected to move in about an hour, when the lunch rush hits. "Right, yeah, OK," he says, paying more attention to Will Smith's rap in his headphones. An hour passes, people begin flooding in, and Allen begins to panic. Trying to carry a tray full of salads too quickly, he slips on the tile floor and lands flat on his back, knocking himself unconscious. Unless you are careful, you could be Allen. If you too don't want to end up in the emergency room on your first day here, you need to be aware of the potential dangers in working at a deli.

Thesis sentence

5. **Definition:** Briefly define some important part of your topic.

Hook is underlined

Self-preservation is an instinct that tries to keep animals out of harm's way, and it works pretty well for most of them, except for some humans. These are the people—maybe you know some like this—who refuse to listen to good advice or even to warnings that might save them from much misery. On the other hand, when a reasonable person has the opportunity to learn about job hazards that might endanger her, she listens, that good old self-preservation instinct kicking in. In this restaurant a new employee has to be careful. If you don't want to end up in the emergency room on your first day here, you need to be aware of the potential dangers in working at a deli.

Thesis sentence

6. **Persuasion:** Appeal to your reader's self-interest by showing her what *she* has to gain by reading your essay.

Hook is underlined

There is no reason that you have to be hurt today. No sane person enjoys pain, and few people can afford the recovery time that serious injury on the job requires. All new employees at this restaurant get a careful orientation that includes warnings on how to avoid accidents. Intelligent people pay attention. If you don't want to end up in the emergency room on your first day here, you need to be aware of the potential dangers in working at a deli.

Thesis sentence

7. **Question (s):** Ask several questions of your reader that relate to your thesis.

Hook is underlined

Would you like to keep all of your body parts intact today? How about your eyesight, how much do you value it, or that brain that keeps your body functioning? With all of the activity in a deli, employees rushing about, impatient customers pressuring you to hurry, and management barking orders, accidents can happen when you least expect them. Smashing your head on a slippery tile floor, splashing caustic chemicals into your eyes, and slicing off fingers are just a few of the dangers you can encounter. If you don't want to end up in the emergency room on your first day here, you need to be aware of the potential dangers in working at a deli.

Thesis sentence

8. **Background information:** Mention any information or history about your topic that would help orient your reader or show him why the topic is important to *you*.

Hook is underlined

As a deli manager I like to keep my fellow employees healthy, and as a reasonably good-hearted human being, I don't like to see people suffer. During our peak hours we only run five employees in the front and back of the house, even though we usually need more. In order for the operation to work, everyone has to do his or her job efficiently and with some enthusiasm. If even one person just gets the slows or, worse, is injured, the rest of the crew suffers. To help the restaurant, your fellow workers, and yourself, listen closely to this orientation. You can keep yourself out of the emergency room on your first day here, if you are aware of the potential dangers in working at this deli.

Thesis sentence

9. **Startling information:** Give facts or statistics that might seem unusual or dramatic to your reader. Or create graphic examples that would cause an emotional response in your reader.

Hook is underlined

A day rarely passes without some kind of accident in our deli. Most of the time the problem is small and the hurt to a person slight. But who wants even a little pain? It is bad enough to deal with small glass cuts and scalds from hot coffee, but when business picks up, the big accidents follow. New employees especially run the risk of breaking a wrist or slicing off a body part. If you don't want to end up in the emergency room on your first day here, you need to be aware of the potential dangers in working at a deli.

Thesis sentence

10. **Reversal:** Begin your introduction moving in one direction, but take off in a significantly different direction as you move into your thesis.

Hook is underlined

Working in a deli can be great fun. Employees dress casually, no suits and ties here. Most of us are young adults with plenty happening in our lives. I enjoy listening to Felipe brag about his date last night (knowing that at least half of what he says is a lie) and watching Gabrielle and Nathan pester each other over nothing, like sister and brother. Also, when business picks up, it is a good feeling to work closely as an efficient team, depending on one another as we get the job done. But the work is not all play. There are real, serious hazards in this business. If you don't want to end up in the emergency room on your first day here, you need to be aware of the potential dangers in working at a deli.

Thesis sentence

11. **Combination:** Focus on any one introductory paragraph method to get started, but realize that you may actually be using several methods. For example, number 10, directly above, uses description within the reversal strategy. Number 9 uses a question, description, and cause/effect. Number 8 explains in part through cause and effect. Almost all paragraphs, including those used in introductions, are developed through examples.

As you can see, there are many interesting ways to write introductory paragraphs. The one you choose depends on your topic, purpose, and audience. If you are writing a straightforward business document like a process analysis—how to put together a swing set, for instance—you might want to avoid the more colorful descriptive and narrative methods, favoring instead a simple listing and defining of parts. If, on the other hand, you are writing to persuade someone—say, a group of teens not to smoke—you might need to capture their attention quickly, showing them what value the essay has for them. Your tone (formal/informal), word choices, and explanations in the body of your essay depend on the overall context in which you are writing, and these choices begin in your introduction.

Keep in mind also that lively, interesting introductions rarely just fall from the sky, a gift of the gods. You must bring beginnings to life. So apply the same prewriting methods to this specialty paragraph that you do to the body of the essay: plan on clustering, listing, freewriting, and so forth to discover usable ideas.

Activity 12-2: Creating Interesting Introductions

Select *one* of the thesis sentences you created for Activity 12-1, and write *three* introductory paragraphs of five to seven sentences leading to the thesis. Review the ten methods listed above, and remember that you can often combine several.

1. List the method number: _Answers will vary_

   Begin the first introductory paragraph: _____

   _____

   _____

   _____

   _____

   _____

   _____

   _____

   _____

   Thesis sentence: _____

   _____

   _____

2. List the method number: _Answers will vary_

   Begin the first introductory paragraph: _____

   _____

   _____

   _____

   _____

   _____

   _____

   _____

   _____

   Thesis sentence: _____

   _____

   _____

3. List the method number: *Answers will vary*

Begin the first introductory paragraph: _____

_____

_____

_____

_____

_____

_____

_____

Thesis sentence: _____

_____

_____

Hooks

If the introductory paragraph as a whole is important, establishing the reader's first impression of a writer's work, then the lead sentence in the paragraph becomes that much more so. The first sentence should serve as the "hook" to reel the fish, your reader, in. A reader can become instantly curious in the middle of your first sentence, or instantly bored. To prevent the bored response, keep these points in mind:

1. Do not state the obvious.

2. Do say something that would interest *your* reader.

Looking back at the model "Dangers in a Deli," we can see how the author, Catherine Denning, managed her hook:

> Would you like to keep all of your body parts intact today? How about your eyesight, how much do you value it, or that brain that keeps your body functioning?

Catherine wrote this essay with an audience of newly hired deli employees in mind. While it would be reasonable to assume that most people are interested in keeping all their "body parts intact," the new employee who will soon be operating the meat slicer might feel like paying special attention. Notice that the hook is phrased as a question and that it begins to answer a question most readers ask at one time or another: "What's in it for me? Why *should* I read this essay?" Also note that the hook extends into the next sentence but that it does not need to. For our purposes, we will talk about the first sentence, realizing that it ought to blend easily into the rest of the introduction.

Here are several ways to create hooks:

1. Ask a question.

2. Begin with a line of dialogue.

3. Begin with a quotation.

4. Make a startling statement.

5. Present an unusual fact.

6. Begin a vivid image.

7. Create a comparison (possibly a metaphor or simile).

Teaching Idea
See Chapter 12 in the Instructor's Manual for the hook method used in each essay in *AWW*.

Hooks often overlap, for instance, the deli hook, using a question and a startling statement.

3. Never apologize for what you may not know.

   Here is another ineffective strategy: "Although I do not know much about this topic. . . ." or "There are experts who know a lot more about this subject than I do. . . ." or "I managed to find out a little bit about this subject, and so I can say something about it. . . ." When we write an essay, we are asking a reader to take time from her busy day to listen to us. If we begin by telling her that we do not have much worth saying, why should she waste her time reading our work?

4. Avoid needless repetition of information.

   Try not to begin an introduction this way: "Some students have problems with their schoolwork. When they do their work, it is often difficult for them. The homework and in-class work is hard to complete, and so many students—as hard as they work—find that they have a lot of trouble getting the work done." By now, the reader has gotten the point . . . and is probably sleeping on it. (For more on effective versus ineffective repetition, see Chapter 19.)

5. Eliminate clichés and worn expressions wherever they appear.

   Beware of clichés like these: "Caught between a rock and a hard place, . . ." "After a wait that seemed like an eternity,. . ." "The butterflies in my stomach,. . ." and many more. If a fresh figure of speech does not come to mind, just use a literal phrase. Say, for example, "a difficult situation" in place of the rock cliché from above. (For more on clichés and worn phrases, see Chapter 19.)

6. Avoid overly long or overly short introductions.

   Introductions should be written in proportion to the rest of the work. A book, on one end of the spectrum, might have an introduction of many pages while an essay of ten pages might need a paragraph or two. Our brief essays can easily support a beginning paragraph of five to seven sentences, about a hundred words or so.

Activity 12-5: Recognizing and Revising Weak Introductions

Decide which of the following introductory paragraphs is ineffective, tell why you think so, and then *rewrite* any one of them, using one of the ten methods listed previously or one of your own. You might find several problems illustrated in each of the weak examples.

1. Credit cards can be a real problem for anyone, especially college students. In this essay I will first discuss how much of a problem they can be, and then I will provide some solutions to this situation. Before I am through, I will show—in paragraph four to be exact—how irresponsible it is of the credit card companies to scatter their cards around so that anyone can get one. In my conclusion I will tell the reader where he can go to get more information on the problem.

2. Some people argue that e-mail contributes to bad writing. After all, they say, look at how people dash off those notes, and look at all the obvious errors in them. However, e-mail can actually make people better writers.

3. Many Americans insist on driving new vehicles, even if they do cost an arm and a leg. These people seem to think that new is automatically better, but I think half the time the supposed new technology is just recreating the wheel. Who needs electric windows when a crank will do the same job? Who needs a $500 antenna that pops up and down like a jack in the box? My old '86 Toyota pickup truck with its 115,000 miles is still as good as gold and better than most of the new products on the market. I prefer driving an older vehicle for several good reasons.

4. I don't know a lot about professional sports, but it seems to me that the players make an awful lot of money. Take for instance professional baseball players. They make a ton of money. Why I think I remember reading about a month ago how some pitcher signed a $5,000,000 contact! This seems like too much money for someone who just throws a baseball. And, even though I am no authority, I'll bet it's even worse for football and basketball. I think these guys make even more! All these high salaries are bound to have negative effects on professional sports.

5. Most people want to be happy. They want to feel good about themselves and the world around them. They like to wake up in the morning feeling good, go through the day without many problems, and then come home at night to a relaxing sleep. People don't want a lot of anxiety in their lives; they prefer to be stress free. But not everyone is lucky enough to have a good life. And if a person is not lucky, he needs to take responsibility on his own shoulders, to carry the weight of his own life. The fact is that happiness is not something that just happens for most people; they have to work for it.

6. "Dammit, Jack," the shift manager yelled at me, "that's the third time you burned those fries tonight! Get your head together or get a new job!" I stood there looking at my feet on the greasy tile floor, hating to take it, but apologizing anyway to keep my job. Around me rang out all the noise of a McDonald's Friday night: ovens beeping, warmers buzzing, pans clanging, deep fat fryer popping, Vera calling back for more Big Macs, kids crying up front from waiting too long in this so-called "fast"-food restaurant. That's when I finally decided I had had enough. I had to get a new life. Although coming back to college has been difficult, it is helping me leave the McDonald's days behind forever.

Ineffective paragraphs: _____ *1–5 are ineffective; 6 is effective* _____

Reasons that each introduction is weak: _____ *(1) talks about what the writer will discuss instead of discussing it. (2) is too brief. (3) is full of cliches. (4) is an apology. (5) is overly repetitive* _____

One weak introduction rewritten: _____ *Answers will vary.* _____

Creating Introductory Paragraphs—Summing Up

1. Decide on a working thesis sentence and *write it out*.

2. Skim the introductory paragraph methods.

3. Review the hook.

4. Review how to avoid weak introductions.

5. Prewrite, focusing on one of the ten introductions but allowing others to slip in.

6. Draft your introduction.

Note: You may jump straight into the body of your essay with only a thesis for focus and then write your introduction after you have completed one or several drafts.

BODY PARAGRAPHS

Introductory paragraphs begin to draw a reader into the essay and give her a sense of its direction. Now the writer must make good on his promise to supply interesting reading. As we practiced in Unit Two, we will present most of our information within body paragraphs.

In our single-paragraph assignments, we frequently wrote body paragraphs as long as 300 words—not an unusual length for paragraphs in many kinds of writing, including academic journals. However, most of your college writing calls for shorter paragraphs, between 100 and 200 words. Your essays in this unit will contain two to four body paragraphs of about five to eight sentences apiece.

You will organize your body paragraphs in much the same way as you have been doing, beginning with a topic sentence that states a point, developing it, and concluding in a sentence. However, you will not often need subtopic sentences in your shorter essay body paragraphs, particularly if you have narrowly focused each topic.

The following are the three main parts of body paragraphs:

1. **Topic sentence:** connector + topic + statement (first sentence)

2. **Development:** four to six sentences (middle sentences)

3. **Summary** sentence—*optional*: refers to main idea in topic sentence (last sentence)

Topic and Summary Sentences in Body Paragraphs

Topic sentences help focus what you want to say about your subject, and they help your reader follow your presentation. Each topic sentence should support the overall controlling idea of the essay (thesis) and be clearly connected to each paragraph that precedes it.

Notice how the topic sentence below uses several connectors (boxed) to bridge the gap between paragraphs and clearly links the main example (slicer) to the dangers of deli work mentioned in the thesis.

But the part of the job that is most dangerous is using the meat and cheese slicer. Whether operating the slicer or cleaning it, you risk cutting yourself. The shiny circular blade on the machine is as sharp as a surgeon's scalpel, and you will use it all the time, your hand just inches away from the cutting edge. Everyone knows the kind of damage that can happen; everyone is extra careful, but then business picks up or someone is just too tired to pay attention. The blade doesn't know the difference, a piece of ham or four fingertips. Just one careless slip and you could end up with one less finger.

(margin notes)

Former subtopic sentences = topic sentences

Teaching Idea
If you stress the *subtopic* sentence in its new role as *topic* sentence, most students will remember that their former single-paragraph papers did not need additional organizing sentences within the subtopic examples, just as brief body paragraphs usually do not.

Teaching Idea
See Chapter 12 in the Instructor's Manual for a list of essays using summary sentences.

Topic sentence

Sentence connectors are boxed.

Summary sentence is underlined.

In essays it is particularly important to help your reader move easily between paragraphs. Remember the five ways we hold sentences and paragraphs together: transitional words, repeat words, synonyms, pronouns, and reference to main ideas (to review these terms, see Chapter 3, pp. 52–57).

To conclude longer body paragraphs, writers sometimes create a summary sentence like the one underlined in the deli paragraph above. The benefit of these sentences is that they reinforce the author's message, adding clarity to the writing. The drawback is that, especially in short body paragraphs, they can become repetitive, potentially boring a reader. You must judge for yourself when summary sentences will be most effective in your essays.

Developing Body Paragraphs

Whether you are expanding a former single-paragraph assignment or beginning an essay from scratch, you will need to consider how to artfully develop your main points. Of course, we will use the same strategies to expand ideas in essays that we did in single paragraphs: examples, details, and explanations (see Chapter 3, pp. 41–48).

And we will continue to ask ourselves "How can I more clearly show my reader what I am saying?" One way is with examples that become increasingly specific, one level of example illustrating the next level. You will also connect more solidly with your reader as you add **specific words** and **sensory details.**

Comparing one major example (subtopic) from the paragraph version of "Dangers in a Deli" to one body paragraph in the essay, we can see developing and refining of a main point in operation:

Single-Paragraph Subtopic	*Essay Body Paragraph*
One concern for potential deli workers is slippery floors. If the counter is packed with anxious customers, and workers are hustling about taking care of their orders, a wet floor is not going to take top priority. During the rush what's going to stop an employee from running too fast, which could result in a serious wipeout.	One common hazard for deli workers is slippery floors. Often, especially during the lunch rush, the place gets jammed. Anxious customers crowd into one another and lean over the stainless in your face to call out three more changes to their already late orders. Trying to manage the rush, employees hustle about, carrying checks, prepping sandwiches, carting plates back and forth. When scurrying from the salad case to the register, you might not notice that freshly mopped floor, and before you know it, you are crashing into a wall and banging your head on the slick, hard tile. And if you don't trip yourself up, there are always other employees to run into you, which can also cause a serious wipeout.

Margin notes:

Always use strong connectors between body paragraphs.

Summary sentences can be useful in body paragraphs.

Teaching Idea
You might want to clarify that a summary sentence in a body paragraph does not contain an expanded thought, as the concluding sentence of a one-paragraph paper often does.

Development of ideas relies on examples, details, and explanations.

Subtopic sentence

What does the author mean by "slippery floors"? She explains, naming things and giving details.

How else can she refine her main idea of danger? She can add action. Note the boxed action words.

Topic sentence

How do they manage the rush? like this—**process analysis.**

What happens when they rush? Falling—**cause and effect.**

Notice how the single-paragraph subtopic has grown from 57 words to 121 in the essay body paragraph. The author held her main idea of danger—specifically slippery floors—in mind and discovered more examples, details, and explanations through using several of the prewriting methods in Chapter 1 (clustering, listing, freewriting) and by applying several of the **patterns of development** that we practiced in Unit Two. Note process analysis, cause and effect, and examples in the essay body paragraph. As we move into essay writing, although we will continue to use one pattern to focus the paper in Chapter 14, we should begin to think even more of using multiple methods for developing ideas. Examples are at the heart of all clear communication, but we apply them through the framework of the patterns of development represented in Unit Two and listed below.

1. **Description:** using vivid details to show something about your subject

2. **Narration:** telling a brief story to make a point about your subject

3. **Illustration:** giving examples to illustrate some point

4. **Classification/division:** putting your subject into a group, separating it from others like it

5. **Cause/effect:** telling what actions can affect your subject or effects can flow from it

6. **Process analysis:** telling how your subject works

7. **Comparison/contrast:** showing how your subject is like and unlike similar subjects

8. **Definition:** telling the essential characteristics of your subject

9. **Persuasion:** trying to move someone to agreement with you or to some action

Activity 12-6: Developing Body Paragraphs

Revise the following underdeveloped body paragraphs, using one or several of the patterns of development combined with detailed examples and explanations. Remember that your narrative/descriptive skills can build brief images that include people acting within a setting. Try for paragraphs of six to eight sentences, around 100 to 125 words.

1. Another problem with people who drink and drive is that often you cannot trust them. Sometimes they say they have not been drinking at all. Other times they say that they have only had one or two beverages when it is clear they have had more. Frequently they will go to a party saying that they will not drink at all. Right.

   Revision: _____*Answers will vary.*_____

   _____

   _____

   _____

   _____

   _____

   _____

   _____

   _____

   _____

Topic sentence

2. However, the most annoying habit my younger brother has is fooling with the TV while we are all trying to watch it. Channel surfing is his specialty. He has many ways of sneaking the constant channel changing in. If there is a commercial, watch out. If you leave the room for a snack, it's all over.

Revision: _Answers will vary._ _____

_____

_____

_____

_____

_____

_____

_____

_____

_____

Topic sentence

3. In addition to the other signs of wealth in this country, when I first entered a supermarket, I found the abundance almost dazzling. Americans have more of everything than we have in Russia. The aisles seemed endlessly stocked with anything a person might need.

Revision: _Answers will vary._ _____

_____

_____

_____

_____

_____

_____

_____

_____

_____

Arranging Body Paragraphs within Essays

Positioning body paragraphs in essays follows much the same logic that we used in organizing subtopics within single-paragraph papers. A writer might choose any of these three overall organizational patterns:

- **Spatial:** describing a subject/place from front to back, side to side, top to bottom, and so on. You might write part of a longer essay, or a whole one, describing, say, a lakefront home as seen from a boat in the water. You could focus the first body paragraph on the dock and boathouse, the next on the yard, and the third on the house itself.

- **Chronological:** relating a series of actions that unfold over time. In writing personal narrative, fiction, or process analysis, you would order your paragraphs as the action occurs. First Little Red Riding Hood had to pack her basket of goodies, then walk into the woods, then meet the wolf, then walk to her grandmother's house, and so on.

- **Order of importance:** arranging from least to most (or most to least) dramatic. In much expository and persuasive writing, you will choose this method. For example, the author of "Dangers in a Deli" felt that a fall was the least serious potential hazard her reader might face, so she built her first body paragraph around it. Next came the chemical danger, paragraph two, and the most serious problem, losing a finger, came last. (For more on these patterns, see p. 52.)

Remember, too, that you might need to follow one of these patterns *within* a body paragraph, just as we did in Unit Two. Although "Dangers in a Deli" uses least to most for overall arranging, within the body paragraphs the author relies more on time order, moving from slow business to fast business as the clock ticks and customers arrive. Notice the chronological sequencing in body paragraph number two below:

Topic sentence

Besides the slippery floors, workers also need to be cautious around chemicals. Even when business is slow, it is easy enough to be careless when cleaning the grease and handprints off all the glass, suddenly spraying yourself in the face with ammonia. But it gets worse when the rush begins, and the owner goes into his panic mode: "Get these dishes done! Now, now—we're filling up!" You might think you have a good grip on that slippery platter, until it squeezes out of your hands and splashes into a sink full of pan degreaser and sanitizer. It only takes one faceful of that hot, soapy water to send someone on her way to the emergency room.

Using Outlines

Another aid in the overall arrangement of an essay is the **outline.** In our paragraph assignments we created lists of major examples so we could then combine, delete, and order them. Because even our brief essays in Unit Three are more complex than single paragraphs, we are more likely to go astray now unless we lay out a framework before we wade into the project. A formal sentence outline is probably not needed for short essays, but listing primary examples and several supporting points can be a great help.

Notice how we might create a working outline for "Dangers in a Deli."

Teaching Idea
Some students resist any kind of outlining, no matter how informal, but you can reinforce the idea of outlines by periodically asking students to mention the main points or examples they will include in their essays and then saying, "Good outline."

Informal Working Outline

Thesis	*If you don't want to end up in the emergency room on your first day here, you need to be aware of the potential dangers in working at a deli.*
<u>Topic sentence</u> Supporting examples	I. *One common hazard for deli workers is slippery floors.* A. *Lunch rush* B. *Hurrying employees* C. *Fall on tile floor*
<u>Topic sentence</u> Supporting examples	II. *Besides the slippery floors, workers also need to be cautious around chemicals.* A. *Slow business still dangerous—ammonia* B. *Owner panicking* C. *Platter splashing into sink—degrease and sanitizer*
<u>Topic sentence</u> Supporting examples	III. *But the part of the job that is most dangerous is using the meat and cheese slicer.* A. *Operating or cleaning—dangerous* B. *Sharp blade* C. *People too tired—accident*

However you outline, write your thesis where you can refer to it frequently, and list at least the main examples with supporting examples and details.

▶ CONCLUDING PARAGRAPHS

If the introduction often poses problems for essay writers, then the conclusion frequently creates even more. How in the world can we leave our reader feeling that the promise we made in the thesis has been met, that the essay is decisively completed?

One way to accomplish this is to *plan* a concluding paragraph. Though many longer works require several paragraphs or even a chapter to conclude, we will only need five to seven sentences (around a hundred words or so) for our short essays. And we can make them interesting sentences by using the familiar strategy of the **expanded thought**.

As we draft and revise, we can notice the strong connection between the introductory and concluding paragraphs and be sure to include the following elements:

1. **Lead sentence:** one sentence (connector + link to thesis)

2. **Summary:** one sentence or less

3. **Development:** three to four sentences (often contains expanded thought)

Lead and Summary Sentences

Just as introductory and body paragraphs have a lead sentence (the "hook" and the topic sentence, respectively), so do concluding paragraphs. As writers move from their last body paragraph, they are careful to begin the conclusion with a connector that looks back at the paragraph just left behind. After that link has been made, it is common to touch on the thesis topic and statement. Sometimes a brief summary can also artfully be inserted into the lead sentence, or the summary might be in the second sentence.

We can see how the first sentence of the concluding paragraph from "Dangers in a Deli" is handled:

> Cuts, chemicals, concussions, and other dangers—with all these ways to injure himself, a new person on the job might feel a little overwhelmed.

The author could have written her lead and summary sentences in other ways, for instance, with the connector and link to thesis in the first sentence with a few summary words in the second:

> No employee wants to get hurt while she is working at the deli. So we all do our best to avoid hazards like falls, chemical burns, and cuts, and most of the time we succeed.

The beginning sentences of a concluding paragraph function to ease the reader out of the main stream of your ideas from the body paragraphs and into your final comments, which will do the real wrapping up of the essay.

Developing Conclusions

After we have led the reader into the concluding paragraph, rather than meandering for half a dozen empty, repetitive sentences, we need to end the essay decisively. We can do this with the following strategies, most of which we already know:

1. Frame: return to image, comparison, story, etc., from introductory paragraph

2. Expanded thought:

   A. Express an emotion.

   B. Give a judgment, opinion, or evaluation.

Sidebar notes:

The conclusion should fulfill the promise made in the thesis.

Introductions and conclusions should be tightly linked.

Teaching Idea
Student essays so often fizzle out in their conclusions that it is worth discussing why this happens. You might ask students to speculate on why they have difficulties at the end: deadlines, lack of inspiration, exhaustion, other?

Teaching Idea
Your discussion of causes for weak conclusions might lead naturally into methods for overcoming the problems: organizing and developing.

Statement about topic is shaded.

Connector is boxed.

Summary is underlined.

Effective writing leads readers carefully into the final thoughts.

Teaching Idea
It is useful to reiterate at this point that conclusions and introductions are "specialty" paragraphs with their own purposes: they work differently than body paragraphs.

Teaching Idea
Remind students that they have already practiced the "expanded thought" in their paragraphs. Conclusions just need a bit more development.

C. Show how something has affected your behavior or outlook on life.

D. Ask a related question.

E. Make a reflective statement.

F. Suggest a course of action.

3. Combination of methods

When we "frame" an essay, we return to the introduction and include at least part of the method we used to begin. As we have seen, there are many methods to develop introductory paragraphs (description, narration, comparison/contrast, etc.), so we would simply recall one, trying to add to it. For example, let's look back at the narrative approach in developing an introduction for "Dangers in a Deli":

Narrative introductory paragraph

Teaching Idea
You may or may not want to mention that "frames" can deal with location, emotional state, mental state, and more.

Thesis

Shawn came into the restaurant cracking jokes, kidding customers and fellow employees alike, and generally having a good time. Everyone liked him right away and could see that he would be fun to have around. But in the middle of his third day on the job, during the lunch rush, we lost him for good. I was taking an order at table seven, when all the loud talking, jostling, and eating stopped abruptly. Everyone in the restaurant heard Shawn scream as he lost the first joint of his little finger to the meat slicer. He learned the hard way how dangerous this job can be. If you too don't want to end up in the emergency room on your first day here, you need to be aware of the potential dangers in working at a deli.

We could "frame" the essay by continuing and extending the narrative like this:

Lead and summary

Concluding paragraph using narrative frame

Cuts, chemicals, concussions, and other dangers—there are plenty of ways a person on a job like this can injure himself. When Shawn came to us on that first day, I hoped that he would be careful enough to keep working here for awhile. We need fun people like him to make the job more interesting. But Shawn let himself have too much fun. He stopped by the day after his accident to show us his hand and say goodbye. He didn't blame anything on us, and he said he was sorry to go. His last words as he walked out the door were "Hey, the next time I'll know to listen up." So have fun while you are here, but don't become another Shawn.

Teaching Idea
See Chapter 12 in the Instructor's Manual for the concluding paragraph method each essay in *AWW* uses.

Whether or not you frame the essay, you still want to capture your reader's attention one last time before she puts your paper aside. An effective way to accomplish this is to offer an **expanded thought**, taking your audience one closely related step beyond the ideas in your body paragraphs, extending and broadening your topic. We followed this same strategy in the final sentence of our one-paragraph papers, but now we can develop the expanded thought. Using the deli essay as an example, we can create several possible conclusions on the basis of different expanded thoughts.

Teaching Idea
As with introductions it is worth taking some class time to have students write at least two different conclusions for one of their own essays to show them that there are many strong ways to conclude.

Concluding Paragraphs with Expanded Thoughts

1. **Personal emotion:** Let your reader know how you feel about your topic. What emotional response has it created in you?

Lead and summary sentences combined

Cuts, chemicals, concussions, and other dangers—there are plenty of ways for a person to get hurt on this job. I worried about it for the first month I was here, especially after I saw several other workers get hurt. But I learned that

I could keep myself safe if, when the restaurant began to speed up and people started moving fast, I kept myself at about 75 percent of my maximum speed. I can still get out the orders and keep everyone satisfied without pushing myself into an accident. Nowadays I don't need to worry much about getting hurt. I just pace myself, watch what I'm doing, and have a good time.

2. **Judgment:** Evaluate your topic, or express an opinion.

Cuts, chemicals, concussions, and other dangers—with all these ways to injure himself, a new person on the job might feel a little overwhelmed. But deli work doesn't always make you feel nervous and frazzled; in fact, it can be enjoyable. Whether you are talking to interesting customers or spending time with friends, the deli is usually a fun place to work. It can even be a great place for keeping your mind off problems at home or that algebra exam on Friday. Although accidents can happen, you are a lot less likely to have one if you keep the worst of the hazards in mind.

3. **Outlook or behavior modification:** Show how something has affected your behavior or outlook on life as a result of your experience with the topic.

Cuts, chemicals, concussions, and other dangers—there are plenty of ways for a person to get hurt on this job. Before I came to work here, I used to jump right into an activity without much thought of the consequences. Frying up a skilletful of bacon, chasing a soccer ball downfield, mowing the lawn—I used to rush into and through them all. But now I think twice. I don't want to burn myself with hot grease, sprain an ankle, or lose part of my foot under the mower. And I have found that becoming more cautious has not taken anything from my life but has, in fact, allowed me to participate more fully in everything. Fingers crossed, from now on I won't be standing around on crutches on the sidelines of anything I want to do in life.

4. **Question (s):** Ask one or more questions that might grow from your topic.

With all these ways to injure herself on the job, a person might wonder about working at a deli at all. Why should someone put herself in such a risky situation? The truth is that few jobs are altogether safe. A librarian can fall off a ladder and break her leg as easily as a waiter can slip and fall on a wet tile floor. The only sure way to reduce the chance of injury on the job is to follow the advice lots of parents give their children when they approach streets: stop, look, and listen. Slow down to live longer.

5. **Reflective statement:** Tell your reader something that your topic suggests to you beyond the points made in the body paragraphs. Think of some larger or more general application to the world around you.

Lead and summary sentences separated

With all these ways to injure herself on the job, a person might wonder about working at a deli at all. After all no one wants to be cut, burned by chemicals, or knocked unconscious. But the truth is that no matter how careful a person might be accidents cannot always be avoided. The world is an uncertain place, full of dangers. We like to think we can control our lives and protect ourselves absolutely. However, because this is not possible, perhaps it is best always to hope for, plan for, and work toward the best while preparing for the worst.

6. **Call to action:** Suggest that your reader or someone else act on the information you have presented.

Lead and summary
sentences separated

New employees and old hands alike can have an accident when they get too tired. Falls, scalds, and cuts are not uncommon in the deli as a result. Your best option to protect yourself is to listen to your trainer on your first few days at the job. Sure some of his advice will sound obvious—"Don't put sharp knives into a sinkful of soapy water"—but the time you stop paying attention is the time you will start hurting. So during your training period listen carefully, watch closely, and read thoroughly all the instructions for operating equipment safely. We want to keep you on the job, not in the hospital.

Activity 12-7: Determining an Expanded Thought

To help you create an expanded thought in your own essays, it will be useful to see the expanded thought in other essays. So turn to the essays listed below, locate and write out the thesis sentence in the space provided, and then write out in your own words the final expanded thought that you think the authors wanted to leave their readers with.

Example: "Dangers in a Deli" (pp. 263–264)

Thesis sentence: *"If you don't want to end up in the emergency room on your first day here, you need to be aware of the potential dangers in working at a deli."*

Expanded thought: *Working in a deli is not all danger and unpleasantness. The job can be fun.*

1. "The Jobs from Hell" (pp. 308–309)

   Thesis sentence: *Finally I tore myself out of the nightmare and sat up in bed, remembering all too well these images from the rotten jobs I have worked in my life.*

   Expanded thought: *His current college education is difficult but will pay off in the end.*

2. "A Skill beyond Price" (p. 313)

   Thesis sentence: *Reading is a skill beyond price, and I see people profiting from it daily as they move through various types of reading based on the person's purpose.*

   Expanded thought: *The author reiterates the value of reading and points to books (reading) as the source of all external knowledge.*

3. "I'll Park. You Get the Tickets—Hurry!" (pp. 325–326)

   Thesis sentence: *Some people love to watch films in a theater, but I find that watching them at home is a much more relaxing experience.*

   Expanded thought: *The author discusses the value of seeing films at a theater.*

Activity 12-8: Creating Interesting Conclusions

Return to Activity 12-2, Creating Interesting Introductions, and choose either the introduction you have already written or write another. Next, brainstorm to uncover several main examples that you *could* include in an essay growing from your chosen introductory paragraph. Now, create *two* concluding paragraphs, one using a frame, the other using any one of the six methods for expanding the final thought. Remember that you may combine several methods.

Answers will vary.

1. Concluding paragraph using frame

   Lead sentence: _____
   _____

   Summary sentence: _____
   _____

   Development: _____
   _____
   _____
   _____
   _____
   _____
   _____
   _____
   _____
   _____

You might combine the lead and summary sentences.

2. Concluding paragraph using expanded thought (list one method number: _____)

   Lead sentence: _____
   _____

   Summary sentence: _____
   _____

   Development: _____
   _____
   _____
   _____
   _____
   _____
   _____
   _____
   _____
   _____
   _____

AVOIDING WEAK CONCLUSIONS

Even after learning what makes a strong final paragraph, we sometimes stumble at the end of our essays. Here are several common problems to avoid in conclusions:

1. **Avoid simply summarizing (*and* overrepetition).**

   Some form of summary is used in almost all conclusions: the longer and more complex the essay, the longer and more detailed the summary might be. However, in brief essays, the reader seldom needs an in-depth recapping of examples and points. A sentence or less should be enough, just as the author of "Dangers in a Deli" used. Here is how the author could have over-summarized for a *weak* conclusion:

   > As you can see, there are plenty of dangers around a deli. It is all too easy for a person to slip and get hurt on a wet floor. And there are chemical hazards as well. Also even experienced employees might have a serious problem with the meat and cheese slicer, so everyone needs to be extra careful around it. Because people can be seriously and permanently injured by falls, chemicals, and cuts, they should be alert on the job at all times.

2. **Do not tell your reader that you are getting ready to end your essay.**

   While it *is* important to connect the first sentence of your concluding paragraph to the final body paragraph, avoid doing it with statements like these: "Well, as you can see, my essay is just about wrapped up, so . . ." or "In conclusion, my thesis sentence has already told you . . ." or "In the essay you have just read, I have tried to show . . ."

3. **Do not move into an unrelated or too-loosely related topic.**

   Remember that an expanded thought should grow naturally from the body of the essay, an extension of the thesis, not a different topic altogether. Looking at our deli example again, we can see how to avoid this problem:

   > Cuts, chemicals, concussions, and other dangers—with all these ways to injure himself, a new person on the job might feel a little overwhelmed. But, you know, life is full of danger. People get hurt all the time. Why once when I was mowing a lawn, I wasn't paying attention and sliced off the front of my right tennis shoe. I learned a lesson from that scare—watch what you are doing when you are operating dangerous equipment, especially lawnmowers!

   This conclusion could be revised to make an interesting and strong expanded thought. But as it is, the emphasis has shifted from the deli to lawn mowing.

4. **Avoid overgeneralizing—qualifying where necessary.**

   Expressing opinions and evaluativeng can be effective concluding strategies. However, it is important to *qualify* statements, so a writer does not seem to be asserting more than he can prove. We want to avoid all-inclusive statements like these: "And so you can see, *no one* has a good reason for watching too much television," "*Any* student who tries hard can make good grades," and "*Everybody* loves football." (For more on qualifying, see pp.371, 459.)

5. **Do not fall into an apologizing mode.**

   Here is another ineffective concluding strategy: "Although I do not know much about this topic, I have tried to show you . . ." or "Even though there are experts who know a lot more about this subject than I do . . ." or "Although I am still kind

Avoid oversummarizing in conclusions.

Teaching Idea
If you teach the chapter on persuasive writing, you might remind students of the overgeneralizing problem in conclusions.

of fuzzy about this topic, I hope you have learned something from my essay. . . ." Whether your essay is all you want it to be at this point or not, it is best to appear confident in the conclusion. If you really do have serious doubts about your paper, why not revise?

6. **Avoid clichés and worn expressions.**

Beware of clichés like these: "There were butterflies in my stomach," "All I had left was the shirt on my back," "No one could ever fill her shoes," and many more. If a fresh figure of speech does not come to mind, just use a literal phrase. Say, for example, "nervous" in place of the butterfly cliché from above. (For more on clichés and worn phrases, see Chapter 19.)

7. **Avoid overly long or overly short conclusions.**

> **Teaching Idea**
> Of course there are legitimate reasons for brief conclusions, for example in essay exams.

Conclusions should be written in proportion to the rest of the work. A book, on one end of the spectrum, might have a conclusion of many pages while an essay of ten pages might need a paragraph or two. Our brief essays can easily support an ending paragraph of five to seven sentences, about a hundred words or so.

Activity 12-9: Recognizing and Revising Weak Conclusions

Decide which of the following concluding paragraphs is ineffective, tell why you think so, and then *rewrite* any one of them, using a frame, one of the six methods for creating an expanded thought, or one of your own. You might find several problems illustrated in each of the weak examples.

1. Thesis: Rebuilding a carburetor is difficult, but with the right instructions most people can do it.

> **Lead and summary sentences shaded**

With all of the complicated steps in rebuilding a carburetor, from initially removing it to reinstallation, you might have trouble with it like I did. I got lost in the process myself several times, and I'm not sure that I included all the steps you will need to get the job done right. But I hope that I explained clearly enough and remembered the really important warnings that you ought to follow if you don't want a big mess on your hands. If you think you can rebuild that carburetor now, then all I can say is "Good luck!"

2. Thesis: My two older brothers are as different as two people can be.

> **Lead and summary sentences shaded**

With two brothers whose personalities are this different—one a whirlwind, the other a couch potato—a person might think that I would have a favorite. But that is not the case. I love both of my brothers equally, and I find many activities that we can share—though it's usually as two's company, three's a crowd.

3. Thesis: One way to group friends is by how long you have known them.

> **Lead and summary sentences shaded**

Friends are important in every person's life. There are potential friends, recent friends, and long-time friends, all of whom have their places in the overall category of friends. Potential friends might become friends someday if circumstances are right. Recent friends might be good friends, but they don't have a real track record yet. They might not hold up as good friends over the long haul. But long-time friends have proven themselves time and time again. A person knows that he can depend on long-time friends because they have been around for quite awhile and have shown their loyalty, support, and friendship many times over. For my money the best and most valuable friends are long-time friends.

CHAPTER 13

Revising Essays

Building Better Essays

Material
Organization
Style
Mechanics

REVISING ESSAYS

We revise essays in much the same way that we revised paragraphs—slowly, carefully, and critically. However, in order to produce that final polished draft, we must first adopt the attitude that we *can* rework and improve an essay, that there are clear steps to follow, and that it is worth the effort to do so. This chapter will remind you of many points that you practiced in the paragraph unit and help take you from that first rough collection of ideas through the final proofreading that produces superior work. (For more on revising on your own or within a group, see Chapter 1, pp. 14–16.)

REVISING FIRST-STAGE DRAFTS

With your first draft in hand, you are ready to begin the revision process that will ultimately tighten the essay and help your reader to better understand your ideas. If at this point you feel like your examples are generally geared toward a different audience than you had originally selected, but you like the overall content and shape of your paper, you might just redefine your reader.

Whether or not you need to rethink your *audience profile,* you should be prepared to make substantial revisions in *material* and *organization.* Expect that one or more of the examples are not working at all. Within each example you will probably need to add and delete details. Whenever the connection between the example and your thesis sentence is unclear, you know that you will need to further clarify. Look closely at your *introductory* and *concluding paragraphs.* Are they doing their job? Are they doing it well? If you are developing a writer's attitude toward revision—it is painful but necessary—then your work can do nothing but improve.

Teaching Idea
It can help students see the need for revising if you discuss how hard you work at revising your own writing.

Teaching Idea
As students revise their first essay or two, it helps to briefly review both the introductory and concluding paragraph examples in Chapter 12.

Grammar, spelling, and punctuation are low priority in first drafts.

The following is a list of common problems to watch for in your first rough draft. Keep in mind that the focus is on **content** (the substance of the examples, clarity of explanations, and kind of details) and **organization** (thesis and topic sentences, arrangement of paragraphs, unity, and coherence). In this draft, resist having your attention diverted from larger revision concerns by relatively minor glitches like spelling errors and questionable words. Second-draft revision will focus on those.

Common First-Stage Draft Problems

1. Have you used several major examples to illustrate your thesis?

    If your prewriting has uncovered enough interesting and relevant points to develop your main idea, you should be in good shape here. Still, you may be tempted to stick with, say, one or two major examples when three or four would better illustrate your thesis.

    Longer essays may have dozens of body paragraphs, but our short essays of 500 to 600 words should have at least two body paragraphs and no more than four. If you find that you have written, say, five to eight body paragraphs, you probably have not developed each one adequately, or you are moving into a lengthier essay. (Check with your instructor on the length range of your assignment.)

2. How effective is your thesis?

    Your thesis sentence has two functions: to name the topic and limit it with a statement. The statement may predict an explanation of the topic or express an opinion or attitude.

    If your working thesis sentence is unclear or too general, the essay may be headed for disaster. Be sure that both you and at least one other reader can easily predict where the essay is going based on the thesis. Also, unless you have some compelling reason to locate it elsewhere, position the thesis as the last sentence in your introduction. You may or may not use a forecasting statement. When you begin to revise a clear and focused thesis sentence, you can polish it through specific words, action words, and sensory details. (For more on thesis sentences, see pp. 265–269.)

3. How effective is the opening sentence—the "hook"—of your introductory paragraph?

    Does the first sentence arouse the reader's interest? Have you said something that would connect with your *target* audience? Check to make sure that you have not begun with an obvious statement or worn out expression. (For more on polishing hooks, see pp. 273–274.)

4. How well developed is your introductory paragraph?

    For our short essays an introduction of five to seven sentences should be fine. Have you used one or several of the methods for development listed in Chapter 12, or have you led your reader into your essay using some other strategy? Have you reviewed Avoiding Weak Introductions in Chapter 12? There are so many effective ways to begin an essay that settling for something so-so is a shame. (For more on methods of developing introductions, see pp. 269–272.)

5. Are your body paragraphs logically arranged by space, time, or importance?

    In expository and persuasive writing you will probably be organizing your body paragraphs chronologically or by order of importance, most frequently from least to most important. Whichever method you select, remain consistent and use appropriate transitions to signal that order between paragraphs. (By the way, occasionally your material will be arranged both by time *and* order of importance simultaneously, which is fine.) (For more on methods of arrangement, see pp. 281–282.)

Teaching Idea
If you review these revision lists with students, you might mention again that thesis sentences can be located elsewhere besides the last sentence in the first paragraph and point them to several of the essays in Unit Six as examples.

Teaching Idea
You might also remind students that summary sentences can make short body paragraphs sound a bit repetitive.

Teaching Idea
Lack of specific examples may be the most common flaw in the development of student essays. It sometimes helps gain students' attention to mention this.

Teaching Idea
You can use Journal Entry 13-1 to find out how students are coming with their drafts. It promotes revision, particularly in groups, to have students discuss what they think *might* need to be changed even if they cannot see how to make the change.

6. Have you introduced each body paragraph with a topic sentence?

While not all essay body paragraphs begin with topic sentences, many do. In our essays, for the sake of clarity and focus, each body paragraph ought to contain a topic sentence, and unless there is some good reason to do otherwise, that sentence should be the first one. Topic sentence = transition or other connector + topic + statement linked to thesis sentence statement.

You may sometimes find a summary sentence useful for wrapping up a body paragraph, particularly if the paragraph is fairly long.(For more on topic and summary sentences in essays, see pp. 278–279.)

7. How well developed are your body paragraphs?

All the paragraphs in an essay should be necessary, appropriate to a specific audience, and well developed enough to accomplish the author's purpose. The purpose of each *body* paragraph should be to illustrate one central idea or statement per paragraph (topic sentence), and this is done through detailed examples and explanations. Remember the principle of increasing specificity from the paragraph unit, layering detailed examples and explanations so that one sentence clearly adds to the next. Develop the habit of asking and answering these questions of your examples: "What do I mean by that statement? How can I make it more clear?"

One way to do this is through the elements of vivid scene building where appropriate: specific word choices, sensory details, active verbs, "-ings," dialogue, setting and people description. (For more on development of body paragraphs, see pp. 279–281; for more on narrative/descriptive elements, see pp. 78–81, 108–116.)

8. How well connected are sentences within and between paragraphs?

All sentences in an essay should flow smoothly, one to the next, but strong connections are especially important between paragraphs. Remember the categories of transitional words (words like *first, next, for example, another*) and the other methods for holding sentences together: repeat words, synonyms, pronouns, and reference to main ideas. (For more on sentence connectors see pp. 52–59.)

9. How effective is your concluding paragraph?

Check your concluding paragraph for these three parts:

- **Lead sentence:** one sentence (connector + link to thesis)

- **Summary:** one sentence or less

- **Development:** three to four sentences (containing a frame and/or expanded thought)

The first sentence of your conclusion should clearly connect with the last body paragraph and the thesis of the essay. A few brief summary words to recap main points/examples are also useful. Rather than oversummarizing, you can make the rest of your conclusion interesting by applying any of the methods for developing conclusions in Chapter 12 or by using one of your own. Be sure to review Avoiding Weak Conclusions. (For more on developing conclusions, see pp. 283–290.)

JOURNAL ENTRY 13-1

List three specific changes you have made or feel you ought to make from your first to second rough draft. Refer to the first-stage draft questions and answer them as specifically as possible. (For example: Question 4: "I decided that my introduction was weak, so I rewrote it, using method 9, startling information, that we practiced in Chapter 12.") Next, in a sentence or two say what you like best about the revised draft.

▶ REVISING SECOND-STAGE DRAFTS

Depending on your writing habits, you may find yourself with a fairly complete draft at this stage, or you may still need to spend more time on content and organization. But assuming that you are comfortable with most of the material in this draft, we can work a bit more with **word-** and **sentence-level** revision possibilities.

Common Second-Stage Draft Problems

1. How well have you used specific language?

   Your essay will include both relatively **general** and relatively **specific** terms, but specific words create the sharpest images. You can write about someone wearing old clothes (a relatively general expression), but if it is important to the scene, be more specific, perhaps saying, "old blue jeans and a sweatshirt" or, becoming more specific, "faded Levi's ripped out at the knees and a baggy KU Jayhawk sweatshirt." (For more on specific language, see pp. 78–79.)

2. Have you included some sensory details?

Teaching Idea
Because students will use many personal examples to develop even their expository writing this semester, it helps to review the strategies of specific language, sensory details, and active verbs.

   Some sensory details can be useful in expository and persuasive essays. Often you can get a two-for-one bonus when you use specific words. For instance, in "Sixteen and Mother of Twelve," p. 117, the author writes *camouflage* uniform pants, *black* marching boots, and *brown* T-shirts, placing the visual color in front of the specific article of clothing. Later the author mentions "sweaty faces," adding a touch sensation. Of course, all spoken dialogue creates a sound impression, but linked to active verbs, the sound can become more dramatic as in "What a Joke!" when Linda Blair <u>roars</u> out, "MERRIN!" (For more on sensory details, see pp. 80–81, 97.)

3. Are you choosing the most "active" verbs to describe action?

   Almost all sentences require verbs to make them complete, often conveying a sense of action or movement. But some verbs show action less efficiently than others (*be, do, have,* and *make* are common culprits). Consider these sets of sentences:

   A. Thunder <u>could be heard</u> on the lake.

   B. Thunder <u>shook</u> the lake.

   C. I <u>moved</u> my head around to my left toward the shore.

   D. I <u>jerked</u> my head around to my left toward the shore.

   If you think that sentences B and D create a more vivid image, review your own draft sentence by sentence to see if any can be made more interesting. (For more on active verbs, see pp. 451–452, 485, and for more on passive voice, see pp. 542–543.)

4. Are you using any "-ing" words?

   Participles (one kind of word with an "-ing" ending) can also be useful for conveying a sense of action. Consider these sets of sentences:

   A. My girls <u>made</u> it through all the obstacles.

   B. <u>Running</u>, <u>climbing</u> wooden walls, <u>crossing</u> rope bridges, and <u>playing</u> Tarzan on a rope swing, my girls tore through that course.

   C. In loose white pajamas he was in front of me to scratch on the door.

   D. <u>Wearing</u> loose white pajamas, grandfather was standing in front of me, <u>leaning</u> forward to scratch on the door again.

   If you think sentences B and D create a more vivid image, revise your own sentences, adding "-ing" words wherever they are needed. (For more on "-ings," see pp. 68, 494.)

5. Have you experimented with a comparison like a metaphor or simile?

Metaphors and similes can create fresh and sometimes startling images by comparing two seemingly dissimilar things that share a common property. Consider the following two descriptions:

A. Thunder shook the huge lake, and I could see the water move.

B. Thunder shook the huge lake <u>as if it were a glass of water</u>, vibrating, nearly ready to fall off of some gigantic rock and <u>shatter on the ground</u>.

Comparing the lake to a glass of water is a fresh image (versus a cliché), and the fragile nature of a glass that can be smashed helps set the mood for the later tragedy in the story. If you think that sentence B has more power, then review your own draft sentence by sentence to see if any literal description might benefit from a metaphor or simile. (For more on metaphor and simile, see pp. 473–474.)

6. Are the sentences in your essay varied in length?

Writing can become more or less interesting based on the structure of sentences alone. After you have polished word choices, check the length of sentences (counting the words can help). If you find more than three or four sentences in a row that are roughly the same length (say, fourteen, seventeen, twelve, fifteen words), you can either combine two or divide any overly long one. (For more on overall sentence variety, see Chapter 18.)

7. Are the beginnings of your sentences varied?

If even two sentences in a row begin with the same word or phrase, such as *the*, change an opening or combine sentences to break up the pattern of beginnings. Also look for too many similar openings even if the sentences are widely spaced. For example, you might notice that you have begun eight out of twenty sentences with the word *as*. It is easy to substitute a word or even combine a few sentences to increase the overall readability of the essay. (For more on variety in sentence openers, see pp. 435–446.)

8. Have you repeated a word or phrase so often that it becomes noticeable?

While some repetition of a word or phrase is often useful, too much of the same word group becomes boring. Consider the following two sets of sentences:

A. There were many people on the **lake** waiting to put their boats in the **water** there at Hillside **Lake** on that tragic July afternoon. In my boat on the **lake,** I felt hot and sticky from waiting on the humid **lake water** as I frantically maneuvered my small aluminum boat closer to the ramp by the **lake**shore.

B. There were many people in the **water** waiting to put their boats on their trailers at Hillside **Lake** on that tragic July afternoon. I felt hot and sticky waiting on the **lake,** frantically maneuvering my small aluminum boat closer to the ramp.

If you think that version B is more readable, revise your own sentences, cutting nonessential words. (For more on unnecessary repetition, see pp. 479–480.)

9. Have you included words that serve no purpose?

Everyday speech is full of unneeded words, but writing should not be. Cluttered writing can bore and confuse, while concise writing involves a reader and clarifies ideas. Compare the following two sentences. Which is concise; which is cluttered?

A. The **meat** hotdogs, **long and thin,** sizzle **with a sizzling sound** as they cook, **roasting,** and drip **meaty juices** off the end of the **wooden** stick.

B. The hotdogs sizzle as they cook and drip juices off the end of the stick.

If you think that sentence B is more readable, revise your own sentences, cutting nonessential words. (For more on unneeded words, see pp. 454–464.)

Teaching Idea
Given half a chance, students will reply to revision questions with vague statements or simply fall back on revising for mechanics. Journal Entry 13-2 again asks for specifics and will be most useful if student responses are discussed in class and then collected for review.

> **JOURNAL ENTRY 13-2**
>
> Skimming through the questions on revising second-stage drafts, can you find ways to improve your paper? If you can't, just list several points that you *suspect* might be a problem. If you have managed to revise successfully, list three specific changes you made from the first to the second draft. (Hint: Refer to the questions when you respond. For instance: Question 8: "I noticed that I had used the word *car* fifteen times, so I substituted *vehicle, hot machine,* and *it* to eliminate five of the *car* references.)

Teaching Idea
Try focusing students on one or two errors at a time as they edit these practice paragraphs.

◗ EDITING

With your assignment substantially complete, now is the moment to practice some of the important editing rules that all serious writers must master. The next few hours that you commit to this project, as you work through errors peculiar to your own work, will help to free you from the constant nagging doubts about grammar, spelling, and punctuation that bother so many writers. So with a bit of determination, your textbook in hand, and a friend or two to help, try to polish your paper till a reader can see himself in it.

Teaching Idea
There are four practice paragraphs to help on days when the class edits essays (or for students to do out of class). If you need more, you will find seven shorter practices in Chapter 4.

The following brief paragraphs have a number of these common mechanical errors:

• Misspelled words	• Sentence fragments	• Missing commas	• Pronoun agreement
• Missing words	• Comma splices	• Unneeded commas	• Apostrophes
• Wrong words	• Run-on sentences	• Verb tense shifts	• Capitalizations
• Sound-alike words		• Pronoun reference	

Editing these practice paragraphs will help you with your own revision.

Take a moment to read through each paragraph *slowly* and carefully, putting your finger on every word if necessary, and see how many of the mistakes you catch.

Editing Review 13-1

Panick and fustration our a sure fire recipe, for tears but I fought them of and strugled too remain calm, for my girls. Suddenly I hear a voice, say "Listen I have a cell phone, do you want to call someone to come pick you up". As I turned toward the voice I saw an older gentleman, who looked a lot like my dad. Begining to cry I explained how helples I felt.

(Turn to p. 130 and look at the middle of "Do Unto Others . . ." to see the corrected version of this excerpt.)

Editing Review 13-2

Another important part of true Home is that people can relax their. When we feel safe we can begin to feel at ease in are surroundings. If famly members our considerat of one another they will give each other the space each need they will give each other the time, and opportunity to unwind in, whatever, way works best for each. Some listens to music some watches TV and, some just appreciates laying down on a couch. A true Home encourages relaxation. At the end of a busy stressful day out "there" we all needed to escape the pressure's of being productive.

(Turn to p. 343 and look at "Finding Home" to see the corrected version of this excerpt.)

Editing Review 13-3

"Your'e a dummy and so's your Old Lady and Old Man!" These were fighting words for me as a child and I ended up rolling around in the dirt more than once with the kids from school who said them. Growing up with hearing impaired parents in sixties if I was not fighting some kid in an alley it seems like I was trying to explain to some other child that my family was normal, we just didnt talk much which words. Back then most people didnt no much about the deaf comunity and even, today I, often see people turn, and gawk at the hearing impaired when they are signing each other. Maybe knowing more about the deaf will make them seem less strange to the hearing world.

(Turn to p. 344 and look at "Deaf, Not Dumb" to see the corrected version of this excerpt.)

Editing Review 13-4

Boing in the ocean in scuba gear, is a lot like being in outer space when a diver is floating, in silence above a deep, water coral plateau with a half-mile drop into darkness a few yards away. He is in another world. Depending on the compressed air, in his cylinders, and his regulator to deliver it. Smoothly the diver glides weightlessly, almost effortlessly, through "inner space." Similarly an Astronaut floats in darkness. With the deepest drop imaginble all around him. He also depend on his gear to deliver air protect him from the cold and other extremes tells him how much air he has and Orient him toward his "boat." Most of us will never have the oportunity too voyage into Outer Space but, we can learn a little about the next, best option for inner planetary travel, scuba diving.

(Turn to p. 355 and look at "Get Wet" to see the corrected version of this excerpt.)

Well, how did you do? If you caught all but two or three errors, congratulations; you are a careful editor! If you missed more than five or six, you should simply slow down even more and apply the editing skills you are learning. The following are a few reminders of the errors to look for in your own draft:

Common Editing Problems

1. **Spelling:** Use your spell checker first, and then try to find at least one other reader who is not afraid to say she is a fairly good speller. Remember, too, that the dictionary can help. (For help with spelling problems, see Chapter 27.)

2. **Sound-alike words:** (*there/their/they're, to/too, then/than, your/you're,* and so forth.) Keep adding to your **Improvement Chart** (p. A-21), and try to memorize these repeat errors. It is seldom that a writer has more than a handful that he just keeps repeating—unless he learns them—till doomsday. (For help with sound-alike words, see Chapter 27.)

Teaching Idea
If you have students edit in class, it is useful to list the three major comma categories on the board along with some "cue" words: *because, who/which, and/but.* You will also find selected editing review sheets in the Instructor's Manual.

3. **Missing words:** Read slowly. Sometimes reading a sentence backward—admittedly, a tedious process—can help, and covering the sentence ahead of the one you are editing can keep you from jumping ahead too quickly.

4. **Wrong words:** Be suspicious of words that sound too "writerly." If you often refer to a thesaurus for word choices, you might be using the words incorrectly. You probably already have enough vocabulary to express yourself well, and, honestly, smaller, more common words are frequently the best choices. Your readers can alert you to *possible* poor selections; then you can work with a dictionary and someone else to make the final decisions. (For more on clarity through small words, see pp. 465–466.)

5. **Sentence fragments:** Remember two common types:

    a. Phrase: Running to the store for bread and a six-pack of Coke. (See pp. 525–527.)

    b. Subordinate clause: Because he is the kind of man we want for mayor. (See pp. 527–529.)

6. **Comma splices/run-ons:** Remember there are at least five easy ways to fix these.

    a. Comma splice: The cement is freezing, it instantly numbs my feet.

    b. Run-on: The cement is freezing it instantly numbs my feet. (See pp. 518–524.)

    ▶ In dialogue be careful to avoid this kind of comma splice: Roxanne shouted, "Get out of here, nobody gives a damn about you anyway!" Instead write: Roxanne shouted, "Get out of here! Nobody gives a damn about you anyway!" People frequently speak in short sentences and in fragments. Don't be afraid to show this in your dialogue.

7. **Capitalizations:** Rule of thumb: capitalize a proper noun (a specific/unique person, place, or thing, see pp. 578–579). In your title capitalize most words, even little ones like *is* and *one*. But do not capitalize articles (*a, an, the*), prepositions (*to, on, of, in,* etc.), and coordinating conjunctions (*and, but,* etc.) unless these words begin or end a title or follow a colon.

8. **Apostrophes:** Use to show ownership or mark the omission of a letter in a contraction: Maria's calculator isn't working. (See p. 578.)

9. **The Big Three comma categories:** These categories govern perhaps half of our common comma mistakes:

    a. Use commas to introduce some single words, phrases, and the subordinate adverb clause before a main clause. (See pp. 565–567.)

    b. Use commas to enclose *nonessential* words, phrases, or clauses within a main clause or set them off at the end of a main clause. (See pp. 567–569.)

    c. Use commas to divide main clauses joined by *and/but* (*or, so, yet, for, nor*). (See pp. 570–571.)

10. **Unnecessary commas:** As you learn the handful of rules that help you with comma placement, you will begin to move away from the old standby "I put commas where I hear the pauses." Using your ear can help with punctuation, but only about half the time. Most of us don't want a 50 percent average, so learning a few rules is the way to go. Try to avoid the ear/pause mistakes of unneeded commas in the following examples:

    a. I went to Burger King for lunch, and then to McDonald's for dinner.

    b. I eat three 13-ounce bags of potato chips every day, because I want to have *a* heart attack. (See pp. 573–575.)

Teaching Idea
If you write an example sentence on the board to illustrate a comma dividing compound sentences, you can use the same sentence to show one unnecessary comma by crossing out the subject in a selected second main clause.

After you have done the most thorough job of editing that *you* can do on your draft, it is time to get some help. Every writer—professional and beginner—benefits from having others look closely at her work. You will undoubtedly spend some class time in collaborative editing sessions, but don't stop there. Be willing to work with your instructor, and remember that many schools have writing centers that specialize in helping students through all phases of the writing process.

> ### JOURNAL ENTRY 13-3
>
> Your draft should be in good shape at this point, all the important details in place, words carefully chosen, and sentences flowing in smooth, varied patterns. Review your **Improvement Chart** to focus on pattern errors, and then slooowly, edit your paper, word by word, line by line. List at least three errors from the editing review list that you found in your draft, and then write out the corrections.

▶ PROOFREADING

Teaching Idea
Proofreading is just another name for final editing, and it is amazing how many students skip it. In particular, you might stress number 3, spell checking additional required material and title pages.

Proofreading is the last step in the preparation of your paper. This is where we put on the final polish. Assuming that you have closely edited your last draft and caught all the mechanical errors possible, you will print your final copy, the one you turn in for a grade. At this point you might think the last copy is as finished as you can make it, because, after all, you just spent an hour editing. But there are still common problems that appear in the last draft, ones that you can catch and correct—before your instructor does.

How to Proofread and Prepare Your Final Manuscript

1. Check for typographical errors such as misspelled, run together, and omitted words. Often when fixing errors in the editing stage, we slip up in small ways on the keyboard. **Be sure to spell check once again.**

2. Check the following items carefully: font size (12 point), line spacing (double-space), margins (1 inch), and title (see capitalization of words in Common Editing Problems, number 7).

3. Spell check any additional required material, such as outlines and audience profiles.

4. Staple or paper clip your pages. Avoid putting the paper in a plastic sleeve. (Most instructors don't want to fish around in the sleeve and then try to stuff the paper back into it when they are finished evaluating the paper.)

To see how to format a title page and the first page of your essay, turn to pp. 74–75.

> ### JOURNAL ENTRY 13-4
>
> Reflecting for a moment over your work in and out of class in producing this essay assignment, take about ten minutes to write a page telling your instructor about the challenges you had to overcome, how you dealt with them, and what you think might be the most important strategies to apply to your upcoming writing assignments this semester.

Final-Draft Checklist

__ 1. Have you used several major examples to illustrate your thesis?

__ 2. How effective is your thesis?

__ 3. How effective is the opening sentence—hook—of your introductory paragraph?

__ 4. How well developed is your introductory paragraph?

__ 5. Are your body paragraphs logically arranged by space, time, or importance?

__ 6. Have you introduced each body paragraph with a topic sentence?

__ 7. How well developed are your body paragraphs?

__ 8. How well connected are sentences within and between paragraphs?

__ 9. How effective is your concluding paragraph?

__10. How well have you used specific language, sensory details, active verbs, and "-ings"?

__11. Have you experimented with a comparison like a metaphor or simile?

__12. Are the sentences in your essay varied in length and beginnings?

__13. Have you repeated a word or phrase so often that it becomes noticeable or included words that serve no purpose?

__14. Have you written a title—an interesting one—for the paper? (Check capitalizations.)

__15. Have you prepared your paper according to the format expected by your instructor? (Check to see if you need a title page, be sure to double-space, leave at least a 1-inch margin, use a 12-point font, and be sure to type or word process.)

__16. Have you edited your work as closely as you know how to, including having at least one other person—classmate, friend, family member—proofread closely? Have you checked your **Improvement Chart** for your pattern errors so you can look for them specifically?

__17. Have you looked specifically for the following errors: spelling, sound-alike words, missing words, wrong words, unclear pronoun reference, sentence fragments, comma splices/run-ons, capitalizations, apostrophes, the Big Three comma categories, and unnecessary commas?

Teaching Idea
You might discuss classification more in terms of organizing than in generating material.

Teaching Idea
Because the single organizing principle can be confusing to students, it is especially useful to work through several of the Chapter 8 activities that focus on the SOP.

CREATING AND EXPLAINING GROUPS (CLASSIFICATION)

As we learned in Chapter 8, we often need to divide large ideas or groups of objects and then separate the pieces in ways that make sense. For example, when a family moves from one home to another, they begin a large-scale **division-and-classification** project as they group all their belongings for the move.

When we divide and classify, we need a standard or reason for grouping items, which we will call the **single organizing principle** (SOP). In moving household belongings, we could divide them according to, say, color and shape, grouping everything blue together (living room couch with blue jeans) and everything round together (plates with CDs)—but this would lead to a mess on the other end. More logically, we would want to keep items that belong in one room together, so we could unpack as efficiently as possible on the other end. To do this, we would use the organizing principle of rooms to divide the household, ending with as many groups as there are rooms in the new home.

People divide and classify all the time on the job, at home, and at school as a way of making sense out of large amounts of information. Consider just these few examples and one possible way of grouping each:

1. **Job—retail sales positions at Dillard's:** *group by departments:* men's wear, women's wear, girl's wear, boy's wear, cosmetics, etc.

2. **Home—a filing system for bills:** *group by billing party:* gas, electric, water, trash collection, mortgage, etc.

3. **School—a way to organize class notes:** *group by classes:* math, history, speech, English, etc.

Whether you are coming to this chapter with a paragraph already written from Chapter 8 or are just beginning a classification assignment, you will find that you already have much experience dividing and grouping things.

Note: For a more complete discussion of classifying, turn back to Chapter 8.

CLASSIFICATION ESSAYS: LOOKING CLOSELY AT STUDENT MODELS

The following two student models will help you write effective classification essays. Notice as you read that both essays make the single organizing principle clear in the thesis sentence so that the reader knows the basis for dividing and classifying the topics. "A Skill beyond Price" discusses groups that the author created himself, while "Shopping the Easy Way" subdivides a toy store by using a preestablished system for categorizing. Either approach can work well.

Look especially closely at the introductory and concluding paragraphs in the models, because they are a major component of the essays.

Prereading Exploration for "A Skill beyond Price"

Teaching Idea
To help students avoid the pointless classification, after they have read "A Skill beyond Price," ask them to discuss the author's purpose and point.

Ho-Chul chose a topic based on his strong belief that reading is a key to a successful, happy life. The people he most wants to address are those who do not read much or see any special value in it, some of his fellow students, in particular.

How do you feel about the importance of reading? Do you read frequently or infrequently? Do you think that young adults of college age value reading more or less than their parents' generation? Write your response in the space provided below.

_____

_____

_____

A Skill beyond Price

Frequently it is said, "No one reads anymore." I have read this in newspapers and magazines and heard it on television commentaries. And I have heard teachers at my college complain that their students do not even read the work assigned in their textbooks, much less read for pleasure. But I wonder if this is true. The students I spend most of my time around seem to be reading constantly, and not always just their homework. Reading is a skill beyond price, and I see people profiting from it daily as they move through various types of reading based on the person's purpose. **1**

The first category can be called required reading. Most people have some kind of regular required reading. At home we sort through mail to find which may be valuable and which may be waste. At work many people have to read office communications and even service and labor jobs post memos and warning notices that employees should read if they want to profit or keep themselves from harm. Of course, students are surrounded by books that they are expected to read and prove that they know on exams. Sometimes we resent the have-to part of this kind of reading, and sometimes just the word "required" makes us want to put it aside. However, there is much to be gained in much required reading, and I have often seen the book that one person drags himself through another person happily embrace. **2**

More pleasant for most people is the reading that they choose for leisure and entertainment. Some people enjoy short stories and novels that include literature, western, romance, detective, science fiction, and mystery. Huge bookstores like Borders and Barnes & Noble are filled with people relaxing with their favorite new story. Others prefer magazines that keep them informed on the world, such as *Newsweek* and *National Geographic,* on their profession, or on some special interest or hobby. People read daily newspapers, comic books, and letters from friends. Many people find inspiration in the Bible and other religious publications. The World Wide Web offers chat rooms, list servs, and e-mail, all of which allow people to read and write for fun and knowledge. The greatest difference between reading in this category and that which is required seems to be freedom, the choice to read or not. **3**

The most helpful for many people and the most enjoyable reading for me is the practical information found in how-to books and magazines. After examining this kind of material, people can immediately apply the knowledge to their everyday lives. For instance, they can learn how to cook delicious food, how to make a beautiful garden, how to take photographs well, and how to decorate a house attractively. Because people have a personal interest, a clear goal, in practical reading, they can concentrate on it more than with much required reading. And I have noticed that, as with some required reading, how-to books can be interesting and fun for many people, moving these books into the more-preferred leisure/entertainment category. **4**

People read for many reasons, and if they achieve their goal in any category of reading, then it can be said that they have profited. Even the least-preferred type of reading, that which is required, can be beneficial in many ways. It seems to me that people are still much involved with words and pages in books, magazines, and electronic sources, and how could this be otherwise since reading is the foundation of civilization? We may not like to do some kinds of reading, but all the knowledge that exists outside of one person and the people he can immediately speak to is contained within books. The Internet, which my generation is growing up with, is a vast library that offers a wealth of words to any who will pause to view them. I think truly that we are still in a reading world. **5**

Ho-Chul Sung

Postreading Analysis

Ho-Chul does a fine job of organizing and developing this essay. From the introduction that draws his target audience in, through the body paragraphs that explain a single point clearly, to the concluding paragraph that reinforces his thesis and expands the point, the essay does the job it sets out to do.

The single organizing principle, so important to a classification essay, is specifically mentioned in the thesis and is echoed in each topic sentence. Because the topic of reading can be classified in many different ways (as most of the topics for your essays can be), the author needed to be careful in designating his three groups, to make sure he included all the important categories without overlap. He manages this, at the same time pointing out how a person's attitude might help one type of reading become another.

Why do you think that Ho-Chul ended each body paragraph with the sentences that he has? What would be lost, if anything, were he to cut them?

▶ Prereading Exploration for "Shopping the Easy Way"

Ann Nall works in a local Toys "R" Us and so decided that it would make a good topic for her classification paper. Although many of her fellow students in the class have been in this toy store, she thought that relatively new parents might most appreciate the information she offers, especially the information on items contained within the baby section.

If you have ever been in a Toys "R" Us or another toy store, how did you find your way around? What single organizing principle seems logical to apply to a toy store? Write out below one or more possible methods for dividing and grouping merchandise in a toy store.

_____

_____

_____

To see this essay as a paragraph, turn back to Chapter 8, pp. 167–170.

Shopping the Easy Way

Have you ever entered a toy store and been confused by the masses of toys and cluttered aisles of seemingly endless options? Sometimes you may know exactly what you are looking for but spend half an hour just trying to find the right area to start the real search. Other times you may have only a general idea of what you want, but you still hope to see everything the store has to offer so that special gift does not pass you by. When a person is overwhelmed by shelves crammed so full of toys that she cannot tell one from the other and puts her life in danger as she stumbles over merchandise lying haphazardly on the floor, she is not having a pleasant shopping experience. However, Toys "R" Us is nothing like this. To help customers shop more efficiently, Toys "R" Us is neatly divided into three overall categories: areas for older children, toddlers, and babies.   1

The older children have four major areas—Blue, Pink, R-Zone, and Silver—with piles of toys for everyone. Boys mostly head for the Blue section and items like the GI Joes, superheroes, Hotwheels, and Legos. In no time at all, the boys can have Lego racetracks assembled on the floor and be racing miniature Batmobiles after the "bad guys." Girls, on the other hand, usually go for the Pink section, where there are dozens of different Barbies, complete with friends—Ken, Skipper, Stacie, Kelly, Teresa, Kira—Cabbage Patch Kids, and tea sets that help the girls build fantasies as they pretend they are older. Both sexes enjoy the video games and bicycles in the R Zone and Silver. Although it may seem like gender stereotyping to some, the Blue and Pink   2 sections, especially, do help both children and parents get to the merchandise they are most interested in.

The next group of children, the toddlers, has the Red and Green areas. Toys in these sections are larger than those in the older children's area and do not have as many small pieces, so the toddlers are less likely to choke. Customers shop in Red to find smaller toys such as Play Dough and building blocks to help their children develop fine motor skills. Also Red offers a variety of musical instruments, from simple shakers like maracas and tambourines to the more complicated guitars and electronic keyboards. Large outdoor play sets, made primarily of plastic, and traditional metal swing sets complete with slides and gliders are located in the Green section.

For the smallest children moms and dads shop in Purple, and it surprises many parents that Toys "R" Us offers so much for infants. This part of the store contains most of what parents need to get children through their first year. Each aisle is clearly marked, guiding shoppers to shelves of diapers, wipes, bottles, formula, clothes, rattles, teething toys, eating utensils (mostly spoons), and . . . well, you name it. After the baby's immediate needs have been met, the store can still help with important items like baby carriers, car seats, and strollers.

Shoppers are often confused by disorganized toy stores, but organizing merchandise the way Toys "R" Us does helps people readily find what they need for children of different ages. There are other places to shop for your children—Kmart, Wal-Mart, Target, K B Toys—but finding what you want in these stores can be an ordeal. As frustrating as shopping of any kind can be, with the general confusion, noise, poor service, tight schedules, and money concerns, why not try to make the venture as painless as possible? Good organization is the key to a pleasant and productive shopping experience.

Ann Nall

Postreading Analysis

Ann's essay begins with an introduction geared to her target audience, new parents, addressing them directly with the pronoun *you*. While *you* is often overused and inappropriately used in writing, it can be an effective device for connecting with your reader, particularly if you have a specific audience in mind (for more on using "you" and involving an audience, see pp. 367–369, 554–555). Notice, also, that *you* virtually disappears from the body of the essay—being replaced with words like *parents*, *shoppers*, *children*, and *customers*—reappearing in the conclusion, where Ann wants to speak directly to her reader again.

Each body paragraph is carefully introduced with a topic sentence that guides readers through the paragraph, and each paragraph is tightly linked to a preceding one with connector words. Because this essay grew from a paragraph assignment in Unit Two, the author was able to add even more specific names of merchandise and further explanation to develop her major examples.

Do you think the comment about gender stereotyping at the end of the first body paragraph is a digression from the main point of the paragraph or useful clarification?

Key Elements of Classification Essays

Here are several important points—illustrated by the preceding student models—to keep in mind for your own classification essay:

1. Use a single organizing principle; see pp. 164–166.

2. Avoid overlapping categories; see pp. 166–167.

3. Include all important members of the group; see pp. 167–168.

4. Have a reason for the classification; see p. 171.

Teaching Idea
You might have students who are having difficulty choosing appropriate pronoun case. Contrast the use of "you" in Ann Nall's introduction—where she intends to speak directly to her audience—with the pronoun shift examples in Chapter 24.

Develop a paragraph by adding specific names and more explanation.

Teaching Idea
To help them get beyond surface causes and effects, try having students carry out a causal chain as far as they can imagine it. You might refer them to Alternate Writing Assignment 5 in Chapter 9 for help with this.

EXPLAINING CAUSES AND EFFECTS

As we learned in Chapter 9, when we speculate about the reasons and outcomes of an event, we are dealing with the process of **cause and effect.** For example, suppose a tree falls on a house. What might have caused it? High winds are a likely immediate cause, but perhaps there are other reasons. Insects, disease, or drought may have weakened the tree, contributing to the fall. Wind resistance from the leaves might explain why the tree fell in spring and not winter. Beyond why it happened, homeowners would want to know how the damage would affect them: How would they clean up the mess; who would do it; how much would it cost; would insurance cover it; how long would the repairs take; would the house ever be the same? When we ask and answer questions of this nature, we are dealing with causes and effects.

In the tree example from above, a *likely* effect that would concern the homeowners would be the increase of their homeowner's insurance, and so this effect should be included in an essay. An *unlikely* cause for the tree's weakening might be excessive fertilizer on the lawn the previous week, and so this "cause" should not be included in an essay. Even though insect damage might be a real cause, it might not be a *significant* cause in this case if the insect damage was marginal, and so this cause would also be omitted from an essay. Finally, it would be *oversimplifying* the likely effects if a person wrote that a single call to Allstate would be the primary effect of the damage. An essay might also need to mention other likely effects, such as inconveniencing the homeowners while the repairs are underway and having the lawn damaged from heavy repair equipment.

Teaching Idea
If you teach the chapter on persuasion, you might refer students back to Chapter 9 for help with avoiding the post hoc fallacy.

Whether you are coming to this chapter with a paragraph already written from Chapter 9 or are just beginning a causes or effects assignment, you will find that you already have much experience determining causes and speculating about outcomes.

Note: For a more complete discussion of cause and effect, turn back to Chapter 9.

CAUSE AND EFFECT ESSAYS: LOOKING CLOSELY AT STUDENT MODELS

The first student model that follows, "My Friend Who Gave Up on Life," discusses likely causes for a tragic event, while the second, "The Thousand-Dollar Lesson," deals with the effects of a questionable pastime. Essays are often developed with both causes and effects, as well as many of the other patterns in Unit Two, but you might be better served to choose either causes *or* effects to help focus your brief essay.

Look especially closely at the introductory and concluding paragraphs in the models because they are a major component of the essays.

Prereading Exploration for "My Friend Who Gave Up on Life"

While we often write for a larger audience, sometimes we do write primarily for ourselves. That is the case for Julie Hammond's introspective essay, which she wrote as a way of helping her reflect on her friend's death and in a small way come to terms with her grief.

Teaching Idea
This brainstorming can help students discover useful and interesting topics; however, reassure students that they may choose not to discuss the event.

If you have lost a loved one or had some other tragedy enter your life, undoubtedly you have been concerned with the "why" behind the event. Take a moment to list one unpleasant or painful event in your life and speculate about its causes. Try to list four or more probable reasons behind the event.

_____

_____

_____

My Friend Who Gave Up on Life

On July 14, 1996, at midnight, I was sound asleep when suddenly the phone rang. It was my friend Austin. His voice was soft and shaky as he told me that our friend had committed suicide. The intensity of the information was hard for me to take in at such a late hour, and I didn't want to grasp what I had heard. "OH NO!" rang through my mind over and over; I didn't know what to do or think. I sat alone in the darkness of my room with tears streaming down my cheeks. The thought of Sam following through with his drunken promises made me sick, and still to this day I wonder what could have caused my friend to think his life was not worth living.

Nobody can really know what causes a suicide, but one of Sam's problems was depression. His life seemed always to be falling apart. When he was younger, it wasn't so bad, but as he moved into his teens, he began having problems with his family, friends, and school. He couldn't even get his car to run right. School started calling home about his absences, and he began acting up in classes, one time getting suspended. Most of his friends didn't know how to handle the "new" Sam, and a lot of them just stopped seeing him. His family wasn't much help either, always nagging at him to straighten up. In his parent's eyes he was just another teenager going through a stage. And after the drinking began, his folks grew even harder on him.

By sixteen Sam was definitely an alcoholic, and this must have pushed him closer to the end. Alcohol was a way for him to escape a world going wrong. School, friends, family—everyone seemed to be deserting him. His family could see that he had a drinking problem. Their solution was to stick him in rehab and figure that should take care of it. When he returned, he would be OK for awhile. But it didn't take long for him to start drinking and acting up. This set his family off, and they began yelling at him that he better shape up or else. He never did, so they just sent him away again. Those of us who were left of Sam's friends should have been listening more carefully. When he was drunk, Sam began saying that he was going to kill himself. I guess deep down inside I thought he might do it someday, but I didn't know what to do about it.

The drinking was bad enough, but it led to another serious problem for Sam, probation. In the last year he was drunk all the time; he never seemed to take a night off. And for some reason he always seemed to get caught. Finally, he was stuck with three years of probation. We used to talk about it, and he told me how trapped he felt. The school didn't want him, his family thought he was hopeless, he couldn't keep a job, and now the probation people were hounding him, making him take drug tests that he couldn't pass and watching his every move. Those three years looked like a prison sentence to Sam, and he said he figured that it would just get worse. If it wasn't his mom and dad, it was the law; someone was just waiting to lock him up for good.

I'm not sure if it was the probation that pushed him over, any one reason, all of them combined, or some others that I will never know. When a friend dies this way, people want to know why. Everyone talks about it, trying to figure it out. What caused the suicide; what could we have done to stop it? All of the friends Sam had left heard him talk about killing himself, and no one said they believed him. But I wonder how many of my friends are like me, inside still thinking that they really did believe he might just do it. When a friend dies, don't we all share the blame?

Julie Hammond

Postreading Analysis

This essay explores some likely causes of a tragic event. The author does not know for a certainty that any of the reasons she gives are *the* cause of the suicide, and this is often the case when people speculate about complex issues. However, all of the reasons Julie offers are likely, real, and significant causes, and she is careful not to oversimplify.

The introduction is clear and compelling, leading to a thesis sentence that lets the reader know an essay about causes will follow. Each major reason is introduced by a topic sentence that is firmly linked to the preceding paragraph and that focuses each body paragraph effectively. The concluding paragraph does a fine job of briefly summarizing causes and then expands the scope of the essay.

Although this essay is well developed with detailed examples and explanations, it lacks direct dialogue: Julie only reports conversations. We have seen that using dialogue on occasion can add emphasis and variety to writing. Why do you suppose the author did not use any dialogue? Do you think leaving dialogue out detracts from this essay? If you wanted to include direct dialogue, where might be a good place for it?

▶ **Prereading Exploration for "The Thousand-Dollar Lesson"**

Luke Eimers chose an audience of young adults for this essay, particularly ones who have received a speeding ticket or two and who have had trouble with their auto insurance. Before you read ahead, consider the topic of getting a speeding ticket. If you were to write an essay on this subject, would you lean more toward causes or effects? Do you think that some topics might be better handled as causes *or* effects on the basis of the topic itself and the reader's likely interest? Take a moment to list below four possible reasons why a person might speed.

_____

_____

_____

(To see this essay as a paragraph, turn back to Chapter 9, pp. 193–194.)

The Thousand-Dollar Lesson

Sometimes you just have to drive fast, even when you know you are breaking—maybe even shattering!—the speed limit. It feels great to be on an eight-lane interstate, the traffic sparse, the day clear and dry, and the pedal to the metal. My '85 Camaro can handle the speed. I push her up to ninety (well, a hundred) all the time, and she floats over the pavement like she's riding on some kind of sci-fi antigrav. Other drivers just seem to drift past my windows as I change a lane here and there, leaving even the long-haul truckers in the dust. I wish we had an autobahn like Germany so I could drive as I want to, but we don't, and I guess I have finally found that out. While traveling last spring, I learned about the miserable consequences of my favorite pastime.   1

My first unpleasant experience was actually getting the ticket. I knew I was in trouble from the moment I saw the red flashing lights in my rearview mirror and looked down at the speedometer to see the needle on eighty-five. I knew that I had been driving that slow for at least five minutes, so even though the posted limit was seventy, I thought I might be able to talk my way out of it. But then I saw the Clint Eastwood lookalike Texas highway patrol officer step up to my window. "All right, boy, let me see your license and proof of insurance," he drawled, cutting off my "Gee-I-didn't-realize-I-was-going-that-fast" line. The officer seemed to enjoy every second it took him to write that ticket out, and with an evil smirk he handed it to me, saying, "Have a nice day." I'm pretty sure he was the only one having fun.   2

The next problem was paying the ticket. I didn't want it on my record because it would crank up my insurance rates, and I knew taking care of the ticket would cost plenty. It did. First I had to call all my friends to dig up a lawyer who could make the ticket "disappear" without making what was left of my bank account disappear too. The ticket turned out to be only seventy-five dollars, but the lawyer cost three hundred. Everyone said I got off cheap, and I believe them, but ouch! 3

As bad as that expense was, the next effect was worse. My parents had been paying my insurance because at the time I was still living at home and going to college. However, after they learned of my ticket, they decided to stop helping me with the coverage. They reasoned that if I had enough money to speed, then I had enough money to pay for my own insurance. I never quite figured out their logic, but I got their point. A thousand dollars for a year's premiums is an expensive lesson. 4

Having to cover the insurance on top of the ticket led to the worst consequence of all—work, work, work! I picked up extra hours at my job on the golf course, but that was not enough. So I turned to my parents, who were willing to help, they said, with smiles that reminded me of the Texas highway patrol officer. There were plenty of odd jobs for me to do on the weekends around the house: painting the shed, staining the deck, washing the windows, cleaning out the garage. . . . When I got tired of the labor jobs, they would let me cart my younger sister around town, baby sit, and help her with her homework. My folks were very creative and have given me lots of this kind of "help." 5

The expense and extra work aside, I know that a high-speed accident is the most serious possible consequence of my fast driving. And I don't want to end up with pieces of my car and me (or others) scattered along a highway somewhere, looking like a broken up 737. I think I've learned my lesson. I can't always follow my impulses, even when everything says, "Go, go, go!" As I consider career choices now that I am in college, I have more decisions to make, and I know they should be practical ones. I have always wanted to be a pro golfer, but my parents have questioned the wisdom of this goal. Well, I still have my Camaro, maybe it's not too late to drive a NASCAR (just joking). 6

Lucas Eimers

Postreading Analysis

"The Thousand-Dollar Lesson" is a well-developed essay that clearly illustrates the author's point as stated in the thesis sentence. In order to guide the reader easily through the negative outcome of his speeding, Luke constructed a topic sentence to begin each of the four body paragraphs and firmly linked each paragraph to the one that precedes it. His introductory and concluding paragraphs are well connected and consistent in tone with the rest of the essay.

When we write, readers inevitably form impressions of who we are. Sometimes who we appear to be in writing is not appealing for a particular audience, so we may need to reassess and then readjust our tone and *persona* (the personality a writer takes on in his work). (For more on tone and persona, see pp. 367–369.) What do you think about Luke's persona? Do you find his sense of humor appealing or distracting? Does his final comment in the conclusion conflict with the expanded thought, add to the appeal of the paper, or detract from it? If Luke had presented the essay in a different voice, say an angry and resentful one, how would it affect your feeling about the essay?

Does the dialogue in the first example make it more interesting or memorable to you? Does the comparison to Clint Eastwood help you to better visualize the scene? In the fourth example do you notice an instance of *irony* (meaning the opposite of what you say)? Does it contribute to the paper?

Teaching Idea
To begin a discussion of voice and tone, ask students how the elements of humor, irony, dialogue, and comparison affect the overall "feel" of "The Thousand-Dollar Lesson." Does the essay feel relaxed, casual? How about the writer? How would students characterize him—as someone they might know or want to know?

Details, action verbs, specific words, dialogue, and comparisons can add interest to your essay.

Key Elements of Cause-and-Effect Essays

Here are several important points—illustrated by the preceding student models—to keep in mind for your own cause-and-effect essay:

1. Explore all the likely causes and effects; see pp. 185–187.

2. Develop causes or effects thoroughly; see p. 189.

3. Choose only the real causes and effects; see pp. 189–190.

4. Avoid oversimplifying by thinking critically; see pp. 190–191.

◗ EXPLAINING ACTIVITIES, DOING THEM, UNDERSTANDING THEM (PROCESS ANALYSIS)

Teaching Idea
It is important to help students see the difference between a process to perform and one to understand. You might mention that while processes to understand are often more challenging to write they can also be more interesting to write and read.

As we discussed in Chapter 10, when we tell someone how to perform an activity or how to understand it, we are practicing process analysis. For example, in building a house there are many steps: clearing the ground, pouring the foundation, framing the walls, putting on the roof, and much more. An experienced builder would be able to tell us about each step in the operation. Within the explanation we would hear new words that we would need defined, hear about dangers on the job, and listen to reasons for why one step comes before another or why one material is used and not another. The builder could give us a detailed explanation of how a house is built so that we might simply understand the process, or he could give us specific instructions for how to perform some smaller part of the job, such as shingling the roof. You may take either of these approaches in your essay, writing about either a process to perform or one to understand.

Whether you are coming to this chapter with a paragraph already written from Chapter 10 or are just beginning a process-analysis assignment, you will find that breaking down an activity into organized steps and explaining each step clearly is a powerful tool for learning about what you thought you already knew.

Note: For a more complete discussion of process analysis, turn back to Chapter 10.

◗ PROCESS ANALYSIS ESSAYS: LOOKING CLOSELY AT STUDENT MODELS

The following two student models will help you write effective process-analysis essays. The first, "Jokers Wild," promotes playing practical jokes as an amusing and worthwhile pastime and is one way to write about a process meant to be understood. The second, "A Boy's Best Friend," gives us a look at the author's life as a boy within the context of a process meant to be performed.

Look especially closely at the introductory and concluding paragraphs in the models because they are a major component of the essays and one with which we have so far this semester had little experience.

◗ Prereading Exploration for "Jokers Wild"

Teaching Idea
Students often have difficulty with topic sentences in process essays, so you might have students pay special attention to the ones in these models.

As a nontraditional student returning to college after many years in the workforce, Michael Feldman wanted to comment on how hard he sees so many people working in our society. Being someone who likes to play jokes on friends also, he decided that he could combine the two topics. Rather than writing a how-to-do process analysis detailing one particular joke, as he moved into his prewriting, he discovered that he wanted to focus on a general process to understand. He thought that young, hard-working adults who might be inclined to try pulling a prank themselves would be an appropriate audience.

If you have ever played a joke on someone, from making a crank phone call to setting up a surprise party, how did you go about it? In the space below list six steps that you followed to surprise the person.

_____

_____

_____

Jokers Wild

The world needs an antidote for seriousness. Too many people are bogged down in the day-to-day grind of making a living and taking care of all their RESPONSIBILITIES. Childhood seems to end about the time we get our driver's licenses and can haul ourselves to work. It's either school or work or, for many of us, both. We can't always take the vacations we want—sometimes it's even hard to get a weekend—and between studying, working, and taking care of the people in our lives, we get kind of dried out and wrinkly, like grapes turned into raisins. But there is one partial remedy for this condition, playing pranks. If you have a general understanding of the ground rules for playing pranks on friends, everyone can survive, and most will even have a good time. 1

The first step is to know yourself. If you are shy or introverted, practical jokes may not work for you because you may suddenly, sometimes unpleasantly, find yourself in the spotlight when/if you are discovered. If you are reasonably outgoing and think you can stand the attention, you may still have problems if the prank backfires. For example, when your friend breaks her favorite desk lamp trying to escape from the gerbil you put in her desk drawer, you may find yourself buying a new lamp and apologizing profusely, on both knees if necessary. 2

If you are the right sort for pranking, the next important point is to know your victim. While casual friends make fairly good targets, good friends are often a better choice. First, you know where they work and play, so you can pick a good spot to lay the trap for that singing telegram or surprise birthday party. Second, and more important, if the joke really blows up in your face, a good friend is less likely to hit or sue you. A casual friend, for instance, might not be as tolerant if he discovers the identity of the person who anonymously had a truckload of gravel dumped on his driveway. 3

With a target and suitable prank picked out, you can begin to think about execution—of the plan, not the person. The first rule here is no dangerous jokes. If, for example, you want to drop water on someone, don't put it in a metal bucket over someone's door. Physical pain is not funny, at least to the sufferer. Next, remember that timing is critical. The singing stripper that you have visit a friend at a party might go over well with everyone there, but send her to the church picnic, and you have problems. In general, if you remember that you still have to live around your victim after the joke has passed, your sense of self-preservation should tell you when to quit. 4

No advice on playing pranks would be complete without a few words on the aftermath, or dealing with the fallout. Your primary concern is how well it went over. If all went well, everyone chuckled, and there were no hard feelings, terrific. Then you can accept the credit for the general good times. However, if the response was mixed or poor, and you want to escape, you have several options, depending on how many people are in on the joke (you can't really rely on anyone not to blab over time). First, admire the idea behind the prank but wish that whoever did it had used a little better judgment. Second, inconspicuously 5

Process analysis usually uses time organization.

How-to-do process instructions especially benefit from specific words.

Postreading Analysis

The author manages a personable tone in this process essay, overcoming one of the problems common in how-to writing—reader boredom. By using "I" and personal experience, Steve is able to include some interesting points about his character and background. For example, we learn that he is from a rural area, his folks are probably farmers, and money is scarce. We also gain some insight into the author's character: he is inventive, determined, and bold enough to risk annoying his father to achieve his ends.

Using chronological organization, as is typical of most process descriptions, Steve begins with an engaging introduction and clear thesis that *implies* the how-to-do instructions that follow. Next, he creates solid topic sentences for each of the two body paragraphs, which are the heart of the essay. His concluding paragraph summarizes, frames, and expands the thought. Throughout, the reader is helped to move easily between sentences and paragraphs with connecting words, including transitions. When he moves into the actual construction, Steve is careful to use plenty of specific language, which includes measurements and locator words. Notice, too, several explanations for his actions (for example, why he cut the belt) and one important warning to anyone wishing to build a slingshot.

Key Elements in Process-Analysis Essays

Here are several important points—illustrated by the preceding student models—to keep in mind for your own process-analysis essay:

1. List all the necessary steps; see pp. 210–212.

2. Explain the steps thoroughly, giving reasons and warnings; see p. 213.

3. Define all the terms; see p. 214.

4. Avoid monotonous sentence patterns; see p. 215.

■ EXPLAINING SIMILARITIES AND DIFFERENCES (COMPARISON AND CONTRAST)

As we learned in Chapter 11, comparing and contrasting ideas, people, and things is the process of discovering similarities and differences among them. For example, we might imagine a football game in which we could *contrast* the players with the cheerleaders. The football team is entirely male while the cheerleading squad is mostly female. One group wears pads, helmets, and spiked shoes, while the other wears light clothing and tennis shoes. The expressions on the faces of one group are serious, almost grim, while the faces of the other are smiling and enthusiastic. One group is riveted on the action in the center of the playing field while the other team is turned outward and upward toward the crowd.

On the other hand, we could also *compare* the two groups. For instance, both are the focus of the spectators' attention, both consist of athletes, both work as teams and are dependent on one another for success, both have leaders, both have organized plays or routines, and both are working toward the same goal of winning the game. If we take a moment to think about it, we can uncover many differences and similarities between the two groups.

Longer essays often explore both comparisons and contrasts, and individual paragraphs frequently use brief comparisons as examples to clarify some point. You, also, may choose to compare and contrast, but a brief essay is often easier to focus if you select either comparison *or* contrast and stick with it, as the student model essays in this section have done.

Teaching Idea
Comparing and contrasting are such fundamental methods of development that it is worth frequently reminding students that they will often use brief comparisons and contrasts within other overall organizational patterns. Chapter 15 discusses this at more length.

Whether you are coming to this chapter with a paragraph already written from Chapter 11 or are just beginning a comparison/contrast assignment, you will find that you already have much experience exploring similarities and differences.

Note: For a more complete discussion of comparison and contrast, turn back to Chapter 11.

COMPARISON/CONTRAST ESSAYS: LOOKING CLOSELY AT STUDENT MODELS

The first student model that follows, "I'll Park. You Get the Tickets—Hurry!" focuses on differences in the experience of watching movies at home or in a theater. The second, "Break on Through to the Other Side," again focuses on differences, this time between two stages of the author's life.

Look especially closely at the introductory and concluding paragraphs in the models because they are a major component of the essays and one with which we have so far this semester had little experience.

Prereading Exploration for "I'll Park. You Get the Tickets—Hurry!"

Hugh Edwards, the author of this essay, chose a topic that he thought most people in any movie-going country could identify with, watching movies at home versus going out to a film. To focus the audience, he decided that people would have to be affluent enough to have a television and videotape player and busy enough to look on going out at night as an inconvenience. Of the many possible ways to compare and contrast watching movies at home with going out to the movies, Hugh chose to contrast the *experiences*, focusing on how relaxing each is for him.

Before you read the essay, take a moment to think about your own movie-going experiences, and then list ways in which watching a videotape at home is preferable to going to the movies. How many of your examples matched the author's?

_____

_____

_____

Teaching Idea
Having students list the points the prereading suggests will help focus students when they begin to read Hugh Edwards's essay.

Teaching Idea
This introduction illustrates another example of the intentional use of "you" to connect with the audience. You can contrast this use with accidental pronoun shift on pp. 554–555.

"I'll Park. You Get the Tickets—Hurry!"

The room is warm and inviting, the lighting low, your recliner soft. With a cool drink in hand, you push play, and a great movie appears on the big-screen TV in front of you. Cut to next scene: This room is cold, almost black, your chair sticky with spilled something. Clutching a softening waxed cup of watered-down soft drink, you pull your feet back as someone steps on them again and spills part of a drink on your legs. It is crowded, noisy, and uncomfortable. You can't see well (maybe the film is out of focus), and it is a hundred yards to the nearest restroom. Welcome to Saturday night at the movies, at home or out. Some people love to watch films in a theater, but I find that watching them at home is a much more relaxing experience.   1

There are many good reasons to stay home for movies. One is snacking. When I am home, I have the run of the kitchen, and I am likely to end up with a light meal of cold chicken, green salad, side dishes of black and jalapeno-stuffed olives, whole wheat rolls, and several beverages of my choice. Since my 27-inch TV is only 10 feet from the kitchen, I can easily watch a film while I nibble on my snack. And if I choose to get even more comfortable, I can   2 move to the best seat in the house, my La-Z-Boy recliner, putting my feet up with a TV tray in my lap. With an extra pillow from the bedroom behind my neck, I am in heaven. But even more important than snacking and seating for my movie-watching pleasure is the freedom I have at home. When I have set myself up for the evening, I can choose any time to start, pause, or stop the movie. If I don't like my first choice, "Eject." Then I pop in the next. If it gets too late to finish one, I just save it for the next night. And I never have to miss a minute if another cold beverage or the bathroom calls. The most relaxing part of my home-viewing evening, though, is no people problems. My room-mate is almost never around, so I have the apartment to myself. The only noises I don't want to hear come from the neighbor down below, and I just crank the volume a notch to take care of him.

On the other hand, too often when I see a movie out, I run into problems   3
that kill my fun. First, half the time I spend ten minutes waiting in line to get junky movie-house food: popcorn with something that resembles butter, stale nachos with melted Cheese Whiz, and Jujubes that want to yank out my fill-ings. With this "feast" in hand, spilling popcorn as I go, I have to search for a seat in the dark and usually find one too close to the screen, too far away from it, or at a bad angle. Then comes the balancing act where I usually manage to dump at least a handful of popcorn in my lap to sit on for the next two hours, mystery butter and all. And once I am in my seat, if the theater is crowded and the movie is exciting, I am trapped. In the first place I don't want to walk over people to get to the aisle; it's embarrassing. In the second place there is no pausing the film. Who wants to miss the best scene when that half gallon of Coke finally cycles through, and it's bathroom or bust? Even though *I* don't like to pop back and forth from my seat to the lobby, it seems like everyone else in my row does. It always caps off my night out at the movies to have people yakking in my ear, blocking my view of the screen, and stepping on my toes on their way out. "Sorry, pal, this is the last time."

Watching a movie at a theater can be downright unpleasant. Because we   4
have less control over our surroundings, we have to put up with more annoy-ances than we would ever stand for in the security of our own homes. But despite the potential aggravations, there are some good reasons for aban-doning the La-Z-Boy. First, if you want to see the newest releases, you have to go out. Second, some films, like those with great special effects, are made to be viewed on a huge screen. And finally, seeing movies out can be a good social experience—and a safe first date.

Hugh Edwards

Postreading Analysis

This essay is a good example of the block pattern of organization, as opposed to "Break on through to the Other Side," which uses point by point. You will notice that the author clearly implies the focus and method of arrangement in his thesis sen-tence, just as you should do. The first major block of information, watching movies at home, is introduced by a clear topic sentence that leads readers into the four major examples, arranged from least to most important, used to develop the paragraph. Each primary example is, in turn, stated in a subtopic sentence. For instance, in body paragraph one, the first example begins with "One is snacking." The second major block of information, watching movies in theaters, begins with a transitional phrase that leads into a topic sentence. Four major examples mirror those in the preceding body paragraph and are again introduced by subtopic sentences and ordered from least to most important.

> Body paragraphs often benefit from order of importance organizing.

Teaching Idea
This is a good place to remind
students of the value of their
narrative/descriptive skills.

While expository essays may not use a great deal of sensory detail, sometimes they benefit from it, especially in combination with specific words and active verbs. Notice how the introductory paragraph, for example, uses *cold, black, sticky, spills, noisy,* and *softening* to help build an image of discomfort. Remember that appealing to a reader's senses (sight, sound, touch, smell, and taste) is an effective writing strategy.

▶ Prereading Exploration for "Break on through to the Other Side"

Comparison and contrast papers give us a wonderful opportunity to reflect on our lives, perhaps to gain some perspective on them. Gina Rizzo, the author of "Break on through to the Other Side," decided to divide her life into her "roaring twenties" and her beginning thirties and contrast the two parts for the other members of her writing group, who were just entering their twenties. Gina felt that young adults moving into the years she had just lived through might be particularly interested in her experiences and how they had shaped her recent decisions.

Teaching Idea
Nontraditional students
respond particularly well to
this essay. But even the
youngest students should be
able to identify several stages
or "phases" of their lives.

Before you read any further, take a moment to think back on your own life. Have you ever done anything that surprises you about yourself in retrospect? Have you had moments when you were extraordinarily indifferent, lazy, selfish, or cruel—how about involved, active, generous, or kind? If you have ever felt like a different person than you are now, even briefly, write out a short description of that person below and consider pursuing the topic in a paragraph of contrast.

_____

_____

_____

To see this essay as a paragraph, turn back to Chapter 11, p. 242.

"Break on through to the Other Side"

Raising hell and living for the moment were all I used to care about. I could see through glassy eyes, somewhat clearly, all the way from one day till the next morning. Then when I would roll out of bed hungover and crawl toward the bathroom, I would remind myself how much fun I was having. These were the good old days, the days of my roaring twenties. I had some fun, learned a little, and came through, surprisingly, with few visible battle scars. But now that I am moving into my thirties, life has changed. 1

When I was just entering my twenties, I was still living at home, although nobody would have known it by the way I came and went, telling no one anything. But I have come a long way since then. Despite me being twenty-nine now, my mom knows where I am most of the time, not because she checks up on me but because I want her to know what I am doing. Being in touch with the family has become important to me. 2

As a younger woman, I was always invited to the biggest and craziest parties. There is an old saying, "If you can't run with the big dogs . . ." well, I *was* one of the big dogs. No one could outparty me. I don't recall when it happened, but I have lost the taste for drinking altogether. Somewhere down the road my body started rejecting the soothing liquid that I had begun to rely on too much. I don't go to the big or crazy parties anymore. My friends have quit inviting me, which is just as well. I don't much feel like partying that way now. I would rather remember my life instead of just hearing about it. 3

Another important difference between my younger self and the woman of today is how I think about time. I used to live only in the present, never planning ahead, never saving money. I bartended for a living, so my money was 4 spent just like I made it, one day at a time. I didn't plan vacations; I would decide the day before, and off I'd go, hopping another red-eye to Las Vegas. I would go anywhere I could afford with the money I had in my pocket. However, times have changed. I actually have a savings account now, and I just bought a plane ticket for my coming vacation two months in advance! Being more responsible with money ought to help me get a few more wants out of life, not just my needs.

As I began to think more about a future, maybe the most dramatic change 5 came over me when I finally decided to stop playing follow the leader. Like lots of young people I wanted to be in there doing what everyone else was doing. For me that included becoming a Deadhead after my first Grateful Dead concert. The other Deadheads became my family, and we followed our leaders around the country, living the Dead life, pushing ourselves to the limit, right up to the end on that warm night in August when Jerry Garcia died. His death stopped me short. "Is this what I want?" I asked myself. "Do I also want to 'break on through to the other side'?" I decided no. It was time to make another kind of break, this time with the pack. I was ready to become an individual, to take some responsibility if I expected to survive as an adult. Among other changes I made, the Deadhead has become a college student.

As I look back over my roaring twenties, I see a lot that makes me shake 6 my head at myself, the hiding from my family, the hard partying, the child's sense that there is no tomorrow. But I realize, too, that nobody comes into the world fully grown. Infant, child, teen, adult—we move through stages, learning a little or a lot as we go. I am satisfied with what I have learned so far, and the wild-child-who-was helped to get me here. I hope now that I am on the right path, the one that leads to a long, peaceful, and happy life. But no one can know. We can only think and plan and work for the best. Probably the only thing I can be sure of is that the woman of thirty-nine will be as different from me today as I am from the nineteen-year-old—and as much the same.

Gina Rizzo

Postreading Analysis

This essay uses point-by-point arrangement of main examples, contrasting several of the author's behaviors as a younger woman with those of herself at twenty-nine. Notice that, as in all point-by-point ordering, one point or main example is discussed in each body paragraph about each of the two topics being contrasted before the author takes up the next main point.

Gina tries to capture her readers' interest as quickly as possible in her first sentence (the "hook") with the phrase "Raising hell and living for the moment" and clearly states both her topic and approach to it through contrast. Each body paragraph is introduced by a topic sentence complete with a solid connector (transitional word, repeat word, synonym, pronoun, or reference to main idea), and the author signals an ordering of least to most important with the phrase "maybe the most dramatic change" in her final topic sentence.

As Gina moves into her conclusion, she briefly summarizes and then ends reflectively. What effect do the author's final five words, "and as much the same," have on her expanded thought? Does this addition give you any other insight into Gina's character?

Teaching Idea
Gina Rizzo's final comment can provoke an interesting class discussion on the ease or difficulty of accomplishing fundamental change in behavior and personality. This discussion may encourage some students to choose life changes as topics.

Key Elements in Comparison and Contrast Essays

Here are several important points—illustrated by the preceding student models—to keep in mind for your own comparison and contrast essay:

1. Make a meaningful comparison or contrast; see pp. 234–236.

2. Make an interesting comparison or contrast; see pp. 236–238.

3. Develop each topic thoroughly; see pp. 238–239.

4. Use transitions and other connectors; see pp. 239–240.

Teaching Idea
The questions for analyzing essays are fairly generic, to cover the five patterns of development in the chapter, but you will find points more specific to each essay in the postreading analyses.

Teacher Idea
Chapter 12 of the Instructor's Manual includes lists that identify methods used in AWW essays for introductions, conclusions, hooks, and summary sentences.

> **Questions to Help You Analyze and Write Effective Essays**
>
> Apply these questions to the student model essays in this chapter.
>
> 1. What is the thesis sentence of this essay, and where is it located? Does the thesis clearly predict what the essay will be about?
>
> 2. Is the hook effective, and which of the Chapter 12 hooks has the author used? (For more on hooks, see pp. 273–274.)
>
> 3. What method(s) from Chapter 12 has the author used to develop the introductory paragraph? (For more on developing introductions, see pp. 269–272.) Is the introduction effective for the audience as stated in the Prereading Exploration—why/ why not?
>
> 4. Is the lead sentence in the concluding paragraph effective—why/why not? (For more on lead and summary sentences, see p. 283.)
>
> 5. What method(s) from Chapter 12 has the author used to develop the concluding paragraph? What is the expanded thought? (For more on developing conclusions, see pp. 283–290.) Is the conclusion effective for the audience as stated in the Prereading Exploration—why/why not? (Consider the conclusion's connection with the introduction.)
>
> 6. What do you think is the author's reason for writing this essay; what point is he or she making?
>
> 7. Write out each of the topic sentences. Next, underline the <u>topic</u> to be discussed once and the <u>statement</u> made about it twice. Circle any connecting words. (For more on connecting sentences, see pp. 52–57.)
>
> 8. How are the body paragraphs arranged: chronologically or by order of importance? What connector words reveal this?
>
> 9. Choose one *body* paragraph and tell how the author's explaining of an example helps you understand his or her meaning.
>
> 10. Choose *any* paragraph in the essay, and explain why you think it is well written. (Consider elements like topic sentences, connecting words, sensory details, specific words, action description, dialogue, metaphors and other comparisons, sentence variety, and clear explaining.)
>
> 11. List at least five uses of specific language. (For more on specific language, see pp. 78–79.)

■ EXPLAINING THE WRITING ASSIGNMENT

◗ SUMMARIZING THE ASSIGNMENT

Teaching Idea
You can work through the next few pages concurrently with Chapter 12 to move students more quickly into their first essay assignment.

Whether you are coming to this assignment chapter with a paragraph already written or are beginning a new topic, our goal is the same: to write a clear, well-organized, and thoroughly developed essay of approximately 500 to 600 words. As soon as you have chosen a topic, you must decide what you want to say about it and then do so in a thesis sentence. Practically speaking, you should plan on a paper of four to six total paragraphs, of which two to four will be in the body. Because introductory and concluding paragraphs are such crucial elements in essays, you will want to pay particular attention to them, and, of course, introduce each body paragraph with a strong topic sentence. (For more on introductions and conclusions, see Chapter 12.)

ESTABLISHING AUDIENCE AND PURPOSE

> Writing to a specific audience helps focus material.

We all are experienced in speaking to different audiences—don't we, for example, speak differently to a close friend than to someone we have just met at work? But when it comes to writing, we sometimes just want to say it for ourselves because . . . well, after all, we know what we mean, right? However, since in writing we are removed from our audience, we get no feedback on their reactions. Do they understand, are they interested, have we offended someone? So it becomes even more important to visualize a person who might really care about our message. The added benefit of writing to a specific audience is that you will often be able to select ideas, explanations, and even individual words with them in mind. The result is that you have another powerful tool for focusing your essay. Having a target audience can help you write more quickly and efficiently.

You may have several purposes as you write—to entertain, inform, or persuade—but clearly communicating ideas should take priority.

WORKING THROUGH THE WRITING ASSIGNMENT

Discovering Ideas

Any of the prewriting methods (clustering, listing, freewriting, etc.) that we have worked with this semester can be useful for uncovering an initial topic for your essay or expanding examples from your former paragraph. To review prewriting techniques, turn back to pp. 5–10 in Chapter 1. For topic lists specific to each pattern of development, use the following page references:

- Illustration: Topic Lists; pp. 148–149
- Classification: Topic Lists; p. 172
- Cause and Effect: Topic Lists; pp. 196–197
- Process Analysis: Topic Lists; pp. 220–221
- Comparison and Contrast: Topic lists: pp. 244–245

> **Teaching Idea**
> Some students will want to abandon a former paragraph topic and begin with a new topic for their essay. However, there is value in developing the former paragraph, not the least of which is that students have to make substantial material additions—real revision.

You may find that your former paragraph examples are just right for your current essay project and simply need to be developed, or you may want to change or add an example, group, cause, or step. However, check with your instructor before you make major material changes. He or she may want you to work with the content of your former paragraph as much as possible.

Organizing Ideas

> Thesis and topic sentences are the keys to solid organization.

Your thesis sentence is essential to keep your essay on track, so you should carefully write one at the top of your paper before you begin to draft. If you already have a topic sentence from a former paragraph assignment, it may work as is, but, again, you may need to revise it first, particularly if you have added or dropped major examples. Remember too that topic sentences are just as important in your essay body paragraphs as they were in your former one-paragraph papers.

Use connecting words between sentences and paragraphs.

Teaching Idea
You might direct students back to pp. 308–309 in this chapter to see the remainder of "The Jobs from Hell," a well-developed illustration essay.

Tips for more efficient drafting

Ask questions of your statements to help develop them.

Teaching Idea
Comparing these two excerpts graphically illustrates how to expand a former subtopic. During group work with essay drafts, have peer reviewers compare an author's former subtopics with his or her current body paragraphs to see if there has been substantial revision.

For overall arrangement of body paragraphs, you will probably use either time or order of importance. Whichever method seems most appropriate for your topic, be sure to include transitions and other connectors throughout your essay but especially *between* paragraphs. (For more on connecting sentences and paragraphs, see pp. 52–57.)

Drafting

As you begin to develop your examples, remember the principle of layering that we began working with in Chapter 3, that is, adding sufficient examples, details, and explanations to help your reader see exactly what you mean. In this excerpt from the illustration essay "The Jobs from Hell," we can see how the author layered meaning:

> When I was a senior, I found another job that, at first, looked promising. Dr. Lawn paid well, but I had to mow lawns for six to eight hours a day in the July heat, with temperatures running into the nineties. One day on the job I grew sick to my stomach and feverish and literally collapsed in back of a walk-behind mower. My manager would not let me go home because we had come in a car pool, and if I had left, it would have affected the other five people working. When I finally made it home, my dad found that I had a 105-degree fever, and we both decided that no job was worth my health.

What does Eric mean by "sick"? His stomach ached, he had a 105-degree fever, and he collapsed on the job. Why would he become ill? He had to mow lawns for six to eight hours a day in ninety-degree heat. Why was his illness a special problem? His boss wouldn't let him go home. As you ask and answer questions of your own examples, more material will emerge, and all your paragraphs will grow.

To see how you might develop part of a former paragraph assignment, read through the following excerpts taken from the student illustration model "Teaching with Whips," first as a subtopic in a paragraph and then as a fully developed body paragraph in an essay. The added material has been shaded:

Single-Paragraph Excerpt: 71 Words (Complete Paragraph on pp. 143–144)

> My moral education teacher was one of these cruel educators. He was short and fat like the whip he carried to enforce his every whim. "I see you haven't done your homework, Jeong," he would say. He ordered me to hold my palms up, and then he began to whip my hands harshly. Somehow the pain ended with me crying and begging, "I will do it next time, teacher. I promise!"

Essay Body Paragraph: 157 Words (Complete Essay on pp. 310–311)

> As I entered middle school, I was surprised when I encountered the first painful moment with my moral education teacher, a short fat man who carried a short fat whip to enforce his every whim. His manner of speaking somehow did not make it seem urgent for me to thoroughly complete all the homework. Then one day he noticed that I was not prepared and made an example of me to show the class how harsh he could be to defiant students. "I see you haven't done your homework, Jeong," he said, his angry red face shaking. Straining with fear, the class was dead quiet, wondering what was going to happen at that frightful moment. "Jeong, stand up!" he ordered. His chalk-dusty hands held my two shaky little hands palms up and aimed at them as if they were targets. The punishment ended with me crying and begging, "I will do it next time, teacher. I promise!"

Jeong Yi developed this body paragraph through additional explaining, examples, and details. You can do the same if you continue to ask yourself the critical question "What do I mean by what I have just said?" and answer it with a specific reader in mind.

Revising Drafts

In addition to the stages of revision we have practiced with body paragraphs in Unit Two, now we need to pay close attention to introductory and concluding paragraphs. As you revise for material and organizational concerns, look closely at your introduction. Does it have a strong lead sentence ("hook"), three to five sentences to interest a reader, and a thesis sentence that contains the main point of your essay? Next, examine your concluding paragraph. Does it contain a lead sentence with a connector word and a link to your thesis? Have you briefly summarized main examples? Does the final paragraph use a framing device and/or expand the thesis?

If you take the time to revise your essay in several stages, dealing with the larger issues of content and organization and working toward style and editing concerns, you will produce a superior final draft.

For step-by-step suggestions for revising, editing, and proofreading your essay drafts, turn back to Chapter 13.

■ ALTERNATE WRITING ASSIGNMENTS

For additional writing assignments, turn back to the chapter in Unit Two featuring the appropriate pattern of development.

CHAPTER 15

Defining Terms, Clarifying Ideas

◖ WHAT ARE WE TRYING TO ACHIEVE AND WHY?

Setting the Stage

Most of us will immediately recognize the object in the picture above: a box. We probably view the word *box* as uncomplicated, its meaning clear. But how simple is it?

If we thumbed through a dictionary, we would find a number of definitions. Do we mean "a container typically constructed with four sides perpendicular to the base and often having a lid or cover"? How about a "square or rectangle," or a "compartment . . . in a theater"? If we were British, we might mean a "gift or gratuity" or a "predicament." We might mean "slap or hit" (as in "to box his ears"). If we were collecting sap for making maple syrup, "*to* box" might mean "to cut a hole (in a tree)," or if we were painting, we might mean "to blend (paint) by pouring alternately between two containers." Or maybe we just want to put a few old clothes in storage—"to box them up."

Still seem simple? Whenever we try to limit the meaning of a word, to clarify and to separate one meaning from many, we are **defining**. This is the essence of Chapter 15. As we move through the chapter, we will see how brief definitions can work with the patterns of development from Unit Two to develop definition essays. (For more on the patterns of development, see pp. 8–9, 341–342, 348–349.)

Linking to Previous Experience

In our own lives we define daily. At home your six-year-old son wants to know what you mean by *responsibility,* so you tell him about the jobs people have, providing several examples to illustrate. At work the waiter you are training knows nothing about wine, so you find yourself defining terms like *cabernet, pinot noir,* and *chenin blanc.* In school you might have to define terms like *democracy, republican,* and *free enterprise.* Whenever we have to explain a word with another word, a phrase, a comparison, or an example, we are defining.

Teaching Idea
To overcome the frequent student reaction that definition consists of one sentence in a dictionary, you can emphasize the broader sense of *extended* definitions, pointing out the defining students have done all semester in their assignments.

In this text we have defined in one form or another in every chapter. Narration is used by Lani Houston in Chapter 6 to reveal what *leadership* means to her. To define *mall crashers,* Chanthan Srouch classifies three groups and then develops each using examples. Contrast in Dave Harrison's Chapter 11 paragraph helps define the meaning of *hard work* in college. All the patterns of development that we have worked with this semester can be seen as forms of definition, and each of these, of course, depends on examples to grow.

The essential concept of the Language Line, which we explored in Chapter 5—that words can be relatively general or relatively specific—continues to apply here. When we define, we limit the meaning of a term, making it more specific. Also, as we work our way through examples, we continue to ask and answer the question "What exactly do I mean by that word or statement?" This, too, is definition.

Determining the Value

Teaching Idea
You can link defining of terms to the process-analysis assignment here.

Words that are quite clear to us because we have lived with them for years are not always clear to someone else. If you talk about rebuilding an engine, using terms like *overhead cam, stroke, compression* and *valve clearance,* mechanics understand without a second thought, but the uninitiated soon become lost. Murky meanings can generate serious problems: think of the trouble vague language like "employer will *contribute* to moving costs" could cause in an employment contract. Clear definition can help satisfy all parties.

And, of course, writing out definitions is valuable in helping us understand our own ideas. We may not feel as strongly as the novelist E. M. Forster, who said, "How do I know what I think until I see what I say?" but writing allows us the time to examine significant words carefully until we are sure we know our own mind.

Teaching Idea
Journal Entry 15-1 can help students see the need for a reason behind their definitions.

JOURNAL ENTRY 15-1

Think about instances during the past week when you have defined something or when you have heard someone else doing so (a friend, a radio announcer, a teacher, for example). What was being defined—a technical term like *website,* a personal term like *loved one,* a job like *veterinary technician,* or perhaps an abstract term like *beauty?* What was the reason for the definition—to inform, entertain, persuade? Did the definition accomplish its purpose? In a few sentences summarize one instance of definition from school, work, and home.

DEVELOPING SKILLS, EXPLORING IDEAS IN DEFINITION ESSAYS

We have all defined words and ideas before and so have some strategies for doing it effectively. However, there are a number of specific techniques worth trying that work well in almost every situation. As we prepare to write a definition essay, we will practice writing the following kinds of definitions:

Teaching Idea
If pressed for class time, you can have students do the activities out of class and then discuss the work in class.

1. Brief definitions:

   - Synonyms (similar words)

   - Negation (not that, but this)

   - Comparisons (metaphor/simile)

   - Formal (grouping and detailing)

2. Extended definitions: patterns of development (description, narration, illustration, etc.)

Groundwork for Activity 15-1: Defining with Synonyms

One effective method for developing a definition is to use a synonym, or a word that is roughly equivalent to the one being defined. If we say, "Granddad is feeling *cantankerous* today," we might substitute *grouchy* or *disagreeable* to achieve a similar meaning. However, if we used *angry*, we would be saying something different—intensifying his irritable mood. Words often have subtle shades of meaning, so writers must take care when choosing substitutes from their own vocabulary, a dictionary, or a thesaurus.

When choosing a synonym, we always want to pick one that is easier for our reader to understand or more common than the word we are trying to define.

> Choose an easier synonym than the word being described.

Collaborative

Activity 15-1: Defining with Synonyms

Using a dictionary, find two workable synonyms (one can be a phrase) for each italicized word in the following sentences. Next, consulting with group members and using your dictionary, find at least one synonym that's *almost* there but that alters the meaning of the original. Now tell why the "almost" synonym is *different* from the original word.

Example: Because Jason has difficulty listening to others, I would call him a *maverick*.

Synonyms: *dissenter, independent in thought and action*

Inaccurate synonym: *radical.*   Reason: *Radical suggests "extreme" behavior,*
and Jason can be independent without being extreme (although he might be extreme too).

Answers will vary.

1. Nobody trusts Mark anymore; he's a *weasel*.

    Synonyms: *weasel/person who is sneaky or treacherous*

    Inaccurate synonym: *cruel.*   Reason: *Mark can be sneaky without*
    also being cruel.

2. Sonya spends too much time making decisions, *vacillating* continually.

    Synonyms: *wavering/indecisive*

    Inaccurate synonym: *fearful.*   Reason: *A person may vacillate for*
    other reasons than fear.

3. Angelina's accident *ruined* her Subaru.

    Synonyms: *ruined/destroyed*

    Inaccurate synonym: *damaged.*   Reason: *Damage is only partial; to*
    ruin is to damage beyond repair.

4. Isabella's *premonition* about her uncle's death was correct.

    Synonyms: *foreboding/feeling/forewarning*

    Inaccurate synonym: *guess.*   Reason: *A guess implies volition,*
    whereas a premonition is involuntary.

5. The virus *mutated* in less than a year.

    Synonyms: *changed/altered*

    Inaccurate synonym: *grow.*   Reason: *Mutations do not necessarily*
    cause growth.

Teaching Idea
These prereading prompts can help students choose topics that they have a real interest in.

▶ Prereading Exploration for "Deaf, Not Dumb"

Bruce Hayworth has a clear purpose in this essay about the hearing-impaired. He thought that people who have little experience with the deaf could use the information he provides, but he particularly wanted to speak to fellow college students.

Are you a part of a group that is little understood and possibly misrepresented? Consider racial or ethnic minorities, groups drawn together by a common interest (heavy metal, knitting, book club), or cliques in high school. List one group and three inaccurate statements you have heard made about it.

Answers will vary.

Possibilities: knitting group: inaccurate statements: only old women knit.

not many people knit. knitting takes patience but not much creativity

Deaf, Not Dumb

Teaching Idea
Paragraph two uses cause/effect and comparison/contrast. Paragraph three uses process analysis and comparison/contrast. Paragraph four uses cause/effect.

"You're a dummy and so's your old lady and old man!" These were fighting   1
words for me as a child, and I ended up rolling around in the dirt more than once with the kids from school who said them. Growing up with hearing-impaired parents in the sixties, if I was not fighting some kid in an alley, it seemed like I was trying to explain to some other child that my family was normal. We just didn't talk much with words. Back then most people didn't know much about the deaf community, and even today I often see people turn and gawk at the hearing-impaired when they are signing to each other. Maybe knowing more about the deaf will make them seem less strange to the hearing world.

Everyone knows that deaf means the inability to hear, but not everyone knows   2
what causes it or to what degree it can affect people. First, not all hearing-impaired people have profound or complete hearing loss. There are many degrees of partial hearing loss, with some occurring progressively as people get older. Those who have been able to hear somewhat from birth are more likely to articulate well, while those completely deaf from birth onward have problems speaking clearly. Hearing loss might be caused by congenital nerve damage or by diseases like meningitis, rubella, and chickenpox, especially in early childhood. Worldwide there are 300 million people with some form of hearing impairment.

Many, though not all, of these people communicate through some form   3
of sign language. In the United States most of the deaf learn American Sign Language (ASL), which differs from sign used in other countries like England or Japan. ASL communicates primarily through gestures and signs made with the hands and arms but also frequently adds the fingerspelling of words, using letters from the English alphabet. Signing is visual, often theatrical, and can be beautiful, depending on how skilled the signer is. People express their personalities in how they sign. Some are reserved, their signing and body language economical. Others are expansive, exaggerating their gestures and body language to make the "listener" laugh. Some signers can be as entertaining as professional mimes, and even nonsigners can follow and enjoy the story.

Teaching Idea
To help students see the writer/reader connection, ask them how the main example in paragraph four relates to Hayworth's stated audience.

ASL serves the deaf community well, but their most serious communica-   4
tion problems are in the hearing world. Few hearing people sign, so most of the hearing-impaired have learned to read lips, but this has its limitations. Often only part of the message gets across because the speaker says the words too quickly or turns away, requiring the deaf person to frequently ask for clarification or miss the point. When, for instance, this noncommunication happens often enough in a classroom, the hearing students sometimes think

the deaf student is unintelligent, rather than merely missing the words spoken so clearly to those who can hear. If hearing-impaired students have enough difficulties in a classroom that cannot or will not understand them, their education suffers, which affects their future employment prospects and so the rest of their lives.

The deaf have many difficulties to overcome to compete in the larger world   5 of those who hear. Maybe knowing something about the causes of hearing impairment, how widespread it is, how the deaf "speak," and how they can be helped or hurt by the hearing, will make the general public more sensitive to this minority. In the same way that we might go out of our way to be courteous to a nonnative speaker, say, a visitor from Russia or Thailand, we should do so for the hearing-impaired. Sometimes we do need to slow our lips down or at least allow them to be seen. Being willing to write and read notes can also help, and learning a little basic ASL is a way to welcome the non-native "speaker" into our hearing world. In a society as privileged as ours, is a moment's worth of consideration for those who have so much to offer too much to ask?

Bruce Hayworth

Postreading Analysis

Bruce has also written a well-organized and developed extended-definition essay. Beginning with a narrative hook, the introduction leads the reader to a clearly written thesis, and the body paragraphs flow smoothly, helped along by strong transitions and other connectors. As in the other student essays in this chapter, the author uses several patterns of development within each paragraph, including illustration through examples, classification, comparison/contrast, cause/effect, and process analysis. You will also find brief definitions (through negation, synonyms, and simile). Notice that the simile in paragraph three, comparing ASL signers to mimes, is not explicitly stated, as in "some signers are *like* mimes," but is instead slipped unobtrusively into the sentence. Metaphors and similes are often most effective when they do not draw attention to themselves (for more on this, see pp. 473–474).

The concluding paragraph begins with a strong lead sentence and summary, moves into an expanded thought that calls on the reader to act, and ends with a rhetorical question (a statement disguised as a question that produces a predictable response from a reader). Do you find the final sentence effective? How does it help or hurt the essay?

Teaching Idea
See Chapter 12 of the Instructor's Manual for lists that identify methods used in *AWW* essays for introductions, conclusions, hooks, and summary sentences.

Questions to Help You Analyze and Write Effective Definition Essays

1. What is the thesis sentence of this essay, and where is it located?

2. Is the hook effective, and which of the Chapter 12 hooks has the author used? (For more on hooks, see pp. 273–274.)

3. What method(s) from Chapter 12 has the author used to develop the introductory paragraph? (For more on developing introductions, see pp. 269–272.) Is the introduction effective for the audience as stated in the Prereading Exploration—why/why not?

4. Is the lead sentence in the concluding paragraph effective—why/why not? (For more on lead and summary sentences, see p. 283.)

5. What method(s) from Chapter 12 has the author used to develop the concluding paragraph? What is the expanded thought? (For more on developing conclusions, see pp. 283–290.) Is the conclusion effective for the audience as stated in the Prereading Exploration—why/why not? (Consider the conclusion's connection with the introduction.)

6. What do you think is the author's reason for writing this definition essay; what point is he or she making?

7. Write out each of the topic sentences. Next, underline the <u>topic</u> to be discussed once and the <u>statement</u> made about it twice. Circle any connecting words. (For more on connecting sentences, see pp. 52–57.)

8. How are the body paragraphs arranged: chronologically or by order of importance? What connector words reveal this?

9. Choose one *body* paragraph and tell how the author's explaining of an example helps you understand his meaning.

10. What patterns of development or brief definition strategies has the author used? Tell how any three of these help you further understand the term being defined.

11. Choose *any* paragraph in the essay, and explain why you think it is well written. (Consider elements like topic sentences, connecting words, sensory details, specific words, action description, dialogue, metaphors and other comparisons, sentence variety, and clear explaining.)

12. List at least five uses of specific language. (For more on specific language, see pp. 78–79.)

■ EXPLAINING THE WRITING ASSIGNMENT

▶ SUMMARIZING THE ASSIGNMENT

Teaching Idea
You might want to stress here that students are still developing their essays through detailed examples and explaining. The developmental patterns simply help generate ideas.

In this assignment we will define a term as completely as possible within a 500 to 600 word essay. The word you choose might be a concrete, physical object, place, activity, group, or person. As long as you are interested in the subject and can sufficiently focus it for a brief essay, you have many options. You may also choose a **concept,** that is, a general idea or abstraction not knowable through the senses. Ideas, emotions, and qualities fall into this category: terms like freedom, love, and goodness. A major goal in this chapter is for us to more consciously manipulate many of the patterns of development from Unit Two (such as, description, narration, and illustration) rather than treating them in artificial isolation. Quality writing grows from diverse developmental strategies.

Practically speaking, you should plan on a paper of five to six total paragraphs, of which three to four will be in the body. Because introductory and concluding paragraphs are such crucial elements in essays, you will want to pay particular attention to them, and, of course, introduce each body paragraph with a strong topic sentence.

▶ ESTABLISHING AUDIENCE AND PURPOSE

Teaching Idea
You might reiterate that people often write for several audiences, a more general one (students' favorite) and the smaller group within it that is usually more help in focusing material.

Writing effective definitions depends on knowing your audience. How will you be able to determine what they need or want to know about your terms if you do not know who they are? How much might a writer overexplain *aerobic exercise* if he forgot that his reader commonly jogs twenty miles and rides her bicycle one hundred miles each week? On the other hand, if a person wrote this formula:

$$\overset{\text{light}}{6CO_2 + 12H_2O \rightarrow C_6H_{12}O6 + 6O_2 + 6H_2O}$$

and began to discourse on light energy, chemical energy, carbohydrates, carbon dioxide, and chlorophyll, not realizing that his reader had little knowledge of biology and no chance of identifying the formula as that for photosynthesis, he might expect soon to lose his audience's attention, through confusion or disinterest. Furthermore, how can a writer know when a brief definition using negation might be useful if she has no sense for what the reader might think the term is? What synonyms might work best? What metaphor or simile might the reader respond well to? Having a clear sense of audience will help you select material a reader will be interested in and understand.

As usual you may have several purposes in mind as you write—to entertain, persuade, or inform—but *defining* clearly should be the top priority.

▶ WORKING THROUGH THE WRITING ASSIGNMENT

Discovering Ideas

As you search for definition topics, remember the distinction between **abstract** and **concrete** terms. Abstract terms are those that cannot be known through the senses. Qualities, ideas, and emotions fall into this category. Concrete terms, on the other hand, have weight, texture, color, and so forth. A rose is a concrete term: it has color, fragrance, shape, and weight, and if you grab one too quickly, you may feel the prick of its thorns. You might define *rose* as a concrete term and develop an extended definition around it, but you could also treat it as a specific example to help illustrate a more abstract term, say, *beauty* or *symmetry*. The Topic List gives you suggestions for both concrete and abstract terms, with most of the abstractions in the concepts group.

Whether you choose a term from the lists or from your own experiences and interests, a good place to start your prewriting is the dictionary. However, if your term has multiple meanings, for the sake of focusing your essay, select only one meaning to develop.

Teaching Idea
Concepts often make more interesting writing and reading than object definitions, and students will choose them more readily if you show students how to develop the concepts through examples.

Choose only one meaning of your term.

Topic List

1. **Family:** mother, father, brother, sister, uncle, aunt, grandmother, grandfather, husband, wife, son, daughter, baby, toddler, child, teenager

2. **Occupations:** doctor, nurse, lawyer, architect, engineer, accountant, realtor, minister, salesperson, coach, counselor, teacher, musician, carpenter, brick mason, welder, machinist, mechanic, firefighter, mail carrier, paramedic

3. **Professional fields/careers:** welding; paralegal; nursing; emergency medical technician; dental hygiene; occupational therapy; fashion merchandising; hospitality management; travel; veterinary technician; fire science; cosmetology; early childhood education; electronics technology; grounds and turf management; heating, ventilation, and air conditioning

4. **Groups:** sports teams, marching band, choir, debate team, Boy Scouts, Girl Scouts, Shriners, clubs (gun club, book club, Trekkies, Dead Heads, sewing circle), PTA, African Americans (Irish, Asian, Hispanic, Native), Democrats, Republicans, Independents, gang, minority

5. **Places:** zoos, parks, sports arenas, rivers, lakes, beaches, swimming pools, cemeteries, amusement parks, national parks, websites, hotels, vacation spots, radio stations, retail stores, restaurants, libraries, schools (any kind), homes, office buildings, arcades, apartments, automobile dealerships, hospitals

6. **Activities:** dating, shopping, driving, moving, playing sports (baseball, football, climbing, hiking, diving, etc.), traveling, landscaping, dancing, aerobics, vacationing

7. **Behavior:** kind, cruel, responsible, irresponsible, truthful, deceptive, generous, selfish, charitable, courageous, cowardly, loyal, honorable, disciplined, sexist

8. **Personal adornment:** jewelry, makeup, tattoos, piercing, hair coloring, hair styling, fingernail polishing

9. **Illnesses/dysfunctions:** AIDS, smallpox, diphtheria, malaria, measles, mumps, chickenpox, cancer, meningitis, alcoholism, cirrhosis, herpes, common cold, headache, migraine headache, arthritis, ulcers, angina, stroke, heart attack, osteoporosis, cataracts, diabetes

10. **Concepts:** credit, health, confinement, freedom, culture, subculture, counterculture, pop culture, marriage, divorce, family, vision, environmentalism, ecology, energy source, organic food, vegetarianism, capital punishment, emotional states (love, hate, envy, joy, depression), beauty, good, evil, God, devil, hero, villain, con artist, fun, work, charity, discipline, home, addiction, music, communication skills, old age, middle age, childhood, employer, employee, co-worker, perfectionist, neighbor, winner, loser, bore, success, failure, leader, follower, man, woman, art (drawing, painting, sculpture, pottery, metal work, textiles, photography), education, initiative, disability, charity, health, window treatments, interior design, electricity, blood circulation, water table, color, pet, assisted living, maturity, work, play, body language, slang, intelligence, sex appeal, fashion, peer pressure, Baby Boomers, generation X, self-esteem, discrimination

Prewriting Suggestions

After you have chosen several terms to explore, use any of the prewriting methods from Chapter 1, along with the brief definition strategies we have practiced in this chapter, to develop your material.

Methods for Developing Extended-Definition Essays:

1. Brief definitions:

   • Synonyms (similar words)

   • Negation (not that, but this)

   • Comparisons (metaphor/simile)

   • Formal (grouping and detailing)

2. Extended definitions: patterns of development

   • Narration: telling a brief story to make a point about the term

   • Description: using vivid details to show something about the term

   • Examples: giving examples to illustrate some point about the term

   • Comparison/contrast: showing how the term is like and unlike other similar terms

   • Classification: putting the term into a group or separating it from others like it

   • Cause/effect: telling what actions can affect the term and what effects can flow from the term

   • Process analysis: telling how some part of the term works

It is helpful to phrase the above points as questions and then apply them to a topic. For example, if we used the term *scuba* from the annotated essay model "Get Wet," we could ask questions like these:

Teaching Idea
You can link these Prewriting Suggestions with Activity 15-5 to generate material for students' topics.

Teaching Idea
It helps students understand the patterns as prewriting if you work through a topic or two in class.

Teaching Idea
After students review the prewriting cluster, have them skim part of the final draft of "Get Wet" to show how the prewriting might translate into an essay.

1. What is a **synonym** for *scuba?* Answer: diving.

2. What is *scuba* **not** like? Answer: swimming in a pool.

3. What **metaphor or simile** could describe *scuba?* Answer: space flight.

4. What is the **formal definition** of *scuba?* Answer: "A portable apparatus that contains compressed air and is used for breathing under water."

Another approach is clustering:

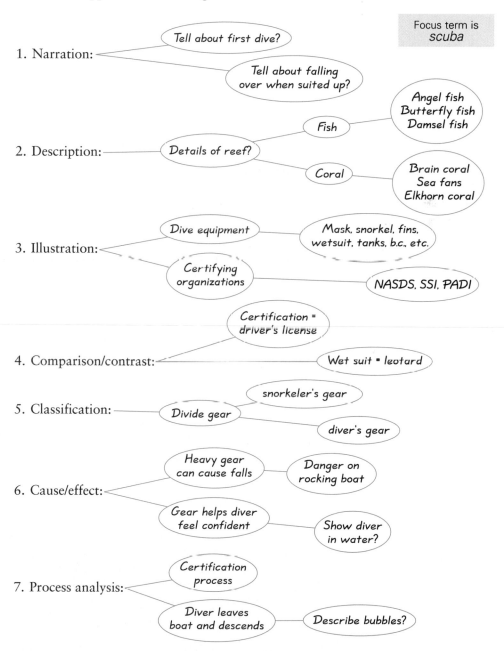

Because one important goal of our extended definition is to use several patterns, thinking about all of them during the initial brainstorming, as illustrated above, can move you quickly into a substantial first rough draft.

To see how the author of "Get Wet" used the material gathered from questioning and clustering in his essay, turn to pp. 355–357.

Prewriting—Summing Up:

1. Choose several topics from the list, or choose several of your own.

2. Consider defining a concept rather than a concrete term.

3. Try both questioning and clustering, using the methods discussed above.

4. Decide on a purpose and point for your extended definition.

Teaching Idea
Journal Entry 15-2 is a good checkpoint to see if students have a reason for their definition.

JOURNAL ENTRY 15-2

Write a paragraph telling why you have chosen your term. What about it intrigues you or makes you want to explore it further through definition? Who do you think would be interested in reading your essay, and what would you like to tell them about your term? What words in your definition do you think you will need to explain?

Organizing Ideas

To stay focused before going further, write out a **thesis** sentence. Remember to name the term and make a statement about it that lets your reader know a definition is forthcoming. You might use a form of the word *definition* (as in "one way to *define* XYZ is . . .") or follow your term with the verbs *is* or *means* (see sentence 3 below). Also, you might imply an extended definition. Here are several sample thesis sentences from the chapter models:

1. Maybe knowing more about the deaf will make them seem less strange to the hearing world.

2. Most of us will never have the opportunity to voyage into outer space, but we can learn a little about the next best option for inner planetary travel, scuba diving.

Forecasting
statement

3. Home is a place where a person feels safe, relaxed, and loved.

A note of caution: Although you may want to use a formal definition of your own devising or as quoted from a dictionary, resist the temptation to include it in your thesis in this overworked way: "As stated in Webster's New World Dictionary, home is. . . ."

For overall organization of the essay, you will probably choose either time or order of importance, with importance used most often. However, if you choose one pattern to develop a whole body paragraph, you might order your material differently within that paragraph than you do in the larger essay. For example, the body paragraphs might be organized from least to most important or dramatic, but one process analysis or narrative paragraph might be ordered chronologically.

Remember to begin each body paragraph with a topic sentence linked to the preceding paragraph by connectors like the transitions listed below (for more on connectors and a complete list of transitions, see pp. 52–57).

- Locating or moving in space: above, against, around, behind, below, on, in

- Moving in time: after, at last, awhile, first, immediately, next, now, often, then

- Adding material: again, also, and, in addition, furthermore, as well as

- Giving examples: for example, for instance, another, one reason, in fact

- Comparing: alike, also, both, in the same way, similarly
- Contrasting: in contrast, although, but, differs from, even though, however
- Cause/effect: and so, as a result, because, consequently, since, so, then
- Summarizing/concluding: finally, in brief, in other words, in short, to summarize

Organizing—Summing Up:

1. Create a rough thesis sentence to help focus your material.

2. Limit body paragraphs to three or four.

3. Arrange body paragraphs by order of importance or time.

4. Plan on using a topic sentence to introduce each body paragraph.

5. Review the list of transitions above

Teaching Idea
After students have done the prewriting cluster with the patterns, you might have them write Journal Entry 15-3 in class and then discuss it in groups.

JOURNAL ENTRY 15-3

Write out your thesis sentence. Does it mention the term and indicate that a definition will follow? Create a rough outline that includes your major points and several supporting examples/details for each body paragraph (to review outlines, see p. 282). List each developmental pattern that you plan to include so far in your first rough draft. Do you feel like you have enough material to thoroughly define your term?

Drafting

With the preliminary work out of the way, you are almost ready to write a first rough draft. But before moving ahead, take a moment to review the Drafting suggestions in Chapter 1, pp. 12–14, and to think about the following points:

1. Negation may be useful in your introductory paragraph (see "Finding Home," p. 342).

2. Synonyms and phrase defining can be easily inserted in your sentences, using commas, parentheses, and, occasionally, dashes (see "Get Wet," pp. 355–357).

3. You may use a single overall pattern of development for a given body paragraph or, as the essay models in this chapter do, mix several. But be sure to rely on specific, detailed examples.

4. Focusing your term is crucial. If you limit your term too much, you will soon run out of words to define it; if you don't limit it enough, you will write a book.

5. Even exciting topics can be made boring by a writer who has little interest in them. One reason the essay models in this chapter can hold an audience's attention is because each one has a point to make. One writer has an opinion to express about home, what she considers to be a good home. Another is excited about the sport of scuba diving and lets us know it. The third writer hopes to encourage people to become more sensitive toward the needs of the hearing impaired. If your first draft lacks a clearly discernible point, the writing will lack energy and interest.

Tips for more efficient drafting

JOURNAL ENTRY 15-4

After writing your first rough draft, skim through it and ask yourself whether or not it feels like the assignment the chapter is asking for. Is this a definition essay that uses several patterns of development, or simply a single narrative, process analysis, or other pattern? If your term has multiple meanings, have you focused on one? Are all paragraphs adequately developed with detailed examples and clear explanations? Are topic sentences in place? What part of this draft do you like best, what part least? Answer in a paragraph.

Revising Drafts

To review the detailed lists for revising drafts, turn to Chapter 13.

■ ANNOTATED STUDENT MODEL

Teaching Idea
When having students compare these drafts, focus them on the text boxes first, which point out many revisions, and then ask students how the revisions strengthen the essay.

Seeing where someone else has struggled through the process of producing a final text can help you avoid obstacles in your own drafts. If you read carefully through the Annotated Student Model, you will save yourself a few headaches and probably clarify questions you didn't even know you had.

First-Stage Draft

For this essay, Kyle Jennings chose an audience of people who are interested in scuba diving but have not yet tried it. He assumed they would know a little about the sport and that they may have been snorkeling in the ocean, so they would be familiar with terms like *mask, fins,* and *snorkel.* Because he is a certified diver and enjoys the sport, he decided to tell his reader about the basics and help them see how exciting scuba diving can be.

With material gathered from asking and answering questions and clustering with the patterns of development (see p. 349), Kyle wrote a rough thesis, chose the following three points for a brief outline, and then wrote this first rough draft.

Teaching Idea
To help students with introductions and conclusions, have them compare the paragraphs from the first and final drafts of "Get Wet," explaining which they think are more interesting.

Working thesis

This essay will try to let the reader know a little about scuba diving.

Working Outline

1. *Discuss gear.*
2. *Tell about certification process.*
3. *Describe a dive in the ocean.*

A Definition of Diving

Begins comparison

Being in the ocean in scuba gear is a lot like being in outer space. In the ocean 1 *you are weightless just like in space, and you depend on specialized gear to keep you safe. An astronaut has a helmet and breaths air; a diver has a face mask and breaths compressed air from special tanks on his back. Both situations often involve the people being in darkness.* <u>This essay will try to let the reader know a little about scuba diving.</u>

First draft lacks several patterns, examples, details, and explanations

Creates working thesis

Lists some equipment

A snorkeler needs a face mask, swimming fins, and a snorkel. But a diver also 2 wears a wet suit, heavy cylinder of air for breathing with an attached regulator, weight belt, diving vest, gauges for monitoring air and time, and a compass. If this seems like a lot of equipment, it is. It's a pain to haul around and expensive.

Tells about certification process

The next thing to know about scuba is certification. Divers need to learn the 3 rules of the ocean and how to operate the equipment. Without basic certification diving is dangerous, and only a few money-starved dive operations or so-called resort dive operations will take uncertified divers out on their boats. There are many professional dive groups, and a person can become certified in a matter of weeks; so there is little reason not to get the training. If a person is in good health and can swim, the process is easy. You just splash around in a pool for a few weeks, and then you are ready for open water, which becomes more interesting.

Describes process of ocean dive

Uses examples and descriptive details

Picture yourself on a dive boat out in the ocean on your way down for that 4 final checkout dive. You jump into the ocean and feel good. You are part of the water world with all the gear that feels so uncomfortable on land. But now it's different. In the water the gear makes you feel like a fish. Down you go, clearing the pressure, trailing bubbles, till you hang a few feet above the reef. Stretching in every direction are forests of tall, jagged corals. Brain coral of all sizes dot the sandy bottom with sea fans around. Scattered throughout the water are saltwater fish: brown and white damsels; orange and white clowns; butterfly fish; green and blue angels. You are overwhelmed and glad you shelled out the cash to get here.

Uses fish simile

Overuses you

Rough conclusion lacks summary and single focus

Scuba is a great sport that everyone should try. It's a sport for all ages, from 5 twelve to seventy. Once you are in the water, it doesn't take a lot of strength to get around; your equipment does the work for you, so the young and old both can do it. Also diving is a good sport because it brings people together. Because everyone helps one another on and off with gear and talks about things they saw on the dive, they become friendly. It's not uncommon to go out to a restaurant or bar with a newfound dive buddy after the boat docks. Diving is a wonderful sport that no one should miss.

Second-Stage Draft

Most first drafts are underdeveloped, lacking sufficient concrete, specific examples, details, and explanations. And they can also be unfocused. Kyle's first draft is strong, with most of the basic ideas from his prewriting in place, but he knew he had material to add and some problems connecting paragraphs.

A Definition of Diving

Introduction reworked, adding descriptive details to strengthen the comparison

Being in the ocean in scuba gear is a lot like being in outer space. When 1 a diver is floating in deep water, he is in another world. He depends on the compressed air in his cylinders and his regulator to deliver it smoothly. The diver swims weightlessly through "inner space." Similarly an astronaut floats in darkness with the deepest drop imaginable all around him. He also depends on his gear to deliver air, protect him from the cold and other extremes, tell him how much air he has, and orient him toward his "boat." <u>Most of us will never have the opportunity to go into outer space, but we can learn a little about the next best option for inner planetary travel, scuba diving.</u>

Thesis revised

Topic sentence added

To understand something about scuba as a sport, we can take a look at some of the gear. Basic diving equipment can be divided into two categories. The first is gear for a snorkeler, and the second is gear for a diver. A snorkeler or breath-hold diver needs a face mask, swimming fins, a snorkel, and sometimes a wet suit, depending on the temperature of the water. The wet suit is a skin tight cov-erall of rubber used to keep warmth in. Putting one on is a pain. It is much like squeezing into a really tight leotard that stretches from the neck to the ankles. A scuba diver most often wears a wet suit of varying degrees of thickness (there is a dry suit for really cold water), and in addition to the snorkelers' gear wears a heavy cylinder (or tank) of air with an attached regulator for delivering the air, weight belt, diving vest, gauges for monitoring amount of air and time under-water, and a compass. If this seems like a lot of equipment, it is. And until a diver gets into the water, the diver is overloaded, uncomfortable, and prone to falling down. A complete set of scuba equipment is expensive (more than a thousand dollars), but many certified divers own only snorkeling gear and rent the rest.

2

Classification added

Comparison added

Examples of equipment added with explanations

Cause and effect added

Transition added to topic sentence

Aside from the gear, people wanting to know more about scuba diving should be aware of the certification process. Just as a person has to learn the rules of the road and pass a driving exam before she gets her driver's license, so too must divers learn the rules of the ocean and how to operate the equipment safely. Without basic certification diving is dangerous. Few reputable dive shops will rent equipment to or take uncertified divers out on their boats. There are many professional dive groups (PADI, SSI, NASDS), and the course fees are nominal. Also a person can become certified in a matter of weeks; so there is little reason not to get the training. If a person is in good health, can swim, and is not inclined to panic in the water, the process is easy. After classroom instruc-tion and study in a text, divers move to a pool and practice with the equipment until they are ready for a lake or ocean journey. Then the real fun begins.

3

Comparison added

Examples added

Explanation added

Topic sentence added

The most exciting part of scuba diving, naturally, is being in the water. The pool may have seemed fascinating at first, but it pales by comparison to open water, especially the waters of a reef. Teetering on the dive boat, all gear in order, the diver "strides" out and splashes into the ocean, and the diver feels in her element. The equipment she is wearing makes her part of the environ-ment, like she belongs, something of a fish. Down the diver sinks, clearing the pressure in her ears, trailing bubbles, equalizing buoyancy till she is floating, weightless, above the reef. Stretching in every direction are forests of tall, jagged corals. Light-brown brain coral ranging in size from basketballs to boulders dot

4

You pronoun replaced

Gender pronoun he shifted to she

Examples, details, action words added

the pale sandy bottom with purple sea fans rocking at their feet. Scattered throughout the coral are the cousins of all those captive saltwater aquarium fish: brown and white damsels; orange- and white-striped clowns; yellow butterfly fish; lime-green and blue angels. The new diver hovers, amazed by the beauty of inner space, eager to see more.

Brief summary added

Scuba is a wonderful sport that only requires the right equipment and proper training to open a new world to the diver. It is a safe sport for all ages, and one that brings people together. Because a number one rule in diving is to pair up before going under, people meet quickly. They help each other with their gear. Then they dive together and share their experiences back on board. "Did you see the size of that lobster?" "How about those amber jacks?" "The mantas looked like flying saucers!" This is the essence of scuba diving: people cooperating and sharing their excitement as they explore the new world of inner space. 5

Conclusion rewritten to focus the point—sharing.

> **Special Points to Check in Revising from First to Second Drafts**
>
> 1. **Introduction:** hook, engaging support sentences, thesis
> 2. **Body paragraphs:** topic sentence with connector
> 3. **Overall development:** examples, details, explanations (brief definitions and pattern of development)
> 4. **Conclusion:** connector, summary, expanded thought

Third-Stage Draft

With most of the organizational and material concerns out of the way, it is time to look more closely at the essay to strengthen style. In this draft you can look even more closely at word choices and sentence patterns and think about punctuating for emphasis.

Get Wet

Title revised

More specific words added

Being in the ocean in scuba gear is a lot like being in outer space. When a diver is floating in silence above a deep-water coral plateau, with a half-mile drop into darkness a few yards away, he is in another world. [Depending on the compressed air in his cylinders and his regulator to deliver it smoothly, the diver glides weightlessly, almost effortlessly, through "inner space."] Similarly, an astronaut floats in darkness with the deepest drop imaginable all around him. He also depends on his gear to deliver air, protect him from the cold and other extremes, tell him how much air he has, and orient him toward his "boat." Few of us will have the opportunity to voyage into outer space, but we can learn a little about the next best option for inner planetary travel, scuba diving. 1

More precise words substituted

Sentences combined for variety

To understand something about scuba (self-contained underwater breathing apparatus) as a sport, we can take a look at some of the gear. [Basic diving equipment can be divided into two categories: gear for a snorkeler and gear 2

Defining in parentheses

Sentences combined for variety

More specific words added

for a diver.**]** A snorkeler or breath-hold diver needs a face mask, swimming fins, a snorkel, and sometimes a wet suit, depending on the temperature of the water. The wet suit is a skin-tight coverall of neoprene rubber (rubber filled with millions of bubbles of nitrogen) used to keep warmth in. Putting one on is a pain. It is much like squeezing into a really tight, thick leotard that stretches from the neck to the ankles. A scuba diver most often wears a wet suit of varying degrees of thickness (there is a dry suit for really cold water), and in addition to the snorkelers' gear wears a heavy cylinder (or tank) of compressed air with an attached regulator for delivering the air, weight belt, diving vest, gauges for

Synonym replaces overused words

monitoring amount of air and time underwater, and a compass. If this seems like a lot of equipment, it is. **[**And until a diver gets into the water, ~~the diver~~ **she** is overloaded, uncomfortable, and prone to falling down.**]** A complete set of scuba equipment is expensive (more than a thousand dollars), but many certified divers own only snorkeling gear and rent the rest.

Aside from the gear, people wanting to know more about scuba ~~diving~~ **3** should be aware of the certification process. Just as a person has to learn the rules of the road and pass a driving exam before she gets her driver's license, so too must divers learn the rules of the ocean and how to operate the equipment safely. **[**Without basic certification diving is dangerous, and few reputable dive shops will rent equipment to or take uncertified divers out on their boats.**]**

Sentences combined for variety

Synonym replaces overused word

[There are many professional ~~dive groups~~ **scuba organizations** (PADI, SSI, NASDS), the course fees are nominal, and a person can become certified in a matter of weeks; so there is little reason not to get the training.**]** If a person is in good health, can swim, and is not inclined to panic in the water, the process is easy. After classroom instruction and study in a text, ~~divers~~ people move to a pool and practice with the equipment until they are ready for a lake or ocean journey. Then the real fun begins.

More precise locator phrase added

The most exciting part of scuba diving, naturally, is being in the water. The **4** pool may have seemed fascinating at first, but it pales by comparison to open water, especially the clear waters of a reef. Teetering at the end of the dive boat, all gear in order, the diver "strides" out and splashes into the ocean.

Sentence divided for emphasis

More specific words added

Immediately, she feels in her element. The equipment she is wearing makes her part of the marine environment, ~~like she belongs~~, something of a fish. Down

Redundant phrase is removed

the diver sinks, clearing the pressure in her ears, trailing bubbles, equalizing buoyancy till she is floating, weightless, a few feet above the reef. Stretching in every direction are forests of tall, jagged staghorn and elkhorn corals. Light-brown brain coral ranging in size from basketballs to boulders dot the pale sandy bottom with green and purple sea fans rocking at their feet. Scattered

Synonym replaces overused word

throughout the ~~coral~~ **seascape** are the cousins of all those captive saltwater aquarium fish: sassy brown and white damsels; orange- and white-striped clowns; yellow butterfly fish; stately lime-green and blue angels. The new diver hovers, amazed by the beauty of inner space, eager to see more.

Scuba is a wonderful sport that only requires the right equipment and proper ₅ training to open a new world to the diver. It is a safe sport for all ages, and one that brings people together. Because a number one rule in diving is to pair up before going under, people meet quickly. [They help each other with their gear, dive together, and share their experiences back on board.] "Did you see the size of that lobster?" "How about those amber jacks?" "The mantas looked like flying saucers!" This is the essence of scuba diving: people cooperating and sharing their excitement as they explore the new world of inner space.

Kyle Jennings

Special Points to Check in Revising from Second to Third Drafts:

1. Added specific words are boxed.

2. More precise or audience-appropriate word substitutions are shaded.

3. [Sentences combined for variety are bracketed.]

4. **Synonyms and phrases replacing clutter and repeat words are bolded.**

5. ~~Unneeded words are lined through.~~

CHAPTER SUMMARY

1. Definition is the act of limiting and clarifying the meaning of a word, of separating it from other similar terms.

2. We define daily at home, school, and work.

3. Brief definitions—synonyms, negation, comparisons, formal—are often part of a paragraph or essay being developed with a single pattern, such as process analysis or comparison and contrast.

4. Brief definitions may be a single word or a short phrase, often enclosed by commas, parentheses, or dashes.

5. Extended-definition essays often use brief definitions and several patterns of development.

6. Definition depends on thoroughly explained and detailed examples.

7. Transitional words and other connectors are especially important in bridging the gap between paragraphs.

8. Definition essays can be organized chronologically but are frequently arranged by order of importance.

9. A thesis sentence is a critical first step in focusing an extended definition essay.

10. Outlining even a brief essay is a logical and valuable prewriting technique.

11. Topic sentences are an essential part of a coherent body paragraph.

12. Writing is never complete until it has gone through several revisions and careful editing.

■ ALTERNATE WRITING ASSIGNMENTS

Teaching Idea
When introducing students to the chapter Topic List, you might also point out these alternate assignments.

The following assignment options may help you focus your extended definition.

> Remember to observe these points:
>
> • Review brief definitions and the patterns of development, and use several methods to develop your essay.
>
> • Have a reason for your definition, and make the reason clear to your reader.
>
> • Write to a specific audience.
>
> • Review methods for creating introductions and conclusions in Chapter 12.
>
> • Create controlling topic sentences for each body paragraph.

1. Write an extended definition of the term "home" that either adds to or differs from the one in "Finding Home," pp. 242–243. Perhaps you don't agree with April Griffin's feeling that a home requires more than one person or that a family should be involved. Brainstorm for ideas based on your personal experience, and if you plan to disagree with points from "Finding Home," consider using negation in your introduction to show how your definition will differ from the author's.

2. Write an extended definition that treats a term as the best or worst of its kind. For instance, you might discuss a person and tell what makes for a terrific or terrible boss, leader, co-worker, parent, child, grandmother, athlete, or neighbor. Or you could choose a place like an amusement park, stadium, or beach. Perhaps an activity like a vacation, sporting event, or a date seems interesting. You will probably draw on personal experiences, perhaps using narrative as one method of development.

3. Write an extended definition that reacts to some term regularly applied to you individually or as a representative of a group. For example, perhaps your friends have often called you "out-of-control" just because you love high-risk activities like freeclimbing, hang gliding, sky diving, and bungee jumping. If you agree with them, write an essay that clarifies what "out-of-control" means in your life. If you disagree, either define "out-of-control" at length or offer another term to describe your lifestyle, and then develop it through definition.

Another approach to this assignment is to agree or disagree with a term someone applies to you as a member of a group. For example, you may be tired of hearing generation Xers referred to as "politically apathetic," the Irish as "alcoholics," or feminists as "radical." As in the other option above, define the term at length as *you* see it, or define an alternative term that better describes your group.

4. Write an extended definition of a term important in a career you are interested in, or define the career itself. For example, if you are thinking about computer science as a career, you might want to know more about terms like "RAM," "ROM," "mother board," or "modem." Or you might want to learn about the education required, employment prospects, or potential salary. If you choose to research the career, remember that you will need to limit your findings to three or four significant points.

5. Write an extended definition of one word that best describes you. You might know immediately what that word is—hard working, athletic, lazy, funny, loyal—or you might struggle with two or three before you pin it down. If you are not sure yourself, try asking a good friend or family member. One of them may surprise you with the defining word. Another approach is to imagine a setting and audience. If you were in a job interview and asked to define yourself in a word, what would you say? How would you support your definition? Presuming you want the job, you would select your word with care, knowing that the employer does not want to hear words like "irresponsible," "lazy," "timid," or "hostile."

CHAPTER 16

Writing Persuasively

WHAT ARE WE TRYING TO ACHIEVE AND WHY?

Setting the Stage

Do the illustrations above have something in common? In the courtroom, a lawyer questions a witness while a judge weighs the evidence. Next, two politicians present their positions, challenging one another's statements and defending their own. The third illustration is filled with advertising. And the last picture shows a family eating dinner, enjoying each other's company and at some point perhaps talking over the day's events. If it's a typical conversation, the parents want the kids to do more around the house, the kids want to do more almost anywhere *but* in the house, and the dog just wants a few more table scraps.

Each of the above illustrations involves **persuasion**: the attempt to convince someone to accept an idea or policy (as with the politicians) or to take some action—find a defendant innocent, buy a product, clean a room, or feed a dog. This is the focus of Chapter 16.

In this chapter, we will discuss persuasion in this broader sense, but we will also look at a particular form of persuasion known as **argument.** When we speak of arguing, we are not referring to raised voices and fists pounding on the table, but rather a reasoned exchange of ideas between two or more parties who hold differing opinions on an issue. As we move through the chapter, we will learn how to select and focus arguable topics (issues), frame our position on the issue, explore it through **reasons** backed by **evidence**, expand our argument with several patterns of development, and finally influence an audience to accept or at least respect our position on the issue.

Linking to Previous Experience

Trying to get what we want from life is a basic human preoccupation. As soon as a baby learns that food is forthcoming if the infant cries loudly enough, persuasion begins. During childhood we quickly learn what strategies work with mom and dad to get the things we want. We appeal to them unconsciously on all three levels that operate in more formal argumentation: mind, heart, self. "If we are going to get the bike, now is the time because it's on sale for 50 percent off" (appeal to the mind with a bargain). "I need a new bicycle because the brakes are shot on my old one, and I might get hurt" (appeal to the parents' heart). "You promised that if I did well this term in school you would buy the bike" (appeal to the parents' sense of fairness).

Of course, our parents are not the only targets of our persuasive attempts. We work on (and are worked on by) other family members, friends, significant others, fellow employees, employers, teachers, merchants, and even the police officer about to write us a speeding ticket. Sometimes we are successful, sometimes not.

In this text although we have focused primarily on communicating ideas and explaining clearly, many of us have already written papers with at least partially persuasive intent. When we created a dominant impression in describing a place, for example, we selected details that would encourage readers to see and feel what we wanted them to. When we created a story line in the personal narratives, we manipulated plot, dialogue, and description so the audience would feel suspense and understand the story's significance to us. In establishing causes and effects, we may have influenced our readers to avoid some kind of behavior because of possible negative results. In short, much of what we have already written in *A Writer's Workshop* has been mildly persuasive, but now persuasion becomes our primary purpose.

Determining the Value

It is clear that people regularly try to influence one another, and those who are good at it profit. Persuasive skills can help us land the job we want, negotiate a purchase, and lead us to that significant other who ultimately becomes a spouse. But becoming aware of persuasive strategies can also help us view the arguments of others more critically, to resist the professional persuaders—politicians, salespeople, advertisers, and others—and make reasoned decisions rather than manipulated ones. The process of examining and constructing arguments can help us think more clearly.

Further, as people living in a society, we need to think clearly about the many issues that divide and bind us. Should abortion remain an option for women? Do we support capital punishment? Do we need stricter gun control laws? Should sex education be taught in schools? We can arrive at reasoned positions on these issues through discussion and debate. We may be uncomfortable at times during the process: we may see our own logic fail and find that we must alter or reverse a position, and we may see tempers flare on occasion; but argument—a reasoned exchange of ideas—is essential for people who live together. Through argument we discover more of who we are and more of what we would like our society to be.

JOURNAL ENTRY 16-1

Think for a moment about instances during the past week when you tried to persuade someone or saw persuasion in action. Maybe you wanted to see one film while a friend favored another? Perhaps you tried to talk your boss into a raise, time off, or a shift change? Maybe you watched a teacher try to persuade her class to find value in a subject under discussion? Summarize one instance of attempted persuasion from home, work, and school. Did the persuader accomplish his or her purpose? If so, why? If not, why not?

🔳 DEVELOPING SKILLS, EXPLORING IDEAS IN PERSUASIVE ESSAYS

Teaching Idea
To help students understand a split audience, you might draw stick figures on the board, showing them at podiums with an audience off to one side. If you are a rotten artist like I am, your illustration will get a few laughs but will also allow you to show with arrows the interaction of the two debaters and the audience. This is a good device for clarifying possible audience objections versus an opponent's counterreasons.

As you work through the activities that follow, remember that argument implies not only the audience you are trying to persuade but also those who already disagree with you. How you deal with that "opposition" is a large part of effective persuasion.

1. Define the issue and clarify terms.

2. Present reasons and support.

3. Connect with the audience.

4. Avoid errors in logic.

5. Qualify.

6. Counter opposing reasons and audience objections.

Groundwork for Activity 16-1: Defining the Issue

Many arguments fail because the writer and reader see the issue differently. For instance, what does the following thesis sentence actually mean? "Minors who break the law should get the same treatment that adults do." Does "minors" mean any young person from three to seventeen? And what exactly does "get the same treatment that adults do" mean? Should minors be prosecuted the same way adults are? If this were the case, a reader might imagine these arguments: "Five-year-olds who are caught taking a piece of candy from a store, should have to appear in court and be prosecuted for the misdemeanor" or "If a thirteen-year-old is caught 'joyriding' in a stolen car, she should be prosecuted as an adult and imprisoned with other adult criminals."

Because arguments can easily be misinterpreted, a writer must carefully limit her issue and define all terms.

Teaching Idea
If students have written a process analysis, you can remind them that the same care they gave to defining terms for their process they should continue with their argument.

Collaborative

Activity 16-1: Defining the Issue

The following thesis sentences are unfocused and might be misinterpreted by an audience. Rewrite each of them to clarify the issue and define unclear terms. Write out a thesis that you think you could support in your own argument.

Teaching Idea
Ask students which terms need to be clarified in Activity 16-1 to focus the arguments.

Example:

Unfocused issue: Children should be able to leave school whenever they want to.

Focused issue (thesis): _Students who have parental consent should be allowed to quit school by the age of sixteen._

Answers will vary.

1. **Unfocused issue:** Birth control should be available to anyone who wants it.

   Focused issue (thesis): _Birth control should be available in high school to students with parental consent._

2. **Unfocused issue:** Schools should have fewer rules.

   Focused issue (thesis): _High schools should not require school uniforms._

_____

3. **Unfocused issue:** Playing sports is bad for young people.

    Focused issue (thesis): *Playing contact sports like football is bad for children under twelve.*

4. **Unfocused issue:** People should be protected from television violence.

    Focused issue (thesis): *Parents should protect their children from television violence.*

5. **Unfocused issue:** Everyone should value the environment more.

    Focused issue (thesis): *If people want to preserve air quality, they should buy fuel-efficient cars.*

Teaching Idea
The term *evidence* can sound difficult to students, so you might refer to it as *support,* a term which is accurate and one they should be familiar with.

Groundwork for Activity 16-2: Presenting Reasons and Providing Support

After we have selected and focused an issue, we must be able to present **reasons** and offer **evidence** for supporting our stand on the issue. Reasons are the main points we will make about the issue; evidence supports those points. For example, if we wanted to argue that fireworks should be outlawed in the United States, we could brainstorm and come up with several reasons like the following:

1. Fireworks hurt people.

2. Fireworks cause property damage.

3. Fireworks annoy many people.

Each of these reasons is still just an unsupported assertion and, as such, not very convincing. However, as soon as we add specific evidence, an argument begins to take shape. For instance, if we focused on reason 1, harm to people, we could state a **statistic** that 17,000 people were injured last year by fireworks. Next, we could add an **example,** saying that the red-hot wires from sparklers burn people. And we might continue with an **anecdote** (a brief story, first- or second-hand) about the time a younger brother shot someone in the face with a Roman candle. There are several forms of evidence useful for developing arguments, and we have been working with them in one form or another all semester. Note the following list:

Kinds of evidence used to support reasons

1. **Facts/statistics:** commonly accepted truths in words and numbers

2. **Authorities:** people who are generally recognized as experts in their field

3. **Examples:** specific instances to illustrate general statements

4. **Anecdotes:** brief stories

5. **Scenarios:** what-if situations, speculating about causes and effects

6. **Logical interpretations:** explanations that help the reader understand how the reasons and evidence work to support a thesis

As you explore your argument, you will probably find several sound reasons to support your position and quite likely develop a body paragraph around each. However, occasionally a single reason is so compelling that an entire argument may rest on it. When this is the case, the rest of the essay will be evidence to support the reason and/or refutation of the "opposition's" reasons.

Teaching Idea
If students choose an issue like removing handguns from homes with young children, the primary reason—safety of the children—may be the only reason they need to support (of course including refutation of the main counterreason— protecting the home).

Collaborative

Activity 16-2: Presenting Reasons, Providing Support

After reading the groundwork material for this activity, discuss with group members each of the following topics. Look closely at the thesis and reason given to support the thesis. Now imagine that each one of the issues is an argument that you are building, and create *three* kinds of acceptable evidence to support each reason.

Teaching Idea
Tell students that they may manufacture facts and authoritative statements to fit the issue they choose in Activity 16-2.

Example:

Topic: Outlawing fireworks

Thesis: Fireworks should be prohibited in this country.

Reason: Many children are injured by them each year.

Evidence:

- **Fact:** _Last year there were 17,000 injuries nationally on July 4th._
- **Authority:** _Dr. Horace Caruthers, director of the Johns Hopkins Trauma Center, has stated that bottle rockets alone are responsible for hundreds of eye injuries on July 4th._
- **Example:** _Even relatively harmless fireworks like sparklers can cause severe burns when children grab the glowing wires in their hands or step on them with bare feet._
- **Anecdote:** _When my younger brother was nine years old he shot me in the face with a Roman candle._
- **Scenario:** _Imagine your eleven-year-old son teased into holding and throwing lit cherry bombs or M-80s. Now imagine how you would feel if his hearing was damaged, his fingers were blown off, or if he was blinded._
- **Logical interpretation:** _Because children get caught up in the moment and so often don't think of consequences, they will continue to be injured by fireworks._

Answers will vary.

1. Topic: Freedom of choice in high school curriculum

   Thesis: High school students should be allowed to choose more of their own curriculum.

   Reason: If students are more interested in their studies, they will perform better.

   Evidence:

   - _I chose a senior English class that emphasized poetry and have carried this interest into college._

   - _During our senior year my best friend chose a real estate course and was so excited about it that he did better in all his courses, knowing that his improved grades might help him get a job with a realtor._

   - _The Tech Prep courses at my high school have saved half the people I know from dropping out._

2. Topic: Teachers accepting late homework

   Thesis: Teachers should accept late homework from students with legitimate excuses.

Reason: Students who have worked hard on homework assignments are demoralized and angered when they cannot turn them in for credit.

Evidence:

- *I have seen more than one confrontation at the beginning of a class session between a teacher and a student who had been absent.*

- *Teachers are always telling students that half the educational battle is won through attitude, but when teachers undercut a student's positive attitude by policies that seem unfair, the teachers are setting their students up for failure.*

- *My friends tell me that many of their other teachers accept late work with legitimate excuses, so my friends feel that not accepting homework is unfair.*

3. Topic: Changing sports teams' names

   Thesis: Professional sports teams that feature ethnic names should change them.

   Reason: Many Native Americans feel demeaned by some team names.

   Evidence:

   - *Washington Redskins, Kansas City Chiefs, Atlanta Braves, Cleveland Indians*

   - *Behavior and stereotypes: the " tomahawk chop" "Chief Wahoo"*

   - *Several Native American groups have spoken against the use of Indian names.*

4. Topic: Privacy of HIV victims versus need to know by parents

   Thesis: Parents should be informed of any child carrying HIV in their children's school.

   Reason: Parents should know of any potential danger to their children.

   Evidence:

   - *In many cities parents can learn when convicted child molesters move into the neighborhood.*

   - *Children get cuts while playing, and blood can pass the HIV virus.*

   - *HIV is so deadly that parents have the right to know even if the chance of infection is minute.*

5. Topic: Length of workweek

Thesis: My company should allow flexible scheduling to create four-day workweeks.

Reason: Four-day workweeks would boost morale.

Evidence:

- *A study by the National Business Consortium in 1999 listed five-day workweeks as one of the top five reasons employees are dissatisfied with their jobs.*

- *Many major corporations, hospitals, and universities allow four-day workweeks, in part to boost employee morale.*

- *Seven out of ten fellow employees that I polled on this issue said that they would be more satisfied with their job if they could redistribute their forty hours over four days.*

Groundwork for Activity 16-3: Connecting with the Audience

Having an issue, reasons, and evidence is a good start to your argument; now we must consider how best to connect with an audience. We have already discussed how to use evidence to develop essays; and, of course, we want to explain the reasons and evidence as completely as possible, defining any term that our reader might not know. This careful presentation of ideas will in itself go a long way toward persuading an audience. However, there are two other major points to consider when writing an argument: **presenting ourselves** effectively and **influencing a reader's emotions**. The figure below shows the three overlapping elements so important in persuasive writing.

Communication Triangle

Text

Are the reasons and evidence—facts, examples, etc.—effectively presented?

Writer/ Speaker

Reader/ Listener

How is the writer perceived by the reader—as someone who is knowledgeable, honest, fair, open, and reasonable?

How does the reader react to the writer? Does she view the writer positively? How does the reader react to the examples and other evidence the author provides? Do the reader's emotional responses favor the writer's position?

Most of us respond more positively to others if we perceive them to be reasonable, fair, honest, good people. In writing, we create an impression of ourselves by what we say and how we say it. If our **persona,** this perception a reader has of the writer, is a good one, it advances our argument; if not, it hinders it. For example, if a person

---

Teaching Idea
Students usually have the most difficulty with ethos and pathos in argument, but this simplified graphic, along with the two following examples, will help them see the impact of persona and the need to consider the reader's emotional response.

Teaching Idea
For more help with the concept of persona, create some scenarios for students where they would consciously try to manipulate their image. For example, how might they dress for an important job interview for a corporation like Sprint? Why wouldn't they wear faded blue jeans, an old sweatshirt, and unlaced tennis shoes?

Teaching Idea
It is helpful to emphasize the *overlapping* nature of the three appeals.

Persona: the image a writer presents of himself or herself wanted to argue that drivers over seventy should take an annual physical and driving exam, which of the following statements reveals the most positive persona:

1. Old farts shouldn't be on the road any longer if they can't handle a grown-up's responsibility. They don't deserve to drive, and I hate it whenever I'm stuck near one in traffic.

2. Though many of our senior citizens have driven responsibly for years, when through no fault of their own the aging process diminishes their capacity to drive safely, in order to protect them and others, we ought to ask them to take an annual physical and driving exam.

> It is always a mistake to antagonize the reader you are trying to persuade.

Clearly, statement number 1 reveals an unsympathetic, even antagonistic, persona, and a reader might suspect the writer's motives for proposing the driving exam. On the other hand, statement number 2 reveals a writer who seems to respect the older driver and regrets having to propose an annual exam but does so because it serves the greater good.

Along with persona a writer should consider the **emotional responses** of a reader and choose examples that cause the reader to respond favorably to an argument. Using the annual exam for elderly drivers again, consider which of the following paragraphs would be more likely to influence an audience that includes people with seniors in their family:

1. Like I said, these old fogies have got to go. They aren't capable anymore, they get in the way, and they cause accidents. Blue hairs and other semi-geriatric cases belong more in wheelchairs than automobiles. If they have a hard time getting out to buy their Geritol and Depends without driving, let the city foot the bill for taxis or let their families do the driving. However we get them off the road, the sooner the better.

Teaching Idea
Paragraph 2 is the conclusion of the chapter Annotated Student Model. You might remind students of Activity 16-3 if you work them through the model, pointing out the revisions the author made to create a more persuasive persona.

2. Neither of my grandfathers wants to endanger anyone, and they both have to get from place to place just like everyone else. But their failing physical and mental health made them unsafe drivers, so they finally stopped driving, luckily before anyone was seriously injured. As a result, my folks and I and the rest of our family are pitching in to shuttle our grandparents around. It *is* inconvenient. And family members are annoyed by the chore on occasion. But this "chore" has the benefit of bringing us more often in contact with each other. I see all of my grandparents more frequently now than before they stopped driving. The family profits because we are sharing a task that is right. Our older generation took care of their children and their children's children in their time. Now it is our time to take care of them.

Most of us would probably choose the second paragraph because it evokes a more sympathetic emotional reaction in the reader. When we develop arguments, it is critical to have a specific audience in mind and to use both our persona and the readers' emotional responses to our advantage.

Activity 16-3: Connecting with the Audience

Collaborative

Teaching Idea
Tell students that they can add or delete material to improve persona in Activity 16-3.

Discuss with group members the Communication Triangle and the appeals of persona and emotion. Next, choose *one* of the following three paragraphs and rewrite it on a separate sheet of paper, making the persona more positive and trying for emotional appeals that would influence the *stated audience*. Consider including yourself in the audience as in the paragraph excerpt above on elderly drivers and using pronouns like *we, us,* and *our.*

Answers will vary.

1. Issue and position: Schools should enforce dress codes.

   Audience: Public high school students

   It should be obvious to anyone that these high school students ought to be wearing uniforms. Just look at what they are doing to one another in their own schools! They beat each other up for a pair of tennis shoes and form packs like animals to hunt each other down. And teachers have to suffer from it too. If they are not risking their lives breaking up knife fights in the halls, they are having to beg the students to stop admiring each other's new sunglasses and pay attention to the lesson. I know that some students are going to whine about personal identity and freedom, but who ever said school was supposed to be a democracy after all?

2. Issue and position: People should only use cell phones for urgent business while driving.

   Audience: Owners and frequent users of cell phones

   Telephones have almost no business in cars. Aside from the rare emergency call, people just yak away while they buzz down the highway, paying little attention to the traffic and other drivers around them. And what are these pressing conversations that can't wait five minutes till the driver gets to his or her destination? "Hi, Judy, remember to bring the potato salad to Jan's on Friday." "Hello, dear, would you be sure to defrost the hamburger for dinner?" "Bill, it's killin' me. I gotta know the name of the lead in *Brave Heart.*" Cell phone addicts are a menace on the road as they weave in and out of traffic, speed up, slow down, and cut off other drivers as the phone freaks swerve to make almost-missed exits. My request to cell phone owners is this: "Shut up. Even your friends don't want to hear from you that much."

3. Issue and position: Andrea Hoffman wants a raise from eight to nine dollars an hour at Family Tree Nursery.

   Audience: Andrea's immediate supervisor

   Dear Mr. T. Ightwad:

   I have been working at this dive for a year now, and I've made it to work most of the time. When I'm here you can ask anyone—well, you better ask Glen or Annette—and they will tell you I work hard. Whenever you need someone to come through for you with overtime or weekend work, I am right there sometimes, and I stayed late twice last year. Besides, I need the money. I took two classes at the community college last year, and my books were almost a hundred dollars (what a rip-off!). I really do like working at the nursery all right, and I'll probably stick around for awhile, so I hope you will consider giving me the raise that I really do deserve.

   P.S. No hard feelings if you don't give me what you owe me. Besides I know where you park your Lexus. Ha, ha, just kidding.

Groundwork for Activity 16-4: Avoiding Errors in Logic

Logical reasoning is another important part of persuasive writing. If readers don't think what we are stating makes sense, even if we have plenty of good evidence, they are not likely to believe us. Below you will find listed several common errors in logic, mostly mistakes in reasoning caused by oversimplifying and underqualifying.

Besides the health issue children suffer from too much exposure to the wrong messages on TV. There has been much debate about whether violence on television influences children to behave in aggressive or violent ways. Some say that TV violence allows kids to release frustration and anger in the fantasy acts of cartoon characters, instead of punching their brothers and sisters, so at least some TV violence is good for children. Perhaps. But when I watch my own children, nieces, and nephews practice karate kicks on one another and slash away with stick swords after seeing the same behavior on TV, it makes me suspicious. Aside from the violent behavior that kids at least model after their cartoon heroes, there are all kinds of sexual, racial, and ethnic stereotypes shaping kids' views of themselves and others. My daughter does not now look like Barbie and never will. Why should she feel this is an image to live up to?

3

What most disturbs me about excessive television for children is the negative effect it has on their learning. Of course there are many good programs available, the Discovery Channel, Animal Planet, Nickelodeon, Travel, and others, that expose children to new ideas. But the truth is that most kids are more attracted to the action/role-playing programs than to a History Channel documentary on the life of Lincoln. When children are unsupervised, they can easily spend four to six hours a day—the national average— watching junk, leaving little time for homework or other learning activities. Schools practically beg parents to spend time with their children reading, learning math, and helping with other course work. How can this happen when TV has captured the audience? And schoolwork is not all that suffers. Don't we as parents want to involve our children in other learning activities like music, dance, and sports?

4

Television is a mixed blessing. In small doses it does not have to have the negative effects on our children's health, behavior, and learning that it often has in large amounts. In fact most of us enjoy watching TV ourselves and with our family; and, let's face it, we often need a break from the kids that the box can provide. But, as tiring as it can be, we need to keep fighting the TV battle with our kids. We need to monitor what they watch and how much. Children cannot see very far down the road. They want what they want when they want it, regardless of the consequences. It is part of our job as parents to protect them from themselves.

5

Marisa Youmbi

Postreading Analysis

Marisa touches an issue close to many parents. Instead of directly stating her thesis at the end of the introductory paragraph, she uses a question, which she then goes on to answer in the rest of the essay. In trying to persuade a fairly resistant or even hostile audience, a writer will sometimes delay her thesis or even avoid stating it directly, implying it instead. However, by the end of any argument, the reader should clearly know what the author's position on the issue is.

The essay is well organized with clear topic sentences, plenty of strong connectors, and both an introduction and conclusion that are effectively arranged. As in many arguments the body paragraphs are built around primary reasons for supporting the author's position on the issue and then arranged by order of importance, saving the strongest reason for last.

Throughout her essay the author makes good use of the argument strategies we have practiced in this chapter. The issue and her position on it are quickly made clear. Beginning in the introduction, Marisa offers material that would interest her audience and continues to show herself as part of her readership as she presents her reasons. This appeal to her audience by identifying with them can be powerfully persuasive, and she carries this out in part by using accommodation pronouns (*we, us, our*), in part by the

Teaching Idea
"Just Say No" is a strong example of shaping an argument for a target audience. Ask students to evaluate the appeals directed to the parent audience. Are the appeals effective, and if so why?

homey examples, and in part by anticipating her readers' possible objections to her reasons. Notice the strong emotional appeals she uses in addressing her readers as fellow parents who want the best for their children.

▶ Prereading Exploration for "Something for Nothing?"

Teaching Idea
You might want to mention assumptions in argument at this point and link the discussion with Matt Smith's assumption about his audience already favoring allowances. You can frame the discussion as another method for focusing an argument.

Matt Smith chose to discuss another family issue: allowances. Drawing on personal experience rather than outside sources, Matt directs his argument toward middle- to lower-income parents who are wondering about giving allowances to their children and are not sure whether to insist that the children complete various chores to earn the money. He assumes that the parents already favor giving allowances in some form, so he does not need to argue this point, which helps with the essay's focus.

Assumptions that we make about our readers—their values, knowledge, and experiences—can help or hurt our arguments, so we should assume with care. How do you feel about another of the author's assumptions that money can be a powerful motivator for young people from "six to sixteen," that it might incline them to work around the house more than, say, the prospects of pleasing a parent, helping the family, or being deprived of something they value?

Answers will vary.

_____

_____

_____

Something for Nothing?

"Josh, congratulations, you don't have to work any more if you don't want to. You just come in whenever you please, and I'll keep writing you a paycheck every month for at least the next ten years. What do you say?" I don't know about you, but if I were Josh, I'd be thanking the Lord and not planning on many more visits to the job site. Paying a child an allowance is not quite the same as an employer paying an employee wages; but there are some similarities, and a child is likely to react like most adults would on hearing he is about to get something for nothing—take the money and run. Parents who believe in allowances for their children should consider making their children work for the money.   1

One good reason for expecting children to work for extra spending money is that most families need the help. While there are plenty of wealthy folk in this country, most of us are not, and households run on people power. Both of my parents worked as I was growing, so neither had a lot of extra time to keep the house running smoothly. They still carried a lot of the load, but my brothers and sister and I were expected to wash dishes, vacuum, do laundry, carry out the trash, rake and mow the lawn—all the routine chores, and if we expected an allowance, we did the work. I remember my youngest brother at six helping rake leaves with his big brothers. He was proud to be a "big kid," and we all got along pretty well together.   2

Another point in favor of paying children for what they earn is the motivation factor. Most parents expect their children to help out around the house, whether they give the children an allowance or not. A lot of the minimal jobs are supposed to be "understood," putting toys away, keeping clothes on hangers, putting books back on shelves, and making up a bed. But by the time children are six or so, many parents begin leaning pretty hard on them to do the daily chores. I have seen adults shout at their kids, call them names, and spank the youngest ones for not doing their jobs. I say rather than making kids mind by punishing them why not reward them for doing what they should? Earned allowances can be a positive motivator for young people from six to at least sixteen, especially when they can buy whatever they want with the money.   3

The most important reason for tying allowances to performance is that it gives children an early clear view of the real world. People have to work and produce for a living, almost everyone. Whatever we want to call it—a paycheck, grades on a report card, praise from someone we respect, or an allowance—the world turns on people putting out effort and being rewarded, sometimes, for it. Why shouldn't children learn this lesson early in life? If they learn it well, maybe they will carry it through to other areas as they grow older, areas like good performance at work and school. I know that some might think a ten-year-old shouldn't have to think of the pressures of the "real world," that kids should be allowed just to be kids. But I am not talking about slave labor here, just a regular routine of chores that kids can reasonably be expected to handle in any day, without taking too much time from their schoolwork, or probably even their TV time.   4

Expecting children to do some work for what they are given just makes sense to me. Aside from the reasons of helping the family, positive motivation, and teaching a realistic view of the world, I think that helping children learn to work, and see the benefit in it, instills values in a child. Too many kids are going bad today, trying to take the easy way out—cheating in school, scraping by at low-status jobs they hate, drifting off into a cloud of drugs. Maybe as simple a decision by a parent early in a child's life as teaching the youngster to earn what he gets, that the world owes him nothing, maybe this lesson will help send a son or daughter off onto the road to succcess.   5

Matt Smith

Postreading Analysis

> Reiterate your thesis several times during an argument.

Matt's argument works well on several levels. First he is careful to clarify his issue not only in the thesis (in which he also includes a bit of audience definition) but several times within the essay. And he also repeats variations on his thesis at strategic points—a standard strategy in argument—including a summing-up sentence to end body paragraph two.

He connects with his audience by using accommodation pronouns (*we, us, our*), specific examples with which the reader can identify, qualifiers (*some, many, maybe, most*), and a **disclaimer** ("I'm not talking about slave labor here, just a regular routine of chores. . . ."). His body paragraphs are each clearly introduced with a well-focused topic sentence, and he uses solid connectors, particularly between paragraphs. Like the other model essays in this chapter, "Something for Nothing?" is arranged by importance, with the strongest reason saved for last, where it may have the most impact on the reader.

> **Teaching Idea**
> If you discuss rhetorical questions in argument, you might link Matt Smith's use of them in body paragraph three with Marisa Youmbi's use of them in body paragraphs two and three of her essay.

In his third body paragraph Matt acknowledges the objection that some members of his audience might have ("kids should . . . just be kids") to earned allowances. After giving examples and explaining his reasoning, the author uses a rhetorical question, "Why shouldn't children learn this lesson early in life?" Do you think this question is an effective strategy at this point? Do you tend to agree with the author (meaning the strategy worked as planned), or does an objection to his point come to your mind? Remember that rhetorical questions are useful argument tactics, but you must carefully calculate the response they will evoke in your audience.

> **Teaching Idea**
> After students have analyzed a model essay, ask who was or wasn't persuaded by the author and why. Then remind students that even well-written arguments don't always succeed.

Questions to Help You Analyze and Write Effective Persuasive Essays

1. What is the thesis sentence of this essay, and where is it located? Does the author sufficiently *clarify the issue* in the thesis? If not, where else within the essay does the author refine the issue (look for clarifying points in several paragraphs)?

2. Where has the author reiterated the thesis in the essay? How does this mention of the author's main point help the argument?

3. Is the hook effective, and which of the Chapter 12 hooks has the author used? (For more on hooks, see pp. 273–274.)

4. What method(s) from Chapter 12 has the author used to develop the introductory paragraph? (For more on developing introductions, see pp. 269–272.) Is the introduction effective for the audience as stated in the Prereading Exploration—why/why not?

5. Is the lead sentence in the concluding paragraph effective—why/why not? (For more on lead and summary sentences, see p. 283.)

6. What method(s) from Chapter 12 has the author used to develop the concluding paragraph? What is the expanded thought? (For more on developing conclusions, see pp. 283–286.) Is the conclusion effective for the audience as stated in the Prereading Exploration—why/why not? (Consider the conclusion's connection with the introduction.)

7. Write out each of the topic sentences. Next, underline the <u>topic</u> to be discussed once and the <u>statement</u> made about it twice. Circle any connecting words. (For more on connecting sentences, see pp. 52–57.)

8. Where has the author acknowledged an opposing reason or objection to his or her own reasons? Has the author refuted or diminished the strength of the opposing reason or objection—in what way?

9. Name at least three places in the essay where the author tries to connect with his or her audience (consider pronouns of accommodation—*we, us, our*—mentioning shared experiences or values, and emotional appeals).

10. Choose any paragraph in the essay, and explain why you think it is well written. (Consider elements like patterns of development, persuasive use of appeals, topic sentences, connecting words, sensory details, specific words, action description, dialogue, metaphors and other comparisons, sentence variety, and clear explaining.)

11. List at least five uses of specific language. (For more on specific language, see pp. 78–79, 451–452.)

12. Has the author succeeded in his or her purpose in writing the essay? What was the most persuasive reason to you and why?

■ EXPLAINING THE WRITING ASSIGNMENT

▶ SUMMARIZING THE ASSIGNMENT

Teaching Idea
You may find that students write stronger arguments at this level by avoiding research, instead choosing topics that they can develop from their own experience.

In this assignment we will tackle an issue (a debatable topic), taking a clear position and defending it in an essay of approximately 500 to 600 words. Issues abound in all of our lives, and we all have opinions on how parts of our world should run, especially when it seems that the machinery of life is running poorly. You may choose an issue that you might be unfamiliar with, such as drug testing in the workplace or selective admission policies in universities, and then read to find out about it. But you may be better off focusing on an issue from your own life, one that you can argue based on personal experience or general knowledge, for example, balancing education with work or helping a friend control a bad habit.

Practically speaking, you should plan on a paper of five to six total paragraphs, of which three to four will be in the body. Because introductory and concluding paragraphs are such crucial elements in essays, you will want to pay particular attention to them, and, of course, introduce each body paragraph with a strong topic sentence.

ESTABLISHING AUDIENCE AND PURPOSE

Argument is, arguably, the mode of writing that requires the most sensitivity to audience. Because we are asking something from our readers besides understanding—to think or act differently than they are now doing—we should expect our jobs as writers to be tougher. After all, how do you react when people call to solicit your time or money? How anxious are you to pull out your wallet or prolong a conversation with telemarketers?

When considering an audience in persuasive writing, we need to ask questions like "How resistant are they to my position? What can I reasonably expect to accomplish in my argument? How far can I move them to action or agreement?" Or maybe you will decide the best you can do is talk them out of throwing a rock at you the next time you pass by. Successful argument depends on discovering the reasons your reader finds convincing, countering opposing reasons, overcoming objections to your own reasons, and appealing to the audience's mind and heart, partly by showing yourself to be a credible person, a writer whose work is worth reading.

WORKING THROUGH THE WRITING ASSIGNMENT

Discovering Ideas

As you explore issues for this assignment, look to your own life for inspiration. We all lead rich lives full of potential topics for argument, particularly when we react to situations we are not happy about. At home perhaps we would like more help with the housework; how can we make this happen? Who can we persuade to help? At school you need an extension on a class project. How do you persuade your instructor to grant it? At work you know that you deserve a raise. How will you talk your boss into it?

Aside from these practical issues, you may want to explore a topic that you are interested in as a way of learning more about it, perhaps something about which you already have strong *feelings* but not perhaps a logical *position*. For example, you may oppose spanking children as a method of discipline but have no clear position against it based on reasons. In conversation with others who see nothing wrong with it, you may have found yourself reduced to responding, "I don't know. It just rubs me the wrong way. There must be a better way." This essay will give you a chance to find out "a better way."

Keep in mind that a topic is not necessarily an issue but that most topics can become issues with a little thought. For example, here is a topic:

Topic: *"When husbands and wives divide chores in a marriage, men often do the yard work."*

This statement is merely a topic because it is not arguable. It is a truth with which no reasonable person can disagree. However, we can frame it as an issue like this:

Issue: *"Men ought to do most or all of the yard work in a marriage."*

Now we have a potential argument because more than a few people might disagree with the statement, offering reasons to prove their point. The following Issue Lists may help you choose an issue. Although the issues are framed as assertions, many will need to be further *focused* with your interests and audience in mind.

Teaching Idea
You might mention that arguments asking for a small—but real—concession or change of behavior/attitude are often more effective than those that try for sweeping changes.

Teaching Idea
Beginning a discussion of issues by first treating them as topics will help clarify for students what is arguable and what is not.

Teaching Idea
These issues are written as assertions to help students move more quickly into an argument, and most of them can be developed through a student's personal experience.

Issue Lists

Issues from Family Life

1. Parents ought to control their children's access to television.

2. Parents should not spank children because there are more effective methods for managing children.

3. "Allowances" for children and teens should be directly tied to how much work they save their parents.

4. Parents who can afford to give their children allowances should do so without considering how much work the child performs.

5. Teens of high school age should be allowed to set their own curfews until they abuse the privilege.

6. By the age of sixteen, a young person should be allowed to choose which family functions she attends.

7. Once children become teenagers, parents should expect to have serious conflicts with them and see their teens drift apart from the family.

8. Dividing household chores along gender lines is a bad idea.

9. Parents should begin informing their children about sex issues before they reach middle school.

10. Parents should remove handguns from their house.

11. People should limit their families to three children or less.

12. Parents should have more than one child.

13. Parents should not pretend to their children that fantasy beings like Santa Clause and the Easter Bunny are real.

14. Families should visit their older members more often who are in assisted-living situations or who can no longer drive themselves.

Issues from Personal Life

1. Your parents should pay for any one of the following: all your college tuition, a car, your auto insurance, or a vacation.

2. Your parents should reconsider their negative attitude toward one of your friends.

3. One of your friends should reconsider his negative attitude toward another friend.

4. One of your friends should change one behavior toward you or others: anger, caustic humor, selfishness, indifference.

5. A friend should see a movie you favor.

6. A friend should stop or reduce some self-destructive behavior: drinking, smoking, overeating, bingeing and purging, gambling, couch potatoitis.

7. More people should eat organic foods.

8. In the winter the best vacation is the beach.

9. In the summer the best vacation is in the mountains.

10. A police officer who has just pulled you over for speeding should not give you a ticket.

11. A salesperson should reduce the price of any purchase you are interested in: stereo, computer, sports equipment, house, etc.

12. A best friend (wife, fiancée, boy/girlfriend, son, daughter) and you should communicate more openly about issues that annoy you both.

13. It is a grandparent's responsibility to intervene in his or her grandchildren's upbringing if the grandparent thinks that the parents are seriously mishandling the children.

Issues from School

1. Students who are not interested in high school should be allowed to drop out, rather than required by law to remain in until they are sixteen.

2. High school students, like college students, should be allowed to choose more of their own curriculum.

3. College students who have demonstrated a sincere commitment to their education based on a minimum of thirty hours at a 3.0 should be able to base their GPA on that record, effectively eliminating past poor performance from their record.

4. Teachers should be more lenient on any of the following: tardiness, absences, late homework (persuade one of your teachers).

5. Teachers should always drop at least one of their students' lowest grades (persuade one of your teachers to do this).

6. Colleges should provide more support services for nonnative speakers.

7. Kindergarten through high school should run a full year instead of nine months.

8. Any school with gang-related violence should institute a dress code.

9. Campus security should be required to issue one-dollar fines to any smoker who throws a cigarette on the ground.

10. No student should graduate from high school without first passing an exit exam.

11. Colleges and high schools should hold coaches accountable for the academic performance of their athletes.

12. Colleges should pay their athletes to play.

13. Your college needs to provide more parking.

14. Colleges should allow an American Sign Language course to fulfill a language requirement.

15. Your college ought to provide free day care to students with young children.

Issues from the Workplace

1. Women often overreact to sexual harassment on the job.

2. Women do not react strongly enough to sexual harassment on the job.

3. Your boss should give you more time off.

4. Your company should change some existing policy (offer an alternative).

5. Your boss should give you a raise.

6. Employee X should be fired (or hired).

7. Your company should provide on-site day care.

8. Your company should provide health insurance.

9. Your company should allow four-day workweeks.

Issues from the Community

1. When drivers reach the age of seventy, they should be required by law to pass an annual physical and driving exam to prove that they can competently handle their vehicles.

2. We should eliminate the drinking age in this country.

3. People who do not want to serve on juries should not have to.

4. Giving ethnic names to children is an important and beneficial practice in American communities.

5. Sports teams that use ethnic names should change them.

6. Parental consent should be needed for minors to obtain birth control.

7. Parents should be informed of any child carrying HIV in their children's school.

8. People should only use cell phones in their cars for emergencies or other urgent business.

9. Halloween is too dangerous a holiday and should be dropped as a national pastime.

10. Your local swimming pool should remain open till fall for parents with pre-schoolers.

11. People convicted of drunk driving the first time should serve a minimum jail term.

12. Animals like pit bulls that are known to attack children should be banned from urban areas.

13. Penalties should be greater for fathers who are delinquent on child support payments.

14. People should support at least one environmental group.

15. Assisted-living establishments should allow their residents to have pets.

Prewriting Suggestions

After you have chosen several topics, it is time to generate reasons. First, double-check to be sure you have real issues. Can you make a statement about them with which people might reasonably disagree? For instance, if we chose the topic "single children" and said, "An only child has a different experience growing up than children with brothers and sisters," we would have a topic—a factual statement. But if we say, "An only child is *less prepared* for life than children coming from families with more than one child," we have an issue.

Next, create a list of reasons favoring and opposing a position on the issue. If we chose the topic of elderly drivers, we could assert that "Drivers over seventy should be required by law to pass a physical exam and driving test annually to keep their driver's license." Now we would brainstorm to create a list of reasons favoring and opposing the assertion:

> Creating a for/against list of reasons is an essential prewriting strategy.

Reasons Favoring Assertion	Reasons Opposing Assertion
1. *Injury of older drivers*	1. *Discrimination toward elderly*
2. *Injury of other people*	2. *Unfair treatment of elderly*
3. *Inconvenience of other motorists*	3. *Unnecessary law*
4. *Failing mental abilities*	4. *Transportation problems*
5. *Failing physical abilities*	5. *Infringes on civil liberty*

We can focus our general list of reasons in two ways: (1) *define an audience* and (2) *find supporting evidence*. Erica Hood, the author of the chapter Annotated Student Model, focused her prewriting by choosing an audience of primarily urban drivers with older family members who could be at risk behind the wheel. With these readers in mind, Erica included the counterreasons "discrimination" and "transportation problems." By establishing that older drivers *are* more at risk because of failing physical and mental health, she was able to refute the discrimination counterreason; and to meet the transportation counter, she offered a list of possible alternatives for helping seniors get around who have lost their licenses.

As you gather ideas for your argument, select the strongest reasons in light of your evidence and audience, and be sure to refute any serious opposition.

Prewriting—Summing Up

1. Choose several topics from the lists, or choose several of your own.

2. Focus the topic as an issue.

3. Create a list of favoring and opposing reasons.

4. Select favoring and opposing reasons based on your evidence and audience.

5. Develop several reasons with evidence.

> **JOURNAL ENTRY 16-2**
>
> Who would oppose your position on this issue? What is one reason they would give? How will you deal with that reason? Can you refute it with one of your own reasons or show how the reason is faulty in some way? Perhaps the logic is flawed (see fallacies, pp. 370–371) or perhaps poorly supported by evidence (see p. 364).

Organizing Ideas

Before moving ahead, be sure to write out your thesis, stating your issue and position. You may choose to imply the thesis or frame it as a question within your draft (see "Just Say No," pp. 375–376), but for now state your mind directly. Most of us will place the thesis as the last sentence in the first paragraph. Remember to **qualify** and focus the thesis, and you may use words like *should, ought to, must,* and *need to* to clarify your position. Here are two strong thesis sentences drawn from the chapter student models:

1. Parents who believe in allowances for their children **should** consider making their children work for the money.

2. Not testing the competency of older drivers annually could be a dangerous oversight.

There are two points to avoid in the introduction in general and in the thesis in particular: (1) inappropriate use of *you* and (2) alienating the audience. Because we are often asking an audience to change some attitude or behavior, we can easily sound critical of them. To avoid this impression (even if, in fact, it is true), do not use *you* but do include yourself in the audience if possible. Contrast the following thesis sentence with number 1 above.

- Unless *you* want to keep raising lazy kids who don't much care about *you* or their family, *you* ought to wise up and make the kids do their fair share around the house to earn their allowance, rather than *you* continuing to spoil them.

As you can see, one of these thesis sentences is more likely than the other to work with the target audience of parents.

Order of importance is probably the best arrangement for your body paragraphs, presenting your reasons from least to most strong. Building each body paragraph around a single reason is a clear way to organize your points. You may then deal with counterreasons or objections to your reasons within the paragraph, or you may create one separate paragraph to refute counterreasons (see the Annotated Student Model for a separate paragraph counter).

Remember to begin each body paragraph with a topic sentence linked to the preceding paragraph by connectors like the transitions listed below (for more on connectors and a complete list of transitions, see pp. 52–57).

Organize essay by order of importance

- **Locating or moving in space:** above, against, around, behind, below, on, in

- **Moving in time:** after, at last, awhile, first, immediately, next, now, often, then

- **Adding material:** again, also, and, in addition, furthermore, as well as

- **Giving examples:** for example, for instance, another, one reason, in fact

- **Comparing:** alike, also, both, in the same way, similarly

- **Contrasting:** in contrast, although, but, differs from, even though, however

- **Cause/effect:** and so, as a result, because, consequently, since, so, then

- **Summarizing/concluding:** finally, in brief, in other words, in short, to summarize

Organizing—Summing Up:

1. Create a rough thesis sentence to help focus your material.

2. Focus and qualify your thesis, and check to be sure you are not offending your reader.

3. Arrange body paragraphs by order of importance.

4. Plan on using a topic sentence to introduce each body paragraph.

5. Review the list of transitions and other connectors above (for more, see pp. 52–57.)

JOURNAL ENTRY 16-3

Write out your thesis sentence. Does it clarify your issue and position? Now, create a rough outline that includes your major reasons and any necessary counterreasons (to review outlines, see p. 282). List any evidence you will use to support each reason.

Drafting

With the preliminary work out of the way, you are almost ready to write a first rough draft. But before moving ahead, take a moment to review the Drafting suggestions in Chapter 1, pp. 12–14, and to think about the following points:

1. A disclaimer ("I don't mean that, I mean this"—similar to negation in definition) is often used in argument (see "Something for Nothing?" paragraph 4 and "Should Our Grandparents Be Driving?" paragraph 4).

2. Reiterate your thesis in each body paragraph.

3. Clarify the issue in the first and second paragraphs, but refine your position throughout the essay, including *defining terms*.

Tips for more efficient drafting.

Teaching Idea
Students often forget in *writing* an argument to use the appeal of self-interest, even when they usually remember it outside a classroom.

4. Use pronouns of accommodation where appropriate (*we, us, our*).

5. Select evidence and use appeals—your **persona** and the audience's **emotional response**—based on your audience.

6. Remember that most people are interested in and moved by knowing how the issue affects them. Think, "What's in it for my audience?" and then tell them.

> **JOURNAL ENTRY 16-4**
>
> Respond to this journal entry soon after writing your first rough draft. Skim the draft and ask yourself the following: Is this an argument that includes reasons and evidence and that counters opposing reasons/objections? Are topic sentences in place? What part of the draft do you like best, what part least—why? Answer in a paragraph.

Teaching Idea
By this point in the semester, students are probably in the habit of turning back to the revision chapters when they begin their drafts, but you might still need to remind them to do so.

Revising Drafts

To review the detailed lists for revising drafts, turn to Chapter 13.

■ ANNOTATED STUDENT MODEL

Teaching Idea
If you use the Annotated Student Model to replace one of the other chapter models, you can easily devise a list of questions to help students analyze the drafts as homework.

Help yourself to avoid obstacles in your drafts by carefully reading through the Annotated Student Model. Doing this will save you at least a few headaches and probably help clarify questions you didn't even know you had.

First-Stage Draft

Erica Hood remembered several examples of her own grandparents in danger while driving, and so she decided to define her audience as other people like her, who have elderly relatives at risk on the road. She thought it would help her readers identify with her if she could show them that she, too, had relatives who would be affected by her proposal. After creating a list of reasons favoring and opposing an annual exam for the elderly, she wrote this scratch outline to organize her main reasons (for more on outlining, see p. 282):

Working Thesis

For everyone's safety, including their own, older drivers should be willing to take a test each year to see if they are still capable of driving safely.

Teaching Idea
You might want students to see the prewriting for/against list that Erica Hood wrote for this first rough draft—located in Prewriting Suggestions.

Working Outline
1. *Reason 1: failing health*
2. *Reason 2: failing reflexes*
3. *Reason 3: other illnesses*
4. *Proposal with refutation of counterreason*

An Argument against Older Drivers

First draft contains reasons but lacks several counters and specific examples as evidence.

Older drivers can have a hard time of it on the road. Their reflexes slow down, 1 *their eyesight deteriorates, and their hearing goes. Although some can handle their cars competently, many are accidents waiting to happen. For everyone's safety, including their own, older drivers should be willing to take a test each year to see if they are still capable of driving safely.*

Working thesis

Topic sentence unfocused

My first point is that elderly drivers are often in poor health. They have trouble 2 moving, their joints ache, getting in and out of a car is a problem, and they neither see nor hear well. Getting behind the wheel is dangerous if these senses are impaired. When traffic is heavy, people need to see the cars all around them and hear if someone leans on the horn. Even drivers in good health with all their senses intact can drift out of their lane and only be brought back to reality by a loud horn honk.

Reflex time also slows down as people get older. This creates other difficulties 3 and problem for drivers. There are many situations where people have to react quickly while driving like when an ambulance wants by or when a car slows down drastically in front of a person. In order to help out their slow reaction time, many old folks slow down, but slower driving can be as dangerous as fast driving. During rush hour when cars are racing past, you can see the older driver, poking along at forty miles an hour. This can cause accidents.

Needs further qualifiers throughout

As people age, many catch illnesses that lead to dangerous driving. My older 4 grandfather on my mother's side has Alzheimer's, and the disease began lowering his competency long before he stopped driving. No one in our family knew that he had Alzheimer's, and he was driving on the very day that he was diagnosed. I am not trying to discriminate against the elderly. However, when a driver frequently endangers himself, putting himself at risk and others, steps must be taken to ensure everyone's safety.

Disclaimer

We all want to protect our grandparents and ourselves from harm. To do this 5 we need to support an annual driving exam and physical checkup for older drivers. Some might oppose such a law on the grounds that once an older driver loses their license, they become housebound. But in the city there are busses and taxis. In rural areas, people can carpool, and family members can take care of their grandparents by driving them. If people want to protect and care for their grandparents' needs, they can insist on more and better public transportation. Our lawmakers can accomplish this.

Begins to refute counterreason

Elderly drivers are creating problems for everyone in society because they have 6 such a hard time driving. Their failing health puts them in danger too. Although seniors will certainly be inconvenienced and so will their family members who have to cart them around, there really is no alternative. When a person is a proven menace, through no fault of his or her own, that person must give up certain privileges for the greater good.

Conclusion needs work to improve persona

Second-Stage Draft

First drafts of arguments are often underdeveloped, lacking reasons, counter-reasons, sufficient evidence, details, and explanations. When there is enough evidence, and it is clearly explained, there may also be difficulties with **emotional appeals** and the writer's **persona**. Erica knew that her first draft was solid but that she needed more material, a stronger connection with her audience, and a more effective introduction and conclusion. This second draft goes a long way toward correcting those concerns.

Teaching Idea
Student arguments so often suffer from underqualifying that it is worth stressing the additional qualifiers that Erica added to her second draft.

An Argument against Older Drivers

Introduction is revised with personal anecdote to connect with audience.

Last year my grandfather drove through the back of the garage and into the garden behind it. Of course, this can happen to anyone, but since his reflexes are so slow, half his car went through the garage wall before he was able to stop. Maybe my grandfather should no longer be driving, but once people in America take a driving test, they are usually turned loose until the day they die. Not testing the competency of older drivers annually—especially by age seventy—could be a dangerous oversight.

Accommodation pronouns added: *we, us, our*

Qualifiers added throughout

Thesis revised

Clarifies age group of drivers

We all know that eyesight and hearing almost always worsen as people age. For various reasons some older people don't like to admit it. Driving is dangerous if these senses are impaired. When a solid wall of cars stops during rush hour, a driver better be able to see it, and when a semi blows its horn announcing that it is changing lanes, a driver better be able to hear it. Sometimes eye wear or even surgery cannot correct vision enough for the elderly to drive safely. And sometimes hearing aids are turned off or their batteries are low. These are just two reasons why people over seventy should take driving tests every year.

Topic sentence revised

Further explaining

Reiterates thesis

Personal example added as specific evidence and link to reader

Reflex time also slows as people get older. This creates other difficulties and problems for drivers. My grandfather might not have caused as much damage to his car or garage if he had reacted faster. There are many situations where people have to react quickly while driving. Sometimes an emergency vehicle needs by. And then there are times when a car abruptly slows in front of another. Also, a hazard like a piece of lumber or truck tread might appear on the highway, or a child might run out into the road. In order to compensate for their slow reaction time, many elderly reduce their overall speed, but slower driving can be as dangerous as fast driving. During rush hour when cars are racing past, that old car with someone's grandmother in it who is barely able to see over the steering wheel, poking along in the high-speed lane, can cause accidents.

Examples added as evidence

Specific details added to example

Reveals personal response to increase persona

As people age, many contract debilitating illnesses that can lead to dangerous driving. My older grandfather on my mother's side has Alzheimer's, and the disease began lowering his competency long before he stopped driving. No one in our family knew that he had Alzheimer's, and he was driving on the very day that he was diagnosed. It frightens me to think that he might not have been able to find his way back home while driving or, worse, become disoriented and had a high-speed accident. I am not trying to discriminate against older drivers. My own young adult age group is often, and sometimes justifiably, bashed for reckless driving. However, when a driver frequently endangers himself, putting himself at risk and others, even though it is not through his own fault, steps must be taken to ensure everyone's safety.

More explaining as evidence

Evidence added—persona

We all want to protect our grandparents and ourselves from harm. To do this ⁵ we need to support an annual driving exam and physical checkup for older drivers. Some might oppose such a law on the grounds that once an older driver loses his license, he becomes housebound, unable to take care of his needs. But in the city there are busses and taxis and in some cities the subway. In rural areas, people can carpool, and family members can take care of their elderly by driving them. If we as citizens and children of our grandparents seriously want to protect our grandparents and care for their needs, we can insist on more and better public transportation. Our lawmakers can accomplish this.

Adds facts as evidence

Neither of my grandfathers wants to endanger anyone, and they both have ⁶ to get from place to place just like everyone else. But their failing health made them unsafe drivers, so they finally stopped driving, luckily before anyone was seriously injured. As a result, my folks and I and the rest of our family are pitching in to shuttle our grandparents around. It is inconvenient. And family members are annoyed by the chore on occasion. But this "chore" has the benefit of bringing us more often in contact with each other. I see all of my grandparents more frequently now than before they stopped driving. The family profits because we are sharing a task that is right. Our older generation took care of their children and their children's children in their time. Now it is our time to take care of them.

Conclusion revised to increase persona and appeals to readers' emotions

Teaching Idea
This second-draft conclusion is such an improvement on the first attempt that it is worth noting to students, especially those who seem regularly to lose their inspiration at the end.

> **Special Points to Check in Revising from First to Second Drafts**
>
> 1. Introduction: hook, engaging support sentences, thesis (clear issue and position)
> 2. Body paragraphs: topic sentence with connector
> 3. Overall development: reasons: evidence (detailed examples, clear explanations, facts/statistics, anecdotes, scenarios, authorites)
> 4. Appeals of persona and emotion (connecting with audience—*we, us, our*)
> 5. Counterreasons and objections (logical fallacies)
> 6. Qualifying
> 7. Conclusion: connector, summary, expanded thought

Third-Stage Draft

With most of the organizational and material concerns out of the way, a writer can focus more on style. In this draft notice how Erica improved her word choices and sentence patterns.

Teaching Idea
If you are bringing students to this assignment at the end of the semester, you may be focusing a bit more on matters of style. This third draft can help students with common style problems that are within the ability of many developmental writers to improve.

Should Our Grandparents Be Driving?

Title revised to correct negative tone—our added

Last year my seventy-five-year-old grandfather drove through the back of the ¹ garage and into the garden behind it. Of course, an accident like this can happen to anyone, but since his reflexes are so slow, half his car went through the garage

More specific words added

More precise words substituted

wall before he was able to stop. Maybe my grandfather should no longer be driving, but once people in America take a driving test at sixteen, they are usually turned loose until the day they die. Not testing the competency of older drivers annually could be a dangerous oversight.

Sentences combined for variety

[We all know that eyesight and hearing almost always worsen as people age, even though some older people don't like to admit it.] ~~Driving~~ **Getting behind the wheel** is dangerous if these senses are impaired. [When a solid wall of cars stops on I-435 during the 5:30 rush hour, a driver better be able to see it. When a semi blows its air horn announcing that it is changing lanes, a driver better be able to hear it.] Sometimes eye wear or even surgery cannot correct vision enough for the elderly to drive safely. And sometimes hearing aids are turned off or their batteries are low. ~~These~~ Poor eyesight and hearing are just two reasons why people over seventy should take driving tests every year.

2

Phrase replaces overused word

Sentence divided for emphasis

More precise words substituted

Sentences combined for variety

[Reflex time also slows as people get older, creating ~~other difficulties and~~ another problem for drivers.] My grandfather might not have caused as much damage to his car or garage if he had reacted faster. [There are many situations where people have to react quickly while driving: when an emergency vehicle needs by, when a car abruptly slows in front of another, when a hazard like a piece of lumber or large chunk of truck tread appears on the highway, or when a child runs out into the road chasing a ball.] In order to compensate for their slow reaction time, many elderly reduce their overall speed, but slower driving can be as dangerous as fast driving. During rush hour when cars are racing past at seventy-five miles per hour, that old Chrysler with someone's grandmother in it who is barely able to see over the steering wheel, poking along at forty in the high-speed lane, can cause accidents.

3

Redundant phrase removed

More specific words added

Sentences combined for variety using colon with list

As people age, many contract debilitating illnesses that can lead to dangerous driving. My older grandfather on my mother's side has Alzheimer's, and the disease began lowering his competency long before he stopped driving. No one in our family knew that Grandpa Miller had Alzheimer's, and he was driving on the very day that he was diagnosed. It frightens me to think that he might not have been able to find his way back home ~~while driving~~ or, worse, become disoriented and had a high-speed accident. I am not trying to discriminate against ~~older drivers~~ the **elderly.** My own young adult age group is often, and sometimes justifiably, bashed for reckless driving. However, when a driver frequently endangers himself ~~putting himself at risk~~ and others, even though it is not through his own fault, steps must be taken to ensure everyone's safety.

4

Synonym replaces overused word

Unneeded phrases removed

[If we want to protect our grandparents and ourselves ~~from harm~~, we need to support an annual driving exam and physical checkup for ~~older drivers~~ the **elderly**.] Some might oppose such a law on the grounds that once an older driver loses her license, she becomes housebound, unable to take care of her needs. But in the city there are busses and taxis and in some cities the subway. In rural areas,

5

Sentences combined for variety

Gender pronoun alternated

Synonym replaces overused word

people can carpool, and family members can take care of their elderly by driving them. If we as citizens and children of our ~~grandparents~~ **older generation** seriously want to protect our grandparents and care for their needs, we can insist on more and better public transportation. Our lawmakers can accomplish this.

Neither of my grandfathers wants to endanger anyone, and they both have 6 to get from place to place just like everyone else. But their failing physical and mental health made them unsafe drivers, so they finally stopped driving, luckily before anyone was seriously injured. As a result, my folks and I and the rest of our family are pitching in to shuttle our grandparents around. It *is* inconvenient. And family members are annoyed by the chore on occasion. But this "chore" has the benefit of bringing us more often in contact with each other. I see all of my grandparents more frequently now than before they stopped driving. The family profits because we are sharing a task that is right. Our older generation took care of their children and their children's children in their time. Now it is our time to take care of them.

More specific words added

Italicizing *is* for emphasis

Erica Hood

Special Points to Check in Revising from Second to Third Drafts

1. Added specific words are boxed.

2. More precise or audience-appropriate word substitutions are shaded.

3. [Sentences combined for variety are bracketed.]

4. **Synonyms and phrases replacing clutter and repeat words are bolded.**

5. ~~Unneeded words are lined through.~~

CHAPTER SUMMARY

1. Persuasion is the act of moving someone to accept an idea or perform an action.

2. Argument is a more formal persuasion that tries to move a target audience, using reasons supported by evidence and refuting opposing reasons.

3. Persuasive speaking and writing are a regular part of our daily lives.

4. Argumentation requires a clearly defined issue and position.

5. Aside from appeals to the mind of evidence, an argument benefits from emotional appeals and persona.

6. Arguments should avoid errors in logic, including oversimplifying and under-qualifying

7. A writer can connect with her audience by showing that she is part of it, understands what readers need to know, and shares in their beliefs and concerns.

8. Insulting or trying to intimidate an audience is a poor persuasive strategy.

9. Argument essays are frequently arranged by order of importance.

10. Writing is never complete until it has gone through several revisions and careful editing.

◼ ALTERNATE WRITING ASSIGNMENTS

The following alternate writing assignments may help you discover topics. Remember to observe these points as you begin any of the options:

- Review the points in the Skills section.
- Define your issue and position clearly for a specific audience.
- Create a chart of reasons favoring and opposing your position.
- Review the Communication Triangle—all three appeals.
- Review methods for creating introductions and conclusions in Chapter 12.

1. Write an argument that refutes an editorial from a newspaper or magazine. You might choose a local issue like when to open or close a pool for summer swimming or select a larger issue like poor voter turnout in state elections. As you read through the article, locate and list the author's reasons and evidence for supporting her position. Also, note counterreasons and objections the author tries to deal with. Would any of the counterreasons work as reasons to support your position? If the author has failed to dispose of objections to her reasons, you might use the objections as part of your refutation. Consider challenging some of the author's evidence, the way she interprets it, or the conclusions she draws from it.

2. Write an advertisement for a product, service, or place, persuading a target audience to buy it. There are a zillion possibilities: a brand of running shoes, a sports car, an upcoming concert, a brand of frozen yogurt, a dating service, a lawn care service, a place to live, or a great vacation spot, to name a few. You might model your ad on one that you think is particularly effective, describing any film clip that might reinforce your message, or including a picture. Remember to deal with possible concerns and objections from the audience, such as *price,* quality, dependability, service, availability, and safety. You might include a competing product and show how yours is superior. Feel free to use emotional appeals, as most advertisers do, but remember that *logical fallacies* can hurt your appeal. Solid evidence is useful even in the world of sales.

3. Write an argument to a highly resistant audience who you will persuade to listen to and perhaps respect someone else's point of view. Playing the role of an arbitrator, you will try to bring one side of a controversial issue closer to the other. For example, you might try to help an activist pro-life group understand that being pro-choice does not necessarily imply favoring abortion. (See the Unit Six essay "Abortion, Right and Wrong," pp. 642–645, for help with this.)

Here are some other possibilities: NRA/pro-gun control groups, tobacco companies/antismoking groups, loggers or ranchers/environmentalists, pharmaceutical companies/animal rights activists, pro-nuclear energy supporters/supporters of renewable resources, gays and lesbians/gay and lesbian bashers. Try showing what the two groups actually have in common, dispelling misconceptions that each might have about the other and showing how both can profit from reducing the friction between them.

4. Write an argument asking for more tolerance toward a group with which you are associated that is discriminated against or misunderstood. You might choose a group based on racial or ethnic discrimination or on some other reason. For instance, high school social groups are divided in many ways, with a more mainstream group often deriding a smaller group. Perhaps you are overweight and feel discriminated against as a result. You may have spent time in prison or know someone who has.

Maybe you have a physical or mental disability, or spend time with a person who has. You may be hearing impaired, dyslexic, ADHD, clinically depressed, or blind. How will you persuade a target audience to become more tolerant? Try dispelling misconceptions and stereotypes, of showing the ordinary human side of the marginalized person. Let your reader see how the behavior of the mainstream population can help or hurt fellow human beings.

5. Write an argument that tries to convince a high school graduate who is already making a satisfactory income that education is still important, that he should consider going to college. You might try the appeal of profit—that is, try to persuade him that the income he is currently making might not satisfy him in a few years. Or you can show how his ability to change jobs in the future will be limited with just a high school education. Another approach would be to promote the learning experience of college, how much knowledge is available, how other life interests may be revealed, and how education can help a person to think more effectively. Be sure to deal with predictable counterreasons and objections like "I'll lose too much money if I go back now," "I was never any good at studying," and "I've been out too long. I've forgotten how to study."

CHAPTER 17

Taking Essay Exams

WHAT ARE WE TRYING TO ACHIEVE AND WHY?

Setting the Stage

Looking at the illustration above, you will probably notice a familiar scene—a class of students taking an exam, the clock ticking, sweat dripping. We have all at one time or another lived through this scenario, sometimes with only mild anxiety and other times in a state of near panic. Few people like to take tests, even those who are good at it, and for those of us who are not as successful as others and/or have high "test anxiety," the experience can be miserable. Perhaps the most dreaded exam is the in-class essay, a task that requires analysis, synthesis, and evaluation—all under the pressure of the ticking clock. Helping you with this common academic chore is the purpose of Chapter 17.

Two important aspects of essay examinations distinguish them from our other writing assignments this semester: **process limitations** and **audience.** To be successful on in-class essays, a student must be particularly well prepared because she must write quickly with little time for revision. Although most instructors consider time constraints when they evaluate an essay-exam response, they still expect a well-written essay. Second, for perhaps the first time this term, you will be consciously writing to your teacher as a *primary* audience. Knowing the material *and* knowing what your instructor expects you to know will help you succeed.

Linking to Previous Experience

We have all taken multiple-choice, matching, and fill-in-the-blank tests before. Essay exams require much the same preparation and come in several familiar forms, of which short-answer (a paragraph), long-answer (an essay), and take-home exams are perhaps the most common. To develop a paragraph or essay-length response, we use the same composition skills that we have practiced all semester: unearthing ideas, organizing, drafting, and revising/editing, as time permits. Sometimes a single pattern is called for, such as comparison or contrast; but often several patterns work together, as we have seen in the rest of *A Writer's Workshop* but particularly in writing extended definitions and arguments.

As in most writing, you will be dealing with a target audience, one who you want something from—in this case, a superior grade. So keep your instructor in mind, and be sure to explain, illustrate, and define for him or her just as you have been doing for each specific audience you have chosen this term.

Determining the Value

Being able to perform well on essay exams has obvious benefits in your school-work; everyone likes to make good grades. But there are many other writing situations in life out of school that require people to quickly organize and draft a response: lawyers writing reports to their clients, nurses writing ward reports, police officers writing accident reports, firefighters reporting the cause of a fire, veterinary technicians describing surgeries, businesspeople drafting interoffice memos, and more. Being able to produce readable writing quickly is a "real-world" asset.

The process of *preparing* for an essay exam is also valuable. How often have you thought that you understood a concept until you had to explain it to an audience? Preparing for an essay exam—memorizing, questioning, making connections, and drawing conclusions—is one good way to explore a topic so that you truly understand it. And learning to remain calm under stress, or to calm yourself in spite of the high anxiety that essay exams can produce, is an ability that you will use repeatedly in school and out.

JOURNAL ENTRY 17-1

Think for a moment about your essay-exam experiences. How well, in general, have you done on them in the past? Do you have a strategy for preparing? Which of the following (if any) do you usually do to prepare?

- Carefully study the material on a weekly basis

- Ask questions in class

- Annotate your text

- Link related ideas

- Take thorough notes

- Participate in class discussions

- Memorize key terms

- Create practice questions

- Wait until the last minute and cram?

What is one change you could make in your preparation habits?

▶ DEVELOPING SKILLS, EXPLORING IDEAS IN WRITING FOR ESSAY EXAMS

Although we all are experienced in answering test questions, there are ways to improve. Aside from attending class daily, doing the homework, reviewing regularly, and reviewing intensively several days before an exam, you can practice the following strategies to help as the clock begins ticking:

1. Analyze the exam question.

2. Write relevant, specific responses.

3. Write brief but effective introductions.

4. Write brief but effective conclusions.

Teaching Idea
Few people like to write under a time constraint, and students may question the value or fairness of in-class essay exams. You might emphasize the preparation process as one of learning and the testing process as one of efficiency.

Teaching Idea
Journal Entry 17-1 helps students see that doing well on essay exams requires a strategy.

Groundwork for Activity 17-1: Analyzing the Question

To take essay exams successfully, a student must first understand the **question** being asked. This might seem easy enough, until a vaguely written or complicated question comes along; then life becomes more difficult. For example, this first essay-exam question from an American history class seems straightforward enough:

- In brief, relate the economic conditions of the South in the years immediately preceding the Civil War.

But what exactly does *relate* mean, and what is the professor's purpose in asking the question? You might be expected to show a **causal link** between the economic conditions in the South and the start of the war. A brief essay response would require summarizing the economic conditions.

Sometimes verbs of command like *discuss, examine, explore,* and *relate* are open to interpretation. When in doubt, do not hesitate to ask your instructor for clarification.

The next essay question, on the same topic, is more precise but also requires analysis to determine the correct response:

- The causes that led to the War between the States are complicated. While many people have been taught that the primary issue was slavery, we have learned otherwise in this class. List the three most important factors leading to the Civil War, but focus on the one that seems clearly to be the most significant (as we have discussed it in class). Be sure to include the names of people prominent in each of the causes and tell something about their contribution toward the ultimate declaration of war.

This question gives more specific directions if we know how to interpret them. First we note the words "causes" and "factors" combined with the key phrase "list the three" we see that causes are important and that we will structure the response in three body paragraphs. "Focus on one" suggests a least-to-most method of arrangement with the most space given to the last, most important, reason (which the question tells us is *not* slavery). Within each paragraph we would explain the primary cause, giving at least one specific example, identify at least one important person, and then summarize ("tell") what the person did or said that helped bring about war.

When you analyze an essay question, circle key words and phrases that tell you **what** to write about, **how** to write about it, and **how many** parts should be included. Often the question will also indicate how to organize your response. Below you will find a list of common phrases used in essay questions and how they connect with the patterns of development we have worked with this semester.

Teaching Idea
Remind students that professors sometimes write ambiguous exam questions, and it is the student's responsibility to clarify the question's meaning.

Teaching Idea
You might clarify that these are not the only phrases for indicating exam question development.

General Category	Phrases to Look for in Essay Questions
1. Description	Create a verbal picture of the event so that . . .
2. Narration	Trace the beginning of the event. . . . Tell how . . .
3. Illustration	Give several examples of the incident. . . . Describe. . .
	Discuss the XYZ. . . . Explore the XYZ. . . . Explain. . . .
4. Division/classification	Divide XYZ. . . . Group or categorize XYZ. . . .
5. Cause/effect	What caused (reasons/factors) XYZ? What were the results of XYZ? . . .
6. Process analysis	Explain (list the steps) how the XYZ works . . . .
7. Comparison/contrast	Explain the similarities and differences between . . .
8. Definition	Explain the meaning of XYZ. . . . Identify. . .

9. Persuasion	Argue in favor of. . . . Take a stand on. . . . Show how X is better than Y. . . . Defend the position of XYZ. . . .
10. Analysis	Look closely at each part of the XYZ. . . . Break down the role of XYZ and examine each of its parts. . . .
11. Synthesis	Using elements from XYZ, show how. . . . Drawing on sources from XYZ, explain how. . .
12. Evaluation	Judge the merit of the XYZ argument. . . .
13. Summary	In brief, tell how XYZ. . . . Sketch out the beginning . . . . Give the main points and briefly discuss them. . . .

Collaborative

Activity 17-1: Analyzing the Question

Analyze the following essay questions: circle the key words, list the general category of question, and then explain how students are expected to respond. Include how many parts the answer should have and how to organize it—if the question gives you these hints.

Example:

Compare and contrast the major advantages and the major disadvantages of the North and the South as they began the Civil War. Consider such factors as population size, economy, geography, political structure, and the military.

General category: _comparison/contrast_

To complete the essay response: _Students are expected to explain similarities and differences between the North and the South that might have helped them win as they began the Civil War. Students should focus on the five points listed. The essay might be structured by either the block or point-by-point method._

Answers will vary.

1. Explain who Pocahontas was and what her contributions were to the history of the United States. Be sure to mention all figures prominent in the Pocahontas myth and explain how the reality might have come to resemble the romantic myth. (history)

   General category: _illustration_

   To complete the essay response: _Students are to explain and give specific examples to show that they understand who Pocahontas was, how she is important in U.S. history, and how the myth developed. The essay might have two body paragraphs, the first dealing with Pocahontas and several key figures (John Smith, Powhatan, etc.) and the second discussing the transformation of reality into myth._

2. Discuss the nature versus nurture debate in psychology. First define the terms, and then explore the history and most recent thinking on the subject. (psychology)

   General category: _illustration_

   To complete the essay response: _Use specific examples to explain the nature versus nurture debate, when it began and how it continues today. Students might define the key terms in their introductions and then create two body paragraphs, one discussing the conflicting opinions historically and the other dealing with current thought. Students should name prominent supporters of both sides._

3. Explain the process of balancing a ledger. (business)

General category: _process analysis_

To complete the essay response: _Students should list the steps necessary to balance a ledger. If they can divide the steps into several body paragraphs, they should and then arrange chronologically._

4. Explain how males and females become socialized to perform within certain fairly clearly defined gender roles. (sociology)

General category: _illustration_

To complete the essay response: _Students should use examples and clear explanation to illustrate how males and females are influenced by the world around them—family, school, friends, media—to behave in ways considered by a given society to be typically male or female. Paragraphing is not suggested, but either chronological or order of importance could work well for overall organization._

5. Explain the principal components of the eukaryotic cell and how they function. Consider dividing your explanation into these three parts: the outer membrane, the components in the cytoplasm, and the nucleus. (biology)

General category: _process analysis_

To complete the essay response: _Students should define the cell parts and then explain how they work. Overall organization calls for spatial arrangement, the first body paragraph being the outer membrane, the next, the cytoplasm, and the last, the nucleus. Each body paragraph would be arranged chronologically, explaining the living process—taking in food, producing energy, eliminating waste, and so on._

6. Discuss the similarities and differences that exist among the human brain, a library, and a computer as they function in terms of storage of data, recovering/processing the information, and presenting the material so people might work with it. (computer science)

General category: _comparison/contrast_

To complete the essay response: _Students should explain and use examples to show that they understand how a computer functions, specifically how it stores, retrieves, and presents information. Students might organize by the block or point-by-point method, being sure to include the human brain and library subjects to highlight how a computer works._

Groundwork for Activity 17-2: Writing Relevant, Specific Responses

When writing an exam response, you are not likely to fool your instructor into thinking that you know the material if you don't. So try to answer the question as clearly and succinctly as possible. Meandering responses that ignore length requirements and those full of empty "padding" are poor strategies for doing well.

Teaching Idea
Activity 17-2 is a good review of topic sentences, unity, and specific supporting examples. While some students do consciously pad essay responses, hoping that length will substitute for substance, others have not yet learned to use what they do know to answer a question. You might stress using a forecasting statement to help students stay on track.

As with any writing, your paragraph will need a clearly stated *point*. An effective response to a short-answer exam question includes a *topic sentence* that in most cases *rephrases* the exam question and *forecasts* an answer to it.

Of the following two paragraph responses to an exam question, which is likely to score well, and which sounds like the student is going under?

> **Exam Question:** Explain in a paragraph why Abraham Lincoln is particularly well suited to be an American hero. Give specific examples to illustrate your answer. (American history)

A. Irrelevant first sentence and unfocused topic sentence

Several reasons listed but not explicitly linked to essay question

Response full of empty phrases and several factual inaccuracies

Why not just say "slaves"?

The quote is inaccurate and has nothing to do with the question.

A. This is a good question that more people should ask instead of just taking it for granted that Abraham Lincoln is some kind of saint or something. There really are very good reasons why most people think of Lincoln as an important figure in history, mostly because of the many things he did while he was president of our country. He accomplished many great deeds. For example, he helped to free African Americans, <u>who were brought to this country against their will and who up until this point in time were bound to work for the white majority for no pay and with no civil rights</u>. Also, Lincoln was president during the Civil War, which started around 1860 and continued until approximately 1865. And he is famous for writing things like the Gettysburg Address, which begins, "Four score and seven years ago our ancestors made a new nation on this continent for all people to be free and equal." Many people think that the Gettysburg Address is one of the most well-written pieces of writing in this country's history and that the person who wrote it had to be a genius. There is no doubt about it. Abraham Lincoln is a great man and our country is lucky to have had him for a president once upon a time.

B. Clear topic sentence with forecasting statement

B. Lincoln has become a hero in our democracy for several reasons: his humble origins, rise to leadership, leadership during crisis, and tragic death. Americans value the "common man," and Lincoln embodies this principle. Born in rural Kentucky and raised on a farm, he was able to educate himself, overcoming poverty and lack of social advantage to rise to the presidency. He is the poor boy who so many people like to say can "grow up to be president someday." Because the Civil War began during his presidency, Lincoln was called on to lead the nation through its most perilous war since the Revolution, not only to win a war of secession, but also to reconcile the North and the South afterward. As commander-in-chief of the North, Lincoln welcomed the South back into the fold, showing the magnanimous nature that many Americans prize. Finally, his tragic assassination by John Wilkes Booth on April 14, 1865, made many people view him as a martyr, one who had given his life to save his country. For these and other reasons Lincoln has become one of America's most revered heroes.

While many of us have written exam responses like A, we usually knew that we would not score well. Instead of staying closely to the question of why Lincoln is considered to be an American hero, version A talks about several of Lincoln's accomplishments in office but then fails to connect them with the point of the question. Also, the author tries to "fill up the space" with empty expressions, repetition, and pointless filler information. To further damage his credibility, the author misquotes part of the Gettysburg Address and reports the beginning date of the Civil War inaccurately. When answering exam questions, if you are not sure about a fact, it is best not to include it.

Collaborative

Teaching Idea
As students work through the poor response model in Activity 17-2, you might join their groups for a few minutes and/or have the groups discuss the problems with the response before they begin their paragraph rewrite. Check to see that students are creating a brief outline and including a forecasting statement in their topic sentence.

Activity 17-2: Writing Relevant, Specific Responses

Analyze the exam question below, circling key terms. Next, read the one-paragraph response that follows the essay question, and then discuss with group members how to improve it. Look in particular for unnecessary repetition and "filler" material, missing specific examples and details, and elements that lack connection to the topic sentence. Next, on a separate sheet of paper, and drawing from the information provided below, draft your own *one-paragraph* response to the question. Remember to *include part of the exam question* in your topic sentence, and forecast the four points you have chosen.

Exam Question: Name and explain four reasons why the Civil War, next to the Revolutionary War, has been the most significant war in the history of the United States. Give specific examples to illustrate your answer.

Information from Which to Write a One-Paragraph Response

1. Casualties: Civil War: 620,000 dead; 400,000 wounded
   • Twice as many deaths as in WWII
   • Proportionate to the population: eight times as many dead as WWII, eighteen times as many as WWI, seventy times as many as the Vietnam War

2. Preserved the union of the country

3. Resulted in the Thirteenth Amendment: abolition of slavery in 1865

4. Exhausted one-half of the country's resources (the South's) while stimulating the economy of the other (the North)

5. Contributed to the passing of new legislation that would affect westward expansion and education in particular:
   • The Homestead Act of 1862: 160 acres after five years of residence
   • Extensive land grants to railroads headed to the Pacific Coast
   • The Morrill Act: provided financing for land-grant colleges (many state universities throughout the country; e.g., Iowa State, Michigan State, Ohio State, Cornell)

Poor Response: Well, we have had lots of wars since the Revolutionary War, which was fought by our forefathers and mothers for our independence from England. But the Civil War was definitely important because many good people died from both the northern part of our country and from the southern part of our country. Besides the fact that thousands of people died, many also were wounded, and lots of the wounded died from their injuries at some later point in time. Hospitals back then weren't as good as they are today, and many soldiers died from infections and just plain bleeding to death. Even though lots of good doctors (good for what they knew back then, I mean) tried hard on both sides to save the soldiers, because of poor facilities, infection, and lack of medical supplies, the doctors often failed, and so the soldiers died. Another result of the Civil War, also called the War between the States, the War of Secession, and the War of the Rebellion, depending on what part of the country you are from, was that the African Americans who were living in this country against their will as slaves were freed by a proclamation from Abraham Lincoln, who was president at that time.

names and dates, instead relying on explanations and examples to answer its question. The Annotated Student Model—untitled, as some essay responses will be if the writer runs out of time and inspiration—defines several concepts fundamental to photography and uses process narration to explain how the concepts work. Here are the other patterns of development you will find in the models: description, narration, illustration, cause/effect, process analysis, definition, and comparison/contrast.

▶ Prereading Exploration for "Clinging by Their Fingers"

Adam Fletcher wrote this essay in response to a question from an exam in his U.S. History to 1877 class. He had the luxury of choosing among several questions and the time to revise because this was a take-home exam.

Before you read the essay, take a moment to circle all the key terms in the exam question below, and then write out what you think Adam's history professor expected in a response.

Question: The colonizing of the United States was neither rapid nor easy. In fact, there were a number of disasters that led some to abandon the effort altogether. Summarize the efforts at establishing English colonies in the New World, beginning with the attempts of Sir Humphrey Gilbert and Sir Walter Raleigh in 1578.

To complete the response: Explain in brief about as many attempts to

establish colonies in the New World as the time permits. Tell whether the

colonies succeeded or failed and why. Don't get carried away by the later

history of the colonies; remain focused on the earliest years.

Clinging by Their Fingers

Huddled together in tiny dark windowless shacks, the first English settlers in the New World struggled to survive the winter. Having little experience at rough living conditions, planning poorly, and often being led by those unqualified for the job, the colonists in most of the early settlements suffered terribly, many dying their first year from starvation, illness, injury, and conflicts with Native Americans. Beginning with the "lost colony" of Gilbert and Raleigh, and progressing through the Massachusetts Bay Company, early English attempts at colonizing the New World met with disaster.   1

Sir Humphrey Gilbert and his half-brother, Sir Walter Raleigh, were the first adventurers to try colonizing America. Obtaining permission from Queen Elizabeth in 1578 to "inhabit and possess" any land in the New World not claimed by a "Christian ruler," they both tried and failed several times. Gilbert, after two attempts, was drowned in passage, and Raleigh had to abandon two more colonies in 1585. Raleigh's final attempt was in 1587 with the infamous "lost colony," settled by more than a hundred people on Roanoke Island, near the coast of North Carolina. It vanished without a trace within three years.   2

After Gilbert and Raleigh colonization efforts stopped until 1607 when James I allowed two companies, the London and Plymouth, to try again, but neither, at first, met with success. The London Company financed the first attempt (to be called Jamestown), which from the start ran into problems. On the four-month voyage across the Atlantic thirty-nine Englishmen died. Not knowing any better, the survivors located Jamestown near swampy ground that bred mosquitoes and malaria. Instead of preparing for winter by planting and storing enough food, the mainly gentlemen settlers searched for gold. As a result many starved to death during the winter, and others died from disease. By 1608 only thirty-eight colonists were alive. Although Jamestown began to prosper after 1630, between 1607 and 1624 eighty percent of the colonists—thousand of men, women, and children—died.   3

The Plymouth Company had even worse luck than the London Company. 4 The merchants of the Plymouth group tried to settle a colony in Maine in 1607, without success. One problem was poor leadership. George Popham, the president of the plantation, was bad tempered, alienated the Native Americans, and could not hold his group together. Expecting a warm, tropical winter, the colonists were not prepared for the extreme cold of Maine. After many died during their first winter, the colony was abandoned. The Plymouth Company next granted land to the small group of Pilgrims and others who sailed on the *Mayflower*, arriving at Plymouth in 1620. They too were decimated by illness and starvation, losing half of their people during the first winter.

The last large group of early English settlers, the Massachusetts Bay Company, also got off to a shaky start. A group of 400 Puritans who founded Salem, Massachusetts, arrived in America in 1628. Their first winter was not much better than that of the Plymouth colony. Half the Puritans died. However, they were met in 1630 by a fleet of eleven ships and 700 new settlers who were far better supplied and prepared for their new life than any previous colonists had been. Even so, 200 of the new arrivers starved to death during the first winter. In 1631, with more supply ships landing, the Massachusetts Bay Colony received the reinforcements and materials they needed to prosper.

Colonizing the New World was no easy task. In the nearly fifty years that it 6 took for the settlements to finally gain a secure foothold, thousands of English men, women, and children died in a world that must have seemed to many of them a nightmare. Some were motivated by greed, some by religion, others by a sense of adventure, but, incredibly, they kept coming, as new immigrants still do today, maybe one day to fill the whole continent.

Adam Fletcher

Postreading Analysis

In answering essay exam questions, the important point is to stick closely to the intent of the question and after establishing a thesis to remain consistent throughout. In this case, the question does not spell out *exactly* what should be included in the response, asking only that the student summarize "efforts at establishing English colonies."

Adam *could* have chosen to emphasize the successes of the early colonies, included other settlements than he did, or focused more on one colony than another, but he took a cue from his professor's phrase "number of disasters." Throughout the essay he emphasizes the negative side of colonization (stated in his thesis), focusing on the hardships and deaths of the settlers in several colonies.

Adam's thesis is clear and incorporates key terms from the exam question, and each body paragraph is introduced with an appropriate topic sentence. Careful not to "dump" information just because he happens to remember it, Adam still includes plenty of specific examples, including facts, statistics, dates, and names. This specific information is crucial to the success of most essay-exam answers.

▶ Prereading Exploration for "Natural Selection"

Emma Perez wrote this essay as a practice response for her upcoming final exam in Principles of Biology. Even though it is written for her biology professor, who would know the specialized vocabulary and references she makes, she primarily relies on plainspoken English and ordinary examples to help with her definition.

As you read, even if you are not particularly interested in science concepts, see how well you can follow her explanations. Important concepts do not have to be cloaked in the jargon of a discipline to be effectively discussed.

Teaching Idea
"Clinging by Their Fingers" is a good example to show that students will sometimes need to interpret an essay-exam question.

Teaching Idea
Before students read this essay, ask them to explain what they currently know about natural selection, have them read the essay, and then ask them to evaluate Perez's explanation. Does her response thoroughly answer the essay question?

Question: Explain Charles Darwin's theory of natural selection, and discuss two weaknesses in it that science has since resolved.

Natural Selection

"Charles Darwin effected the greatest of all revolutions in human thought," wrote Sir Julian Huxley, "greater than Einstein's or Freud's or even Newton's...." This praise refers to Darwin's theory of evolution, which is a cornerstone for the biological sciences. At the heart of this theory is the concept of natural selection, which, with the exception of two points, convincingly explains organic evolution.   1

First, Darwin said, all organisms show variation, meaning that no two creatures are identical. No mouse is exactly alike another even from the same litter; no person is an exact replica of another. Organisms differ in height, weight, color, intelligence, behavior, personality, and in many other ways. He cited the breeding of domesticated animals and cultivated plants as instances of human beings taking advantage of inherited variations to shape a species. If people can engineer the selection of desirable traits, then so can nature, and so the term "natural selection."   2

Next, Darwin discussed the struggle within a species that favors creatures with beneficial variations. He noted that all living things reproduce more of themselves than the original parents. Even a slowly reproducing species like the elephant can, mathematically, produce millions of offspring from a single pair given enough time, much less a plant species like an elm tree that produces tens of thousands of seeds each season. If all of them survived, the species would crowd itself into extinction. However, it is clear that not all or even most offspring survive, especially when resources become scarce. Members of a species must compete for limited resources, as in two elm seedlings competing for the same nutrients in the soil or two lions struggling for the same gazelle. Because *variation* has already been established, the creature with the most favorable variation will ultimately win this contest for limited resources and pass its characteristics down to succeeding generations, and so the term "survival of the fittest."   3

Finally, to explain the emergence of new species, Darwin explained that when the environment of a species changes, members of the species will gradually change as their variations allow them to exploit the new resources, as did the Galápagos finches, for example. Over time, as the members of a species diverge more widely, they eventually become new species.   4

Science has come to accept Darwin's theory of natural selection as he explained it in 1859, but since that time two points have been further clarified. Darwin knew that characteristics could be passed from one generation to the next, but he did not know how it was done. The science of genetics has accounted for the "how" of traits being passed on. Darwin also did not know of the concept of mutation, by which a gene carrying a variant trait could be passed along, thus fueling natural selection. Although he noted that isolation of a species, as in the Galápagos, contributed to speciation, Darwin did not give it the weight that biologists do today, who call it an "essential element" in the development of a new species.   5

Beneficial variations (genetic mutations), competition among members of the same species, reproduction, and time are the ingredients of the natural selection (and evolution) recipe. Darwin's theory has stood the test of time, and is now almost universally accepted among scientists. Over the years some   6 have criticized Darwin's work on the grounds that it is merely a theory, as in a nonscientist's guess. But as we have discussed in class, Darwin's theory is as close to fact as science gets most of the time and belongs with the other "mere" theories that the world runs on, such as the "theory" of numbers or gravity.

Emma Perez

Postreading Analysis

This essay takes a close look at a concept and develops it in terms that most people can understand. The exam question uses the term "explain," but as we have practiced in Activity 17-1, "explain" can call for several kinds of response, including this one of definition. The author sticks closely to the intent of the exam question, using strategies from the definition chapter and developing much of her essay through cause-and-effect explanation and examples. Emma creates clear thesis and topic sentences and uses strong connectors between and within paragraphs.

One strategy for introducing any essay is to use a quotation. When preparing for an essay exam, it can be useful to memorize several key quotations that might come in handy, as Emma did with the Huxley quotation. If you are allowed to bring a chapter or even your essay outline, it is a good idea to write down several usable quotes. As the author concludes, she brings up the issue of criticism of Darwin's findings, noting that the criticism had been discussed in class.

While we can assume that her instructor would follow her reference to "theory" and the debate that surrounds it, do you? Does the theory of evolution belong in the same category as the theories of numbers and gravity? What is at least one of the author's purposes in raising this point at the end of her essay?

Teaching Idea
Perez shows that she considers the concept of evolution to be scientific fact. One of her purposes is to show her instructor that she is aware of the debate and has thought it through to the point where she can take a position on it.

Questions to Help You Analyze and Write Effective Essay-Exam Responses

1. What is the thesis sentence of this essay, and where is it located? Does the author include parts of the exam question in it?

2. Is the hook effective, and which of the Chapter 12 hooks has the author used? (For more on hooks, see pp. 273–274.)

3. What method(s) from Chapter 12 has the author used to develop the introductory paragraph? (For more on developing introductions, see pp. 269–272.) Would the introduction be effective for the instructor listed as the audience in the Prereading Exploration—why/why not?

4. Is the lead sentence in the concluding paragraph effective—why/why not? (For more on lead and summary sentences, see p. 283.)

5. What method(s) from Chapter 12 has the author used to develop the concluding paragraph? What is the expanded thought? (For more on developing conclusions, see pp. 283–286.) Is the conclusion effective for the instructor listed as the audience in the Prereading Exploration—why/why not? (Consider the conclusion's connection with the introduction.)

6. Write out each of the topic sentences. Next, underline the <u>topic</u> to be discussed once and the <u>statement</u> made about it twice. Circle any connecting words. (For more on connecting sentences, see pp. 52–57.)

7. Choose one *body* paragraph and tell how the author's explaining of an example (including definition) helps clarify some part of the essay question. Do all body paragraphs stick closely to the point of the question?

8. How well has the author used information from his or her source text to answer the exam question? Comment on statistics, dates, specific names, and quotations. Does any information seem "dropped in," perhaps related to but not specifically supporting the answer to the exam question?

9. Choose any paragraph in the essay, and explain why you think it is well written. (Consider elements like patterns of development, topic sentences, connecting words, sensory details, specific words, comparisons, sentence variety, and clear explaining.)

10. List at least five uses of specific language. (For more on specific language, see pp. 78–79, 451–452.)

11. Has the author successfully answered the essay question—why/why not?

■ EXPLAINING THE WRITING ASSIGNMENT

▶ SUMMARIZING THE ASSIGNMENT

Teaching Idea
If you introduced this assignment to students at the beginning of the semester, they are more likely to have an exam question in hand from another discipline. If they create their own, you might refer them to Alternate Writing Assignment 5 in this chapter and help them focus the question.

Using composition skills we have practiced all semester, write an essay of 500 to 600 words in response to an exam question. This question may come from several sources, including your instructor, yourself, the Topic List, or, perhaps the best choice, another class (math, nursing, psychology, other). A question from another discipline will help you prepare for an actual exam—good motivation—or simply learn the material more completely. If you don't have an exam coming up soon, you might ask an instructor from one of your other classes if he or she would create a question for you to answer as extra credit.

Teaching Idea
You might treat this assignment as an in-class final essay, giving students a real test environment to prepare for.

You should plan on studying the information from which you will compose your essay, create a detailed outline, and then write the essay *in class* within one period, just as you would during an actual timed essay exam. You will include a brief, but effective, introduction and conclusion and several body paragraphs. Because this is an in-class project, preparation is critical to your success.

▶ ESTABLISHING AUDIENCE AND PURPOSE

Your instructor is, of course, the audience for an essay-exam response, and your purpose is to show him or her what you know. So here are several points to keep in mind as you brainstorm for material:

1. First, remember that your teacher's goal in creating the exam is to see what you have learned and how you can apply it. Not everything you have read or studied will be on the exam, so part of your preparation ought to be finding out as clearly as possible what the exam will focus on.

2. Second, your writing does not have to be eloquent, but it does have to be clear and specific. If you think you need to define a term for your audience, do so, but spend most of your creative energy explaining how your examples fit together and how they help develop the question.

Teaching Idea
This is a good point at which to review tone in writing and how to avoid common lapses from an academic voice like use of *you*, slang, and inappropriate contractions.

3. Finally, control your tone. Most disciplines in college expect a fairly formal academic voice on an essay exam, even if the atmosphere of your classroom is informal and relaxed on most occasions.

▶ WORKING THROUGH THE WRITING ASSIGNMENT

Discovering Ideas

Almost all of your material for this essay will come from a textbook and class notes. Therefore, you should plan on studying outside of class, even if the essay is open book. Trying to piece together a strong answer from several chapters you are not familiar with while minutes trickle away is a discouraging experience.

Prewriting out of Class

No matter how diligently we study and review on a weekly basis, test time demands more from us. If the exam covers several chapters or a unit, the review may seem overwhelming—and might be if you had to know every fact and detail. However, this is not the case. Your instructor will almost always help focus your studying, generally by indicating significant pages in the text, handing out study sheets, and offering practice (or actual) essay questions.

If you feel uncertain about any part of the exam, you should ask questions in class, but if you still are having trouble, visit your instructor outside class. She may be able to clarify any conceptual problems and give you some further direction for studying.

Ideally, you will have a study guide that includes trial questions, but if not, you can create your own. Look to your text's chapter headings, subheadings, introductions, conclusions, summary boxes, and bold and italicized fonts for important information from which to write practice questions. (See Chapter 2 for tips on effective reading.)

In your notes, look for points that appear several times, indicating their significance to your instructor, and you will probably notice an occasional broad hint, such as: "Remember this for the exam." As you study, drill yourself on key terms, ideas, and definitions, and use them by name. You may not like saying *phloem* and *xylem* or *cretaceous,* but if these are likely candidates for the exam, you should become comfortable with them—including the spellings. Remember too that linking ideas is important, so try to cross-reference main points wherever possible in reviewing. Also, memorize a few short quotations that can be applied to several possible questions.

After you have prepared yourself by studying as much as your time and energy permits, try to relax. Pretest jitters are commonplace; almost everyone has them. If you can avoid "cramming" late into the night, you will, of course, be more rested and better able to think clearly during the exam. One useful technique to calm yourself the night before is to imagine yourself taking the test. Mentally put yourself in your accustomed seat in the classroom; visualize the room, the students, the teacher; and imagine that you are taking the test, doing great. The words are flowing, no problem. Often this relaxation technique will help control "test anxiety."

Prewriting in Class

After you arrive in class to write your exam, there are several strategies that will help you do well:

1. Anticipate that some class time will be spent explaining the exam.

2. While papers are being distributed, ask any unanswered question, but don't expect the teacher to summarize three weeks of classroom instruction in sixty seconds or less.

3. When you get the exam, listen carefully to any instructions, and then again ask questions if you need any point clarified.

4. Skim the exam, all of it, to be sure you understand the questions and their point value. Decide on how much time to spend on each question, considering their point

Teaching Idea
You might want to review part of the chapter on active reading at this point and remind students that focus in preparing for an essay exam is another way of saying "I need a thesis that I can support."

Outline, annotate, summarize.

Know the terminology of your discipline.

Memorize the spelling of key terms.

Teaching Idea
You can emphasize that these prewriting suggestions will help students control their nervous reaction to essay exams, and that if they feel more in control, they are likely to perform better.

Plan on less than the regular length of your class session to write your response.

Use your time efficiently: skim the exam, choose your questions, and monitor your time.

total; write out the time by the question, and try to stick to it (this can be diffi-cult). If you have no idea how to answer a high-point question, do not give up on it, but let the question rest in your mind as you answer the others questions, hop-ing that they or some part of the exam information will stimulate your memory.

5. Analyze each question (as we practiced in Activity 17-1). Circle key words and phrases, number the parts of the question that need to be answered, and pay spe-cial attention to the command verbs, such as *define, divide, contrast*, or *evaluate*. If the question is confusing, ask your instructor to clarify.

However, do not ask this way: "Can I answer this question any way I want to?" rather tell your teacher precisely how you have interpreted the question, and see how he or she responds.

Ask questions to clarify the intent of the exam question.

6. Check the time periodically as you write so you do not get swept up in one ques-tion while losing precious minutes for others.

The following topic list may help you in writing your own exam question, or you may simply want to choose and answer one. Most of the questions contain cues to help you arrange and develop the answers.

Topic List

1. Describe the seven major categories in the taxonomic classification system of Carolus Linnaeus. (biology)

2. Discuss the similarities and differences that exist among the human brain, a library, and a computer as they function in terms of storage of data, recovering/processing the information, and presenting the material so people might work with it. (com-puter science)

3. Define the term "ecosystem" and develop several examples with specific details. (environmental science)

4. Name and explain the five factors that must be controlled in providing heating, ventilation, and air conditioning for human beings. (HVAC)

5. Define the term "social stratification" and explain the systems it is based on, giv-ing a specific example for each. (sociology)

6. Name and explain the four primary arguments offered by Noam Chomsky and others in favor of a "universal grammar." (linguistics)

7. Define the term "harmony" and explain how it relates to chord progressions. (music)

8. Explain how the AIDS virus suppresses a human being's immune system and dis-cuss several common effects of the virus. (nursing)

9. Explain the four basic steps in the process of balancing the general ledger of a small company that uses a cash-based accounting system. (accounting)

10. List and explain the three physical states of matter and then classify the three forms that matter is found in. (chemistry)

11. Describe what is meant by Impressionism, name three significant artists repre-sentative of the movement, list one important work from each, and explain why the work falls into the category of Impressionism. (art history)

12. Define mitosis in relation to meiosis. Next, group and explain each of the four major phases of mitosis. (zoology)

13. Explain the relationship between aperture diameter and shutter speed in controlling the amount of light entering a lens. Next, describe three photo shoots where the light varies significantly and explain what settings to use for f-stop and shutter speed to achieve the effect you hope for. (photography)

14. Describe the water cycle, being sure to include statistics of where water is stored. Include specific examples that illustrate the terms *precipitation, transpiration, percolation, runoff,* and *evaporation.* (botany)

15. Explain the differences and similarities among the red wines of France, Italy, and the United States. (hospitality management)

16. Define "timber management" and explain the process. Be sure to include the three factors a forest manager must take into account when he or she first analyzes a new forest, and include the major problems the manager is likely to encounter. (forestry)

17. Explain what is meant by class "A," "B," and "C" fires, describe what kind of fire extinguishers are effective on them, and explain the rating system used to determine how large a fire each extinguisher can control. (fire science)

18. Explain the major features of "cultural change and development," choose one of the communities we have discussed this semester, and show how well-meaning intervention with that culture can have negative results. (sociology)

19. As we have discussed in class, the Internet has affected the way news is written and disseminated. Choose any major story that we have discussed this semester and compare/contrast its print versus electronic coverage. Be sure to include both the depth of coverage and the updating of breaking news in your response. (journalism)

Prewriting Suggestions

After circling key terms, you may need to prewrite to shake loose a few ideas. Many techniques can work, but clustering and listing can be especially helpful. For example, when the author of the Annotated Student Model got the following question, he circled key terms and then listed possible responses:

Essay Question. Define the three essential elements of photography and explain how they combine to create an esthetically pleasing photograph. (photography)

Shape	~~Form~~
Tone	~~Texture~~
Color	~~Pattern~~

The time you take up front with your response will save you time and trouble at the end. Doug was going to plow into his answer by throwing all six terms into his essay but realized after listing them that his instructor classed *form, texture,* and *pattern* as *subcategories* of the first three terms.

> ### Prewriting—Summing Up
>
> 1. Prepare for the exam out of class: review, create practice questions, ask your instructor to help focus your efforts.
>
> 2. Prepare for the exam in class: skim the entire exam, ask questions, allocate your time.
>
> 3. Analyze the question for key terms and command verbs.
>
> 4. Prewrite on paper to uncover ideas.

Take time to prewrite on paper if you are not sure of your main ideas.

JOURNAL ENTRY 17-2

Write a brief paragraph explaining your essay question. What does it ask you to do? What are the key terms? Have you been able to locate enough material from your textbook and class notes to thoroughly answer the question? What one point has your instructor stressed to the class that should be included in your response?

Organizing Ideas

Now, write a thesis using key terms from the essay question. You may also include some parts of the question in your introductory paragraph, and you may forecast what your essay will cover, although this is not always necessary. The following three sentences from the student models in this chapter demonstrate effective thesis statements:

> Use key terms from the essay question in your thesis.

1. At the heart of this theory is the concept of natural selection, which, with the exception of two points, convincingly explains organic evolution.

> 1. No forecasting

2. Beginning with the <u>"lost colony" of Gilbert and Raleigh and progressing through the Massachusetts Bay Company</u>, early English attempts at colonizing the New World met with disaster.

> 2. Partial forecasting

3. When skillfully combined, the three essential elements—<u>shape, tone, and color</u>—can produce aesthetically pleasing pictures.

> 3. Complete forecasting

Whichever method you choose, placing the thesis as the last sentence in your first paragraph maximizes clarity.

> Locate thesis as last sentence in introduction.

Sometimes essay questions are ambiguously written, and you will need to interpret them. For example, the question that generated "Clinging by Their Fingers" allows for several possible approaches (see Postreading Analysis, p. 405), so the student had to shape a response. When in doubt, write out a thesis, and then ask your professor.

Arrangement of body paragraphs depends largely on the essay question. You may organize spatially if the question calls for description, say, of a machine, building, or painting. More often you will use time order, as in the history model essay "Clinging by Their Fingers," or an order that shows progression of thought, as in the model "Natural Selection." Sometimes order of importance is called for, as in the Annotated Student Model. So look to the question for guidance, and if you see indicators like "compare and contrast" (use the block or point-by-point method) or "describe the process of" (chronological method), your knowledge of the patterns of development will help you organize the essay.

If you have been able to bring a prewritten outline to class, great, but if not, writing a **scratch outline** will help (see the Annotated Student Model). Include the main point of each body paragraph and one or two supporting examples. If there are several questions to answer, you might skim the exam, select questions, and jot down a scratch outline for each answer while the information is still in mind from that last-minute review session.

> Prepare a scratch outline.

Remember to begin each body paragraph with a topic sentence linked to the preceding paragraph by connectors like the transitions listed below (for more on connectors and a complete list of transitions, see pp. 52–57).

- **Locating or moving in space:** above, against, around, behind, below, on, in

- **Moving in time:** after, at last, awhile, first, immediately, next, now, often, then

- **Adding material:** again, also, and, in addition, furthermore, as well as

- **Giving examples:** for example, for instance, another, one reason, in fact
- **Comparing:** alike, also, both, in the same way, similarly
- **Contrasting:** in contrast, although, but, differs from, even though, however
- **Cause/effect:** and so, as a result, because, consequently, since, so, then
- **Summarizing/concluding:** finally, in brief, in other words, in short, to summarize

Organizing—Summing Up

1. Analyze the essay question, and use parts of it in your thesis.

2. Be alert to the possible need to *interpret* the question.

3. Look to the question to help organize your response.

4. Write a scratch outline.

5. Plan on using a topic sentence to introduce each body paragraph.

6. Review the list of transitions and other connectors above (for more, see pp. 52–57.)

Teaching Idea
When reviewing Journal Entry 17-3, you might mention that teachers often begin to evaluate content in an essay-exam response by circling facts, statistics, dates, names, etc., that they expect to see.

JOURNAL ENTRY 17-3

Write out your thesis sentence. Does it use key terms from the essay question? Create a rough outline that includes your major points and several supporting examples. Be specific with names, dates, facts, and statistics (to review outlines, see p. 282).

Specific examples and clear explanations are crucial.

Teaching Idea
Remind students that misspelling key discipline terms gives the impression—often a wrong one—that the student does not know the material well.

Tips for more efficient drafting

Try to reserve time for brief revision and editing.

Do not plan on recopying.

Out of time? Outline.

Drafting

With the preliminary work out of the way and an outline in hand, you are almost ready to draft. Plan on leaving wide margins (1 1/2 inches) and skipping lines so you can revise as time permits. Do not be overly concerned with matters of style, but do try for clearly written and connected sentences. Strive for completeness of ideas—including specific *names, dates, facts, statistics,* and *quotations*—and connect them soundly with your thesis. Using numbered lists can save time.

Throughout drafting keep the audience in mind. What points has your instructor stressed? Where would she expect you to clarify an idea or define a term, where not? Are you using the accepted language of the discipline and maintaining an academic tone?

Near the end of the exam time, there are several ways to improve your essay score:

1. Reserve a few minutes to revise and edit. You may not have to add or cut much, but even clarifying one major example can help a lot (see the Annotated Student Model). Number anyplace in the text where you might need to insert additional sentences and key the number to notes at the end of your essay (see Annotated Student Model). Do your best to correct spelling errors, especially for *key discipline terms,* and major grammar and punctuation problems.

2. If time runs out, you might still get partial credit for sketching a quick outline of any points you were not able to cover.

Here are several additional concerns that students often have during essay exams:

- Having an anxiety attack, feeling like you know nothing on the exam: If you have reviewed even a fair amount and attended class regularly, it is unlikely that you know *nothing* on the exam. Take a few deep breaths, slow your breathing, and refocus.

You may need to leave the class for a moment to regroup, after asking for your instructor's permission. Come back to the exam, skim the questions again, locate one that you can say something about, and begin an answer. Remind yourself that in the larger scheme of life, this exam will disappear. It will not be a deathbed regret.

- Worrying about other students completing their essay first: Often early completion of an exam means that the student did not do well, rather than the reverse. Take every available minute to write and revise your work.

- Worrying about time running out: Remind yourself that you have taken all possible steps to deal with this: You have reviewed thoroughly, skimmed the exam, allotted time for each question, and monitored your progress. You know that you can outline any part that you cannot answer in complete sentences. There is nothing else left to do.

- Wondering whether or not to use uncertain information: If you are not reasonably sure of important facts, statistics, quotations, and so on, leave them out.

- Wondering what to do about a question when no ideas are coming: The truth is that sometimes we don't know or cannot remember important information. Try to realize when you cannot move forward on even an important question and leave it behind. You may come back to it before time is up and maybe not. Sometimes it is best to cut your losses and move on.

> **JOURNAL ENTRY 17-4**
>
> If you have prepared for this in-class essay by writing a rough draft, respond to this journal entry as soon after writing it as possible. Does your response answer all parts of the exam question? Is each paragraph clearly centered around a topic sentence? Have you provided specific, detailed examples with names, dates, facts, statistics, and quotations as needed? Have you avoided "padding"? Do your introduction and conclusion work as they should; are they brief but compelling? What part of this draft do you like best, what part least—why? Answer in a paragraph.

Revising Drafts

To review the detailed lists for revising drafts, turn to Chapter 13.

■ ANNOTATED STUDENT MODEL

The two drafts that follow will help you with drafting and the minimal revising essay exams allow.

Teaching Idea
Encourage students to write simple, clear topic sentences. Remind them that transitional words like *first, second, next,* and so forth, are easy for them to write and the instructor to follow.

First Draft

Doug Cunningham wrote this essay response to a question provided by his photography instructor. Because his instructor is an expert in his field, Doug knew that he would not need to explain concepts or define terms common to photography in general, but that he would need to clarify any term or point as it related to his understanding of the course material. He brought a brief outline with his thesis sentence and knew what he wanted to say in the introduction and conclusion.

Essay Question

Circling key terms

Define the three essential elements of photography, and explain how they combine to create an aesthetically pleasing photograph. (photography)

Thesis

Thesis with key terms included and forecasting points

When skillfully combined, the three essential elements—*shape, tone, and color*—can produce aesthetically pleasing pictures.

Working Outline

1. *Shape: define—show how it creates quality pictures*
2. *Tone: define—show how it creates quality pictures*
3. *Color: define—show how it creates quality pictures*

No title

Brief introduction

While much about photography is subjective, both in the eye of the composer 1 and the viewer, there are some features that can be found in all photographs. These features combine to create other artistic elements, in the process adding depth and complexity to the field of photography. When skillfully combined, the three essential elements—shape, tone, and color—can produce aesthetically pleasing pictures.

Thesis incorporates key word in question

Clear topic sentence

Shape is the outline or contour of a subject. It is the most important element 2 in a photograph, particularly black and white. On a dark, overcast night we still can find our way through a landscape because we can see the shape of the tree trunk, bush, or car in front of us. In photography the size and placement of shapes within a frame help create balance and draw a viewer's eye to one point or another. Striking images can be formed using silhouettes (*a darkened shape with few, if any, features recognizable*). One reason shapes handled in this way are so interesting is because they simplify what the viewer sees. Without other visual cues, the eye focuses on the central shape.

Specific examples

Definition essential to question

Unneeded definition

Clear topic sentence

The second essential element in a photograph is tone, the contrast between light and dark portions of a picture. Tone gives definition to shape. Without the contrast 3 between light and dark, shapes appear flat; in fact, they are silhouettes. The photographer who chooses black and white film specializes in shape and tone, in the absence of color. Black and white pictures may contain very little tonal difference or may run the full range of the light/dark spectrum. Photographs that use tone effectively can create depth and mood, in some instances more effectively than in color. In general, darker images tend to create darker moods, giving a picture a sense of "mystery or menace." On the other hand, lighter tones can give a feeling of "freedom, space, and softness." Experienced photographers work with tonal qualities of film to cause emotional responses, and they are careful not to clash meaning with tone, for example, shooting a joyous wedding in dark, somber shades.

Definition essential to question

No defining of terms instructor knows

Explaining supported by specific example

Clear topic sentence

Color is the last essential element in photography and is linked to tone. Together 4 they give depth and substance, or form, to shapes in a picture. Color, like tone, affects a viewer's emotional response to an image. Bright, warm colors—reds, oranges, yellows—can convey a sense of liveliness and fun; cooler colors—blues, purples, greens—can create a more quiet, reflective tone. Handling color in photography is another matter of selection rather than just pointing the lens at any jumble

Cause and effect development

of colored objects and clicking the shutter. The most aesthetically pleasing color images try for a single dominant color with other colors harmonizing. To achieve harmony in a photograph, the photographer composes a picture using colors closely related on the color wheel, for instance, shades of blue and green as they merge with the bordering yellow and purple. When too many muted or too many bold colors are combined within the same frame, the image can become confusing, with shapes "flattening," which damages the feeling of depth.

These three essential features—shape, tone, and color—come together to produce 5 *form, texture, and pattern, all of which together can produce beautiful pictures. However, as we have discussed in class, there are few unbreakable rules for combining these basic features of photography. Sometimes, for instance, a photographer wants to use many primary colors to deliberately create a sense of confusion. Some of the strongest images ever recorded on film break many of the "rules," and, after considering their artistic options, people should learn to trust their own subjective response to an image.*

Doug Cunningham

First Draft with Minor Revisions and Editing

Unlike out-of-class essays, the in-class essay cannot be substantially revised. However, you should try to reserve some time for clarifying main points, eliminating unneeded material, and editing. If you have double-spaced and left wide margins, you can add a word, phrase, or brief explanation at the appropriate spot. But if you need to add more than just a few words, number the location in your answer and then write the information at the end of your essay.

First Draft with Minor Revisions and Editing

While much about photography is subjective, both in the eye of the composer 1 *and the viewer, there are some features that can be found in all photographs. These features combine to create other artistic elements, in the process adding depth and complexity to the field of photography. When skillfully combined, the three essential elements—shape, tone, and color—can produce aesthetically pleasing pictures.*

Shape is the outline or contour of a subject. It is the most important element 2 *in a photograph, particularly black and white.[1] On a dark, overcast night we still can find our way through a landscape because we can see the shape of the tree trunk, bush, or car in front of us. In photography the size and placement of shapes within a frame help create balance and draw a viewer's eye to one point or another. Striking images can be formed using silhouettes (~~a darkened shape with few, if any, features recognizable~~) with varying degrees of backlighting to create full or semisilhouettes. One reason shapes handled in this way are so compelling is because they simplify what the viewer sees. Without additional visual cues, the eye focuses on the central shape.*

Margin notes:

Specific examples given

Conclusion contains brief summary, expanded thought, and link to classroom instruction.

Explaining links to "aesthetic" point in question

The author never added a title. Would it help to have one? What might you suggest?

[1] Note added

Explaining added to show full knowledge of silhouettes

Unneeded defining eliminated

The second essential element in a photograph is tone, the contrast between light 3 and dark portions of a picture. Tone gives definition to shape. Without the contrast between light and dark, shapes appear flat; in fact, they are silhouettes. The photographer who chooses black and white film specializes in shape and tone, in the absence of color. Black and white pictures may contain very little tonal difference or may run the full range of the light/dark spectrum. Photographs that use tone effectively can create depth and mood, in some instances more effectively than in color. In general, darker images tend to create darker moods, giving a picture a sense of "mystery or menace." On the other hand, lighter tones can give a feeling of "freedom, space, and softness." Experienced photographers work with tonal qualities of film to cause emotional responses, and they are careful not to clash meaning with tone, for example, shooting a joyous wedding in dark, somber shades.

Color is the last essential element in photography and is linked to tone. Together 4 they give depth and substance, or form, to shapes in a picture. Color, like tone, affects a viewer's emotional response to an image. Bright, warm colors—reds, oranges, yellows—can convey a sense of liveliness and fun; cooler colors—blues, purples, greens—can create a more quiet, reflective tone. Handling color in photography is another matter of selection rather than just pointing the lens at any jumble of colored objects and clicking the shutter. The most aesthetically pleasing color images try for a single dominant color with other colors harmonizing. To achieve harmony in a photograph, the photographer composes a picture using colors closely

[² Note added]

related on the color wheel², for instance, shades of blue and green as they merge with the bordering yellow and purple. When too many muted or too many bold colors are combined within the same frame, the image can become confusing, with shapes "flattening," which damages the illusion of depth.

These three essential elements—shape, tone, and color—come together to produce 5 form, texture, and pattern, all of which together can produce beautiful pictures. However, as we have discussed in class, there are few unbreakable rules for combining these basic features of photography. Sometimes, for instance, a photographer wants to use many primary colors to create a feeling of confusion. Some of the strongest images ever recorded on film break many of the "rules," and, after considering their artistic options, people should learn to trust their own subjective response to an image.

Doug Cunningham

Notes
¹ Because shape occupies the most space within a frame, and it draws a person's attention immediately, even in the absence of tone and color

² Note on color wheel: Photographers should be aware of the primary and secondary colors, how they mix, complement, and contrast with one another to create pleasing images (and other effects).

Special Points to Check in Revising Essay-Exam Response

1. Introduction: hook, engaging support sentences, thesis (includes key terms from question)

2. Body paragraphs: topic sentence with connector

3. Overall development: detailed examples, clear explanations, patterns of development (all supporting essay question)

4. Conclusion: connector, summary, expanded thought

CHAPTER SUMMARY

1. Successfully taking an essay exam requires sufficient out-of-class preparation, including active review of textbooks and class notes, annotating, summarizing, outlining, anticipating questions, and often writing practice responses.

2. In-class preparation can help with essay-exam responses: skimming the exam for an overview, allocating time to questions based on point value and knowledge, analyzing the exam questions, outlining, and monitoring time while drafting.

3. In-class essay exams differ from our out-of-class writing assignments in several ways, including the expert audience (your instructor), limited revision possibility, and reduced introductions and conclusions.

4. Essay-exam responses are similar in most respects to our other major writing projects including the need for prewriting, organizing, drafting, and whatever revising and editing that time allows.

5. Essay-exam responses usually involve several patterns of development and rely on specific, detailed examples with clear explanations. Names, dates, facts, statistics, and quotations are often called for.

6. Analyzing the essay question and answering all its parts are crucial to a successful essay-exam response.

7. The thesis sentence should contain key terms from the essay question and will often forecast what the essay will discuss.

8. Introductions and conclusions for essay-exam responses should be concise but well written, with a target audience in mind.

9. Transitional words and other connectors are especially important in bridging the gap between paragraphs.

10. An overall organizational pattern may be suggested by the essay question.

11. Revising and editing, even briefly, will improve the essay-exam response.

■ ALTERNATE WRITING ASSIGNMENTS

Teaching Idea
When discussing ideas for the students' essay questions, you might also point out these Alternate Writing Assignments.

To give you some alternatives to the chapter Topic List and a bit more focus, you might be interested in the following assignments.

Remember to observe these points as you begin any of the options:

- Review the points in the Skills section.

- Prepare by active reading: questioning, annotating, summarizing, and outlining.

- Construct a thesis sentence with key terms from the essay question.
- Know how you will begin and end your essay.
- Use specific examples and explain succinctly.

1. Question: Drawing on information in Chapter 1, list and define the seven methods for discovering ideas. Next, choose any two that you have used this semester, and tell why they have been particularly effective for you. Use specific examples from the text to illustrate the methods, but also use examples from your own writing experiences this term.

2. Question: Drawing on information from Chapter 1, define what it means to revise a text. Next, explain the process of group revision, categorizing the information by help the writer can give the reader and by help the reader can give the writer. Illustrate your response with personal examples.

3. Question: Using the information in Chapter 3, list and define the four elements of support found in body paragraphs. Rely primarily on the text for examples.

4. Question: Drawing on information from Chapter 5, define the concept of "general versus specific language." Illustrate your response with examples from the text, and then compare the concept with developing sufficient support in Chapter 3, the concept of "increasing specificity."

5. Create your own essay question and then answer it. Whether or not you will take an essay exam this semester, you almost certainly will at some point in college. So learning how to answer a specific question at some length will have practical value. However, you might want to create a question that involves an interest outside of school. For example, you may be curious about lightning, what causes it, what it consists of, and what its effects can be. After reading about the subject, you could fashion an essay-exam question and then answer it on the basis of your reading. If you choose this option, you will become your own teacher—a fine goal for anyone. Remember that you should choose a topic that requires some reading and learning.

Note: You are likely to have some initial difficulty in focusing the question and making it interesting enough to want to answer. For help with this, review the general category of questions in Activity 17-1 and the Topic List. Instead of simply "listing and explaining," you might want to add comparing or contrasting, evaluating, taking a position, or one of the other categories of questions. Here is an example:

A. Question: Define the term "lightning" and explain its effects.

B. Question: Define the term "lightning," explaining the process by which it is generated, categorizing the types, explaining its most damaging effects, and explaining how people might protect themselves from lightning injury.

As you read and learn about your topic, you will find that you could write many pages on it—or narrow the focus. Experiment with your question until you think you have just what you need for an essay response of 500 to 600 words.

Polishing Style

CHAPTER 18

Creating
Sentence Variety

Building
Sentence Variety

- Length
- Type
- Coordination
- Subordination
- Beginnings
- Inversion

Teaching Idea
This chapter may be best used after students have been introduced to basic sentence grammar in Chapter 20. However, both chapters can help students understand and overcome punctuation problems, and you might find it helpful to assign this chapter in small pieces over a five-six week period.

WHAT ARE WE TRYING TO ACHIEVE AND WHY?

Looking at the military formation above, we see lines of soldiers dressed alike, all with similar serious expressions on their faces, standing in a similar posture, unmoving, at attention. When we look at this image, we see little to mark one person from the other. Uniformity is the goal; individual expression is not. However, most of us will find our eyes more drawn to the fans at the football stadium, dressed (or undressed) as they are in a variety of clothes and colors, smiling, cheering, gesturing, in short, behaving differently. One of the reasons we are interested in the football fans is contrast. Because there are clear differences among them, our eyes fix on one person and then on another, seeing something new at each resting point. In general people want contrast and difference in their lives, at least in small doses.

The same principle holds true in our writing. Sentence after sentence constructed the same way, stretching throughout a paragraph and then into an essay, will, like the company of soldiers above, tend to lose the reader's interest, no matter how exciting the ideas contained within those sentences. The point of Chapter 18, then, is to give you some practical suggestions for involving your readers in your ideas as you structure sentences in a variety of ways.

We will work on the following points for help with sentence variety: *length, type, openers,* and *word order.*

VARYING THE LENGTH OF SENTENCES

Sometimes when we write, particularly when we draft in a hurry, we find our sentences becoming similar in length. It may be that we have a paragraph with ten short sentences or maybe six or seven longer ones. However, short, medium, or long, if we string too many sentences of the same length together, they can become monotonous. For example, what is your reaction to the following paragraph?

Music brings simple enjoyment. It also affects our lives in many ways. One song can bring out specific memories. It can change a person's mood from happy to sad. Music is so much more than just a rhythmic combination of sounds. It is a marvelously powerful experience. It is universal in cultures. Music bridges the cultural gap. It brings people closer together. Can you think of a society where music was or is not a part of people's lives?

If you think the paragraph above feels "choppy," you are right. The ten sentences are too close in length, creating a start-stop feeling, not unlike being in a car with someone learning how to use a clutch, alternately lurching down the street and slamming on the brakes. We could revise the paragraph this way, combining sentences to vary their length and create smoother flow:

> Besides the simple enjoyment that music brings, it also affects our lives in many ways. It is amazing how hearing one song can bring out specific memories and how it can change a person's mood from happy to sad or vice versa. Music is so much more than just any rhythmic succession or combination of sounds. It is a marvelously powerful experience that is universal in cultures, bridging the cultural gap, bringing people closer together. Can you think of a society where music was or is not a part of people's lives?

The revised version has only five sentences, but notice the variety in length: 1 = 15 words, 2 = 27 words, 3 = 14 words, 4 = 19 words, and 5 = 17 words. The object in length variation in a paragraph is not to jump from long to short to medium in some preset pattern. It is—when revising for style in a second or third draft—simply to interrupt a string of sentences that are similar in length. A good rule of thumb is to alter the length of the third or fourth sentence in a series of roughly the same word count.

Activity 18-1: Combining Sentences for Variety in Length

Revise the paragraph below to increase its readability by combining sentences. You will end up with a mix of sentence lengths, but do not eliminate all the shorter ones. A short sentence can be especially emphatic when following a series of longer ones and so draw the reader's attention to it. You may need to drop or add a word or two as you combine.

> "If you use a little imagination, Aaron," mother said, "this bathtub can be an ocean full of adventure." This sounded like a good idea to Aaron. He climbed into the tub. Then he pretended to head out across the vast ocean in search of pirates. He also looked for valuable sunken treasure. Mother began washing him and lathering his hair. Soapsuds fell into the water. They became islands to sail his ship around. His mother washed his hair. Then she said, "OK, time for a rinse." Aaron didn't mind this time. He pretended to swim under his ship. There he would look at all the ocean creatures. He saw a school of huge blue whales. He saw a giant octopus squirting a cloud of black ink. He saw hundreds of pink jellyfish trailing long stinging tentacles.

Answers will vary.

Revised paragraph:

"If you use a little imagination, Aaron," mother said, "this bathtub can be an ocean full of adventure." This sounded like a good idea to Aaron, so after he climbed into the tub, he pretended to head out across the vast ocean in search of pirates and valuable sunken treasure. Mother began washing him and lathering his hair. When the soapsuds fell into the water, they became islands to sail his ship around. After his hair was washed, mom said, "OK, time for a rinse." Aaron didn't mind this time. He pretended to swim under his ship to look at all the ocean creatures. He saw a school of huge blue whales, a giant octopus squirting a cloud of black ink, and hundreds of pink jellyfish trailing long stinging tentacles.

Teaching Idea
Stress the point that sentence variety does not require some arcane patterning of sentences.

Teaching Idea
Some students misinterpret sentence variety to mean no short sentences, so you might anticipate and correct this misimpression.

Teaching Idea
If you have several students read their revised paragraphs aloud in Activity 18-1, you can quickly list on the board common sentence structures they are using (such as participial phrases, adverb clauses, and relative clauses) and tally them to show similar sentence variety solutions. Alternately, you might have students in pairs or groups exchange and discuss revised paragraphs.

VARYING THE TYPES OF SENTENCES

Another way to create sentence variety is by using different **types** of sentences. We can classify types of sentences by **rhetoric** (where the main idea is located), **function** (statements, questions, commands, and exclamations), and **grammar** (what kinds of clauses they contain). (You will read more about this in Unit Five.) Here are the four kinds of sentences classified by *grammar:*

1. Simple: Aaron likes ice cream.

2. Compound: Aaron likes ice cream, *so he eats a lot of it*.

3. Complex: Aaron likes ice cream *because it tastes sweet*.

4. Compound–complex: Aaron likes ice cream because it tastes sweet, so he eats a lot of it.

Our interest in the grammatical sentence types in relation to sentence variety centers around the concepts of **coordination** and **subordination**. When we create a *compound sentence*, we join **coordinate** sentence parts, and so tell our reader that the parts are equal. We indicate this with one of seven words called **coordinating conjunctions** (*and, but, or, so, yet, for, nor*), as in the compound sentence, number 2, above. When we **subordinate** sentence parts, we tell our reader that one part is less important than another, as in the *complex sentence*, number 3, above. Both coordination and subordination are valuable tools for expressing our thoughts in sophisticated ways, and they help us achieve sentence variety. (For more on coordination and subordination, see Chapters 20 and 21.)

Teaching Idea
This is a good point at which to mention the unnecessary comma students often use with compound verbs.

COORDINATING WORDS IN SENTENCES

As we have just seen in number 2, above, a compound sentence has at least two equal parts, each a separate simple sentence joined by a coordinating conjunction (and, but, etc.). In our writing we often create compound or two-part sentences for among other reasons to reduce the number of simple sentences in our paragraphs (as many of us probably did in Activity 18-1). However, we do not always need to create a *complete* compound sentence. In fact, we often use **two-part** subjects, verbs, and other words to add variety to our sentence structures and eliminate unneeded words. For example, we might combine two simple sentences into a complete compound sentence *or* create a compound subject:

A. Simple sentences: My grandmother lived into her nineties.

   My grandfather also lived into his nineties.

1. Compound **sentence:** My grandmother lived into her nineties, *and* my grandfather also lived into his nineties.

2. Compound **subject:** My grandmother and grandfather lived into their nineties.

Or we might combine sentences with a **two-part** verb as in the following:

B. Simple sentences: Jody smashed the ball over the left field fence.

   She triumphantly rounded the bases to home.

1. Compound **sentence:** Jody smashed the ball over the left field fence, *and* she triumphantly rounded the bases to home.

2. Compound **verb:** Jody smashed the ball over the left field fence and triumphantly rounded the bases to home.

When you revise for sentence variety, you will sometimes write complete compound sentences and sometimes only compound subjects, verbs, and other words. Remember to use a comma before the coordinating conjunction in a compound sentence but *not* to use a comma with a compound subject or verb. (For more on coordination, see pp. 508–510.)

Activity 18-2: Combining Sentences by Compounding

Combine the following sets of sentences first as compound sentences separated by a comma and an *and* or a *but*. Next, reduce the compound sentence by using *either* a two-part subject or verb, eliminating any unneeded words, making necessary changes in words, and removing the comma.

Teaching Idea
Activity 18-2 will help students having a problem with commas and compound verbs.

Comma

No comma

Example:
Simple sentence: Muhammad Ali was a great fighter in his day.
Simple sentence: Sugar Ray Leonard was also a great fighter in his day.

- Compound **sentence:** *Muhammad Ali was a great fighter in his day, and Sugar Ray Leonard was also a great fighter in his day.*

- Compound **subject:** *Muhammad Ali and Sugar Ray Leonard were great fighters in their day.*

1. Simple sentence: My best friend won a lot of money in Las Vegas.

   Simple sentence: I also won a lot of money in Las Vegas.

   Compound sentence: *My best friend won a lot of money in Las Vegas, and I also won a lot of money in Las Vegas.*

   Compound subject: *My best friend and I won a lot of money in Las Vegas.*

2. Simple sentence: My great Aunt Martha sailed to Bimini on Friday.

   Simple sentence: My cousin Ellen also sailed to Bimini on Friday.

   Compound sentence: *My great Aunt Martha sailed to Bimini on Friday, and my cousin Ellen also sailed to Bimini on Friday.*

   Compound subject: *My great Aunt Martha and my cousin Ellen sailed to Bimini on Friday.*

3. Simple sentence: Beth approached the counter at Best Buy.

   Simple sentence: She asked for a refund on her DVD player.

   Compound sentence: *Beth approached the counter at Best Buy, and she asked for a refund on her DVD player.*

   Compound verb: *Beth approached the counter at Best Buy and asked for a refund on her DVD player.*

4. Simple sentence: Jack learned a lot from his DWI conviction.

   Simple sentence: He has given up drinking altogether.

   Compound sentence: _Jack learned a lot from his DWI conviction, and he has given up drinking altogether._

   Compound verb: _Jack learned a lot from his DWI conviction and has given up drinking altogether._

5. Simple sentence: The wedding plans finally came together.

   Simple sentence: They had seemed headed for disaster.

   Compound sentence: _The wedding plans finally came together, but they had seemed headed for disaster._

   Compound verb: _The wedding plans finally came together but had seemed headed for disaster._

6. Simple sentence: This century humanity will spread through our solar system.

   Simple sentence: After that they will colonize the stars.

   Compound sentence: _This century humanity will spread through our solar system, and after that they will colonize the stars._

   Compound verb: _This century humanity will spread through our solar system and after that will colonize the stars._

7. Write three sentences of your own that are either compound or that contain a two-part subject or verb (use commas correctly).

   A. _Answers will vary._ _____

   _____

   B. _____

   _____

   C. _____

   _____

Teaching Idea
Students often want to skip writing sentences of their own, but you might remind them that this is the most important part of the exercise.

SUBORDINATING WORDS IN SENTENCES

Aside from coordination and creating compound sentences, we can achieve sentence variety through **subordination,** that is, placing a word, phrase, or clause in a position of less prominence in a sentence. Subordination allows us to deal with shades of meaning and complex ideas in sentences, often by setting information off with commas, parentheses, and dashes.

We will focus here on the **complex** sentence (simple sentence plus one or more subordinate clauses), and the **adjective** (or *relative*) and **adverb clauses.**

Teaching Idea
For simplicity's sake, it helps focus students on these most common relative pronouns: *who, which,* and *that.*

Adjective Clauses—Nonessential

Adjective clauses are usually easy to spot, because most of them begin with one of these three relative pronouns: *who*, *which*, and *that*. This kind of clause tells us something about the noun or pronoun it follows. Focusing for a moment on *who* and *which*, we can see what these clauses look like (for more on nonessential clauses, see pp. 499–500, 512):

A. Jason, *who is really a very bright guy*, is flunking out of college.

B. Jason has a drug problem, *which keeps him from focusing on his studies*.

The "who" clause in sentence A comments about Jason being "a very bright guy," adding information about the noun "Jason." The "which" clause in sentence B explains one effect of "focusing on his studies," adding information about the noun "problem."

Adjective clauses used in this way are said to be **nonessential** because they are not needed to clarify the meaning of the main part of each sentence. In both examples if we remove the relative clauses, the main clauses left would still communicate the central idea. Note that *commas* are used to set off these subordinate clauses.

> **Note:** To avoid ambiguity with "which" clauses, it is usually best to position them next to a single noun or pronoun rather than expecting them to describe several words or ideas.
>
> **Not this:** Jason has a drug problem and is also dyslexic, which keeps him from focusing on his studies. (Is it the drug problem, the dyslexia, or both that are affecting the studies?)

Activity 18-3: Combining Sentences with Nonessential Adjective Clauses

Combine the sets of sentences listed below by crossing out the unneeded noun or pronoun in the second sentence and replacing it with either "who" or "which." Use "who" to refer to *people* and "which" to refer to *animals* or *things*. Use a comma to set off these subordinate clauses.

Example: Eric refused to talk with anyone at the party except Simone.
~~He~~ had been treated for clinical depression last year.

Combined: *Eric, who had been treated for clinical depression last year, refused to talk with anyone at the party except Simone.*

1. Governor Bush will run for president against Al Gore in 2000.
   Bush has the blessing of the Republican Party.
   Combined: *Governor Bush, who has the blessing of the Republican Party, will run for president against Al Gore in 2000.*

2. AIDS is still spreading worldwide.
   It is a debilitating and usually fatal disease.
   Combined: *AIDS, which is a debilitating and usually fatal disease, is still spreading worldwide.*

3. Lucille Ball will be appearing on a stamp in 2001.
   She has been called "America's favorite redhead."
   Combined: *Lucille Ball, who has been called "America's favorite redhead," will be appearing on a stamp in 2001.*

4. Brown recluse spiders have a dangerous and painful bite.
They have a violin shape on their heads and backs.

Combined: *Brown recluse spiders, which have a violin shape on their heads and backs, have a dangerous and painful bite.*

5. Tiger Woods makes a fortune through endorsements.
He is one of the finest golfers in the world.

Combined: *Tiger Woods, who is one of the finest golfers in the world, makes a fortune through endorsements*

6. A classical guitar uses nylon strings.
It has a wider neck than other acoustic guitars.
The nylon strings give the instrument a more mellow tone.

Combined: *A classical guitar, which has a wider neck than other acoustic guitars, uses nylon strings, which give the instrument a more mellow tone.*

7. Write three of your own sentences that contain a nonessential adjective clause. Remember to use commas, and be especially careful with the "which" reference.

A. *Answers will vary.*

B. _____

C. _____

Adjective Clauses—Essential

As we have seen, adjective clauses can be nonessential to the meaning of the main part of a sentence, in which case we use commas to set them off. However, they can also be **essential**; that is, if we left the clause out, the meaning in the main part of the sentence would be unclear or distorted.

Compare the following two sentences (for more on essential clauses, see pp. 499–500, 512):

A. Governor Bush, <u>who has the blessing of the Republican Party</u>, will run for president against Al Gore in 2000.

B. A politician <u>who has the blessing of the Republican Party</u> will run for president against Al Gore in 2000.

In the first sentence once we have named Governor Bush, there can be no doubt about who will run for the presidency; therefore, the relative clause "who has the blessing . . ." becomes nonessential and so is set off with commas. However, in the second sentence we do not know who will have the opportunity to run for president until we read the relative clause. We ask the question "Who gets to run for the office?" and we answer it with the essential clause, the politician "who has the blessing of the Republican Party."

Determining the difference between nonessential and essential clauses can be difficult sometimes and often depends on the author's intent. In general, the pronoun "that" (*not* "which") is used in essential clauses (though you will see both). We will continue to use "who" to refer to people.

Teaching Idea
To further clarify the essential/nonessential question, try using family members. For example: "My mother, who loves to windsurf, . . ." or "My brother who works at the hospital. . . ."

Teaching Idea
Perhaps the best way to show how the author's intent can affect the restrictive or nonrestrictive nature of a sentence element is to point out the word group in students' own writing and ask what the student intends to say.

Activity 18-4: Combining Sentences with Essential Adjective Clauses

Combine the sets of sentences listed below by crossing out the unneeded noun or pronoun in the second sentence and replacing it with either "who" or "that." Use "who" to refer to people and "that" to refer to animals or things. Remember that the adjective clause should follow a noun or pronoun in the first sentence so it can clearly say something about it. Also, do *not* use a comma to set off these subordinate clauses because they are essential to the meaning of the main part of the sentence.

Example: AIDS is a debilitating and usually fatal disease.
~~It~~ is still spreading worldwide.

Combined: _AIDS is a debilitating and usually fatal disease that is still spreading worldwide._

Teaching Idea
You might point out to students that if they position the *who* clauses in sentences two, four, and six immediately after the subjects, they will have created *non*essential clauses, which *do* require a comma.

1. A grant allowed Wales to build a national botanical garden.
   The grant was given by the Millennium Commission.

   Combined: _A grant that was given by the Millennium Commission allowed Wales to build a national botanical garden._

2. Jim is a bus driver in Kansas City.
   He has no complaints about his job.

   Combined: _Jim is a bus driver in Kansas City who has no complaints about his job._

3. The arctic tern is a wide-ranging bird.
   It can fly as many as 22,000 miles during the round-trip of its annual migration.

   Combined: _The arctic tern is a wide-ranging bird that can fly as many as 22,000 miles during the round-trip of its annual migration._

4. J. K. Rowling is an author of children's books.
   She has become phenomenally popular in the past few years with her Harry Potter series.

   Combined: _J. K. Rowling is an author of children's books who has become phenomenally popular in the past few years with her Harry Potter series._

5. The tickling sensation turned out to be a cockroach.
   I felt it on the back of my neck.

   Combined: _The tickling sensation that I felt on the back of my neck turned out to be a cockroach._

6. Martin Luther King, Jr., was a highly influential civil rights leader.
   He won the Nobel Peace Prize in 1964.

   Combined: _Martin Luther King, Jr., was a highly influential civil rights leader who won the Nobel Peace Prize in 1964._

7. Write three of your own sentences that contain an essential adjective clause: (Hint: To avoid confusion, review the *non*essential clauses from Activity 18-3. Remember essential clauses do *not* need commas.)

A. *Answers will vary.* _____

_____

B. _____

_____

C. _____

_____

Adverb Clauses

Another form of complex sentence commonly used for sentence variety combines an **adverb clause** with a main clause. Adverb clauses, like single adverbs, answer the questions *when, where, why, how,* and *to what extent* something was done. Here is a brief list of words called **subordinating conjunctions**, which begin adverb clauses (for a more complete list, see p. 488):

after	**because**	since	when
although	before	though	where
as	if	until	while

A. **Because** Jeremy stayed out too late last night, he overslept his 8:00 class.

B. Jeremy overslept his 8:00 class **because** he stayed out too late last night.

We ask ourselves the question "Why did Jeremy miss his 8:00 class?" and answer it with the adverb clause, "because he stayed out too late last night." Adverb clauses, like adjective clauses, are subordinate or dependent on a main clause to complete their meaning. Standing alone, they are fragments, but combined with main clauses, they add variety to style.

Notice that adverb clauses, like single adverbs and adverb phrases, are flexible sentence parts, easily repositioned in a sentence to suit the writer's meaning and word flow. When adverb clauses begin a sentence, use a comma, but do *not* generally use a comma when they come after the main clause. (For more on adverb clauses, see p. 500.)

Activity 18-5: Combining Sentences with Adverb Clauses

Choosing from the list of subordinating conjunctions, above, combine the following sets of sentences by adding a subordinating conjunction to the *second* sentence in each pair. Write two versions, the first with the adverb clause beginning the sentence and the second with the clause ending the sentence. Be careful with the comma.

Example: I had never seen such a huge alpine lake.
I visited Lake Tahoe.

- *Before I visited Lake Tahoe,* I had never seen such a huge alpine lake.

- I had never seen such a huge alpine lake *before I visited Lake Tahoe.*

Teaching Idea
Having students memorize a single subordinating conjunction like *because* can help them remember the larger category of subordinators.

Subordinating conjunctions

A. Yes comma

B. No comma

Adverb clauses are easy to move around.

Teaching Idea
You might want to remind students of the potential fragment problem with adverb clauses and the unnecessary comma error.

Yes comma

No comma

Answers will vary.

1. I can now get to work on time.
   The city has finally synchronized its stoplights along major thoroughfares.

   Adverb clause beginning sentence: *Because the city has finally synchronized its stoplights along major thoroughfares, I can now get to work on time.*

   Adverb clause ending sentence: *I can now get to work on time because the city has finally synchronized its stoplights along major thoroughfares.*

2. The mudslides will soon begin.
   It does not stop raining in northern California.

   Adverb clause beginning sentence: *If it does not stop raining in northern California, the mudslides will soon begin.*

   Adverb clause ending sentence: *The mudslides will soon begin if it does not stop raining in northern California.*

3. The major cigarette companies settled lawsuits in excess of a billion dollars.
   They were dragged to court.

   Adverb clause beginning sentence: *When they were dragged to court, the major cigarette companies settled lawsuits in excess of a billion dollars.*

   Adverb clause ending sentence: *The major cigarette companies settled lawsuits in excess of a billion dollars when they were dragged to court.*

4. Sydney, Australia, prepares to receive the crowds.
   The world heads toward the 2000 Olympics.

   Adverb clause beginning sentence: *As the world heads toward the 2000 Olympics, Sydney, Australia, prepares to receive the crowds.*

   Adverb clause ending sentence: *Sydney, Australia, prepares to receive the crowds as the world heads toward the 2000 Olympics.*

5. Air pollution will become manageable.
   Automobile manufacturers finally eliminate gasoline-powered engines.

   Adverb clause beginning sentence: *When automobile manufacturers finally eliminate gasoline engines, air pollution will become manageable.*

   Adverb clause ending sentence: *Air pollution will become manageable when automobile manufacturers finally eliminate gasoline engines.*

6. We came across a website dedicated to Puff the Magic Dragon.
   We were surfing the Net.

   Adverb clause beginning sentence: *While we were surfing the Net, we came across a website dedicated to Puff the Magic Dragon.*

   Adverb clause ending sentence: *We came across a website dedicated to Puff the Magic Dragon while we were surfing the Net.*

7. Write three sentences of your own that contain an adverb clause. (Remember to use a comma only with *beginning* adverb clauses.)

A. _Answers will vary._ _____

_____

B. _____

_____

C. _____

_____

▶ WORKING WITH FUNCTIONAL SENTENCE TYPES

Teaching Idea
Remind students that questions can be quickly *overused.*

Aside from variety through grammatical sentence types, we can also use **functional sentence types:** *declarative* (makes a statement), *interrogative* (asks a question), *imperative* (makes a command), and *exclamatory* (expresses strong emotion). We use declarative sentences most often in writing, but occasionally mixing one or more of the other three can make our work more interesting.

Questions

The questions we ask readers come in two varieties: the **rhetorical question,** which is a disguised statement, and the question that we ask and then answer.

A rhetorical question looks like this: "Do we really want our ten-year-olds addicted to crack?" No sane person would respond with a yes. The question actually is this statement: "We do not want our ten-year-olds addicted to crack." Rhetorical questions help move readers to agree with us, and we use them especially in persuasive writing. Here is an excerpt from the Chapter 16 argument essay "Just Say No."

Rhetorical questions

> Schools practically beg parents to spend time with their children reading, learning math, and helping with other course work. How can this happen when TV has captured the audience? And schoolwork is not all that suffers. Don't we as parents want to involve our children in other learning activities like music, dance, and sports?

Both rhetorical questions evoke a predictable response in the reader. The question that we ask and then answer, on the other hand, does not call for agreement from the reader but promises further information. Here is an example from the Chapter 15 definition essay "Finding Home."

Question to ask and answer

> What makes the home happy? Is it the house decorated in warm, inviting colors, furnished with all the modern conveniences, or is it the people who live inside? I believe a home is not defined by the physical structure but by the people who live in it. Home is a place where a person feels safe, relaxed, and loved.

After posing questions, the author gives additional information. These kinds of questions are particularly useful in introducing paragraphs and developing ideas within them.

Commands and Exclamations

Questions create variety in a text by encouraging a more active response from a reader than merely processing the information in declarative sentences. *Command* and *exclamation sentences* work in much the same way. Even a mild command asks for

We might also use two adverbs to open a sentence:

- Swiftly and gracefully, Florence climbed the rope to the top of the tent.

While some writers omit the comma after single adverbs beginning sentences, most often the comma is used, and paired adverbs should always be set off with a comma.

Activity 18-7: Creating Variety in Sentence Beginnings with Adverbs

Rewrite the following sentences with the adverb or adverb pair at the beginning. Remember to use a comma.

Example: Sonya dragged herself <u>slowly</u> out of bed.
   <u>Slowly</u>, Sonya dragged herself out of bed.

1. Lillith whispered softly into her ex-husband's ear, "You can have the car, but I get the house."
   Softly, Lillith whispered into her ex-husband's ear, "You can have the car, but I get the house."

2. The wrecking ball effortlessly leveled the building.
   Effortlessly, the wrecking ball leveled the building.

3. The Border collie instantly leaped into the air and snared the Frisbee.
   Instantly, the Border collie leaped into the air and snared the Frisbee.

4. Juan's best friend shouted angrily at him and left the party.
   Angrily, Juan's best friend shouted at him and left the party.

5. Aunt Diana slowly and patiently explained to her five-year-old niece why the frog could not sleep under the pillow.
   Slowly and patiently, Aunt Diana explained to her five-year-old niece why the frog could not sleep under the pillow.

6. The winds from the storm last night blew violently and continuously until 4:00 A.M.
   Violently and continuously, the winds from the storm last night blew until 4:00 A.M.

7. Write three sentences of your own that begin with one or more adverbs.
   A. *Answers will vary.*

   B. _____

   C. _____

▶ PHRASES

The sentence parts that can help us most with variety in beginnings are **phrases,** a group of words working together but lacking a subject or a verb. There are six phrases in English, all of which can be placed in various positions within a sentence, including the beginning. We will work with the following phrases: **prepositional, participial** (*present/past*), **absolute** (*present/past*), **infinitive,** and **appositive.**

Prepositional Phrases

Prepositional phrases are the workhorses of our paragraphs—we can scarcely write a sentence without one—and are easy to spot once we know a few cue words. Every prepositional phrase begins with a preposition (often a word that tells location) and ends with a noun or pronoun. These phrases function as either adjectives or adverbs to describe other words in a sentence, and the adverb forms can be moved from one location to another. Here is a brief list of common prepositions (for more, see pp. 487–488):

above	behind	in	over
across	below	of	to
at	by	on	with

Single prepositional phrases often begin sentences:

- *Above* the door you will find the house key.

The preposition "above" connects the noun "door" to the sentence. Together the three words "above the door" tell where the key is located, so the prepositional phrase functions as an adverb. Notice that we could shift the phrase to the end of the sentence: "You will find the house key *above* the door."

When using two or more prepositional phrases to begin a sentence, set them off with a comma:

- *Above* the door *on* the north side *of* the house, you will find the house key.

Activity 18-8: Combining Sentences with Prepositional Phrases

Combine the following sets of sentences by crossing out the unneeded words at the *beginning* of the second and third sentences. Reposition the remaining prepositional phrases at the beginning of the first sentence. Remember to use a comma.

Example: You will find the reference section.

- ~~It is~~ on the first floor.
- ~~The floor is~~ of the library.

On the first floor of the library, you will find the reference section.

1. I witnessed a terrible four-car pileup.

- The accident was at the intersection.
- The intersection was of 85th and Metcalf.

At the intersection of 85th and Metcalf, I witnessed a terrible four-car pileup.

2. I watched the hotel under construction rise to completion seemingly overnight.

   • I watched through a hole.

   • The hole was in a wooden fence.

   Through a hole in a wooden fence, I watched the hotel under

   construction rise to completion seemingly overnight.

3. Jake set off to seek his fortune in the land of his dreams—California!

   • He set off with only twenty-five dollars.

   • The money was in his pocket.

   With only twenty-five dollars in his pocket, Jake set off to seek his

   fortune in the land of his dreams—California!

4. John Wayne holds a special place.

   • That place is in the hearts of fans.

   • They are fans of the mythic West.

   In the hearts of fans of the mythic West, John Wayne holds a special

   place.

5. Sycamore trees grow that date back to the Civil War.

   • The trees are in the old cemetery.

   • The old cemetery is on the east side of Troost.

   In the old cemetery on the east side of Troost, Sycamore trees grow

   that date back to the Civil War.

6. A single determined cricket kept Bruce awake far into the night.

   • The cricket was outside a bedroom window.

   • The window was on the north side of the house.

   Outside a bedroom window on the north side of the house, a single

   determined cricket kept Bruce awake far into the night.

7. Write three sentences of your own that begin with at least *two* prepositional phrases. Be sure to use a comma.

   A. *Answers will vary.*

   _____

   B. _____

   _____

   C. _____

   _____

Participial Phrase—Present Tense

Participial phrases consist of a participle—a verb form with an *-ing*, present tense, or *-ed, -en, -n* ending, past tense—and words that describe a noun or a pronoun. As single-word openers, participles can be effective:

Teaching Idea
Students are sometimes more comfortable saying *-ing words* rather than participles. As long as students don't confuse gerunds and the present progressive tense with participles, this *-ing* reference can be useful.

Teaching Idea
For more on misplaced modifiers, see Chapter 25.

Beware of misplaced and dangling modifiers.

- *Singing,* Andrew enjoyed the sound of his voice echoing in the shower.

    Who is singing? Andrew. The participle tells us about a noun. Or we might want to add an adverb to create a brief phrase:

- *Singing* happily, Andrew enjoyed the sound of his voice echoing in the shower.

    To give even more information, we could include a prepositional phrase:

- *Singing* happily and with great volume, Andrew enjoyed the sound of his voice echoing in the shower.

    Participial phrases can be used at the beginning, in the middle, or at the end of a sentence and usually come directly before or after the noun or pronoun they are describing. However, a participial phrase placed next to a word that it does not intend to describe is called a **misplaced modifier.** Confusing and sometimes amusing sentences can result, as in the following:

- Andrew enjoyed the sound of his voice echoing in the happily singing shower. While it is true that pipes can sometimes make a ringing sound, it is not likely that Andrew's voice would be coming from them.

Activity 18-9: Combining Sentences with Participial Phrases (Present Tense)

Combine the sets of sentences listed below by changing the first part of the *second* sentence into a participial phrase. Locate the verb in the second sentence, and then convert it into a present participle by adding *-ing.* Next, cross out any unneeded noun or pronoun, and attach the resulting participial phrase to the front of the first sentence. Use a comma.

Example: Lori daydreamed of the warm sands and tropical weather of Ft. Lauderdale. ~~She~~ smiled at the thought of Spring Break.
Smiling at the thought of Spring Break, Lori daydreamed of the warm sands and tropical weather of Ft. Lauderdale.

1. Angelina asked herself again if Katy was really right for her younger brother. Angelina worried about the upcoming wedding.
    Worrying about the upcoming wedding, Angelina asked herself again if Katy was really right for her younger brother.

2. Jeff decided it was better off in the long run to at least be friendly enemies. He held out his hand to a man he did not much like.
    Holding out his hand to a man he did not much like, Jeff decided it was better off in the long run to at least be friendly enemies.

3. Richard screamed "Aaggh!" when he grasped what felt like a handful of wriggling snakes. He reached blindfolded into the box.
    Reaching blindfolded into the box, Richard screamed "Aaggh!" when he grasped what felt like a handful of wriggling snakes.

4. Crosby, Stills, Nash, and Young surprised many people by not just being alive but still being fine musicians.
   They jammed hard for three straight hours.
   Jamming hard for three straight hours, Crosby, Stills, Nash, and Young surprised many people by not just being alive but still being fine musicians.

5. The boys threw down their icy snowballs and tore down the alley.
   They tried to escape from an angry driver with a dented door.
   Trying to escape from an angry driver with a dented door, the boys threw down their icy snowballs and tore down the alley.

6. Isabella bent the speed limit in several places.
   She hoped to catch the 8:00 ferry to Victoria.
   Hoping to catch the 8:00 ferry to Victoria, Isabella bent the speed limit in several places.

7. Write three of your own sentences that begin with a present participial phrase. Remember to use a comma.
   A. *Answers will vary.* _____
   _____
   B. _____
   _____
   C. _____
   _____

Participial Phrase—Past Tense

Just as with the present participle, the **past participle** can help with sentence beginnings. Past participles are formed with an *-ed* on the end of a regular verb (excite = excit*ed*, play = play*ed*, frighten = frighten*ed*). Single-word participles can be effective sentence openers:

- *Overjoyed,* Samantha made a beeline for the bank with her three-thousand-dollar tax refund.

Who is overjoyed? Samantha. The participle tells us about a noun. Or we might give even more information with two prepositional phrases:

- *Overjoyed* by the size of her check, Samantha made a beeline for the bank with her three-thousand-dollar tax refund.

As with the present participial phrase, be sure to set off the past participle with a comma, and avoid creating dangling or misplaced modifiers by keeping the participle next to the noun or pronoun that it modifies.

Activity 18-10: Combining Sentences with Participial Phrases (Past Tense)

Combine the sets of sentences listed below by changing the *second* sentence into a past participial phrase. Cross out the subject (noun or pronoun) and helping verb (*am, was, were*), and attach the resulting participial phrase to the front of the first sentence. Be sure to use a comma.

Example: I basked like a walrus on the cement at the pool's edge.
~~I was~~ <u>chilled</u> after a dip in the cool water.

<u>*Chilled after a dip in the cool water*, I basked like a walrus on the cement at the pool's edge.</u>

1. We went to bed without unpacking.
   We were exhausted after the long drive home.

   Exhausted after the long drive home, we went to bed without
   unpacking.

2. Mitch promised himself that he would actually buy textbooks next term.
   He was disappointed by his semester grades.

   Disappointed buy his semester grades, Mitch promised himself that he
   would actually buy textbooks next term.

3. Mark could barely sleep for a week.
   Mark was excited by the opportunity to intern at Channel 9 News.

   Excited by the opportunity to intern at Channel 9 News, Mark could
   barely sleep for a week.

4. One of the bank tellers actually tried to eat some paper money.
   The teller was locked in the vault for forty-eight hours.

   Locked in the vault for forty-eight hours, one of the bank tellers
   actually tried to eat some paper money.

5. Paula watched her planned vacation slowly begin to crumble.
   She was handed a subpoena in the airport just before her flight.

   Handed a subpoena in the airport just before her flight, Paula watched
   her planned vacation slowly begin to crumble.

6. Tens of thousands of people have donated money to help preserve their environment.
   The people are impressed by the Nature Conservancy's plan to protect land and wildlife by owning and leasing the land.

   Impressed by the Nature Conservancy's plan to protect land and wildlife by owning and leasing
   the land, tens of thousands of people have donated money to help preserve their environment.

7. Write three sentences of your own that begin with a past participial phrase. Remember to use a comma.

   A. *Answers will vary.* _____

   _____

   B. _____

   _____

   C. _____

   _____

Absolute Phrase

The **absolute phrase** is closely related to the participial phrase and consists of a noun or pronoun placed in front of a participle. In the following examples, the nouns are boxed and the endings of the participles are shaded:

- The 737 encountering severe turbulence, passengers without seatbelts fastened were tossed about like loose bales of hay.

- Its brown moss–covered fur blending with the surrounding foliage, a three-toed sloth is difficult to spot.

- Our expectations shattered, we left New York and headed back to Philadelphia.

- The tips of his skis pointed straight downhill, Eric started his run for the bottom of the mountain.

Absolute phrases modify the main clause they are attached to and are always set off with commas, whether they appear at the beginning, middle, or end of a sentence.

Any of the above absolute phrases would become stand-alone sentences by adding a helping verb like *is, are, was* or *were*. For example, "The 737 *was* encountering severe turbulence" or "The tips of his skis *are* pointed straight downhill." When we create absolute phrases, we deliberately leave the helping verb out to create variety in sentence structure, rather than stringing a series of simple sentences together.

Activity 18-11: Combining Sentences with Absolute Phrases (Past and Present Tense)

Combine the sets of sentences listed below by changing the *second* sentence into an absolute phrase. Cross out any unneeded helping verb (*am, are, was, were*), and attach the resulting absolute phrase to the front of the first sentence. Be sure to use a comma.

Example: The singer croaked out a few measures before she gave up.
Her throat ~~was~~ aching from laryngitis.

Her throat aching from laryngitis, the singer croaked out a few measures before she

gave up.

1. Enrique decided it was time to take it to the shop.
The car was stalling at every other intersection.
   The car stalling at every other intersection, Enrique decided it was

   time to take it to the shop.

2. Ellen greeted her friends at Union Station.
Her hand was waving frantically.
   Her hand waving frantically, Ellen greeted her friends at Union Station.

3. Frank let himself dream for a moment about world unity.
The flags from dozens of countries were rippling together in front of the UN building.
   The flags from dozens of countries rippling together in front of the UN

   building, Frank let himself dream for a moment about world unity.

Absolute phrases with present participles

Absolute phrases with past participles

How to identify and create absolute phrases

Teaching Idea
Students often have difficulty devising their own absolute phrases. You might want to show them on the board how to create a simple sentence with a helper verb and then delete the helper to form the phrase.

4. Skyscrapers collapsed weeks after the earthquake.
Their internal support was weakened.

Their internal support weakened, skyscrapers collapsed weeks after the earthquake.

5. Its contents were strewn about the room.
The suitcase was emptied in a hurry.

The suitcase emptied in a hurry, its contents were strewn about the room.

6. Florence wondered, "Since when does being nine month's pregnant make me communal property?"
Her stomach was constantly patted by people she hardly knew.

Her stomach constantly patted by people she hardly knew, Florence wondered, "Since when does being nine month's pregnant make me communal property?"

7. Write three sentences of your own that begin with an absolute phrase. Remember to use a comma.

A. *Answers will vary.*

_____

_____

B. _____

_____

C. _____

_____

Infinitive Phrase

Infinitive phrases, which appear in various positions within a sentence, also help with variety in sentence beginnings. Infinitives are easy to spot because they always attach the word *to* to the present tense of a verb (*to love, to laugh, to run*). Infinitives can function as nouns, adjectives, and adverbs, but we will concentrate on them as adverbs, telling *why, where, when, how,* and *to what degree or extent.* Here is a two-word infinitive opener:

- <u>*To think*</u>, Rachel needed quiet.

Why did Rachel need quiet? To think. The infinitive works as an adverb. Notice that we could also position the infinitive at the end of the sentence: Rachel needed quiet <u>*to think*</u>.

Or we can add an adverb:

- <u>*To think*</u> deeply, Rachel needed quiet.

To give even more information, we could include a prepositional phrase:

- <u>*To think*</u> deeply about her future, Rachel needed quiet.

Infinitive phrases used at the beginning of sentences, like participial phrases, sometimes do not clearly attach themselves to an intended word. Be careful not to construct sentences like the following:

Teaching Idea
You might reiterate how maneuverable adverbs can be.

Beware of
misplaced and
dangling modifiers.

- *To think* deeply about her future, the radio must be turned off, or Rachel will be distracted.

    While the radio can be good entertainment, it does not generally have much on its mind.

Activity 18-12: Introducing Sentences with Infinitive Phrases

Complete each of the following infinitive phrases by attaching a main clause of your own choosing. Be careful not to follow the infinitive immediately with a verb like *is* or *was*, which would turn the infinitive into a subject rather than a describing phrase. Be sure to use a comma.

Example: To approach the president in public,

Not this: To approach the president in public *is* a dream of mine.
But this: To approach the president in public, people must first clear themselves with the Secret Service.
Answers will vary.

1. To scale the last two thousand feet of the mountain,
   the climbers needed oxygen.

2. To make it to the store before it closes,
   Harry ran two red lights.

3. To enjoy the concert,
   I always arrive an hour early.

4. To beat the heat on a scorching summer day,
   people flock to the pool.

5. To bake the most delicious chocolate chip cookies,
   you need fresh ingredients.

6. To adjust to a new culture,
   many people begin reading about it before they visit the country.

7. Write three sentences of your own that begin with infinitive phrases. Be careful to create infinitives that describe rather than infinitives as subjects, and be sure to use a comma.
   A. *Answers will vary.*

   B.

   C.

Teaching Idea
Students sometimes confuse appositive with participial phrases, so you might reiterate the *-ing/-ed* ending for the participles and the synonym for the appositive.

Appositive Phrase

The **appositive phrase,** a word group that renames a noun or pronoun, also helps with sentence variety. *Nonessential* appositives are set off by a comma wherever they occur in a sentence: beginning, middle, or end. Here is a brief opening appositive:

- *A bodybuilder,* Arnold Schwarzenegger had greater ambitions.

What was Schwarzennegger? a bodybuilder. The appositive phrase tells about a noun. Notice that the phrase could also follow the subject: Arnold Schwarzenegger, *a bodybuilder,* had greater ambitions.

Or we could add several other descriptive words:

- A *former award-winning* bodybuilder, Arnold Schwarzenegger had greater ambitions.

For more information we could add a prepositional phrase:

- A former award-winning bodybuilder *of international fame,* Arnold Schwarzenegger had greater ambitions.

To stuff in about as much information as the opening of a sentence will bear, we could include an essential relative clause as well:

- A former award-winning bodybuilder of international fame *who won the Mr. Olympia title seven times,* Arnold Schwarzenegger had greater ambitions.

Appositive phrases may contain just a bit of information or brief comment or may hold as much information as a writer feels she can effectively place in them without interfering with the main thought.

Activity 18-13: Combining Sentences with Appositive Phrases

Combine the following sets of sentences by crossing out the unneeded subject and verb in the *second* sentence and attaching the remaining appositive phrase to the front of the first sentence. Remember to use a comma.

Example: Tae kwon do is practiced by many Americans who want to stay physically fit. ~~It is~~ a Korean martial art.

A Korean martial art, tae kwon do is practiced by many Americans who want to stay physically fit.

1. Rap is misunderstood by many "mainstream" Americans.
   It is a musical style that focuses on beat.

   A musical style that focuses on beat, rap is misunderstood by many "mainstream" Americans.

2. My grandmother is still overjoyed to welcome a new grandchild into the world.
   She is a woman who has given birth to fourteen of her own children.

   A woman who has given birth to fourteen of her own children, my grandmother is still overjoyed to welcome a new grandchild into the world.

3. The coach demanded maximum performance but earned maximum respect.
   He was a man who did not much like teenagers.

   A man who did not much like teenagers, the coach demanded maximum performance but earned maximum respect.

4. Frank's Toyota pickup is just beginning to look middle-aged.
   It is a vehicle with a hundred thousand miles on it.
   A vehicle with a hundred thousand miles on it, Frank's Toyota pickup is
   just beginning to look middle-aged.

5. The police officer did not look fit for action.
   She was a woman fifty pounds overweight.
   A woman fifty pounds overweight, the police officer did not look fit
   for action.

6. Professor Northam guides his students slowly to appreciate the beauty of words.
   He is a teacher with a deep knowledge of British literature.
   A teacher with a deep knowledge of British literature, Professor
   Northam guides his students slowly to appreciate the beauty of words.

7. Write three sentences of your own that begin with an appositive phrase. Be sure
   to use a comma.
   A. *Answers will vary.*

   B. _____

   C. _____

INVERTED SENTENCES

Teaching Idea
It is helpful to discuss inversion
as a way to create variety *and*
emphasis.

Another method for creating variety in sentence structure is to change the common order of sentence parts, a process called **inversion.**

The typical arrangement of words in English sentences is subject, verb, object as in "Mark hit the ball." However, sometimes we alter the pattern. When we ask questions—"Where is your brother?"—we reverse the subject and verb positions. And when we begin sentences with words like *there* and *here,* we push the subject farther into the sentence: "There are dark clouds overhead." "Here rests an old friend."

To vary sentence openers, we can shift a prepositional phrase or phrases to the front part of the sentence and then move the subject closer to or all the way to the end of the sentence. Shifting the subject closer to the end can help emphasize it. Compare the following sentences:

A. The terrified kitten fell from the third-story window of the apartment building.

B. From the third-story window of the apartment building fell the terrified kitten.

A. The welcoming sight of a campground was at the end of the road.

B. At the end of the road was the welcoming sight of a campground.

When we move the subjects to the ends of the B sentences, the reader's focus shifts to the "terrified kitten" and the "welcoming sight" of the campground.

Activity 18-14: Creating Sentence Variety through Inversion

In the following sentences underline the <u>subject</u> once and the <u>verb</u> twice. Next, invert the sentences, moving the prepositional phrases to the beginning and switching the positions of the subjects and verbs. Note that inverted sentences do *not* call for a comma to set off the introductory prepositional phrases.

Example: Two innocent <u>bystanders</u> <u><u>cowered</u></u> in the middle of the angry crowd.

In the middle of the angry crowd <u><u>cowered</u></u> two innocent <u>bystanders</u>.

1. A rattlesnake slithered into a hole in the ground.

   Into a hole in the ground <u><u>slithered</u></u> a <u>rattlesnake</u>.

2. A fundamental truth about human nature lies at the heart of this story.

   At the heart of this story <u><u>lies</u></u> a fundamental <u>truth</u> about human nature.

3. A fisherman nodded underneath a willow tree on the banks of the Mississippi River.

   Underneath a willow tree on the banks of the Mississippi River <u><u>nodded</u></u> a <u>fisherman</u>

4. A stroller with a baby in it rolled down Johnson Drive and through a busy intersection.

   Down Johnson Drive and through a busy intersection <u><u>rolled</u></u> a <u>stroller</u> with a baby in it..

5. Great white sharks often lurk in the deep, cold water of Monterey Bay.

   In the deep, cold water of Monterey Bay often <u><u>lurk</u></u> great white <u>sharks</u>.

6. New life patiently awaits within the cool earth under an icy blanket of snow.

   Within the cool earth under an icy blanket of snow patiently <u><u>awaits</u></u> new <u>life</u>.

7. Write three inverted sentences of your own. Follow the pattern of the previous six sentences, and begin with at least one prepositional phrase.

   A. *Answers will vary.*

   B. _____

   C. _____

CHAPTER SUMMARY

1. Variety in sentences depends primarily on length, types, and beginnings.

2. Sentences should be a mix of lengths: short, medium, and long. Three or four sentences in a row may be roughly the same length, but the next one should be shorter or longer.

3. Sentences can be compound with a subject and verb on both sides of a coordinating conjunction (*and, but, so, or, for, nor, yet*): I <u>like</u> 7-Up, and I <u>drink</u> a quart a day.

4. Sentences may contain several parts connected by *and*, such as a compound subject: <u>Jim</u> and <u>I</u> both like 7-Up. Or verb: I <u>like</u> 7-Up and <u>drink</u> a quart a day.

5. Sentences may subordinate ideas in many ways, including with adjective clauses, which are often introduced by *who, which,* or *that.* Essential (*that* and *who*): The baseball game <u>that we saw tonight</u> was boring. Nonessential (*which* and *who*): My mother, <u>who calls me every evening</u>, says she wants me to become more independent.

6. Sentences may subordinate information through adverb clauses: <u>*Because* I was late</u>, I missed the last ferry.

7. Sentences may begin with transitional words (*first, second, however, next*) and adverbs (*-ly* words: happi*ly*).

8. Question, command, and exclamation sentences can create sentence variety.

9. Phrases create sentence variety and can be especially useful in shaping beginnings.
   a. Prepositional phrase: <u>In the drawer</u> <u>next to the file cabinet</u>, you will find the hammer.
   b. Participial (present): <u>Slipping on the wet tile</u>, Maria wrenched her back.
   c. Participial (past): <u>Thrilled by his good fortune</u>, Dale carried the trophy home.
   d. Absolute (present): <u>The train leaving ahead of schedule</u>, Vito missed his ride.
   e. Absolute (past): <u>Their foundations weakened</u>, buildings collapsed in the earthquake.
   f. Infinitive: <u>To run a marathon</u>, Keith had to train for a year.
   g. Appositive: <u>Beautiful but aggressive birds</u>, blue jays swarmed my feeders last winter.

10. Inverting sentences can create variety and emphasis: In the deep, cold water of Monterey Bay often <u>lurk</u> <u>great white sharks</u>.

Use a comma

No comma

Use a comma

Use a comma

Collaborative

Activity 18-15: Revising for Sentence Variety

Review the chapter summary, and skim back through the methods for creating sentence variety. Now revise the following student narrative on a separate sheet of paper. Think in particular about restructuring the paragraph to vary sentences in length, type, and beginnings. You will need to add or drop an occasional word, but keep the organization and content largely intact.

Teaching Idea
If you don't have time to complete the whole paragraph, you might have students revise half of it.

Answers will vary.

The Clown Princess

My daughter Monique is four. She is the most comical child I know. Sometimes I have a bad day. She will find a way to make me laugh. I remember one day I was in the kitchen cooking. All of a sudden, I heard the television volume go up. The volume went up in the living room. Monique had put in her favorite noncartoon movie. The name of the movie is *Hope Floats.* My son was there.

His name is Marquise. Baby Mariah was there too. They were also watching the movie. Next, I heard Monique run to her room. I wondered what on earth she was doing. A few minutes later she made her dramatic entrance. She was decked out in high-heels and a purple boa. She also had on a purple skirt. She held a fuzzy purple fan. On her head was a bright fuchsia hat with a purple feather. But the articles that got the most attention were her Marilyn Monroe elbow-length white gloves. She also had a strand of fake pearls. Now was the time for her favorite song. The song was from the movie. Sandra Bullock sang to her sad daughter "I Just Want to Get Next to You." Monique sang the same song to Mariah and Marquise. "I can make a gray sky blue. I can make it rain whenever I want to. I can make a ship sail on dry land. I can make a castle out of a single grain of sand. But the reason I'm so sad and blue is because I can't get next to you." Monique fluttered her hands. She wiggled her fingers to show rain falling. She dipped her hands up and down to pantomime ocean waves. She pinched her fingers together. She pretended she was holding a grain of sand. She strummed an imaginary banjo during the rest of the song. She sang, "ohh-ohh, wooo." Her song was finished. With a bow, she ever so politely said, "Oh thank you very much." I watched smiling from the kitchen. Then she blew a kiss. She waved goodbye to her brother and sister. She made her exit to her room. Mariah and Marquise may still be too young to appreciate how much joy their older sister brings into the house. My little clown princess can always brighten our day with her silly, fun ways.

CHAPTER 19

Choosing the Most Effective Word

Building Style

Specific and Concrete
   Words
Concision
Levels of Formality
Tone
Figures of Speech

◗ WHAT ARE WE TRYING TO ACHIEVE AND WHY?

In the first picture above we see a young man dressed in blue jeans and a T-shirt, seated between casually dressed friends who are enjoying themselves. In the next illustration we see the young man wearing a suit, conferencing with colleagues in his law office. In both scenes he looks at home; no one would remark otherwise. However, were we suddenly to transport him from his backyard to the office or vice versa, he would suddenly seem out of place. Why? He would be the same man, in the company of people who know him well. The difference would be his clothing. He would appear out of place in the more formal setting of his office dressed for play and vice versa.

Our writing is not unlike the young man in variable attire. We can express the same thoughts in different ways, depending on the circumstances. When we choose different words and different ways of arranging them based on the subject, our feelings about it, and the audience's likely reaction to it, we are dealing with **writing style**. If our style is appropriate to the context, our work stands a better chance of being well received. This chapter offers some advice on how to select the most specific, concrete, concise, and artful expressions possible with which to communicate your ideas.

◗ SPECIFIC AND CONCRETE LANGUAGE

Choosing Specific Words

One of the most important elements of style is the choice of **general** or **specific** words. Language consists of words that are either relatively general or relatively specific, each with an appropriate place in our writing. The more general a word the larger the category that contains it, and, conversely, the more specific the word, the smaller the group that it belongs to. We have already seen this concept illustrated as a "Language Line" like the one below:

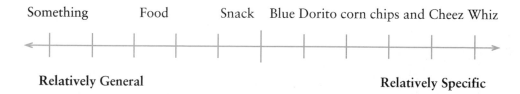

Something   Food   Snack   Blue Dorito corn chips and Cheez Whiz

Relatively General   Relatively Specific

If a friend asked you to go to the store to pick up "something," what would you come back with? How about if he said "food," would you need to know more? A snack? If your friend really has a preference, maybe he should specify the "large bag of blue Dorito corn chips and small can of Cheez Whiz." When we want to create a clear image, we choose the most specific words possible, particularly nouns and verbs. By narrowing the group to which the word belongs, we more clearly communicate our meaning.

In first drafts we often overrely on general language, perhaps in part because our own thoughts are not yet clear. However, when revising for word choice, we should search our vocabulary, sometimes supplementing with a dictionary or thesaurus, for the word that conveys the most precise meaning. Besides nouns like "food" from the example above, we often initially choose *verbs* that lack strength, as in the following sentences:

A. Jennifer made an attempt to say she was sorry.

B. Lilah is sleepy as she gets into the van.

C. Sam does hard work when he gets the hay up on the wagon.

These sentences are clear enough, but they lack punch, largely because of inexpressive verbs. Here is one way to revise them:

D. Jennifer stuttered, "I . . . I . . . I'm sorry."

E. Lilah's eyelids droop as she fumbles her way into the van.

F. Sam struggles with fifty-pound hay bales as he hoists them into the wagon.

When we revise, we can be especially alert to forms of the verbs *be, do, have, make,* and *get,* all of which can dissipate the energy in a sentence.

Along with using general nouns and verbs, we sometimes fall into the "very, really, extremely" habit. We say, "It's very hot out," "She's really smart," and "He is extremely mean." To be more specific, we might say, "scorching," "brilliant," or "brutal." Typically, four out of five of these empty intensifiers in a draft should simply be eliminated, and often they can be replaced with more precise words.

Other overly general words that say little are ***thing, nice, pretty, handsome, good looking, good, bad, interesting, fun, great, young, old, happy,*** and *sad.* Here is a sentence built from vague words:

- A very nice young man, who used to be happy but now is sad, no longer has much fun and has few interesting things to say.

We could try this version, replacing most of the general terms:

- John Kelley, a sophomore in high school, used to be optimistic and happy but was devastated when his parents were divorced. He no longer talks to even his closest friends about his feelings and has become a virtual recluse.

Collaborative

Activity 19-1: Revising for Specific Word Choice

Discuss the differences between relatively general and relatively specific terms. Next, revise the following sentences to improve their interest and clarity by choosing more specific words. Pay particular attention to the subjects and verbs, but be on the lookout for any other vague word, and either delete or replace the "very" words.

Example: The person's child very often got into her lap.

Revised: _Anita's three-year-old daughter often crawled up into her mother's lap._

Answers will vary.
1. Someone made contact with an object, and it went over some part of a fence somewhere out there.
   Jack smashed the baseball over the left-field fence.

2. A person moved very quietly toward an animal standing near some vegetation.

    Ethan crept up on a deer grazing near a clump of birch trees.

3. A man was occupying himself in a boat on a really small body of water.

    An old man was bait fishing from a rowboat on a pond.

4. At the place where the big machines do jobs, one that pushes earth around had a problem with the gas flow and quit running.

    At a construction site a bulldozer stalled from a clogged fuel line.

5. In a building full of interesting books and other great things, some young people made conversation in extremely quiet voices.

    Three teenagers were whispering in the library.

6. Some time ago the structure was damaged in a natural disaster.

    Last year the Pacific Grove water tower sprang a leak in an earthquake.

7. The person's job hanging in the balance, she got to work very fast and did the paperwork that was really very late.

    Sheila's job hanging in the balance, she raced to her law firm and finished the Dobson contract that was three days overdue.

8. Feeling the situation was hopeless, the nice person made an attempt to control himself, but had to sit down and let his emotions get out.

    Feeling hopeless, Brian tried to control himself but collapsed in a chair and sobbed.

Choosing Concrete Words

Teaching Idea
To give students additional practice with the concept of abstract versus concrete, see Chapter 5, Activity 5-2.

Just as we can choose specific words to clarify ideas and images, we can favor **concrete** over **abstract** terms. Abstractions are ideas, qualities, emotions, and processes—terms like *equality, friendship, happiness,* and *evolution,* general terms that we come to know through specific examples. When we think of *friendship,* for instance, most of us picture a scene, say, of a group of people talking and laughing, or an act of kindness performed. Without specific examples abstract terms remain remote.

To help illustrate abstract terms, we rely not only on specific words but also *concrete* ones. Concrete terms we come to know through our senses: sight, sound, touch, smell, and taste. We might hold a can of Sprite, feeling the coolness and slick aluminum sides. We see that the can is green, feel that it weighs about 12 ounces, and taste the sweet soda in it. Popping the top, we hear it; splashing the liquid into a glass, we see and hear the bubbles rising. Sprite is clearly a concrete term. So is a handshake, whereas friendship is not. Tears too are concrete but not the abstract term sorrow.

Abstractions are necessary for thinking and communicating because they establish large ideas quickly, often acting as the framework for the more specific and concrete examples we use to illustrate them.

Writing can be immediate and compelling when it relies on concrete and specific words to develop more abstract terms. Compare the two following paragraphs, the first with most of the abstract terms underlined. Which paragraph seems most vivid? Which one best communicates the concept of intense activity?

Teaching Idea
To help students understand how concrete words often develop abstractions, ask them to give some examples of a term like *democracy* in action (people voting, congressional debates, etc.). Ask what words in their example can be known through the senses (voting: punch cards and stylus, people standing in long lines, etc.).

A. When the ocean recedes, leaving the tide pool behind, a beautiful and deadly world is revealed. Sea creatures struggle for life and often find death. They battle with one another, challenging each other's power in their quest for existence and continuity. This community is alive with marine animals moving about their world, chasing and escaping one another, searching for mates, trying to evade each other's snares. Large and small, brilliantly colored and drab, slow moving and graceful, frantic and powerful—the tide pool is a study in intense and frenzied life.

B. But when the tide goes out, the little water world becomes quiet and lovely. The sea is very clear and the bottom becomes fantastic with hurrying, fighting, feeding, breeding animals. . . . Starfish squat over muscles, and limpets attach their million little suckers and then slowly lift with incredible power until the prey is broken from the rock. And then the starfish stomach comes out and envelops its food. Orange and speckled and fluted nudibranchs slide gracefully over the rocks, their skirts waving like the dresses of Spanish dancers. And black eels poke their heads out of crevices and wait for prey . . . . Hermit crabs like frantic children scamper on the bottom sand. . . . Here a crab tears a leg from his brother. The anemones expand like soft and brilliant flowers. . . .

Teaching Idea
To see the rest of the Steinbeck *Tidepool* excerpt, turn to Unit Six.

If you prefer paragraph B, then try to use the same strategies in your own work that John Steinbeck uses so well of illustrating through concrete and specific examples.

Collaborative

Activity 19-2: Revising for Concrete Words

With group members read through paragraph B, above, discuss the differences between concrete and abstract terms, and then underline all the concrete terms.

▶ WRITING CONCISELY

Another important concept in revising for style is **concision**—saying what we mean with no wasted words. In the rush of getting our first ideas onto paper, we often include everything that pops into our minds. Our drafts often resemble this:

A. *Let me tell you for a moment about what it means to communicate clearly to other people in words when you are going to a job interview where you hope to find work. Some kinds of advice are more worth listening to than others, and I have always thought the best sort of advice that one person can give to another is the kind of suggestions that get straight to the point.*

When we revise for concision, we can eliminate unnecessary repetition, imprecise words, and stalling phrases to get to the point:

B. *Communicating clearly will help you do well in a job interview.*

By shrinking the wordy passage from seventy-three words to eleven, the writing gains in economy and clarity. Now the writer can move ahead with his job interview advice. The point in trimming deadwood from sentences is not to cut *all* repetition—we often use repetition for emphasis—and not merely to write short sentences. We simply want to keep words out of the way that interfere with meaning. In revising for economy and clarity, we can reduce the following:

- Redundant expressions
- Padded phrases
- Excessive qualifiers and emphasizers
- Unnecessary detail
- Inflated clauses and phrases

Redundant Expressions

Some unnecessary words creep into our sentences as **redundant expressions,** words that say virtually the same thing several times as in the following example:

A. <u>Currently</u> today, as we gather <u>and come together</u> as a <u>group</u> of unemployed <u>people who are out of work</u>, although our numbers are few and <u>there are not many of us</u>, we can still push for decent jobs.

If we eliminate the redundant phrases, we are left with a more clear, concise sentence:

B. Today as we unemployed gather, although we are few, we can still push for decent jobs.

Here are several categories to watch for as you revise:

Redundant Pairs, Modifiers, and Categories

adequate enough	first and foremost	intentionally try	return again
circle around	free gift	link together	small in size
climb up	gather together	old antiques	square in shape
continue on	heavy in weight	past history	sum total
cooperate together	hopes and wishes	proceeded to go	terrible tragedy
each and every one	if and when	red in color	true facts
few in number	important essentials		

Activity 19-3: Revising to Eliminate Redundant Expressions

Using the chart above, revise the following sentences to eliminate redundancy. Be careful not to cut any important ideas.

Example: ~~In this day and age each and~~ every one ~~of us~~ today has the right to affordable health care ~~that is inexpensive enough that no one is left without it~~.

Revised: _Everyone today has the right to affordable health care._

Answers will vary.

1. If everyone in this country would cooperate together, we could overcome our past history of failure to meet the needs of our poor.

   If everyone in this country would cooperate, we could overcome our history

   of failure to meet the needs of our poor.

2. Although Horace is small in stature, he is aggressive, and he skates well enough and with sufficient skill to be on the team.

   Although Horace is small, he is aggressive, and he skates well enough to be on

   the team.

3. If we return again to the Lake of the Ozarks for the presentation on time-share condos, we are guaranteed to get a free gift this time.

   If we return to Lake of the Ozarks for the presentation on time-share

   condos, we are guaranteed a gift.

4. Scaling back the space program would be a terrible tragedy for humanity and all the people living on earth because space research continues to make critically essential discoveries that affect everyone's life on the planet.

   Scaling back the space program would be a tragedy for humanity because

   space research continues to make essential discoveries that affect everyone.

5. Heavy in weight but mostly full of liquid water, watermelons are best eaten when their pink color deepens to a red color.

   Heavy but mostly full of liquid, watermelons are best eaten when their pink

   deepens to red.

6. Everyone on the committee, meaning all the people who are discussing the issue, continues to circle around the first and foremost problem.

   Everyone on the committee, continues to circle the foremost problem.

7. Missing her children terribly, Margaret had fond hopes and wishes to gather them together again once more on Christmas Eve to celebrate as they once had.

   Missing her children terribly, Margaret hoped to gather them to celebrate

   Christmas Eve.

8. If the sum total of all the true facts of the awful tragedy were known, people would finally cooperate together to demand closer official government inspection of tainted meat.

   If all the facts of the tragedy were known, people would finally cooperate to

   demand closer government inspection of tainted meat.

Empty and Padded Phrases

Beyond mere repetition of words and redundant phrases, we often bog readers down with **empty** and **padded phrases**. *Empty words* and phrases are best simply deleted. The following list gives a few common words and phrases that can be dropped from a sentence most of the time without altering the meaning in any way:

Teaching Idea
You might want to reiterate that there are good reasons to use some of these terms on occasion.

Empty Words and Phrases

absolutely	certain	in kind	really
actually	character of	in terms of	situation of
area of	definitely	kind of	sort of
aspect of	element of	manner	thing
awfully	extremely	nature of	type of
basically	factor	quite	very

Padded phrases are stock expressions that use more words than needed to make their point, for example, *due to the fact that*, meaning *because*.

- <u>Due to the fact that</u> we are understaffed, no one goes home early.

- <u>Because</u> we are understaffed, no one goes home early.

The word "because" is a simple, concise replacement for the padded phrase. Below is a list of common padded phrases with more concise substitute words:

Padded Phrases	Concise Substitutes
at the present time, at this point in time, at the present moment, in this day and age	now, today
during that time, in the time when, in those days	then, when
at all times	always
despite (regardless of) the fact that	although
due to the fact that, the reason is because, for the reason that, considering the fact that	because
located close by	near
in the event that	if
by means of	by
form a consensus of opinion	agree
a large number of	many
few in number	few
aware of the fact that	know
refer back	refer
in the final analysis	finally
sufficient amount of	enough
make contact with	contact, meet
for the purpose of	for
in a situation in which, in the event that	when, if
is in a position to, has the opportunity to	can
it is important (crucial/critical) that	must
there is a chance that	may
during the time that	while
all of a sudden	suddenly

Activity 19-4: Revising to Reduce Empty and Padded Phrases

Revise the following sentences by crossing out the empty and wordy phrases and substituting more concise ones from the lists above.

Example: ~~Considering the fact that~~ summer is almost over, we will ~~actually very~~ soon be back in school ~~again~~.

Revised: *Because summer is almost over, we will soon be back in school.*

Answers will vary.

1. If the committee would form a consensus of opinion on this one issue, we could, in the final analysis, be out of this situation of constant debate and all go home.

   If the committee would agree on this issue, we could finally go home.

2. Some of the team members may not be aware of the fact that there is a chance the coach has an ulcer.

   Some of the team may not know that the coach may have an ulcer.

3. Located close by the intersection of I-435 and Nall is a jogging trail that a large number of people run on daily considering the fact that they need exercise.

   Near the intersection of I-435 and Nall is a jogging trail that many

   people run on daily.

4. It is absolutely essential that Sheila and Maureen make contact with their supervisor despite the fact that it is after working hours.

   Sheila and Maureen must contact their supervisor, although it is after

   working hours.

5. In a situation in which CO_2 and other greenhouse gases continue to rise, the earth will warm by several degrees, which is a sufficient enough increase in heat to cause catastrophic coastal flooding.

   If CO_2 and other greenhouse gases continue to rise, the earth will

   warm by several degrees, causing catastrophic coastal flooding.

6. At this point in time, currently, it is the consensus of opinion among many political commentators that Dick Cheney, a kind of low-key politician, will become George Bush's vice presidential running mate.

   Many political commentators agree that Dick Cheney, a low-key

   politician, will become George Bush's vice presidential running mate.

Excessive Qualifiers and Emphasizers

Teaching Idea
You can save the material on qualifiers and emphasizers for your work in the chapter on persuasive writing.

Even when we have thoughtfully revised redundant and empty expressions from our work, we can still have difficulties with **qualifiers** and **emphasizers**. Qualifying words, such as *often, usually,* and *frequently,* are important in writing, especially in persuasion, because they soften our tone and keep us from overstating our case. But qualifiers can be overused, cluttering a text and making a writer seem unsure of himself. Consider the following sentences:

A. *In my opinion, we should probably lower the drinking age to maybe eighteen or possibly nineteen because, for the most part, young adults are responsible enough to choose when, where, and how much they drink, most of the time, except for when they are not being responsible, which they are not, admittedly, some of the time.*

B. *We should lower the drinking age to eighteen because most young adults are responsible enough to choose when, where, and how much they drink.*

Sentence A clearly overqualifies, bogging the reader down, whereas B is direct and concise yet still qualifies sufficiently. Below is a list of common qualifiers. (For more on qualifying, see pp. 369–371.)

Common Qualifiers

almost	for the most part	maybe	often	seldom
apparently	frequently	might	perhaps	sometimes
can	in my opinion	more or less	possibly	try
could be	may	occasionally	seemingly	usually

Emphasizers, words such as *of course, clearly,* and *obviously,* are also important when we write because they help us direct our reader's attention to points we want to stress. However, as with overqualifying, we can unnecessarily clutter a text, and instead of sounding unsure, as we do with excessive qualifiers, we often sound arrogant. Consider the following sentences:

A. *As everyone knows, eighteen-year-olds are obviously considered adults in the eyes of the law, and as anyone can plainly see, the simple fact that eighteen-year-olds have to assume adult responsibilities means that, of course, they should be, inevitably, allowed to legally drink.*

B. *Because eighteen-year-olds are considered legal adults and have to assume adult responsibilities, they should be allowed to drink.*

Sentence A clearly overemphasizes, bogging the reader down and possibly irritating him, whereas B is direct and concise yet still makes its point. Below is a list of common emphasizers:

Common Emphasizers

all	crucial	invariably	unequivocally
always	definitely	never	undoubtedly
certainly	every time	obviously	unmistakably
clearly	everyone can see that	of course	unquestionably
critical	inevitably	plainly	vital

Collaborative

Activity 19-5: Removing Unneeded Qualifiers and Emphasizers

Discuss the following sentences and revise them by removing qualifiers and emphasizers wherever you feel that they might be over- or understating the writer's case. You may need to add an occasional word or restructure a sentence, but keep the main ideas intact.

Example: When enough time has passed, most Americans ~~inevitably~~ forget the broken campaign promises of politicians and, ~~unquestionably, as anyone can see,~~ will ~~certainly~~ reelect the greatest liars of the bunch.

Revised: _When enough time has passed, most Americans forget the broken campaign promises of politicians and will reelect the greatest liars of the bunch._

Answers will vary.

1. Although it seems to me that most people would like to feel safe in their homes, keeping fully loaded handguns on their bedside tables, for most people, might not be the very best possible solution to their safety concerns, in my opinion.

   Although people want to feel safe in their homes, keeping loaded handguns on their bedside table is not the best way to ensure their safety.

2. Imprisoning people for smoking marijuana might just possibly waste taxpayer's money, may be an injustice to some of those imprisoned, and could drain some of the resources for dealing with at least a few of the serious crimes.

   Imprisoning people for smoking marijuana wastes taxpayer's money, is an injustice to those imprisoned, and drains resources for dealing with serious crimes.

3. Most people who love one another might find it helpful in their relationship to try to communicate as often as they can stand to about issues that they are not likely to agree on, unless they don't think they can talk about a really tough issue, in which case it might be all right for them to skip it occasionally.

   People who love one another should communicate most clearly on the issues they are least likely to agree on.

4. It should be obvious to any clear thinker that state lotteries are legalized gambling and that supporting the system will inevitably lead to greater state involvement in gaming, with racetracks and, undoubtedly, riverboat gambling in the near future.

   State lotteries are legalized gambling, and supporting the system often leads to greater state involvement in gaming, such as racetracks and riverboat gambling.

5. I think that everyone will agree that parents should definitely be held responsible for their children's education, and the way to deal with this critical issue, obviously, is to withhold tax credits from all parents who allow their children to fail subjects in school.

   Parents should be held responsible for their children's education, and one way to do this is to withhold tax credits from parents who allow their children to fail subjects in school.

6. As anyone can plainly see, year-round schooling is a critical issue that certainly requires action, and it is vitally important that we give our undivided support to change the school system in this respect, or students' academic performance will inevitably continue to decline.

We should support year-round schooling to help students' academic

performance.

Unnecessary Examples, Details, and Explanations

Along with unnecessary repetition we sometimes create wordy writing by including more **examples**, **details**, and **explanations** than our subject warrants. Often this happens when we are swept along in the initial act of composing, and one sentence just seems to demand painstaking detailing and explanation by the next. Also, when we lose sight of our audience, what they already know about the subject or what they need to know, we can drown a reader in unneeded detail.

Consider the following paragraph response written to remind an *adult* of what to check before mailing a letter.

> Look closely at the front of the envelope, in the general area of the center, to see if you have remembered to write the proper and complete address where you want the letter to go. Remember to put the person's, company's, school's, or any other institution's name at the top of the outgoing address; and then on the very next line under the first line, put the street address with numbers first, that is, before the name of the street, road, boulevard, or drive. Then on the bottom line, under the middle line, write out the destination, beginning with the city and progressing through the state and possibly country if you are sending the letter out of the United States. Also be sure to write out all the numbers of the zip code (those numbers that help the post office route your mail properly). When you have accomplished this task, repeat it in more or less the same way as you check your return address, which should be in the upper left corner of the envelope you want to mail. Find a stamp that you have to lick or one that already has adhesive on the back, lick or in some other way, possibly using a sponge, dampen the stamp that needs to be wet in order for it to stick; and then affix it to the upper right-hand corner of the envelope. The final step is to seal the envelope, which you can do again by licking or using the same sponge, or you might have envelopes that already have adhesive on them if you are lucky. Now seal it, and you are finished with the job.

If this process paragraph seems a bit overlong, it is because the writer has lost sight of what his audience needs and wants to know. Here is a concise revision:

- Address the envelope properly, include your return address, stamp the envelope, and seal it.

The longer version might serve as a rough draft of an explanation to children who have never before addressed an envelope. However, even for this audience the writer would need to eliminate much of the digressive explaining and many of the examples. As we draft, we should be open to new ideas and feel comfortable including many specific examples; but, clearly, there is a time to check the flow.

Collaborative

Read through the following paragraph, and, on a separate sheet of paper, revise it to remove unneeded examples, details, and explanations. The purpose of the paragraph is to *briefly* explain how to light a charcoal fire to an adult. As you read, ask yourself "How much of this information would *I* need to start a charcoal fire?"

To successfully light a charcoal fire for grilling, there are four basic steps, but there is a lot to know about each one. First off, what kind of grill do you have? If it is a gas or electric grill, you have an easy task. Just turn it on. If, on the other hand, you have a small Weber or other type of grill that has to use the kind of fuel you can buy in almost any supermarket, meaning charcoal, then the process becomes more complicated. Do you want to buy matchless charcoal or the kind of charcoal that requires charcoal starting fluid and a match or some other lighting device? Of course, there are several brands of charcoal, but if you choose the kind that requires fluid and a match, then pay for the bag, take it to your car, drive home, and take the charcoal out onto your deck or patio or driveway or wherever you plan to do your grilling. After you get there, open the bag with a knife or a pair of scissors or maybe you can just pull that little string that hangs down, but I can never seem to get the darned thing to work right. Next, cover the bottom of the grill on the inside with some kind of fire-resistant material like aluminum foil and pour the briquettes (small pieces of charcoal that are sort of square and rough around the edges) out of the bag so that the charcoal covers the bottom of the grill. Now pour just enough fluid on the briquettes so that a film of the liquid covers most of the top at least (but don't obsess over covering every square centimeter!). Now you are ready to manipulate the charcoal so that it becomes a pile that has roughly the shape of a pyramid, meaning a pile about 6 inches high at the pointed top tapering down to a kind of round-shaped base. The final step is to stand back at least at arm's length and, using a match, lighter, or a piece of paper that you have rolled up and lit with a match or lighter, carefully light the edge of the pile of charcoal. Be sure to stand back immediately so that you won't run the risk of having the flames leap up and possibly scorch your hand or arm or even your face.

Answers will vary.

Inflated Clauses and Phrases

As we have seen in Chapter 18, phrases and clauses are easy to manipulate. We cannot only often move them from one place in a sentence to another but also expand or reduce them. When we revise for concision, we often reduce clauses to phrases and phrases to single words.

Reduce Phrases to Single-Word Modifiers

1. Hannah ran to answer the phone ~~in an~~ eager ~~way~~.
   Hannah <u>eagerly</u> ran to answer the phone.

2. The wolf could not blow down the house <u>built of bricks</u>.
   The wolf could not blow down the <u>brick house.</u>

3. Most people appreciate the beauty ~~of~~ a sunset.
   Most people appreciate a <u>sunset's beauty.</u>

Teaching Idea
These clause/phrase reductions can also serve as a quick reminder about essential versus nonessential word groups.

Reduce Clauses to Phrases

4. Ernest Hemingway, ~~who is~~ <u>a well-known writer</u>, was a big-game hunter.
   Ernest Hemingway, <u>a well-known writer</u>, was a big-game hunter.

5. The man ~~who is~~ <u>wearing a red vest</u> is my grandfather.
   The man <u>wearing a red vest</u> is my grandfather.

6. Elephants, ~~which are~~ <u>the largest land animals</u>, may weigh five tons.
   Elephants, <u>the largest land animals</u>, may weigh 5 tons.

7. The painting ~~that is~~ <u>hanging in the library</u> is from the nineteenth century.
   The painting <u>hanging in the library</u> is from the nineteenth century.

8. The wolf could not blow down the house ~~that was~~ <u>built of bricks</u>.
   The wolf could not blow down the house <u>built of bricks (or brickhouse)</u>.

9. Eleanor has a dance style ~~that is~~ <u>graceful</u>.
   Eleanor has a graceful dance style.
   (Eleanor dances gracefully.)

10. <u>While she waited in the lobby</u>, Paula occupied herself by counting roses on the wallpaper.
    <u>Waiting in the lobby</u>, Paula occupied herself by counting roses on the wallpaper.

Activity 19-7: Reducing Clauses and Phrases

Revise the following sentences by reducing the underlined clauses to phrases and phrases to single-word modifiers.

1. The journalist <u>who was interviewing Kevin Bacon</u> seemed interested in Bacon's childhood.
   The journalist ~~who was~~ interviewing Kevin Bacon seemed interested in Bacon's childhood.

2. Labor Day, <u>which is a well-deserved national holiday</u>, falls on the first Monday in September.
   Labor Day, ~~which is~~ a well-deserved national holiday, falls on the first Monday in September.

3. <u>Because the summer drought is deepening</u>, lawns are beginning to die.
   ~~Because~~ the summer drought ~~is~~ deepening, lawns are beginning to die.

4. After the storm the sun shone <u>in a bright fashion</u>.
   After the storm the sun shone brightly.

5. Madeline had always wanted <u>a couch covered in leather</u>.
   Madeline had always wanted a leather-covered couch (or leather couch).

6. Many people are attracted to the style and performance <u>of a sports car</u>.
   Many people are attracted to a sports car's style and performance.

7. <u>Of female swimmers who competed in international meets during the 1990s</u>, Jenny Thompson is the most decorated.
   Of female swimmers competing internationally during the 1990s, Jenny Thompson is the most decorated.

8. <u>After Lutz had visited Kenya</u>, he flew back home to Germany.
   After visiting Kenya, Lutz flew back home to Germany.

▶ CHOOSING LANGUAGE FOR TONE

Beyond eliminating nonessential words, we need to consider other elements of language that affect the **tone** of our work, that is, the *attitude* the writer reveals toward her subject and audience. Consider the following sentences and in what circumstances you would be likely to hear or say them:

A. Because Charley was busted by his butthead boss gettin' out the door, he was stuck on the line burnin' orders till 10:00.

B. Because Charley was caught by the shift manager as Charley was leaving the restaurant, he had to cook until 10:00.

C. Because Charles was discovered by his employer as Charles was departing the restaurant, he was required to prepare entrees until 10:00 P.M.

Teaching Idea
Try having different students read the three tone examples to produce a few smiles and make a point about manipulating tone.

If you decided that sentence A is the most informal and C the most formal, there are reasons for it. Sentence A uses several slang words (*busted, butthead, burnin' orders*), drops letters (*gettin'/burnin'*), uses the common word *boss*, and is unclear with the "he" pronoun reference. Sentence B substitutes mainstream American English diction like *caught* for *busted* and *cook* for *burnin' orders*. B also chooses the more specific words *shift manager* over *boss* and eliminates the pronoun reference error. Sentence C favors longer words: *discovered* for *caught, departing* for *leaving, required* for *had*, and *entrees* for *food*. Also *Charley* has become *Charles*.

Teaching Idea
Encourage students to see tone as an element they can control and one that truly depends on the rhetorical context of writer, reader, and occasion.

A writer chooses his tone on the basis of his topic and audience and how he feels about both. Many of us speak very informally when we are excited, in a hurry, and relaxing with friends. Our tone is generally personable, unpretentious, and spontaneous. Informal writing contains slang on occasion, colloquialisms, idiomatic expressions, contractions, personal pronouns, and shorter words than formal style.

The midrange of the formal/informal spectrum that sentence B represents is typical of the style that many college students use in their academic work. In general, as a writer moves farther along the spectrum toward a formal tone, informal elements decrease: contractions, informal idioms, and personal pronouns are minimized; slang is eliminated; sentences become more heavily subordinated; and words grow longer.

Sentence C illustrates the most formal style, used extensively in the academic community and in many professions, including law, science, medicine, and business.

The way we structure sentences and select vocabulary largely determines the style and tone of our writing. In the next few pages we will look closely at language to learn some suggestions for controlling tone.

~~Polysyllable~~ Big Words

Relatively formal writing uses more multisyllable words than does relatively informal writing. Sometimes the larger words are needed to express a complicated idea, sometimes not. Often writers simply fall into a habit of choosing a larger word when a smaller one will do, *terminate* instead of *end, numerous* instead of *many;* and carried to extremes, this habit can produce difficult reading. Consider the following sentence:

- A continuous regimen of nutritional intake of the electronic medium most revered by the great mass of Americans can effect a deleterious transformation in the organ responsible for a human being's cerebration, producing intellectual obesity.

If your response is "huh?" it is justified. Stringing multisyllable words together generally produces writing that is hard to understand. The above sentence is an extreme form of "thesaurus" writing—exotic word hunting—and it obscures rather than clarifies meaning.

Here is a revised version:

- A steady diet of television can make the brain flabby.

Your choice of words depends on the **writing context.** If you are writing for an audience highly knowledgeable in a certain field—doctors, mechanics, restaurant managers—you will frequently use specialized terms that they understand, though the terms might be unfamiliar to others. Not many people, for example, writing to the medical community would define terms like "otoscope" or "platelets." And sometimes we choose a longer word for variety (*additionally* in place of *also* or *and*). So there are good reasons to use some "big" words. However, as a general rule, favoring the more common, often smaller, word will make your writing more clear.

In the following passage how many words of more than one syllable did the author Joseph Ecclesine need to express himself?

- "Small words move with ease where big words stand still—or worse, bog down and get in the way of what you want to say. There is not much, in all truth, that small words will not say—and say quite well."

Collaborative

Activity 19-8: Revising Unneeded Big Words

Discuss the following sentences, and then revise them by "translating" the unneeded big words into more everyday language. Be sure to keep all the ideas intact.

Example: The Boy Scouts gathered their <u>paraphernalia</u> and prepared themselves for the coming <u>arduous adventure into the wilderness</u>.

Revised: _The Boy Scouts gathered their gear and prepared for their backpacking trip._

Answers will vary.

1. Shannon attempted to purchase an automobile yesterday but did not succeed.
   Shannon tried to <u>buy</u> a car yesterday but <u>failed</u>.

2. Those who obtain a proficiency with computers can anticipate increased marketability.
   Learning computer skills will make a person more <u>marketable</u>.

6. Jackie will be a freshman at JCCC this year.
   (first-year student)
   _____

   _____

7. If we had more manpower in this office, we could finish the job on time.
   (personnel)
   _____

   _____

8. Congressman Andrea Cambiano will now take questions from the newsmen.
   (representative/press)
   _____

   _____

Contractions

Teaching Idea
Students are often told never
to use contractions in writing,
but clearly there are legitimate
reasons for using them.
Perhaps this discussion will
help students strike a
reasonable balance.

Contractions are a small but contributing element to tone in writing. When we contract two words, of course, we join them using an apostrophe to mark the omitted letters (isn't = is not). Contractions are common in everyday speech and informal writing but are largely absent from more formal writing, particularly much of the academic writing in college. However, there is a good reason for not banishing the contraction altogether from your writer's toolkit. Some constructions sound awkward and stilted without combining two words, so we must accept the odd sound, revise the sentence, or use a contraction. Consider the following sentences:

A. Would not this sentence seem somewhat stilted if I did not use a contraction?

B. Will not you come with me to the ballgame?

C. Do not you feel like ice cream tonight?

Question sentences like these sound more natural using contractions. Compare "Won't you come with me to the ballgame?" to version B above.

Another valid reason for using contractions on occasion in even relatively formal writing is that they can add a welcome moment of informality in an otherwise serious paragraph. Like other markers of informal style, such as personal pronouns, dialogue, revealed thought, and plain words to name a few, contractions can contribute to a more relaxed tone.

With that said, do be cautious about overusing any stylistic device. In particular avoid these contractions: *could've, would've, should've, they'd, I'd, we'd,* and *when's.*

Activity 19-13: Revising Contractions

Assume that the following sentences have been written in college essays trying for a middle style, neither distant nor chummy. Examine the contractions, keep any that seem appropriate, and revise the rest.

1. They'd have made it to the summit if they could've.
   (They would have/could have)
   _____

   _____

2. When's the last time a president was impeached in this country?
   (when is)
   _____

3. What's the CIA think they could've accomplished through covert means that the Pentagon hasn't been able to achieve?

(What does/could have/has not)

_____

_____

4. I can't give you an answer if you haven't a proper question.

(can't or cannot/haven't)

_____

_____

5. Shouldn't the storm have passed by now?

(shouldn't)

_____

_____

6. Aren't you the one who said he wasn't interested in video games?

(aren't/wasn't or was not)

_____

_____

USING FIGURES OF SPEECH

Figures of speech are expressions that convey their meaning in a nonliteral way or that reinforce their meaning through the arrangement of words in a sentence. They can create comparisons, like metaphor, simile, and personification; play with meaning, like overstatement, understatement, and irony; and position words for effect, like emphatic repetition. Figures of speech are a natural, regular part of our language, contributing much to its strength, clarity, and color. When we use expressions like "Sam's a couch potato" and "Mall shopping is a breeze," we are using figures of speech that have become embedded in the language—so well liked and overused by people that the figures have become barely noticed clichés.

Because figures of speech are such a valuable resource for writers, helping with concision and audience rapport, we should try to gain more conscious control over them. As elements of style that draw attention to themselves, figures of speech should also be used with discretion: a little spice is welcome, a lot, is not.

Metaphor, Simile, and Personification

Metaphor and **simile** are perhaps the most useful and widespread word figures in writing, often, along with **personification**, slipping into our expressions unnoticed. Metaphor says that one thing is another, whereas simile uses *like* or *as*. A sports reporter writes, "Luis Figo is a $56 million man, soccer's most expensive diamond," a metaphor. If he had written "as expensive" or "like a diamond," we would have a simile. The literal meaning of the metaphor is that Luis Figo is a valuable and well-paid soccer player, but notice how the figure of speech adds interest to the writing. Here are several other metaphors and similes:

Metaphors

- Dunn's knee was done for, a hinge with the pin pulled, not much good to anyone.

- Her life had become an empty house, a chain on the front door, windows boarded shut, and a sign nailed to the front door saying: "Nobody home."

Teaching Idea
Encourage students to see figures of speech like metaphor and simile as "mainstream" expressions, not special literary devices reserved for poetry.

Teaching Idea
To help students see how figures of speech abound in everyday writing, have them bring in newspaper and magazine articles that include examples of metaphor, simile, and personification. The sports section of a newspaper is one good place to look.

Teaching Idea
Tell students that metaphors and similes often occur *after* they have written a literal expression that establishes a context, so they may find themselves consciously adding a figure of speech when polishing a draft.

Similes

- His illness crept upon him, barely noticed, draining his life like the fall stealing green from the trees.

- Jeb shouted downstairs to his son, "That damn noise sounds more like a chainsaw cuttin' galvanized tin than music!"

When creating figurative comparisons, avoid clashing images called **mixed metaphors,** for example:

A. Seeming to escape the web of her misfortune, at the last possible moment she slammed into the wall of her destiny.

The metaphor becomes more unified if we consistently use the spider web imagery:

B. Seeming to escape the web of her misfortune, at the last possible moment a strand of her destiny pulled her back down into the spider's lair.

Personification gives human attributes to animals and things, thereby creating a comparison and often establishing a mood. When we say that the sky looks angry or threatening, we are personifying, attributing emotions to the sky. Here are several other examples of personification:

Personification

A. Tired from the weight of years, the old barn leaned hard to one side.

B. The Concorde, heavy with fuel and feeling its age, seemed reluctant to leave the runway.

C. Having missed breakfast and lunch, I heard my stomach urging me to find food.

D. The golden arches seemed to smile at me, saying, "Come on in. The fries are hot."

When we work with figures of speech like metaphors, similes, and personification, we should watch for **clichés** and worn expressions. Clichés are metaphors and similes that have had the life sucked out of them by overuse, for example: "he stood still as a statue" or "her heart pounded like a drum."

Teaching Idea
You might point out that spotting clichés in our own writing can be difficult because we have grown so used to them. Another pair of eyes is often required.

Worn phrases are similar but do not always use a comparison, for example "live life to the fullest" or "a cut-and-dried solution." Because even old figures of speech have a vestige of power and because they have become so embedded in our casual speech, they occasionally sneak into our writing. However, since they are second-hand expressions, we should guard against them. Here is a brief list of some common clichés and worn expressions:

Clichés and Worn Expressions

sent chills down my spine	get the ball rolling	right on the money
seemed like an eternity	moved like lightning	handed on a silver platter
couch potato	out in left field	bundle of energy
roll with life's punches	hot as hell	cold as ice
sparkle (gleam, spark, glint) in his eye	like a chicken with its head cut off	butterflies in my stomach
is a tower of strength	like two peas in a pod	a perfect little angel
thin as a rail (stick)	security blanket	pounded like a drum
is a breeze	still as a statue	glued to
velcroed to	iron out the wrinkles	step in the right direction

the white glove test	window of opportunity	see the light
makes my blood boil	pushing the envelop	a pat on the back
fill her shoes	get a handle on	a slap on the hand
make the project fly	live life to the fullest	few and far between
no strings attached	take things one day (one step) at a time	life flash before her eyes
between a rock and a hard place	last but not least	winning isn't everything
through thick and thin	seemed like only yesterday	up bright and early
hated with a passion	go with the flow	brushed him off
break a sweat	set in stone	

Collaborative

Activity 19-14: Revising Clichés and Worn Expressions

Discuss the following sentences and then revise them to eliminate clichés and worn expressions. You may "translate" the cliché into literal language or try for a fresh metaphor or simile.

Example (cliché): As I waited to take my algebra final, I felt butterflies in my stomach.

Revised (simile): _As I waited to take my algebra final, I felt like a beginning skier about to plunge down her first black slope._

Revised (literal language): _As I waited to take my algebra final, I was nervous._

Answers will vary.

1. I wish Sam would have the guts for once to say no.
   (courage)

2. They should act quickly, for their days are numbered.
   (their time is limited)

3. While driving on the highway, you can lose your life in the blink of an eye.
   (instantly)

4. Their relationship was doomed from the start.
   (poorly matched) (not likely to succeed)

5. We need more jobs where money isn't everything.
   (is less important)

6. Everyone else was right on target, but Jason didn't have a clue.
   (did not know)

   _____

   _____

7. It's about time that somebody drew a line in the sand to say here but no farther.
   (somebody said no) (refused to cooperate)

   _____

   _____

8. The last thing I want to do is to end up another statistic.
   (dead)

   _____

   _____

Collaborative

Teaching Idea
As in Activity 19-15, writers can discover similes by ending a thought with like or as: "Connor's depression left him feeling like _____."

Activity 19-15: Creating Metaphors and Similes

Discuss with group members possible metaphors or similes for the following sentences, trying several comparisons before you choose one. Often it helps to imagine a scene that might contain an image you can work into the figure of speech. For instance, in the example below you might visualize a car with a wobbly wheel and then search for images that suggest a spinning object: pinwheel, Ferris wheel, carousel, Frisbee, blender blades—or the drum of a washing machine. Our minds often offer only clichés at first when we try for figurative comparisons, but with a little effort we can push past exhausted images. In number 7 create a metaphor or simile for any subject or situation that comes to mind, and explain how the figure of speech helps convey your meaning.

Example: The blown tire on Mayfield's car wobbled like *a washer with an uneven load*.

Meaning: *The wheels on a racing car move at high speeds, so does the drum inside a washing machine, and both are subject to stress. People can relate to a washer clonking around from an uneven load of clothes and see how the wheel might need the same immediate attention.*

Answers will vary.

1. My life today is like *an approaching thunderstorm.*

   _____

2. She fell down the stairs like *a sack of wheat, rolling heavily, her dress splitting at the seams.*

3. The car skidded like *a flat rock across a lake, spinning and then dropping out of sight.*

4. After pumping iron for six years, Mark had become a *swollen giant, muscles straining at his clothing like a child's super hero action toy.*

5. The grease burn felt like *someone had removed the skin with a scalpel.*

   _____

6. When people came in late for their shift, the boss became a *simmering stew* *pot ready to boil over if anyone dared turn up the heat.*

7. Your metaphor/simile *Answers will vary*

How it conveys your meaning: *number 6: People are often described as* *"heating up" when they become angry. The boss is angry but controlling* *himself—until a few more annoyances cause him, like the stew pot, to* *"boil over."*

Collaborative

Activity 19-16: Personifying

Discuss the options below for personifying, and then create sentences that include personified imagery, trying for original expressions. In number 7 explain how the personification of any one of the previous six phrases helps convey your meaning.

Example: a boring baseball game

Personification: *After the seventh inning the game just limped along till the misery* *was finally over.*

Meaning: *When there is little hitting and base running, baseball can slow to a crawl.* *A person with a limp moves slowly and is often in pain, just the way I feel when I'm stuck* *in a slow game.*

Answers will vary.

1. A mountain ridge covered with snow and ready to avalanche
   It was a threatening ridge, eager to send icy death rumbling down onto *the unwary.*

2. The entrance to a mortuary when you are attending the funeral of a loved one
   The doors were cold and distant, indifferent to the man within, whose *body had once contained the life of a husband and father.*

3. The sun setting over the ocean as seen from a comfortable perspective (dock, restaurant, cruise ship)
   It was a satisfied sun, fat and full of itself, content with the day *well done.*

4. A 1968 Volkswagen Beetle with the running boards rusted off
   The old Beetle was forlorn, a ragged survivor from happier days when *the streets were filled with her kind.*

5. A large building crane carrying a steel beam to a fifth floor
   He was a well-muscled crane with steel sinews, confidently carrying *any load the world wanted to bring his way.*

6. A litter of six-week-old beagle puppies playing with a knotted towel

   The puppies were like children on a playground, eager, happy, and

   inexhaustible.

7. How one of the above personifications conveys your meaning:

   The old VW could be characterized as a survivor and symbol of the

   '60s generation. Just as production of the Beetle stopped, so too did

   the "production" of the '60s flower children who so often drove them.

Overstatement, Understatement, and Irony

Other figures of speech that affect tone are overstatement, understatement, and irony. **Overstatement** is exaggeration for special effect, for example: "When they see this speeding ticket, my parents are going to murder me." We can hope that the parents will be a little less drastic. **Understatement** pretends to reduce the significance of a situation, thereby drawing even more attention to it. The comment in this paragraph "We can hope that the parents will be a *little less* drastic" is understatement—we hope that the parents will be a *lot* less drastic than murder. **Irony** is stating the opposite of what a person really means. For example, in the hall before your algebra final exam, you might remark to a friend, "This is going to be fun." You both know what you really mean. Irony can be useful in writing because it reflects on the author's persona, often revealing a sense of perspective and humor, and establishes shared knowledge, in effect saying to the reader: "I know that you understand my intended meaning." Here are more examples of each of these figures:

Overstatement

A. After his high school win, Terri felt like the best golfer on the planet.

B. To you it was just a summer shower; to me it was a typhoon!

Understatement

A. Robert DeNiro's character in the film *Backdraft* after he has been impaled on a wrought iron fence: "Hey . . . a, kid, I think I gotta little problem here."

B. Your comment to a friend's uncle who has just bought a Dodge Viper: "That must have set you back a little bit."

Irony

A. Dilated to 6 centimeters, dripping sweat, and twisting on the hospital bed, Alice gasped between contractions, "Tell me . . . again . . . about the joys of motherhood."

B. While Alice suffered through another round of contractions, her brother-in-law, in the waiting room, suffered his own agony—missing the playoff game between the Lakers and the Bulls.

Collaborative

Activity 19-17: Creating Overstatement, Understatement, and Irony

Discuss how you might revise the following sentences for overstatement, understatement, and irony. As you revise the sentences, expect that it will take some work to create figures of speech that are interesting. You may notice irony also working in understatement. Try to avoid worn phrases and clichés.

Example: I don't feel appreciated at work.

Overstatement: _If I died tomorrow and fell on the floor, people would just step around me till they got tired of the nuisance, and then they would toss me in the dumpster out back._

Answers will vary.

1. Registering for classes can seem complicated.

   Overstatement: _Registering for classes can't be done by mere humans._

2. Freddy Krueger, from the *Nightmare on Elm Street* movies, is a spooky character.

   Overstatement: _Freddy Krueger and his goalie mask make me never want to go to another hockey game._

3. Bill Gates is worth sixty-five billion dollars.

   Understatement: _Bill Gates has piled up a little spare change in his time._

4. Drunken driving kills thousands of people annually.

   Understatement: _Drunken driving has become something of a problem in this country._

5. A friend is doing poorly in college. He has not bothered to buy textbooks, seldom goes to class, and never studies for exams.

   Irony: _If you want to do well in school, you are going about it in the right way._

6. Elaine works hard, helps her friends, gives to charity, and is active in her community. She also is overly meticulous. Comment on this habit.

   Irony: _Now there is a serious character flaw for you._

Emphatic Repetition

Repetition can be a useful figure of speech that underscores meaning and helps guide a reader through our work. Of course, repetition can also be useless, boring a reader who wonders why the same word or phrase keeps repeating itself endlessly. Which of the following two paragraphs illustrates harmful and which, helpful repetition?

A. **Television** is a mixed blessing. In small doses **television** does not have to have the negative effects on our **kid's** health, behavior, and learning that **TV** often has in large amounts. In fact most of us enjoy watching **TV** ourselves and with our **kids;** and, let's face it, we often need a break from the **kids** that the **TV** can provide. But, as tiring as it can be, we need to keep fighting the **TV** battle with our **kids.** We need to monitor what the **kids** watch on **TV** and how much. **Kids** cannot see very far down the road. **Kids** want what **kids** want when **kids** want it, regardless of the consequences. It is part of our job as parents to protect our **kids** from too much **TV.**

B. **Television** is a mixed blessing. In small doses *it* does not have to have the negative effects on our *children's* health, behavior, and learning that *it* often has in large amounts. In fact most of us enjoy watching **TV** ourselves and with our family; and, let's face it, we often need a break from the **kids** that the *box* can provide. But, as tiring as it can be, <u>we need to</u> keep fighting the **TV** battle with our **kids.** <u>We need to</u> monitor what *they* watch and how much. *Children* cannot see very far down the road. *They* <u>want</u> what they <u>want</u> when they <u>want</u> it, regardless of the consequences. It is part of our job as parents to protect *them* from *themselves.*

Paragraph A bogs the reader down and bores through unneeded repetition. On the other hand, paragraph B uses synonyms and pronouns to minimize unneeded repetition, keeping only what is useful for coherence. The author also creates special emphasis with the words "we need to" and "want."

In your own work consider occasionally repeating a word or phrase that you want to specially emphasize. Concluding paragraphs are a good place to work toward emphatic repetition, with the repeat words at the beginnings of sentences and the clauses within them, as in paragraph B.

Teaching Idea
For more help with effective repetition, see Creating Coherence in Chapter 3.

Teaching Idea
For more practice to illustrate unnecessary repetition, have students compose a paragraph of four or five sentences and then deliberately revise it, overrepeating one or two words. Have them exchange versions and read each other's aloud in pairs or groups.

Activity 19-18: Revising for Emphatic Repetition

Read through the following brief narrative paragraph, and on a separate sheet of paper, revise it for effective repetition. Replace any word that you think is repeated unnecessarily, restructuring a sentence slightly if you think it is needed. Next, underline any *effectively* repeated phrase and explain how the repetition adds to the meaning of the paragraph.

Answers will vary; effective repetition: too tired

Martin dragged into the house at the end of another exhausting workday. Martin had slept little the night before, and Martin had been kept on the job two hours past his regular quitting time. Martin collapsed on the sofa. Staring down at his work boots, Martin thought about unlacing his boots; his feet hurt. But he was too tired to manage it. Martin was too tired to unlace his boots, too tired to think about dinner, and far too tired to cope with the stack of unpaid bills on his dining room table.

CHAPTER SUMMARY

1. Style in writing consists largely of word choices and arrangement.

2. Writers choose their words on the basis of their subject, their attitude toward it, and their sense for what the audience wants or needs to know.

3. General and abstract words are necessary for framing larger ideas, particularly in thesis and topic sentences, but specific and concrete terms are essential to develop the more general words.

4. Writing concisely requires eliminating words that serve little purpose in a sentence. Sentences, paragraphs, and essays may be concise *and* still long.

5. We can improve concision by controlling these elements:

   - Redundant expressions: *each and every one, true facts*

   - Padded phrases: *very, thing, in terms of*

   - Excessive qualifiers and emphasizers: *sometimes, maybe/certainly, obviously*

   - Unnecessary detail: postage stamp *that is rectangular and placed in the corner*

   - Inflated clauses and phrases: *in an eager way = eagerly*

6. Writers vary their tone on the basis of how they feel about their topic and how they regard their audience.

7. Multisyllable words can easily be overused. Generally, rely on the more common word: *numerous = many, terminate = end, edifice = house.*

8. Eliminate slang from relatively formal writing and use colloquial expressions judiciously: *bummed = depressed, psyched up = excited, kid = child.*

9. The connotation of words often affects tone: *child = innocence, happiness, freedom.*

10. Avoid biased language, including sexual bias, in writing: *all men = everyone.*

11. Contractions should be used sparingly in relatively formal writing.

12. Figures of speech can enrich writing, helping in concision, color, and emphasis.

   • Metaphor: *Her life was an empty house.*

   • Simile: *Her life was <u>like</u> an empty house.*

   • Personification: *the angry sky*

   • Overstatement: *My parents will murder me!*

   • Understatement: *AIDS is a disease that could use a bit of research.*

   • Irony: *"If you want to keep them safe, let the children have loaded guns."*

   • Emphatic repetition: *"<u>I stand</u> here in the name of law; <u>I stand</u> here in the name of justice; and <u>I stand</u> here in the name of human decency."*

13. Avoid clichés and worn expressions: *sent chills up my spine.*

Practicing Sentence Sense

CHAPTER 20

Working with Sentence Parts

Teaching Idea
Because this is a foundational
chapter, you might find it
helpful to begin working
students through it the first
week of class and continue in
small bits as the semester
progresses until you finish it.

WHAT ARE WE TRYING TO ACHIEVE AND WHY?

Most of *A Writer's Workshop* has focused on helping you discover, organize, develop, and revise ideas. However, once those ideas are in place, we must take the next step by expressing them in sentences that an audience readily understands. By learning the fundamental parts of sentences, we can begin to manipulate them more confidently; and as we see the relationship the parts have to one another, we will begin to punctuate more effectively as well.

PARTS OF SPEECH

All of the words we use in sentences fall into eight traditional categories on the basis of how they function:

1. **Verbs:** express an action or state of being: *run* or *is*.

2. **Nouns:** name a person, place, thing, concept, or quality: *Tom, Idaho, ant, freedom, pleasure.*

3. **Pronouns:** stand in place of a noun: *he, her, they, who, their, it.*

4. **Adjectives:** describe nouns and pronouns: *hard* chair.

5. **Adverbs:** describe verbs, adjective, and adverbs: running *quickly, very* angry, *too* busily.

6. **Prepositions:** shape nouns and pronouns into phrases: *on* the table, *near* her.

7. **Conjunctions:** connect words, phrases, and clauses: cats *and* dogs, *because* we left.

8. **Interjections:** emphasize emotions: *Oh! Ouch!*

Teaching Idea
AWW treats articles
as adjectives.

We seldom use all of these parts of speech in any one sentence, but we frequently use many of them in our commonest expressions, as in the following sentence:

```
  7       2      1      2    6  3     2         5        1    3      4        2
Because Timmy threw water on him, Tom immediately chased his younger brother
  6       4      2      7    6      2
through the house and into the street.
```

Once we have become familiar with examples from each category and realize how each one works, we will be able to tell where sentences begin and end and work more effectively with larger sentence units.

Verbs

Verbs, along with nouns, are the core of sentences. While nouns (and pronouns) perform or receive the action in a sentence, verbs express that action or state of being. Verbs come in several varieties:

1. **Action verbs:** show something happening, a physical, mental, or emotional action:

   • Zeus *hurled* a lightning bolt across the sky.

   • Aristotle *reflected* on the cause.

2. **Being verbs (linking):** tell about an existing state or make a statement:

   • Sheryl *is* an intelligent woman.

Forms of the verb *to be* are the most common variety (*am, are, is, was, were, been, being*). Others being verbs are *look, sound, taste, smell, appear, feel, seem, become, remain, get, grow:*

- Max *seemed* calm but was nervous.

- Hot chocolate with marshmallows *tastes* good in the winter.

3. **Helping verbs:** help a main verb express its meaning and so create verb units of several words called **verb phrases.** Here are some common helping verbs: *be, do, have, may, might, must, can, could, should, would.*

- Martin <u>*should have*</u> thought more carefully about his decision.

- Melanie <u>*might have*</u> finished the race, but she sprained her ankle.

Verbs have a base or infinitive form (*to run, to laugh, to love*), and several tenses that show action as occurring in the present, past, or future: John *laughs* today, *laughed* yesterday, and *will laugh* again tomorrow. (For more on verbs, see pp. 530–544.)

Nouns

Nouns, along with verbs, form the backbone of our sentences. They can be relatively specific and concrete (*snow*) or relatively general and abstract (*cold*) (for more on specific/general, concrete/abstract see pp. 451–454). Nouns create images and tell who or what is doing or receiving the action in a sentence. Here are five categories:

1. **Common nouns:** name a general person (*woman*), place (*city*), thing (*statue*), concept (*religion*), or quality (*width*).

2. **Proper nouns:** name a specific person (*Maria Gonzalez*), place (*Kansas City*), thing (*Statue of Liberty*), or concept (*Judaism*).

3. **Count nouns:** name objects that can be quantified or enumerated: *rocks, trees, Tinker Toys, cars.* They generally form their plurals by adding an *-s* or *-es.*

4. **Noncount nouns:** name objects that cannot be counted: *sunlight, music, coffee, air.* They have no plural form.

5. **Collective nouns:** name a group that is considered as a unit and so is grammatically singular: *team, family, gathering, band.* (For more on collective nouns and agreement, see p. 543.)

Nouns are frequently introduced by articles, the words *a, an,* and *the. A* and *an* refer to general nouns (*a* flock of sparrows) while *the* refers to a specific noun (*the* flock of sparrows that damaged my rice crop). We use the article *a* in front of nouns that begin with a consonant (*a* rock) and the article *an* in front of nouns that begin with a vowel (*an* egg). Occasionally we use nouns with lead consonants that sound like vowels or with vowels that sound like consonants. When this occurs, use the article that matches the **sound** of the first letter (*an* F in chemistry, *an* hour, *a* united workforce *a* used car).

Pronouns

Pronouns are words that take the place of nouns. They can and often do perform the action in a sentence as subjects (*She* ran up a horrendous credit card debt) or receive the action (Anna kicked *it* [the ball] downfield). Because pronouns have no identity on their own, they must refer back to a noun. Readers can easily be confused if a writer does not *always* make the link between a pronoun and noun clear. Pronouns fall into the following categories: (For more on pronouns, see pp. 545–555.)

1. Personal pronouns: *I, you, he, she, it, we, they, me, her, him, them*

2. Indefinite pronouns: *all, any, anybody, anything, both, each, everybody, everyone, everything, few, many, more, most, much, nobody, none, no one, one, several, some, somebody, someone, something*

Hint: Memorizing *who, which,* and *that* will help you identify relative clauses.

3. Relative pronouns: **who, which, that,** *(what, whatever, whichever, whoever whom, whomever, whose)*

4. Interrogative pronouns: *what, who, which, (whatever, whichever, whoever, whom, whomever, whose)*

5. Demonstrative pronouns: *this, that, these, those*

6. Reflexive and intensive pronouns: *myself, yourself, herself, himself, itself, oneself, ourselves, yourselves, themselves*

7. Reciprocal pronouns: *each other, one another*

8. Possessive pronouns: *my, mine, your, yours, her, hers, his, its, our, ours, their, theirs*

Adjectives

Adjectives are words that describe nouns or pronouns by answering the following questions: which one; how many; what kind, shape, color, texture; and so on. An adjective usually comes directly before the word it modifies and comes in degrees of intensity: *good, better, best; big, larger, largest; loud, louder, loudest.* (For more on adjectives, see pp. 556–557.)

- Jonathan was the *best* child in the room.
- The *huge* Great Dane drooled on my arm.

Adverbs

Adverbs are words that describe verbs, adjectives, or other adverbs by answering the questions *when, where, why, how,* and *to what degree or extent.* An adverb is a flexible modifier, appearing immediately before or after the word it describes and sometimes is separated from that word by an entire sentence:

- Antonio scaled the ladder *too quickly* for safety.
- *Too quickly* for safety, Antonio scaled the ladder.

Many adverbs are created by adding -*ly* to an adjective *(bold/boldly, happy/happily),* but many do not end in -*ly* *(then, sometimes, very, too).* (For more on adverbs, see pp. 557–560.)

Prepositions

Prepositions are words that link nouns and pronouns to sentences to form prepositional phrases. Often prepositions indicate location *(in, on, near)* but not always *(during, except, despite)* as the shaded column below indicates. Prepositional phrases function as adjectives (the skateboard *with* the broken wheel) and as adverbs (hiked *up* the mountain path).

Prepositions that show location

Prepositions that do *not* show location

above	beyond	onto	despite
against	by	opposite	during
ahead of	down	out of	except
along	from	outside	for
alongside	in	over	in addition to
among	in front of	past	instead of
around	inside	through	till

at	into	to	until
at the side (end)	near	toward	with
behind	next to	under	without
below	off	up	
beside	on	upon	
between			

Hint: Memorizing several prepositions will help you identify prepositional phrases.

Conjunctions

Conjunctions (like prepositions) connect sentence parts and come in two varieties: coordinating and subordinating. The seven **coordinating conjunctions** are used to show an equal relationship among single words, phrases, and clauses:

Hint: Use the acronym *FANBOYS* to help remember the coordinating conjunctions.

for	and	nor	but	or	yet	so

- Jesse *and* Frank James were outlaws.
- On the playing field *and* in the classroom, we will do our best.
- Florence works at IHOP, *but* Greg works at Dillard's.

Note: Use a comma before coordinating conjunction between two main clauses.

Correlative conjunctions also join sentence parts and work in pairs. Here are several common pairings: *both/and, either/or, neither/nor, not only/but also.*

- Neither eggs nor whole milk will clog arteries if consumed in moderation.

Conjunctive adverbs can link main clauses or comment on some part of a sentence:

- I'm going to the symphony; *however*, Allen is going to the Pearl Jam concert.
- I'm going to the symphony. Allen, however, is going to the Pearl Jam concert.

Note: semicolon is required before a conjunctive adverb between main clauses.

Here is a list of common conjunctive adverbs: *however, therefore, nevertheless, in fact,* and *consequently.*

Subordinating conjunctions connect subordinate (dependent) clauses to main (independent) clauses. These conjunctions signal an unequal relationship between the sentence parts. The dependent clause introduced by the conjunction may contain interesting and relevant information, but it is of less importance in the sentence and cannot stand alone. Dependent clauses "depend" on main clauses to complete their meaning.

Hint: Memorizing a conjunction like *because* will help you remember the larger group of conjunctions.

- <u>*Because* it is ninety-five degrees out</u>, I am heading for the pool.
- I am heading for the pool <u>*because* it is ninety-five degrees out</u>.

Here is a list of common subordinating conjunctions:

Note: Use a comma after a beginning subordinate clause but usually not when a subordinate clause follows the main clause.

after	as though	in order that	so that	whenever
although	**because**	now that	though	where
as	before	once	till	whereas
as if	even though	rather than	until	wherever
as long as	if	since	when	while

Interjections

Interjections are words used to express strong emotion. Mild interjections are set off with a comma (*Well*, I won't be going to the movie), and more emphatic interjections are punctuated with an exclamation point (*Oh, no*! Sophie forgot the tickets).

▶ WORD SHIFTS

Many of the parts of speech that you have just reviewed are fairly easy to spot, and memorizing some of the "cue" words listed will help you identify them. However, many words also shift their identity on the basis of how they function. For example, we can *light* a fire (verb), turn on a *light* (noun), feel a *light* breeze (adjective), or even walk *lightly* (adverb). In order to recognize a part of speech to help with structuring and punctuating sentences, the most reliable approach is to determine how the word *functions*: does it name, describe, show action or being, connect, or express emotion?

Activity 20-1: Using Parts of Speech

After reviewing the material on the parts of speech, fill in the blanks below with the type of word indicated in parentheses at the end of each sentence.

Example:

My whole family _____ to go to the Renaissance Festival. (action verb)

My whole family ___*loves*___ to go to the Renaissance Festival. (action verb)

Answers will vary.

1. Sharks ___*swim*___ in the deep, cold water of Monterrey Bay. (action verb)

2. During the storm a ___*branch*___ broke from the elm tree in our front yard. (noun)

3. The sound from the furnace would ___*mysteriously*___ disappear and then begin again. (adverb)

4. Hang gliding is a ___*dangerous*___ sport. (adjective)

5. Wild Bill Hickok was shot and killed ___*in*___ Deadwood ___*at*___ the age of thirty-nine. (prepositions)

6. Adolph Hitler was a dictator. ___*He*___ was responsible for the deaths of millions. (personal pronoun)

7. Honduras ___*and*___ Guatemala are both Central American countries. (coordinating conjunction)

8. Benjamin Franklin, ___*who*___ was one of the founding fathers, lived to be eighty-four. (relative pronoun)

9. ___*Although*___ football is popular in America, soccer has more followers worldwide. (subordinating conjunction)

10. Just before the performance Pavarotti ___*seemed*___ like he was not feeling well. (being verb)

▶ VERBS, SUBJECTS, AND SIMPLE SENTENCES

Teaching Idea
Being able to identify subjects
and verbs is critical for students
struggling to overcome
sentence boundary and internal
punctuation problems. Even
after you leave this chapter
behind, it helps to periodically
ask students in class to identify
the subjects and verbs in their
sentences.

Being familiar with the parts of speech should make sentences seem less mysterious and, perhaps, less intimidating. To form sentences, of course, we do not need all the parts of speech, or even most of them. In fact, we can create a one-word sentence— "Stop!" As long as we have both a **subject** (in this case, *you* is understood to be the subject), a **verb** *and* a **complete thought,** we have a sentence. Because we are already acquainted with nouns and pronouns, which are often subjects in sentences, and verbs, now we will see how they work together to form simple sentences (sentences with one main clause and perhaps accompanying phrases).

Simple sentences in English are usually ordered with the subject close to the beginning, followed by a verb, and then followed by a word that receives the action (direct object).

<pre>
      S   V   O
</pre>

- Eric cooked dinner.

We look for the verb first, in this case an action verb; and then, to find the subject, we ask who or what is performing the action. Who is cooking? Eric. When we ask what he cooked, we see that it is "dinner," the receiver of the action. Knowing this word order will give you a place to start when you are uncertain about the subject and verb in any group of words.

Recognizing Verbs

As we have seen under parts of speech, verbs can be action words (*to run*), state-of-being words (*is*), and helping words (*be, do, have*). They can be single words or made up of several.

To locate verbs, aside from asking which word in a sentence conveys action or state of being, we can ask which words have tense: present, past, or future. If we look at the sentence "Michael plays with his children," we can test the word *plays* by including these words: *today, yesterday,* and *tomorrow.*

To test for verbs, try
tense.

A. Today, Michael *plays* with his children.

B. Yesterday, Michael *played* with his children.

C. Tomorrow, Michael *will play* with his children.

Because *plays* changes form, it has tense and is therefore a verb.

Verbs can sometimes surprise us when we find more than one in a sentence. We frequently use **compound** or two-part verbs to create variety and concision (as we have seen in Chapter 18), but these divided verbs are sometimes difficult to spot:

No comma used with
compound verbs

- Margaret decided to skip her lunch *but* later regretted it.

When you compose sentences, be particularly alert to the coordinating conjunctions *and* and *but, w*hich may signal a compound verb or subject.

As we saw in the parts of speech, verbs often use helpers, words like *be, do, have, may, might, must, can, could, should, would.* These helping verbs form verb phrases such as <u>*might have been* singing</u> or <u>*will be* starting</u> that sometimes become divided in our sentences. Life gets even more complicated when we split our verb phrases and compound our verbs. When trying to determine sentence boundaries by finding your subjects and verbs, keep an eye out for sentences like the following:

A. I will soon be starting back to college and will probably enjoy all my classes.

B. Elaine may still arrive at the movie on time but will have run a dozen red lights in the process.

Note: Try to keep verb phrases intact unless the intervening word sounds most natural when placed within the verb parts. For example, "Brian has quickly forgotten every answer on the exam" sounds less stilted than "Brian quickly has forgotten every answer on the exam."

There are other word groups (called verbals) that are also easy to mistake for verbs because they look much like them. Notice that the italicized words in the following sentences are *not* verbs:

A. Jennifer has barely escaped *dieting* herself into a coma.

B. Victor comforted his *crying* baby.

C. We are often told *to fend* for ourselves.

Teaching Idea
You might want to mention the present progressive tense here to head off possible confusion with the participial phrase.

We will discuss these verbals later in the chapter in relation to phrases, but for now just remember that these kinds of words, often recognized by an *-ing* ending (*dieting*) or a *to* beginning (*to* fend), are *never* the verbs in a sentence.

Another potentially confusing sentence for sorting out subjects and verbs is the simple sentence that becomes more complicated with the addition of one or more clauses.

Subordinate clause | Main clause (simple sentence)
- Although Arthur did not jog in the marathon, he watched it on TV.

When we discuss sentence types later in this chapter, we will look again at locating subjects and verbs in multiple clauses. (For more on finding verbs, see pp. 539–544.)

Recognizing Subjects

Subjects in sentences are usually nouns or pronouns located in front of a verb and answering the question who or what is performing the action.

      S   V
- Glenda saved Dorothy from a sleeping spell.

Who saved Dorothy? Glenda. Glenda is the subject of the sentence.

Although subjects are frequently one word, they can be more than one word as in this two-part (compound) subject: (For more on compound subjects, see p. 540.)

A. *Dorothy* and the *lion* became friends.

Sometimes even more words fill the subject position:

B. *Dorothy*, the *lion*, the *scarecrow*, and the *tin man* became friends.

Sometimes subjects have describing phrases attached:

C. *Dorothy*, a young girl from Kansas, the *lion*, the *scarecrow*, and the *tin man* became friends.

We might also construct a sentence with one or more phrases functioning as the subject:

A. *To return* to Kansas was Dorothy's dream.

B. *Returning* to Kansas was Dorothy's dream.

Finally, we often write simple sentences with one or more clauses added (changing the sentence type):

Subordinate clause | Main clause (simple sentence)
- Although the *lion* tried to frighten Dorothy and her friends at first, *Dorothy* and the *lion* became friends.

In all of these instances where the added words might cause some initial confusion, rely on the who/what question: "Who or what is doing the action (or making a statement)?" The answer might be more than one word, but as long as those words are functioning as a unit, you have found the subject.

There are several other situations that can make locating subjects more difficult. In command sentences, for instance, we often omit the subject:

- Pass the salt, please.

In this sentence the subject is understood to be *you*, the person who is expected to perform the command or request.

When we begin sentences with the words *there* and *here* and ask questions, we place the subject after all or part of the verb:

A. There are four boys in the courtyard.

B. Here lies my best friend.

C. Will you come with me?

In this instance simply rearrange the sentence mentally, putting the subject back into its usual slot.

A. Four boys are there in the courtyard.

B. My best friend lies here.

C. You will come with me.

Finally, we can mistake as subjects the nouns and pronouns contained within prepositional phrases attached to the subject:

A. The bitter taste *of lemon peels* makes him want to spit.

B. One *of the girls* wants anchovies on her pizza.

In these sentences the nouns *peels* and *girls* cannot be subjects because they are contained within prepositional phrases. Since subjects *never* appear within prepositional phrases, one way of locating subjects is by mentally crossing out any prepositional phrases in the subject part of the sentence. (For more on finding subjects, see pp. 539–544.)

(For more on finding subjects, see pp. 539–544.)

Teaching Idea
Subject confusion in prepositional phrases is so common that you might want to write several more examples on the board. Students will find more help under Subject/Verb Agreement in Chapter 23.

Activity 20-2: Locating Verbs and Subjects

In the following sentences underline the subject or subjects once and the verb or verbs twice. Look for the word(s) that expresses action or being, and then ask the question who or what is performing the action or making the statement.

Examples:

A. Over the years Clint Eastwood has become a fine director.

B. Since he first appeared in the series *Rawhide,* Clint Eastwood has become a fine director.

1. The United States still welcomes people from all over the world.

2. There are three good reasons not to take this trip.

3. Protecting the watershed of the river will help protect the river itself.

4. One of the team's most outstanding players was awarded a scholarship to Michigan State.

5. To pilot commercial jets has always been Teresa's dream.

6. Gore/Lieberman and Bush/Cheney seem to be well-matched political teams.

7. Montana and Wyoming are fighting more than the typical fires of a dry summer and are hoping for a quick end to their troubles.

8. Why has Hollywood seemingly lost interest in making classic westerns?

9. Warren might have quickly started the car but, in his nervousness, dropped the keys.

10. Please open the blinds and raise the window.

11. Hanging by one hand from a seventh-story windowsill, the stunt double hoped that the airbag would break his fall.

12. Residents of Central America and South America sometimes wonder about and resent the habit of many United States' citizens of referring to themselves as Americans.

▶ PHRASES

Knowing which words function as subjects and which as verbs will help us distinguish between **clauses** and **phrases,** the two word groups from which sentences are constructed.

A *clause* consists of a subject and a verb, whereas a *phrase* may have either a subject or a verb form, but not both. Because phrases function as nouns, adjectives, or adverbs, knowing these parts of speech will help you identify and manipulate phrases. Being able to work with phrases will increase your sentence fluency and help you resolve punctuation difficulties.

The six phrases we will explore are the **prepositional, infinitive, participial, gerund, absolute,** and **appositive.**

Prepositional Phrases

A prepositional phrase begins with a preposition (*in, on, of, by*), ends with a noun or pronoun, and functions as an adjective or adverb. We identify the phrase just as we identified single adjectives and adverbs.

Adjective

A. The pickup truck *with* the cracked windshield is mine. (tells which one)

B. The girl *in* the blue silk blouse is my date. (tells who)

Adverb

A. Houdini escaped many times *from inside* a locked safe. (tells where)

B. Arthur talked *during* the whole movie. (tells when)

C. I struggled out of bed this morning *with* great difficulty. (tells how)

Teaching Idea

To reinforce comma usage—particularly for beginnings, middles, and ends—you can frequently point out how the rules apply to the phrases and clauses students are studying.

Teaching Idea

Students often feel like sentence grammar is incomprehensible because sentence parts seem to have "no logic," that they can be moved here and there at random. It helps to stress that adverbial modifiers are the most maneuverable ones and that they can be identified by their function, answering the questions *when, where, why, how,* and *to what extent.*

We use prepositional phrases frequently; in fact, it would be difficult to write even a medium-length sentence without one or more. The adverb form, like single adverbs, is often easy to move, allowing greater sentence variety as a writer locates the phrase for clarity and emphasis. Notice that we could reposition any of the three adverb prepositional phrases in the sentences above, as in sentence C:

A. *With* great difficulty I struggled out of bed this morning.

B. I struggled out of bed *with* great difficulty this morning.

If you begin a sentence with two or more prepositional phrases, be sure to use a comma.

Infinitive Phrases

Infinitive phrases, along with gerunds and participials, are known as **verbals,** meaning that they use a verb form that carries a sense of action but does not function as a verb.

Infinitives are marked by the word *to* in front of any base verb, for instance, *to run, to love, to climb.* To create a phrase, the infinitive includes several describing words: *to run* a marathon, *to love* one's country, *to climb* a ladder. Infinitives function as adjectives, adverbs, or nouns:

Adjective

A. Paula has a proposal *to present*. (describes the noun *proposal*)

Adverb

B. We practiced long hours *to win* the basketball game. (describes the verb *practiced*)

Noun

C. *To reach* the top was his driving ambition. (is the subject of the sentence)

As with the adverb prepositional phrase, the infinitive adverb form can often be moved from one part of a sentence to another to add flexibility to your expression. For example, we could recast sentence B like this: "*To win* the basketball game, we practiced long hours." Often the adverb infinitive phrase is a pairing down of the phrase *in order to*: "*In order to win* the basketball game. . . ." Be sure to use a comma with introductory adverb infinitive phrases.

Participial Phrases

Participial phrases begin with either a present or past participle (base verb form ending with *-ing* or *-d/ -ed/ -n*). They often include prepositional phrases and function as adjectives. As single-word modifiers they might look like this: *struggling* soldiers, *crashing* waves, *wrinkled* jacket, or *forgotten* memory. Here are several phrases within sentences:

Present Participial Phrase

A. *Skimming* close to the ground, the swallow caught a cricket in midhop.

B. Jamie bought fifty more lottery tickets, *praying* for a miracle.

C. The sales clerk *chewing* gum was the one who ignored me for ten minutes.

Past Participial Phrase

A. *Exhausted* from three final exams in one day, Marilyn fell asleep in her seat.

B. Devin vowed to play his hardest, *thrilled* to finally be on the team.

C. A bluegill *caught* on ultralight tackle can put up quite a battle.

Nonessential phrases, as in sentences A and B, require a comma.

Essential phrases, as in both C sentences, do not use a comma.

Participial phrases can be *essential* to the meaning of the word they are describing, as they are in sentences C above, or *nonessential,* as they are in sentences A and B.

When they are nonessential, we set them off with a comma, and we often have a great deal of freedom with their placement in a sentence. For example, we might recast the past participial phrase in sentence B in these ways:

A. *Thrilled* to finally be on the team, Devin vowed to play his hardest.

B. Devin, *thrilled* to finally be on the team, vowed to play his hardest.

When shifting nonessential participial phrases, be careful not to place them too close to another noun that they might appear to describe. For example, the present participial phrase in sentence A might seem to describe the cricket if recast this way:

• The swallow caught a cricket in midhop, *skimming* close to the ground.

Also be wary of dangling and misplaced phrases that clearly modify the wrong word, for example:

• *Skimming* close to the ground, the cricket was caught by a swallow in midhop.

Gerund Phrases

The gerund, the last of the three verbal phrases, is a verb form ending in *-ing* that is used as a noun, for example, *backpacking, swimming,* or *laughing.* Gerund phrases consist of an *-ing* verb form with whatever describing words accompany them, and these phrases may appear in several places in a sentence. Note the following examples:

No comma is used with gerunds.

A. Backpacking is a strenuous sport. (one-word subject)

B. *Backpacking* in the Bob Marshall Wilderness is an unforgettable experience. (phrase subject)

C. Ellen enjoys *laughing* at life's idiotic moments. (phrase as object)

While the gerund *-ing* looks like a participle, the gerund functions as a noun rather than an adjective. Notice that the gerunds in sentences A and B are subjects, and the gerund in C is an object. To compare the gerund with a participial phrase, note the following sentences:

• **Participial phrase***: Backpacking* in the Bob Marshall Wilderness, Pauline learned the meaning of rugged.

• **Gerund phrase:** *Backpacking* in the Bob Marshall Wilderness is an unforgettable experience.

Sentence 1 uses *backpacking* as an adjective that tells about Pauline, the subject of the main part of the sentence; therefore, the phrase is a participial. Sentence 2 uses *backpacking* as the subject, so it is a gerund. Whereas the participial phrase requires a comma, the gerund does not.

Absolute Phrases

The absolute phrase resembles a participial phrase in that it uses a present (*-ing*) or past participle (*-d,- ed, -n*), but it differs in an important respect: a noun or pronoun always precedes the participle. Absolute phrases are said to describe the rest of the sentence that they are attached to, rather than modifying any single word, so they can be positioned in several places within a sentence. Here are several examples:

Absolute Phrase—Present

Absolute phrases require a comma.

A. [The wind *blowing* steadily from the south,] we knew that the warm weather would last.

B. Coco said goodbye to her homeland forever, [her eyes *streaming* tears.]

Absolute Phrase—Past

C. Adam tried to appear at attention, [his <u>arm</u> *raised* in a stiff salute].

D. [The <u>thief</u> finally *locked* in a cell,] everyone felt more at ease.

You can easily create an absolute phrase by omitting the helping verb from a sentence. For instance, we could insert *is* or *was* in sentence A above and have a stand-alone sentence rather than an absolute phrase: "The <u>wind</u> is <u>blowing</u> steadily from the south."

Absolute phrases are often used with participial phrases to convey a sense of action as in the following example:

Absolute phrase   **Participial phrase**

- [Her <u>eyes</u> *streaming* tears,] desperately *clutching* the deck rail, Coco said goodbye to her homeland forever.

Absolutes, like nonessential participial phrases, must be set off with a comma.

Appositive Phrases

The last phrase we will discuss here is called an appositive, a word group that renames a noun or pronoun. Appositives usually follow the word they are describing, but as we saw in Chapter 18, appositives can be useful as sentence openers.

Most appositives are nonessential, giving useful additional information but not information critical to understand the meaning of the sentence. Therefore, as with all nonessential material, we use commas. Here are several examples:

A. The dolphin, *a mammal*, lives in family units called pods.

B. The dolphin, *a mammal* known as a cetacean, lives in family units called pods.

C. The dolphin, *a mammal* known as a cetacean that is still killed in large numbers by tuna fishers, lives in family units called pods.

In each case the underlined appositive tells the reader a bit more about dolphins. These phrases are a handy way to add ideas or comments without distracting the reader too much from the main flow of thought.

Activity 20-3: Identifying Phrases

Identify each of the underlined phrases below by writing the name over each. Do not be confused when you find several phrases within a word group. We name the overall structure on the basis of how the words function as a unit. For example, "<u>Slipping on the ice</u>, Ben fell" contains a participle, *slipping*, and a prepositional phrase, *on the ice*, but overall we would call the word group a participial phrase. Look for these phrases: prepositional, infinitive, participial, gerund, absolute, and appositive.

Infinitive phrase
Example: <u>To make it through her study session</u>, Jody drank two pots of coffee.

Participial phrase
1. <u>Perched on Jasmine's shoulder</u>, her cockatiel always felt secure.

Gerund   *Prepositional*
2. <u>Jumping out of a plane</u> is not Ethan's idea <u>of a relaxing weekend</u>.

Infinitive
3. <u>To find better jobs</u>, many adults long out of school are returning.

Participial phrase   *Prepositional*
4. The new Corvette, <u>redlining at 7,000 rpms</u>, smoked <u>down the interstate</u>.

Participial phrase
5. <u>Having climbed to the top of the tree</u>, the kitten could not climb back down.

> How to build an absolute

> Appositives usually require commas.

Appositive

6. Robert Downey, Jr., <u>a man with questionable judgment and bad luck</u>, is out of prison and looking for work.

Prepositional

7. <u>On a trip from Chicago to Denver</u>, Joanne was stranded in airports for thirty-six hours.

Appositive   *Infinitive*

8. Internet advertising, <u>mostly obnoxious junk mail</u>, continues <u>to flood into our homes</u>.

Gerund

9. <u>Having clear goals in life</u> helps people succeed.

Participial phrase   *Absolute*

10. <u>Stepping quietly into the room</u>, <u>his pipe glowing dimly</u>, Holmes surveyed the scene

Prepositional

<u>of the murder</u>.

Activity 20-4: Creating Phrases

After reviewing the information on phrases and working Activity 20-3, create phrases to complete the following sentences. Notice how commas are used to set off phrases at the beginning, in the middle, and at the end of the sentences.

Example: Lilly sat (prepositional phrases) _____ and waited.

Lilly sat ___*at the end of the pier*___ and waited.

Answers will vary.

1. In the morning Anna went (prepositional phrases) ___*out to the edge of the dock.*___

2. ___*Dancing until 3:00 a.m.*___ (participial phrase), Lauren and Roy had the best evening of their lives.

3. ___*His stomach rumbling loudly*___ (absolute phrase), Roger was so hungry that he nearly fainted.

4. ___*To reach their base camp*___ (infinitive phrase), the climbers had to struggle up the cliff face till nearly dusk.

5. ___*Jogging for thirty minutes*___ (gerund) is good aerobic exercise.

6. Michael Jackson, (appositive phrase) ___*a talented but strange human being*___, bought the rights to almost all of the Beatles' music.

7. ___*In the middle of the field*___ (prepositional phrases), the children found six baby bunnies in a nest.

8. Charleton Heston would like to legalize assault weapons, and perhaps any other weapon that can fire a projectile, (participial phrase) ___*proving his lunacy.*___

9. ___*To keep his credit rating*___ (infinitive phrase), Frank finally wrote a check to the gas company.

10. Whales communicate through body language and song, (absolute phrase) ___*their music echoing across miles of ocean.*___

Example:

Main clause

Children love to draw and paint from the earliest ages, and *Adverb clause* if adults continue to

Main clause

encourage them, children will often carry their artistic interests into adulthood.

____Compound-complex____

1. *Adverb* Although swimming is not the best sport for losing weight, *Main* it can be a great aerobic workout. ____Complex____

2. *Main* Carp are said by some to be delicious, but *Main* a person must know how to prepare the fish properly. ____Compound____

3. *Main* Large companies in the United States regularly profit from the misery of foreign labor. ____Simple____

4. *Main* Trial lawyers are experts at bending the truth to help their clients.
____Simple____

5. *Adverb* Because scooters are becoming popular again, *Main* skateboarders and roller bladers will have to make more room on the sidewalks and in the streets for them. ____Complex____

6. *Main* I used to think that *Noun* David was slow moving until *Adverb* I saw him jump up from his chair to shake a centipede off his bare arm. ____Complex____

7. *Main* Playing an instrument is a good way to learn music and bring joy into a person's life. ____Simple____

8. *Main* Fireflies, which are also *Adjective* called lightning bugs, produce their *Main* glow through a process known as bioluminescence. ____Complex____

9. *Adverb* When the weather permits, *Main* I love to grill just about anything out on my deck, but *Main* my favorite food is hamburgers. ____Compound-complex____

10. *Main* Jet planes cannot glide well, so if *Adverb* the engines malfunction, *Main* the plane is likely to crash. ____Compound-complex____

Collaborative

Activity 20-8: Using Phrases and Clauses to Improve Readability

Review the phrases, clauses, and sentence types summarized in the chart at the end of this chapter, and then discuss how you can improve the clarity and flow of sentences in the following brief narrative. Keeping the main ideas intact, on a separate piece of paper, revise the narrative by combining sentences and adding whatever connecting words might be needed (prepositions, such as *in, on, near;* conjunctions, such as *because, when, and, but;* and relative pronouns, such as *who, which, that* will be particularly useful). Also try using *-ing* phrases ("clos*ing* the car door"). Leave the dialogue alone, keep some of the short sentences for emphasis, and check your commas.

Example: Shaded excerpt from "America's Dumbest Criminal," which follows, rewritten like this:

Teaching Idea
To expedite Activity 20-8, be sure that students review the sentence grammar chart, and then you can list several "cue" words on the board—prepositions, conjunctions, and relative pronouns. After students have written part or all of a paragraph, you might have them read their version aloud while you note similar sentence-combining strategies on the board.

To help with punctuation, you can give students the comma editing sheet included in the Instructor's Manual.

- *My older brother Jason should be on a special show called America's Dumbest Criminals. One night in May of 1988, Jason and his best friend, Ken, found a new white Datsun with the keys left in the door in the neighbor's driveway. This was temptation they could not resist.*

Answers will vary.

America's Dumbest Criminal?

My older brother Jason should be on a special show called *America's Dumbest Criminals.* One night in May of 1988, Jason found a new white Datsun. His best friend, Ken, was with him too. The car was in the neighbor's driveway. The car had the keys left in the door. This was temptation they could not resist.

"Hey, look at this," Jason said. "What an idiot to forget your keys."

"Yeah, it's their own fault if we borrow their car," replied Ken.

Both boys jumped in the car. Jason sat on the garage door opener. The door raised.

"Oh, crap!" Jason yelled. They leapt out of the car. Then they ran back home.

They watched the neighbors' house. They didn't see anyone reacting. Jason and Ken thought they were safe to try again. This time they figured they would be smart. They would bring along gloves to mask fingerprints. They climbed back into the car. Once again Jason sat on the garage door opener.

"Dammit, man!" Ken said. They were hiding in some nearby bushes. Still no one was stirring in the house. They tried for the Datsun again. This was the third time. This time they succeeded. So, off they went on their "well-planned" expedition.

They reached the major roads. Ken began to get paranoid. "Man, we just passed a cop. We're gonna get caught!"

"Shut up, dude," ordered Jason. "We're cool. How are they gonna know? The people are still asleep, remember?"

"Uhh . . ." said Ken, "because we're driving around with white gloves on, and it looks a little odd, don't you think?"

"Well then, we'll just take them off," Jason replied.

"Yeah, but when they get the car back, our fingerprints will be all over it."

Jason and Ken idled at a stoplight for a minute. My brother came up with his next brilliant suggestion. They would buy some Armor-All. Then they would wipe off all their fingerprints. Then they would park the car a few blocks from the owner's house. Well, they managed to clean the car half way up. They congratulated themselves on getting away with it. They taped the car key to the hood. Then they walked home.

But Jason had forgotten his gloves. Jason panicked. They went back to the car for them. But someone had called the police. The boys were arrested. Their situation got worse. They had parked across a city line. So they were prosecuted by two cities.

Older brothers and sisters are supposed to set an example. This is one older and "wiser" brother I learned never to follow.

▶ A WRITER'S BASIC SENTENCE GRAMMAR

Having had the opportunity to read through and practice the basic sentence elements in this chapter, you now know what you need to know to control your sentences. Words (parts of speech) build phrases, phrases grow into or are attached to clauses, clauses are sentences or are attached to them. With this knowledge of how words function—primarily to express action or state of being, name, describe, or connect words—you will be able to manipulate phrases and clauses confidently, knowing where to put the commas and how to shift the sentence parts to best express your meaning.

The following chart summarizes key sentence parts:

◼ A WRITER'S BASIC SENTENCE GRAMMAR

Words (8 Kinds)

noun, pronoun, verb, adverb, adjective, preposition, conjunction, interjection

Phrases (6 Kinds)

participial, gerund, absolute, infinitive, prepositional, appositive

1. <u>Participial</u>: phrase beginning with "ing" or "ed" word—used as an adjective
   Example: *Running fast,* Erik made it to class on time.

2. <u>Gerund</u>: phrase beginning with an "ing" word—used as a noun
   Example: *Running fast* always wore Erik out.

3. <u>Absolute</u>: phrase made of noun + "ing" or "ed" word—describes whole sentence
   Example: Erik raced toward class, *the door closing just in front of him.*

4. <u>Infinitive</u>: phrase made of "to" + verb—used as a noun, adjective, or adverb
   Example: *To arrive at class on time,* Erik finally set his alarm.

5. <u>Prepositional</u>: phrase beginning with a preposition and linking nouns and pronouns to sentences—used as adjective or adverb
   Example: *Down the hall and through the door,* Erik ran to class.

6. <u>Appositive</u>: phrase that renames a noun or pronoun—used as an adjective
   Example: Erik, *a chronic oversleeper,* raced down the hall as the bell rang.

Words that begin **prepositional phrases**: *to, of, on, near, under, around, beside, against, at, by, in,* etc.

Clauses (2 Kinds)

main and subordinate (3 kinds): noun, adjective, and adverb

1. <u>Main</u>: clause with subject, verb, and complete thought—stands by itself
   Example: Fran likes cheese pizza.

2. <u>Subordinate</u>: clause without a complete thought—stands with a main clause

   - <u>Noun</u>: clause used as subject, object, or complement
     Example: *That Fran likes cheese pizza* is obvious to everyone.

   - <u>Adjective</u>: clause that follows and describes a noun or pronoun
     Example: Fran, *who is a close friend of mine,* likes cheese pizza.

   - <u>Adverb</u>: clause that describes verbs, adjectives, and adverbs
     Example: *When she goes to Italian Delight,* Fran likes to eat cheese pizza.

Words that begin **adjective clauses**: *who, which, that*

Words that begin **adverb clauses**: *because, as, if, although, since, when, while, after, before, until,* etc.

Sentences (4 Kinds)

simple, compound, complex, compound–complex

1. <u>Simple</u>: Aaron likes ice cream.

2. <u>Compound</u>: Aaron likes ice cream, *so he eats a lot of it.*

3. <u>Complex</u>: Aaron likes ice cream *because it tastes sweet.*

4. <u>Compound–complex</u>: Aaron likes ice cream because it tastes sweet, so he eats a lot of it.

Words that divide **main clauses**: *and, but, so, or, yet, nor, for*

The type and number of clauses identify a grammatical sentence.

CHAPTER 21

Coordination, Subordination, and Parallelism

WHAT ARE WE TRYING TO ACHIEVE AND WHY?

Chapter 20 helped us to understand the parts of a sentence, what they are and how they function. This chapter takes us one step further, helping us understand the vital role **coordination, subordination,** and **parallelism** play in establishing the importance of our ideas within a sentence.

Not everything we wish to tell a reader has equal weight, so we need to signal our audience when we expect them to pay special attention to some point. **Coordination** gives roughly *equal weight* to ideas, **subordination** *stresses one idea* while deemphasizing another, and **parallelism** uses *similar structures* to achieve clarity and emphasis. In Chapter 21 we will discuss reasons and means for using each of these devices.

COORDINATION

Using Coordination

Coordination in writing is a balancing method that primarily relies on *coordinating conjunctions* to link roughly equivalent sentence parts: words, phrases, and clauses. When we say, "I'm going to the store to pick up some bread *and* milk," we are coordinating the two words *bread* and *milk* by using the word *and*. The two items are equally important. We might also use the conjunction *or* to link two single words: "I'm going to the store to pick up Coke *or* Sprite, whichever is on the shelf." Again the linked words, *Coke* and *Sprite*, have the same value.

We regularly coordinate phrases as well as single words as in the following sentences: "I'm in the mood to crank up the stereo *and* to rock till dawn." The infinitive phrases beginning with *to crank* and *to rock* are joined by the word *and*. Or we might say, "I am going to vote in the morning *or* in the evening." In this sentence *or* links two prepositional phrases.

But few of us have problems in writing with the linking of a word or phrase here and there; however, clauses can present more difficulties. In Chapter 20 we discussed the coordinating conjunctions *and, but, or, so, yet, for,* and *nor,* practicing their use with compound subjects and verbs and with compound sentences. When we coordinate sentences with two or more main clauses—unless the clauses are only several words long—we should use a comma before the coordinating conjunction as in the following examples:

A. Hitchhiking used to be looked on as an adventure, *but* it was always a risky business.

B. Many of the Marlboro men have given up smoking, *or* they have died from it.

C. The Concorde supersonic jets are proving too expensive to maintain, *so* they may soon be phased out.

It is important to choose the correct conjunction to express the relationship you want to establish between the main clauses. While *yet* and *but* are often interchangeable (as in sentence A), there are clearly wrong choices. For example, sentence A would not communicate well if we tried to use *and, or, so, for,* or *nor* in place of *but* as a coordinating conjunction.

Sometimes, instead of using a coordinating conjunction, we can express a coordinate relationship between two closely related main clauses with a *semicolon*:

• He quit his job; he was not fired.

Another option we have is to use the semicolon with a word called a **conjunctive adverb,** such as *however, therefore, nevertheless, in fact,* and *consequently.* Conjunctive adverbs add emphasis or a small bit of explanation, as in the following sentence:

• He was not fired; *in fact,* he quit his job. (Note semicolon before and comma after *in fact*).

Teaching Idea
You might want to discuss coordination and subordination in terms of general intellectual development. Children begin speaking and progress into writing, relying heavily on coordination. As they mature and their communication becomes more sophisticated, they begin to subordinate more. Of course excess in either coordination or subordination can make for difficult reading.

Note: Usually use a comma before the coordinating conjunction in a compound sentence.

Activity 21-1: Coordinating Sentences

After reading the preceding information, select the most appropriate coordinating conjunction for the following sentences, and write it in the space provided.

Example: My sister adopted a Korean baby, _____*and*_____ both of them have been happy ever since.

1. Living life as a single person has many rewards, _____*but/yet*_____ it can be terribly lonely.

2. Michael Johnson strained a hamstring, _____*so*_____ he will not run the 200-meter in the Sydney Olympics.

3. Danny does not regret his decision to leave town, _____*nor*_____ does Elaine regret her decision asking him to.

4. Skin cancer is frightening, _____*for*_____ once the disease penetrates the lymph nodes, it is difficult to cure.

5. Does Coca-Cola add caffeine to its soft drinks to improve the flavor, _____*or*_____ does the company add caffeine to help "hook" consumers on the drug?

6. There are many die-hard Mac users out there, _____*but/yet*_____ PCs are still more flexible.

7. "Latisha, you have a choice: either you can brush your teeth regularly, _____*or*_____ you can expect to have the dentist drill out the cavities."

8. Florence likes to talk and talk and talk about herself, _____*so*_____ she is not in great demand.

9. Credit card companies shower students with credit cards like so much confetti, _____*and*_____ then the companies wait patiently for the 20 percent interest charges that so often will be coming their way.

10. SUVs have become the stationwagon of the new century, _____*and*_____ upwardly mobile types are crowding the freeways with them.

Excessive Coordination

While coordination is a vital device for balancing meaning in sentences, like any other writing strategy, it can be overworked. What is your reaction to the following paragraph constructed entirely of compound sentences?

A. Comedians are important in a culture, *and* they help people release their frustrations with one another. Comics can be mean spirited, *and* they can truly injure the people they are lampooning. Often comedians express the irritation of millions of people, *and* these people have often been disappointed by some segment of society, *and* an example of a group who regularly disappoints others is politicians. Billy Crystal *or* Jay Leno parodies Bill Clinton *or* George W. Bush, *and* there is usually some truth behind the barbs, *and* recognizing this truth makes us laugh.

If the above paragraph seems a bit tedious, you can immediately see that the *and/and/and* sentence pattern makes the paragraph monotonous. If we keep some of the compounding and add more *subordination,* we can clarify meaning and increase the overall readability like this:

> B. Comedians are important in a culture *because* they help people release their frustrations with one another. *Even though* comics can be mean spirited, truly injuring people they are lampooning, often comedians express the irritation of millions of people *who* have been disappointed by some segment of society, for instance, politicians. *When* Billy Crystal or Jay Leno parodies Bill Clinton or George W. Bush, there is usually some truth behind the barbs, and recognizing this truth makes us laugh.

SUBORDINATION

Coordination helps us to achieve clarity and sentence variety, but as we can see from paragraph A above, coordination alone is not enough to create readable writing. When we add **subordination** to our work, however, we help the reader discriminate among our ideas, to see which points to pay most attention to.

We can use single words as subordinate expressions, such as, "Fortunately, Jim made the team," and we might use subordinate phrases as in the following sentences:

A. With the right front fender missing and the windshield cracked, the old Chevy had seen better days.

B. At the bottom of my purse in the zipper pouch, you will find my lipstick.

C. Alfredo Calderella, a magnificent baritone, is vice president of First National Bank.

Each of the underlined phrases above adds useful information to the sentences, but the main thought is reserved for the main clause. For instance, in sentence C we appreciate that Alfredo is a good baritone, but the sentence wants to highlight his position as a bank vice president.

Adverb Clauses

We also frequently subordinate whole clauses, as we discussed in Chapters 18 and 20, that function as nouns, adjectives, and adverbs. The **adverb clause** (a clause beginning with words like *because, if, although, etc.*) is particularly useful in clarifying relationships among ideas in complex sentences. For example, we could write the following sentences and leave the reader to make his own connections:

A. Janice hid the Oreos from her husband. He has a sweet tooth and would eat the whole bag.

Or we could subordinate the second sentence by adding the conjunction *because,* thereby making the cause-and-effect relationship clear:

B. Janice hid the Oreos from her husband *because* he has a sweet tooth and would eat the whole bag.

Adverb clauses function like single adverbs, answering the questions why, when, where, how, and to what extent or degree something was done. Why did Janice hide the Oreos? Because her husband has a sweet tooth.

When we begin sentences with adverb clauses—unless they are only a few words long—we set them off with a comma. However, when we position the adverb clause after the main clause we usually do not use a comma. Here are several examples:

A. *Because* he has a sweet tooth and would eat the whole bag, Janice hid the Oreos from her husband.

B. No comma

A. Comma needed

B. *While* temperatures soared past 100 degrees, I lived at the community pool.

C. *Until* we fix the beat-up old air conditioner, we are back to fans and misting our-selves with spray bottles of water.

Here is a list of words (called subordinating conjunctions) that begin adverb clauses and help clarify the relationship of the subordinated information to the main point of the sentence. (For more on adverb clauses, see pp. 500–502.)

Subordinating Conjunctions

after	as though	in order that	so that	whenever
although	**because**	now that	though	where
as	before	once	till	whereas
as if	even though	rather than	until	wherever
as long as	if	since	when	while

Activity 21-2: Subordinating with Adverb Clauses

Fill in the blanks in the following sentences with appropriate clauses that work with the given subordinating conjunction. To be sure that you have written a subordinate **clause,** underline the verb in each clause twice and the subject once.

Example: Whenever _____, I will give you a call.

Whenever _____ *I finish my homework* _____, I will give you a call.

Answers will vary.

1. If _____ *Donald makes it through the last mile of the half marathon without collapsing from a heart attack* _____, he swears he will hang up his running shoes for good.

2. After _____ *the rest of you get to my house* _____, we will party till the refrigerator is empty.

3. Although _____ *I have never thought of myself as much of a writer* _____, this composi-tion class has given me new hope.

4. Once _____ *Shawn's mom gets the sump pump working* _____, we can unflood the basement.

5. I didn't realize that Gary Larson was truly demented until _____ *I saw his cartoon of the chicken carrying a baby toward the chicken pen.* _____

6. _____ *Hugh is majoring in business* _____, so that he will be marketable when he graduates.

7. As _____ *Western medicine continues to advance* _____, some practi-tioners are looking to medicine of the East for solutions.

8. Write three sentences from your own imagination that contain an adverb clause: (Remember to use a comma only to set off adverb clauses that begin sentences).
Answers will vary.

A. _____

B. _____

C. _____

Adjective Clauses

Almost as useful as adverb clauses for subordinating ideas within sentences are **adjective (relative) clauses,** which generally begin with the relative pronouns *who, which,* or *that.* While adverb clauses function as adverbs (telling when, why, where, how, and to what degree or extent), adjective clauses function as adjectives, meaning that they describe nouns and pronouns, answering the questions which one; how many; and what kind, shape, color texture, or condition.

Adjective clauses may be *essential* or *nonessential* to the meaning of a sentence but in both cases help compress information, making sentences more economical and fluid. Here are several examples: (For more on essential versus nonessential adjective clauses, see pp. 499–500.)

Nonessential Adjective Clauses

> Nonessential clauses require commas.

A. The mockingbird has an amazing range of musical voices.
   The mockingbird is common to the Midwest.

   • The mockingbird, <u>*which* is common to the Midwest</u>, has an amazing range of musical voices.

B. Paul Bunyan is said to have created the Grand Canyon by dragging his ax along the ground one day.
   Paul Bunyan is a giant out of folklore.

   • Paul Bunyan, <u>*who* is a giant out of folklore</u>, is said to have created the Grand Canyon by dragging his ax along the ground one day.

Neither of the underlined adjective clauses above is essential to the meaning of the main part of the sentence, so they are enclosed with commas.

Essential Adjective Clauses

> Essential clauses do not use commas.

A. The woman is my sister.
   The woman is wearing a bright red scarf.

   • The woman <u>*who* is wearing a bright red scarf</u> is my sister.

B. The Camaro ended up on its side in a ditch.
   The Camaro almost got away from the highway patrol.

   • The Camaro <u>*that* almost got away from the highway patrol</u> ended up on its side in a ditch.

Both of the underlined adjective clauses above are essential to the meaning of the main part of the sentence, so they are *not* enclosed with commas.

Activity 21-3: Subordinating with Adjective Clauses

Fill in the blanks in the following sentences with an appropriate clause. Notice that commas are used to set off the nonessential clauses but that essential clauses do not use commas.

Example: My best friend, who _____, will graduate from college in the spring.

My best friend, _who has put himself and his children through school_, will graduate from college in the spring.

Answers will vary.

1. Paul Newman, who _has given a great deal of money to charity_, is still a fine actor.

2. Baseball is still the game that _most defines the United States_.

3. Babe Ruth is a baseball icon who _hit sixty home runs in 1927_.

4. SUVs that _come equipped with four-wheel drive_ are driven by many people who would never consider taking them off-road.

5. The Trojan Horse, which _allowed the Greeks to enter Troy_, was left outside the walls of Troy and presumed by the Trojans to be a gift from the gods.

6. Ireland is a country that _has given birth to many fine poets, singers, and songwriters_.

7. The Three Stooges were slapstick comedians who _took hundreds of falls to entertain their public_.

8. Write three sentences from your own imagination that contain an adjective clause: (Remember to use commas only to set off *non*essential adjective clauses).

Answers will vary.

A. _____

B. _____

C. _____

Excessive Subordination

As with coordination, subordination can be too much of a good thing. Sometimes we are tempted to put more ideas into a sentence than the reader can manage to sort through. When this is the case, our writing becomes dense and difficult. The easy solution to the problem is simply to "unpack" a few of the sentences, often splitting them into two or even three parts. Here is an example of overly subordinated writing along with a revision:

A. People *who* are worried about the high risk of heart attack, *which* can strike both men and women even in their twenties, have several alternatives *that* can keep them healthy *as long as* they are willing to abide by some sensible rules for managing their lives *in such a way as* to bring their LDL cholesterol to within tolerable limits, *which* can be done through regular exercise and a low-fat diet, neither of *which* is beyond anyone's capabilities, *although* having to give up favorite foods can seem like a terrific sacrifice to many people *who* have made food a central part of their lives.

B. People who are worried about heart attacks have several alternatives for remaining healthy. If they are willing to abide by some sensible rules (regular exercise and a low-fat diet), they can bring their LDL cholesterol to within tolerable limits. It is true that giving up favorite foods can seem like a terrific sacrifice to many people who have made food a central part of their lives.

Notice that aside from becoming more clear, version B is also shorter, more concise, without sacrificing any ideas.

▶ PARALLELISM

Parallelism is a form of coordination that repeats similar grammatical units for clarity and emphasis. The words may be in a series, list, or pair, and often use a coordinating conjunction like *and* or *but* to balance the grouping.

Series

A. Be sure to pick up <u>milk, eggs, bread,</u> *and* <u>coffee</u>. (nouns)

B. I will <u>swim, bike,</u> *and* <u>climb</u> my way through my vacation. (verbs)

C. Daryl plans to spend his vacation <u>reading, watching television,</u> *and* <u>sleeping</u>. (gerunds)

D. <u>On the playground, in the halls,</u> *and* <u>in the classroom</u>, the children played nonstop. (prepositional phrases)

Items in a series should be similar grammatical units, nouns following nouns, verbs following verbs, and so forth, although slight variations are fine as in sentence C above with "watching <u>television</u>." However, you should avoid this kind of nonparallel construction:

- **Nonparallel:** Daryl plans to spend his vacation reading, watching television, and <u>he wants to sleep</u> in as much as possible.

We might either rewrite the sentence as three parallel gerunds as in C above, or we could break the series into a parallel pair and a separate main clause like this:

- **Parallel:** Daryl plans to spend his vacation reading and watching television, and he wants to sleep in as much as possible.

Lists and Outlines

Related to items in a series are **lists**, especially in the form of **outlines**. All outlines should be in parallel form. A sentence outline contains all sentences. A phrase outline contains all phrases—the same kind of phrases (prepositional, participial, and so on):

I. Mimicry in nature
  A. Avoidance by predators
  B. Ratio of mimics to models
  C. Occurrence of predation

This brief outline uses prepositional phrases, so parallelism would lapse if we substituted, for example, an infinitive phrase like "to avoid predators."

Pairs

Another useful and common form of parallelism is **pairing.** Rather than listing objects or ideas in a series, we balance two, usually with a coordinating conjunction as in the following examples:

A. Bart loved to <u>fish</u> *and* <u>backpack</u>.

B. As a child Maryanne learned <u>to whistle like a train</u> *and* <u>hoot like an owl</u>.

C. Ping pong requires <u>fast reflexes</u> *and* <u>long arms</u>.

D. <u>I am going to Seattle by train</u>, *but* <u>Jenny is traveling to the city by boat</u>.

Notice that sentence D is a compound sentence linking two main clauses that mirror one another in grammatical structure: subject, verb, and two prepositional phrases. When clauses are paired this way, the sentence is said to be *balanced,* the parallelism emphasizing ideas in each clause.

We also use a few word groups called **correlative conjunctions** to pair ideas, as in the following sentence:

With my tax refund I will <u>have *either* the house painted *or* the driveway paved</u>. Here are several common correlative pairs:

- either . . . or

- both . . . and

- neither . . . nor

- not only . . . but also

Whenever we create parallel phrases and clauses, we need to include the correct words to balance both parts of the expression, and we do not want to leave any necessary words out. Note the following nonparallel examples, A with an unneeded infinitive, *to make,* and B missing the word *long.*

A. **Nonparallel:** Martin wanted <u>recognition</u> for his hard work *rather than* <u>to make money</u>.

   Parallel: Martin wanted <u>recognition</u> for his hard work *rather than* <u>money</u>.

B. **Nonparallel:** Ping-pong requires <u>fast reflexes</u> *and* <u>arms</u>.

   Parallel: Ping-pong requires <u>fast reflexes</u> *and* <u>long arms</u>.

We do not have to include every word in a grammatical pairing or list, and we frequently choose to exclude some words that begin phrases and clauses for variety or economy, as in the following examples:

A. The new beagle puppy chewed <u>on</u> magazines, (on) table legs, and (on) shoes.

B. Marlene ordered <u>a</u> chocolate shake, (a) hamburger, and (a) plate of fries.

C. I learned early in life to trust <u>my</u> parents, (my) close relatives, and (my) best friends.

D. I hope <u>that</u> my education encourages me to look inward, (that it) guides me onward, and (that it) carries me upward.

Note that in sentence A above it would be incorrect to write "on magazines, on table legs, and shoes," dropping the final *on*. If you commit to the first two *ons,* you must finish the series using *on*.

Whether or not to include the words in parentheses above is an issue of style. Repetition can often help emphasize a point, and some people might find, for example, that sentence D above is more forceful with the *thats* left in.

Activity 21-4: Creating Parallelism

After reading the preceding information on parallelism, complete the following sentences with words, phrases, and clauses that are parallel.

Example: Margaret loves to dance, to ice skate, and _____.

Margaret loves to dance, to ice skate, and _____*to bowl*_____.

1. Singing, writing, and _____*painting*_____ are art forms.

2. Jerome will go either to the mall tonight or _____*to the movies*_____.

3. We all feel at times that we are unappreciated and that _____*life should give us more*_____
*than it does*_____.

4. Brett wanted to spend his days surfing rather than to _____*be chained to a desk*_____.

5. Michelle is a woman who works harder than most and who _____*is likely to*_____
*succeed as a result*_____.

6. Neither the football team nor _____*the basketball team*_____ made the play-off
this year.

7. The horse bolted from the stable and then _____*headed for the hills*_____.

8. Write three sentences from your own imagination that contain parallel constructions:
Answers will vary.

A. _____

B. _____

C. _____

Run-Ons, Comma Splices, and Sentence Fragments

Building Complete Sentences

Run-On Sentences
Comma Splices
Sentence Fragments
  Phrase Fragments
  Subordinate Clause
    Fragments

WHAT ARE WE TRYING TO ACHIEVE AND WHY?

Chapter 22 will focus on two common problems in our writing: improperly divided and incomplete (fragmented) sentences, errors that often occur in rough draft. When the time comes to edit our work, we sometimes find that ideas have lapped over onto one another and that it is difficult to determine where one main thought ends and another begins.

The key to pinning down sentence boundaries, and so controlling **run-ons, comma splices,** and **fragments,** is locating *verbs* and *subjects*, as we practiced in Chapter 20. As you work through the information in this chapter, make a habit of looking for the action (or state-of-being) word(s) in each sentence—the verb—and then asking yourself who or what is performing the action—the subject.

RUN-ON SENTENCES AND COMMA SPLICES

If we have let two main clauses run together as a single sentence, without any punctuation, we have a **run-on** or **fused** sentence. If we have simply divided two sentences with a comma, we have created a **comma splice.**

Both kinds of error can present problems for readers, as in the following example:

A. Greg says he will take all three of my shifts next week so I can go to the lake if my dad is in a good mood, he might give me the keys to the boat.

B. Greg says he will take all three of my shifts next week so I can go to the lake, if my dad is in a good mood, he might give me the keys to the boat.

When we reach the end of the first main thought with the final word, *lake,* we need to mark the spot with strong enough punctuation so the reader knows that a new main thought is beginning. We cannot do this with a comma alone, but we can use one of the following four methods:

1. Period (question mark and exclamation point)

2. Comma with a coordinating conjunction (*and, but, so, or, yet, for, nor*)

3. Semicolon

4. Subordination (words, phrases, clauses)

Fixing Run-Ons and Comma Splices with End Punctuation

The easiest fix for these errors is dividing the sentences with a period or other **end punctuation** (a question mark or exclamation point, for example).

Fixed: Greg says he will take all three of my shifts next week so I can go to the lake. If my dad is in a good mood, he might give me the keys to the boat.

However, a period is not always the best solution: if the sentences that are run together are short, using a period may create a "choppy" effect, as in the following example:

• Paul Moller has been working on an air car for thirty-seven years he is still not close to seeing it lift off the ground. He hopes to have it operational in his lifetime, most people do not think he will make it.

Revised but "choppy": Paul Moller has been working on an air car for thirty-seven years. He is still not close to seeing it lift off the ground. He hopes to have it operational in his lifetime. Most people do not think he will make it.

For more on problems with sentence variety, see Chapter 18.

Teaching Idea
Searching for a quick fix to their problems, many students will try to rely entirely on a period or comma with a coordinating conjunction to correct comma splices and run-ons. Encourage students to experiment with several methods, including subordination, so they don't end up repairing one problem only to create another—poor sentence variety.

A. Run-on sentence

B. Comma splice

• Run-on and comma splice

Fixing Run-Ons and Comma Splices with Coordination

If a period is not the best choice, you might find that using a **coordinating conjunction** like *and, but, or, so, yet, for,* and *nor* works better. These conjunctions are useful connecting words that help readers understand the relationship between clauses.

For example, *and* says that the clauses are roughly equivalent and not dependent on each other. *But* and *yet* point out contrast, and *so* shows cause and effect. Revising our example from above, we can eliminate a run-on and a comma splice by using coordinating conjunctions:

Fixed: Paul Moller has been working on an air car for thirty-seven years, *and* he is still not close to seeing it lift off the ground. He hopes to have it operational in his lifetime, *but* most people do not think he will make it.

For more on coordinating sentences, see Chapter 21.

Fixing Run-Ons and Comma Splices with Semicolons

A **semicolon** sometimes works as an alternative to coordinating conjunctions for dealing with run-ons and comma splices. If the main ideas are closely related, then a semicolon might be a good choice.

A. Knitting is not just for old folks many young people enjoy it too.

B. Knitting is not just for old folks, many young people enjoy it too.

Fixed: Knitting is not just for old folks; many young people enjoy it too.

While we could easily use a period or a comma with *and,* a semicolon is probably the best choice because the second main clause completes the statement made in the first clause. These two sentences work as a single unit of thought.

Another option is using a semicolon before a *conjunctive adverb* followed by a comma. Here is an example:

- Western medicine has much to offer; *however,* Eastern medicine is also a valuable resource.

Notice that we sometimes use the conjunctive adverb *within* rather than between a main clause, in which case we do not use a semicolon:

- Western medicine has much to offer. Eastern medicine, *however,* is also a valuable resource.

Here is a list of common conjunctive adverbs: *however, therefore, nevertheless, in fact,* and *consequently.*

Fixing Run-Ons and Comma Splices with Subordination

A method for avoiding run-on and comma splice errors *and* helping with concision (eliminating unneeded words) is **subordination.** When we subordinate one main clause to another, we focus the reader's attention on the idea contained within the main clause. For more on subordination, see Chapter 21.

Notice the following examples:

A. Jamie bought fifty more lottery tickets he was praying for a miracle.

B. Jamie bought fifty more lottery tickets, he was praying for a miracle.

Fixed

1. Jamie, <u>*who* was praying for a miracle</u>, bought fifty more lottery tickets. (adjective clause)

2. Jamie, <u>*praying* for a miracle</u>, bought fifty more lottery tickets. (participial phrase)

3. Jamie, <u>*praying*</u>, bought fifty more lottery tickets. (participle)

A. Run-on
B. Comma splice

A. Run-on
B. Comma splice

Each of the revised sentences corrects the error—and eliminates unneeded words. Here are several other examples showing subordination to fix problem sentences:

A. Run-on
B. Comma splice

A. Some Christmas carolers came to our house we served them hot chocolate.

B. Some Christmas carolers came to our house, we served them hot chocolate.

Fixed

1. _When_ some Christmas carolers came to our house, we served them hot chocolate. (adverb clause)

2. Some Christmas carolers _coming_ to our house, we served them hot chocolate. (absolute phrase)

A. Run-on
B. Comma splice

A. The pickup truck over there is mine it has a cracked windshield.

B. The pickup truck over there is mine, it has a cracked windshield.

Fixed

1. The pickup truck over there _that_ has a cracked windshield is mine. (adjective clause)

2. The pickup truck over there _with_ a cracked windshield is mine. (prepositional phrase)

A. Run-on
B. Comma splice

A. We practiced long hours we wanted to win the basketball game.

B. We practiced long hours, we wanted to win the basketball game.

Fixed

1. _Because_ we wanted to win the basketball game, we practiced long hours. (adverb clause)

2. _Wanting_ to win the basketball game, we practiced long hours. (participial phrase)

3. _To win_ the basketball game, we practiced long hours. (infinitive phrase)

4. _To win_, we practiced long hours. (infinitive)

A. Run-on
B. Comma splice

A. The dolphin lives in family units known as pods it is a mammal called a cetacean.

B. The dolphin lives in family units known as pods, it is a mammal called a cetacean.

Fixed

1. The dolphin, _which_ is a mammal called a cetacean, lives in family units known as pods. (adjective clause)

2. The dolphin, a mammal called a cetacean, lives in family units known as pods. (appositive phrase)

A. Run-on
B. Comma splice

A. I had an unforgettable experience it was backpacking in the Bob Marshall Wilderness.

B. I had an unforgettable experience, it was backpacking in the Bob Marshall Wilderness.

Fixed

1. I had an unforgettable experience, _which_ was backpacking in the Bob Marshall Wilderness. (adjective clause)

2. I had an unforgettable experience, backpacking in the Bob Marshall Wilderness. (appositive phrase)

3. _Backpacking_ in the Bob Marshall Wilderness was an unforgettable experience. (gerund phrase)

For help with these phrases or clauses, review Chapters 18 and 20.

Activity 22-1: Recognizing Run-Ons and Comma Splices

Examine each of the following sentences to determine whether it is correct, a run-on, or a comma splice. In order to see where one main clause ends and another begins, underline each <u>verb</u> twice, ask yourself who or what is doing the action, and then underline each <u>subject</u> once. You will find main clauses and a few subordinate clauses. Draw a line where the main clauses meet, and then in the blank at the beginning of each sentence, indicate RO for run-on, CS for comma splice, or C for correct.

Example: ___RO___ <u>I</u> <u>was having</u> a great time | <u>I</u> <u>didn't want</u> to go home.

1. _____ I think that I must have eaten too much I'm feeling a little sick.

2. _____ The family will be having dinner at Cindy's house, she has prepared a feast.

3. _____ Although some think Jamie is kindhearted, he has a cruel streak.

4. _____ Truck drivers are often away from home, this must make them lonely.

5. _____ My daughter learned to swim this summer, I can't keep her out of the pool.

6. _____ Fifty percent of the marriages today end in divorce I am sure that mine will not.

7. _____ The book left me feeling nervous I think that I will sleep with the light on.

8. _____ My uncle used to live in Hawaii, but he moved back to Kansas last year.

9. _____ Some people give good advice others just give lots of it.

10. _____ Harbour Island has beautiful pink sand beaches we will go there again one day.

Activity 22-2: Fixing Run-Ons and Comma Splices

In each of the main clauses in the numbered sentences below, underline each <u>verb</u> twice, and then underline each <u>subject</u> once. You will find main clauses and a few subordinate clauses. In the blank at the beginning of each sentence, indicate RO for run-on and CS for comma splice. Next, correct each of the sentences, using *each* of the four methods we have discussed: end punctuation, coordination, semicolon, and subordination.

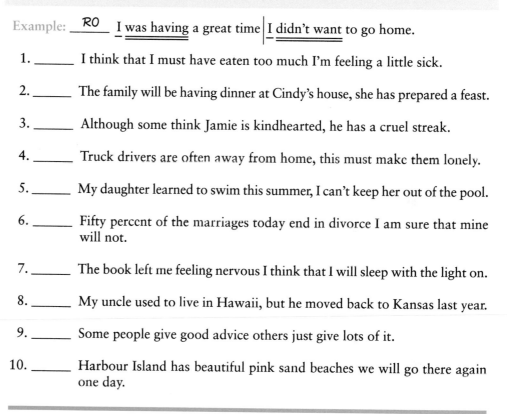

Example: ___CS:___ <u>Wal-Mart</u> <u>can sell</u> cheaper than small stores, many little <u>retail stores</u> in small town <u>are going</u> out of business.

   A. Period: *Wal-Mart can sell cheaper than small stores. Many little retail stores in small towns are going out of business.*

   B. Coordinating Conjunction: *Wal-Mart can sell cheaper than small stores, so many little retail stores in small towns are going out of business.*

   C. Semicolon: *Wal-Mart can sell cheaper than small stores; therefore, many little retail stores in small towns are going out of business.*

   D. Subordination: *Because Wal-Mart can sell cheaper than small stores, many little retail stores in small towns are going out of business.*

1. _____ Some people believe in astrology, others think that it is complete nonsense.

Period: _____

_____

Coordinating conjunction: _____

_____

Semicolon: _____

_____

Subordination: _____

_____

2. _____ Chen loves to draw Virginia prefers to paint.

Period: _____

_____

Coordinating conjunction: _____

_____

Semicolon: _____

_____

Subordination: _____

_____

3. _____ Children are naturally active they learn to become sedentary from those around them.

Period: _____

_____

Coordinating conjunction: _____

_____

Semicolon: _____

_____

Subordination: _____

_____

4. _____ A finish carpenter is a master artisan, he or she can bring wood to life.

Period: _____

_____

Coordinating conjunction: _____

_____

Semicolon: _____

_____

Subordination: _____

_____

5. _____ Bees are an essential part of agriculture, they pollinate thousands of species of fruits and vegetables.

Period: _____

_____

Coordinating conjunction: _____

_____

Semicolon: _____

_____

Subordination: _____

_____

6. _____ Unicorns are mythological creatures, many children wish they were real.

Period: _____

_____

Coordinating conjunction: _____

_____

Semicolon: _____

_____

Subordination: _____

_____

7. _____ The Mongol warrior of Genghis Khan's army was a superb rider, he could turn almost completely in the saddle to accurately fire an arrow at an enemy.

Period: _____

_____

Coordinating conjunction: _____

_____

Semicolon: _____

_____

Subordination: _____

_____

8. _____ Halley's comet returns to earth every seventy-six years few people see it twice in a lifetime.

Period: _____

_____

Coordinating conjunction: _____

_____

Semicolon: _____

_____

Subordination: _____

_____

9. _____ Hockey is a sport that requires strength, speed, and agility, it also helps if a player can duck fast.

Period: _____

_____

Coordinating conjunction: _____

_____

Semicolon: _____

_____

Subordination: _____

_____

10. _____ Robert E. Lee and Ulysses S. Grant were the finest generals in the Civil War they fought on opposite sides.

Period: _____

_____

Coordinating conjunction: _____

_____

Semicolon: _____

_____

Subordination: _____

_____

◼ SENTENCE FRAGMENTS

Run-ons and comma splices occur when we cannot clearly see where one sentence ends and another begins. For similar reasons we sometimes have difficulty with **sentence fragments.** In order for a sentence to stand alone, it must have a *verb* and a *subject,* and it must express a *complete thought.* If a sentence lacks one or several of these requirements, a reader will often have difficulty understanding the writer's thought, as in the following examples:

Phrases	Clauses
1. Trying desperately with all his might.	5. When his aching muscles let him try again.
2. Tired beyond belief but happy.	
3. To win the pennant after fourteen years.	6. Who arrived there late but made it.
4. A hard worker and good-hearted person.	

None of these examples can stand alone because they all lack a finished thought. Sentences in the left-hand column are *phrases*—they lack both subjects and verbs. Numbers 5 and 6 are *clauses.* They come the closest to free-standing sentences because they *do* have a subject and verb, but they lack a main clause to complete their meaning.

One of the reasons that sentence fragments slip into our writing is that they can look and sound like complete sentences within the context of our paragraphs, as in the following example:

Fragments

Fragments fixed

- Trying desperately with all his might. Walter jerked 200 pounds of free weight above his head. Tired beyond belief but happy. He promised himself to make 220. When his aching muscles let him try again.

Fixed: Trying desperately with all his might, Walter jerked 200 pounds of free weight above his head. Tired beyond belief but happy, he promised himself to make 220 when his aching muscles let him try again.

Sentence fragments can frequently be fixed by attaching them to the sentence that precedes or follows them, often using a comma as in the corrected version above. When this does not work, we must replace any missing words, usually subjects or verbs.

The key to dealing with fragments is recognizing *verbs* and *subjects* so we can identify sentence boundaries. The rest of this chapter will focus on the two most common kinds of fragments—phrases and subordinate clauses.

Phrase Fragments

In Chapter 20 we learned that by definition a phrase can have a verb form or a noun but not both a subject and verb. Phrases are sentence fragments and must be attached to a main clause to express their full meaning. There are two ways to fix phrase fragments:

- Connect them to a main clause.

- Add words (including subjects and verbs) to turn the phrases into main clauses.

---

1. **Prepositional phrase fragment:** We finally made it to the stadium. *After* a long, boring delay *in* traffic.

A. **Fix by attaching:** We finally made it to the stadium *after* a long, boring delay *in* traffic.

B. **Fix by adding words:** We finally made it to the stadium. The <u>traffic</u> <u>caused</u> a long, boring delay.

---

2. **Infinitive phrase fragment:** <u>*To enter* the water cleanly from a high dive</u>. A diver must keep arms and legs straight, fingers and toes pointed.

A. **Fix by attaching:** <u>*To enter* the water cleanly from a high dive</u>, a diver must keep arms and legs straight, fingers and toes pointed.

B. **Fix by adding words:** There <u>is</u> a <u>method</u> to entering the water cleanly from a high dive. A diver must keep arms and legs straight, fingers and toes pointed.

---

3. **Participial phrase fragment (present tense):** <u>*Pushing* hard to get through the sweaty bodies.</u> Shawn struggled to escape from the mosh pit.

A. **Fix by attaching:** <u>*Pushing* hard to get through the sweaty bodies,</u> Shawn struggled to escape from the mosh pit.

B. **Fix by adding words:** <u>Shawn</u> <u>pushed</u> hard to get through the sweaty bodies. He struggled to escape from the mosh pit.

---

4. **Participial phrase fragment (past tense):** <u>*Tired* beyond belief but happy.</u> Walter promised himself to make 220 when his aching muscles let him try again.

A. **Fix by attaching:** <u>*Tired* beyond belief but happy,</u> Walter promised himself to make 220 when his aching muscles let him try again.

B. **Fix by adding words:** <u>Walter</u> <u>was tired</u> beyond belief but happy. He promised himself to make 220 when his aching muscles let him try again.

---

5. **Absolute phrase fragment:** <u>The *earth shaking* violently beneath their feet</u>. Samita and Lane were knocked flat.

A. **Fix by attaching:** <u>The *earth shaking* violently beneath their feet,</u> Samita and Lane were knocked flat.

B. **Fix by adding words:** The <u>earth</u> <u>was shaking</u> violently beneath their feet. Samita and Lane were knocked flat.

6. **Appositive phrase fragment:** <u>A hard worker and a good-hearted person</u>. Allison was often taken advantage of by her co-workers.

A. **Fix by attaching:** <u>A hard worker and a good-hearted person,</u> Allison was often taken advantage of by her co-workers.

B. **Fix by adding words:** <u>Allison</u> <u>was</u> a hard worker and a good-hearted person. She was often taken advantage of by her co-workers.

Activity 22-3: Recognizing and Fixing Phrase Fragments

Decide which of the following sentences are fragments, and then correct the error by rewriting the sentence in the space provided. You may attach a phrase or add words to the fragment, whichever method seems best to you. When you combine the phrase with a main clause, be sure to punctuate correctly. (To review punctuating phrases, see pp. 493–496.)

Example: Singing with great power and feeling. Pavarotti received a standing ovation from the audience.

Fixed: *Singing with great power and feeling, Pavarotti received a standing ovation from the audience.*

1. The pancakes were not appetizing. Burned on the bottom and raw on top. They made Elaine want to go out for breakfast.

   _____

   _____

2. Streaking down field, shaking off tackles as he went. Allen charged toward the end zone thirty yards away.

   _____

   _____

3. We were supposed to meet them. Across the street and down the gravel road by the railroad tracks.

   _____

   _____

4. Ahsan and Fatima spend more time with their children than anyone I know. They have a truly happy family.

   _____

   _____

5. Although it is expensive, it is a special treat. To eat at the American Restaurant.

_____

_____

6. Two flight attendants were thrown onto the laps of passengers. The plane encountering heavy turbulence.

_____

_____

7. The funniest child in the family. Cicely seemed to have a joke for every occasion.

_____

_____

8. Fishing in his pocket for a handkerchief. Martin finally found one. Buried underneath his car keys, wadded-up dollar bills, and rent statement. He handed the handkerchief to his fiancée, who was feeling depressed. Remembering how adamantly her parents were opposed to this marriage.

_____

_____

_____

_____

Subordinate Clause Fragments

While phrases contribute a great deal to sentence fragments so do **subordinate clauses.** As we discussed in Chapter 20, a subordinate clause contains a subject and a verb but not a complete thought. These clauses depend on a main clause to finish the thought they start.

Subordinate clauses come in three varieties—noun, adjective, and adverb—but the most common fragment problems come from adverb and adjective clauses. To identify adverb clause fragments, be alert to this list of common subordinating conjunctions:

Subordinating Conjunctions

after	as though	in order that	so that	whenever
although	**because**	now that	though	where
as	before	once	till	whereas
as if	even though	rather than	until	wherever
as long as	if	since	when	while

Adverb clause fragments can be fixed either by attaching them to the main clause or dropping the subordinating conjunction to create another main clause, as in the following example:

Adverb Clause Fragment

Because the Midwest drought and heat wave has lasted for a month. Much of what was once green is now withered.

A. **Fix by attaching:** Because the Midwest drought and heat wave has lasted for a month, much of what was once green is now withered.

B. **Fix by dropping the subordinator:** The Midwest drought and heat wave has lasted for a month. Much of what was once green is now withered.

Adjective clause fragments can usually be identified by one of these three common relative pronouns:

who	which	that

Adjective clause fragments can be fixed either by attaching them to the main clause or by dropping the relative pronoun and replacing it with a noun or pronoun as in the following example:

Adjective Clause Fragment

The first decent bicycle I bought was a Trek. _Which has given me years of good service_.

A. **Fix by attaching:** The first decent bicycle I bought was a Trek, _which has given me years of good service_.

B. **Fix by dropping the relative pronoun and adding a noun:** The first decent bicycle I bought was a Trek. This _bike_ has _given_ me years of good service.

Activity 22-4: Recognizing and Fixing Subordinate Clause Fragments

Decide which of the following sentences are fragments, and then correct the error by rewriting the sentence in the space provided. You may attach the fragment to a main clause or add an appropriate subject, whichever method seems best to you. When you combine the subordinate clause with a main clause, be sure to punctuate correctly. (To review punctuating clauses, see pp. 498–500.)

Example: When the Renaissance Festival begins to advertise. I begin to think of all the food I will end up eating. While I am there.

Fixed: _When the Renaissance Festival begins to advertise. I begin to think of all the food I will end up eating while I am there._

1. If Morgan joins the eco tour in Brazil. She will see some breathtaking rain forest canopy.

   _____

   _____

2. We took the course in emergency CPR for children. Even though our daughter is grown. Because we hope to have grandchildren sometime soon.

   _____

   _____

3. While the daytime world sleeps. The creatures of the night gather to feed and hunt.

   _____

   _____

4. For family pets many people favor Labradors. Which have a reputation for being friendly and gentle.

_____

_____

5. Rather than stay in a dead-end job that you don't like, why not go back to college, retrain, and find a new life?

_____

_____

6. The Bible is full of interesting stories, including the tale of Methuselah. Who was reputed to have lived 969 years.

_____

_____

7. We hope to get all the new windows installed in the house. Before winter begins.

_____

_____

8. Once we finally get the last kitten of this litter out of the house. I am taking Maizey on a little trip. We're not going far, and I'm sure that she will enjoy the ride. Which will end at the vet's. Although Maizey has never really warmed to Dr. Scott. By the time he is through with her tubal ligation, I am sure they will have formed a lasting bond.

_____

_____

_____

_____

_____

Activity 23-4: Distinguishing Simple Past from Past Progressive

After reading the information on the simple past and past progressive tenses, decide which verb form is correct in the following sentences and underline it. Remember that simple past tells that an action has been completed in the past whereas the past progressive tells that the past action is ongoing.

Example: I (worked/was working) in the back of the store when you called.

I (worked/<u>was working</u>) in the back of the store when you called.

1. We (went/<u>were going</u>) to the store when mom was pulled over for speeding.

2. Jessica (typed/<u>was typing</u>) her composition at the moment her computer crashed.

3. The men (smoothed/<u>were smoothing</u>) out the last section of sidewalk as the children (scratched/<u>were scratching</u>) their initials in the first section.

4. We (ate/<u>were eating</u>) at Rio Bravo when we heard the news about Paul's accident.

5. We (<u>ate</u>/were eating) at Rio Bravo last week, and this week we will try Margarita's.

6. Allen said, "I (hoped/<u>was hoping</u>) that you would see *Casablanca* with me."

7. Virginia (spoke/<u>was speaking</u>) when you interrupted her.

8. Create three sentences of your own that use the past perfect tense:
   Answers will vary.
   A. _____

   B. _____

   C. _____

Irregular Verbs

Regular verbs in English form their past tense by adding *-d* or *-ed* to the base or dictionary form (*walk/walked*), but **irregular verbs** are not so easy on us. The past tense and past participle of irregular verbs are usually spelled differently than the base form—sometimes just changing a vowel, but sometimes changing consonants, and sometimes not changing at all! You might use any of the following spellings for the base, past, and past participle: *begin/began/begun, eat/ate/eaten,* or *cut/cut/cut.* The only way to handle these forms in your own writing is to memorize them and then refer to a dictionary whenever you are uncertain of which to use.

The most important irregular verb in English is *to be.* Because we use this word so often as a helper (*is* speaking) and on its own as a linking verb (John *is* a strong man), we should learn its seven forms (*am, are, is, was, were, been, being*):

To Be	Singular	Plural
Present	I am	we are
	you are	you are
	he, she, it is	they are
Past	I was	we were
	you were	you were
	he, she, it was	they were

To Be	Singular	Plural
Past Participle	I had been	we had been
	you had been	you had been
	he, she, it had been	they had been

Here is a list of the principal parts of some common irregular verbs:

Common Irregular Verbs

Present Tense	Past Tense	Past Participle	Present Tense	Past Tense	Past Participle
awake	awoke	awoke/ awakened	hear	heard	heard
become	became	become	hide	hid	hidden
begin	began	begun	hit	hit	hit
bite	bit	bitten	hold	held	held
blow	blew	blown	keep	kept	kept
break	broke	broken	kneel	knelt	knelt
bring	brought	brought	know	knew	known
build	built	built	lay (put)	laid	laid
buy	bought	bought	lead	led	led
catch	caught	caught	leave	left	left
choose	chose	chosen	let	let	let
come	came	come	lie (recline)	lay	lain
cost	cost	cost	light	lit (lighted)	lit (lighted)
creep	crept	crept	lose	lost	lost
cut	cut	cut	pay	paid	paid
dig	dug	dug	prove	proved	proven
dive	dived/dove	dived	ride	rode	ridden
do	did	done	ring	rang	rung
draw	drew	drawn	rise	rose	risen
drink	drank	drunk	run	ran	run
drive	drove	driven	say	said	said
eat	ate	eaten	see	saw	seen
fall	fell	fallen	set	set	set
feel	felt	felt	shake	shook	shaken
fight	fought	fought	show	showed	shown
find	found	found	sing	sang	sung
fly	flew	flown	sit	sat	sat
forget	forgot	forgotten	sleep	slept	slept
freeze	froze	frozen	speak	spoke	spoken
get	got	got/gotten	steal	stole	stolen
give	gave	given	swim	swam	swum
grow	grew	grown	swing	swung	swung
go	went	gone	take	took	taken
hang	hung	hung	tell	told	told
hang	hanged	hanged	write	wrote	written

Problem Verbs

Aside from the partial list of irregular verbs above, there are several verbs that are especially tricky: *lie/lay, sit/set,* and *rise/raise.*

Base Form	Past Tense	Past Participle	Present Participle	-s Ending
lie	lay	lain	lying	lies
lay	laid	laid	laying	lays
sit	sat	sat	sitting	sits
set	set	set	setting	sets
rise	rose	risen	rising	rises
raise	raised	raised	raising	raises

- *Lie* means to rest or recline, as in "I'm tired. I think I <u>will *lie*</u> down now."
- *Lay* means to place something, as in "I <u>will *lay*</u> the book on the table."

- *Sit* means to be seated, as in "I <u>will *sit*</u> in the chair."
- *Set* means to place something, as in "I <u>will *set*</u> the cup on the counter."

- *Rise* means to go up, as in "The balloon <u>is *rising*</u> in the sky."
- *Raise* means to lift, as in "I <u>will *raise*</u> the window to get some air."

Verb Tense Sequences and Unneeded Tense Shifts

When we write, we often combine verb tenses, speaking in the present, past, and future. As we move from a subordinate clause to a main clause, however, we should be sure that the verb tenses indicate a logical time relationship so we do not confuse the reader. We can show many time relationships by combining tenses, including the following:

A. Amy *spends* time with her grandparents because she *loves* them. (present/present)

B. Amy *spent* time with her grandparents because she *loved* them. (past/past)

C. Amy *spent* time with her grandparents because she *loves* them. (past/present)

D. Amy *spends* time with her grandparents because she *loves* them, and they *will be* gone soon. (present/present/future)

In sentence A Amy is still spending time with her grandparents, who she still loves. In sentence B she used to spend time with them because she used to love them but may not any more. Sentence C says that Amy once spent time with the old folks but may not any more, even though she still loves them. Sentence D explains that Amy spends time with the grandparents because she loves them and because she realizes they may die soon.

However, there are also illogical tense relationships that we want to avoid as in the following:

- Amy *spends* time with her grandparents because she *will love* them. (present/future)

In this sentence it is unlikely that Amy is spending time with her grandparents because she will love them someday.

Another practice that is apt to confuse your reader is needlessly shifting from one tense to another, usually between present and past. Notice how the following passage begins in the present, shifts to the past, and then shifts back to the present.

- *Here we <u>are</u> at the stadium, looking forward to a great game. Then Brent <u>told</u> me that he had forgotten the tickets! I <u>was</u> understandably <u>annoyed</u>. How <u>were</u> we <u>going</u> to get into the sold-out game without tickets? I <u>try</u> not to scream at my idiot friend, but it <u>is</u> hard not to.*

To solve the problem, simply change the tenses so that they are consistent through-out. Either past or present will do, although past is used in narrative passages more often. Here is the revision:

● *There we* <u>were</u> *at the stadium, looking forward to a great game. Then Brent* <u>told</u> *me that*

he <u>had forgotten</u> *the tickets! I* <u>was</u> *understandably* <u>annoyed</u>*. How* <u>were</u> *we* <u>going</u> *to get into*

the sold-out game without tickets? I <u>tried</u> *not to scream at my idiot friend, but it* <u>was</u> *hard*

not to.

▶ SUBJECT/VERB AGREEMENT

Another important part of understanding the verbs in our sentences is knowing how they **agree** with their subjects. Singular verbs should be paired with singular subjects and plural verbs with plural subjects. Although it might seem confusing, the -*s* ending on a present tense verb usually marks it as **singular** whereas the same ending on a sub-ject marks it as **plural.** Ordinarily we do not think much about this distinction but observe it naturally when we speak and write, as in the following two examples:

A. My <u>cat</u> <u>sleeps</u> in bed with me.

B. My <u>cats</u> <u>sleep</u> in bed with me.

Sentence A is singular: one cat sleeps. Sentence B is plural: several cats sleep. As we begin to write more complicated sentences than those about sleeping cats, we sometimes have difficulty finding subjects and verbs and then making them agree in number. The rest of this chapter lists common situations in which subject/verb agree-ment can be a problem.

Intervening Words

<u>One</u> of the most frequent trouble spots in our sentences <u>occurs</u> when dealing with a verb separated from its subject by a number of words (as in this sentence, for instance). We often try to connect the verb with the closest noun (in this case, *sentences*) instead of the actual subject (<u>one</u>). Here are several examples with the subjects under-lined once and the verbs twice:

A. *Terminator II*, one of the decade's many action-packed spectacles, <u>stars</u> Arnold Schwarzenegger.

B. The <u>movie</u> that we enjoyed more than all of the others <u>is</u> *Terminator II.*

C. <u>Figures</u> released yesterday from the Whitehouse <u>explain</u> the president's proposal.

D. A <u>box</u> with thirteen rolls or doughnuts <u>is called</u> a baker's dozen.

E. The defense <u>attorney</u>, along with union members, <u>is protesting</u> the judge's ruling.

In each of these sentences, locating the action or state of being word and then ask-ing the question who or what is doing the action or "being" will help you make the subject and verb agree. For example, in sentence A what stars? *Terminator II* stars. In sentence C what explains? *Figures* explain. Notice that sentence D has a prepositional phrase, *with thirteen rolls or doughnuts,* dividing the subject and verb. Subjects are never found within a prepositional phrase (for more on subjects with prepositional phrases, see p. 492).

Also note that sentence E uses the phrase *along with,* one of this small group of phrases that do not affect the number of the subject: *in addition to, as well as, along with, plus, including,* and *together with.*

| Subjects are never found within prepositional phrases. |

Activity 23-5: Agreement with Divided Subjects and Verbs

After reading the preceding information on divided subjects and verbs, underline the correct verb in parentheses twice and its subject once.

Example: The cars on this lot (cost/costs) much more than I can afford.

The cars on this lot (cost/costs) much more than I can afford.

1. The undercover officer standing among the teens at the concert (blends/blend) easily with the crowd.

2. Some of the most interesting sculptures in the museum and one made entirely of soap (is/are) on the third floor.

3. Music therapy along with other holistic healing methods (is/are) helping many people to overcome stress.

4. The red-tailed hawk in high winds (needs/need) to fly above them or land.

5. The sound of piston rods knocking (makes/make) most car owners a little sick.

6. A stack of red composite shingles (sits/sit) in Harold's pickup truck.

7. One of the cat's paws (has/have) a nasty infection.

Compound Subjects

Often we use a **compound** or **two-part subject,** in which case the verb usually becomes plural:

A. Firestone and Ford are accusing each other in the latest round of blame fixing over blown tires.

However, be careful of a seeming two-part subject when in fact the subject is singular:

B. My best friend and older brother, Robert, has helped me through tight spots all my life.

Another confusing combination is a singular indefinite pronoun attached to a subject of two or more parts. These sentences require singular verbs:

C. Every man, woman, and child deserves equality under the law.

Indefinite Pronouns

The singular indefinite pronouns in the following list require singular verbs when the pronouns are used as subjects:

anybody	each	everyone	none	somebody
anyone	either	neither	no one	someone
anything	everybody	nobody	one	something

A. Nobody wins if everyone is destroyed in the battle.

B. Anyone who thinks she can do better is welcome to try.

C. Everybody listens closely to wolves howling in the distance.

However, indefinite pronouns like *all, more, most, any,* and *some* can be singular or plural, depending on the meaning of the sentence:

A. From the whipped cream topping to the bottom crust, <u>all</u> of the key lime pie <u>was</u> delicious.

B. <u>All</u> of the band's instruments <u>were</u> stolen last night.

Activity 23-6: Agreement with Indefinite Pronouns

After reading the preceding information on subject/verb agreement with indefinite pronouns, underline the correct <u>verb</u> in parentheses twice and its <u>subject</u> once.

Example: Everyone (is/are) here who is going to make it.

<u>Everyone</u> (<u>is</u>/are) here who is going to make it.

1. <u>Some</u> of Julio's best friends (is/<u>are</u>) majoring in business.

2. <u>Nothing</u> (<u>tastes</u>/taste) as good as an ice-cold Coke on a hot summer day.

3. <u>Each</u> of the girls on the team (<u>has</u>/have) a twenty-minute warm-up routine.

4. <u>None</u> of the buildings that faced the full wrath of the hurricane still (stands/<u>stand</u>).

5. <u>Neither</u> of the candidates in the presidential race (<u>has</u>/have) gone into full mud-slinging mode—yet.

6. <u>Most</u> of Sarah's friends (thinks/<u>think</u>) that she is a hard worker.

7. Every <u>animal</u> from the smallest creepy crawlers to the largest African mammals (<u>deserves</u>/deserve) enough space to live.

Or, Either/Or, Neither/Nor

When we use *or, either/or,* and *neither/nor* to connect compound subjects, we have three possibilities for subject/verb agreement:

A. When the subjects are both singular, the verb will be singular.

B. When the subjects are both plural, the verb will be plural.

C. When subjects are singular and plural, the verb agrees with the one **closest** to it.

A. *Either* <u>Tim</u> *or* <u>Diane</u> <u>wins</u> the gold, not both of them.

B. <u>Apples</u> *or* <u>peaches</u> <u>make</u> my favorite pies.

C. *Neither* the <u>minister</u> *nor* the <u>members</u> of his congregation <u>want</u> to abandon school prayer.

Relative Pronouns as Subjects

The relative pronouns *who, which,* and *that* (among others) are the subjects of relative clauses. Because they are pronouns, they must refer back to nouns for their identity. These pronouns are singular or plural based on the noun they refer to.

A. A <u>person</u> *who* <u>rides</u> motorized scooters says they are fun and safe.

B. <u>People</u> *who* <u>ride</u> motorized scooters say they are fun and safe.

C. An SUV *that* blows a tire is more likely to roll over than a car.

D. SUVs *that* blow tires are more likely to roll over than cars.

Linking Verbs

Linking verbs should agree with their subjects, not their complements.

A. A deciding factor in many elections today is women.

B. Women are a deciding factor in many elections today.

Often we will write sentences like A above that sound a bit awkward whether or not they are grammatically correct. When this is the case, it is best to revise them, as sentence A has been revised in B.

Changing the Order of Subjects and Verbs

Although the usual order of words in English sentences is subject, verb, object (*Eric threw the ball*), we sometimes change this order for variety, emphasis, and clarity. When we change these standard word locations, especially reversing subject and verb, we sometimes have trouble with subject/verb agreement. Here are four ways we redistribute sentence parts:

1. **Inversion** moves the subject of a sentence close to or all the way to the end of a sentence, thus emphasizing the final word. Compare sentence A, in standard order, with sentence B, inverted. (For more on inversion, see pp. 446–447.)

   A. A rattlesnake slithered into a hole in the ground.

   B. Into a hole in the ground slithered a rattlesnake.

2. **There/here** sentences push the subject past the verb.

   A. *There* are three good reasons for exercising regularly.

   B. *There* is a terrible noise coming from the washing machine.

   C. *Here* are the leftovers from last night's dinner.

3. **Questions** can also reverse the ordinary positions of subject and verb.

   A. Are you coming to the game with me?

   B. Where is the map of Missouri?

   It helps to locate the verb and subject by rearranging the sentence part as a statement, for example: You are coming to the game with me.

Teaching Idea
You might also want to mention passive voice in the context of concision.

4. **Passive voice** is a way of constructing a sentence so as to downplay or eliminate the active agent, the real subject. This is done by shifting the subject and direct object, adding a preposition and a form of the verb *to be* as a helper, and often by eliminating the subject altogether. Compare sentence A, in **active voice,** to B, in passive voice:

   A. Jenny climbed the tree.

   B. The tree was climbed by Jenny.

Sentence A clearly has the intended subject, Jenny, climbing the tree, the direct object. Sentence B shifts the direct object to the subject position, making the tree the grammatical subject. If passive voice sentences seem confusing when you are trying to find a subject, try asking the question who or what is having something done to it.

Remember that when the doer of an action is relatively unimportant or unknown, the passive voice can be an effective choice, but active voice works best when—as in most cases—you want your real doer of the action to receive full attention. However, here are two examples of effective passive sentences, both of which seek to emphasize the words in the subject position:

A. My friend's <u>home</u> <u>was broken</u> into last night. (A thief did it, but the focus is on the violation of the home.)

B. Six million <u>Jews</u> <u>were exterminated</u> during World War II. (The Nazis did it, but the focus is on the deaths rather than the perpetrators of the crime.)

Activity 23-7: Agreement with Reordered Sentences

After reading the preceding information on agreement with relocated subjects and verbs, find the <u>verb</u> in each sentence and underline it twice, and then underline the <u>subject</u> once.

Example: In the middle of an angry crowd cowered two innocent bystanders.

In the middle of an angry crowd <u>cowered</u> two innocent <u>bystanders</u>.

1. From the back of the old Chevy stationwagon <u>clung</u> three young <u>boys</u>, hitching a ride on their sleds.

2. This <u>mess</u> <u>was made</u> by someone.

3. When <u>is</u> Louis <u>going</u> to take the bar exam?

4. By the side of the road <u>was</u> a <u>Ford Explorer</u> with a flat tire.

5. Here <u>are</u> the best <u>facilities</u> for losing weight and toning up.

6. When my <u>flight</u> <u>was delayed</u> by the ice storm, <u>I</u> <u>waited</u> six hours for the next flight.

7. There <u>is</u> a <u>hole</u> in the ozone over Antarctica that <u>gets</u> bigger with each passing year.

Collective Nouns

We use some words that group things, animals, and people in a way that we consider to be a single unit. Even though there are many members, if they are seen to be acting together, we treat them as grammatically singular, for example: *army, committee, team, band, class, audience, crowd, gathering, group, herd, school,* and *flock.*

A. The <u>group</u> <u>feels</u> that its decision was just.

B. Our <u>committee</u> <u>has beaten</u> this issue to death.

However, if the members of the group are acting individually, it often sounds more natural to revise the sentence to reflect this, for example: The <u>members</u> of our group <u>are divided</u> in their judgment.

Plural Nouns/Plural Verbs

While some nouns are collectively singular, others are always plural, for example: *scissors, pants, clothes,* and *fireworks.*

• The <u>scissors</u> <u>are</u> in the drawer.

"False" Plural Nouns

Some nouns that end in -s are not plural, for example: *mathematics, physics, athletics, economics, statistics, measles, mumps, politics, ethics,* and *pediatrics.* Though titles may contain plural nouns–for example, *All Creatures Great and Small* or *The Last of the Mohicans*—they take singular verbs. Sums of money, distances, measurements, and time units may also look plural, but when they are being used as a unit, they, too, are grammatically singular.

A. Mathematics is my favorite subject.

B. Thirty minutes is too long to spend listening to Dr. Parrish lecture.

C. Twenty-five thousand dollars sounds like too much to spend on a car.

However, notice that in certain contexts we might also use number subjects as singular:

- Ten dollars in ones were lying on the counter.

Activity 23-8: Agreement with Plural and Collective Nouns

After reading the preceding information on agreement with plural and collective nouns, locate the verb in parentheses and underline it twice, and then underline the subject once.

Example: Fireworks (is/are) a wonderful spectacle to many Americans on July Fourth.

Fireworks (is/are) a wonderful spectacle to many Americans on July Fourth.

1. *Jaws* (is/are) a movie that made many people reluctant to swim in the ocean.

2. The whole gathering (believes/believe) in the eminent destruction of the planet.

3. The audience (applauds/applaud) enthusiastically, hoping for one more encore.

4. A whole flock of Canadian geese (is flying/are flying) through the airspace above La Guardia airport.

5. Five hundred dollars (is/are) too much for this guitar.

6. Athletics (brings/bring) many people together who otherwise might not meet.

7. The only pants I have (is/are) in the dryer.

8. Five hundred flat miles across Kansas (is/are) way too many to drive to reach the Rockies.

CHAPTER 24

Pronouns

Reference, Agreement, and Form

Building Agreement

Reference
Agreement in Number
Pronoun Case
Common Problems
Consistency in Person

Teaching Idea
You might want to frame the discussion of pronouns as writer- versus reader-based prose. The writer usually knows who or what she is referring back to, but the reader often does not.

WHAT ARE WE TRYING TO ACHIEVE AND WHY?

Like verbs and nouns, **pronouns** are a commonly used and important part of speech. Pronouns like *he, this, who, myself, everyone* stand in the place of nouns and are useful for creating variety in our sentences.

Without pronouns to replace nouns, we might be stuck with paragraphs like A below:

A. The *leopard* crept stealthily through the dry grass, stalking the *leopard's* prey. As the *leopard* neared the antelope, the *leopard's* ears flattened, and the *leopard's* tail began to twitch in anticipation. Pausing for a moment, seeming to hold the *leopard's* breath, the *leopard* sprang from hiding to land on the antelope's back.

Clearly, the repetition of *leopard* becomes monotonous. To solve the problem, we can rely on pronouns as in the following paragraph revision:

B. The leopard crept stealthily through the dry grass, stalking *her* prey. As the leopard neared the antelope, the leopard's ears flattened, and *her* tail began to twitch in anticipation. Pausing for a moment, seeming to hold *her* breath, the leopard sprang from hiding to land on the antelope's back.

For more on variety and coherence through pronouns, see p. 56.

Teaching Idea
For a complete list of pronouns, see pp. 486–487.

As useful as pronouns are, they present a built-in problem. Because they have no identity by themselves, they must refer to a noun to gain meaning. When someone says, "It was a horrible experience," we respond, "What was horrible?" We cannot know until the person says, "Having a *root canal* was horrible." Now we know what *it* referred to because we have named the horrible experience with a noun, *root canal*.

Whenever we use pronouns, we must be sure that the reader knows what they are referring back to, and we must be careful of the pronoun form. Chapter 24 will help us explore both of these areas.

REFERRING TO THE ANTECEDENT

A pronoun refers to an **antecedent,** a word that the pronoun substitutes for—most often a noun, but occasionally another pronoun or phrase. The antecedent is usually located before the pronoun, either within the same sentence or within a nearby sentence, as for example in the following: "<u>Jim</u> drinks <u>hot chocolate</u>. <u>He</u> likes <u>it</u> a lot." The words *he* and *it* take the place of *Jim* and *hot chocolate*.

The farther the pronoun is removed from its antecedent, the more likely is the chance for confusion. Consider the following sentences:

A. Eileen told Isabella that *she* would never be happy until *she* stopped relying on men to define her existence.

B. After *she* made this statement, *she* apologized, not wanting to sound like *she* was unkind.

In sentence A we are not sure who needs to stop relying on men. The confusion escalates when we move to sentence B. Who has said what? We can only guess. To clarify the meaning, we could recast the sentences this way:

C. Eileen told Isabella that Isabella would never be happy until she stopped relying on men to define her existence.

D. After Eileen made this statement, she apologized, not wanting to sound like she was unkind.

Now we can readily understand the writer's intended meaning.

Pronouns that can be particularly confusing to readers are *it, they, them, this, that, these, those,* and *which.* When we use these words, they should usually refer to a specific noun rather than a general idea, and they should be positioned closely to the noun they stand for, or we could have ambiguities in meaning as in the following examples:

A. *They* rudely informed Jenna and Craig at the grocery store that *they* were out of mangoes.

Who informed Jenna and Craig—perhaps a store employee? The employee probably did not tell Jenna and Craig that the two of them were out of mangoes; the store was out.

Revised: An <u>employee</u> at the grocery store rudely informed Jenna and Craig that the <u>store</u> was out of mangoes.

B. *It* made Jenna and Craig unhappy.

What made them unhappy, the lack of mangoes, the rudeness of the employee, or both?

Revised: The <u>rudeness</u> of the employee and the <u>lack of mangoes</u> made them unhappy.

C. *This* taught *them* to prepare further in advance for parties, *which* will help *them* prevent *this* in the future.

What taught Jenna and Craig a lesson: the rude behavior, the lack of mangoes, or both? Is *which* referring to the parties—the closest noun—or the idea of preparing in advance? Is *them* referring to the parties—again, the closest noun—or to Craig and Jenna? What is the final *this* referring to?

Revised: This <u>unhappy shopping experience</u> taught Craig and Jenna to prepare farther in advance for parties. The <u>lesson</u> will help the couple to avoid future <u>unpleasant surprises</u> when planning parties.

Pronouns are necessary and useful in our writing, but we must be careful that they clearly link with their intended antecedent. Often the best fix for ambiguous pronoun reference is simply to replace the pronoun with a noun, as in the revised examples above.

Activity 24-1: Clarifying Pronoun Reference

After reading the preceding information, revise the following sentences for unclear pronoun reference by replacing the pronouns with likely nouns and writing the revised sentence in the space provided.

Example: When I finally reached the admissions office, they told me my transcripts had been lost.

Revised: *When I finally reached the admissions office, <u>an employee</u> told me my transcripts had been lost.*

1. On Brian's office door it says, "Don't bother knocking. I'm not home."

On Brian's office door a sign says , "Don't bother knocking. I'm not home."

2. My first vacation with Rob will be backpacking in a wilderness area, which frightens me to think about.

My first vacation with Rob will be backpacking in a wilderness area.

Going with Rob on any kind of vacation frightens me.

3. Many teachers have become aware that they have unconsciously discouraged girls from excelling in science and math. This is why they should now do better.

Because many teachers have become aware that they have unconsciously

discouraged girls from excelling in science and math, the teachers will correct

their former habits, and the girls should now do better.

4. Large asteroids seldom hit the earth, but when they do, they cause terrific destruction, which is a relief to me.

Though asteroids can cause terrific destruction, because they seldom

hit the earth, I feel relieved.

5. Sylvia plays the guitar beautifully, although she has never had a lesson in it.

Sylvia plays the guitar beautifully, although she has never had a guitar

lesson.

6. Florence was talking to Abby when she saw the accident in the parking lot.

Florence was talking to Abby when Florence saw the accident in the

parking lot.

7. After the painters spoke with Jim and Kristi in their dining room, they moved the dining room table and then painted it.

After the painters spoke with Jim and Kristi in the dining room, the

painters moved the dining room table and then painted the room.

8. Rainbow trout rest behind rocks in streams to conserve their energy and because they channel food toward them.

Rainbow trout rest behind rocks in streams to conserve their energy

and because the rocks channel food toward them.

9. Sheila only needed wire cutters or pliers to strip the insulation from the wire, so she asked her husband to hand it to her.

Sheila needed only wire cutters or pliers to strip the insulation from

the wire, so she asked her husband to hand the wire cutters to her.

10. Meat and dairy products are high in saturated fats and often have toxic chemicals in them. But they taste good and also have many valuable nutrients. For these reasons, many people are trying to cut down on their consumption.

Meat and dairy products are high in saturated fats and often have toxic chemicals in them. But these foods taste good and also have many valuable nutrients. Because of the potential health hazards, many people are trying to cut down on their consumption of meat and dairy products.

AGREEING IN NUMBER WITH THE ANTECEDENT

Not only must pronouns be clearly linked to their antecedents, but also they must agree in **number:** singular nouns take singular pronouns; plural nouns take plural pronouns. Consider the following examples:

A. *The Night of the Living Dead* is a classic horror film, but there is much in *it* that is laughable.

B. Many *films* have tried to capture the essence of Mary Shelley's Frankenstein, but few of *them* have succeeded.

In sentence A the singular pronoun *it* refers to the singular film. In sentence B the plural pronoun *them* links with the plural noun *films*.

Difficulties with pronoun–antecedent agreement often fall into one of the following three categories: **indefinite pronouns, collective nouns,** and **compound antecedents.**

Indefinite Pronouns

Indefinite pronouns as antecedents can be a problem because they do not refer to a specific person or thing. Although most are singular, a few are plural, and several (all, any, enough, more, most, none, some) can be either singular *or* plural, depending on what noun they connect with. Note the following list:

Indefinite Pronouns			
Singular			**Plural**
anybody	everybody	none	both
anyone	everyone	one	few
anything	neither	somebody	many
each	no one	someone	others
either	nobody	something	several

Notice how we might use these pronouns in sentences:

A. *Everyone* at the party was having a good time.

B. *Someone* is knocking at the front door.

C. *Many* are called, but *few* are chosen.

Sentences A and B use singular indefinite pronouns while C uses two plural pronouns. If A, B, and C above seem straightforward, not presenting any difficulty, here are two sentences that might be more puzzling:

A. *Each* of the *rock bands* plays until midnight, and then *it* moves onto the next gig.

B. *Neither* of the *players* deserves to be benched for defending *himself*.

In sentence A above, the pronoun *each* is the singular subject, requiring a singular verb, and even though the noun *bands* is plural, the singular pronoun *it* refers back to *each*. Sentence B uses the singular pronoun *neither* as its subject, requiring a singular verb, and even though the noun *players* is plural, the singular pronoun *himself* refers back to *neither*.

It would be incorrect to write these sentences in the following manner:

C. *Each* of the *rock bands* play until midnight, and then *they* move onto the next gig.

D. *Neither* of the *players* deserve to be benched for defending *themselves*.

> Here are several more examples illustrating correct pronoun agreement:
>
> A. *One* of the shoppers was trying to find *her* checkbook.
>
> B. *Anyone* can learn to play a musical instrument if *he* or *she* practices long enough.
>
> C. *Many* of the athletes failed *their* drug tests.

Notice that sentence B uses the pronouns "*he* or *she*" to overcome gender bias in pronoun usage. For a more thorough discussion of this, turn to Chapter 19, pp. 470–471.

Collective Nouns

We use some words that group things, animals, and people in a way that we consider to be a single unit. Even though there are many members, if they are seen to be acting together, we treat them as grammatically singular, for example: *army, committee, team, band, class, audience, crowd, gathering, group, herd, school,* and *flock*. Pronouns that refer to singular collective nouns must also be singular

A. The *group* feels that *its* decision was just.

B. Our *committee* has discussed the proposals, and *it* has decided to accept the low bid.

However, if the members of the group are acting individually, the noun becomes plural and so does the pronoun, for example:

- The *group* are divided in *their* judgment, *all* members arguing strenuously for *their* position.

Compound Antecedents

We often use two-part or **compound** nouns connected with the conjunctions *and, or,* and *nor*. When the antecedent is connected by *and*, it is usually plural, requiring a plural pronoun, as in the following examples:

A. *Wind and sun* suck moisture from the earth, and *they* can devastate a corn crop.

B. My *daughter and I* will be on *our* favorite float river by this time tomorrow.

When the antecedent is linked by *or* or *nor,* the pronoun should agree with the nearest part, as in the following examples:

A. Either Mark *or* Luke will bring *his* Frisbee to the park.

B. Mark or his *brothers* will bring *their* Frisbees to the park.

C. Neither Mark nor his *friends* remembered to bring *their* Frisbees to the park.

For smoother-sounding sentences, when you use a plural and a singular compound antecedent, put the plural word second, as in the following example:

Awkward: Neither the fans nor the *coach* could control *his* anger at the referee's decision.

Revised: Neither the coach nor the *fans* could control *their* anger at the referee's decision.

Activity 24-2: Creating Pronoun Agreement

Underline the antecedent in each of the following sentences, and then write an appropriate pronoun in the blanks. Remember that you are making decisions about indefinite pronouns, collective nouns, and compound antecedents.

Example: We are often told that anybody can be successful in this country if _____ is willing to work hard.

We are often told that <u>anybody</u> can be successful in this country if *he or she* is willing to work hard.

Answers will vary.

1. <u>Everyone</u> would like a job that makes ___*him or her*___ happy.

2. A <u>flock</u> of Canadian geese was on ___*its*___ way south for the winter.

3. Carl knew that the success of his latest CD depended on <u>many people</u> and that ___*they*___ deserved recognition for ___*their*___ help.

4. <u>Each</u> player, giving ___*his or her*___ utmost, makes a team a winner or loser.

5. <u>Nobody</u> was able to move ___*his or her*___ vehicle from the crowded stadium parking lot.

6. <u>Several</u> of the people at my party called the next day to say that ___*they*___ had had a great time.

7. The <u>audience</u> broke into wild applause, and then ___*it*___ pleaded for one more curtain call.

8. <u>Every one</u> of the girls should know that ___*she*___ has an equal shot at the job.

9. <u>Either</u> of the boys will clean up the mess ___*he*___ made if you bribe ___*him*___ with candy.

10. Neither the director nor <u>any</u> of the actors thought that ___*they*___ would complete the scene on schedule.

Teaching Idea
Refer students back to pp. 470–471 to discuss gender bias in language and ways to prevent it.

▶ CHOOSING PROPER PRONOUN CASE

Even after we have clearly indicated the antecedent of a pronoun and checked the pronoun for agreement in number, we can still run into problems in **case.** Pronoun case is one of three forms a pronoun can take to show how it functions in a sentence: as subject, object, or possessor.

Subjective Case

Pronouns used as **subjects** or subject complements are in the *subjective case.*

A. *She* <u>runs</u> six-minute miles. (pronoun as subject)

B. <u>We</u> <u>are</u> lucky to walk a ten-minute mile because <u>we</u> <u>are</u> so out of shape. (pronouns as subjects)

C. The <u>person</u> to thank for breakfast <u>is</u> *she*. (pronoun as complement)

Objective Case

Pronouns used as **objects** (receiving the action of verbs), objects of prepositional phrases, and subjects of infinitives are in the *objective case*.

A. The whole <u>family</u> happily <u>greeted</u> *her*. (pronoun as direct object)

B. <u>Emily</u> <u>kicked</u> the ball to *him*. (pronoun as indirect object)

C. <u>Alex</u> <u>wanted</u> to share the secret only with *you* and *me*. (pronouns as object of <u>preposition)</u>

D. <u>Patty</u> <u>asked</u> *him* to bring a green salad. (pronoun as subject of infinitive)

Possessive Case

Pronouns used to show **ownership** are in the *possessive case*.

A. Is that *your* umbrella?

B. No, that one is not *mine*.

The following pronoun case chart will help when you have trouble choosing the correct pronoun form.

Note:
its, whose, and *your* are possessive pronouns; *it's, who's,* and *you're* are contractions.

Pronoun Case Chart			
Singular	**Subjective**	**Objective**	**Possessive**
First person	I	me	my, mine
Second person	you	you	your, yours
Third person	he, she, it, who whoever	him, her, it, whom, whomever	his, her, hers, **its,** whose
Plural	**Subjective**	**Objective**	**Possessive**
First person	we	us	our, ours
Second person	you	you	your, yours
Third person	they, who	them, whom	their, theirs, whose

▶ SOLVING COMMON PROBLEMS

Pronoun case does not generally cause us too many problems, but there are three categories into which the most common uncertainties fall: **compounds, comparisons,** and *who/whom.*

Compounds

Compound (two-part) case difficulties occur when two pronouns, two nouns, or a noun and a pronoun are linked by *and* and *or,* as in the following examples:

A. Subjects: *Jerry* and *I/me* went to the Royals' game last night.

B. Objects: The <u>game</u> <u>disappointed</u> *him* and *I/me.*

C. Objects of preposition: So we left early, and <u>this</u> <u>was</u> all right with *him* and *I/me.*

In each of these sentences, confusion sometimes results from the pairings. If we mentally cross out one of the pair, the remaining word will often guide us to the correct case:

A. ~~Jerry and~~ *I* went to the Royals' game last night.
   Jerry and *I* went to the Royals' game last night.

B. The game disappointed ~~him and~~ *me*.
   The game disappointed *him* and *me*.

C. So we left early, and this was all right with ~~him and~~ *me*.
   So we left early, and this was all right with *him* and *me*.

Being able to locate the verb and subject in your sentence will also help determine case. By process of elimination, if the pronoun you are dealing with is not a subject and does not show possession, it is in the objective case.

Comparisons

We frequently make noun/pronoun and pronoun/pronoun comparisons using the words *than* and *as*. These comparisons can be confusing because they often involve implied words, that is, words left out of the sentence, as in the following examples:

A. Pauline sings more beautifully than *I/me*.

B. Arthur is as competent as *he/him*.

If we add the implied verbs to sentences A and B above, it becomes easier to determine the correct pronoun case. With the verbs in place, we can see that the pronouns *I* and *he* are subjects and therefore must be in the subjective case.

A. Pauline sings more beautifully than *I* (sing).

B. Arthur is as competent as *he* (is).

Using the same strategy of adding the implied words to the following sentences, we can see that the pronouns *her* and *him* are the correct choices as direct objects:

C. This study guide will help you more than *her/she*. (it will help)

D. Loud music distracts Jessica as much as *him/he*. (it distracts)

C. This study guide will help you more than it will help *her*.

D. Loud music distracts Jessica as much as it distracts *him*.

Sometimes choosing the pronoun case will affect the meaning of your sentence, as in the following example:

• Ian cares for football more than me. (more than he cares for me)

• Ian cares for football more than I. (more than I care for football)

Who/Whom

The relative pronouns *who/whoever* and *whom/whomever* are another source of occasional confusion in selecting pronoun case. *Who/whoever* are used as subjects and *whom/whomever* have been traditionally used as objects, as in the following sentences:

Subject: *Who* will give Jenny a ride to the game?

Object: I should give your house keys to *whom*?

Although the distinction between *who* and *whom* has been steadily fading from the language—*who* often used in place of *whom*—you can signal a note of formality in usage if you observe it. If the objective use of *whom* seems awkward or contrary to the tone of a piece of writing, you can always recast the sentence so that the relative pronoun is unneeded or sometimes just drop it, as in the following example:

• The fastest swimmer *whom* Brandon had to face was his archrival from Shawnee Mission South.

• The fastest swimmer Brandon had to face was his archrival from Shawnee Mission South.

Activity 24-3: Choosing Pronoun Case

Underline the correct form of the pronoun within parentheses in each sentence. You are making decisions about two-part constructions, comparisons, and *who/whom*. Remember that locating verbs and subjects will help you decide between subjective and objective case. Also, try the strategies of crossing out one member of the pair and supplying the implied words.

Example: We finally found a babysitter so that my wife and (me/<u>I</u>) could have a night out.

1. It made George furious to hear (she/<u>her</u>) and Jason laughing together.

2. Anna is the girl (who/<u>whom</u>) Tomas is taking to the prom.

3. My platoon sergeant pointed at Carlos and (I/<u>me</u>) and said, "You are volunteering."

4. During the recital Lewis could see that Amy was more bored than (him/<u>he</u>).

5. Few people have reacted as violently as (<u>they</u>/them).

6. The gold medal belongs as much to the rest of the team as (she/<u>her</u>).

7. My older brother and (me/<u>I</u>) started skateboarding before we discovered surfing.

8. My boss offered Richard and (she/<u>her</u>) a raise.

9. April is a girl (whom/<u>who</u>) never gives up.

10. (<u>She</u>/Her) and her friend will leave the party by midnight.

▶ REMAINING CONSISTENT IN PERSON

As we noticed on the Pronoun Case Chart, p. 552, pronouns have number (singular or plural) and *person* (first, second, or third). **Person** is the perspective the author assumes when he or she writes: first person (*I, we*), second person (*you*), and third person (*he, she,* or *they*). Within a single-paragraph paper or essay, we should remain consistent in both number and person.

The most frequent shift error is from the first person *I* or third person *they* to the second person, *you*, as in the following examples:

Teaching Idea
To help students understand appropriate pronoun shift, you might have them turn to the Unit Six essay "What Is Biodiversity and Why Should We Care about It?" Ask them why the author shifts to second person in paragraphs five and six.

A. *I* looked out the window as *I* sat in a huge jet cutting through the clouds. *You* could see tiny green irrigation rings on the ground 25,000 feet below, reminding *me* of the drought still in progress.

   Fixed: *I* looked out the window as *I* sat in a huge jet cutting through the clouds. <u>*I*</u> could see tiny green irrigation rings on the ground 25,000 feet below, reminding *me* of the drought still in progress.

B. To improve *their* lives, immigrants to America have often traveled westward. If *you* wanted to farm, ranch, or mine, the West was the place for *you*.

   Fixed: To improve *their* lives, immigrants to America have often traveled westward. If <u>*they*</u> wanted to farm, ranch, or mine, the West was the place for <u>*them*</u>.

Use *you* only when there is a good reason to directly address your reader.

Writers often mix persons in their work, but there should always be a legitimate reason for doing so. The *I* of personal experience is sometimes used in introductions and conclusions but then avoided in the body paragraphs of an essay (unless a personal anecdote is being used for support). When we want to directly address the reader, we can use *you*, as we do on occasion in introductions and conclusions and extensively in process-analysis instructions (as in textbooks like this one). *We, us,* and *our* are useful pronouns for establishing a link to an audience, especially helpful in persuasive writing. However, a writer needs to control shifts in person, especially avoiding the ones listed in A and B above.

When using the slightly more formal third person, we have several options to avoid slipping into an inappropriate second-person "you." We can use third-person pronouns (*he, she, they*), nouns that stand in their place (*people, students, employees*—whatever noun describes the subject), or leave the pronoun out altogether. Note the following examples:

Inappropriate Pronoun Shift:

- Australia was first colonized by English convicts. <u>You</u> would have worked hard in those early settlements.

A. **Fixed (pronoun-third person):** Australia was first colonized by English convicts. <u>They</u> would have worked hard in those early settlements.

B. **Fixed (noun):** Australia was first colonized by English convicts. The <u>colonists</u> would have worked hard in the early settlements.

C. **Fixed (pronoun deleted):** Working hard in the early settlements, English convicts first colonized Australia.

Activity 24-4: Avoiding Shifts in Person

Read through the following brief paragraphs, cross out the inappropriate pronouns, write in the appropriate word in the space above it, and change any verb affected by a pronoun substitution.

Answers will vary.

A. When I lived on the farm, I had to help with a lot of chores. I had to take care of my animals, help my dad irrigate in the morning and evening, and I also had to help in the kitchen. When ~~you~~ moved to the city, ~~you~~ ended up with fewer responsibilities. All I have to do now is help my father with his lawn and landscaping business and help around the house. ~~You~~ don't have all of the extra responsibilities in the city that ~~you~~ had on the farm.

B. People who downhill ski often love the sport and regularly risk terrible injury pursuing it. ^{*Some*} ~~You~~ might think that ^{*they*} ~~you~~ are too tough to get hurt, but skiers frequently break bones and, worse, rip their knee joints apart. Hurtling downhill at forty to fifty miles an hour, ^{*a person*} ~~you~~ can easily run into a tree or another person, sending ^{*both people*} ~~you~~ ~~both~~ to the hospital. Skiers say that a fast run down the mountain is a lot like flying, but ^{*there are not*} ~~you don't have~~ all those trees, boulders, and people to dodge up in the sky.

CHAPTER 25

Adjectives and Adverbs

Words that Describe

Building Description

- Adjectives
- Adverbs
- Comparative Forms
- Superlative Forms
- Overused Modifiers
- Dangling and Misplaced Modifiers

◗ WHAT ARE WE TRYING TO ACHIEVE AND WHY?

One of the ways that we add information to sentences is to use **adjectives** and **adverbs,** words that *describe* or *modify.*

Adjectives tell us about *nouns* and *pronouns:* the *red* Mustang. **Adverbs** tell us about *verbs, adjectives,* and other *adverbs:* she sings *melodiously.* Although we usually locate these modifiers close to the word they tell about, adverbs in particular may be separated by some distance from the words they modify. The problems we generally have with adjectives and adverbs are choosing the right ones, using them selectively, and attaching them clearly to the words they intend to describe.

◗ ADJECTIVES

Adjectives describe nouns and pronouns, telling how many; which; or what kind, color, shape, size, texture, or age the person or thing is. Adjectives can be single words, phrases, or clauses, as in the following examples:

A. **Single word:** A *tall* sycamore tree stands in my yard. (tells size)

B. **Phrase:** A sycamore tree *with an eagle's nest* stands in my yard. (tells which one)

C. **Clause:** The sycamore tree *that fell on my house last night* was 110 years old. (tells which one)

We place the single adjective, as in sentence A, directly in front of the word *sycamore.* However, in sentences B and C the adjective phrase and clause follow the noun *sycamore.* When we use a linking verb (*be, seem, feel,* etc.), as in the following example, the adjective is separated from the noun or pronoun by the verb:

- Louis feels *sick.*

- He is *kind.*

◗ ADVERBS

Adverbs describe verbs, adjectives, and other adverbs, telling when, where, why, how, and to what degree or extent (something was done). Adverbs, like adjectives, can be single words, phrases, or clauses, as in the following examples:

A. **Single word:** Arthur *quietly* entered the room. (tells how)

B. **Phrase:** *On his tiptoes* Arthur entered the room. (tells how)

C. **Clause:** *When everyone was sleeping,* Arthur entered the room. (tells when)

Adverbs are the most maneuverable modifier, often allowing us a great deal of freedom with placement. For example, we could recast the three sentences above in several ways, including these:

D. **Single word:** Arthur entered the room *quietly.* (tells how)

E. **Phrase:** Arthur entered the room *on his tiptoes.* (tells how)

F. **Clause:** Arthur entered the room *when everyone was sleeping.* (tells when)

One way to identify adverbs is to look for the -*ly* ending that is frequently attached to adjectives to form adverbs (bad/bad*ly,* happy/happi*ly,* sweet/sweet*ly*). However, this method is not foolproof, because there many adverbs that do not have the -*ly* ending (*soon, too, very, already, often, quite, then, always, there*). Knowing how a word *functions* is the best way to determine what part of speech it is.

Teaching Idea
This chapter offers another opportunity to reinforce the value of knowing the function of phrases and clauses so that students can recognize and manipulate these structures. You might want to link the discussion on this page with the information on phrases and clauses in Chapter 20.

Many adverbs are formed by adding -*ly* to the end of an adjective.

9. Josh swore that if they came for him he would not go ~~quiet~~ to jail. ___*quietly*___

10. Handle the crystal ~~careful~~ or you will break it. ___*carefully*___

◼ DANGLING AND MISPLACED MODIFIERS

Teaching Idea
You will find other references to misplaced modifiers in Chapter 18.

Besides choosing the correct form for adjectives and adverbs, we sometimes have problems clearly connecting them to the word they intend to describe. When a single modifier or a word group at the beginning of a sentence describes the wrong following word or no word at all, it is said to *dangle*. Here are several examples:

Note: participial phrases are especially prone to dangling.

A. After finishing the meal, my eyelids grew heavy, and I dozed off.

B. Worn to a frazzle, the final exam had sucked out the last of Amy's energy.

C. To make it to the peak, the weather would need to favor the climbers.

D. As a civilian, his family had always come first.

As you can see, the leading phrase in each sentence appears to describe the first noun that follows it. But in all four sentences this meaning would be silly or nonsensical. To correct the dangling modifier, we can either insert a subject into the leading phrase or place the intended noun immediately after the phrase, at the beginning of the main clause, as in the following examples:

1. After I finished the meal, my eyelids grew heavy, and I dozed off.

2. After finishing the meal, I felt my eyelids grow heavy, and I dozed off.

3. Amy was worn to a frazzle, the final exam having sucked out the last of her energy.

4. Worn to a frazzle, Amy felt that the final exam had sucked out the last of her energy.

Misplaced modifiers also appear to modify an unintended word, again creating confusion for a reader, as in the following examples:

A. John called to the beagle in his slippers.

B. Paula especially liked the calendar on her office wall covered with nature pictures.

C. The machinist drilled a hole in a piece of metal that was 1/2 inch in diameter.

D. We saw a herd of cows from our car grazing in a harvested wheat field.

E. My daughter decided that we should eat at Burger King, which I later regretted.

F. Billy only drank a glass of Pepsi.

Teaching Idea
If example F seems puzzling to students, you might mention that in this sentence Billy didn't drop or spill, he only drank the Pepsi. In the clarified version F, Billy drank only a glass of Pepsi and not a Coke or chocolate milk.

To correct the misplaced modifier, we need to move it closer to the word it is supposed to describe, and sometimes we must add a word or two. Notice the following examples:

A. In his slippers *John* called to the beagle.

B. Paula especially liked the *calendar* covered with nature pictures on her office wall.

C. The machinist drilled a *hole* that was 1/2 inch in diameter in a piece of metal.

D. From our car we saw a herd of *cows* grazing in a harvested wheat field.

E. My daughter decided that we should eat at Burger King, a *decision* which I later regretted.

F. Billy drank only a *glass* of Pepsi.

Teaching Idea
Because punctuating correctly so often depends on being able to locate subjects and verbs, this is a good point at which to review subjects and verbs in Chapter 20.

THE BIG TH[...]

Commas are pr[...]
in a sentence by fir[...]
asking the questic[...]
located a main cl[...]
within, and after [...]
account for perha[...]
categories.

Commas are ne[...]

1. **introduce** main[...]

2. **enclose** nonesse[...]

3. **divide** main cla[...]

Commas That In[...]

We often begin[...]
be separated from[...]

Single Words

1. *However*, I ho[...]
   pp. 488, 508)[...]
   (Some commor[...]

2. *Unfortunately*[...]
   pp. 557–562)[...]

3. *Next*, the cat [...]
   (Some commo[...]
   ple, of course,[...]

4. *Smiling*, Bobb[...]

5. *Excited*, Susie[...]

6. *Yes*, I would l[...]

7. *Well*, someon[...]

Phrases

1. *Near the fen[...]
   phrases, see p[...]

Teaching Idea
Linking these phrases to those in Chapters 18 and 20 is useful reinforcement.

2. *Diving for th[...]
   participial ph[...]

3. *Thrilled by tl[...]
   phrase, see pp[...]

4. *The car runn[...]
   phrase, see p.[...]

5. *His boat cou[...]
   absolute phra[...]

Activity 25-2: Correcting Dangling and Misplaced Modifiers

After reading the preceding information, rewrite the following sentences, adding whatever words might be needed to correct the dangling and misplaced modifiers.

Example: Trying his best to make the team, Isaac's sweat-soaked shirt was proof of his effort.

Revised: *Isaac was trying his best to make the team, and his sweat-soaked shirt was proof of his effort.*

Answers will vary.

1. Rain soaked the highway that was pouring from the sky.
   Rain pouring from the sky soaked the highway.

2. Banging two pans together to wake him up, Tim groaned as his mother clanged them together once again.
   As Tim's mother banged two pans together to wake him up, Tim groaned, and his mother clanged them together once again.

3. To vote in national elections, polling booths should be open to people until midnight.
   So that people can vote in national elections, polling booths should be open until midnight.

4. I felt sorry for the kitten at the pet store meowing in its cage.
   I felt sorry for the kitten meowing in its cage at the pet store.

5. At the age of seventy-three, Maria watched her grandfather run in the Boston Marathon.
   Maria watched her seventy-three-year-old grandfather run in the Boston Marathon.

6. Walking through the produce section, the peaches looked delicious.
   Walking through the produce section, I thought that the peaches looked delicious.

7. I read about an insect in a magazine that is born, mates, and dies all in one day.
   In a magazine I read about an insect that is born, mates, and dies all in one day.

8. Vito rode on the subway wearing only shorts and a T-shirt.
   Wearing only shorts and a T-shirt, Vito rode on the subway.

Teaching Idea
Students often feel (sometimes rightly so) that punctuation is arbitrary, pretty much wherever the current teacher says it is supposed to be, even when this advice conflicts with what teachers in their past have said. It can help to discuss punctuation as an imperfect but *self*-imposed system for achieving clarity.

WHAT ARE \

After we have lab
task as writers—to
ics) support our ha
marks such as semi
our ideas into easily
punctuation, even t

For example, no
letters, based on pu

  A. Dear John:

    I want a man
    thoughtful. P
    You have rui
    soever wher

    Susan

  B. Dear John:

    I want a mar
    thoughtful—
    rior. You hav
    whatsoever.

    Yours,
    Susan

Our work is no
mas, but we *are* li
our work if we c
cause us the most

COMMAS

Aside from en
mark. Because w
ing this mark, an
ideas. The system
reasonably well,
usage convention
needs. There *is* a
than ear. Writing
and edited versio
will only help a
of us are happy
Learning to pu
parts, which we
ordinate clause a
make sense to yo
and the few seco
had with comma

Teaching Idea
Because most students rely heavily on the "pause-and-punctuate" method, it is worth acknowledging that it does work *part* of the time.

Teaching Idea
Long after students have forgotten participial phrases and adverb clauses, they may remember the five-to-six-word rule of thumb for applying introductory commas.

Five to six words
before a main clause?
Use a comma.

Two-part sentences?
Punctuate the second
half just like the first.

6. *To play lead guitar in the band*, <u>Tanya</u> <u>knew</u> that she would need to practice hard. (infinitive phrase, see p. 494)

7. *An athlete with much experience*, <u>Leslie</u> <u>could see</u> that the game was headed for disaster. (appositive phrase, see p. 496)

Clause

***Because** fall had arrived in full force*, <u>Bernie</u> <u>was raking</u> his twentieth bag of leaves. (adverb clause)

One quick method for identifying adverb clauses is to memorize a few "cue" words, subordinating conjunctions, like the word *because* that begins the sentence above. Here are a few more common ones: *if, since, when, after, until, while, as, although, before, so that* (see p. 488).

Notice in each of the phrase and clause examples above that the word groups add meaning to the main clause, in effect, introducing the main idea of the sentence. Whether or not you can identify the phrases and adverb clause above, if you can find the subject of the **main** clause and notice that there are five to six or more words in front of it, you probably need a comma.

Problems with Introductory Word Groups

When words come in front of our "cue" words, we sometimes have trouble punctuating introductory word groups.

- This morning *before I went to school*, I ate breakfast at IHOP.

In the sentence above, the introductory adverb clause begins with the subordinating conjunction *before* but the two words *this morning* might cause a person to miss the clause if she is only looking for subordinating conjunctions as the first word in the sentence.

Another instance in which we sometimes overlook introductory word groups is with compound and compound–complex sentences. To use the comma correctly, we treat the second half of the sentence, the one coming after the coordinating conjunction (*and, but, so, or, yet, for, nor*) as if it were the beginning of the sentence, as in the following examples:

A. <u>I</u> <u>have</u> to work this weekend, and *even though I have a math test on Monday*, <u>I</u> probably <u>won't be</u> able to study much for it.

B. <u>Brianna</u> <u>ended</u> up with a terrible sunburn, but *having spent most of the afternoon under an umbrella*, <u>I</u> <u>was</u> only pink.

Sentence A uses an introductory adverb clause after the *and*. Because this sentence has two main clauses, a comma is required after the word *Monday*. Sentence B is another two-part sentence, this one using two prepositional phrases after the *but*. Therefore, we use a comma.

One other point to consider in punctuating your sentence beginnings is that a single prepositional phrase does not require a comma, and neither does an adverb clause that is only three or four words long:

- *In this house* both parents are the bosses.

- *If we go* we will probably have fun.

For more help with identifying phrases and clauses, see Chapter 20.

Activity 26-1: Commas after Introductory Word Groups

Punctuate the following sentences, using commas to separate introductory word groups from main clauses. Before you place the comma, locate the verb and subject in the main clause, underlining the verb twice and the subject once. If a sentence is correct, do not insert a comma. In number 10 create three sentences that begin with introductory word groups requiring a comma.

Example: If we get this job done we can meet everyone at the party.

Corrected: If we get this job done, we can meet everyone at the party.

1. When we get to the top of the hill, we can see all of Monterey Bay.

2. Slipping on a slice of tomato, Darin fell flat on his back.

3. To have fun at the lake, a person only needs sunblock and a towel.

4. In the backseat you will find the new Radiohead CD.

5. Of the cell phones on the warning list, the Ericsson T28 World produces the highest level of radiation.

6. His lungs eaten away by cancer, the last Marlboro Man dropped from the saddle today.

7. Nevertheless, RU 486, the abortion pill, has finally arrived in the United States.

8. Frightened by a legal system that finally decided to care, deadbeat dads are beginning to pay their child support.

9. Climbing to the fifth floor of her walk-up apartment was a daily ordeal for Kendra.

10. Create three of your own sentences that begin with a phrase or adverb clause that needs to be set off from the main clause with a comma. (Underline the verb of the main clause twice and the subject once.)

   A. _Answers will vary_ _____

   _____

   B. _____

   _____

   C. _____

   _____

Teaching Idea
For more information on essential versus nonessential elements, you can direct students to Chapters 18, 20, and 21.

Commas That Set Off Nonessential Word Groups

The second major reason for using commas is to enclose **nonessential** word groups within main clauses or to set off the nonessential material at the end of the clause. *Nonessential* means that a word, phrase, or clause is not needed to complete the meaning of the main clause to which it is connected. If the unneeded material is removed from the sentence, the main idea is still clear. Let's compare nonessential to *essential* word groups:

A. The Dodge Caravan *that is leaking gasoline* is mine.

B. Dodge Caravans, *which are roomy family vehicles,* have convenient hatchback doors.

In sentence A we need the *that* clause to tell us which Dodge Caravan the writer is speaking about. In sentence B the *which* clause simply adds a comment that is not essential to the meaning of the main clause.

Which clauses frequently signal nonessential material, and when they do, they require commas to enclose or set them off at the ends of sentences. *That* clauses signal essential material and so do not take commas.

C. A bicyclist *who has survived cancer* might work even harder at his sport.

D. Lance Armstrong, *who has survived cancer,* is one of the best bicyclists in the world.

In sentence C the *who* clause identifies which bicyclist might work harder, not all cyclists, but perhaps those who have survived cancer. Sentence D uses a proper noun, Lance Armstrong, which identifies the athlete beyond question; therefore, the *who* clause that follows is nonessential and so is enclosed with commas.

We frequently use nonessential word groups within and at the ends of our sentences to enrich our writing, adding useful information and creating sentence variety. When we do, we should signal our reader with commas that the material is of secondary importance. Following, you will see examples of nonessential single words, phrases, and clauses. Notice that the nonessential introductory word groups from our previous comma category still require commas when shifted into the main clauses.

Single Words

1. I hope, *however,* to make it to the bank before it closes. (conjunctive adverb)

2. Gail, *unfortunately,* doesn't have enough money to buy that computer. (adverb)

3. The cat, *next,* decided to claw the new curtains. (transitional word)

4. Bobby, *smiling,* cradled his new catcher's mitt. (present participle)

5. Susie, *thrilled,* ran to meet her mother. (past participle)

Phrases

1. Wayne, *diving for the football,* snatched it from the air with one hand. (present participial phrase)

2. Susie, *excited by the sight of presents,* ran to meet her mother. (past participial phrase)

3. Latashia coasted into her driveway, *the car running on fumes.* (present absolute phrase)

4. Terry, *his boat covered with a tarp,* felt it would survive the hailstorm. (past absolute phrase)

5. Tanya knew, *to play lead guitar in the band,* that she would need to practice hard. (infinitive phrase)

6. Leslie, *an athlete with much experience,* could see that the game was headed for disaster. (appositive phrase)

We sometimes confuse essential with nonessential participial phrases within and at the ends of sentences, leading to misused commas. Compare the participial phrases that end the following two sentences:

A. We took great pleasure in the cottonwood leaves *rustling in the wind.*

B. <u>We</u> <u><u>took</u></u> great pleasure in the cottonwood leaves rustling in the wind, *hoping the day would remain fair.*

Sentence A tells us which leaves the people took pleasure in. We could rewrite the phrase into an essential adjective clause that reads, the cottonwood leaves *"that were rustling in the wind."* Sentence B, on the other hand, ends with a nonessential participial phrase, one that merely adds a comment. Notice that we could easily shift the phrase *hoping the day would remain fair* to the beginning of the sentence because it describes the subject *We.* However, the phrase *rustling in the wind* is fixed in place next to the word it describes, *leaves.* To shift the *rustling* phrase to the beginning of sentence A would create a dangling modifier. (For more on dangling modifiers, see p. 560.)

Clauses

1. <u>Dimitri</u> <u><u>stayed</u></u> at the Marriott Hotel, *which is one of the finest in the city.*

2. <u>Slobodan Milosevic</u>, *who contributed to the deaths of thousands,* <u><u>is</u></u> no longer in power in Yugoslavia.

In both of the above sentences, the underlined adjective clauses are clearly nonessential because they follow proper nouns. The same logic applies to another adjective clause that begins with the word *where* and can be either essential or nonessential, as in the following examples:

A. <u>Gary</u> <u><u>was</u></u> not as popular in Topeka as he is in the city *where he now lives.*

B. <u>Gary</u> <u><u>was</u></u> not as popular in Topeka as he is in St. Louis, *where he moved last summer.*

In sentence A the *where* clause completes the meaning of the main clause, telling which city he is now popular in. Sentence B uses the proper noun *St. Louis,* so the *where* clause becomes nonessential and is therefore set off with a comma.

For more on nonessential versus essential word groups, see pp. 499–500.

Activity 26 2: Commas with Nonessential Word Groups

Punctuate the following sentences, using commas to set off nonessential word groups within and at the ends of main clauses. Before you place the commas, locate the verb and subject in the main clause, underlining the <u>verb</u> twice and the <u>subject</u> once. If a sentence is correct, do not insert commas. In number 10 create three sentences that use nonessential word groups.

Example: Kelcey chased after the soccer ball running at full speed.

Corrected: <u>Kelcey</u> <u><u>chased</u></u> after the soccer ball, running at full speed.

1. The <u>motorcycle</u> that is blowing oily smoke <u><u>needs</u></u> a ring job. *C*

2. *<u>Smithsonian</u>* <u>magazine</u>, which has Al Gore on its board of regents, <u><u>is</u></u> <u><u>filled</u></u> with interesting articles.

3. <u>Dustin</u>, reacting quickly, <u><u>managed</u></u> to save the child from falling overboard.

4. <u>Eboni</u>, exhausted, <u><u>dragged</u></u> herself into the shower at 6:30 A.M.

5. The <u>wind</u>, which had blown continuously for three days, <u><u>whipped</u></u> the edge of the flag to ragged tatters.

6. The boxer, hoping desperately for an opportunity to attack, continued to backpedal around the ring.

7. At midnight, a time known as the "witching hour," Halloween parties reach their height.

8. Gail's pediatrician, who looked like she had bad news, walked slowly toward us.

9. I couldn't help but notice the purple bruise developing under his left eye. *C*

10. Create three of your own sentences that include nonessential word groups. Be sure to set off the unneeded material with commas. (Underline the <u>verb</u> of the main clause twice and the <u>subject</u> once.)

A. *Answers will vary* _____

_____

B. _____

_____

C. _____

_____

Memorizing *and/but* will help you remember to edit for commas in two-part sentences.

Commas That Divide Main Clauses

The last major reason for using commas is to separate main clauses within a sentence that uses a coordinating conjunction (***and, but**, or, so, yet, nor, for*). Here are several examples:

1. Five-year-old Addie wanted to climb the sweet gum tree in her backyard, *and* her mother wanted to stop her.

2. Jacob wanted to explain to his girlfriend what he was doing at the movies with another woman, *but* he couldn't think of a convincing excuse.

3. You can pay me now, *or* you can pay me later.

4. People can listen to radio over the Internet, *so* now they can tune in to other countries and other cultures.

5. Terrorists destroyed the World Trade Center on September 11, 2001, yet with this act they also began the destruction of their own organization.

Notice that in each sentence there is a subject and a verb on *both* sides of the coordinating conjunction. If you try to place a comma before every coordinating conjunction in a sentence, you will have a mess on your hands. Do not punctuate like this:

- The willow trees were blowing in the wind, and losing leaves, so quickly that the trees would soon be bare. (no comma needed)

The sentence above has only one main clause with a two-part verb, *were blowing* and *losing*. Remember, use a comma before a coordinating conjunction when you have two separate sentences that could be divided with a period but instead are being separated with a comma.

One other point that sometimes puzzles us is the subordinating conjunction *so that*, which can look just like the coordinating conjunction *so* when we drop the *that*, as in the following example:

- Cinderella's cruel stepmother locked her in a room so (that) one of the stepmother's daughters might wed Prince Charming. (no comma needed)

Teaching Idea
It is worth stressing this misuse of a comma with a coordinating conjunction because it is so frequent in student writing, particularly when students are focusing on commas with compound sentences. You might direct students who are having trouble with this error back to Coordination in Chapter 18 and to Unnecessary Commas in this chapter.

When one or both of the main clauses are only a few words long, some writers omit the comma, as in the following example:

• This deal stinks and you do too.

Activity 26-3: Commas to Divide Compound Sentences

In the following sentences, put commas before the coordinating conjunctions (*and, but, or, so, yet, nor, for*) wherever needed. Before you place the commas, locate the verb and subject in the **main** clause, underlining the <u>verb</u> twice and the <u>subject</u> once. If a sentence is correct, do not insert commas. In number 10 create three sentences that use coordinating conjunctions in compound sentences.

Example: Nina asked her grandfather a question but he did not hear her.

Corrected: <u>Nina</u> <u>asked</u> her grandfather a question, but <u>he</u> <u>did</u> not <u>hear</u> her.

1. The <u>California sea otter</u> and the <u>Chinese panda</u> <u>are</u> on the endangered species list. *C*

2. <u>Sending</u> large robots to distant planets <u>is</u> too expensive, but <u>sending</u> miniature ones <u>is</u> not.

3. <u>Lois</u> <u>tried</u> for three years to play piano, yet <u>she</u> <u>could</u> not <u>master</u> the bass line.

4. <u>Pagers</u> in college classrooms <u>can be viewed</u> as a blessing to those who need them or a curse to those who are <u>startled</u> by the beeping. *C*

5. The <u>principal</u> <u>cried</u> out in the midst of his nightmare and <u>drifted</u> back into dreams of being chased through the halls by students. *C*

6. Some <u>people</u> <u>feel</u> that college athletes should maintain at least a C average, or the athletes <u>should be benched</u> until they raise their grades.

7. At first <u>Cecelia</u> <u>favored</u> the Republican candidate, but then <u>she</u> <u>discovered</u> what his real priorities were.

8. <u>Russ</u> <u>was</u> on his way to Madison Middle School, and <u>he</u> fervently <u>hoped</u> that Max, the class bully, would be absent again that day.

9. <u>Angie</u> <u>wanted</u> to win the lottery so she could quit her job at the GM plant. *C*

10. Create three of your own compound sentences, being sure to use a comma before the coordinating conjunction. (Underline the <u>verb</u> of the main clause twice and the <u>subject</u> once.)

   A. _Answers will vary_ _____

   _____

   B. _____

   _____

   C. _____

   _____

◼ SECONDARY COMMA CATEGORIES

While the Big Three comma categories account for most comma errors, the secondary group that follows can also cause some confusion.

Items in a Series

When we list three or more single words or word groups in a row, we should follow each word group with a comma:

A. I'm going to Payless to buy some lumber, paving stones, and cement. (nouns)

B. We ran for the bus stop, missed the bus, and then chased it all the way to the next stop. (verb phrases)

C. Harry did the research, Albert organized all the sources, and Terry wrote most of the first draft. (main clauses)

Coordinate Adjectives

Teaching Idea
Students will find more information on ordering adjectives in Chapter 28.

When we use two or more adjectives in front of a noun (or pronoun), and those adjectives equally describe the noun (or pronoun), we place a comma between the adjectives:

A. It was a *long, hard* hike to get to the top of the mountain.

In the sentence above we could easily have used the word *and* in place of the comma, or we could reverse the two adjectives, saying *a hard, long hike*. Contrast sentence A above, which uses coordinate adjectives, with sentence B, which uses cumulative adjectives:

B. *Two tired old* men sat on a park bench.

The noun *men* is being described by the words *two tired old*, but we could neither insert *and* between the words nor reverse them and still make sense. Cumulative adjectives that do not require commas fall into these categories: number, judgment, size, age, color, location, and material. (For more on cumulative adjectives, see p. 603.)

Another question that we sometimes have about adjectives are those that are connected to two-word nouns, as in the following sentence:

• Melanie changed the *filthy* furnace filter.

In this sentence *furnace filter* functions as a single unit, so no comma is needed.

Contrasting Expressions

We often contrast ideas in a sentence using the word *not*:

• Frank, not Tony, deserves the promotion.

Misleading Expressions

If a word might be misinterpreted without a comma, either restructure the sentence or insert a comma:

Misleading: Without hunting deer would soon overpopulate and die from starvation.

Comma: Without hunting, deer would soon overpopulate and die from starvation.

Rewriting: Deer would soon overpopulate and die from starvation if there were no hunting season.

Numbers, Addresses, Place Names, Dates, Direct Address

When we use numbers, addresses, place names, dates, and direct address we should follow the conventions of standard comma placement:

- **Numbers:** 3,985,041
- **Addresses:** Joanne lives at 4593 Connell Lane, Overland Park, Kansas.
- **Place names:** Most of my relatives live in Forth Worth, Texas.
- **Dates:** On October 13, 2000, the dreaded Friday the 13th appeared on the calendar.
- **Direct address:** "Stefanie, would you please close the window?"

Activity 26-4: Commas with Secondary Categories

After reading the preceding information, put commas wherever you think they are needed in the following sentences. Do not insert any commas if you feel that the sentence is correct.

Example: Everyone I know is going on to college trade school or the service.

Corrected: Everyone I know is going on to college, trade school, or the service.

1. Five young trick-or-treating children came jostling up to the front door. *C*

2. Wallace stood on shaky, weak legs that would carry him no farther.

3. Estefana wanted to go to Mardi Gras, not the mountains.

4. The wedding will be on May 14, 2001, at the Episcopal church at 4966 Birch, Mission, Kansas.

5. The overworked Canon BubbleJet printer began to run out of ink. *C*

6. Canoeing on Ozark rivers, rafting on the Colorado River, and kayaking in the ocean are three of Omar's favorite pastimes.

7. "Brianna, I hope you are done with your homework," said her mother.

8. At sixteen, teenagers are finally able to drive.

9. Tammy and her friends decided not to go to the show after all. *C*

10. Anthony has the stereo cranked full blast, his sister is channel surfing, and little Amy is banging away on the piano—both parents have surrendered, retreating to the porch for a few moments of quiet.

Unnecessary Commas

Having just reviewed the three main uses and the secondary uses of the comma, you probably have a good idea of where most commas belong. However, we are still sometimes tempted to insert commas without a specific rule to guide us, or sometimes we misinterpret an example, leading to comma confusion. Following are four common instances where we misuse commas:

Separating Subject from Verb or Object

Unless you are enclosing nonessential word groups, avoid putting a comma between the subject and the verb or the verb and its object. Here are several examples of incorrectly punctuated sentences:

A. All of Andy's friends, went to see him in the hospital. (subject separated from verb)

B. How the child managed to force his head through the bars, was a mystery to everyone. (subject separated from verb)

C. Our team finally won, an important away game. (verb separated from its object)

D. Several times that day Myndi hoped, that she had turned the oven off before she left the house. (verb separated from its object)

No comma in these sentences

Separating Compound Constructions

One of the Big Three comma categories stresses putting a comma before a coordinating conjunction (*and, but, or, so, yet, for, nor*) between two **main** clauses (stand-alone sentences). However, unless there is a subject and a verb on *both* sides of the conjunction—except for items in a series—you do not need a comma. Here are several examples of incorrectly punctuated sentences:

A. Marta thought that she would see Bruce Springsteen in concert at Sandstone, *but found out* that he had canceled the tour. (compound verb: no subject after *but*)

B. T. E. Lawrence survived many hardships and much combat between the years 1916 and 1918, *and died in* his home country of England from a motorcycle accident. (compound verb: no subject after *and*)

C. Some long-overdue recognition from his boss, *and* the promise of an immediate pay raise helped Raymundo decide to stay at his job. (compound subject: one verb)

D. The skiers rocketed *down the icy slopes,* and *then along the narrow trail* that connected Fantasy to Suicide Run. (compound prepositional phrases)

No comma in these sentences

In sentences A and B we sometimes mistake the second half, the part after the coordinating conjunction, as a complete main clause. Sentence C could treat the phrase *and the promise of an immediate pay raise* as a nonessential word group, but to do this, the phrase would need to be enclosed in commas. Sentence D might also want to treat a phrase as nonessential—*and along the narrow trail*—but the phrase is necessary to complete the meaning of the sentence.

Separating Essential Word Groups

Sometimes we confuse our readers by separating essential information from a sentence with commas. Here are several examples of incorrectly punctuated sentences:

A. Stephen King's novel, *Salem's Lot,* has several frightening vampire scenes. (Essential appositive: King has many novels, not just one, so the commas in this sentence are misleading.)

B. The motorcycle, *that has no mufflers,* wakes everyone in the neighborhood. (Essential adjective clause: the clause *that has no mufflers* is needed in the sentence to point out which motorcycle is waking everyone.)

C. The squirrel, missing half a tail, is the one that keeps getting into my bird feeders. (Essential participial phrase: the phrase *missing half a tail* is needed to tell which squirrel is invading the feeders.)

No comma in these sentences

D. The Chile's restaurant, in the Oak Park Mall Shopping Center, is the one with the best chicken sandwich in town. (Essential prepositional phrase: the phrase *in the Oak Park Mall Shopping Center* is needed to tell which Chile's has the best chicken sandwich.)

Note: Remember to use two, not just one, commas to enclose nonessential material.

Separating Adverb Clauses after Main Clauses

A final comma convention that can trip us up says to avoid commas before adverb clauses (clauses beginning with words like *because, if, since, when, until, while, as*) that come *after* main clauses in sentences. Perhaps in part because we are beginning to remember to follow the first main comma rule that calls for the setting off of introductory adverb clauses—subordinate clauses that come before main clauses— we generalize the comma to any place in a sentence where we spot an adverb clause. Here is an example of a misused comma:

Not this: We went to the hockey game, *because we like the Blades.*

But this: *Because we like the Blades,* we went to the hockey game.

Note: Adverb clauses that begin with *although, though,* and *even though* usually do use a comma even when they follow a main clause because these subordinating conjunctions announce strong contrast.

Activity 26 5: Removing Unnecessary Commas

Cross out any incorrectly used comma in the following sentences. Before you make the correction, underline the <u>verb</u> of the main clause twice and the <u>subject</u> once. If the sentence is correct, leave the commas intact.

Example: While Roxanne tried on a new dress, her friend wandered around the department store, and finally decided to buy a new purse.

Corrected: While Roxanne tried on a new dress, her <u>friend</u> <u><u>wandered</u></u> around the department store and finally <u><u>decided</u></u> to buy a new purse.

1. Wandering listlessly, across the front yard, Helen felt that she had seen her better days pass her by, and wondered, if there was a chance that she still had a future.

2. Everyone, in the class thought, that singular pronouns like *everyone* should be plural.

3. The Saturn, missing its left rear taillight, was being followed closely by a highway patrol car. *(keep commas or delete both)*

4. The Suzuki Grand Vitara, costing less than several of its competitors, has a zippy, six-cylinder engine.

5. Arturo knew, that he was in trouble, when the conductor stopped practice the second time, and pointed at him.

6. Bruce Willis performed well in the movie, *Armageddon.*

7. The stillness in the air, and the sudden absence of animal activity made Gloria think a big storm might be on the way. *(delete comma or add one after "activity")*

8. Dennis could see that quitting his job, and moving out of the city would not help him forget his first lost love.

9. The temperatures will remain in the hundreds, if the Jet Stream does not dip back down into the Midwest.

10. The insane engineer blew the whistle for five nonstop minutes as his train rumbled past the crossing, waking residents at 3:00 A.M. who grumbled into their pillows and then dropped back into restless sleep. C

OTHER PUNCTUATION AND MECHANICS

Commas are our main punctuation mark but not the only one. We frequently use other marks—such as semicolons, colons, dashes, and parentheses—to group and separate ideas. And sometimes we wish to emphasize a word through bolding or italicizing.

Semicolon

If we think about periods as full stops in sentences, bringing the reader to a temporary halt, we might think of commas as half stops, split-second pauses that give the reader a rest and a chance to process information. Semicolons might be thought of as three-quarter stops, marks midway between a comma and a period. We use semicolons in two primary ways: to divide (or link) main clauses without using a coordinating conjunction (such as *and/but*) and to separate word groups in a series that contain commas.

Dividing Main Clauses

A. Jakob Dylan is following in his father's footsteps; Bob Dylan is proud of his son.

B. Many books have been written about the Beatles; however, *The Beatles Anthology* has been written by the surviving Beatles themselves.

> Note: semicolons are one method for correcting comma splices and run-on sentences.

In both A and B while a period could be used to separate the main clauses, each second main clause is so closely related to the first that the semicolon is a good choice. You might notice that sentence B uses a conjunctive adverb, *however*, between the two main clauses as well as a semicolon. Other common conjunctive adverbs used to join main clauses this way are *therefore, nevertheless, then, in fact,* and *consequently*. The semicolon used to divide main clauses is one option for eliminating a comma splice or a run-on sentence. (For more on comma splices and run-ons, see Chapter 22.)

Separating Word Groups in a Series

• When we go to the Renaissance Festival, we end up *devouring* turkey legs, sausages, and meat pies; *watching* the jousting, acting, and juggling; and *shopping* for clothing, art work, and musical instruments.

In the sentence above there are three primary word groups in a series, *devouring, watching, shopping*. However, each main phrase has other words within it that are separated by commas. To avoid confusion, we use semicolons to separate the main word groups.

Colon

The colon has three primary uses: to begin a formal list (as this sentence does), to separate closely related main clauses (as does the semicolon), and to mark a formal appositive (nonessential describing word or phrase) at the end of a sentence. We also use the colon sometimes to introduce quotations (John Smith claimed: "There is no gold in the New World.") and after the salutation of a business letter (Dear Professor Hastings:).

Formal List

- Maria will bring the following items: potato chips, soda, and pasta salad.

When introducing a list, the colon should be viewed as end punctuation: like a period it ends one grammatical sentence and begins the list. You do not need a colon in a sentence that includes the series of items within it, like this:

- **Unnecessary colon:** Maria will bring: potato chips, soda, and pasta salad.

Separating Main Clauses

Lowell finally understood why his girlfriend would not return his calls: she had decided that they were through.

Similar to a semicolon, a colon can be used to divide closely related main clauses as in the sentence above. To use a colon, however, the second clause should restate or complete the meaning of the first.

Appositive

- If you want a candid look at the Beatles, buy *The Beatles Anthology*: a book written by Paul, George, and Ringo.

The sentence above ends with a formal appositive, which describes the noun it follows, *The Beatles Anthology*.

Dash

The dash is a versatile punctuation mark that can help writers in several ways: to set off a series that begins a sentence, to indicate an abrupt break in thought within a sentence, to enclose items in a series that contain commas, and to emphasize a word or word group at the end of a sentence. Avoid overusing dashes; try to keep to one or two per page. (Note: A dash [—] is longer than a hyphen [--]. Use two hyphens on your keyboard to create a dash.)

Beginning series: Three novels, one anthology of short stories, and two how-to books—my summer reading list is complete.

Break in thought: I will arrive at the party—if Tony shows up to drive me—around midnight.

Items in a series: Last night Carrie packed all her necessities—clothes, shoes, and toiletries—but forgot to include her hair dryer.

Note possible confusion without the dashes: Last night Carrie packed all her necessities, clothes, shoes, and toiletries, but forgot to include her hair dryer.

Emphasize final word group: Javier had worked hard at Sprint and deserved some recognition—and a salary increase.

Parentheses

We use parentheses primarily to add nonessential material to a main clause, much as we use commas to set off similar unneeded but useful material. Sometimes commas and parentheses are interchangeable in a sentence, but writers usually reserve parentheses for more loosely related material. Avoid overusing parentheses; usually once or twice a page is enough.

- There were too many players on the team (and coaches for that matter).

Quotation Marks

Quotation marks are used primarily to enclose spoken and written words, either as dialogue or a quote from a text. We occasionally use quotation marks when refer-

Teaching Idea
End dashes can also help students with some fragment problems.

Teaching Idea
You might suggest the dash to students who want to use a comma to separate compound elements at the ends of sentences. Of course, they should reserve the dash for special emphasis.

ring to a word used as a word (the word "dinosaur" means monstrous lizard) and to enclose the titles of short creative works: stories, essays, poems, newspaper and magazine articles, songs, and episodes on television.

Dialogue: "I'll get Jamie out of the bath," said Albert.

Quotation from text: In *The Voyage of the Beagle* Charles Darwin writes, "In five little packets which I sent him, he has ascertained no less than sixty-seven different organic forms!"

Notice that the comma after *bath* and the exclamation point after *forms* are both placed **inside** the quotation marks.

Apostrophe

Apostrophes have two primary functions: they mark the omission of letters in contractions and show ownership.

Contractions: Here are some common contractions: *wouldn't* (would not), *won't* (will not), *let's* (let us), *it's* (it is), *you're* (you are), *who's* (who is/has).

Be careful when using contractions not to mistake *it's, you're,* and *who's* for these sound-alike words: *its, your,* and *whose.*

It's, you're, and *who's* are different words than *its, your,* and *whose.*

Possession: To show ownership, we use the apostrophe like this: John's book, Stefanie's car keys, the cloud's shadow. If we want to indicate plural possession, we place the apostrophe after the *s:* Adam and Darin owned the lemonade stand. It was the boys' stand.

Some words that require an apostrophe to show possession are not as obvious as others, for example, an hour's wait, a dollar's worth of chocolate raisins, a whole season's rain in one week. Restating the possessive word as an "of" phrase usually clarifies the need for the apostrophe: the car keys of Stefanie, the wait of an hour, the rain of a whole season.

Capitalization

We capitalize proper names—specific, unique individuals or things—and words derived from them. Here are several categories:

1. **Names of people, things, trademarks:** Mark, Statue of Liberty, Coca-Cola

2. **Professional titles:** Professor Oden, Doctor Franklin, Senator Jorgenson

3. **Organizations, sports teams, companies:** the United Way, Kansas City Chiefs, Sears

4. **Nationalities and races:** German, Russian, French, Korean, Syrian, African American, Hispanic, Asian

5. **Languages:** Spanish, Mandarin, Swahili, Portuguese, English

6. **Religions, deities, and holy books :** Catholic, Protestant, Buddhist, Hindu; Lord, Allah, Yahweh; Bible, Koran, Talmud

7. **Historical documents, periods, events:** the Constitution, the Renaissance, the Vietnam War

8. **Geographic names:** the Ozark Mountains, St. Louis, Pacific Northwest, Middle East

9. **Days, months, holidays:** Saturday, April, Christmas

10. **First word in a direct quote:** Margaret said, "No one will agree with you."

11. **Titles:** books, stories, films, magazines, newspapers, poems, songs, and works of art: *The Catcher in the Rye,* "A Perfect Day for Bananafish," *Newsweek*

Note: Capitalize all words in titles except prepositions (*on, in, by,* etc.), coordinating conjunctions (*and, but, or, so, yet, nor, for*), and articles (*a, an, the*)—unless any of these words follow a colon in the title, begin, or end the title (*Sleepwalking: A Comedy*).

What not to capitalize: seasons (spring), plants (rose, oak), animals (robin, aardvark), school subjects (biology, economics). Also, note that we capitalize a person's professional title but not the general profession: *Doctor* Johnson versus Abby Johnson, who is a *doctor*. Southwest *High School* versus Tom's *high school*.

Hyphen

Hyphens are used to join words and to show where words are divided into syllables.

Prefixes: ex-athlete, anti-Communist, self-respect, pro-democracy

Compound words: son-in-law, go-between, look-alike, twenty-seven

Compound adjectives: *well-respected* machinist, *good-looking* quarter horse, *hard-fought* contest, *problem-solving* attitude, *hard-to-catch* outlaw

Note: When the compound adjective follows the noun, no hyphen is used: The machinist is *well respected*. Jesse James was *hard to catch*.

Numbers

Some writers prefer to use numerals to indicate numbers instead of letters in most cases. However, a more traditional treatment calls for spelling out numbers of one or two words (*three, fourteen, fifty-six*) and then using numerals for numbers of three words or more (*101; 2,098; 5,980,746*). Here are several other conventions for number use:

- **Numbers in dates:** January 3, 2001 (*-st, -d, -th* are not needed after dates.)

- **Numbers in series:** The driveway was 140 feet long, 12 feet wide, and 6 inches deep. (Be consistent using numerals or letters.)

- **Beginning sentences with numbers:** One hundred and thirty passengers died in the crash. (Spell out the number at the beginning of a sentence or recast the sentence.)

- **Percentages and decimals:** The solution was 95 percent common water. (Use numerals.)

- **Pages of books:** The authors state on page 34. . . . (Use numerals.)

- **Identification numbers:** room 14, Interstate 35, channel 41

Underlining and Italicizing

We underline words to draw the reader's attention to them (italicizing as an option in word processing), and most of the underlining or italicizing that we do is for titles. The following list shows what categories of words to underline or italicize:

- Titles:

Books: *The Ox-Bow Incident*	Long poems: *Beowulf*
Plays: *Hamlet*	Periodicals: *Newsweek*
Pamphlets: *Treating Lower Back Pain*	Published speeches: *Gettysburg Address*
Musical works: *Tapestry*	Movies: *The Abyss*
Television and radio programs: *60 Minutes*	Works of art: *David*

- Names of specific airplanes, trains, ships, and satellites: the space shuttle *Challenger*
- Words and letters referred to as such: The word *very* is usually expendable.

It can also be useful to occasionally italicize a word for emphasis, similar to raising your voice when you say the word aloud. Use this stylistic device sparingly, maybe once in an entire essay, but don't be afraid to experiment with it:

- Luann said that she would *never* marry a man for money.

Activity 26-6: Practicing Mechanics

Correct the errors in the following sentences. Before you make any correction, underline in the main clauses the <u>verb</u> twice and the <u>subject</u> once. Check for semicolons, colons, dashes, quotation marks, apostrophes, capitalization, hyphens, numbers, and underlining/italicizing.

Example: The essay that Tony wrote called Diminished Capacity was praised by his teacher, who said, This essay should win the school's literary competition.

Corrected: The essay that Tony wrote called "Diminished Capacity" was praised by his teacher, who said, "This essay should win the school's literary competition."

1. Harvey said, there are many well intentioned people maybe the majority who vote for a president based on a single issue.

2. Here are just a few of the car Manufacturers who have gotten into the mini-SUV line: toyota, subaru, suzuki, and nissan.

3. The recent arrival of the hybrid gasoline/electric cars is a hopeful sign for the environment; these cars might significantly reduce air pollution.

4. Some forget that its the peoples will that is supposed to govern a democracy.

5. Juliet loves cool Spring days (though she dislikes the rain) and says after the earth has slept all winter, I cant wait for the first of Springs Daffodils.

6. 43 sailboats set out for key west, Florida, but only 39 made it through the *Hurricane*.

7. Thirty year old Alex Carroll has written a best selling book called Beat the Cops: The guide To Fighting Your Traffic Ticket And Winning. (Italic)

8. No till farming has become an established method for conserving the soil.

9. The AARP organization begins sending out it's membership applications to people when they turn 50.

10. Madonna's latest CD, Ray of Light, was overseen by French Producer Mirwais Ahmadzai.

CHAPTER 27

Spelling and Sound-Alike Words

Building Correct Spelling

Spelling Help
Vowels and Consonants
Patterns
Spelling Lists
Frequently Misspelled
  Words
Sound-Alike Words

Teaching Idea
Students who have special problems with spelling (such as those who are dyslexic) have often all but given up hope of dealing with the situation and also have often labeled themselves as unintelligent. It encourages these students in particular if you stress spelling as only one skill among many and one which they can improve.

WHAT ARE WE TRYING TO ACHIEVE AND WHY?

In conversation we often demonstrate our ability to communicate clearly and forcefully, impressing the people around us as we make a point. However, the same explanation or argument offered in writing can become less convincing, if not discredited altogether, based on nothing more than misspelled words. Although spelling has low priority when we are composing, at some point it should become an important concern, not so much because unconventional spelling affects people's understanding as because the misspelled words affect people's perception of us. For example, even the brightest, most well-qualified applicant for a job who submits a résumé littered with words like *there* instead of *their*, *resumay* instead of *résumé*, and *exsellent communnication skils* instead of *excellent communication skills* will have a difficult time getting an interview.

English spelling is quirky at best, and everyone misspells words on occasion because of this. Sounding a word out helps frequently but many times is no help at all. A language that produces words like *knight, sign, sugar,* and *ocean* is bound to frustrate its writers. But there are a number of regularities in our spelling rules, patterns that we can depend on to answer many spelling questions. This chapter will help you improve your spelling with several basic rules, lists of commonly misspelled words, and lists of sound-alike words.

SOME SUGGESTIONS FOR HELP WITH SPELLING

1. **Make a decision to work on your spelling.** If you want to improve, you can.

2. **Develop the dictionary habit.** Write with a dictionary close at hand. Put a question mark by words that you are unsure of as you draft, and then use your dictionary to find the correct spelling. If you try several letter combinations and still cannot find the correct spelling, mark the word and ask someone for help, perhaps a person in your editing group.

3. **Buy an electronic dictionary** that is programmed to find approximate spellings.

4. **Take advantage of the spell-check feature** of your word-processing software, realizing that it is only a simple-minded device that can help, not solve, spelling problems. (For more on spell check, see pp. A14–A15.)

Teaching Idea
After students have turned in their first evaluated assignment, you might encourage them to track their errors, including spelling and homonyms, and list them on the Improvement Chart, Appendix 2.

5. **Begin a personal spelling list** of words you are unsure of or have misspelled in compositions. Pay particular attention to the ordinary words that you use regularly and to sound-alike words (*it's/its, their/there, then/than*). These words create far more problems for us than multisyllable or uncommon words. If we need to write words like *photovoltaic* or *conundrum*, because they are uncommon, we are alerted to the need to check their spelling. It is the common, small misspelled words that are more likely to plague us.

6. **When you begin to edit, look closely at *every* word in every sentence,** pausing to sound the word out syllable by syllable.

7. **Try to remember pattern words** that have similar consonant/vowel arrangements and the same number of syllables. If, for example, you are unsure of whether to double the *p* in the word *hopped* but are fairly sure about the double *p* in *stopped*, the similarity in syllables and consonant/vowel arrangement will often help you make the right decision.

8. **Test yourself with the lists of commonly misspelled words and sound-alike words in this chapter.** List any word that you misspell on your spelling chart along with the correct spelling. It often helps to pronounce the word aloud several times, exaggerating the stresses on syllables, such as *soph-O-more* or *math-E-mat-ics.*

9. When you discover a misspelled word, look up the correct spelling, and then write the word several times, preferably within a sentence.

10. Study the spelling patterns listed in this chapter.

■ REVIEWING VOWELS AND CONSONANTS

Much of spelling hinges on being able to break words into **syllables** and to recognize **vowels** and **consonants**. *Syllables* are simply units of sound—the way a word is divided in the dictionary, for example: *syl-la-ble* or *base-ball*. *Vowels* and *consonants* are the names that we give to the two groups of letters into which we divide the twenty-six letters of our alphabet.

Vowels: *a, e, i, o, u*

Consonants: *b, c, d, f, g, h, j, k, l, m, n, p, q, r, s, t, v, w, x, y, z*

The letter *y* can function as either a vowel or consonant, depending on the word it is in and its placement in the word.

Y as a vowel: *pretty* (the *y* sounds like *ee*) and *fly* (the *y* sounds like *i*).

Y as a consonant: *yes*

■ SOME USEFUL SPELLING PATTERNS

Doubling the Final Consonant

To know when to double the final consonant of a word when adding a suffix (a brief ending like *-ed* or *-ing*), look for the three following points:

1. Is the word one syllable (*pot = potted*), or is it accented on the last syllable (*oc-cur = oc-curred*)?

2. Does the suffix begin with a vowel (*spin + ing = spinning*)?

C V C
3. Are the last three letters of the word consonant/vowel/consonant (s-*h-o-p* = *shopping*)?

If all three of these conditions are met, double the final consonant, as in the following lists:

Single-Syllable Words	Words Accented on the Final Syllable
stun + ing = stunning	oc-cur + ing = occurring
stop + ed = stopped	sub-mit + ing = submitting
plan + er = planner	com-mit + ed = committed
hot + est = hottest	pre-fer + ed = preferred

Double final consonant

If any of the three conditions are lacking, do *not* double the final consonant. Notice that the following words fulfill conditions 1 and 2 but not 3. None of the following words end in consonant/vowel/consonant:

Single-Syllable Words	Words Accented on the Final Syllable
crawl + ing = crawling	despair + ing = despairing
stoop + ed = stooped	pretend + ing = pretending
plain + er = plainer	attend + ed = attended
slight + est = slightest	appear + ed = appeared

Do **not** double final consonant

Dropping or Keeping the Final *e*

As a general rule drop the final *e* from a word ending in *e* if the suffix begins with a **vowel.** Common suffixes: *-ing, -al, -able, -ence, -ance, -ion, -ous, -ure, -ive,* and *-age.*

come + ing = coming	congregate + ion = congregation
survive + al = survival	fame + ous = famous
excite + able = excitable	seize + ure = seizure
precede + ence = precedence	create + ive = creative
guide + ance = guidance	plume + age = plumage

Here are several exceptions to this rule: *noticeable, courageous, manageable, dyeing, mileage.*

If the word ending in *e* adds a suffix beginning with a **consonant,** usually keep the *e.* Common suffixes: *-ly, -ment, -ness, -less, -ty,* and *-ful.*

definite + ly = definitely	taste + less = tasteless
advertise + ment = advertisement	entire + ty = entirety
like + ness = likeness	waste + ful = wasteful

Here are several exceptions to this rule: *acknowledgment, ninth, truly, wholly, argument.*

Changing or Not Changing the Final *y* to *i*

When a word ends with a *y* preceded by a **consonant,** change the *y* to *i* when you add a suffix, as in the following list:

sky + es = skies	happy + ness = happiness
rely + ance = reliance	healthy + est = healthiest
marry + ed = married	merry + ment = merriment
pity + less = pitiless	mercy + ful = merciful

When a word ends with a *y* preceded by a **vowel,** keep the *y* and add the suffix, as in the following list:

enjoy + able = enjoyable	play + ful = playful
deploy + ed = deployed	employ + ment = employment
joy + ous = joyous	gay + ly = gayly
coy + est = coyest	essay + ist = essayist

Here are several exceptions to this rule: *paid, said, laid, daily, gaily.*

Note: When a word ends in *y,* and you want to add the suffix *-ing,* always keep the *y: crying, studying, enjoying, laying, playing, saying.*

Forming Plurals: *-s* or *-es*

Most nouns form their plurals by adding *-s* or *-es* (*birds, bears, bees*). If the word ends in *ch, sh, ss, x,* or *z* use the *-es:*

snitch + es = snitches
brush + es = brushes
miss + es = misses

box + es = boxes

waltz + es = waltzes

If the noun ends in *y* preceded by a **vowel,** add -*s:*

holiday + s = holidays

Friday + s = Fridays

monkey + s = monkeys

But if the word ends in *y* preceded by a **consonant,** change the *y* to *i* and add -*es:*

theory + es = theories

sky + es = skies

fly + es = flies

Words that end in *o* may form their plurals with either an -*s* or -*es*. Here are a few common ones that might be helpful to memorize:

O Words Ending in -*s*	O Words Ending in -*es*
pianos	tomatoes
memos	potatoes
solos	heroes
radios	mosquitoes

Using *ie* or *ei*

In most instances use i before *e*, except after *c*, unless the *ei* sounds like *ay* as in *neighbor* and *weigh*.

ie	
believe	piece
niece	yield

Here are several exceptions: *caffeine, seize, height, leisure, neither, either, weird, foreign.*

ei after *c*	
conceive	receive
deceive	ceiling

ei That Sounds Like *ay*	
eighth	reign
weight	vein

List of Frequently Misspelled Words

a lot	adolescence	already	break
accept	advice	argument	breathe
accommodate	advise	beginning	business
acquaint	affect	believe	calendar
acquire	all right	beside	cannot

capital	field	necessary	since
career	foreign	ninety	sophomore
character	forty	noticeable	strength
choice	fourth	obstacle	subtle
choose	friendliness	occasion	success
chose	fulfill	occurred	suppose
completely	government	occurrence	surprise
conceive	governor	occurring	temperature
conscience	grammar	opportunity	than
conscientious	guarantee	parallel	their
conscious	height	particular	then
controlled	heroes	passed	there
controlling	hypocrite	past	therefore
convenience	immediately	perform	they're
council	independent	personnel	threw
counsel	interest	piece	through
counselor	interfere	possess	to
criticism	interrupt	practical	too
criticize	it's	precede	transferred
curiosity	its	preferred	truly
curious	jewelry	prejudice	unconscious
definitely	judgment	principal	unfortunately
dependent	knowledge	principle	until
desirability	led	privilege	usually
despair	leisure	proceed	vacuum
disappoint	length	professor	vegetable
disastrous	license	quiet	weight
discipline	likelihood	receive	weird
effect	liveliest	referring	where
eighth	loneliness	relieve	whether
environment	lonely	reminisce	whole
equipped	lose	rhythm	whose
exaggerate	maintenance	roommate	without
except	marriage	sense	woman
experience	mathematics	separate	written
fantasies	mischief	sergeant	yield
fascinate	moral	shining	you're
fictitious	morale	similar	your

SOUND-ALIKE WORDS

1. **A, an, and**

   The letter *a* is used before a word beginning with a consonant or consonant sound:

   * *A* rose is a beautiful flower.

   The word *an* is used before a word beginning with a vowel or vowel sound:

   * *An* iris is also a beautiful flower.

   The word *and* links words:

   * A rose *and* an iris are both beautiful flowers.

2. **Accept/except**

   The word *accept* means to receive:

   * Olga *accepted* the silver medal.

   The word *except* means excluding, other than, or but:

   * Olga proudly *accepted* the silver medal, *except* she still longed for the gold.

   * Every member of the gymnastics team *except* Marina received a medal.

3. **Advice/advise**

   The word *advice* means an opinion or suggestion:

   * Brent had some good *advice* to give to his younger brother.

   The word *advise* means to counsel or give a suggestion:

   * Brent *advised* his younger brother not to take their dad's car again.

4. **Affect/effect**

   The word *affect* means to influence or change:

   * Graduating from high school *affected* Matthew's career plans.

   The word *effect* means the result—and occasionally means to cause something:

   * The *effect* of Matthew's graduation was to change his career plans.

5. **All ready/already**

   The words *all ready* mean prepared:

   * Are you *all ready* to go to the beach?

   The word *already* means before or by this time:

   * Everyone was *already* prepared to go to the beach.

6. **Are/our**

   The word *are* means to be—it is the plural form:

   * Wallace and Lupe *are* working on the proposal.

   The word *our* means belonging to us:

   * Wallace and Lupe *are* working on *our* proposal.

7. Beside/besides

The word *beside* means next to:

- Brent sleeps with his cell phone *beside* him.

The word *besides* means in addition to or except for:

- *Besides* his cell phone Brent also sleeps with his pager.

8. Brake/break

The word *brake* means to stop or names a device for stopping:

- Most people *brake* when they approach a red light.

The word *break* means to separate something into pieces or destroy it:

- Please don't *break* the vase.

9. Breath/breathe

The word *breath* means the air we inhale:

- Having climbed five flights of stairs, Austin was out of *breath*.

The word *breathe* means the act of filling our lungs with air:

- Having climbed five flights of stairs, Austin needed to *breathe* deeply.

10. Choose/chose

The word *choose* means to select:

- "Sylvia, which mutual fund will you *choose?*"

The word *chose* is the past tense of *choose*:

- Sylvia *chose* the environmentally friendly fund.

11. Clothes/cloths

The word *clothes* means something to wear:

- Allyson is wearing business *clothes* this morning.

The word *cloths* means fabric:

- We will need several damp *cloths* to get the baby's face clean.

12. Conscience/conscious

The word *conscience* means an inner sense of ethical behavior:

- Natasha's *conscience* troubled her when she took the promotion.

The word *conscious* means to be awake or aware:

- Natasha was *conscious* of her *conscience* troubling her.

13. Do/due

The word *do* means to perform:

- When she discovered her error, Gabriel had to *do* the budget again.

The word *due* means something owing or expected to arrive:

- Javier was *due* at 3:00 P.M.

14. Farther/further

The word *farther* means distance:

- It's *farther* to your house than it is to mine.

The word *further* means additional:

- I would like *further* practice before I embarrass myself onstage.

15. Hear/here

The word *hear* means sensing a sound:

- At the Eagles' concert you are sure to *hear* "Hotel California."

The word *here* means a place:

- Next month the Eagles will play *here* in this city.

16. Its/it's

The word *its* means ownership by a thing or animal:

- The horse hurt *its* hoof.

The word *it's* means the contraction *it is*:

- The horse hurt *its* hoof, but *it's* going to recover soon.

17. Lead/led

The word *lead* means metal, to guide, or to be in front of:

- *Lead* is heavier than iron.
- Marco has been here before, so he will *lead* the way.

The word *led* is the past tense of *lead*:

- Marco had been here before, so he *led* the way.

18. Loose/lose

The word *loose* means unrestrained:

- I had a pocketful of *loose* change.

The word *lose* means to misplace:

- If you are not careful with all that *loose* change, you are likely to *lose* it.

19. Past/passed

The word *past* means time before now:

- Michael spends too much time thinking about the *past*.

The word *passed* is the past tense of the verb *to pass,* to go by:

- Haven't we *passed* this Dillard's sometime in the *past*?

20. Quiet/quite

The word *quiet* means silent:

- At the end of the dock, all was *quiet*.

The word *quite* means very:

- At the end of the dock, all was *quiet* and *quite* still.

21. Sit/set

The word *sit* means to be seated:

- If you don't mind, I will *sit* on the counter.

The word *set* means to place something:

- Please don't *sit* on the counter where we are going to *set* the plates.

22. Suppose/supposed (to)

The word *suppose* means to assume or guess:

- I *suppose* Carmaletta will skate today.

The word *supposed* can be the past tense of *suppose* but, combined with *to,* usually means ought to:

- Carmaletta is *supposed to* skate today.

23. Their/there/they're

The word *their* means ownership by more than one:

- Cofia and Travis own that house. It is *their* house.

The word *there* means a place:

- Cofia and Travis live in that house over *there*.

The word *they're is* a contraction meaning *they are*:

- Cofia and Travis own that house. *They're* living in it.

24. Then/than

The word *then* means afterward or at that time:

- Jocelyn went to the art exhibit and *then* went home.

The word *than* means a comparison is being made:

- Jocelyn likes impressionist paintings better *than* pop art.

25. Through/threw/thru

The word *through* means moving from one side to another or finished:

- Harvey drove *through* the parking lot at McDonald's.

The word *thru* is a commercial shortening of *through* and means a place of doing business as you briefly pass by. *Thru* should not be used as a synonym for *through:*

- Harvey drove *through* the drive-*thru* at McDonald's.

The word *threw* is the past tense of throw:

- When Harvey drove *through* the drive-*thru,* he *threw* five dollars to the cashier.

26. To/too/two

The word *to* means toward or marks an infinitive (*to* talk):

- Ashley went *to* the bank.

The word *too* means also or very:

- Ashley arrived at the bank *too* late *to* get any money from a teller.

The word *two* is a number:

- Ashley was *too* late *to* get the *two* hundred dollars she needed.

27. Use/used

The word *use* means to operate or work with something (*used* is the past tense):

- I will *use* the lawnmower today that my aunt *used* yesterday.

The word *used*, followed by *to,* means to be accustomed to:

- I am not *used to* the loud noise the lawn mower makes.

28. Whose/who's

The word *whose* shows ownership:

- Maxine found fifty dollars in the street but did not wonder long *whose* it was.

The word *who's* is a contraction meaning *who is* or *who has:*

- Maxine found fifty dollars, so she is the one *who's* buying lunch.

29. Were/where

The word *were* is the past tense of *are:*

- The clowns *were* squirting water all over the ring.

The word *where* means a place:

- The clowns *were* squirting water only *where* they *were* supposed to.

30. Your/you're

The word *your* shows ownership:

- Is that *your* Jeep?

The word *you're* is a contraction meaning *you are:*

- Oh, *you're* driving a rental.

Activity 27-1: Editing for Spelling and Sound-Alike Errors

The essay excerpt below has many spelling and sound-alike errors. Applying the rules from this chapter—and using a dictionary—find each error, cross it out, and write in the correct spelling in the space above it.

Huddled
Hudled together in tiny dark windowless shacks, the first English settlers in

the New World struggled to survive the winter. Having little expereince at rough *[experience]*

living conditions, planing poorly, and often being led by those unqualified for *[planning]*

the job, the colonists in most of the early settlements suffered terribly, many

dieing there first year from starvation, illness, injury, and conflicts with Native *[dying]* *[their]*

Americans. Begining with the "lost colony" of Gilbert and Raleigh and progresing *[Beginning]* *[progressing]*

thru the Massachusetts Bay Company, early English attempts at colonizeing the *[through]* *[colonizing]*

New World met with disaster.

Sir Humphrey Gilbert and his half-brother, Sir Walter Raleigh, *were* where the first
adventurers   *colonizing*
adventures to try colonizeing America. Obtaining permission from Queen
possess
Elizabeth in 1578 to "inhabit and posses" any land in the New World not claimed
by
buy a "Christian ruler," they both tried and failed several times. Gilbert, after

two attempts, was drowned in passage, and Raleigh had to abandon two more
colonies
colonys in 1585. Raleigh's final attempt was in 1587 with the infamous "lost

colony," settled by more than a hundred people on Roanoke Island, near the

coast of North Carolina. It vanished without a trace within three years.
                                                        stopped   *until*
After Gilbert and Raleigh, colonization efforts stoped untill 1607 when
                                companies
James I allowed two companys, the London and Plymouth, to try again, but
neither   *success*
niether, at first, met with succes. The London Company financed the first
                                                                into
attempt (to be called Jamestown), which from the start ran in to problems.

On the four-month voyage across the Atlantic, thirty-nine Englishmen died. Not

knowing any better, the survivors located Jamestown near swampy ground
                mosquitoes   *preparing*
that bred mosquitos and malaria. Instead of prepareing for winter by planting
        storing
and storeing enough food, the mainly gentlemen settlers searched for gold.
                                to
As a result many starved too death during the winter, and others died from

disease. By 1608 only thirty-eight colonists were alive. Although Jamestown

began to prosper after 1630, between 1607 and 1624 eighty percent of the
            thousands
colonists—thousand of men, women, and children—died.

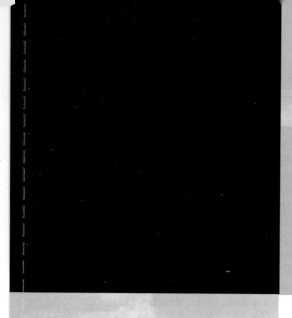

CHAPTER 28

ESL Concerns

Building Clarity

Nouns
Articles
Verbs
Prepositions
Adjectives

The following chart summarizes article usage:

Count/Noncount Noun	General	Specific
Singular count noun: car, bird, apple	Use *a* or *an*	Use *the*
Plural count noun: cars, birds, apples	Use no article	Use *the*
Noncount noun: weather, advice, flour	Use no article	Use *the*

Activity 28-2: Articles

Locate the article errors in the following paragraph. Cross out any incorrect articles and supply those that are missing by writing them in the space above the line.

This was my first trip aboard *a* jet and my first trip to another country. I was excited to be up in ~~an~~ *the* air with only five more hours till we would be landing in ~~a~~ *A* Munich, Germany. Flight attendant walked by and offered me ~~the~~ *a* Coke. "Yes, please," I said, trying not to look too excited, but the truth was that I could hardly wait to touch down. My parents had promised me this trip as *a* reward for finishing in *the* top third of my graduating class, and now we were finally here together at 30,000 feet, a few hours away from *a* week-long adventure.

◼ VERBS

As we discussed in Chapter 23, **verbs** are the heart of our writing, combining with subjects (nouns or pronouns) to create grammatical sentences. All sentences in English require a verb and a subject (though the subject may only be implied in a command, as in "<u>Leave</u> the room!"). Verbs have three simple tenses—past, present, and future—and must agree in person and number with their subject: "<u>Ronnell</u> <u>leaves</u> tonight. Her <u>friends</u> <u>leave</u> tomorrow." Chapters 20 and 23 will help you to identify and use verbs correctly, but this section will give you several other suggestions for handling questions common to nonnative speakers of English.

Word Order

- Verbs generally come after subjects in sentences: <u>Sasha</u> <u>dances</u> well.
- Helping verbs precede action verbs in a verb phrase: <u>Sasha</u> <u>*will*</u> <u>dance</u> this evening.
- A verb phrase may be separated by another word: <u>Sasha</u> <u>will</u> *not* <u>dance</u> this evening.

Three Irregular Verbs— *to Do, to Have,* and *to Be*

Two irregular verbs that can function as either helper verbs or action verbs are *to do* (forms: *do, does, did,* and *done*) and *to have* (forms: *have, has, had*).

Action verb: I *did* the dishes right after dinner. (meaning *completed* the job)

Helper verb: Olya *did* pay her credit card balance this month. (emphasizes *pay*)

Action verb: Ramon *had* only 500 dollars to spend on the guitar. (meaning *possessed*)

Helper verb: At one time he *had* hoped to have 1,000 dollars. (past perfect tense)

When used as a helping verb, *to do,* in all its forms, can help with questions, express a negative, and emphasize an action verb:

- **Question:** When *do* you plan on arriving?
- **Negative:** I *do* not intend to answer the question.
- **Emphasizer:** Leona *does* want to come to the party.

The irregular verb *to be* (forms: *am, are, is, was, were, been, being*) can function as either a verb that expresses state of being (linking verb) or a helping verb:

State of being: Em *is* in a good mood today. (links the subject, Em, to the feeling)

Helper verb: She *is* planning a party for fifteen friends. (present progressive tense)

Activity 28-3: Choosing Forms of *to Be, to Do,* and *to Have*

In the spaces below write the correct form of the verbs *to be, to do,* and *to have.*

Example: Sam ___*did*___ (to do) his homework last night before he went to bed.

1. Enrique ___*did*___ (to do) the laundry this morning.

2. Chen ___*did*___ (to do) send me a check last week.

3. Francesca ___*was*___ (to be) feeling wonderful yesterday.

4. Ms. Pollard ___*was*___ (to be) the best algebra teacher I ever had.

5. Coco ___*has*___ (to have) the letter of recommendation from her history professor.

6. We all ___*have*___ (to have) worked hard to make the performance succeed.

Modals

Other verbs that function as helpers are often called **modals:** *may/might, can/could, will/would, shall/should, must.* These helping verbs express requests, doubt, capability, necessity, and advisability:

- **Request:** *Would (will, could, can)* you pass the salt?
- **Doubt:** I *might (may)* go to the concert this weekend.
- **Capability:** I *could (can)* ask Mae to come with me.
- **Necessity:** Jade *must* meet her deadline or lose the contract.
- **Advisability:** You *should* arrive at the airport at least one hour before your flight.

The modals help refine the meaning of our primary verbs and are especially useful in softening requests. For example, while eating dinner we might easily say, "Pass the salt," with a tone of voice that sounds like a command. Or we could reduce the command to a request, using one of the modals: "Would you pass the salt?"

Note: The base form of a verb always follows the modal, so be careful not to use the past tense or an infinitive:

Not this: Francesca <u>should called (to call)</u> her mother this weekend.

But this: Francesca should call her mother this weekend.

Teaching Idea
You might point out how important modals are in English for addressing one another courteously.

Activity 28-4: Practicing Modals

In the following sentences write the correct modal.

1. The sun is in my eyes. Please, _____ *will* _____ you close the blinds? (request)

2. Ashwinder _____ *might* _____ be able to visit her parents in New Delhi over Christmas. (doubt)

3. Crystal _____ *can* _____ pick you up by 6:00 if you are ready to go. (capability)

4. If you want to do well on the exam, you _____ *should* _____ study the whole unit. (advisability)

5. I _____ *must* _____ make it to the bank by 5:00 if I want to get the loan. (necessity)

Stative Verbs

> Stative verbs do not use the present progressive tense.

Stative verbs indicate that a subject will remain constant, unchanging, for a certain time, for example, "Ashwani *understands* calculus better than I ever will." This sentence tells us that Ashwani knows calculus, and we assume that he is not likely to forget it in the near future. *Understand* is a stative verb. We should be careful not to use the present progressive with this kind of verb. It would be incorrect to write, "Ashwani *is understanding* calculus better than I ever will."

Here is a list of some common stative verbs:

be	hate	love	resemble
believe	have	mean	think
belong	know	need	understand
cost	like	own	weigh

Several verbs can be either stative or *active,* depending on their meaning, such as *weigh* and *look.* When this is the case, they can use the present progressive tense, for example:

• **Active use:** Tony *is weighing* himself to see how many pounds he must lose.

• **Stative use:** Tony *weighs* so much that he knows he must lose some pounds.

Activity 28-5: Recognizing Stative Verbs

In the space provided in the following sentences write *C* if the verb is correct and *I* if it is incorrect.

1. _*C*_ I believe that everything will turn out fine in the end.

2. _*I*_ Felipe is liking Maria and plans to tell her so.

3. _*I*_ I am hating the idea of taking another exam today.

4. _*C*_ Canadian geese are flying north as the weather begins to warm.

5. _*I*_ Rita has told us more than once that she is needing some money for tuition.

6. _*C*_ Neeva understands how to balance her checkbook.

Phrasal verbs are often informal and idiomatic.

Teaching Idea
Knowing phrasal verbs is invaluable to nonnative speakers in understanding informal language use, but students should know that informal and idiomatic expressions are usually not appropriate to academic discourse.

Two-Word (Phrasal) Verbs

Another verb that can be confusing is the **two-part** or **phrasal verb,** which consists of a verb followed by a preposition or adverb. For example, when we say that Leon will *look over* the report, we do not mean that he will try to see across the report to something on the other side; we mean that he will read and think about the report. Phrasal verbs usually express a different idea than the verbs would have without the attached preposition or adverb, so they can be difficult to understand if you consider only the literal interpretation. Dictionaries list phrasal verbs, and native speakers of English can help clarify meaning.

Most phrasal verbs consisting of a main verb and an adverb can be split or remain attached, as in the following example:

A. Travis will *drop* his sister *off* at school.

B. Travis will *drop off* his sister at school.

However, when a pronoun is used as the object it must be placed *between* the two verb parts, as in sentence C below:

C. **Correct:** Travis will *drop* <u>her</u> *off* at school.

D. **Incorrect:** Travis will *drop off* <u>her</u> at school.

Many phrasal verbs consisting of a main verb and a preposition are nonseparable, as in the following example:

• After that, Travis will *drop in* on his best friend.

We use many phrasal verbs in informal conversation that we would avoid in more formal academic writing, often finding a more concise substitute, for example:

• **Phrasal verb:** Professor Allen *drags out* class sessions with pointless anecdotes.

• **Substitute:** Professor Allen *prolongs* class sessions with pointless anecdotes.

For more on idiomatic and overworked expressions, see Chapter 19. Here is a list of some common two-part verbs:

Separable Two-Part Verbs		
ask out	invite on a date	Gabriel *asked* Sergei *out* to a movie.
ask over	invite to a place	Javier *asked* Marta *over* to his home.
back up	support	I hope my friends will *back* me *up*.
blow up	destroy	The construction crew had to *blow* the bridge *up*.
break down	disassemble	Sveta *broke* her tent *down* in the morning.
bring back	return	Frederick had to *bring* the videos *back*.
call off	cancel	The promoters had to *call* the concert *off*.
call up	telephone	Hector was too nervous to *call* Elena *up*.
carry out	do	The Marines *carried* their mission *out*.
cover up	hide	Politicians are always trying to *cover* something *up*.
drag out	prolong	Dad *dragged* the lecture *out* for an hour.
figure out	solve	Let's *figure* these bills *out*.
fix up	repair	We can *fix* this house *up* if we work hard.
get across	explain	Mom tried to *get* the message *across* to me.

give up	quit	Gebdao would like to *give* smoking *up*.
hand in	submit	The students all *handed* their homework *in*.
help out	assist	Friends *help* each other *out* in times of need.
lead on	entice, deceive	The salesperson *led* his customer *on*.
look up	search for	*Look* the number *up* in the phone book.

Nonseparable Two-Part Verbs

call on	visit, ask someone	Professor Sung *called on* Amy to answer.
catch up (with)	reach	I *caught up* with the bus at the corner.
come across	discover	Jesus *came across* a great CD sale.
drop by	visit	My cousin *dropped by* unexpectedly.
drop out	leave	Too many teenagers are *dropping out* of school.
get along (with)	coexist	Everyone *gets along with* Alex.
get in	enter	Tomas *got in* the car.
get off	leave	The passengers *got off* the plane.
get on	enter	The passengers *got on* the plane.
get out of	leave, avoid	Ho Chul *got out of* the final exam.
get over	recover from	Marco *got over* the reprimand from his boss.
get through	complete	The work crew *got through* with the road.
get up	arise	I *got up* late for class this morning.
go over	review	*Go over* your packing list before the bus arrives.
look after	take care of	Tasha said that she would *look after* the baby.
look into	investigate	Principal Alvarez said he would *look into* it.
look out (for)	care for, alert to	Rabbits must *look out for* foxes.
run into	meet accidentally	Kristin *ran into* Jamie at the hardware store.
run out (of)	finish a supply	We *ran out of* bread this morning.

Activity 28-6: Recognizing Phrasal Verbs

In the following sentences underline the phrasal verb(s). Remember that sometimes the verb parts will be separated.

1. While driving my truck yesterday, I ran into a shopping cart.

2. Ping worked hard to fix his motorcycle up for the Saturday race.

3. I promised my father that while he was gone I would look after my younger brother.

4. Sasha has decided to give all fried food up till he loses ten pounds.

5. Maria's boss got <u>over</u> his anger by the time the crew got <u>through</u> with the job.

6. Professor Capelli told his students that they could not <u>cover</u> their lack of knowledge <u>up</u> by "padding" their essay exam responses.

◼ PREPOSITIONS

Prepositions are words used to link nouns and pronouns to sentences. As in the phrasal verbs in the preceding section, prepositions are often part of *idiomatic expressions* (phrases that may ignore grammar rules and that have a meaning beyond the literal definition of the words used). Many prepositions help show location (*near, around, against, beside, below,* etc.), some indicate time (*until, till, during, for, since*), and some can represent either time or location (*on, in, by, at*).

Deciding which preposition to use can be tricky because idioms are often involved and because some prepositions can have several meanings. We will look at the common problem areas of overlapping *place and time* prepositions (*on, in, by, at*) and then note some common idiomatic phrases.

For more on prepositions, see Chapter 20.

Prepositions of Place

There are many prepositions of location, but the ones that can most often cause us problems are *on, in, by, at*.

On tells about a surface on which something rests:

- The pitcher is *on* the table. (rests on a surface)

- His watch is *on* his wrist. (rests on the arm)

- David's apartment building is *on* the corner of 119th and Quivera. (rests on the street)

  In tells that something is contained, surrounded, or enveloped:

- The guinea pig was *in* its cage. (contained by the bars)

- Maxine was outside *in* a drenching rain. (surrounded by the rain)

- Harold was *in* a perpetual state of depression. (enveloped by the emotion)

  By tells that one person or thing is next to another.

- Prudencio is standing *by* the gate.

- The beagle walks *by* my front porch every night at dusk.

  At tells about one person or thing in relation to another:

- This evening Jorge was *at* home.

- Joseph left his truck *at* Paul and Randy's Car Place.

Prepositions of Time

There are only a few prepositions that indicate time (including *until, till, during, for,* and *since*), but the ones that are particularly troublesome are those that overlap with location: *on, in, by,* and *at*.

On tells about a specific day or date:

- Your dental appointment is *on* October 17.

- We will arrive in Miami *on* Sunday morning.

In tells about relatively specific time periods, such as mornings, afternoons, evenings, minutes, hours, days, months, years, and seasons.

- I will wake you early *in* the morning.

- *In* about five minutes we will be ready.

    By tells "at this point in time."

- Roberto will be here *by* 3:00.

- If he is not here *by* midnight, we will have to leave him.

    At tells about a specific time:

- Angie hoped the game would start *at* 7:00 P.M.

- We were supposed to meet *at* noon by the rose garden.

Idiomatic Phrases

Convention has established the use of certain prepositions to follow adjectives and verbs, and when we substitute a differing preposition, the phrase becomes nonstandard English. The only way to become fluent with idiomatic phrases is to listen carefully to native speakers, read extensively, and memorize the phrases that are new to you or that your instructor marks on your papers. Below is a list of some common phrases using the correct prepositions.

Prepositional Phrases

abide *by* a decision	apologize *for* a mistake	concerned *about (with)* crime
abide *in* New York	arrive *at* home	independent *of* each other
accuse *of* theft	aware *of* a fact	interested *in* politics
afraid *of* horror films	bored *with* TV	proud *of* yourself
agree *with* a wife	capable *of* reading	responsible *for* a child
agree *to* a proposition	charge *for* an oil change	rewarded *by* an employer
angry *with* a friend	comply *with* an order	rewarded *for* work

Activity 28-7: Using Prepositions Correctly

In the following sentences determine whether or not the prepositions are used correctly. If all are right in a sentence, mark C in the space provided. Otherwise, cross out the incorrect preposition and write the correct one above it.

1. _____ Kim agreed *with* ~~by~~ her husband that they could afford to add a family room to their house.

2. _____ Ellie was proud *of* ~~in~~ herself that she had won first place with her oil painting.

3. __C__ This afternoon we will ride on the ferry to Vancouver Island.

4. _C_ Marta's art class was supposed to meet at the Nelson Art Gallery on Friday morning.

5. _____ The neighbor's Siamese cat stands *by, under, beneath, near* over my porch swing until I reach down to pet her.

6. _____ Susumu promised that he would arrive *at* to home by 6:00.

ORDERING ADJECTIVES

Adjectives are words that describe nouns and pronouns and that generally come in front of them (*strong* horse, *blue* sky). When we use more than one adjective, the resulting word group is said to accumulate meaning as it moves closer to the noun or pronoun it is describing (a *huge old deserted* mansion).

There are several categories of adjectives with a preferred arrangement to follow when using multiple adjectives:

1. **Determiners:** *this, these, that, the, a, an, some, many, my, our, your, all, both, each, several, one, two,* etc.

2. **Adjectives of judgment:** *unusual, interesting, impressive, ugly, beautiful, inspiring, hopeful, smart, funny*

3. **Adjectives of size:** *large, massive, small, tiny, heavy, light, tall, short*

4. **Adjectives of shape:** *round, square, rectangular, wide, deep, thin, slim, fat*

5. **Adjectives of age:** *young, adolescent, teenage, middle-aged, old, ancient*

6. **Adjectives of color:** *white, black, blue, red, yellow, green*

7. **Adjectives derived from proper nouns:** *American, German, Kansan, Parisian, Gothic*

8. **Adjectives of material:** *wood, plastic, cloth, paper, cardboard, metal, stone, clay, glass, ceramic*

Here are several combinations of adjectives:

- *The beautiful tall ancient* redwoods should stand forever.

- *Our brilliant young* daughter amazes people wherever we travel.

- *Five amusing fat brown* squirrels chased each other through the trees.

The adjective groups in each of the above sentences gather meaning as they approach the noun, and so no comma is needed to separate them. Remember that adjectives that modify or describe equally are said to be **coordinate** and *do* require a comma between them (*happy, hard-working* firefighter). In general, avoid "stacking" adjectives in front of nouns and pronouns. If you use more than two or three modifiers at one time, the word they are describing becomes overloaded. Try spreading the modifiers around within several sentences for better effect.

For more on single-word adjectives, adjective phrases, and adjective clauses, see Chapter 25.

Activity 28-8: Ordering Adjectives

In each of the following sentences, either mark C for correct in the space provided or rearrange the adjectives so their order is appropriate.

1. _____ This green large cardboard box _This large green cardboard box_____

2. _____ My Asian young friend _My young Asian friend_____

3. _____ Each ceramic beautiful tiny bird _Each beautiful tiny ceramic bird_____

4. _____ Four old shrunken men _Four shrunken old men_____

5. _____ A Parisian wide boulevard _A wide Parisian boulevard_____

6. __C__ A well-written big paperback book _____

UNIT SIX

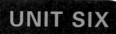

Additional Readings

The student models in the assignment chapters are excellent resources for helping you create paragraphs and essays. However, this unit offers a brief look at how professional writers incorporate the patterns of development in their writing, relying on detailed examples and explanations to produce memorable prose. As you read through these models, consider the elements of good writing we have practiced and see how many you can spot in the work of these authors. Do not be surprised if a topic or thesis sentence seems "out of place" occasionally. As we have noted previously, not all body paragraphs begin with a topic sentence and not all introductory paragraphs end with a thesis sentence.

▶ DESCRIPTION

The following two paragraphs are excerpts from John Steinbeck's novel *Cannery Row*, set in northern California. In this selection he describes a tide pool at the edge of Monterey Bay. Whether you have seen a tide pool before, or been in the ocean, does this description leave you feeling like you have seen a tide pool now?

To review the elements of descriptive writing, turn back to Chapter 5.

The Great Tide Pool

John Steinbeck

Doc was collecting marine animals in the Great Tide Pool on the tip of the Penin-   1
sula. It is a fabulous place: when the tide is in, a wave-churned basin, creamy with foam, whipped by the combers that roll in from the whistling buoy on the reef. But when the tide goes out the little water world becomes quiet and lovely. The sea is very clear and the bottom becomes fantastic with hurrying, fighting, feeding, breeding animals. Crabs rush from frond to frond of the waving algae. Starfish squat over mussels and limpets, attach their million little suckers and then slowly lift with incredible power until the prey is broken from the rock. And then the starfish stomach comes out and envelops its food. Orange and speckled and fluted nudibranchs slide gracefully over the rocks, their skirts waving like the dresses of Spanish dancers. And black eels poke their heads out of crevices and wait for prey. The snapping shrimps with their trigger claws pop loudly. The lovely colored world is glassed over. Hermit crabs like frantic children scamper on the bottom sand. And now one, finding an empty snail shell he likes better than his own, creeps out, exposing his soft body to the enemy for a moment, and then pops into the new shell. A wave breaks over the barrier, and churns the glassy water for a moment and mixes bubbles into the pool, and then it clears and is tranquil and lovely and murderous again. Here a crab tears a leg from his brother. The anemones expand like soft and brilliant flowers, inviting any tired and perplexed animal to lie for a moment in their arms, and when some small crab or little tide-pool Johnnie accepts

the green and purple invitation, the petals whip in, the stinging cells shoot tiny narcotic needles into the prey and it grows weak and perhaps sleepy while the searing caustic digestive acids melt its body down.

Then the creeping murderer, the octopus, steals out, slowly, softly, moving like 2 a gray mist, pretending now to be a bit of weed, now a rock, now a lump of decaying meat while its evil goat eyes watch coldly. It oozes and flows toward a feeding crab, and as it comes close its yellow eyes burn and its body turns rosy with the pulsing color of anticipation and rage. Then suddenly it runs lightly on the tips of its arms as ferociously as a charging cat. It leaps savagely on the crab, there is a puff of black fluid, and the struggling mass is obscured in the sepia cloud while the octopus murders the crab. On the exposed rocks out of water, the barnacles bubble behind their closed doors and the limpets dry out. And down to the rocks come the black flies to eat anything they can find. The sharp smell of iodine from the algae, and the lime smell of calcareous bodies and the smell of powerful protean, smell of sperm and ova fill the air. On the exposed rocks the starfish emit semen and eggs from between their rays. The smells of life and richness, of death and digestion, of decay and birth, burden the air. And salt spray blows in from the barrier where the ocean waits for its rising-tide strength to permit it back into the Great Tide Pool again. And on the reef the whistling buoy bellows like a sad and patient bull.

Questions for Analysis

1. **What is the dominant impression of these two paragraphs? Does the author state it in a topic sentence, if so where?**
   Answer: Paragraph 1: "the bottom becomes fantastic with hurrying, fighting, feeding, breeding animals . . ." Or in students' own words: dominant impression: action, struggle, life rushing about its business.

2. **Name five specific words. How do these words contribute to the description?**
   Answer: Starfish, mussels, limpets, nudibranchs, eels, etc. All relatively specific names can create images.

3. **Choose any image that seems clear to you and tell how the details and explanation make the image appealing.**
   Answer: Answers will vary. One possibility: "a fabulous place . . . wave-churned basin, creamy with foam": the author tells his feeling ("a fabulous place") so that we understand what the author wants us to feel, and we can all easily see the commonplace image of a foamy basin.

4. **How does the description of action add to the dominant impression?**
   Answer: In this selection, action *is* the dominant impression.

5. **In the second paragraph Steinbeck personifies (gives human attributes to) an octopus, calling it a "murderer." How does this description of the octopus add interest to the paragraph and help reinforce the dominant impression? (For more on personification, see pp. 473–474.).**
   Answer: Using the term *murderer* arouses our curiosity as does the description of stalking and killing prey.

6. Whether or not you are familiar with some of the creatures Steinbeck names, how do the metaphors and similes help you visualize them? What can you conclude about the value of comparisons in building description? (For more on metaphor/similes, see pp. 473–476.)

Answer: Answers will vary: One possibility: *Nudibranchs*, sea slugs, is a term that few in the class will know, but with the Spanish dancer and skirt image, most would now be able to pick out the animal in an aquarium. Comparisons add color and clarity to images.

▶ NARRATION

This personal narrative, by freelance writer Roger Hoffman, tells how the author as a twelve-year-old took a dangerous dare. Though the event occurred many years in the author's past, he is able to recall a number of specific details of the setting, particularly the train, and some significant dialogue. As you read the story, ask yourself how Hoffman holds the reader's attention, maintaining suspense until the end.

To review the elements of narrative writing, turn back to Chapter 6.

The Dare

Roger Hoffmann

The secret to diving under a moving freight train and rolling out the other side   1 with all your parts attached lies in picking the right spot between the tracks to hit with your back. Ideally, you want soft dirt or pea gravel, clear of glass shards and railroad spikes that could cause you instinctively, and fatally, to sit up. Today, at thirty-eight, I couldn't be threatened or baited enough to attempt that dive. But as a seventh grader struggling to make the cut in a tough Atlanta grammar school, all it took was a dare.

I coasted through my first years of school as a fussed-over smart kid, the   2 teacher's pet who finished his work first and then strutted around the room tutoring other students. By the seventh grade, I had more A's than friends. Even my old cronies, Dwayne and O. T., made it clear I'd never be one of the guys in junior high if I didn't dirty up my act. They challenged me to break the rules and I did. The I-dare-you's escalated: shoplifting, sugaring teachers' gas tanks, dropping lighted matches into public mailboxes. Each guerrilla act won me the approval I never got for just being smart.

Walking home by the railroad tracks after school, we started playing chicken with   3 oncoming trains. O. T., who was failing that year, always won. One afternoon he charged a boxcar from the side, stopping just short of throwing himself between the wheels. I was stunned. After the train disappeared, we debated whether someone could dive under a moving car, stay put for a 10-count, then scramble out the other side. I thought it could be done and said so. O. T. immediately stepped in front of me and smiled. Not by me, I added quickly, I certainly didn't mean that I could do it. "A smart guy like you," he said, his smile evaporating, "you could figure it out easy." And then, squeezing each word for effect, "I . . . DARE . . . you." I'd just turned twelve. The monkey clawing my back was Teacher's Pet. And I'd been dared.

As an adult, I've been on both ends of life's implicit business and social I-dare-you's, although adults don't use those words. We provoke with body language, tone of voice, ambiguous phrases. I dare you to: argue with the boss, tell Fred what you think of him, send the wine back. Only rarely are the risks physical. How we respond to dares when we are young may have something to do with which of the truly hazardous male inner dares—attacking mountains, tempting bulls at Pamplona—we embrace or ignore as men. **4**

For two weeks, I scouted trains and tracks. I studied moving boxcars close up, memorizing how they squatted on their axles, never getting used to the squeal or the way the air fell hot from the sides. I created an imaginary, friendly train and ran next to it. I mastered a shallow, head-first dive with a simple half-twist. I'd land on my back, count to ten, imagine wheels and, locking both hands on the rail to my left, heave myself over and out. Even under pure sky, though, I had to fight to keep my eyes open and my shoulders between the rails. **5**

The next Saturday, O. T., Dwayne and three eighth graders met me below the hill that backed up to the lumberyard. The track followed a slow bend there and opened to a straight, slightly uphill climb for a solid third of a mile. My run started two hundred yards after the bend. The train would have its tongue hanging out. **6**

The other boys huddled off to one side, a circle on another planet, and watched quietly as I double-knotted my shoelaces. My hands trembled. O. T., broke the circle and came over to me. He kept his hands hidden in the pockets of his jacket. We looked at each other. BB's of sweat appeared beneath his nose. I stuffed my wallet in one of his pockets, rubbing it against his knuckles on the way in, and slid my house key, wired to a red-and-white fishing bobber, into the other. We backed away from each other, and he turned and ran to join the four already climbing up the hill. **7**

I watched them all the way to the top. They clustered together as if I were taking their picture. Their silhouette resembled a round-shouldered tombstone. They waved down to me, and I dropped them from my mind and sat down on the rail. Immediately, I jumped back. The steel was vibrating. **8**

The train sounded like a cow going short of breath. I pulled my shirttail out and looked down at my spot, then up the incline of track ahead of me. Suddenly the air went hot, and the engine was by me. I hadn't pictured it moving that fast. A man's bare head leaned out and stared at me. I waved to him with my left hand and turned into the train, burying my face in the incredible noise. When I looked up, the head was gone. **9**

I started running alongside the boxcars. Quickly, I found their pace, held it, and   10
then eased off, concentrating on each thick wheel that cut past me. I slowed
another notch. Over my shoulder, I picked my car as it came off the bend, locking
in the image of the white mountain goat painted on its side. I waited, leaning forward like the anchor in a 440-relay, wishing the baton up the track behind me. Then
the big goat fired by me, and I was flying and then tucking my shoulder as I dipped
under the train.

A heavy blanket of red dust settle over me. I felt bolted to the earth. Sheet-metal   11
bellies thundered and shook above my face. Count to ten, a voice said, watch the
axles and look to your left for daylight. But I couldn't count, and I couldn't find left
if my life depended on it, which it did. The colors overhead went from brown to
red to black to red again. Finally, I ripped my hands free, forced them to the rail,
and, in one convulsive jerk, threw myself into the blue light.

I lay there face down until there was no more noise, and I could feel the sun   12
against the back of my neck. I sat up. The last ribbon of train was slipping away in
the distance. Across the tracks, O. T. was leading a cavalry charge down the hill,
five very small, galloping boys, their fists whirling above them. I pulled my knees
to my chest. My corduroy pants puckered wet across my thighs. I didn't care.

Questions for Analysis

1. Summarize the story's primary action in several sentences and identify the climax.
   Name several word groups the author uses to keep the action connected from one
   paragraph to the next. (For more on time transitions, see p. 53.)
   Answer:
   • Group of boys walking by a train track
   • O. T. daring the author to dive between the moving wheels
   • The author watching the trains and learning how to make his move
   • The author preparing to make the dive, making the dive, and surviving the dare
   Climax: Hoffman rolling out from under the train
   Time transitions: *after school, for two weeks, next Saturday*, etc.

2. Showing and telling are crucial to effective storytelling (for more on showing versus telling, see p. 112). What does Hoffman show us in paragraph 7, and how does
   this affect the suspense in the story?
   Answer: Hoffman shows how frightened he and O. T. are and heightens suspense by
   transferring Hoffman's property to O. T. The dangerous dive will be easier without the
   wallet and keys, and if the author does not make it, his best friend has the property,
   an impromptu will, perhaps.

3. What do you think the meaning of this story is for the author, and where in the
   story does Hoffman make this clear?
   Answer: The author marvels at what people will do for approval, though he does not
   moralize or shake a finger at those who take dares. Paragraphs 1, 2, and 4 discuss this.

4. If you think the introductory paragraph is effective, what makes it work? Look
   especially at the first sentence. Write out the thesis sentence.
   Answer: The hook is well chosen to telegraph that a story involving danger will follow. Students
   will identify the thesis as the first or last sentence of this paragraph, but the last is a better choice.

5. If you think the concluding paragraph is effective, what makes it work? How does the last sentence reflect on the author and the need for approval that drove him to accept the dare?

   Answer: The concluding paragraph creates several strong images that pull the story together. Although the twelve-year-old Hoffman might have been highly embarrassed any other time at wetting his pants, coming after this close brush with death, he "didn't care" what the boys thought of his accident—at least temporarily above the need for peer approval.

6. Hoffman uses metaphors and similes in several places. Choose any two and explain how they add to the story. Does he also include any overly used metaphors (clichés) that he might have avoided? (For more on figures of speech, see pp. 473–476.)

   Answer: Answers will vary: Two possibilities: silhouette = round-shouldered tombstone: association with death; cavalry charge = the group of boys: triumphing over the enemy train, completing the dare. Clichés: teacher's pet, monkey on back.

7. Specific words, sensory details, and active verbs are critical to effective storytelling. List several of each in paragraph 11 and tell how they add to the story.

   Answer: Specific words (*blanket of red dust, sheet-metal bellies*, etc.), sensory details (*thundered, settling dust, bolted to the earth*, etc.), and active verbs (*settled, thundered, shook, count, watched, ripped, forced, threw*) help to put the reader under the train with Hoffman here at the climax of the story.

▶ ILLUSTRATION

"Rambos of the Road," an essay written by Martin Gottfried for *Newsweek* magazine, illustrates with two extended examples and many shorter ones an assertion about people's driving habits. As you read through this essay, imagine that Gottfried has just said to you, "I think drivers in America are getting crazier and more violent by the minute," and you have responded, "Show me what you mean." Does the author provide enough detailed examples and explanations to help you understand his position?

To review the elements of illustrating through examples, turn back to Chapter 7.

Rambos of the Road

Martin Gottfried

The car pulled up and its driver glared at us with such sullen intensity, such 1 hatred, that I was truly afraid for our lives. Except for the Mohawk haircut he didn't have, he looked like Robert DeNiro in *Taxi Driver*, the sort of young man who, delirious for notoriety, might kill a president.

He was glaring because we had passed him and for that affront he pursued us 2 to the next stoplight so as to express his indignation and affirm his masculinity. I was with two women and, believe it, was afraid for all three of us. It was nearly midnight and we were in a small, sleeping town with no other cars on the road.

When the light turned green, I raced ahead, knowing it was foolish and that I 3 was not in a movie. He didn't merely follow, he chased, and with his headlights turned off. No matter what sudden turn I took, he followed. My passengers were silent. I knew they were alarmed, and I prayed that I wouldn't be called upon to protect them. In that cheerful frame of mind, I turned off my own lights so I couldn't be followed. It was lunacy. I was responding to a crazy *as* a crazy.

I'll just drive to the police station," I finally said, and as if those were the magic   4
words, he disappeared.

Elbowing fenders: It seems to me that there has recently been an epidemic of   5
auto macho—a competition perceived and expressed in driving. People fight it out over parking spaces. They bully into line at the gas pump. A toll booth becomes a signal for elbowing fenders. And beetle-eyed drivers hunch over their steering wheels, squeezing the rims, glowering, preparing the excuse of not having seen you as they muscle you off the road. Approaching a highway on an entrance ramp recently, I was strong-armed by a trailer truck so immense that its driver all but blew me away by blasting his horn. The behemoth was just inches from my hopelessly mismatched coupe when I fled for the safety of the shoulder.

And this is happening on city streets, too. A New York taxi driver told me that   6
"intimidation is the name of the game. Drive as if you're deaf and blind. You don't hear the other guy's horn and you sure as hell don't see him."

The odd thing is that long before I was even able to drive, it seemed to me that   7
people were at their finest and most civilized when in their cars. They seemed so orderly and considerate, so reasonable, staying in the right-hand lane unless pass-ing, signaling all intentions. In those days you really eased into highway traffic, and the long, neat rows of cars seemed mobile testimony to the sanity of most people. Perhaps memory fails, perhaps there were always testy drivers, perhaps—but everyone didn't give you the finger.

A most amazing example of driver rage occurred recently at the Manhattan end   8
of the Lincoln Tunnel. We were four cars abreast, stopped at a traffic light. And there was no moving even when the light had changed. A bus had stopped in the cross traffic, blocking our paths: it was normal-for-New-York-City gridlock. Perhaps impatient, perhaps late for important appointments, three of us nonetheless accepted what, after all, we could not alter. One, however, would not. He would not be helpless. He would go where he was going even if he couldn't get there. A Wall Street type in suit and tie, he got out of his car and strode toward the bus, rapping smartly on its doors. When they opened, he exchanged words with the driver. The doors folded shut. He then stepped in front of the bus, took hold of one of its large windshield wipers and broke it.

The bus doors reopened and the driver appeared, apparently giving the fellow 9
a good piece of his mind. If so, the lecture was wasted, for the man started his car
and proceeded to drive directly *into the bus.* He rammed it. Even though the point
at which he struck the bus, the folding doors, was its most vulnerable point, ram-
ming the side of a bus with your car has to rank very high on a futility index. My
first thought was that it had to be a rented car.

Lane merger: To tell the truth, I could not believe my eyes. The bus driver 10
opened his doors as much as they could be opened and he stepped directly onto
the hood of the attacking car, jumping up and down with both his feet. He then
retreated into the bus, closing the doors behind him. Obviously a man of action,
the car driver backed up and rammed the bus again. How this exercise in absurd-
ity would have been resolved none of us will ever know for at that point the traffic unclogged and the bus moved on. And the rest of us, we passives of the world,
proceeded, our cars crossing a field of battle as if nothing untoward had happened.

It is tempting to blame such belligerent, uncivil and even neurotic behavior on 11
the nuts of the world, but in our cars we all become a little crazy. How many of us
speed up when a driver signals his intention of pulling in front of us? Are we resentful and anxious to pass him? How many of us try to squeeze in, or race along the
shoulder at a lane merger? We may not jump on hoods, but driving the gauntlet,
we seethe, cursing not so silently in the safety of our steel bodies on wheels—
fortresses for cowards.

What is it within us that gives birth to such antisocial behavior and why, all of a 12
sudden, have so many drivers gone around the bend? My friend Joel Katz, a Manhattan psychiatrist, calls it, "a Rambo pattern. People are running around thinking
the American way is to take the law into your own hands when anyone does anything wrong. And what constitutes 'wrong'? Anything that cramps your style."

It seems to me that it is a new America we see on the road now. It has the men- 13
tality of a hoodlum and the backbone of a coward. The car is its weapon and hiding
place, and it is still a symbol even in this. Road Rambos no longer bespeak a self-
reliant, civil people tooling around in family cruisers. In fact, there aren't families in
these machines that charge headlong with their brights on in broad daylight,
demanding we get out of their way. Bullies are loners, and they have perverted our
liberty of the open road into drivers' license. They represent an America that derides
the values of decency and good manners, then roam the highways riding shotgun
and shrieking freedom. By allowing this to happen, the rest of us approve.

Questions for Analysis

1. How many paragraphs are devoted to the introduction, and which of the introductory methods that we practiced in Chapter 12 is being used? Is the introduction effective—why/why not?

   Answer: Paragraphs 1 to 4 use a narrative method. Effective: arouses the reader's curiosity and gives her a sense of the essay's direction.

2. The introduction contains one extended example to illustrate the author's thesis; which paragraphs contain the second extended example? Write out the topic sentence that begins this example. How does the example develop the author's thesis?

   Answer: Paragraphs 8 to 10. "A most amazing example of driver rage. . . ." The idiocy and frustration that Gottfried wants us to see is quite clear in this futile and pointless face-off.

3. In which paragraphs does the author reiterate his thesis? Is this pointless repetition, or does it strengthen the essay, if so, how?

   Answer: Paragraphs 6, 7, 8, 11, 12, 13. Strengthens: Reminding the reader of an essay's main point increases clarity and should be done periodically.

4. Which of the patterns of development is used to expand paragraph 7, and how does this paragraph strengthen the essay (for more on PODs, see pp. 8–9)?

   Answer: Comparison/contrast. The contrast of the way it was (or should be) and the way it is now, makes the current antisocial driving habits seem all the more extreme.

5. List several specific words and action verbs in the narrative description of paragraphs 8 to 10. How do they strengthen these paragraphs?

   Answer: Specific words: *Manhattan, Lincoln Tunnel, New York City, Wall Street,* etc. Active verbs: *strode, folded, stepped, broke, wasted, started, rammed,* etc. Both sharpen the picture so we can see the anger and senselessness of the confrontation, thus supporting the author's thesis.

6. What effect do the questions and the pronouns *we, our,* and *us* in paragraph 11 have on a reader? (For more on questions, see p. 433. For more on personal pronouns and audience, see pp. 367–369.)

   Answer: Questions are a good strategy for connecting with an audience and creating sentence variety. These pronouns are especially useful when a writer needs to even mildly criticize his audience.

7. How does the reference to *Rambos* in the title and paragraphs 12 and 13 reinforce the thesis?

   Answer: Most students will recognize the reference to the movie *First Blood* and Sylvester Stallone as the unstable Vietnam special forces's veteran.

8. Why does the author use a dash in paragraphs 7 and 11 to set off the last few words in each sentence (for more on the dash, see p. 577)?

   Answer: For emphasis.

◗ CLASSIFICATION

   In the essay "The Ways of Meeting Oppression," Martin Luther King, Jr., classifies the ways people react to oppression and argues that one method is superior. As you read, notice how clearly the author states the methods and develops them through specific examples, several of which are biblical references. Are you convinced after reading this essay that King's method of choice is the best one?

   To review the elements of classification, turn back to Chapter 8.

The Ways of Meeting Oppression

Martin Luther King, Jr.

Oppressed people deal with their oppression in three characteristic ways. One way is acquiescence: the oppressed resign themselves to their doom. They tacitly adjust themselves to oppression, and thereby become conditioned to it. In every movement toward freedom some of the oppressed prefer to remain oppressed. Almost 2800 years ago Moses set out to lead the children of Israel from the slavery of Egypt to the freedom of the promised land. He soon discovered that slaves do not always welcome their deliverers. They become accustomed to being slaves. They would rather bear those ills they have, as Shakespeare pointed out, than flee to others that they know not of. They prefer the "fleshpots of Egypt" to the ordeals of emancipation.

There is such a thing as the freedom of exhaustion. Some people are so worn down by the yoke of oppression that they give up. A few years ago in the slum areas of Atlanta, a Negro guitarist used to sing almost daily: "Been down so long that down don't bother me." This is the type of negative freedom and resignation that often engulfs the life of the oppressed.

But this is not the way out. To accept passively an unjust system is to cooperate with that system; thereby the oppressed become as evil as the oppressor. Noncooperation with evil is as much a moral obligation as is cooperation with good. The oppressed must never allow the conscience of the oppressor to slumber. Religion reminds every man that he is his brother's keeper. To accept injustice or segregation passively is to say to the oppressor that his actions are morally right. It is a way of allowing his conscience to fall asleep. At this moment the oppressed fails to be his brother's keeper. So acquiescence—while often the easier way—is not the moral way. It is the way of the coward. The Negro cannot win the respect of his oppressor by acquiescing; he merely increases the oppressor's arrogance and contempt. Acquiescence is interpreted as proof of the Negro's inferiority. The Negro cannot win the respect of the white people of the South or the peoples of the world if he is willing to sell the future of his children for his personal and immediate comfort and safety.

A second way that oppressed people sometimes deal with oppression is to resort to physical violence and corroding hatred. Violence often brings about momentary results. Nations have frequently won their independence in battle. But in spite of temporary victories, violence never brings permanent peace. It solves no social problem; it merely creates new and more complicated ones.

Violence as a way of achieving racial justice is both impractical and immoral. It   5
is impractical because it is a descending spiral ending in destruction for all. The old
law of an eye for an eye leaves everybody blind. It is immoral because it seeks to
humiliate the opponent rather than win his understanding; it seeks to annihilate
rather than to convert. Violence is immoral because it thrives on hatred rather than
love. It destroys community and makes brotherhood impossible. It leaves society
in monologue rather than dialogue. Violence ends by defeating itself. It creates bitterness in the survivors and brutality in the destroyers. A voice echoes through time
saying to every potential Peter, "Put up you sword."* History is cluttered with the
wreckage of nations that failed to follow this command.

If the American Negro and other victims of oppression succumb to the temp-   6
tation of using violence in the struggle for freedom, future generations will be the
recipients of a desolate night of bitterness, and our chief legacy to them will be an
endless reign of meaningless chaos. Violence is not the way.

The third way open to oppressed people in their quest for freedom is the way   7
of nonviolent resistance. Like the synthesis in Hegelian philosophy, the principle
of nonviolent resistance seeks to reconcile the truths of two opposites—the acquiescence and violence—while avoiding the extremes and immoralities of both. The
nonviolent resister agrees with the person who acquiesces that one should not be
physically aggressive toward his opponent; but he balances the equation by agreeing
with the person of violence that evil must be resisted. He avoids the nonresistance
of the former and the violent resistance of the latter. With nonviolent resistance, no
individual or group need submit to any wrong.

It seems to me that this is the method that must guide the actions of the Negro   8
in the present crisis in race relations. Through nonviolent resistance the Negro will
be able to rise to the noble height of opposing the unjust system while loving the
perpetrators of the system. The Negro must work passionately and unrelentingly
for full stature as a citizen, but he must not use inferior methods to gain it. He must
never come to terms with falsehood, malice, hate, or destruction.

Nonviolent resistance makes it possible for the Negro to remain in the South and   9
struggle for his rights. The Negro's problem will not be solved by running away. He
cannot listen to the glib suggestion of those who would urge him to migrate en
masse to other sections of the country. By grasping his great opportunity in the
South he can make a lasting contribution to the moral strength of the nation and
set a sublime example of courage for generations yet unborn.

*The apostle Peter had drawn his sword to defend Christ from arrest. The voice was Christ's, who
surrendered himself for trial and crucifixion (John 18:11).

By nonviolent resistance, the Negro can also enlist all men of good will in his 10
struggle for equality. The problem is not a purely racial one, with Negroes set against
whites. In the end, it is not a struggle between people at all, but a tension between
justice and injustice. Nonviolent resistance is not aimed against oppressors but
against oppression. Under its banner consciences, not racial groups, are enlisted.

Questions for Analysis

1. Classification requires a single organizing principle for focus. What is the SOP (single organizing principle) in this essay? Name two other possible ways to classify oppression.
   Answer: SOP: How people react to oppression. Other possible SOPs: levels of brutality, levels of freedom, length of bondage, that which is oppressed (physical, mental, emotional, spiritual), etc.

2. Having a reason for a classification is important. What is King's purpose in writing this essay? What sentence is this most clearly stated in?
   Answer: King is strongly advocating nonviolent resistance as the best hope of achieving civil rights. First sentence of paragraph 8.

3. Classification essays can be organized by space, time, or importance. Name the major categories in this essay and method of arrangement, and then explain why you think King chose this organization.
   Answer: Arrangement: order of importance. King discusses nonviolence last to emphasize it most.

4. Is the introductory paragraph effective—why? Where is the thesis located?
   Answer: Effective: The introduction begins with the thesis, which works as a solid hook, and then offers background information that would interest King's audience.

5. Essays are usually developed through several patterns, such as cause/effect, comparison/contrast, and definition. Tell which of the patterns of development is used in paragraph 5 and how effectively.
   Answer: Cause and effect. Effectively: The effects mentioned help make King's case that violence is a bad choice, in turn leading to his proposal of nonviolence.

6. Paragraphs 4 to 6 deal with the issue of violence in responding to oppression. Why does King discuss violence at this length? What groups in his audience might be especially interested in King's message?
   Answer: Violence is a natural response to oppression, and King constantly had to defend his position against the objections of more radical leaders like Malcolm X. His nonviolent message is directed to African Americans but also to the white community, reassuring them of King's nonviolent intent and perhaps thereby diminishing some opposition.

7. Is the concluding paragraph effective—why? What is King's expanded thought?
   Answer: Effective: King repeats "nonviolent" as a connector, touches on his strongest point, and adds the thought of the struggle being between "justice and injustice."

CLASSIFICATION

Margot Mifflin finds many different categories of boring people in this essay, "The Ten Most Memorable Bores." To avoid having her own essay lapse into tedium, Mifflin chooses an interesting organizing principle—level of irritation—and writes in an informal, humorous voice, which would be engaging to many in her target audience, readers of *Cosmopolitan* magazine. As you read the essay, notice how many specific examples, anecdotes (brief stories), and references to popular culture the author includes. Do you know any people like the boring ones Mifflin describes?

The Ten Most Memorable Bores

Margot Mifflin

Exactly what *is* a bore? According to comic Henny Youngman, he's "a guy with 1 a cocktail glass in one hand and your lapel in the other."

Boring people can't be diverted by polite interjections or gaping yawns—they just 2 go on happily torturing anyone who's unwittingly jumped onto their tedium treadmill. And although *Winnie the Pooh* author A. A. Milne divided bores into two classes— "those who have their own particular subject, and those who do not need a subject"— they actually come in many flavors. Here are the ten most irritating types.

1. Gasbag Bores

Gasbags can't abide a second of silence, so they fill the air with their own obser- 3 vations, relevant or not. Agonizingly thorough in their descriptions, which include recaps of entire film plots and blow-by-blows of recent jaunts to Disneyland or the Amish country, their attention to detail borders on the pathological. Brand names, proper names, prices embellish their every tale. The gasbag bore is a species that takes its name from the *Honeymooners* episode in which Ralph makes his long-winded "king of the castle" speech, proclaiming his superiority in the Kramden home, to which Alice responds, "Now that your gasbag has been filled, why don't you float away?"

2. Vain Bores

You may be wondering why that blond dinner guest is sitting across the table from 4 you, blowing smoke rings at some unseen camera lens and delivering one-line responses to everything you ask her. Are you boring her? Get it straight—*you're* doing all the work; *she's* the bore, and for all her self-importance she's about as personable as the preop Bride of Frankenstein. At parties, such dreary sorts are inevitably a few inches taller that you are—just enough to graze the top of your head with their vacant gazes and make you feel, well, short. But then they'll drop a comment like "Cyndi Lauper didn't get famous until she was thirty; that's probably what'll happen to me," revealing their mental midgetry.

3. Shy Bores

These special paralytics honestly can't help it. Too reserved to inquire about your 5
life, too modest to satisfy inquiries about their own, shy bores are a difficult and
pitiable brood. They were born without a love of anecdotes or a command of adjectives, and they'll greet your own stories with a blank stare or polite smile that asks,
"Is that the punch line?"

Capable of boring the dead, the bashful bores reduce you to conversational idiocy 6
by forcing you to keep things moving. You find yourself frantically scraping the bottom of your salad bowl saying, "I myself have always loved arugula. Do you love
arugula?" If you have to spend any length of time with a shy bore, for God's sake,
go to the movies.

4. Pontificating Bores

This category includes the righteous (they have an ax to grind), and the academic 7
(they insist on using ridiculously self-conscious words like *copacetic*). Pontificating
bores have a point to make, whether you want to hear it or not, and often work their
theories out in public. *Your* opinion, however, has no value in the development of their
theses. For academic bores, all the world's a classroom, the bore is the professor,
and you're the unlucky student. Similarly, righteous bores occupy an invisible
podium, and their index fingers wag perpetually.

Righteous bores often have a religious mission, but increasingly they tend to man- 8
ifest themselves as self-help advocates intent on convincing you that you're hopelessly messed up and in need of Adult Children of Alcoholics or Jack LaLanne. It
never occurs to them before embarking on, say, an animal-rights diatribe that you
may be president of the Humane Society. *You*, sucker, are gonna get educated.

5. Monotone Bores

When author Laurence Peter said, "a bore is a fellow talker who can change the 9
subject to his topic of conversation faster than you can change it back to your own,"
he was describing a monotone bore. They've elevated the construction of run-on
sentences to an art form, which lets them ramble without interruption for hours.
Because of this expertise in tedium, they're immune to a victim's desperate escape
maneuvers, which makes them especially trying on the telephone. "My husband
has just been thrown from his exercise bike and is lying unconscious on the piano—
gotta go!" you exclaim, calmly filling in the last blank of a crossword puzzle. And
they drone on, unfazed.

Monotone bores are unique in that they appear to bore even *themselves*. Yet 10
they persist, bridging topics from underarm razor burn to turmoil in the Middle East,
and *nothing* can stop them.

6. Hyperbolic Bores

Let's call this person Harry. First he's describing a woman whose nose is the size 11 of Mount Rushmore, next he's discussing his teenage son, who hasn't bathed since his fifth birthday. The hyperbolic bore is like the boy who cried wolf—no one believes a word of it, even when he's *not* exaggerating.

7. Chemically Altered Bores

These weekend Dionysians assume that whatever they've been smoking or drink- 12 ing, you have smoked and drunk too. Drunken bores usually just drool, mumble, and repeat themselves, while people reacting to more exotic intoxicants will march right up to you and say, "I've been trance-channeling with a light being named Ariel who lives on the outer ring of Mars." When you come back with, "But Mars doesn't *have* rings," the response is invariably (snort, giggle) "Gosh, don't be so literal!"

The worst chemically altered bores are couples in a mutual daze. At any given 13 moment, one of them will point at some stationary object and the pair will dissolve into helpless laughter (you may even discover that you are the source of their amusement). When you retreat, they *will* be offended . . . but they *won't* remember a thing in the morning.

8. Techno-Bores

Techno-bores are like chemically altered bores in that their condition (infatuation 14 with technology—often computers) blinds them to the possibility that *your* reality simply isn't theirs. Details about the latest software or synthesizer are lost on you.

The curious thing about computer-obsessed bores is that their behavior appears 15 to have been directly influenced by the machines they love—you can see little floppy disks spinning in their eyes when they speak; their sentences roll out in a robotic cadence. Don't even consider launching a personal question in the direc- tion of a techno-bore—you may cause a short circuit.

9. Slow-Talking Bores

In the time it takes them to finish one thought and start another, you've redeco- 16 rated your living room, planned a trip around the world, married and raised a family. These are the people French author Jules Renard once described as "so boring that they make you waste an entire day in five minutes." On first meeting, slow talkers appear to be hard of hearing. They will return your questions with long silences, and stare stubbornly at the carpet, dredging a response from the depth of their souls— inevitably a strained "Yeah."

Like shy bores, slow talkers seem to be in some sort of pain, so initially, at least, 17 have pity on them. Wait it out and you *may* find a little pot of gold at the end of their tongue-tied silences.

10. Boring Relatives

There's the great-aunt who's about to tell you for the tenth consecutive Christ-   18
mas about her 1957 trip to Alaska, the uncle for whom World War II never ended,
the cousin who's bent on giving you annual reports on her kid's learning disabili-
ties. Boring relatives have a little refrain they like to incant: *"Isn't* that wonderful!"
. . . whether you've just described a recent subway mugging or been told you have
lipstick on your teeth.

The perils of boring relatives is that, like it or not, you're just as boring to *them*   19
as they are to *you.* When you're pulling into the driveway thinking "God, how will
I survive this?" be assured that the feeling is mutual. The only relief from this ennui
is family scandal, and if none exists, it's *your* duty to create it . . . even if you have
to get a little, well, *hyperbolic.*

Questions for Analysis

1. Comment on the introduction (paragraphs 1 and 2). What do you like about it?
   What seems to be working? How does the author draw you into the essay? Where
   do you find the thesis?
   Answer: Answers will vary. This is an effective introduction using a question as a
   hook, referencing several people who would be familiar to many in her audience, and
   ending with a clear thesis.

2. Comment on the conclusion. The author does not try to summarize all of the boring people she categorizes in the body of the essay, but which group does she refer
   to? Explain her expanded thought and tell why or why not you feel that it satis-
   factorily ends the essay.
   Answer: Answers will vary. The hyperbolic bores. The final thought extends Mifflin's groups to
   include the reader and presumably herself. Perhaps she is trying to reduce the finger-pointing
   nature of the rest of the essay by showing that we all might be bores at one time or another.

3. Dialogue is one method we use for development and emphasis, and we sometimes
   invent imagined dialogue. Notice the instances of imagined dialogue in paragraphs
   4, 5, and 9, and—disregarding the quote—explain what the author accomplishes
   with it.
   Answer: Mifflin adds to the humor and clarity of the essay.

4. Mifflin describes the "hyperbolic bores" (those who exaggerate) in paragraph 11
   but then goes on to use hyperbole or overstatement herself in several places. Is she
   becoming one of the bores she categorizes by using exaggeration—why/why not?
   What effect does the author achieve with her overstatement in paragraph 16? (For
   more on overstatement, see p. 478.)
   Answer: She is not becoming boring because she uses hyperbole with discretion. Her
   comments in paragraph 16 reinforce how long the "slow-talking bores" can hold an
   audience captive.

5. Name the metaphor used in paragraph 2 and explain how it supports the main
   point of the paragraph.
   Answer: "tedium treadmill." Treadmills require much energy to use and can run
   indefinitely, much like some of the bores Mifflin describes.

6. Choose one category of bore and explain why you think it is interesting, entertaining, true, or all three.
   Answer: Answers will vary.

▶ CAUSE AND EFFECT

"Two by Two, We'll Fill the Planet," by Benjamin Zuckerman, first appeared in the *Los Angeles Times* in October of 1991. The author raises a question that concerns us all—overpopulation. If we believe his statistics, human overpopulation of the planet is inevitable unless people control how many children they bring into the world. How accurate do you think the author's projections are? Are there any other factors that he has not mentioned that might offset the population explosion? Must couples at some point limit themselves to only two children—the "replacement level"—to save the human race from a miserably overcrowded planet or even extinction?

To review the elements of cause and effect, turn back to Chapter 9.

Two by Two, We'll Fill the Planet

Benjamin Zuckerman

HOW MANY angels can dance on the head of a pin? This is a type of question 1 that people asked in the not so distant past when religion reigned supreme, and science and technology played a negligible role in everyday life. Now that the rise of science and technology has enabled enormous increases in the human population, we must face the question: How many people can live on the surface of the Earth?

The rate of growth, that is, the percentage increase per year, of the human population is at an all-time high. Many politicians, economists and religious leaders 2 regard rapid population growth as "natural" and extol its virtues. For example, we often read that population growth stimulates the economy and is, therefore, good. This may be true if one's vision is expressed in units of four years and limited to a few decades at most. However, life has existed on Earth for at least 3.5 billion years and human beings for a few million years. So the very rapid population growth of the past 100 or so years is not natural.

If the current rate of growth of world population, about 2% per year, were continued into the year 3400, then each person now alive would have 1 trillion descendants 3 and the total human population would be about 10,000,000,000,000,000,000,000 (10 sextillion). This is 10% of the total number of stars in the entire observable universe. Well before 3400, the average amount of land per person would have diminished to less than one square inch.

Broken down into shorter intervals, we are talking about a tenfold increase in 4 just over a century. So by about the year 2100, at current rates, there would be 50 billion people on Earth. And 500 billion not long after the year 2200.

What about covering all the deserts and oceans with people? That would only 5 delay the inevitable need for zero population growth by a century at the very most. How about shipping off the extra people (net difference between the number born and the number who die) to outer space? At current growth rates that would mean sending 10,000 people up every hour of every day. And we have trouble launching a few shuttles per year safely.

The issue is not whether an economy that is stimulated by population growth 6 is good, bad or indifferent. The above calculations show that growth is impossible except in the very short run. The real issue is what kind of world will the people of the present and next few generations leave for the people and other creatures of the next few millennia.

According to UCLA professor and biologist Jared Diamond, the coming century 7 will witness one of the worst extinctions in the history of life on Earth. Roughly one-half of the 30 million species that are estimated to end will become extinct, courtesy entirely of human beings. If yet additional population and economic growth of the sort that some people espouse actually occurs, then the extinction rate will be even worse. A combination of far too many people, greed and unbridled technological power is destroying the natural world.

Each person plays a role in the population equation. If you and your spouse have 8 two children and four grandchildren then you are reproducing at replacement levels (zero population growth). But if you have four children and they, in turn, each have four children so that you have 16 grandchildren then that is roughly equivalent to the 2% per year growth rate that characterizes the world as a whole.

Each of us has his or her own system of values. For me, a planet with relatively 9 few people, each of whom can live with dignity and a high quality of life, is far superior to a world where too many people, awash in pollution stretch resources to the breaking point, and where billions struggle to survive at mere subsistence levels.

Questions for Analysis

1. If you think the introductory paragraph is effective, what makes it work? Look especially at the hook (first sentence) and the thesis sentence. Write out the thesis sentence.

   Answer: Effective: The question as a hook draws the reader in and begins to introduce the issue of religion, one source of conflict with the author's position. The thesis is another question that delays the persuasive intent of the essay: couples should limit themselves to two children.

2. What is the author's purpose, is it stated or implied, and what paragraph reveals it most clearly?

   Answer: Implied: Zuckerman's essay is persuasive, largely relying on logical appeals to move people to limit the number of children they have. The clearest statement of the thesis is in the conclusion.

3. Writers sometimes use a transitional paragraph to summarize part of their essay and then move readers into the next discussion point. Which paragraph in Zuckerman's essay functions this way, what is it transitioning from, and what point is it moving the reader to? What effect does any statement in this paragraph have on the thesis?

   Answer: Paragraph 6: moves from the population statistics to the effect of animal extinction. The last sentence ("The real issue is what kind of world. . . .") clarifies the issue and the author's position.

4. If you think the concluding paragraph is effective, what makes it work? How does the author try to connect with the reader?

Answer: Effective: The author shows conviction for his position without becoming strident or confrontational. His use of "for me" is effective qualifying, and the ethical appeal of what is best for all people is another strong concluding appeal.

5. Is this primarily an essay dealing with causes, effects, or both? What effects are discussed in paragraphs 3 and 4 and in 7?

Answer: Effects. Paragraphs 3 and 4: explosive population growth measured in statistics; paragraph 7: the accelerated rate of species extinction.

6. Cause-and-effect essays often explore problems and solutions. What paragraph is developed this way, and what is the author's point in this paragraph?

Answer: Paragraph 5: Zuckerman anticipates objections to his argument, potential solutions, and shows that they will not work.

7. The author addresses his audience in the third person ("people") and first person ("we") but also speaks to them in the second person ("you"). In what paragraph does Zuckerman speak to his readers as "you," and what effect is he trying to achieve? Is this use of second person effective or might it alienate his audience—why?

Answer: Paragraph 8: the author is trying to emphasize that his audience is part of the problem—but also part of the solution. He is careful not to accuse his reader but to include them. This use of "you" is effective, and you might contrast it with the pronoun shift problems illustrated in Chapter 24.

CAUSE AND EFFECT

Brent Staples is a journalist who writes about the negative effects—as an African American male—he has on the people around him. Staples uses a number of well-illustrated examples to show these effects and points out that men of his race are themselves often endangered simply by being black. As you read this essay, try to put yourself in the author's shoes. Have you ever been frightened by someone who appears menacing? Have you ever perceived yourself to be frightening to others? How have these experiences altered your behavior?

Black Men and Public Space

Brent Staples

My first victim was a woman—white, well dressed, probably in her early twenties. I came upon her late one evening on a deserted street in Hyde Park, a relatively affluent neighborhood in an otherwise mean, impoverished section of Chicago. As I swung onto the avenue behind her, there seemed to be a discreet, uninflammatory distance between us. Not so. She cast back a worried glance. To her, the youngish black man—a broad six feet two inches with a beard and billowing hair, both hands shoved into the pockets of a bulky military jacket—seemed menacingly close. After a few more quick glimpses, she picked up her pace and was soon running in earnest. Within seconds she disappeared into a cross street.

That was more than a decade ago. I was twenty-two years old, a graduate stu- 2
dent newly arrived at the University of Chicago. It was in the echo of that terrified
woman's footfalls that I first began to know the unwieldy inheritance I'd come
into—the ability to alter public space in ugly ways. It was clear that she thought
herself the quarry of a mugger, a rapist, or worse. Suffering a bout of insomnia,
however, I was stalking sleep, not defenseless wayfarers. As a softy who is
scarcely able to take a knife to a raw chicken—let alone hold one to a person's
throat—I was surprised, embarrassed, and dismayed all at once. Her flight made me
feel like an accomplice in tyranny. It also made it clear that I was indistinguishable
from the muggers who occasionally seeped into the area from the surrounding
ghetto. That first encounter, and those that followed, signified that a vast, unnerving
gulf lay between nighttime pedestrians—particularly women—and me. And I soon
gathered that being perceived as dangerous is a hazard in itself. I only needed to
turn a corner into a dicey situation, or crowd some frightened, armed person in a
foyer somewhere, or make an errant move after being pulled over by a policeman.
Where fear and weapons meet—and they often do in urban America—there is
always the possibility of death.

In that first year, my first away from my hometown, I was to become thoroughly 3
familiar with the language of fear. At dark, shadowy intersections, I could cross in
front of a car stopped at a traffic light and elicit the *thunk, thunk, thunk, thunk* of
the driver—black, white, male, or female—hammering down the door locks. On
less traveled streets after dark, I grew accustomed to but never comfortable with
people crossing to the other side of the street rather than pass me. Then there were
the standard unpleasantries with policemen, doormen, bouncers, cab drivers, and
others whose business it is to screen out troublesome individuals *before* there is
any nastiness.

I moved to New York nearly two years ago and I have remained an avid night 4
walker. In central Manhattan, the near-constant crowd cover minimizes these one-
on-one street encounters. Elsewhere—in SoHo, for example, where sidewalks are
narrow and tightly spaced buildings shut out the sky—things can get very taut
indeed.

After dark, on the warrenlike streets of Brooklyn where I live, I often see women 5
who fear the worst from me. They seem to have set their faces on neutral, and
with their purse straps strung across their chests bandolier-style, they forge ahead
as though bracing themselves against being tackled. I understand, of course, that
the danger they perceive is not a hallucination. Women are particularly vulnerable
to street violence, and young black males are drastically overrepresented among

Lee was tidewater Virginia, and in his background were family, culture, and tra- 5
dition . . . the age of chivalry transplanted to a New World which was making its own
legends and its own myths. He embodied a way of life that had come down through
the age of knighthood and the English country squire. America was a land that was
beginning all over again, dedicated to nothing much more complicated than the rather
hazy belief that all men had equal rights and should have an equal chance in the world.
In such a land Lee stood for the feeling that it was somehow of advantage to human
society to have a pronounced inequality in the social structure. There should be a
leisure class, backed by ownership of land; in turn, society itself should be keyed to
the land as the chief source of wealth and influence. It would bring forth (according
to this ideal) a class of men with a strong sense of obligation to the community; men
who lived not to gain advantage for themselves, but to meet the solemn obligations
which had been laid on them by the very fact that they were privileged. From them
the country would get its leadership; to them it could look for the higher values—of
thought, of conduct, of personal deportment—to give it strength and virtue.

Lee embodied the noblest elements of this aristocratic ideal. Through him, the 6
landed nobility justified itself. For four years, the Southern states had fought a desperate war to uphold the ideals for which Lee stood. In the end, it almost seemed
as if the Confederacy fought for Lee; as if he himself was the Confederacy . . . the
best thing that the way of life for which the Confederacy stood could ever have to
offer. He had passed into legend before Appomattox. Thousands of tired, underfed,
poorly clothed Confederate soldiers, long since past the simple enthusiasm of the
early days of the struggle, somehow considered Lee the symbol of everything for
which they had been willing to die. But they could not quite put this feeling into
words. If the Lost Cause, sanctified by so much heroism and so many deaths, had
a living justification, its justification was General Lee.

Grant, the son of a tanner on the Western frontier, was everything Lee was not. 7
He had come up the hard way and embodied nothing in particular except the eternal toughness and sinewy fiber of the men who grew up beyond the mountains.
He was one of a body of men who owed reverence and obeisance to no one, who
were self-reliant to a fault, who cared hardly anything for the past but who had a
sharp eye for the future.

These frontier men were the precise opposite of the tidewater aristocrats. Back 8
of them, in the great surge that had taken people over the Alleghenies and into the
opening Western country, there was a deep, implicit dissatisfaction with a past that
had settled into grooves. They stood for democracy, not from any reasoned conclusion about the proper ordering of human society, but simply because they had

grown up in the middle of democracy and knew how it worked. Their society might have privileges, but they would be privileges each man had won for himself. Forms and patterns meant nothing. No man was born to anything, except perhaps to a chance to show how far he could rise. Life was competition.

Yet along with this feeling had come a deep sense of belonging to a national 9 community. The Westerner who developed a farm, opened a shop, or set up in business as a trader, could hope to prosper only as his own community prospered— and his community ran from the Atlantic to the Pacific and from Canada down to Mexico. If the land was settled, with towns and highways and accessible markets, he could better himself. He saw his fate in terms of the nation's own destiny. As its horizons expanded, so did his. He had, in other words, an acute dollars-and-cents stake in the continued growth and development of his country.

And that, perhaps, is where the contrast between Grant and Lee becomes most 10 striking. The Virginia aristocrat, inevitably, saw himself in relation to his own region. He lived in a static society which could endure almost anything except change. Instinctively, his first loyalty would go to the locality in which that society existed. He would fight to the limit of endurance to defend it, because in defending it he was defending everything that gave his own life its deepest meaning.

The Westerner, on the other hand, would fight with an equal tenacity for the 11 broader concept of society. He fought so because everything he lived by was tied to growth, expansion, and a constantly widening horizon. What he lived by would survive or fall with the nation itself. He could not possibly stand by unmoved in the face of an attempt to destroy the Union. He would combat it with everything he had, because he could only see it as an effort to cut the ground out from under his feet.

So Grant and Lee were in complete contrast, representing two diametrically 12 opposed elements in American life. Grant was the modern man emerging; beyond him, ready to come on the stage, was the great age of steel and machinery, of crowded cities and a restless burgeoning vitality. Lee might have ridden down from the old age of chivalry, lance in hand, silken banner fluttering over his head. Each man was the perfect champion of his cause, drawing both his strengths and his weaknesses form the people he led.

Yet it was not all contrast, after all. Different as they were—in background, in per- 13 sonality, in underlying aspiration—these two great soldiers had much in common. Under everything else, they were marvelous fighters. Furthermore, their fighting qualities were really very much alike.

Each man had, to begin with, the great virtue of utter tenacity and fidelity. Grant 14 fought his way down the Mississippi Valley in spite of acute personal discouragement and profound military handicaps. Lee hung on in the trenches at Petersburg after hope itself had died. In each man there was an indomitable quality . . . the born fighter's refusal to give up as long as he can still remain on his feet and lift his two fists.

Daring and resourcefulness they had, too; the ability to think faster and move **15** faster than the enemy. These were the qualities which gave Lee the dazzling campaigns of Second Manassas and Chancellorsville and won Vicksburg for Grant.

Lastly, and perhaps greatest of all, there was the ability, at the end, to turn quickly **16** from war to peace once the fighting was over. Out of the way these two men behaved at Appomattox came the possibility of a peace of reconciliation. It was a possibility not wholly realized, in the years to come, but which did, in the end, help the two sections to become one nation again . . . after a war whose bitterness might have seemed to make such a reunion wholly impossible. No part of either man's life became him more than the part he played in their brief meeting in the McLean house at Appomattox. Their behavior there put all succeeding generations of Americans in their debt. Two great Americans, Grant and Lee—very different, yet under everything very much alike. Their encounter at Appomattox was one of the great moments of American history.

Questions for Analysis

1. Essays that compare and contrast organize material by the block or point-by-point method and sometimes both. In this essay which paragraphs are devoted exclusively to Lee and which to Grant? Are these paragraphs comparing or contrasting?
   Answers: Lee, 5 to 6 and 10; Grant, 7 to 9 and 11. Contrasting.

2. Which paragraphs discuss the similarities of the two generals? Has the method of organizing shifted? Are the comparison paragraphs arranged by the block method or point-by-point?
   Answer: 12 to 16. Yes. Point-by-point.

3. Transitional words are particularly important when moving from one paragraph to another in comparison/contrast essays. Identify the transitional words in the first sentences of paragraphs 9 to 13.
   Answer: *yet, and that, on the other hand, so, yet.*

4. Identify the topic sentence in paragraph 5 and explain if it is effective or not. Which example uses cause and effect for development?
   Answer: First sentence. Effective: the examples and explanations in the paragraph clearly support the topic sentence. The leisure class will bring about several effects. . .

5. Contrast the views of Lee and Grant toward their communities as discussed in paragraphs 5 and 9. What is the fundamental difference between the two men?
   Answer: Lee's community is rural, agricultural, and local; Grant's community is the nation.

6. If you think the concluding paragraph is effective, what makes it work? What final thought does Catton leave us with?
   Answer: Effective: connector, brief summary, and expanded thought. Grant and Lee's behavior set the tone for reconciliation.

■ COMPARISON AND CONTRAST

Russell Baker is a well-known columnist and essayist noted for his humor and insight into human behavior. In "A Nice Place to Visit" Baker contrasts Toronto with New York City, using irony and overstatement extensively to make his point (for more on these figures of speech, see Chapter 19). You might notice that many of the author's paragraphs are brief, a convention of articles appearing in newspaper columns. As you read the article, how do you respond to Baker's humor? How do you think a resident of New York City would respond?

A Nice Place to Visit

Russell Baker

Having heard that Toronto was becoming one of the continent's noblest cities, we 1 flew from New York to investigate. New Yorkers jealous of their city's reputation and concerned about challenges to its stature have little to worry about.

After three days in residence, our delegation noted an absence of hysteria that 2 was almost intolerable and took to consuming large portions of black coffee to maintain our normal state of irritability. The local people to whom we complained in hopes of provoking comfortably nasty confrontations declined to become bellicose. They would like to enjoy a gratifying big-city hysteria, they said, but believed it would seem ill-mannered in front of strangers.

Extensive field studies—our stay lasted four weeks—persuaded us that this fail- 3 ure reflects the survival in Toronto of an ancient pattern of social conduct called "courtesy."

"Courtesy" manifests itself in many quaint forms appalling to the New Yorker. 4 Thus, for example, Yankee fans may be astonished to learn that at the Toronto baseball park it is considered bad form to heave rolls of toilet paper and beer cans at players on the field.

Official literature inside Toronto taxicabs includes a notification of the proper 5 address to which riders may mail the authorities not only complaints but also compliments about the cabbie's behavior.

For a city that aspires to urban greatness, Toronto's entire taxi system has far 6 to go. At present, it seems hopelessly bogged down in civilization. One day a member of our delegation listening to a radio conversation between a short-tempered cabbie and the dispatcher distinctly heard the dispatcher say, "As Shakespeare said, if music be the food of love, play on, give me excess of it."

This delegate became so unnerved by hearing Shakespeare quoted by a cab dis- 7 patcher that he fled immediately back to New York to have his nerves abraded and his spine rearranged in a real big-city taxi.

What was particularly distressing as the stay continued was the absence of 8
shrieking police and fire sirens at 3 A.M.—or any other hour, for that matter. We
spoke to the city authorities about this. What kind of city was it, we asked, that
expected its citizens to sleep all night and rise refreshed in the morning? Where
was the incentive to awaken gummy-eyed and exhausted, ready to scream at the
first person one saw in the morning? How could Toronto possibly hope to maintain a robust urban divorce rate?

Our criticism went unheeded, such is the torpor with which Toronto pursues true 9
urbanity. The fact appears to be that Toronto has very little grasp of what is required
of a great city.

Consider the garbage picture. It seems never to have occurred to anybody in 10
Toronto that garbage exists to be heaved into the streets. One can drive for miles
without seeing so much as a banana peel in the gutter or a discarded newspaper
whirling in the wind.

Nor has Toronto learned about dogs. A check with the authorities confirmed that, 11
yes, there are indeed dogs resident in Toronto, but one would never realize it by
walking the sidewalks. Our delegation was shocked by the presumption of a town's
calling itself a city, much less a great city, when it obviously knows nothing of either
garbage or dogs.

The subway, on which Toronto prides itself, was a laughable imitation of the real 12
thing. The subway cars were not only spotlessly clean, but also fully illuminated.
So were the stations. To New Yorkers, it was embarrassing, and we hadn't the heart
to tell the subway authorities that they were light-years away from greatness.

We did, however, tell them about spray paints and how effectively a few hundred 13
children equipped with spray-paint cans could at least give their subway the big-
city look.

It seems doubtful they are ready to take such hints. There is a disturbing distaste 14
for vandalism in Toronto which will make it hard for the city to enter wholeheartedly
into the vigor of the late twentieth century.

A board fence surrounding a huge excavation for a new high-rise building in the 15
downtown district offers depressing evidence of Toronto's lack of big-city impulse.
Embedded in the fence at intervals of about fifty feet are loudspeakers that play
recorded music for passing pedestrians.

Not a single one of these loudspeakers has been mutilated. What's worse, not 16
a single one has been stolen.

It was good to get back to the Big Apple. My coat pocket was bulging with candy 17 wrappers from Toronto and—such is the lingering power of Toronto—it took me two or three hours back in New York before it seemed natural again to toss them into the street.

Questions for Analysis

1. What is the author's thesis, and where do you find it? Name several places in which Baker reiterates it.

   Answer: Paragraph 1: Toronto is a more civilized, relaxed, cleaner city than New York City. Baker reiterates his thesis with each point he raises, for example, courtesy, cab drivers, baseball behavior, noise, and garbage.

2. How is this article arranged, by the block or point-by-point method? If the author had chosen the other method, would the presentation be as effective—why or why not?

   Answer: Point-by-point. Because Baker wants to discuss a number of points primarily by developing the Toronto side of the comparison, point-by-point is probably a better choice. The block method would be more likely to produce a well-developed paragraph or two on Toronto but underdeveloped paragraphs on New York City, unless Baker added more material.

3. List the points that the author compares between the two cities. Explain how any one of these points is developed, including the use of specific details.

   Answer: Main points: level of hysteria, courtesy, baseball behavior, sirens, garbage, dogs, subway, vandalism, consideration of pedestrians. Answers will vary: Baker supports his point about the limited vandalism in Toronto by citing the undamaged subway and speakers attached to the board fence.

4. Baker presents an ironic, humorous persona in this article (for more on persona, see pp. 367–368). Choose one instance of irony—saying one thing but meaning the opposite—and explain how it adds to your appreciation (or dislike) of the article.

   Answer: Answers will vary: Baker discusses the "failure" of Toronto residents to be ill tempered and confrontational due to an "ancient pattern of social conduct called 'courtesy.'" Baker uses irony to gently jab at the New Yorker who might be rude, approving of behavior like throwing beer bottles and toilet paper at baseball games.

5. Overstatement, exaggerating for effect, is used in many places in this article. Choose one instance of it and explain how it adds to your appreciation (or dislike) of the article.

   Answer: Answers will vary: Paragraph 4: "Yankee fans may be astonished to learn. . . ." Paragraph 7: "This delegate . . . fled immediately back to New York." Paragraph 8: "the absence . . . of sirens" at any hour. The overstatement that favors Toronto diminishes the implied criticism of the New Yorkers' behavior because the criticism is viewed in part as a joke, although Baker wants his essential points to be taken seriously.

6. Comment on the author's use of the dash and the rhetorical questions in paragraph 8. What does Baker accomplish with each?

   Answer: The dash adds emphasis and heightens the overstatement. In answering the rhetorical questions, the readers respond as Baker wants them to. "What kind of city was it . . . ?" a wonderful city. "Where was the incentive" to behave badly? Not in Toronto.

7. What do you think of the conclusion? Of course it is brief (a journalistic convention), but is it effective? Is irony still operating in this paragraph? What is the expanded thought?

Answer: We might believe that after the positive experiences Baker has had in Toronto he is less than happy to be back in New York. The final sentence can be interpreted in several ways: it is difficult to change a person's behavior; people need positive reinforcement from those around them to behave well; at heart Baker *is* a New Yorker, and he is affirming this in the end.

▶ DEFINITION

Sydney J. Harris is a well-known columnist and essayist who has collected many of his essays in books like *Clearing the Ground*, from which "Opposing Principles Help Balance Society" is taken. You might notice that the paragraphs in this essay are shorter than those of most of the other essays in this unit, brief paragraphs being a convention of newspaper columns. However, even with brevity Harris manages to clearly communicate his definition of "liberal" and "conservative" and how they help create a "balanced society."

To review the elements of definition, turn back to Chapter 15.

Opposing Principles Help Balance Society

Sydney J. Harris

I devoutly wish we could get rid of two words in the popular lexicon: *liberal* and *conservative*. Both are beautiful and useful words in their origins, but now each is used (and misused) as an epithet by its political enemies. 1

Liberal means liberating—it implies more freedom, more openness, more flexibility, more humaneness, more willingness to change when change is called for. 2

Conservative means conserving—it implies preserving what is best and most valuable from the past, a decent respect for tradition, a reluctance to change merely for its own sake. 3

Both attributes, in a fruitful tension, are necessary for the welfare of any social order. Liberalism alone can degenerate into mere permissiveness and anarchy. Conservatism alone is prone to harden into reaction and repression. As Lord Acton brilliantly put it: "Every institution tends to fail by an excess of its own basic principle." 4

Yet, in the rhetoric of their opponents, both *liberal* and *conservative* have turned into dirty words. Liberals become "bleeding hearts"; conservatives want "to turn the clock back." But sometimes hearts *should* bleed; sometimes it would profit us to run the clock back if it is spinning too fast. 5

Radical, of course, has become the dirtiest of words, flung around carelessly and sometimes maliciously. Today it is usually applied to the left by the right—but the right is often as "radical" in its own way. 6

The word originally meant "going to the roots" and was a metaphor drawn from the radish, which grows underground. We still speak of "radical surgery," which 7 is undertaken when lesser measures seem futile. The American Revolution, indeed, was a radical step taken to ensure a conservative government, when every other effort had failed.

Dorothy Thompson was right on target when she remarked that her ideal was 8 to be "a radical as a thinker, a conservative as to program, and a liberal as to temper." In this way she hoped to combine the best and the most productive in each attitude, while avoiding the pitfalls of each.

Society is like a pot of soup: It needs different, and contrasting, ingredients to 9 give it body and flavor and lasting nourishment. It is compound, not simple; not like wine that drugs us, or caffeine that agitates us, but a blend to satisfy the most divergent palates.

Of course, this is an ideal, an impossible vision never to be fully realized in any 10 given society. But it is what we should aim at, rather than promoting some brew that is to one taste alone. It may take another thousand years to get the recipe just right. The question is: Do we have the time?

Questions for Analysis

1. **Well-written essays should capture the reader's interest from the first sentence. Does Harris manage this, and if so how?**
Answer: Answers will vary. Harris creates an interesting hook by expressing a strong emotion and using two specific terms that his reader would be familiar with. The reader is curious as to why the author wants to remove these words from our language.

2. **What three words does the author define in this essay, and how do they relate to the overall thesis?**
Answer: Liberal, conservative, and radical. Harris is calling for more tolerance and less name calling in society. He defines all three terms to show that they all have positive qualities but that people distort them for their own ends.

3. **What simile does Harris develop, and how does it help advance his thesis?**
Answer: He works with the "pot of soup" image, developing it in the final two paragraphs. The author's point in this essay is to call for a balanced vision in our society (as indicated in the title). He sees liberal and conservatives as necessary "ingredients" to the soup of society.

4. **Where does the author use negation in this essay, and what point is he making with it?**
Answer: In the last body paragraph Harris uses negation to reiterate his point that we need diversity in society.

5. **Several patterns of development are commonly used in developing definition essays. In which paragraph does Harris use cause and effect, and what is his point in doing so?**
Answer: Paragraph 4. Harris warns that liberalism or conservatism alone, without the other to balance it, can be self-destructive.

6. **What point does the author reiterate in his conclusion, and what is his expanded thought?**
Answer: Harris calls for a blend of ingredients again, suggests that it will take a long time to find the proper mix, and then raises the question "Do we have time?"

▶ DEFINITION

In the essay "What Is a Dad?" Bob Brannan offers several defining elements of fatherhood. Because this is an extended definition, you will find many of the patterns of development represented, as well as points common to brief definitions: synonyms, negation, comparisons, and formal defining. As you read, ask yourself if the designated audience—young married men who have just learned they are about to become fathers—would be interested in the examples and explanations provided.

What Is a Dad?

Bob Brannan

"Honey, it's going to be a girl!" my wife of ten years said to me as I paused near 1 the top of the living room steps. I looked at the half a dozen pink balloons bouncing on the ceiling and at Beth smiling from above me at the head of the stairs. "Wonderful," I thought, and then immediately, "Oh, no!" Fatherhood was rushing at me like a space shuttle coming in with its payload from outer space, and I wasn't prepared. I dropped my briefcase on the landing, gave her a hug, and lied convincingly: "That's the best news I've heard this year." As we talked over the details of the sonogram, I thought hard about what lay ahead for us and about what I was going to become—a dad. I didn't know then much of what a dad was supposed to be, but I was sure it involved a lot more than just providing food, clothing, and shelter. And that's exactly what the past three years of raising a little girl has taught me: Being a dad is one of the hardest yet most rewarding jobs there is.

I had thought that being a father meant being a child again, just a quick time travel 2 back to the days of bare feet and endless summers, becoming a friend and playmate. Well, I was wrong . . . and right. Fathers can and should play with their children, the more the better. But that's not how I spent the first year with my daughter. No one had prepared me for the seemingly endless routine of feeding, burping, cleaning, rocking, and diaper changing that came with the territory. It wasn't until Lauren was fairly secure on her feet that we were able to play the way I had anticipated. But for the past two years we have been inseparable companions, creating fantasy games, role playing every Disney character that Walt ever helped bring into the world, and both learning to sing lots of drippy songs—God help whoever has to listen.

But becoming a good father requires more than just a willingness and ability to 3 become young again; a man must become fiercely, wholeheartedly protective. Of course we should be alert to the more predictable dangers for our children (put the gate across the stairs, pad all the sharp corners, put the locks on the cabinets, cover all the electrical outlets), but there is another world of potential hurt out there that most of us know next to nothing about. What if your son wakes up at three in the morning coughing uncontrollably? How about the ear infection and runny nose that never seem to go away? What do you do about those angry red welts that appear on, migrate across, disappear from, and then reappear on your little girl's skin? You might think that modern medicine and an enlightened, caring pediatrician could solve the problems. But often this is not so. Fathers and mothers are frequently on their own in this. If we care deeply for our children, we spend a lot of time finding out for ourselves how to help them.

However, the parent's life isn't all *that* dismal. Many fathers have supremely   4
healthy children, which leaves the dads with more time for one of the most important roles he will play in his child's life, teacher. Yes, fathers-to-be, whatever you have done for a living up till this point, now you are a teacher. While some might view themselves more as a boss, benevolent monarch, or dictator, the truth is that we will be spending a large part of the next eighteen years (at least) trying to teach our children how to become happy, healthy, complete human beings. All the areas we work with from the initial ABCs and counting to restraining our anger—often at them!—to appreciating a spring daffodil or majestic sunset, all of these lessons, well taught, mark us as the most crucial teachers there can be. If we do our small jobs well, we slowly remake the world.

So what is a dad, really? As far as I can tell, he is a man who bravely and fool-   5
ishly, with only limited vision, steps into a difficult lifelong role that he begins with almost no experience and ends, if he is lucky, having learned a little. Along the way he has profited immeasurably: he has had an attentive, enthusiastic playmate who laughs at his stupidest jokes and thinks his voice impressions are incredibly brilliant; he has become less selfish, if not selfless, learning to put the needs of another ahead of his own; and he has grown by giving daily without counting of his knowledge and wisdom, whatever they may be, as he teaches his son or daughter to the best of his ability. I suppose, in the end, the true measure of a good father is one who loves his children beyond himself—perhaps all others—and who can hope that the adult he has helped shape will for all her life be able to look back at the man and, at least on occasion, say, "I love you, dad."

Questions for Analysis

1. Extended definitions often grow from several patterns of development. Name two from paragraph 2, and explain how they add to the paragraph.
   Answer: Patterns: comparison/contrast and process analysis. The contrast between baby chores and toddler playtime helps the reader see what fathers face. The process description of the baby chores works the same way—specific examples.

2. If you think the introductory paragraph is effective, what makes it work? Look especially at the hook (first sentence), the author's use of "I," the brief dialogue, revealing thoughts, and the thesis sentence. Write out the thesis sentence.
Answer: Effective: The hook draws the reader in, the "I" of personal experience adds credibility, the dialogue adds interest, and the thesis clearly predicts the direction of the essay.

3. If you think the concluding paragraph is effective, what makes it work? Why does the author use a question as the first sentence? What are the effects of being a father that the author lists?
Answer: Effective: The conclusion uses a connector, summarizes, and adds an expanded thought: fatherhood helps a person to grow. Question serves as transition. Effects: all of sentence 3.

4. Brief definitions often include negation, comparisons (often as metaphor/simile), and synonyms. List each paragraph in which these occur, and explain how they add to your understanding of "fatherhood."
Answer: Introduction: negation shows author's lack of knowledge about parenting. Introduction: Space shuttle simile develops the idea of how new and "alien" the experience felt. The synonyms *parent* and *dad* are used for *father* in several paragraphs.

5. What words in the topic sentence of paragraph 3 relate back to paragraph 2, and are they an effective connector?
Answer: "more than just a willingness and ability to become young again." Yes.

6. Choose any paragraph and explain how the examples help develop the author's points.
Answer: Answers will vary. One possibility, dangers in paragraph 3: Predictable dangers can be controlled; other dangers require a skeptical attitude toward facile answers, a willingness to question and seek out the best solutions.

▶ PERSUASION

In the essay "Abortion, Right and Wrong," Rachel Richardson Smith argues for greater perspective on the issue of abortion. As you read, think about the author's persona—how she presents herself to the audience—and her position on abortion. For an argument to be successful, does it need to convert a listener, or can it merely ask for greater tolerance and respect?

To review the elements of persuasion, turn back to Chapter 16.

Abortion, Right and Wrong

Rachel Richardson Smith

I cannot bring myself to say I am in favor of abortion. I don't want anyone to have 1 one. I want people to use contraceptives and for those contraceptives to be fool-proof. I want people to be responsible for their actions; mature in their decisions. I want children to be loved, wanted, well cared for.

I cannot bring myself to say I am against choice. I want women who are young, 2 poor, single or all three to be able to direct the course of their lives. I want women who have had all the children they want or can afford or their bodies can withstand to be able to decide their future. I want women who are in bad marriages or destructive relationships to avoid being trapped by pregnancy.

So in these days when thousands rally in opposition to legalized abortion, when 3 facilities providing abortions are bombed, when the president speaks glowingly of the growing momentum behind the anti-abortion movement, I find myself increasingly alienated from the pro-life groups.

At the same time, I am overwhelmed with mail from pro-choice groups. They, 4 too, are mobilizing their forces, growing articulate in support of their cause, and they want my support. I am not sure I can give it.

I find myself in the awkward position of being both anti-abortion and pro-choice. 5 Neither group seems to be completely right—or wrong. It is not that I think abortion is wrong for me but acceptable for someone else. The question is far more complex than that.

Part of my problem is that what I think and how I feel about this issue are two 6 entirely different matters. I know that unwanted children are often neglected, even abandoned. I know that many of those seeking abortions are children themselves. I know that making abortion illegal will not stop all women from having them.

Absolutes

I also know from experience the crisis an unplanned pregnancy can cause. Yet I 7 have felt the joy of giving birth, the delight that comes from feeling a baby's skin against my own. I know how hard it is to parent a child and how deeply satisfying it can be. My children sometimes provoke me and cause me endless frustration, but I can still look at them with tenderness and wonder at the miracle of it all. The lessons of my own experience produce conflicting emotions. Theory collides with reality.

It concerns me that both groups present themselves in absolutes. They are com- 8 mitted and they want me to commit. They do not recognize the gray area where I seem to be languishing. Each group has the right answer—the only answer.

Yet I am uncomfortable in either camp. I have nothing in common with the pro- 9 lifers. I am horrified by their scare tactics, their pictures of well-formed fetuses tossed in a metal pan, their cruel slogans. I cannot condone their flagrant misuse of Scripture and unforgiving spirit. There is a meanness about their position that causes them to pass judgment on the lives of women in a way I could never do.

The pro-life groups, with their fundamentalist religious attitudes, have a fear and 10 an abhorrence of sex, especially premarital sex. In their view abortion only compounds the sexual sin. What I find incomprehensible is that even as they are opposed to abortion they are also opposed to alternative solutions. They are squeamish about sex education in the schools. They don't want teens to have contraceptives without parental consent. They offer little aid or sympathy to unwed mothers. They are the vigilant guardians of a narrow morality.

I wonder how abortion got to be the greatest of all sins? What about poverty, 11
ignorance, hunger, weaponry?

The only thing the anti-abortion groups seem to have right is that abortion is 12
indeed the taking of a human life. I simply cannot escape this one glaring fact. Call
it what you will—fertilized egg, embryo, fetus. What we have here is human life.
If it were just a mass of tissue there would be no debate. So I agree that abortion
ends a life. But the anti-abortionists are wrong to call it murder.

The sad truth is that homicide is not always against the law. Our society does 13
not categorically recognize the sanctity of human life. There are a number of legal
and apparently socially acceptable ways to take human life. "Justifiable" homicide
includes the death penalty, war, killing in self-defense. It seems to me that as a society we need to come to grips with our own ambiguity concerning the value of
human life. If we are to value and protect unborn life so stringently, why do we not
also value and protect life already born?

Mistakes

Why can't we see abortion for the human tragedy it is? No woman plans for her 14
life to turn out that way. Even the most effective contraceptives are no guarantee
against pregnancy. Loneliness, ignorance, immaturity, can lead to decisions (or lack
of decisions) that may result in untimely pregnancy. People make mistakes.

What many people seem to misunderstand is that no woman wants to have an 15
abortion. Circumstances demand it; women do it. No woman reacts to abortion
with joy. Relief, yes. But also ambivalence, grief, despair, guilt.

The pro-choice groups do not seem to acknowledge that abortion is not a per- 16
fect answer. What goes unsaid is that when a woman has an abortion she loses
more than an unwanted pregnancy. Often she loses her self-respect. No woman
can forget a pregnancy no matter how it ends.

Why can we not view abortion as one of those anguished decisions in which 17
human beings struggle to do the best they can in trying circumstances? Why is
abortion viewed so coldly and factually on the one hand and so judgmentally on the
other? Why is it not akin to the same painful experience families must sometimes
make to allow a loved one to die?

I wonder how we can begin to change the context in which we think about abor- 18
tion. How can we begin to think about it redemptively? What is it in the trauma of
loss of life—be it loved or unloved, born or unborn—from which we can learn? There
is much I have yet to resolve. Even as I refuse to pass judgment on other women's
lives, I weep for the children who might have been. I suspect I am not alone.

Questions for Analysis

1. A good argument defines its issue early. Where in the first few paragraphs do we learn what the issue is in this essay?
   Answer: Paragraphs 1 and 2.

2. What is the author's position on the issue, and in which paragraph is it most clearly stated?
   Answer: People should recognize the complexity of the abortion issue and become more tolerant of each side—paragraph 8.

3. How would you characterize the author's persona (for more on persona, see pp. 367–368)? What points in the essay make you feel this way?
   Answer: A person who is concerned, sincere, troubled, reasonable, fair. Her position, her self-presentation as a mother (one who has experienced unplanned pregnancy, childbirth, and child rearing), her insight into the feelings of women who decide to have an abortion, etc.

4. Strong arguments require clear terminology and refutation of opposing reasons. In which paragraph does the author define a key term? How does the definition help refute a pro-life reason?
   Answer: Paragraph 13. Richardson Smith refutes the charge that abortion is "murder" by naming three examples of justifiable homicide.

5. In which paragraph does the author deal with the issue of the fetus as human? Does her position support pro-life or pro-choice?
   Answer: Paragraph 12. Pro-life.

6. All arguments grow from assertions supported by detailed examples and explanations. Identify the topic sentence in paragraph 9, and then list the examples the author offers to support her assertion.
   Answer: The second sentence. Pictures of fetuses in metal pans, cruel slogans, misuse of Scripture.

7. What three reasons does the author list in paragraph 6 that support the pro-choice position?
   Answer: Unwanted children, children having children, abortion continuing whether illegal or not.

8. To preserve their credibility by limiting overstatement, writers qualify frequently in argument (using words like *seems, might, often, frequently*). Name three instances of qualifying in paragraphs 5 to 7 (for more on qualifying in argument, see pp. 371, 459).
   Answer: Paragraphs 5, *seems;* 6, *part of, often, all women;* 7, *can, sometimes.*

▶ PERSUASION

"What Is Biodiversity and Why Should We Care About It?" comes from the book *The Global Citizen,* written by Donella Meadows in 1991. The author argues that people do not care enough for their planet, that if we continue to destroy plant and animal habitat we will ultimately destroy ourselves. As you read this article, imagine yourself as part of Meadows's target audience, people who are interested in the environment but not well informed on matters like "biodiversity." Does the author hold your interest and speak persuasively to you, or do you feel alienated at any point, as if the author is reprimanding you?

What Is Biodiversity and Why Should We Care About It?

Donella Meadows

Most of us have grasped the idea that there's a hole in the sky over the South 1
Pole that could give us skin cancer. We are beginning to understand that a global
warming could inundate Miami Beach and make New York even more unbearable
in the summer. There is another environmental problem, however, that doesn't
have a catchy name like "ozone hole" or "greenhouse effect," and that hasn't yet
entered the public consciousness. It's the loss of biodiversity.

Bio-*what?*   2

Biodiversity sounds like it has to do with pandas and tigers and tropical rain 3
forests. It does, but it's bigger than those, bigger than a single species or even a
single ecosystem. It's the whole, all of life, the microscopic creepy-crawlies as well
as the elephants and condors. It's all the habitats, beautiful or not, that support life—
the tundra, prairie, and swamp as well as the tropical forest.

Why care about tundras and swamps? There's one good reason—self-interest. 4
Preserving biodiversity is not something to do out of kindness of our hearts, to
express our fondness for fuzzy creatures on Sunday mornings when we happen
to feel virtuous. It's something to do to maintain the many forms of life we eat and
use, and to maintain ourselves.

How would you like the job of pollinating all trillion or so apple blossoms in the 5
state of New York some sunny afternoon in May? It's conceivable, maybe, that you
could invent a machine to do it, but inconceivable that the machine could work as
efficiently, elegantly, and cheaply as honeybees, much less make honey.

Suppose you were assigned to turn every bit of dead organic matter—from fallen 6
leaves to urban garbage to road kills—into nutrients that feed new life. Even if you
knew how, what would it cost? Uncountable numbers of bacteria, molds, mites, and
worms do it for free. If they ever stopped, all life would stop. We would not last long
if green plants stopped turning our exhaled carbon dioxide back into oxygen. The
plants would not last long if a few beneficent kinds of soil bacteria stopped turning
nitrogen from the air into fertilizer.

Human reckoning cannot put a value on the services performed for us by the mil- 7
lions of species of life on earth. In addition to pollination and recycling, these services
include flood control, drought prevention, pest control, temperature regulation, and
maintenance of the world's most valuable library, the genes of all living organisms, a
library we are just learning to read.

Another thing we are just learning is that both the genetic library and the ecosys- 8
tem's services depend on the integrity of the entire biological world. All species fit
together in an intricate, interdependent, self-sustaining whole. Rips in the biological fabric tend to run. Gaps cause things to fall in unexpected ways.

For example, attempts to replant acacia trees in the Sahel at the edge of the 9
Sahara desert have failed because the degraded soil has lost a bacterium called rhi-
zobium, without which acacia trees can't grow. Songbirds that eat summer insects
in North America are declining because of deforestation in their Central American
wintering grounds. European forests are more vulnerable to acid rain than American forests because they are human-managed, single-species plantations rather
than natural mixtures of many species forming an interknit, resilient system.

Biodiversity cannot be maintained by protecting a few charismatic megafauna 10
in a zoo, not by preserving a few greenbelts of even large national parks. Biodiversity can maintain itself, however, without human attention or expense, without
zookeepers, park rangers, foresters, or refrigerated gene banks. All it needs is to
be left alone.

It is not being left alone, of course, which is why biological impoverishment has 11
become a problem of global dimensions. There is hardly a place left on earth, where
people do not log, pave, spray, drain, flood, graze, fish, plow, burn, drill, spill, or
dump.

Ecologists estimate that human beings usurp, directly or indirectly, about 40 per- 12
cent of each year's total biological production (and our population is on its way to
another doubling in forty years). There is no biome, with the possible exception of
the deep ocean, that we are not degrading. In poor countries biodiversity is being
nickeled and dimed to death; in rich countries it is being billion-dollared to death.

To provide their priceless service to us, the honeybees ask only that we stop sat- 13
urating the landscape with poisons, stop paving the meadows and verges where
bee food grows, and leave them enough honey to get through the winter.

To maintain our planet and our lives, the other species have similar requests, all 14
of which, summed up, are: Control yourselves. Control your numbers. Control your
greed. See yourselves as what you are, part of an interdependent biological community, the most intelligent part, though you don't often act that way. Act that way.
Do so either out of a moral respect for something wonderful that you did not create and do not understand or out of a practical interest in your own survival.

Questions for Analysis

1. Evaluate the introduction. Does the first sentence arouse the reader's curiosity? Do the middle sentences speak to the audience's interests and knowledge? Does the paragraph indicate what the article will be about? What pronouns help connect the writer to the audience?

   Answer: The hook works well as does the other information, establishing a connection with the audience of shared knowledge, and Meadows clearly states the topic of the article. Pronouns of accommodation are *us* and *we*.

2. Effective arguments quickly clarify their issue. One way to do this is by defining terms. In which paragraph does Meadows begin to define her key term, and what specific examples does she use to illustrate her definition? Has the author made a mistake by not also defining the term *ecosystem*—why or why not?

   Answer: Paragraph 3. Meadows cites specific animals and habitats. Students should be able to determine from the introductory audience definition that most of the author's readers would be familiar with the term *ecosystem*.

3. Persuasive writing gives people reasons to accept a writer's position. What is the author's primary reason to support her position, where does she first state it, and how clearly does she explain it? What objection or misconception in this paragraph does she anticipate and counter?

   Answer: Primary reason: self-interest, stated in paragraph 4. Meadows begins to clarify her point by anticipating the potential objection of some who might feel that preserving biodiversity is primarily an act of kindness rather than self-interest.

4. Without support reasons are unconvincing. What paragraphs does Meadows devote to supporting her primary reason? What main examples does she offer for support in paragraphs 5 and 6? Does the author's use of *you* in these paragraphs seem appropriate? Why would she combine *you* with a question as the first sentence in paragraph 5?

   Answer: Support for paragraph 4: paragraphs 5 to 9; paragraph 5: bees and pollination, paragraph 6: recycling organic matter. The pronoun *you* is appropriate because Meadows wants to directly address her audience; neither *we* nor *people* would work as well in this instance. Questions are useful for engaging an audience.

5. Because writers regularly combine the patterns of development in supporting their ideas, you will find several in this article, including cause and effect. Locate two instances of cause and effect and explain how effectively they are used to help make the author's point.

   Answer: Cause and effect in paragraphs 6 and 9. Paragraph 6 effectively establish a causal chain, and paragraph 9 uses three specific examples to illustrate negative effects.

6. All arguments deal with counterreasons and objections to the author's position. What is the counterreason offered in paragraph 10, and how well does Meadows refute it?

   Answer: Counterreason: biodiversity can be maintained with wildlife preserves. Meadows has established in paragraphs 5 to 9 that diversity is essential and that it must be planetwide to avoid chain-reaction extinctions of beneficial species.

7. Connecting paragraphs in essays is important to ease the reader from one idea into the next. What connecting methods does Meadows use to link paragraphs 1 to 4?

   Answer: Paragraph 2 repeats a word and uses a question: "Bio-*what?*" Paragraph 3 repeats *biodiversity*. Paragraph 4 repeats *tundras and swamps*, using a question.

8. How effective is the concluding paragraph? What points does the author remind us of; what is the expanded thought? What device does Meadows use to keep from having to criticize her audience, even though she does use the pronoun *you?*

   Answer: The conclusion is effective. Meadows links the lead sentence to her final body paragraph, connects with her thesis, touches on two strong reasons for supporting her position, and reminds readers that they, too, are part of the biological community. She uses the animal voices to ask for change.

9. The author uses a number of stylistic devices to create clarity and interest, including the dash, italics, questions, metaphor, and personification. Locate an instance of each one of these and explain how it strengthens the writing. (For more on figures of speech, see pp. 473–480.)

   Answers: Answers will vary: Paragraph 4, dash for emphasis. Paragraph 2, italics for emphasis. Paragraph 4, question used to develop a point. Paragraphs 7 and 8, metaphors of "gene library" and "biological fabric" for emphasis and clarity. Paragraph 13, personification of honeybees to promote emotional appeal.

APPENDIX 1

Working with Your Computer

▶ CAN A MACHINE MAKE YOU A BETTER WRITER?

Most of the world's great literature has been written without a computer (or even a typewriter), so we might begin by asking ourselves who needs a computer in the first place. If you have always written your drafts in longhand, why not continue doing so? After all, word processing on a computer requires time and energy to learn even the basics and can be unpredictable—half an essay suddenly vanishing during a power surge or a loose connection to an electrical outlet.

The answer, of course, is that we *can* continue to write in longhand or use a typewriter and write wonderfully. However, a computer, like the typewriter before it—and the quill pen before that!—is another tool for helping us record our thoughts. Word processing allows us to concentrate our energy on creating material rather than copying the same words over and gives us an uncluttered backdrop against which we can better see our thoughts emerge. Computers can help us in every step of the writing process: invention, organization, drafting, revising, and editing.

But it is important also to realize the limitations of computer-assisted composition. Word processing software cannot add ideas or point out where vague statements need more specific examples and explanations to make them clear to a reader. Computers cannot notice when one of our paragraphs begins to drift from a central point or when one statement does not logically follow from another. Computers cannot comment on or help us with the creative spark that marks an interesting introduction or conclusion. In short, it is important for us to view and use our computers as helpful tools but not to expect help that they are incapable of giving. Computers are not smart; they are just incredibly quick.

This chapter is intended for those who are new to word processing and want some help beginning, formatting, and printing a document using Microsoft Word (other software, such as WordPerfect, is similar). For more in-depth questions about how to use your word processing software, you can look to the Help function listed on the main pull-down menu at the top of your screen, the computer lab at your college, a friend, or your instructor—all valuable resources.

Starting Microsoft Word

After you have turned on your computer, you will see a screen similar to the one below, called the desktop. If you have a small picture (called an icon) of Microsoft Word or other word processing software, such as WordPerfect, on your desktop, simply click on it to take you into a Windows screen. If not, follow the steps listed below:

1. At the left bottom of the screen, move the mouse pointer to Start and click once.

2. Next, move the pointer up to Programs, which will become highlighted in blue.

3. Now, move the arrow across to the next column of programs, find **W** Microsoft Word, and click once. This will move you into Microsoft Word so you can begin a new document or open one you have already created.

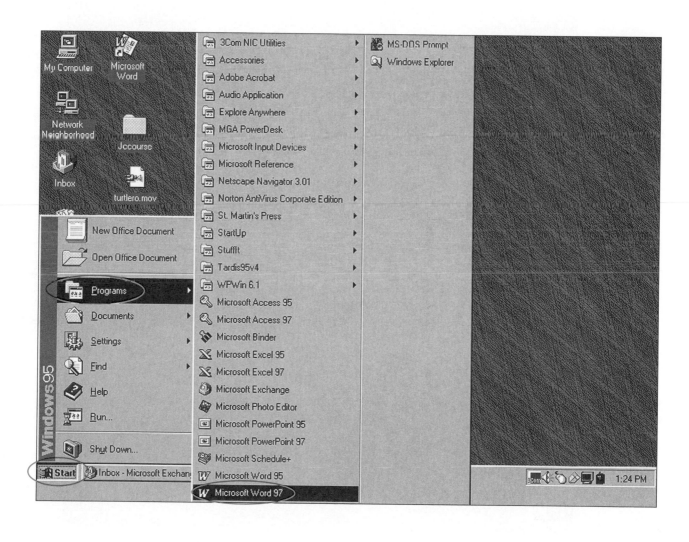

Finding Your Way Around in a Windows Screen

After you have entered Word (or other word processing software), you will see a screen (or window) similar to the one below. To help move around in it, we should learn some basic terminology. The illustration below labels the basic Windows parts that we will talk about in this chapter.

---

*If no toolbars are visible, turn to the next page in this appendix for instructions on inserting them.

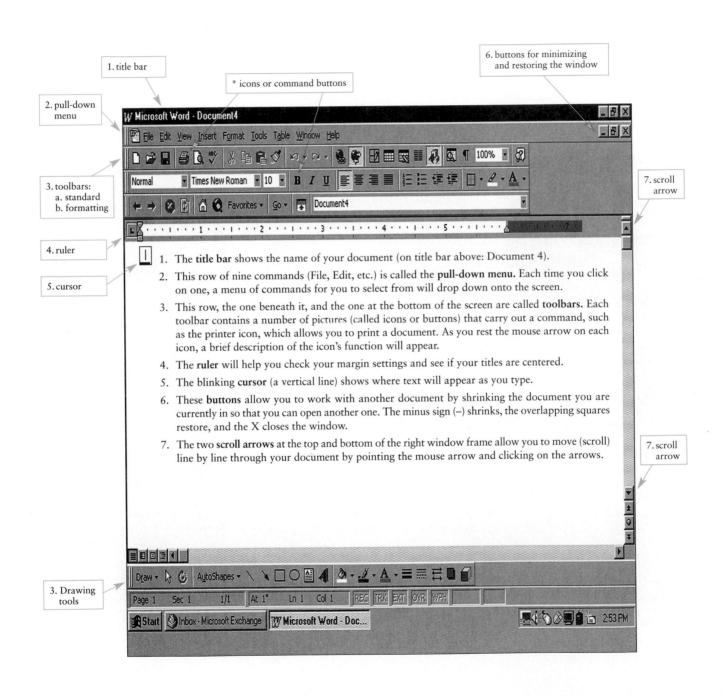

1. title bar

2. pull-down menu

* icons or command buttons

6. buttons for minimizing and restoring the window

3. toolbars:
   a. standard
   b. formatting

7. scroll arrow

4. ruler

5. cursor

3. Drawing tools

1. The **title bar** shows the name of your document (on title bar above: Document 4).

2. This row of nine commands (File, Edit, etc.) is called the **pull-down menu.** Each time you click on one, a menu of commands for you to select from will drop down onto the screen.

3. This row, the one beneath it, and the one at the bottom of the screen are called **toolbars.** Each toolbar contains a number of pictures (called icons or buttons) that carry out a command, such as the printer icon, which allows you to print a document. As you rest the mouse arrow on each icon, a brief description of the icon's function will appear.

4. The **ruler** will help you check your margin settings and see if your titles are centered.

5. The blinking **cursor** (a vertical line) shows where text will appear as you type.

6. These **buttons** allow you to work with another document by shrinking the document you are currently in so that you can open another one. The minus sign (–) shrinks, the overlapping squares restore, and the X closes the window.

7. The two **scroll arrows** at the top and bottom of the right window frame allow you to move (scroll) line by line through your document by pointing the mouse arrow and clicking on the arrows.

7. scroll arrow

Adding Toolbars to Your Window

If your screen does not show toolbars, you will want to add the Standard and probably the Formatting toolbars, as you see shown on the previous page. To accomplish this, refer to the illustration below and follow these instructions:

1. Move the mouse arrow to View on the pull-down menu and click.

2. Move the arrow to Toolbars, and another drop-down menu will appear.

3. Move the arrow across, click on Standard, and this toolbar will appear.

4. Repeat the above steps, click on Formatting, and the formatting toolbar will appear.

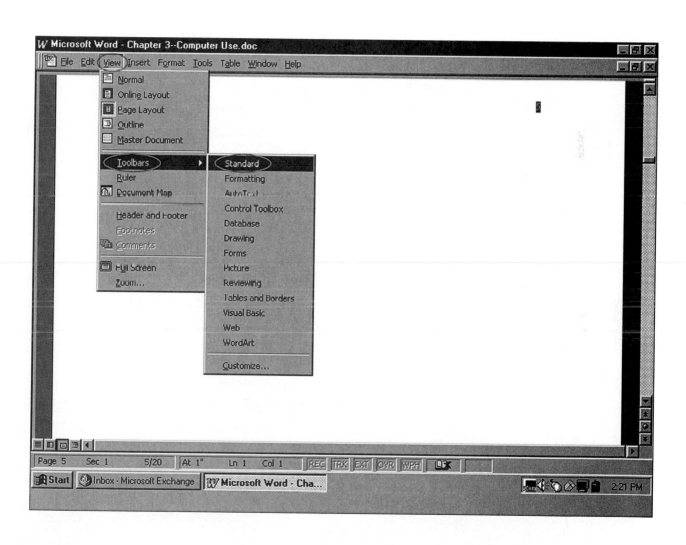

Saving a Document

After entering Word from Start, you can immediately begin typing your document, but it is best to save your work right away so you do not lose any of it (and to continue saving every few minutes as you work). To save a document the first time, refer to the illustrations below, and follow these steps:

1. Move the mouse arrow to File on the pull-down menu and click.

2. On the menu that drops down click Save As.

3. In the Save As dialog box that appears, you have two steps.
   A. Decide where you want to save the file, either to Floppy A (your disk) or some place on your C drive. To choose a location in which to save your file, click on the arrow to the right of the Save in box, select your location (Floppy A or another), and click on it.
   B. Now you will decide on a file name (such as Essay 1), place the mouse arrow in the box next to File name, delete any words that might be there, and type your file name into the box (the illustration uses the file name title Chapter 3—Computer Use).

4. Now click on Save, and your document is saved.

After you have named your file, you can save it periodically by clicking on the disk icon on the pull-down menu.

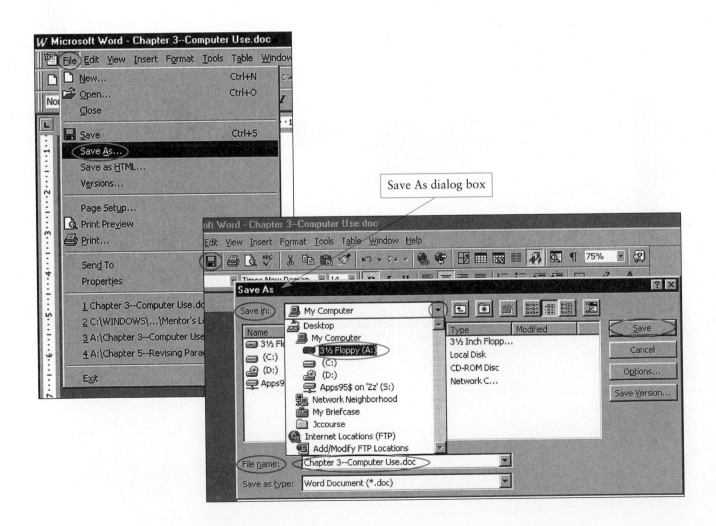

Opening a Document

When you want to return to a file that you have previously closed, you can click on the file folder icon on the toolbar or click on File on the pull-down menu and then click on Open. Refer to the illustrations below and follow the steps listed:

1. Click on Open.

2. When the Open dialog box appears, click on the arrow to the right of Look in.

3. Choose the location from the drop-down list where you previously stored your file (perhaps Floppy A) and click.

4. If you stored your file in Floppy A, you will see it listed along with any other files you have stored there. Click twice on the file, and it will open.

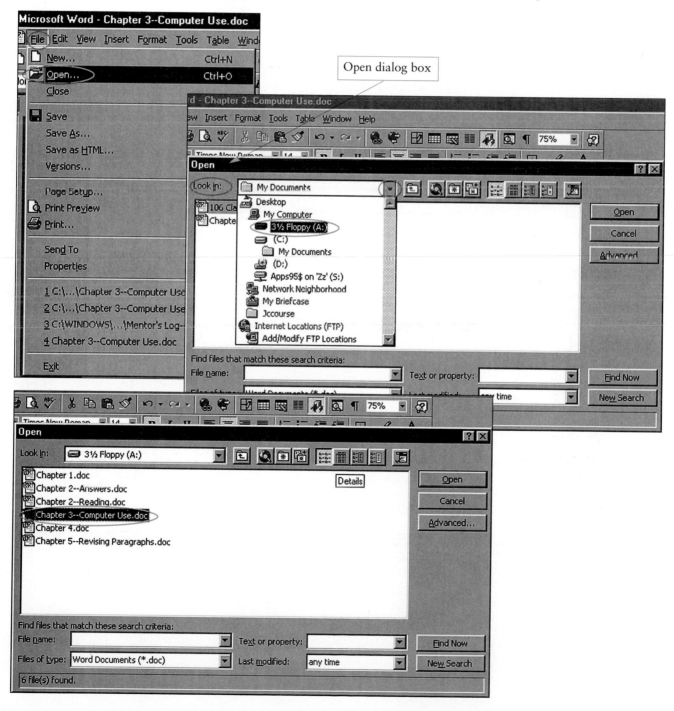

Moving Words and Sentences

There are several ways to move text with a computer. The quickest is simply to highlight whichever words you want repositioned, click on the text and hold the mouse button down while you reposition the mouse arrow. The text will reappear wherever you place the arrow and release the mouse button.

If you want to move larger sections of text from one screen to another, you might want to cut and paste using the icons from your standard toolbar. The following steps and illustration will help you with this task:

1. Highlight the text you want to cut or move.

2. Click on the scissors icon from the toolbar.

3. Reposition the mouse arrow to where you want the text to appear.

4. Click on the clipboard icon from the toolbar to paste in the words.

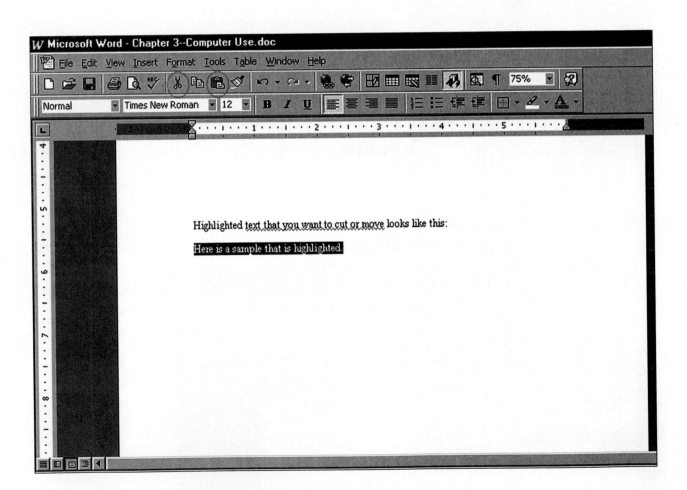

Changing Line Spacing

Your computer single spaces lines to help fit more text into a screen while you are composing. However, before you print paragraphs and essays for your instructor, you will need to double-space so he or she will have room to comment on your paper. Here is how to do it:

1. Highlight the text that you want to double-space by left clicking and dragging with the mouse. (Or if you want to quickly highlight the entire document, you can click on Edit in the pull-down menu and then click on Select All from the menu list.

2. Next, click on Format in the pull-down menu, and then click on Paragraph in the menu list.

3. In the dialog box that appears, labeled Paragraph, you will see the words Line spacing over a box with the word Single showing. Click on the arrow next to the word Single, and a drop-down menu will give you several line spacing options, including Double. Click on the word Double, and then click OK at the bottom of the Paragraph box.

The illustrations that follow will help you with line spacing.

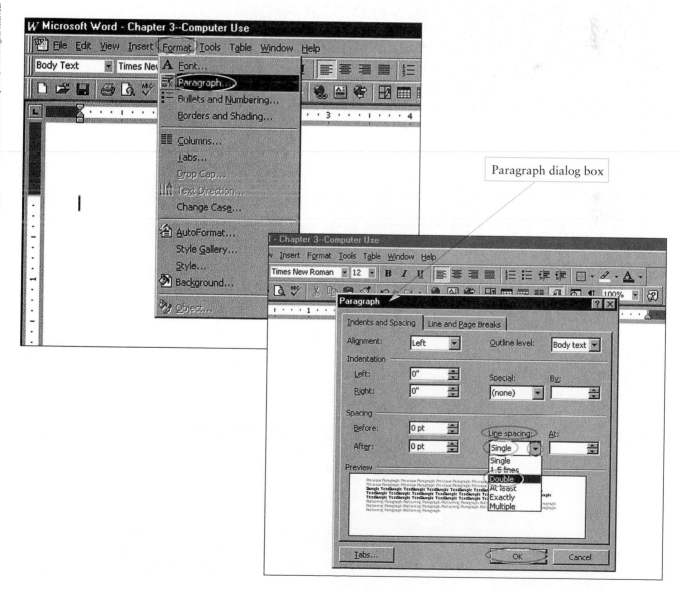

Paragraph dialog box

Setting Margins

Margins are preset by most word processing software, but you may need to change the settings if they are too wide or too narrow. Here is how to accomplish this task:

1. Click on File on the toolbar and then on Page Setup in the drop-down menu.

2. In the dialog box that appears, Page Setup, you will find measurements given in inches for the margins. In Microsoft Word the margins are set for one inch on top and bottom and 1¼ inches for the left and right margins. To change the settings, click on the arrows beside the box with the measurement in it (1" or 1.25"). Each time you click, the measurement will increase or decrease by .1, and you can see the effect on your document in the Preview box to the right of the measurements. When you have the setting you want, click on OK at the bottom of the Page Setup box.

The illustrations below will help you with margin setting.

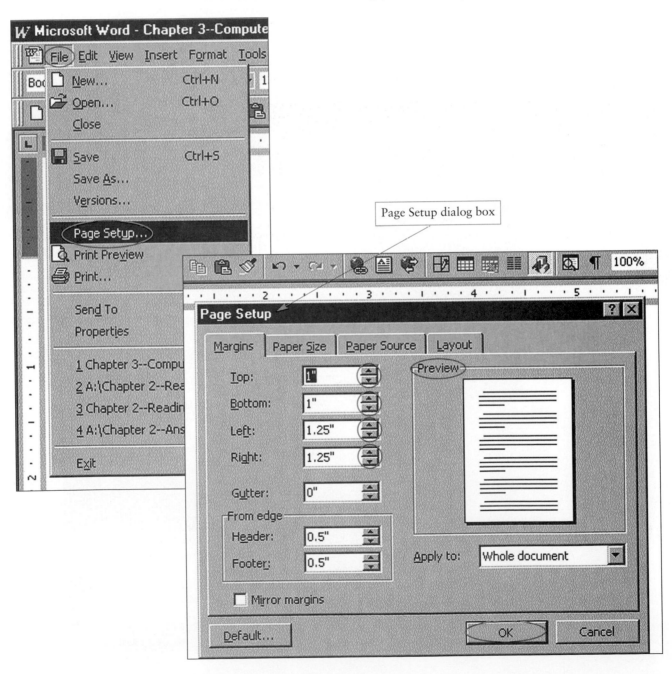

Centering Text

Being able to place text accurately in the center of a page will help you particularly when you title your paragraph or essay. Here is how to do it:

1. Place the cursor next to the text you want to center on the page.

2. Now look for the four icons with horizontal lines in the toolbar at the top of the screen. Click on the second icon, the one showing the horizontal lines centered. Your title should now be centered.

The illustration that follows will help you with centering text.

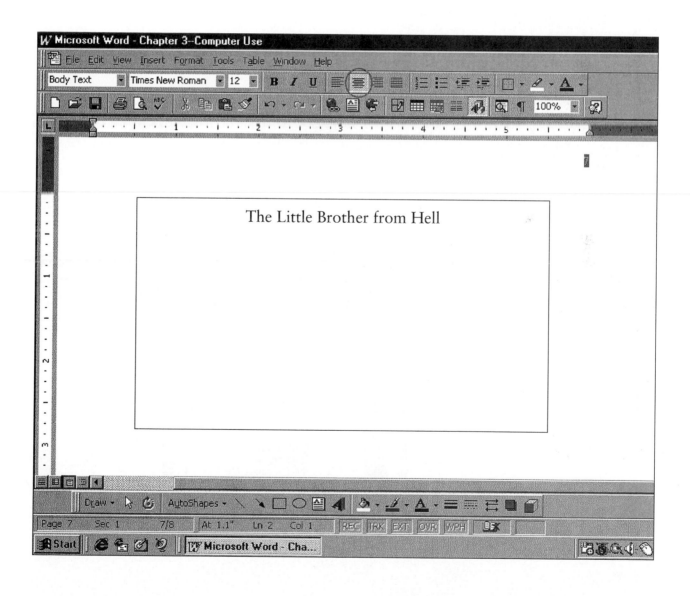

Bolding, Italicizing, Underlining, Changing Font and Typeface

Your computer allows you to change the look of letters in several ways to add emphasis and clarity to your ideas. When you want to bold, italicize, or underline letters, use the icons listed on the formatting toolbar as **B**, *I*, and <u>U</u>.

1. Highlight the word or words that you want to **bold,** *italicize,* or <u>underline</u>, and then click on the icon.

2. To change the letter size from the standard 12-point font, again highlight the letters or words you want changed, and then click on the arrow next to the number box on the formatting toolbar. The pull-down menu will list numbers for letter sizes, one of which you will click on. Once you have changed the font setting, letters will continue in this size until you change the size again. **Note:** Most instructors require a 12-point font and will not want you to try to "save" paper by using 10-point.

3. To change the style of typeface, click on the arrow to the left of the number box. The drop-down menu will list various options, one of which you will then click on. **Note:** Most instructors require a standard business typeface such as Times New Roman.

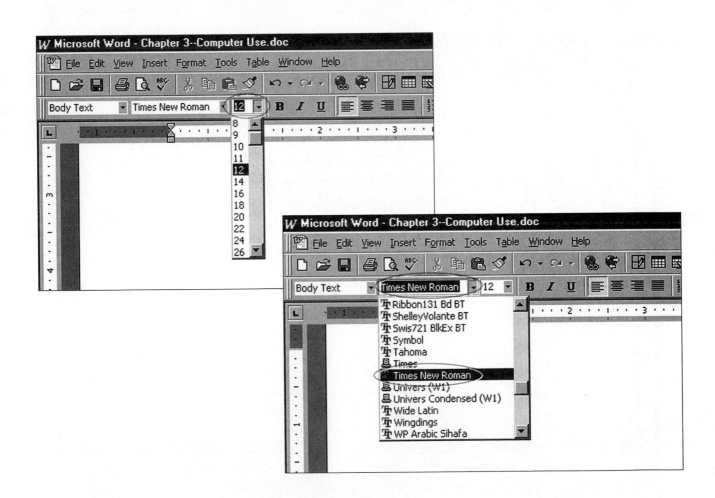

Inserting Page Numbers

If you have a one-page paragraph assignment to turn in, numbering the page does not matter. However, as soon as you begin essay writing, you will need to number pages. Here is one way to do it:

1. From the pull-down menu click on Insert.

2. Next, click on Page Numbers.

3. The Page Numbers dialog box will let you choose how to position your numbers—top or bottom; right, left, or center—and will give you the option of numbering the first page. Choose the location for your page numbers, and then click OK at the bottom of the Page Numbers dialog box.

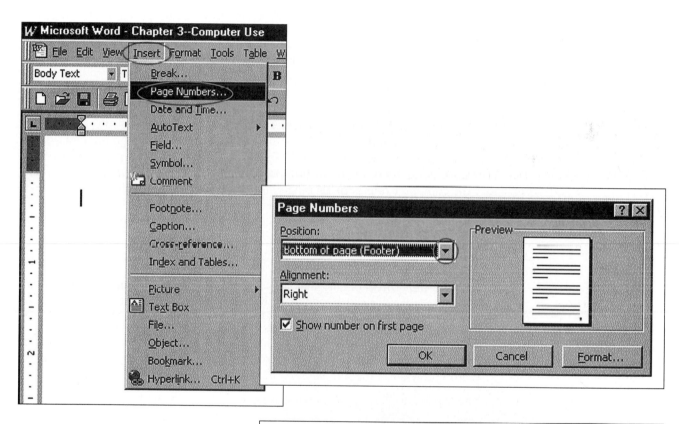

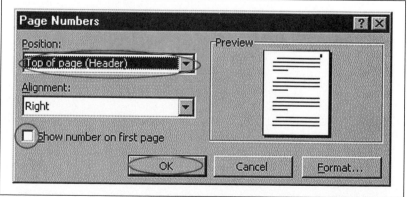

Using Spell Check, Grammar Check, and Word Count

Your computer can help you in several ways as you begin to edit your work, including checking for spelling errors, some grammar problems, and total paper length. Spell check can be particularly useful because it catches many typographical errors as well as repeat words and spacing problems. However, be warned that spell check is not infallible, sometimes simply missing misspelled words and at all times overlooking sound-alike errors such as *their/there/they're* and other wrong word choices. Here is a poem that makes this point. How many errors can you find in it?

Spellbound

I have a spelling checker,
It came with my PC;
It plainly marks four my revue
Mistakes I cannot sea.
I've run this poem threw it,
I'm sure your pleased too no,
Its letter perfect in its weigh;
My checker tolled me sew.

Janet Minor

Grammar check is another mixed blessing, often requiring such sophisticated writing skills to evaluate the "help" being offered that the writers who are best able to use it are the ones who need it least. Grammar check can alert a person to possible problems, but quite often no problem exists. Do not simply follow every suggestion that the computer offers for revising your work. People are much more capable of making informed revision and editing decisions than is computer software.

Word count is a useful tool that will save you some line counting and multiplying when you are thinking about assignment length requirements.

To use spell and grammar check, follow these steps:

1. To begin the process of checking your whole document, click on the ABC icon on the top toolbar. (To check a single word, highlight the word and then click on the icon.)

2. Each time your computer stops at a highlighted word, you can choose to skip it by clicking Ignore. If you want to correct a spelling or grammar error, click on the word you want in the box labeled Suggestions, and then click on Change.

The illustration on the following page will help you with spell and grammar checking.

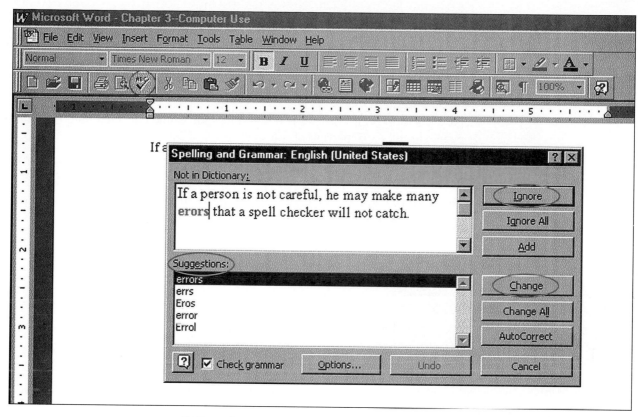

Follow these steps to use Word Count:

1. Highlight the words you want counted (or click on Edit from the pull-down menu and then click on Select All).

2. Click on Tools from the pull-down menu, then Word Count, and you will see your word total.

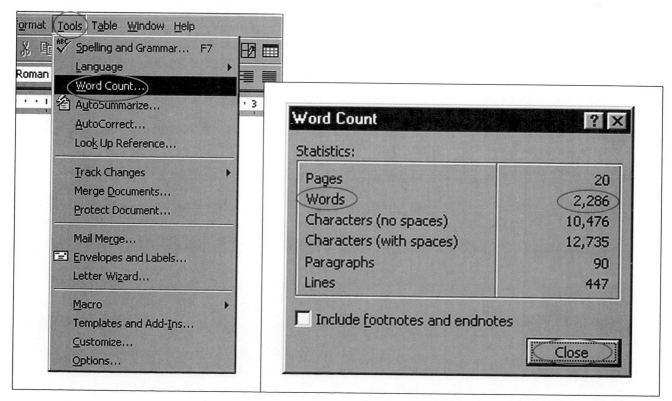

Using Print Preview

Print Preview is a useful option that lets a writer look at her whole document before she prints it, often showing errors in margin settings and page breaks that can then be corrected. Here is how to use Print Preview:

1. Click on File in the pull-down menu.

2. Now click on Print Preview. You will find your whole document laid out in tiny pages shrunk to 10 percent of full size.

3. To look at any portion of a page, place the mouse arrow on it and click. After you have seen the part of the page close up, click again to return to the Preview screen.

4. To return to regular viewing of your document, click on Close in the upper right corner of the Print Preview screen.

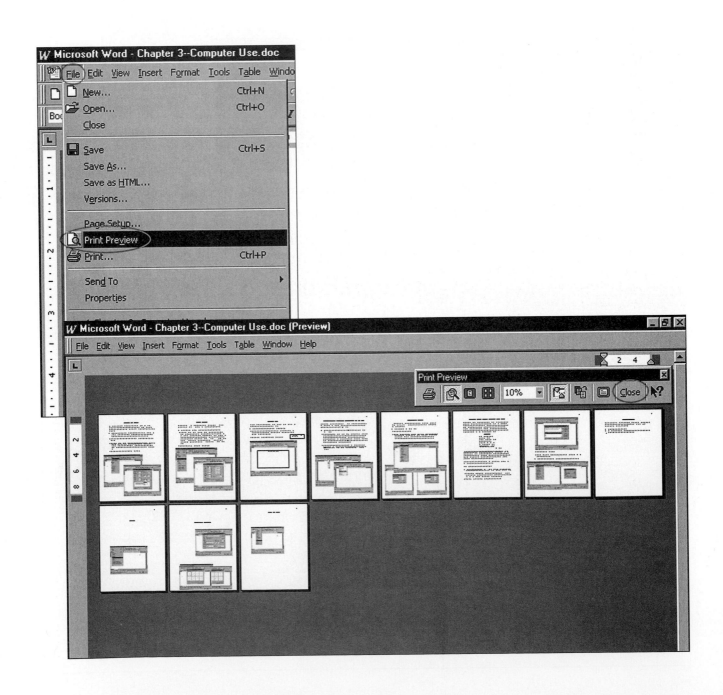

Printing

To print your whole document, you can simply click on the printer icon on the standard toolbar. However, if you want to print only part of the file or multiple copies, you will need to use the pull-down menu. Here is how:

1. Click on File on the pull-down menu.

2. Next, click on Print, and the Print dialog box will appear.

3. If you only want to print part of the document, click on Pages. A blinking cursor will appear in the box next to Pages. Type in whatever page numbers you want to print, separating each with a comma (such as 1, 3, 5) or a hyphen for a range of pages (such as 1-4), and then click OK.

4. If you want more than one copy, click on the arrow next to the box labeled Number of copies. Select the number of copies you want, and then click on OK.

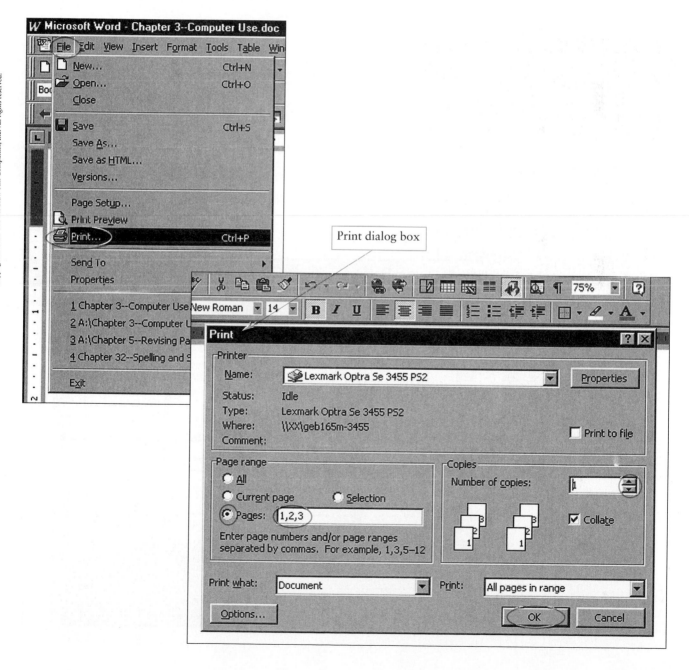

Print dialog box

Bulleting and Numbering

Bulleting and numbering are used for outlines and lists when we prewrite and when we turn in more formal outlines with essays. To bullet or number using the formatting toolbar, simply highlight the text you want to mark, and then click on either the three stacked squares (the bullet icon) or the stacked numbers 1, 2, 3 (the number icon). If you need to change the numbers to letters (as in creating formal outlines), you can do so through the main pull-down menu by following these steps:

1. Highlight the text you want bulleted or numbered.

2. Click on Format on the pull-down menu.

3. Click on Bullets and Numbering.

4. When the Bullets and Numbering dialog box appears, click on the numbers or letters that you want in your outline and then click OK.

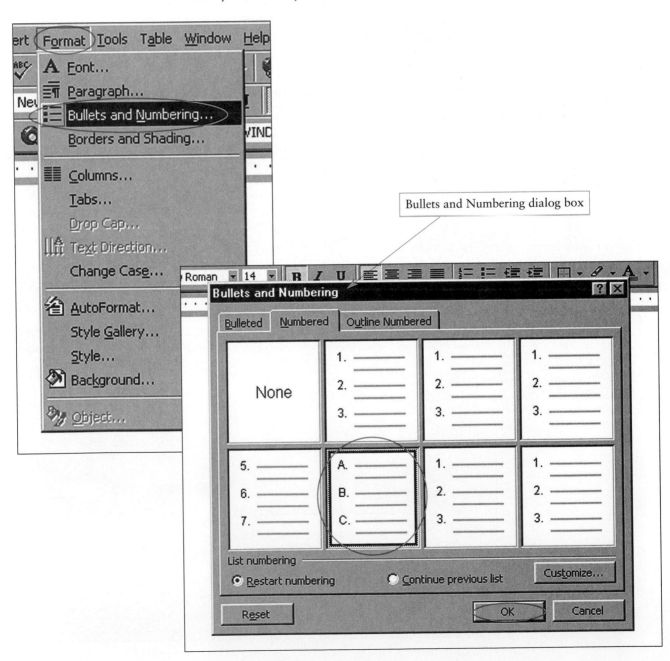

Bullets and Numbering dialog box

Using Text Boxes

Text boxes are small moveable boxes that we jot notes in. They can be particularly useful in prewriting and drafting because we can write notes to ourselves and scatter them in the margins to be viewed after we have finished whatever thought we are working with at the time. You might think of using text boxes as scribbling notes to yourself the same way you would when writing in longhand. Notice the example text box note in the left margin:

Sample Text Box Note:

> Should I explain how to move text boxes here?

If you want to create text boxes, you can either place the drawing toolbar on your Windows screen (see Adding Toolbars to Your Window p. A-5) and click on the icon (a box with an A in it) or use the pull-down menu. To use the pull-down menu:

1. Click on Insert from the pull-down menu.

2. Click on the text box icon.

3. When you move the mouse arrow back into your document, you will see that the arrow has become a plus sign. Stop the sign wherever you want to place the text box and then click. A box will appear with a blinking cursor in it, and you can begin writing your note. Here are three ways to manipulate a text box:

   a. **Changing the size:** When you click on the box, you will notice eight tiny boxes surrounding the main box. If you place the mouse arrow on one of the tiny boxes, the arrow will become two-pointed. Click once with the mouse and drag the dotted edge of the box outward. You can make the box as large or small as you want.

   b. **Moving the box:** Click anywhere on the edge of the box, hold the mouse button down, and drag the box to wherever you want it positioned. **Note:** If you place it over other words in your document, they will be temporarily covered, as if you had laid a sheet of paper over them.

   c. **Deleting the box:** Click on it until the outer edge is surrounded by tiny dots, and then press the delete key on your keyboard or cut with your scissors icon from the formatting toolbar.

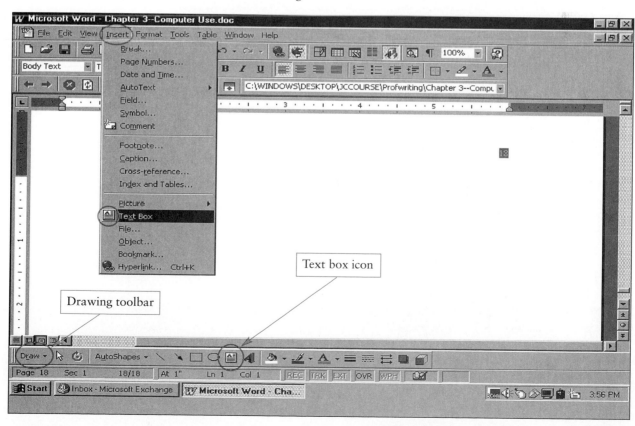

Improvement Chart

IMPROVEMENT CHART

Name: _____

This chart will help you track and correct errors in your major writing assignments. Chapter numbers (in parentheses) follow each error.

	1	2	3	4	5	6	7	8	Spelling	Sound-alike
1. Subject/verb agreement (23)										
2. Verb tense shift (23)										
3. Verb form (23)										
4. Pronoun agreement (24)										
5. Pronoun shift (24)										
6. Pronoun case (24)										
7. Pronoun reference (24)										
8. Parallelism (21)										
9. Misplaced and dangling modifier (25)										
10. Adverb form (25)										
11. Run-on sentence (22)										
12. Comma splice (22)										
13. Sentence fragment (22)										
14. Unneeded comma (26)										
15. Comma to introduce (26)										
16. Comma to enclose/end (26)										
17. Comma to divide (26)										
18. Comma with a series (26)										
19. Comma with coordinate adjective (26)										
20. Comma for contrast (26)										
21. Comma with numbers, dates, addresses, place names, direct address dialogue (26)										
22. Semicolon (26)										
23. Quotation marks (26)										
24. Apostrophe (26)										
25. Capitalization (26)										
26. Hyphen (26)										
27. Spelling (27)										
28. Sound-alike (27)										
29. Wrong word (19)										
30. Missing word (1)										

▶ TEXT ACKNOWLEDGMENTS

Baker, Russell, **"A Nice Place to Visit."** Copyright © 1979 by *The New York Times.*

Catton, Bruce, **"Grant and Lee: A Study in Contrasts."** Copyright © 1958 by U.S. Capitol Historical Society, all rights reserved.

Gottfried, Martin, **"Rambos of the Road."** Copyright © 1986 by Martin Gottfried, author of twelve books, most recently *Balancing Act—The Authorized Biography of Angela Lansbury* and a forthcoming biography of Arthur Miller.

Harris, Sydney J., **"Opposing Principles Help Balance Society."** From *Clearing the Ground* by Sydney J. Harris. Copyright © 1982, 1983, 1985, 1986 by *The Chicago Sun-Times,* Field Newspaper Syndicate, News-America Syndicate and Sydney J. Harris. Reprinted by permission of Houghton Mifflin Company. All rights reserved.

Hoffmann, Roger, **"The Dare."** First published in *The New York Times.* Copyright © 1986 by Roger Hoffman.

Keillor, Garrison, **"How to Write a Letter."** From *We Are Still Married,* published by Viking Penguin Inc. Reprinted by permission of International Paper Company. Copyright © 1987 by International Paper Company. (Originally titled "How to Write a Personal Letter.")

King, Jr., Martin Luther, **"The Ways of Meeting Oppression."** Reprinted by arrangement with the Estate of Martin Luther King, Jr., c/o Writers House as agent for the proprietor. Copyright 1958 by Martin Luther King, Jr. Copyright renewed 1986 by Coretta Scott King.

Meadows, Donella, **"What is Biodiversity, and Why Should We Care about It?"** Permission granted by Island Press. From *The Global Citizen,* copyright ©1991 by Donella H. Meadows.

Mifflin, Margot, **"The Ten Most Memorable Bores."** Copyright © 1990 by Margot Mifflin, who is a contributor at *Entertainment Weekly* and an assistant professor at Lehman College.

Smith, Rachel Richardson, **"Abortion, Right and Wrong."** Copyright © 1985 by Rachel R. Smith.

Staples, Brent, **"Black Men and Public Space."** Copyright © 1986 by Brent Staples, who writes editorials on politics and culture for *The New York Times* and is author of the memoir, *Parallel Time: Growing Up In Black and White*

Steinbeck, John, 2 page excerpt from *Cannery Row.* Copyright 1945 by John Steinbeck. Renewed © 1973 by Elaine Steinbeck, John Steinbeck IV and Thom Steinbeck. Used by permission of Viking Penguin, a division of Penguin Putnam Inc.

Zuckerman, Benjamin, **"Two by Two, We'll Fill the Planet."** Copyright © 1991 by Benjamin Zuckerman, Professor of Physics and Astronomy, UCLA.